THE WORLD'S

BEST COOKING

IN COLOUR

ISBN 0 907305 21 0

First published by Bay
Books
61–69 Anzac Parade
Kensington 2033 NSW

This edition specially produced for
CEEPI Ltd/Dealerfield Ltd in 1988

© Bay Books
© Illustrations Bay Books
© Illustrations "Les Cours de la
    Cuisine A a Z" — "Femmes
    d'Aujourd'hui"

Printed in Singapore

THE WORLD'S
BEST COOKING
IN COLOUR

CAXTON

CONTENTS

Weights and Measures

Quantities are given in Metric, Imperial and US cup/avoirdupois measures. Rarely do exact conversions from Imperial/US measures to Metric measures give convenient working quantities, and so Metric measures have been rounded off to a more handy unit: 1 ounce (oz) = 25 grams (g) (28.5g is the exact conversion of 1 oz). The tables below show recommended equivalents:–

As a general rule 1 kilogram (kg) (1000 g) = about 2 pounds (lb) 3 oz (2.2 lb); 1 litre (1000 millilitres (ml) = about 1¾ pints (1.75 pints). However, in some recipes a more exact conversion has been used to maintain the balance between ingredients.

Notes for American Users
In America the American measuring cup is used in conjunction with the American pint – 16 fluid oz (fl oz). Also in this book, remember that the tablespoon measure used in these recipes differs from the American tablespoon, e.g.:
1 British standard tablespoon holds 17.7 ml
1 American tablespoon holds 14.8 ml.

Notes for Australian Users
Ingredients are given in Metric/Imperial/US cup/avoirdupois measures. In Australia the American 8 oz measuring cup is used in conjunction with the Imperial pint – 20 fluid ounces (fl oz). Also in this book, remember that the tablespoon measure used in these recipes differs from the Australian tablespoon, e.g.:
1 British standard tablespoon holds 17.7 ml
1 Australian tablespoon holds 20 ml. However 1 teaspoon holds 5 ml in both systems.

Remember: follow only one set of quantities for any single recipe, as

Metric/Imperial/US measures are not interchangeable.

WEIGHT

Metric	Imperial
15g	½oz
20g	¾oz
25g	1oz
40g	1½oz
50g	2oz
75g	3oz
100g	4oz (¼lb)
150g	5oz
175g	6oz
200g	7oz
225g	8oz (½lb)
250g	9oz
(¼kg)	
275g	10oz
300g	11oz
350g	12oz (¾lb)
375g	13oz
400g	14oz
425g	15oz
450g	16oz (1lb)
900-1000g	2lb
(1kg)	
1½kg	3lb
2kg	4lb
2½kg	5lb
3kg	6lb
3½kg	7lb
4kg	8lb

VOLUME

Metric	Imperial	US Cup
50ml	2floz	¼
75ml	2½floz	⅓
	3floz	⅜
100ml	4floz	½
150ml	5floz (¼ pint)	⅝
200ml	6floz	¾
	7floz	⅞
225ml	8floz	1
275ml	9floz	1⅛
300ml	10floz (½ pint)	1¼
	11floz	1⅜
	12floz	1½
400ml	14floz	1¾
	16floz	2 = 1 pint (US)
½ litre		
(500-600 ml see recipe)	20floz (1 pint)	2½
750ml	1¼ pints	3
(¾ litre)		
900ml	1½ pints	–
1 litre	1¾ pints	–

BAR MEASURES

Dash	4-6 drops
Teaspoon	⅙floz
Tablespoon	½floz

Pony/liqueur glass	1floz
Jigger	1½floz
Wineglass	4floz
Cup	8floz

LINEAR MEASURE

Metric	Imperial
3mm	⅛in
5mm	¼in
1cm	½in
2.5cm	1in
4cm	1½in
5cm	2in
6.5cm	2½in
7.5cm	3in
10cm	4in
12.5cm	5in
15cm	6in
18cm	7in
20cm	8in
23cm	9in
25cm	10in
30cm	12in (1ft)
35cm	14in
38cm	15in
45cm	18in
60cm	24in
92cm	36in

Equivalent Oven Temperatures

°C	°F	Gas Mark
110	225	¼
130	250	½
140	275	1
150	300	2
170	325	3
180	350	4
190	375	5
200	400	6
220	425	7
230	450	8
240	475	9

SPOONS
(level unless otherwise stated)

Metric	Imperial
1.25ml	¼ teasp.
2.5ml	½ teasp.
5ml	1 teasp.
15ml	1 tablesp.
30ml	2 tablesp. (1floz)

3 teasp.	1 tablesp.
2 tablesp.	1 fl oz
16 tablesp. (US)	1 cup (US)

Key to Symbols

This symbol indicates the average cost of each recipe (it does not allow for seasonal or regional changes in prices)

Inexpensive 🪙   🪙🪙 Expensive

This symbol indicates the degree of difficulty in the preparation and cooking of each recipe

Easy ☆   ☆☆ More difficult

This symbol indicates what time is involved in the preparation and cooking of each recipe

⧗   ⧗⧗   ⧗⧗⧗

Less than 1 hour   1-3 hours   Over 3 hours

Soups

Clear soups, like consommé, are light on the palate and ideal for formal dinner parties. Hearty soups – broths, purées and brews packed with chunks of meat, fish, rice, pasta or vegetables – can easily be meals in themselves. Creamy soups, thickened by the addition of cream, egg yolk or flour, demand greater care in their making

Stocks

A full-bodied flavoursome stock is the basis of so many good dishes but especially of soups – even packet and canned soups can be pepped up and enriched by stock – sauces, gravies and many casserole dishes.

Most of us use ready-made stock preparations like the cubes just to save time, but they are often highly seasoned and very salty, so exercise care when adding seasonings. But if you take the trouble to make your own stock, you'll get a lot more satisfaction from a dish – and a tastier one as well.

There's an economic stock, largely using whatever is to hand, a white or chicken base for light-coloured soups and sauces, a brown base for consommé, dark soups, sauces and gravy, and a fish base.

A really concentrated bone stock sets as a firm jelly (gelatin) when cold, and slow and lengthy cooking is the only way to concentrate the flavours.

Unlike soups to which almost anything can be added, stock must be clear – vital when making consommé or aspic (savoury gelatin) – so avoid using starchy foods like rice and potatoes, or thickened liquids, which will turn it cloudy; and leave out strongly-flavoured vegetables like turnip and cabbage, as well as mutton bones which will give a bitter taste.

Make as large a pan of stock as possible (a pressure cooker will save time and fuel) and, if not using at once, keep stock in the fridge for a couple of days – otherwise boil up daily. Fish stock, however, should always be used the same day.

Household Stock

1 kg (2 lb) raw or cooked meat bones, chopped
1 onion
1 carrot
1 stalk celery, optional
2 litres (3½ pints) (8¾ cups) cold water
1 bouquet garni
5 ml (1 teaspoon) salt
6 peppercorns

1 Wash the bones. Peel, wash and roughly chop the onion and carrot; wash and chop the celery.

2 Put the bones in a large stewpan, add the water, bring to the boil and remove any scum that rises to the surface.

3 Add the chopped vegetables, bouquet garni and seasonings to the pan. Reduce the heat and simmer, with the pan lid on, for about 4 hours.

4 Strain the stock and then leave to cool. When cold remove the fat from the surface.

Makes about 1½ litres (2½ pints) (6¼ cups)

Tip: additions to this stock can include tomato concentrate (paste), meat trimmings and leftovers (but not liver), bacon rinds and cooked ham bones.

Brown Stock

1 kg (2 lb) raw meat bones (beef, marrowbone or knuckle of veal), chopped
½ kg (1 lb) lean stewing beef
2 onions
2 carrots
1 stalk celery
2 litres (3½ pints) (8¾ cups) cold water
1 bouquet garni
5 ml (1 teaspoon) salt
6 peppercorns

1 Wash the bones and meat and dry on absorbent paper. Cut the meat into 3 cm (about 1 in) cubes.

2 Peel, wash and chop the onions and carrots; wash and chop the celery.

3 Put the chopped bones, cubes of beef and the chopped onion in a roasting pan and bake in a moderate oven (180°C, 350°F, gas 4) until well browned.

4 Strain off any fat in the pan, then transfer the bones, beef and onion to a large stewpan. Add the water, sliced carrots and celery, bouquet garni and seasonings. Bring to the boil, remove any scum, reduce the heat, cover the pan, and simmer 5 hours.

5 Strain the stock and then leave to cool. When cold remove the fat from the surface.

Makes about 1½ litres (2½ pints) (6¼ cups)

White Stock

1 kg (2 lb) raw knuckle of veal, chopped or stewing veal
2.3 litres (4 pints) (10 cups) cold water
2.5 ml (½ teaspoon) lemon juice
1 onion
1 carrot
1 bouquet garni
5 ml (1 teaspoon) salt
6 peppercorns

1 Wash the veal bones, then put them in a large stewpan with the water and lemon juice. Bring to the boil and skim off any scum that rises to the surface.

2 Meanwhile peel, wash and slice the onion and carrot.

3 Add the sliced vegetables, bouquet garni, salt and peppercorns to the pan of bones, bring back to the boil, then reduce the heat and simmer, with the lid on, for about 5 hours.

4 Strain the stock and then leave to cool. When cold remove the fat from the surface.

Makes about 1½ litres (2½ pints) (6¼ cups)

Chicken Stock

1-2 raw or cooked chicken
   carcasses and bones
225 g (½ lb) chicken giblets,
   excluding the liver
2 litres (3½ pints) (8¾ cups) cold
   water
2 onions
2 carrots
1 bouquet garni
5 ml (1 teaspoon) salt
6 peppercorns

1 Wash the chicken carcasses, bones and giblets. Put them in a large stewpan, add the water, bring to the boil and remove any scum that rises to the surface.

2 Meanwhile peel, wash and slice the onions and carrots.

3 Add the sliced vegetables and seasonings to the pan, bring back to the boil, then reduce the heat and simmer, with the lid on, for about 3 hours.

4 Strain the stock and then leave to cool. When cold remove the fat from the surface.

Makes about 1½ litres (2½ pints) (6¼ cups)

Variation: to make turkey or game stock, substitute the appropriate carcasses, giblets and feet, if used, for the chicken ingredients.

Fish Stock

1 kg (2 lb) fresh fish heads, or fish
   bones and trimmings
1 carrot, optional
1 onion
1½ litres (2½ pints) (6 cups) cold
   water, or half and half mixture
   of water and dry white wine
5 ml (1 teaspoon) salt
4 peppercorns
1 bouquet garni

1 Wash the fish heads or bones and trimmings well. Peel and cut up the carrot, if used, and the onion.

2 Put the fish pieces in a large pan, add the water, bring to the boil and skim the surface. Add the vegetables, salt, peppercorns and bouquet garni to the pan, bring back to the boil and cover. Reduce the heat and simmer slowly for about 40 minutes when the stock should be reduced.

3 Strain the stock through clean muslin (cheesecloth) or a fine hair sieve (strainer), cover and cool; refrigerate until required.

Makes about 1 litre (1¾ pints) (4½ cups)

Tip: fish stock should always be used the same day it is made.

Stock, other than a fish one, can be frozen up to 6 months. Strain it, cool and skim off any fat. Boiling stock down to one-third its volume concentrates it, and it can then be frozen as single cubes in ice trays and diluted with water for use.

Bouquet Garni

Many recipes call for the use of a bouquet garni, the French name for a small bunch of herbs, either fresh or dried, which is used to flavour dishes. The traditional bouquet garni is made up of a bay leaf, a sprig or two of parsley and thyme, and a few peppercorns, all tied in a small piece of muslin (cheesecloth).

It doesn't matter too much which herbs are used so long as they are aromatic, so you can experiment with different mixtures, incorporating herbs like chervil, basil, rosemary and tarragon.

Ready-made bouquet garnis in muslin (cheesecloth) or paper sachets are available, but the paper ones tend to disintegrate with long cooking.

Hearty Soups

Mulligatawny

Created in the days of the British in India, this soup is basically a rich meat stock flavoured with curry, and can be made with any meat.

500 g (1 lb) lean breast of lamb
1 large onion
1 medium carrot
1 small green tart apple
30 ml (2 tablespoons) oil
15 ml (1 tablespoon) curry
   powder
salt and pepper
15 g (½ oz) (2 tablespoons) flour
1¼ litres (2½ pints) (6 cups) brown
   stock
200 ml (6 fl oz) (¾ cup) milk
5 ml (1 teaspoon) arrowroot
15 ml (1 tablespoon) cold water
5 ml (1 teaspoon) lemon juice

1 Wipe and trim lamb of excess fat; cut into 1-cm (½-in) wide strips. Peel and slice the onion and carrot; peel, core and slice the apple.

2 Heat the oil in a large pan. When hot brown the lamb all over. Take out and add the sliced vegetables and apple and cook, stirring, for about 5 minutes. Stir in the curry powder and cook for a further 2 minutes, then blend in the flour. Add the stock, bring to the boil and return the meat to the pan. Cover and simmer gently for about 1½ hours.

3 Take out the meat and any bones. Rub the liquid through a sieve (strainer) or purée in a blender. Return the purée to a clean pan. Stir in the milk and reheat but do not boil. Blend the arrowroot with the cold water, stir into the soup and heat nearly to boiling point till thick. Check the seasoning and serve.

Serves 6

Beef and Carrot Soup

1 small onion
450 g (1 lb) carrots
1 medium potato
40 g (1½ oz) (3 tablespoons) butter
2.5 ml (½ teaspoon) salt
freshly ground (milled) black
  pepper
2.5 ml (½ teaspoon) sugar
700 ml (1¼ pints) (3 cups) brown
  stock
15 ml (1 tablespoon) chopped
  parsley
5 ml (1 teaspoon) chopped
  chervil or marjoram

1 Peel and chop the onion; peel and dice the carrots and potato.

2 Melt the butter in a heavy saucepan and add the carrots, onion and potato. Add the salt, pepper and sugar. Cover the pan and cook over a low heat for 15 minutes.

3 Add the stock and bring to the boil. Lower the heat, cover the pan and cook for a further 15 minutes. Rub the soup through a sieve (strainer) or purée in a blender.

4 Reheat until hot, then serve, sprinkling over the chopped herbs.

Serves 4

Fresh Pea Soup

1 round (Boston) lettuce
100 g (¼ lb) (½ cup) butter or
  margarine
500 g (1 lb) shelled fresh peas
2.5 ml (½ teaspoon) salt
5 ml (1 teaspoon) sugar
1 litre (good 1½ pints) (4 cups)
  chicken stock
freshly ground (milled) black
  pepper

1 Wash the lettuce, drain well, tear the leaves into pieces.

2 Heat the butter or margarine in a saucepan, add the lettuce pieces, shelled peas, salt and sugar. Cover the pan, reduce the heat and let the vegetables cook gently over low heat for about 10 minutes. Stir in the stock cover and simmer 10 minutes more or until the peas are tender.

3 Purée the soup by rubbing through a sieve (strainer) or work in a blender. Return the pea purée to a clean saucepan, add black pepper to taste and heat again until just simmering. Serve at once.

Serves 4

Minestrone

1 carrot
4 potatoes
1 small white cabbage
½ head celery
100 g (¼ lb) (1 cup) shelled
  garden peas
5 tomatoes
1 clove garlic
175 g (6 oz) bacon
2 onions
30 ml (2 tablespoons) oil
2 litres (3¼ pints) (8 cups) white or
  brown stock
10-15 g (2-3 tablespoons) chopped
  mixed herbs (as available)
salt and pepper
100 g (¼ lb) macaroni
grated Parmesan cheese

1 Peel and dice the carrots and potatoes; trim and cut up the cabbage and celery in small pieces. Wash them well. Skin the tomatoes, then cut them in half and scoop out the seeds. Cut the tomato pulp into small cubes. Peel and crush the garlic. Cut the bacon into strips. Peel and chop the onions.

2 Heat the oil in a large pan and when hot fry the bacon, onion, carrots, cabbage, celery and tomatoes. Add the stock with the crushed garlic, chopped mixed herbs and salt and pepper to taste. Cover and cook for 1 hour over a low heat. Then add the diced potato and the peas and continue cooking for a further 15 minutes.

3 During this time, cook the macaroni in a pan of boiling salted water for about 15 minutes or until just tender. Drain and set aside.

4 When the soup is cooked, add the macaroni and serve immediately with grated Parmesan cheese separately.

Serves 6

Italian Egg Soup

Zuppa Pavese is the Italian name for this very nourishing soup. Instead of poaching the eggs in the stock as we do here, the eggs may be broken into the individual bowls and the boiling stock then poured over. However the eggs tend not to be cooked sufficiently this way. It is such a substantial soup that only a light main course should follow.

500 ml (1 pint) (2½ cups) brown
  stock
500 ml (1 pint) (2½ cups) chicken
  stock
4 slices sandwich loaf
8 very fresh eggs
30 ml (2 tablespoons) oil
60 ml (4 tablespoons) grated
  Parmesan cheese
30 ml (2 tablespoons) chopped
  mixed herbs

1 Mix the 2 stocks together in a large pan and put on a low heat. Cut the slices of bread into small cubes.

2 Break the eggs, one by one, into a saucer and slide them carefully down the side of the pan into the stock. Draw the white back onto the yolk with a fork to get neat, poached eggs.

3 Whilst the eggs are poaching, heat the oil in a frying pan (skillet) and fry the cubes of bread in it. Then drain them.

4 Put 2 poached eggs into each soup bowl. Pour in the stock and divide the cubes of bread, the Parmesan and the mixed herbs between each; serve.

Serves 4

Minestrone is one of Italy's best known soups and easily a meal in itself. Regional variations are many, ranging from the addition of fresh basil and pork to substituting a goat's milk cheese for Parmesan

1 Ingredients: leeks, carrots, turnips, celery, peas, beans, bacon, potatoes, cabbage, butter **2** Peel the carrots and turnips, trim the leeks and dice **3** Sof-

ten the vegetables in the butter **4** Moisten with water or stock. Add the bacon and shredded cabbage; season with salt and pepper and bring to the

boil **5** String and chop the beans **6** Peel and dice the potatoes; place in a bowl of cold water to remove excess starch **7** Drain the potatoes, then add all the vegetables to the pan **8** Take out the bacon and dice; put in tureen **9** Serve the soup, with the croûtons and grated cheese separately.

Farmhouse Soup

2 carrots
2 turnips
white portion of 2 leeks
2 stalks celery
½ green cabbage
50 g (2 oz) (4 tablespoons) butter
500 g (1 lb) lightly salted bacon, in one piece
2 litres (3½ pints) (9 cups) white or chicken stock
salt and pepper
150 g (5 oz) (1¼ cups) runner (snap) beans
2 potatoes
150 g (5 oz) (1¼ cups) shelled peas
75 g (3 oz) (¾ cup) grated Gruyère cheese

1 Peel the carrots and turnips, and wash them. Wash the whites of the leeks and the celery. Cut them all into small cubes. Wash and cut the cabbage into thin strips.

2 Melt the butter in a large pan. Put in the prepared vegetables and soften on low heat for 10 minutes, stirring from time to time.

3 Wash the bacon in cold water, then put it into a saucepan. Cover with cold water, bring to the boil and simmer for 10 minutes on a low heat. Then drain and rinse in cold water.

4 Add the stock to the vegetables, then add the bacon, cabbage and salt and pepper. Bring to the boil, then reduce the heat, cover and simmer very gently for about 1¼ hours.

5 Remove the 'strings' from the beans, wash them and cut into pieces about 4 cm (1½ in) in length. Peel the potatoes. Wash and cut them into tiny cubes. Cover with water and leave to soak.

6 About 20 minutes before the end of the cooking time, drain the potatoes. Add them to the soup with the peas and the green beans. Leave to finish cooking.

7 Heat a soup tureen. Put the grated Gruyère cheese into a bowl. Drain the bacon, cut into cubes and put into the tureen.

Pour on the rest of the soup. Serve the soup with croûtons and the Gruyère cheese served separately.

Serves 4

Rose-coloured Cauliflower Soup

1 small cauliflower
3 potatoes
small bunch chervil
1.3 litres (2¼ pints) (5½ cups) salted water
30 ml (2 tablespoons) tomato concentrate (paste)
salt and pepper
60 ml (4 tablespoons) rice flour
½ litre (scant 1 pint) (2¼ cups) milk
25 g (1 oz) (2 tablespoons) butter

1 Wash the cauliflower and divide it into small florets. Peel and dice the potatoes.

2 Bring the salted water to the boil. Add the cauliflower and diced potatoes to the water and boil gently for 30 minutes. Cool a little, then rub through a sieve (strainer) or purée in a blender.

3 Return the purée to the pan and heat, mixing in the tomato concentrate (paste) and seasoning with salt and pepper.

4 Mix the rice flour to a smooth paste with a little of the milk and then mix in the rest. Add to the soup. Cook for 10 minutes more over a low heat, stirring constantly. Wash, dry and chop the chervil.

5 Put the butter in a heated tureen, pour over the soup, sprinkle over the chervil and serve.

Serves 6

Rose-coloured Cauliflower Soup

Belgian Leek Soup — nourishing and one of the simplest soups

Belgian Leek Soup

40 g (1½ oz) (3 tablespoons) butter
225 g (½ lb) leeks, or 4 onions
450 g (1 lb) potatoes
1½ litres (2½ pints) (6 cups) beef stock
5 ml (1 teaspoon) salt
100 ml (4 fl oz) (½ cup) single cream or milk
4-6 slices toasted French bread

1 Trim and wash the leeks well, then slice or peel and slice the onions. Peel and dice the potatoes.

2 Heat the butter in a large pan, add the prepared leeks or onions and fry gently for 3 minutes. Add the diced potatoes, beef stock and salt, and bring to the boil. Cover with the lid, reduce the heat and simmer for 40 minutes, stirring occasionally.

3 When ready to serve, stir in the cream or milk. Place a slice of toasted bread in each soup bowl and pour over the hot soup.

Serves 4 -6

Normandy Soup

giblets of 2 chickens
100 g (¼ lb) (½ cup) butter
salt and pepper
2 litres (3½ pints) (8¾ cups) white
  or chicken stock
1 small bouquet garni
225 g (½ lb) runner (snap) beans
2 courgettes (zucchini)
4 small carrots
2 turnips
3 potatoes
1 small stalk celery
white part of 2 leeks
1 onion
2 tomatoes
few lettuce leaves
250 ml (8 fl oz) (1 cup) single
  (light) cream

1 Put the washed giblets into cold water, bring to the boil and drain. Heat 50 g (2 oz) (4 tablespoons) butter in a stewpan and lightly fry the giblets in it. Add the salt, pepper, stock and bouquet garni. Bring to the boil, cover with the lid, reduce the heat and simmer for 20 minutes.

2 During this time, remove the 'strings' from the beans and cut them into small pieces. Peel the courgettes (zucchini), the carrots, the turnips and the potatoes, and cut them into small dice. Wash the celery and chop it into tiny slices. Wash and slice the white part of the leeks. Peel and chop the onion.

3 Skin and quarter the tomatoes, remove pips, then cut the pulp into small pieces. Wash and dry the lettuce and shred.

4 Melt the rest of the butter in a saucepan and cook all the vegetables in it until they begin to colour. When the giblets have cooked for 20 minutes, add the vegetables to them and continue simmering for a further hour. Then heat the soup tureen.

5 Remove the bouquet garni. Put the cream into the hot tureen, whisk in the soup and serve.

Serves 6

Tip: During the winter months the runner (snap) beans can be replaced by soaked, dried haricot (navy) beans, and the courgettes (zucchini) left out, or frozen vegetables can be used.

Portuguese Lobster Soup

2 large onions
2 large carrots
3 medium potatoes
3 cloves garlic
1 litre (2 pints) (5 cups) water
225 ml (8 fl oz) (1 cup) dry
  white wine
5 ml (1 teaspoon) salt
12 peppercorns
1 kg (2 lb) live lobster
30 ml (2 tablespoons) oil
225 ml (8 oz) (1 cup) tomato
  concentrate (paste)
175 g (6 oz) (¾ cup) long
  grain rice
5 g (1 tablespoon) finely
  chopped parsley
2.5 ml (½ teaspoon) ground
  (powdered) coriander
freshly ground (milled) black
  pepper
30 ml (2 tablespoons) brandy

1 Peel and finely chop the onions and carrots; peel and dice the potatoes; peel and crush the garlic cloves.

2 Put the water, white wine, half the chopped onions and carrots, the potatoes, salt and peppercorns in a large saucepan and bring to the boil. Reduce the heat and simmer for 30 minutes. Then put in the lobster and simmer again for about 30 minutes or until the lobster is cooked.

3 Heat the oil in another large saucepan until hot; add the remaining chopped onions and carrots and fry until lightly browned. Stir in the tomato concentrate (paste) and draw the pan off the heat.

4 Take out the cooked lobster, strain the cooking liquor and reserve. Split the lobster in half lengthways, crack the claws and take out the meat from the tail shell and the claws; cut it into 1-cm (½-in) pieces. Break the lobster shell into pieces (use either a hammer or nut crackers), put them into a pan with the reserved cooking liquor and simmer for 20 minutes.

5 Strain the liquor again and stir into the tomato mixture. Add the raw rice, parsley, coriander, pepper and garlic and simmer for 30 minutes. Stir in the lobster meat pieces and brandy and simmer for another 5 minutes. Check the seasoning and serve at once.

Serves 8-10

Traditional Meatball Soup

1.4 litres (2½ pints) (6 cups)
  brown stock
100 g (¼ lb) (good ½ cup) minced
  (ground) beef
2.5 ml (½ teaspoon) salt
freshly ground (milled) black
  pepper
15 g (3 tablespoons) finely
  chopped parsley
30 ml (2 tablespoons) oil
5 ml (1 teaspoon) paprika
100 g (¼ lb) (½ cup) long grain rice
2 cloves garlic
50 ml (2 fl oz) (¼ cup) vinegar

1 Put the stock into a large pan and bring to simmering point. Mix the beef with the salt, pepper and 10 g (2 tablespoons) of the chopped parsley. Form into small balls about 2.5 cm (1 in) in diameter.

2 Add the meat balls to the stock and simmer 15 minutes.

3 Heat the oil in a small pan, stir in the paprika and cook for 2 minutes. Stir this into the soup.

4 Add the rice to the soup, cover the pan and simmer 15 minutes or until the rice is tender. Stir in the rest of the parsley, garlic and vinegar. Serve at once.

Serves 6

Normandy Soup — a hearty broth flavoured with chicken

Look 'n Cook French Onion Soup

1 Ingredients: onions, butter, flour, stock, wine, bread, eggs, cheese, salt and pepper **2** Peel and chop onions **3** Brown onions in half the butter

4 Stir in the flour till it browns **5** Add liquid, garlic, salt and pepper, then simmer **6** Toast the slices of bread **7** Poach the eggs and set aside in a bowl of

warm water till required **8** When the soup is cooked, divide between individual flameproof bowls **9** Place a poached egg in each soup bowl

10 Butter the toasted slices of bread and sprinkle with grated cheese **11** Put a slice of bread in each bowl **12** Brown the cheese under a hot grill (broiler)

French Onion Soup

225 g (½ lb) onions
1 clove garlic
80 g (3 oz) (⅓ cup) butter
30 ml (2 tablespoons) flour
¾ litre (1¼ pints) (3¼ cups) stock
¼ litre (8 fl oz) (1 cup) dry white
  wine
salt and pepper
4 large slices white bread
75 g (scant ¼ lb) (scant 1 cup)
  grated cheese
60 ml (4 tablespoons) white
  vinegar
4 eggs

1 Peel and chop the onions. Peel and crush the garlic.

2 Melt half the butter in a sauté pan. Add the onions and cook them. When they are golden, add the flour and stir with a wooden spoon until the flour browns.

3 Add the stock and the wine, mixing in well. Add the crushed garlic. Cook for about 40 minutes. Adjust the seasoning without stinting the pepper.

4 Meanwhile cut the bread into rounds. Toast them or dry in a low oven.

5 Boil some water in a saucepan. Add the vinegar. Break the eggs one by one into a cup, put each carefully into the pan and let them poach just enough to allow them to be removed without breaking. Keep them warm in a dish containing warm water.

6 When the soup is ready, divide it between flameproof bowls.

7 Place a poached egg in each dish. Butter the slices of bread and sprinkle with grated cheese. Put a slice of bread in each bowl and brown quickly under a hot grill (broiler) (the eggs must not continue to cook) under the grill (broiler). Serve piping hot.

Serves 4

Tip: This is a good dish for a small dinner party; if preferred, the poached eggs can be omitted from the soup.

French Onion Soup

Red Pepper and Tomato Soup

(Cover photograph)

1 onion
2 medium red peppers
100 g (¼ lb) tomatoes
1 large leek
50 g (2 oz) (4 tablespoons) butter
5 g (1 tablespoon) finely
  chopped parsley
1 litre (2 pints) (5 cups)
  chicken stock
salt and pepper
25 g (1 oz) (4 tablespoons) flour

1 Peel and chop the onion. Cut the red pepper in half, remove the seeds and white membrane and chop. Skin and cut the tomatoes in half, scoop out the seeds and chop the pulp roughly. Trim the outer leaves of the leek and cut off the root; cut in half, wash well, then slice thinly.

2 Heat half the butter in a large pan, put in the onions, red pepper and leek and cook gently until the onions are soft and translucent. Add the chopped tomatoes and parsley and cook for about 2 minutes.

3 Pour in the stock, add salt and pepper, bring to the boil, cover the pan, reduce the heat and simmer for about 15 minutes or until the vegetables are tender.

4 Soften the remaining butter and, using a fork, blend with the flour to make kneaded butter, then stir this into the soup. Bring to the boil, stirring until the soup thickens. Serve at once.

Serves 6

This classic country hotpot of meat and vegetables in broth hails from France where it is called pot-au-feu. A two-in-one dish — serve the broth first, with toast, then follow with the beef and veg. Turn overleaf for the recipe and photo-strip guide for Hotpot Soup plus a variation using four different meats.

Look 'n Cook Hotpot Soup

1 Tie the beef with string so it holds its shape during cooking **2** Put the beef and bones in a large pot with the water **3** Peel and quarter the carrots and turnips; halve the leeks and celery **4** Add the vegetables, bouquet garni and seasonings and cook **5** and **6** Wrap up the marrowbone, add to pot and cook.

Hotpot Soup
(Pot-au-feu)

2 kg (4 lb) stewing beef, in
  one piece
1-2 beef bones, chopped into
  small chunks
3 litres (5¼ pints) (13 cups) water
1 bouquet garni
¾ kg (1½ lb) carrots
½ kg (1 lb) turnips
¾ kg (1½ lb) leeks
1 bunch celery
2 large onions
2 cloves garlic
4 cloves
1 large marrowbone, about
  10 cm (4 in) long

1 Tie the meat with thin string so it holds its shape during cooking. Place it in a large pot together with the beef bones. Add all the water except for 50 ml (2 fl oz) (¼ cup) and bring slowly to the boil, with the lid off.

2 Meanwhile, if using fresh herbs for the bouquet garni, tie them together. Peel the onions and garlic; stud the onion with the cloves.

3 Peel and quarter the carrots lengthways; peel and quarter the turnips. Trim and cut away the roots of the leeks, then cut in half and wash in several changes of water, fanning out the green stems, so all the dirt is removed. Trim the root end of the celery and discard the green leaves; then quarter and tie the pieces together with the leeks.

4 When the surface of the liquid is covered with scum, draw the pot off the heat; pour in the reserved water and skim at once. Return the pot to the heat, cover with a lid and simmer slowly for 1 hour. Then add the prepared vegetables, bouquet garni, garlic, onions, salt and pepper, and cook slowly for a further 1¾ hours.

5 Wrap the marrowbone in muslin (cheesecloth) or stockinette and tie with string; this will stop the marrow from slipping out of the bone. Put the wrapped bone in the pot 15 minutes before the end of cooking.

6 When the meat is cooked, take it out of the pot, remove the string, slice and place on a heated serving dish. Drain the vegetables, discarding the bouquet garni, and arrange round the meat; keep hot.

7 Slice the bread and toast on both sides. Meanwhile lift out and unwrap the marrowbone, scoop out the marrow, then spread on the hot toast.

8 Serve the broth separately with the toast, followed by the platter of meat and vegetables. Traditional accompaniments include gherkins (dill pickles), pickled onions, mustard and horseradish sauce.

Serves 6-8

Four-meat Hotpot Soup

1½ kg (3 lb) stewing beef
450 g (1 lb) salted belly of pork
1 game bird (pheasant,
    partridge, etc.), with its liver
1 knuckle of veal, with meat on
5 litres (8 pints) (20 cups) water
coarse salt
pepper
¾ kg (1½ lb) carrots
4 onions
3 cloves garlic
4 cloves
¾ kg (1½ lb) leeks
1 celeriac root
1-2 bulbs of fennel
1 bouquet garni

For the forcemeat roll:
225 g (½ lb) belly of pork
1 shallot
3 cloves garlic
225 g (½ lb) fresh white
    breadcrumbs
60 ml (4 tablespoons) brown
    stock
1 egg

1 Wipe the various meats and derind the belly pork. Tie the beef with string. Split the game bird in half and wash the liver. Put the water in a large pot, add a good handful of coarse salt and some pepper; put in the beef, bring to the boil, with the lid off, remove the scum from the surface, cover, reduce the heat and simmer for 1 hour.

2 Meanwhile peel the carrots, onions and garlic; stud the onions with the cloves. Trim and wash the leeks, celeriac root and fennel; cut them in quarters.

3 When the beef has cooked for 1 hour, add the knuckle of veal, the game bird and belly of pork. Bring to the boil again, skim the surface, cover and reduce the heat and cook for 1 hour longer.

4 Meanwhile prepare the forcemeat roll. Cut the belly of pork into tiny dice; peel and finely chop the shallot and remaining garlic. Chop the liver of the game bird. Put all the forcemeat ingredients in a mixing bowl, moisten with the stock and mix together well. Season well with salt and pepper.

5 Sprinkle a piece of muslin (cheesecloth) or stockinette with a little flour. Place the forcemeat in the centre, fold over the cloth and mould into a sausage shape. Tie the ends with string.

6 After 2 hours cooking, put the forcemeat roll into the pot, together with the prepared vegetables, garlic and bouquet garni and simmer for 1 hour longer.

7 Wrap the marrowbones in muslin (cheesecloth) or stockinette and tie securely; put in the pot about 15 minutes before the end of cooking.

8 Serve the Four-meat Hotpot as for Hotpot Soup (see previous page), with the broth served separately, the meats carved into portions on one platter, with the toasted slices of bread round, and the vegetables on another with slices of forcemeat round them.

Serves 6-8

Four-meat Hotpot Soup — a satisfying dish for family appetites

Cockie-Leekie

750 g (1½ lb) medium leeks
100 g (¼ lb) celery
100 g (¼ lb) carrot
1 kg (2 lb) chicken, oven ready
1½ litres (2½ pints) (6¼ cups) chicken stock
25 g (1 oz) (2 tablespoons) butter
salt and pepper
10 g (2 tablespoons) finely chopped parsley

1 Trim the outer leaves of the leeks to within 5 cm (2 in) of the white stems and cut away the roots. Split the leeks in half lengthways, wash them well, then cut into chunks. Wash and cut the celery into 1 cm (½ in) lengths; peel and slice the carrot.

2 Wipe the chicken and wash its giblets well. Put both into a large deep pan, add the stock and simmer for 1 hour or until the chicken is tender. Discard the giblets; take out the bird, remove the skin and take the meat off the bones. Leave the broth to cool, then chill and remove the fat from the surface.

3 Heat the butter in a large pan, put in the leeks, celery and carrot; add salt and pepper to taste. Cover the pan and cook gently until the leeks are soft but not coloured (about 10 minutes). Add the chicken broth and the pieces of chicken meat, increase the heat, cover the pan and simmer for about 15 minutes. Serve at once, garnished with chopped parsley.

Tip: This soup is improved by making the day before and chilling overnight; then remove the fat the next day and complete the recipe.

Serves 6-8

For this traditional Scottish soup, a chicken (cockie) is poached in stock, the meat taken off the bone, returned to the broth with leeks (leekie); celery and carrot may also be added to vary the flavour

Soup Garnishes

Bacon
Crumble crispy-fried rashers and sprinkle over soup.

Pasta
Either cook in the soup towards the end of cooking or cook separately and add to the hot soup.

Croûtes
Remove crusts from slices of French bread, spread with butter (flavoured if liked) or grated cheese on one side and bake until crisp and golden.

Croûtons
Remove crusts from slices of bread, cut into 5-10 mm ($\frac{1}{4}$-$\frac{1}{2}$ in) cubes and either fry in hot lard or oil until golden and crisp, or toast them.

Melba Toast
Remove crusts from 5 mm ($\frac{1}{4}$ in) thick slices of white bread. Toast until a pale brown, then cut through the middle of each to give extra-thin slices. Toast again, white sides up, until golden. Or bake the thinly-cut slices in the bottom of a very slow oven until very crisp and curled; then brown under grill (broiler).

Sippets
Remove crusts from slices of bread, cut into large triangles and bake in a slow oven till dry and very crisp.

Dumplings or Meatballs
Add either plain or flavoured ones to the soup towards the end of cooking and simmer for about 20 minutes.

Herbs and Green Stems
Sprinkle over soups finely chopped herbs, green celery leaves, chives or the green stems of spring onions (scallions), all either snipped with scissors or chopped.

Mushrooms
Thinly slice and gently fry in butter for 5 minutes until soft but not coloured. Sprinkle over just before serving.

Borsch

2 carrots
2 leeks
4 onions
2 cloves
750 g (1½ lb) raw beetroot
1 white cabbage
1 kg (2 lb) beef (chuck, bottom round or rump)
1 marrowbone
1 bouquet garni
1 fennel stalk or pinch ground (powdered) cumin
65 g (2¼ oz) (¼ cup) tomato concentrate (paste)
salt and pepper
500 g (1 lb) cooked garlic sausage
5 or 6 Russian or Polish pickled cucumbers
300 ml (10 fl oz) (1¼ cups) sour cream

1 Scrape the carrots and cut into small rounds. Clean and chop the leeks. Peel the onions, stud 1 whole onion with cloves and cut the other onions into very fine slices. Peel the beetroot and chop finely. Cut away the core and stalks, then shred the cabbage.

2 Bring a large saucepan, two-thirds filled with water, to the boil. Add the meat and the marrowbone, return to the boil and skim off the scum from the surface as it rises. Add the leeks, the carrots, the onions, the bouquet garni, beetroot, cabbage and fennel or cumin.

3 Thin the tomato concentrate (purée) with a few tablespoons of hot soup. Pour this back into the pan, season with salt and pepper and bring to the boil. Cover, reduce the heat and simmer for 2½ hours. Remove the meat and marrowbone from the pot, then chop the beef finely.

4 Slice the garlic sausage and the pickled cucumbers. Add the meat, the garlic sausage and the pickled cucumber to the soup. Cover and simmer for about 30 minutes. Heat a soup tureen.

5 Lift the bouquet garni and the clove-studded onion out of the soup. Pour the soup into the warmed tureen. Serve the cream in a sauce-boat, allowing a generous spoonful per serving.

Serves 4-6

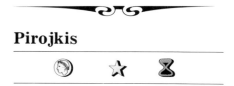

Pirojkis

For the pastry:
300 g (11 oz) (2¾ cups) flour
150 g (5 oz) (⅔ cup) butter
2 eggs plus 1 egg yolk, beaten
pinch salt

For the filling:
3 eggs
200 g (approx ½ lb) cream cheese
2 sprigs parsley
salt and pepper
grated (powdered) nutmeg
100 g (¼ lb) (½ cup) butter

1 To make the pastry: tip the flour onto a board or into a bowl and make a well in the centre. Cut up the butter. Break the eggs and put with the salt and butter into the well. Mix all together to form a firm and elastic dough. Roll this out with a rolling pin several times, folding between rollings.

2 Prepare the filling. Put 2 of the eggs set aside for the filling into a saucepan of cold water. Bring to the boil. Simmer gently for 10 minutes over a moderate heat so the shells do not break. Remove from the boiling water and cool in cold water: they will then be easier to shell.

3 Put the cream cheese into a bowl. Wash and chop the parsley. Add, with the salt, pepper and a little grated nutmeg, to the cream cheese.

4 Put the hard-boiled eggs through a mincer (grinder) and add to the cream cheese. Blend well together to form a smooth even mixture. Put the butter in a bowl and cream well before blending with the cream cheese-egg mixture.

5 Dust the board or the table work surface with flour. Roll out the pastry to a thickness of about

3 mm (⅛ in). Then cut out circles of 6.5-8 cm (2½-3 in) in diameter.

6 On one side of each circle put 30 g (2 tablespoons) of the filling and cover with the other half to form a turnover. Damp the edges and press together to seal. Preheat the oven to 200°C, 400°F, gas 6.

7 Brush the turnovers with the yolk to glaze them. Bake in the oven for 20 minutes. Serve hot as an accompaniment to Borsch.

All varieties of borsch (below), also spelt bortsch and borscht, contain root vegetables: the name comes from the old slavic word for beetroot. The classic accompaniment are pirojkis (also pirozhky and pirozhki — from the old word for feast) often filled with meat from the soup

Onion Soup with Blue Cheese

450 g (1 lb) onions
2 shallots
2 cloves garlic
100 g (¼ lb) (½ cup) butter
30 ml (2 tablespoons) oil
1½ litre (2½ pints) (6¼ cups)
  brown stock
6 rounds French bread
75 g (scant ¼ lb) blue cheese
30 ml (2 tablespoons) brandy
75 g (3 oz) (¾ cup) grated
  cheese
100 g (¼ lb) (1¼ cups) crushed
  walnut kernels
salt and pepper

1 Peel and chop the onions and the shallots; peel and crush the garlic.

2 Heat one-third of the butter and the oil in a sauté pan. Add the chopped onions and shallots and let them brown while stirring with a wooden spoon.

3 When the onions and the shallots are golden, add the stock. Bring to the boil and simmer for 40 minutes.

4 Twenty minutes before it is ready, heat the oven to 200°C, 400°F, gas 6. Put the bread in it to dry. Mash the blue cheese and most of the rest of the butter in a bowl with a fork, reserving a little butter for the bread. Moisten this mixture with the brandy. Heat the grill (broiler).

5 Butter the bread. Spread over the grated cheese.

6 Add the softened blue cheese and the crushed walnuts to the soup. Let it boil for about 3 minutes.

7 Rub the crushed garlic over the inside surface of an earthenware bowl. Pour the soup into it. Adjust the seasoning and be very generous with the pepper.

8 Put the slices of bread on top of the soup and brown quickly under the grill (broiler). Serve piping hot.

Serves 6

Cheesy Mushroom Soup

400 g (scant 1 lb) mushrooms
juice ½ lemon
50 g (2 oz) (¼ cup) butter
salt and pepper
few slices stale bread
1 litre (1¾ pints) (4½ cups) chicken
  stock
100 ml (4 fl oz) (½ cup) port
1 lean slice cooked ham
100 g (¼ lb) (1 cup) grated
  cheese

1 Cut off the ends of the mushroom stalks. Wash the mushrooms carefully without soaking them, then slice them finely. Sprinkle the mushrooms with the lemon juice.

2 Melt the butter in a saucepan and when it is hot, fry the mushrooms carefully for 10 minutes. Season with salt and pepper.

3 Heat the grill (broiler) and toast the bread on both sides.

4 Add the chicken stock and the port to the fried mushrooms. Bring to the boil and cook for 5 minutes. Chop the ham and add it at the end of the 5 minutes.

5 Pour the very hot soup into individual flameproof bowls. Arrange the slices of toast on the surface of the soup and sprinkle generously with the grated cheese. Grill (broil) until the cheese browns. Serve the soup at once.

Serves 4

Crushed walnuts and blue cheese add a delicious zest to onion soup. Top with cheesy croutes to serve.

Corn Chowder

100 g (¼ lb) salt pork
1 onion
2 medium potatoes
2 sticks celery
1 red pepper
25 g (1 oz) (2 tablespoons) butter
½ litre (1 pint) (2½ cups) white stock or water
1 bay leaf (imported)
salt and pepper to taste
15 g (½ oz) (2 tablespoons) flour
½ litre (1 pint) (2½ cups) milk
450 g (1 lb) (2 cups) corn kernels, fresh, canned or frozen and thawed
5 g (1 tablespoon) finely chopped parsley

1 Dice the salt pork, put in a pan with cold water to cover and blanch by bringing to the boil and boiling for about 1 minute; then drain and set aside. Peel and chop the onion; peel and dice the potatoes; chop the celery; cut the pepper in half, remove the seeds and membrane and chop.

2 Heat the butter in a large pan, then put in the diced salt pork and fry till it starts to brown. Add the celery and onion and cook for 1 minute. Add the diced potatoes and red pepper, the white stock or water, the bay leaf and salt and pepper, bring to the boil, cover, reduce the heat and simmer for 15 minutes or until the potatoes are almost tender.

3 Blend the flour to a paste with a little of the cold milk. Stir this into the hot soup. Add the remaining milk and the corn kernels, bring to the boil to thicken, then cover, reduce the heat and simmer for about 10 minutes or until the corn is tender. Remove the bay leaf. Check for seasoning, sprinkle with parsley and serve.

Serves 6

Chowders are thick fish, meat or vegetable soups cum stews from America; the most famous is New England Clam Chowder shown right

New England Clam Chowder

450 g (1 lb) (1 quart) fresh soft shell steamer clams or canned minced clams
3 small potatoes
3 slices bacon
1 medium onion
700 ml (1¼ pints) (3 cups) milk
225 ml (8 fl oz) (1 cup) double (heavy) cream
15 g (½ oz) (1 tablespoon) butter
salt if necessary
freshly ground (milled) black pepper

1 Scrub the fresh clams and soak in three changes of cold water to remove any sand. Steam them over 200 ml (scant ½ pint) (1 cup) water for 8 minutes until they open. Discard the shells and chop the clams into small pieces.

Strain the broth through muslin (cheesecloth) to remove the sand.

2 Peel and dice the potatoes; derind and cut the bacon into small pieces. Peel and finely chop the onion. Boil the potatoes in salted water for 15 minutes.

3 Fry the bacon in a saucepan until 15 ml (1 tablespoon) of fat has run from it. Remove the bacon pieces and set aside, then fry the onion in the fat for 5 minutes. Add the strained clam broth or the liquid from the canned clams. Simmer for 5 minutes. Add the chopped clams, milk, cream, butter and potatoes. Season with salt and simmer for 5 minutes or until the potatoes are tender.

4 Ladle the chowder into individual bowls and garnish each with a sprinkling of black pepper and the bacon pieces.

Serves 6

Sausage and Cabbage Soup

450 g (1 lb) cabbage
1 clove garlic
25 g (1 oz) (2 tablespoons) butter
  or margarine
25 g (1 oz) (2 tablespoons) flour
1 litre (2 pints) (5 cups) chicken
  stock
salt and pepper
6-8 frankfurters

1 Cut away the stalks and core from the cabbage; shred finely. Peel and crush the garlic. Heat the fat in a pan and soften the cabbage and garlic in it – about 10 minutes.

2 Mix in the flour, then gradually blend in the stock, stirring all the time. Bring to the boil, season with salt and pepper, reduce the heat, cover and simmer 1 hour.

3 Meanwhile slice the frankfurters thinly. When the soup is ready, skim any fat off the surface, add the sliced frankfurters, leave 5 minutes to heat through and serve.

Serves 4-6

Lentil Soup

500 g (1 lb) (scant 3 cups) lentils
1 onion
1 carrot
200 g ($\frac{1}{2}$ lb) smoked bacon
100 g ($\frac{1}{4}$ lb) ($\frac{1}{2}$ cup) butter or
  margarine
1 bouquet garni
1 litre (1$\frac{3}{4}$ pints) (4$\frac{1}{4}$ cups) chicken
  stock
salt and pepper

1 Wash the lentils and put them in a pan. Cover them with cold water and bring to the boil. Boil for 1 minute, then drain the lentils. Wash the pan.

2 Peel and chop the onion and the carrot. Cut the bacon into strips.

3 Melt half the butter in the rinsed-out pan and add the bacon, onion and carrot. Fry carefully for 10 minutes, then add the lentils, bouquet garni, salt and pepper. Pour in the stock, bring to the boil, then reduce the heat, cover and simmer for about 50 minutes or until the lentils are soft.

4 When the soup is cooked, take out the bouquet garni and purée the soup in a blender or work through a sieve (strainer) or food mill. When smooth, pour into a pan and then reheat.

5 Just before serving, heat up a soup tureen. Pour the hot soup into it. Cut the rest of the butter into small pieces. Add them to the soup and mix in well. Serve very hot, with bread croûtons, lightly rubbed with garlic and fried in butter.

Serves 4

Tomato and Onion Soup

200 g ($\frac{1}{2}$ lb) medium onions
1 large clove garlic
400 g (scant 1 lb) ripe tomatoes
1 small celery heart
1$\frac{1}{2}$ litres (2$\frac{1}{2}$ pints) (3$\frac{3}{4}$ cups) stock
  (bouillon)
45 ml (3 tablespoons) olive oil
salt and freshly ground pepper
few sprigs chervil
50 g (2 oz) ($\frac{1}{2}$ cup) grated cheese

1 Peel the onions and garlic. Slice the onions finely. Chop the garlic. Skin the tomatoes, then quarter and remove the pips. Trim and chop the celery heart.

2 Bring the stock to the boil. Heat the oil in a pan. Add the onion rings and fry until golden. Add the tomatoes and garlic and cook until soft, stirring with a wooden spoon. Add the celery, and the hot stock. Season to taste.

3 Cook the onion soup slowly with the lid on for about 30 minutes.

4 Rinse, drain and finely chop the chervil. Preheat the oven to 230°C, 450°F, gas 8.

5 When the soup is cooked, add the chopped chervil. Pour it into a casserole, preferably an earthenware one. Sprinkle with grated cheese and brown in the oven for about 10 minutes. Serve immediately.

Serves 4

Scotch Broth

900 g (2 lb) stewing lamb, with
  bones
1.4 litres (2$\frac{1}{2}$ pints) (6 cups) cold
  water
50 g (2 oz) (3 tablespoons) barley,
  washed
2 onions
2 carrots
2 stalks celery
1 bay leaf (imported)
2.5 ml ($\frac{1}{2}$ teaspoon) thyme
15 g (3 tablespoons) finely
  chopped parsley
2.5 ml ($\frac{1}{2}$ teaspoon) salt
freshly ground (milled) black
  pepper

1 Peel and chop the onions; peel and dice the carrots; trim and dice the celery. Trim and wipe the lamb.

2 Put the lamb into a pan with the water. Bring to the boil, reduce the heat, cover and simmer for 1 hour. Then add the remaining ingredients and simmer for a further 1 hour. Add more water if necessary.

3 Discard the bay leaf. Lift out the lamb with a skimmer and separate the meat from the bone. Discard the bones and cut the meat into small pieces. Add the meat to the soup. Simmer for 5 minutes. Serve hot.

Serves 6

Lentils are rich in protein and form the basis of a cheap and filling soup (right). Garnish with garlic-flavoured sippets — triangles of bread baked in the oven

Clear Soups

Consommé is probably the best known clear soup. Prime quality beef, herbs and vegetables are simmered in a well-flavoured brown stock, and the addition of egg whites — sometimes crushed egg shells are used as well — help to clarify the liquid. The mixture is then strained, with the crust that has formed on top during the cooking acting as a filter.

To be sure of making a sparkling clear soup, which all consommés must be, all utensils and ingredients — especially the stock — must be completely free from grease.

You can serve consommé hot or cold (in which case it is lightly jellied (gelled) and usually chopped), and plain or varied by adding different garnishes. A consommé, in fact, takes its name from the garnish, and this should always be cooked or prepared separately and added only at the moment of serving. That way nothing can cloud and spoil the appearance of the soup.

Beef Consommé

1 carrot
1 leek, green part only
2 stalks celery
4 ripe tomatoes, optional
2 egg whites
½ kg (1 lb) minced (ground), very lean prime cut beef
few sprigs chervil and tarragon
2 litres (3½ pints) (8¾ cups) chilled brown stock
150 ml (¼ pint) (⅝ cup) cold water
peppercorns
15 ml (1 tablespoon) sherry, optional

1 Remove all fat from the surface of the brown stock and turn into a large pan. Peel the carrot.

Wash and dry it, together with the leek, celery and tomatoes, if used. Chop or slice them. Wash, dry and chop the herbs.

2 Mix the vegetables with the egg whites in a large bowl; stir in the beef, tomatoes, chopped herbs and the water.

3 Add the vegetable mixture to the stock, mix together, then bring slowly to the boil, stirring to the bottom of the pan to prevent the mixture from sticking. Keep whisking the mixture until a thick froth starts to form.

4 As soon as the mixture starts to boil, turn down the heat and simmer, covered, for about 1½ hours without stirring. From time to time remove any fat which rises to the surface (there should be hardly any at all).

5 At the end of the cooking time, pour the contents of the pan through a scalded cloth over a sieve (strainer), on which the peppercorns have been put, into a bowl underneath. At first hold back the egg white crust with a spoon, then let it slip onto the cloth. Pour the soup through again and over the egg white filter. The consommé should now be completely clear. Reheat, check the seasoning and add the sherry, if liked, to improve the flavour.

Serves 8

Variations:

Consommé Colbert: add 100 ml (4 fl oz) (½ cup) port to the above quantity of hot soup; add cooked diced carrots and turnips, cooked garden peas, as well as a poached egg per serving.

Consommé Julienne: add cooked matchstick-thin strips of vegetables (carrot, turnip, celery) to the hot soup.

Consommé à la Brunoise: add a mixture of cooked small diced carrots, green beans or celery to the hot soup. Substitute chicken stock for the brown stock if liked.

Consommé à la Madrilène: substitute chicken stock for brown stock; blanch a few tarragon leaves in boiling water for 2 minutes, then add to the hot

soup. Float a thin slice of lemon in each bowl.

Consommé au Riz: add a small quantity of cooked long grain rice to the hot soup.

Consommé au Vermicelli: add vermicelli or other tiny pasta (alphabetti, stelletti, pastine, semini, etc.) to the soup while reheating.

Quick Consommé
Heat canned consommé gently in a pan and stir in 15 ml (1 tablespoon) sherry or Madeira or to taste to boost the flavour. Garnish and serve as for homemade consommé.

Watercress Soup

½ bunch watercress
50 g (2 oz) very lean, raw pork
1-2 small spring onions (scallions)
700 ml (1¼ pints) (3 cups) chicken stock
2.5 ml (¼ teaspoon) grated fresh root ginger
2.5 ml (¼ teaspoon) soya sauce
5 ml (1 teaspoon) dry sherry
salt and pepper

1 Wash and dry the watercress. Reserve 4 small top clusters for garnish. Remove the thick stems and cut the rest up roughly. Cut the pork into very small slivers; trim and thinly slice the spring onions (scallions).

2 Put into a pan the chicken stock, root ginger, soya sauce, sherry, the pork, sliced spring onions (scallions) and salt and pepper to taste. Remember the stock is already well seasoned.

3 Bring to the boil, cover and simmer for 15 minutes. Add the watercress and simmer the soup for 3 more minutes. Serve at once, garnishing each bowl with a sprig of watercress.

Serves 4

Look 'n Cook Clarification of Consommé

1 Ingredients: chilled brown stock, carrots, celery, green part of 1 leek, tomatoes, chervil and tarragon, eggs, minced (ground) beef **2** Carefully remove any fat from the surface of the stock **3** Chop or slice the vegetables and tomatoes; wash and chop the herbs **4** Put the prepared vegetables and herbs into a large bowl together with the minced (ground) beef. Add the egg whites only **5** Mix the ingredients together well, adding a little cold water to moisten. Add the vegetable mixture to the pan of stock and heat gently, stirring all the time **6** As soon as it begins to boil, reduce the heat so it is only just simmering. Skim off any fat that rises to the surface – there should be hardly any at all – and cook for 1½ hours without stirring; this will allow a 'crust' to form on top **7** Scald a cloth and place over a large sieve (strainer); put the peppercorns on the cloth, then slowly pour the soup over the vegetable/egg white mixture to clarify **8** and **9** Two garnishes for consommé: vermicelli and chopped tomatoes.

Cold Soups

Cold Spanish Soup (Gazpacho)

1 cucumber
sea salt
100 g (¼ lb) (1½ cups) dry white
  breadcrumbs
3 tomatoes
1 clove garlic
60 ml (4 tablespoons) oil
15 ml (1 tablespoon) lemon juice
½ litre (scant 1 pint) (2¼ cups)
  cold water
salt and pepper
pinch cayenne pepper
2 mild Spanish onions
1 green pepper
bunch chervil
bunch chives

1 Peel the cucumber with a potato peeler. Dice it. Bring a saucepan of salted water to the boil. Add half the diced cucumber and leave to simmer for 10 minutes. Sprinkle sea salt over the rest of the cucumber to draw out some of its moisture.

2 Drain the cooked cucumber. Purée in a blender or food mill or rub through a sieve (strainer). Put the breadcrumbs into a bowl. Add just enough water to moisten them. Skin the tomatoes, then cut half the tomatoes into small pieces.

3 Peel and chop the garlic and put into a mortar. Add a pinch of salt and pound with the pestle. Add the tomato pieces and breadcrumbs. Pound the whole until the mixture is thoroughly blended. Add the oil a little at a time, mixing all the time. Add the lemon juice and cucumber purée. Dilute with the cold water, stirring all the time. Add salt and pepper to taste and a pinch of cayenne pepper. Mix

again, then chill in the refrigerator for at least 2 hours.

4 Chop the rest of the tomatoes into small cubes. Peel the onions and chop roughly. Wash the green pepper. Dry it and cut in half. Remove the seeds and white membrane, then cut the flesh into small cubes. Rinse the cucumber cubes. Squeeze them gently with your hands to make sure they are well drained. Wash and dry the chervil and the chives. Chop them.

5 Arrange the tomatoes, onions, green pepper and cucumber in 4 separate dishes. Divide the soup into 4 individual bowls. Sprinkle the chervil and

chives over them. Serve very chilled.

Serves 4

Tip: Each guest takes a little of all the finely chopped raw vegetables into his soup bowl. It is customary to put an ice cube into each soup bowl at the moment of serving.

Gazpacho, or gaspacho (below), is a Spanish salad-soup made with a purée of cucumber, tomatoes, garlic, breadcrumbs and oil. Served chilled, the soup is garnished with herbs and accompanied by bowls of chopped tomatoes, green peppers, onion and cucumber

Vichyssoise

900 ml (1½ pints) (4 cups) chicken
  stock
2.5 ml (½ teaspoon) salt
4 medium potatoes
3 medium onions
3 leeks (or 1 extra onion)
2.5 ml (½ teaspoon) fresh chervil
  or marjoram
10 g (2 tablespoons) fresh parsley
150 ml (¼ pint) (good ½ cup) double
  (heavy) cream

1 Put the chicken stock in a large pan and bring to simmering point; add the salt. Peel the potatoes and cut into medium chunks. Peel and chop the onions. Prepare, wash, dry and slice the leeks. Add all these vegetables to the stock, bring to the boil, cover, reduce the heat and simmer for about 20 minutes.

2 Cool a little, then put the soup in a blender and blend until smooth or pass through a food mill or sieve (strainer). Chill for at least 2 hours.

3 Wash, dry and finely chop the chervil or marjoram and the parsley. Just before serving add the herbs and cream. If wished, put 2 or 3 over-lapping raw onion rings in the centre of each soup dish when serving.

Serves 6

> **To Store Soup**
> Unthickened soup (no liaison has been added) freezes best and can be frozen in handy quantities for up to 3 months, Cool, then skim off any fat from the surface before freezing a soup; allow about 1 cm (½ in) headspace for expansion.

Vichyssoise (below) is one of the classic French soups. Traditionally garnished with snipped chives, try finely chopped parsley or a few raw onion rings, overlapped, instead

Avocado Soup

2 large and 1 small avocados
2.5 ml (½ teaspoon) salt
pinch white pepper
225 ml (8 fl oz) (1 cup) double
  (heavy) cream
900 ml (1½ pints) (4 cups)
  chicken stock
45 ml (3 tablespoons) dry sherry

1 Peel the 2 large avocados, remove the stone (seed) and cut the flesh into small pieces. Put it into a blender with salt, pepper and half the cream and blend until smooth or work through a sieve (strainer). Then add the remaining cream and blend again until mixed.

2 Heat the chicken stock until it is wam but not hot. Pour in the avocado cream mixture. Taste and adjust the seasoning. Chill this in the refrigerator for 1 hour.

3 Stir in the sherry. Peel the small avocado, remove the stone (seed) and cut it into thin slices. Add to the soup and serve.

Serves 4-6

Tip: Do not make this soup too early in the day. Avocado discolours when exposed to the air so put into a covered container when chilling. A little lemon juice brushed over the flesh helps to prevent discolouration.

Watercress and Potato Soup

1 bunch watercress
25 g (1 oz) (1 tablespoon) butter
1 onion
1 stalk celery
2 medium potatoes
700 ml (1¼ pints) (3 cups)
  chicken stock
15 ml (1 tablespoon) lemon juice
2.5 ml (½ teaspoon) salt
freshly ground black pepper
150 ml (¼ pint) (good ½ cup)
  double (heavy) cream

1 Wash the watercress and reserve some of the leaves for decoration. Chop the remainder and the stems into small pieces.

2 Melt the butter in a saucepan. Peel the onion and chop it finely. Clean the celery and chop it. Peel the potatoes and cut into cubes. Add the onion and celery to the pan and cook for 3 minutes.

3 Add the potatoes, stock, chopped watercress, lemon juice, salt and pepper. Cover and simmer for 30 minutes. Remove from the heat and cool a little.

4 Work through a sieve (strainer) or purée in a blender. Then strain the soup into a container with a lid. Taste and adjust seasoning if necessary. Cover and chill for 2 hours. Just before serving stir in the cream and the reserved watercress.

Serves 4

Cream of Lettuce Soup

3 heads lettuce
25 g (1 oz) (2 tablespoons) butter
7.5 ml (1½ teaspoons) salt
freshly ground black pepper
900 ml (1½ pints) (4 cups) water
150 ml (¼ pint) (good ½ cup)
  double (heavy) cream
juice ½ lemon
6 small spring onions (scallions)

1 Cut the lettuce into quarters, remove the cores and wash the leaves. Cook in boiling, salted water for 10 minutes. Drain and then chop roughly.

2 Melt the butter in a saucepan, add the chopped lettuce, put on the lid, then tip it a little and cook slowly for 5 minutes. Season the lettuce with salt and pepper, add the water and bring to the boil. Cover, lower the heat and simmer for 1 hour. Cool a little.

3 Pour the soup into a blender and blend until smooth, or rub through a sieve (strainer). Taste and adjust the seasoning.

4 Chill the soup very well and, just before serving, stir in first the cream and then the lemon juice.

5 Trim the spring onions (scallions) leaving about 2.5 cm (1 in) of the green part still on them. With a pair of kitchen scissors or a

Avocados, combined with sherry and cream, make an excellent soup

sharp knife, cut this green part downwards, into as many thin strips as possible. Put 1 onion in the centre of each bowl of soup so that the thin strips float.

6 Serve very cold.

Serves 6

Chilled Cucumber and Tomato Soup

1½ litres (2½ pints) (6¼ cups) chicken stock
75 g (3 oz) (⅓ cup) long grain rice
4 very ripe tomatoes
½ cucumber
100 ml (4 fl oz) (½ cup) double (heavy) cream
small bunch chervil
pinch cayenne pepper
salt and pepper

1 Bring the stock to the boil in a saucepan. Wash the rice and add to the vigorously boiling stock; cook 20 minutes.

2 Wash and skin the tomatoes; quarter and squeeze gently to extract the water and pips. Add tomatoes to the stock after the rice has cooked for 20 minutes. Leave to cook 30 minutes longer.

3 Remove the end of the cucumber. Cut in two, lengthways; take out seeds with a small spoon. Cut in thin strips.

4 When cooked, purée the soup in a blender or rub through a sieve (strainer). Stiffly whip and fold in cream. Add cayenne pepper. Mix well together. Taste and adjust the seasoning; cool.

5 When cold, add the cucumber strips. Stir. Chill in refrigerator for at least 3 hours. About 5 minutes before serving, wash, dry and chop the chervil. Ladle the chilled soup into individual bowls. Sprinkle over the chervil and serve.

Serves 4

Chilled Cucumber and Tomato Soup, garnished with strips of cucumber

South Pacific Cold Fruit Soup

450 g (1 lb) black, ripe
  cherries, stoned
2 peaches, peeled, seeded and
  thinly sliced
1 stick cinnamon
4 whole cloves
juice 1 lime
1 litre (1¾ pints) (4 cups)
  water
45 ml (3 tablespoons) honey
15 g (½ oz) (2 tablespoons)
  cornflour
45 ml (3 tablespoons) water
2.5 ml (½ teaspoon) almond
  extract
225 ml (8 fl oz) (1 cup) red
  wine
100 ml (4 fl oz) (½ cup) sour
  cream and 50 g (2 oz) (¼
  cup) slivered browned
  almonds for garnish

1 Simmer cherries, peaches,
cinnamon, cloves, lime juice,
water and honey together in
covered saucepan for 15 minutes. Discard cinnamon and
cloves.

2 Blend cornflour with water
and stir into soup, cooking
over low heat until slightly
thickened. Stir in almond extract and wine and chill
thoroughly.

3 Spoon fruit evenly into
serving plates, pour soup over
and garnish with sour cream
and almonds.

Serves 6

Chilled Custard Apple Soup

2 medium, ripe custard
  apples
500 ml (20 fl oz) (2 cups)
  chicken stock
juice 2 limes
225 ml (8 fl oz) (1 cup) sour
  cream

salt
freshly ground pepper
lemon slices and dill sprigs
  for garnish

1 Scoop out flesh of custard
apple; discard seeds. Purée in
blender or food processor,
gradually adding stock, until
smooth. Blend in lime juice.

2 Transfer mixture to bowl.
Stir in sour cream. Season to
taste with salt and pepper.
Serve in bowls garnished with
lemon slices and dill.

Serves 4

Chilled Blueberry Soup

350 g (¾ lb) (2 cups)
  blueberries
300 ml (½ pint) (1¼ cups)
  water
50 g (2 oz) (¼ cup) sugar
8 cm (3 in) strip lemon peel
1 stick cinnamon
200 ml (¾ cup) sour cream

1 Simmer blueberries, water,
sugar, lemon peel and cinnamon stick for 15 minutes. Allow to stand for 10 minutes,
then discard lemon peel and
cinnamon stick.

2 Purée in blender or food
processor and chill
thoroughly. Just before serving, blend in sour cream.

Serves 6

Chilled Rockmelon Soup

750 g (1¾ lb) rockmelon,
  halved and seeded
200 g (7 oz) seedless grapes
200 g (7 oz) apricots, halved
  and seeded
1 medium apple, peeled,
  cored and sliced

15-30 ml (1-2 tablespoons)
  lemon juice
750 ml (1¼ pints) (3 cups) dry
  white wine
10 ml (2 teaspoons) cornflour
15 ml (1 tablespoon) honey
75 g (3 oz) pine nuts

1 Remove flesh from half the
rockmelon and dice. Using
melon baller, scoop flesh from
other half. Simmer diced
melon, grapes, apricots,
apple, lemon juice and wine
for 20 minutes. Allow to cool
slightly then purée in blender
or food processor. Return
purée to saucepan.

2 Mix cornflour to paste with
a little water. Stir cornflour
and honey into soup and cook
until slightly thickened. Stir
in melon balls and chill
thoroughly.

3 Just before serving, toast
pine nuts by tossing in frying
pan until just starting to
brown. Cool. Ladle soup into 6
bowls and sprinkle with pine
nuts.

Serves 6

Chilled Watermelon Soup

2 kg (4 lb) watermelon flesh,
  seeded
500 ml (20 fl oz) (2 cups)
  sweet white wine
30 ml (2 tablespoons) honey
5 ml (1 teaspoon) garam
  masala
grated rind 1 lemon
225 ml (8 fl oz) sour cream

1 Bring watermelon, wine,
honey, garam masala and
lemon rind to the boil, stirring constantly. Reduce heat
and simmer for 20 minutes.
Allow to cool.

2 Purée in blender or food
processor. Stir in sour cream
and chill thoroughly before
serving.

Serves 6

Creamy Soups

All creamy soups have a smooth, velvety texture achieved by thickening them with cream or egg yolks, flour or some kind of cereal. They can be made with stock or milk or combinations of both.

Green vegetables are popular choices for cream soups; they are usually cooked in milk, then sieved and blended and then thickened.

If both egg yolks and cream are used for thickening a soup, the extra velvety consistency achieved is called a *velouté*.

Bisque is a term applied to shellfish soups only. Often a bisque is enriched by the addition of a special butter made with the fish coral, and in some cases the shells themselves are pounded and incorporated as well to give an extra fishy flavour.

To Thicken Soups

If using cream: put in a bowl, blend in a little of the hot but not boiling soup, then stir back into the pan of soup and reheat but do not boil.

If using egg yolk: blend with a little cold milk or cream in a bowl, mix in a little of the hot soup, then strain back into the pan of soup; reheat very gently but do not boil or else the egg will curdle (if the soup already contains flour/cereal, curdling is less likely to occur).

If using flour or fine cereal: blend with a little cold milk or other liquid in a bowl, mix in a little hot soup, then pour back into the pan, bring to the boil and cook for a few minutes until thickened.

Cream of Spinach Soup

1 kg (2 lb) leaf spinach
1 small onion
25 g (1 oz) (2 tablespoons) butter or margarine
25 g (1 oz) (4 tablespoons) flour
300 ml (½ pint) (1¼ cups) white stock
300 ml (½ pint) (1¼ cups) creamy milk
salt and pepper

1 Wash the spinach well; peel and finely chop the onion. Put the spinach in a large pan with about 30 ml (2 tablespoons) water and cook until tender – about 5 minutes. Drain well and rub through a sieve (strainer) or work in a food mill; set aside.

2 Heat the butter or margarine in a saucepan; put in the onion and cook until soft and transparent. Stir in the flour and blend. Pour in the white stock and milk, a little at a time, stirring continuously until smooth.

3 Stir in the spinach purée, season to taste, cook gently for a few minutes until hot, then serve immediately.

Serves 4-6

Cream of Spinach Soup is a delicious way of serving this under-rated vegetable

Cream of Chervil Soup

40 g (1½ oz) (3 tablespoons) butter
40 g (1½ oz) (5 tablespoons) flour·
1½ litres (2½ pints) (6 cups)
  chicken or white stock
salt and pepper
1 egg yolk
50 ml (2 fl oz) (¼ cup) double
  (heavy) cream
10 g (2 tablespoons) finely
  chopped chervil or parsley

1 Melt the butter in a large saucepan. Blend in the flour to make a roux. Pour in the stock a little at a time, and stir continuously over a medium heat until the sauce is thick and smooth. Season with salt and pepper to taste.

2 Mix the egg yolk with the cream in a bowl; stir in a little of the hot liquid, then pour into the pan of soup, stirring continuously. Add the chervil, or parsley, reheat gently but not boil, and serve at once.

Serves 4-6

Cream of Leek and Potato Soup

3 leeks, white part only
2 large, floury potatoes
25 g (1 oz) (2 tablespoons) butter
  or margarine
2 litres (3½ pints) (9 cups) white
  stock
salt and pepper
1 egg yolk
50 ml (2 fl oz) (¼ cup) double
  (heavy) cream
2 handfuls chervil or parsley

1 Wash the leeks well (this is best done by standing them, green stems down, in a jug of cold water so grit and dirt can float out from between the stems). Drain them and cut into thin slices. Peel the potatoes and cut into quarters.

2 In a pan, melt the butter. When hot add the leek slices. Soften them a little in the covered pan, stirring frequently over a gentle heat.

3 Draw the pan off the heat and pour in the stock. Return to the heat and bring to the boil again. Add salt and pepper. Put in the potato quarters, cover the pan, reduce the heat and simmer about 20 minutes till tender. Then purée in a blender or work through a sieve (strainer) or food mill.

4 In a bowl blend the cream and egg yolk together, then stir in some of the hot soup. Return this mixture to the soup. Stir and adjust the seasoning, adding plenty of pepper. Heat gently for a few moments but do not boil.

5 Meanwhile, wash and dry the chervil or parsley, then chop it finely.

6 Pour the soup into a heated tureen. Sprinkle with the chopped herbs and serve.

Serves 6

Cream of Chicken Soup

40 g (1½ oz) (3 tablespoons) butter
40 g (2½ oz) (5 tablespoons) flour
900 ml (1½ pints) (4 cups) chicken
  stock
75 g (3 oz) (½ cup) finely chopped
  cooked chicken
1.25 ml (¼ teaspoon) salt
freshly ground (milled) black
  pepper

For the liaison:
1 egg yolk
60 ml (4 tablespoons) double
  (heavy) cream

1 Melt the butter in a large pan. Stir in the flour to make a roux and cook for about 1 minute without colouring. Then draw the pan off the heat and gradually blend in the chicken stock, stirring all the time to make a smooth sauce. Return the pan to the heat and bring to the boil.

2 Reduce the heat, then add the cooked chicken, salt and pepper and cook for 2 minutes.

3 Blend the egg yolk and cream together in a bowl. Stir in a little of the hot soup, then return to the pan and reheat gently, stirring all the time, until thickened. Do not allow the soup to boil after the egg yolk is added. Serve at once.

Serves 4

Cream of Mushroom Soup

500 g (1 lb) button mushrooms
1 shallot
50 g (2 oz) (4 tablespoons) butter
15 g (½ oz) (2 tablespoons) flour
1½ litres (2½ pints) (6 cups) brown
  stock
salt and pepper
1 egg yolk
30 ml (2 tablespoons) double
  (heavy) cream
juice ½ lemon

1 Wipe the mushrooms and slice them finely. Peel and chop the shallot.

2 Heat the butter in a large pan; when hot add the shallot and fry quickly till golden. Then add the sliced mushrooms and sauté over a medium heat for about 4 minutes. Stir in the flour and cook for a further 2 minutes, then blend in the brown stock off the heat. Return the pan to the heat, season with salt and pepper to taste and cook gently for about 10 minutes.

3 To thicken the soup, blend the egg yolk with the cream and the lemon juice, then stir into the hot soup. Reheat very gently but do not boil. Serve at once.

Serves 4-6

Cream of Mushroom Soup – as a variation try stirring in plain yoghurt instead of cream

Avgolemono (Greek Egg and Lemon Soup)

1.8 litres (3¼ pints) (8 cups)
  chicken stock
100-175 g (4-6 oz) (½-¾ cup)
  long grain rice, vermicelli or
  other small pasta
3 eggs
juice 2 small lemons
salt and freshly ground (milled)
  black pepper

1 Bring the chicken stock to the boil. Add the rice, vermicelli or pasta and simmer for 15 minutes.

2 Meanwhile, beat the eggs until frothy. Slowly add the lemon juice to the eggs, beating constantly. Add about a quarter of the hot stock, 15ml (1 tablespoon) at a time, beating all the time. Remove the remaining stock from the heat and stir in the egg mixture.

3 Adjust the seasoning as necessary and serve immediately.

Serves 8

Cream of Carrot Soup

2 medium onions
2 medium potatoes
1kg (2lb) carrots
25g (1oz) (2 tablespoons) butter
  or margarine
salt and pepper
2 litres (3½ pints) (8¾ cups) white
  stock
30g (2 tablespoons) raw rice

For the liaison:
1 egg yolk
60ml (4 tablespoons) double
  (heavy) cream

1 Peel and slice the onions. Peel and cut the carrots into strips. Peel and cut the potatoes into tiny dice.

2 Melt half the fat in a large pan. When hot, put in the onions and fry without colouring over a low heat until soft and transluscent.

3 Stir the carrots into the pan. Add the stock and salt to taste, then cover and cook over a moderate heat for 30 minutes.

4 Wash the rice under cold running water. Then add the rice and potatoes to the pan and cook for a further 30 minutes. Purée in a blender or work through a siever (strainer) or food mill.

5 When the soup is cooked, blend the egg yolk with the cream in a bowl. Season generously with salt and pepper and beat again. Stir in a little of the hot soup; then return the egg yolk mixture to the pan of soup. Reheat gently but do not boil. Serve hot.

Serves 6

Chinese Asparagus Soup

2 onions
500ml (¼ pint) (2 cups) chicken
  stock – may be made from a
  cube
30g (2 tablespoons) potato flour
  or cornflour (cornstarch)
1 egg
30ml (2 tablespoons) oil
salt and pepper
15ml (1 tablespoon) white wine
30ml (2 tablespoons) cooked
  tiny peas
3-4 slender, cooked asparagus
  spears per person

1 Peel and chop up the onions so as to obtain the equivalent to 45ml (3 tablespoons). Mix 30ml (2 tablespoons) of cold water with the potato flour. Break an egg into a bowl and beat until blended.

2 Heat the oil in the saucepan, put in the chopped onions and fry slowly until lightly browned. Add the chicken stock with salt and pepper, and mix in the potato flour or cornflour, stirring all the time.

3 Then add the wine and peas and bring it to the boil. When the soup starts to thicken, slowly add the beaten egg, but keep stirring the whole time. When it thickens, remove from the heat.

4 Cut the asparagus into pieces and place them in bowls or soup plates. Add soup and serve.

Serves 4

Cream of Artichoke Soup

3 shallots
6 globe artichokes
juice of 1 lemon
100g (¼lb) (8 tablespoons) butter
  or margarine
60g (2½oz) (7 tablespoons) flour
1 litre (1¾ pints) (4¼ cups) milk
salt and pepper
100ml (4fl oz) (½ cup) double
  (heavy) cream

1 Peel and chop the shallots. Remove the artichoke leaves and hairy choke in the centre (see page 58). Trim the artichoke hearts and rub them in the lemon juice to stop them turning black. Cut them into quarters.

2 Gently heat 25g (1oz) (2 tablespoons) butter or margarine in a pan. Put in the artichoke hearts and the shallots, cover and cook on a low heat for 10 minutes.

3 During this time melt the rest of the butter in another pan. Mix in the flour to make a roux and cook for about 2 minutes, but without letting it brown. Remove the pan from the heat and blend in the milk, little by little, beating continuously with a wooden spoon. When smooth return the pan to the heat and bring to the boil; season with salt and pepper and cook gently for 5 minutes.

4 Pour this white sauce over the artichokes and shallot mixture and simmer 30 minutes. Then remove 2 artichoke hearts and cut them into tiny dice. Purée the rest in a blender or work through a sieve (strainer) or food mill.

5 Heat a soup tureen. Pour in the cream, add the diced artichoke and pour over the hot soup. Stir well and serve immediately.

Serves 4

Cream of Artichoke Soup is an unusual way of serving artichokes

Browned Onion Soup with Madeira

For the bouquet garni:
sprig parsley
good sprig thyme
bay leaf

225 g (½ lb) onions
2 cloves garlic
40 g (1½ oz) (3 tablespoons) butter
30 ml (2 tablespoons) oil
25 g (1 oz) (¼ cup) flour
150 ml (¼ pint) (good ½ cup) dry white wine
salt and pepper
3 egg yolks
60 ml (4 tablespoons) Madeira
½ French loaf
cayenne pepper
100 g (¼ lb) (1 cup) grated cheese

1 Wash and dry the parsley. Tie the parsley, thyme and bay leaf together, making sure that the thyme and bay leaf are inside the parsley. Peel the onions and chop them. Peel the garlic.

2 Heat the butter and the oil in a sauté pan. Add the chopped onions and cook them, stirring from time to time with a wooden spoon. When they are golden, add the flour and let it cook while stirring until it too turns brown.

3 Pour in the white wine. Let it reduce (evaporate) by half, then add the stock or water. Add salt and plenty of pepper. Add the bouquet garni. Crush the garlic and add it as well. Bring to the boil, then skim. Cover the soup and allow to simmer for about 45 minutes. About 15 minutes before it is ready, preheat the oven to 200°C, 400°F, gas 6, to dry out the bread.

4 Mix yolks with the Madeira. Cut the French loaf into thin slices. Spread them on a baking (cookie) sheet and dry out in the oven. Take out the bread. Heat the grill (broiler).

5 When the soup is cooked, take it off the heat and discard the bouquet garni. When it has stopped bubbling, pour a little of the soup into the yolk/Madeira mixture whisking briskly all the time. Then pour it all back into the soup and mix well. Add a hint of cayenne pepper and check the seasoning.

6 Divide the soup between four bowls. Place 2-3 slices of bread in each bowl. Cover the bread with the grated cheese. Stand the bowls in a pan of hot water (bain marie). Heat on the stove until the water is almost boiling, then brown under the grill (broiler).

7 Serve piping hot as soon as the cheese browns.

Serves 4

Tips: If a soup without onion pieces is preferred, sieve it or put through a blender before adding the egg yolks. Don't allow the soup to boil once the egg yolks have been added.

If chopped beetroot leaves and a floury potato are added to the onion whilst frying, the flour would then be unnecessary.

The white wine and Madeira can be replaced with a very full-bodied red wine to produce a 'country' brown soup (gratinée).

Rich Turnip Soup

350 g (¾ lb) small turnips
125 g (¼ lb) semi-salted (mild cure) bacon
30 g (1½ oz) (3 tablespoons) butter
100 g (¼ lb) sorrel
1 litre (1¾ pint) (4¼ cups) chicken stock
few sprigs chervil
1 egg yolk
30 ml (2 tablespoons) single (light) cream
salt and pepper

1 Boil 2 small pans of water. Peel and wash the turnips and cut them into cubes. Slice the bacon into thin strips. Put the turnips into one pan and the bacon strips into the other. Let each boil for 5 minutes, then drain.

2 Melt the butter in a stewpan. Put the turnips and the bacon into the hot butter and leave to brown a little on a low heat for about 15 minutes.

3 Wash the sorrel and chop it. Add it to the stewpan and stir in with a wooden spoon, then pour the stock into it and cook for 20 minutes.

4 Wash, dry and chop the chervil. Pour the egg yolk into the soup tureen, add the cream and mix in.

5 When the bacon strips are cooked, drain them. Purée the soup in a blender or work through a sieve (strainer) or food mill. Taste and adjust the seasoning. Pour the soup into the tureen and beat with a whisk. Add the bacon strips to the soup and sprinkle it with chervil. Serve very hot.

Serves 4

Bulgarian Beef Soup

225 g (½ lb) lean beef
4 large onions
40 g (1½ oz) (3 tablespoons) butter
2.5 ml (½ teaspoon) cumin seeds
mixed fresh herbs for small bouquet garni
1½ litres (2¾ pints) (7 cups) brown stock (use a cube if necessary)
salt and pepper
45 ml (3 tablespoons) sour cream
1 carton natural yogurt
15 ml (1 tablespoon) paprika
15 ml (1 tablespoon) ground rice
100 g (¼ lb) cooked ham
sprigs parsley

1 Dice the beef finely. Peel the onions and cut into quarters.

2 Melt the butter in a big saucepan. Add the diced beef and onions, and fry gently for 20 minutes, stirring frequently.

3 Put cumin seeds in a pepper mill and grind them. Wash and dry the herbs for the bouquet garni, and tie them together.

4 When the beef and onions have cooked for 20 minutes, add the brown stock and bouquet garni. Sprinkle with the ground cumin. Add salt and pepper, bearing in mind the seasoning of the stock, and cook for 20 minutes.

5 Put the soured cream into a bowl with the yogurt, paprika and ground rice. Mix carefully so that lumps do not form, and pour into the soup. Stir with a wooden spoon over a low heat.

6 Put the cooked ham through the mincer (grinder). Wash and dry the parsley sprigs and chop them finely.

7 Add the ham to the soup and cook a further 2 minutes over a low heat.

8 Just before serving, remove the bouquet garni. Taste the soup, and if necessary adjust the seasoning. Pour it into a heated soup tureen, sprinkle with chopped parsley and serve hot.

Serves 6

Bulgarian Beef Soup is a nourishing and spicy meal in itself

1 Ingredients for Shrimp (prawn) Bisque **2** For the sauce, make a roux with butter and flour, then blend in milk **3** Soften shrimps (prawns) and vegetables in oil, add brandy and flame. Add wine and tomatoes, season and cook **4** Take out shrimps (prawns), chop and return to pan **5** Press soup through conical strainer **6** Return to pan, boil, add remaining shrimps (prawns); tip cream into tureen, pour over boiling soup (see opposite page) and serve

Fish Soups

Shrimp (Prawn) Bisque

50 g (2 oz) (4 tablespoons) butter
50 g (2 oz) (¼ cup) flour
1 litre (1¾ pints) (4½ cups) milk
salt and pepper
5 tomatoes
1 shallot
1 small onion
1 stalk celery
225 g (½ lb) unshelled shrimps
  (prawns)
30 ml (2 tablespoons) oil
1 small bouquet garni
50 ml (2 fl oz) (¼ cup) brandy
100 ml (4 fl oz) (½ cup) dry white
  wine

To finish:
50 g (2 oz) (⅜ cup) peeled (shelled)
  shrimps (prawns), fresh or
  frozen
100 ml (4 fl oz) (½ cup) double
  (heavy) cream

1 Melt the butter in a double saucepan and blend in the flour to make a roux. Cook for about 1 minute without letting it colour. Using a wooden spoon, blend in the milk off the heat, then return to the stove and bring to the boil. Season with salt and pepper and cook for 20 minutes over a low heat

2 Skin the tomatoes and cut them in half. Remove the pips and chop the flesh roughly. Peel and finely chop the shallot and onion. Wash and finely chop the celery.

3 Wash and dry both kinds of shrimps (prawns), but keep them separate. Remove the heads and tails.

4 Heat the oil in a pan. When hot add the unshelled shrimps (prawns), the vegetables (but not the tomatoes) and the bouquet garni. Cook gently for about 10 minutes or until the vegetables are soft.

5 Pour in the brandy, heat for about 1 minute, then set alight. When the flames die down, add the tomatoes and white wine. Add salt and season liberally with pepper, then cook for 20 minutes.

6 Remove the shrimps (prawns) from the pan. Crush or chop them and put them back into the pan. Add the white sauce, mix and cook slowly for another 15 minutes. Heat a soup tureen.

7 Pour the soup through a fine conical strainer, pressing down well with a wooden spoon, back into the pan. Bring to the boil again, check the seasoning and add the peeled shrimps (prawns).

8 Pour the cream into the tureen, add the soup, while stirring vigorously, and serve.

Serves 4

Tip: The shrimp shells are used to add additional flavour to the soup. If unshelled shrimps are not available increase the weight of additional shrimps by about 100 g (¼ lb) (⅔ cup).

6

Cream of Mussel Soup

1 litre (1¾ pints) fresh mussels
½ litre (1 pint) (2½ cups) dry white
  wine
½ litre (1 pint) (2¼ cups) water
pepper
1 bouquet garni
4 potatoes
2 carrots
1 onion
2 cloves
700 g (1½ lb) whiting fillets

For the liaison:
2 egg yolks
200 ml (7 fl oz) (⅞ cup) double
  (heavy) cream
15 ml (1 tablespoon) cornflour
  (cornstarch)

1 Scrub and wash the mussels in several changes of water to ensure all the sand is removed. Put them in a large pan and add half the white wine and pepper to taste. Bring to the boil on a high heat. Shake the pan from time to time until the mussels open.

2 Lift out the mussels, discarding any that stay closed; remove the shells. Pass the cooking juices through a fine piece of muslin (cheesecloth). Pour the juices back into the pan. Add the rest of the wine, the water and the bouquet garni. Bring to the boil.

3 Meanwhile peel the potatoes and cut them into even pieces. Peel the carrots and cut them into thin slices. Peel the onion and stud it with the cloves. Add the carrots and onions only to the pan. Bring to the boil, then reduce the heat, cover and simmer for 20 minutes.

4 After 20 minutes' cooking, add the potatoes to the pan and cook for a further 25 minutes.

5 Put the egg yolks in a bowl, add the cream and cornflour (cornstarch) and mix with a fork.

6 Cut the whiting fillets into small pieces and add to the pan; simmer for 5 minutes. Heat a soup tureen.

7 Pour a little of the hot soup onto the egg yolk mixture. Blend well, then return it to the pan.

Add the mussels and reheat the soup gently for 2-3 minutes, without letting it come to the boil.

8 Take out the onion and the bouquet garni. Pour the soup into the tureen and serve hot.

Serves 4

Mock Caviar Soup

1 kg (2 lb) cod or whiting fillets
2 onions
4 cloves
¾ litre (1¼ pints) (3 cups) fish stock
½ litre (1 pint) (2½ cups) dry white
  wine
1 bay leaf, imported
good pinch white pepper
2.5 ml (½ teaspoon) salt

For the liaison:
50 g (2 oz) (4 tablespoons) butter
2 egg yolks
15 g (½ oz) (2 tablespoons) flour
250 ml (8 fl oz) (1 cup) double
  (heavy) cream
100 g (¼ lb) lumpfish roe

1 Cut the fish fillets into small pieces. Peel the onions and stud 1 of them with the cloves.

2 Pour the stock and white wine into a large saucepan. Add the onions, bay leaf, pepper, salt and pieces of fish. Cover and as soon as it comes to the boil, reduce the heat and simmer for about 30 minutes.

3 Beat the butter to soften it. Then beat in the egg yolks, one at a time, and each time with half of the flour and the cream respectively.

4 Work the soup through a sieve (strainer) or food mill, pressing the fish with a wooden spoon to extract all the juice. Pour this fish liquid back into the saucepan.

5 Blend a little of the hot fish liquid with the cream mixture in a bowl; then return it to the pan of soup. Reheat gently but do not boil and cook for about 15 minutes.

6 Heat a soup tureen. Pour in

the soup, add the lump fish roe and stir. Taste and adjust the seasoning and serve at once.

Serves 4

Oyster Bisque

24 fresh large oysters
200 ml (½ pint) (scant 1 cup) water
2 medium onions
50 g (2 oz) (4 tablespoons) butter
30 ml (2 tablespoons) flour
600 ml (1 pint) (2½ cups) milk
salt and pepper
10 g (2 tablespoons) finely
  chopped parsley

1 Open the oysters, retain their juice but discard the shells. Soak the oysters in the water and their juice. Peel and finely chop the onions.

2 Heat 40 g (1½ oz) (3 tablespoons) butter in a pan. Add the onions and fry slowly until they are just beginning to brown. Add the flour and stir with a wooden spoon for 3 minutes. Add one-third of the milk, stir again and cook for 2 minutes.

3 Drain the oysters, keeping the liquid in which they were soaked, and cut them into small pieces.

4 Mix the onion sauce with the rest of the milk and the soaking liquid in a double saucepan (bain marie). Season with salt and pepper to taste.

5 Add the oysters to the pan and leave 20 minutes over a low heat, taking care the mixture does not boil. Add the chopped parsley.

6 Just before serving, stir in the rest of the butter and the paprika. Serve at once.

Serves 4

Cream of Mussel Soup — mussels, once considered the 'oysters of the poor,' are now featured in world-famous dishes. They are in season from March to September and should be bought alive. Test for freshness by sliding the two shells against each other — if they move they are probably full of sand or mud, not mussel

Look 'n Cook Bouillabaisse

1 Wash and clean the fish; cut into pieces 2 Skin, deseed and chop tomatoes; peel and finely chop onions, garlic and parsley; cut fennel and leeks into matchsticks 3 Fry vegetables gently in oil 4 Add saffron, tomatoes, garlic and parsley 5 Add fish pieces 6 Strain broth and add to the pan 7 Pound

together garlic, saffron and cayenne for rouille **8** Blend in egg yolk and oil **9** Spread croûtes on baking (cookie) sheet, pour over oil and bake

10 Season broth with salt and pepper as soon as it boils **11** Rub garlic over croûtes **12** Lift pieces of fish onto serving dish (continued overleaf)

Bouillabaisse started as a very simple fish soup made with spiny scorpion fish (rascasse), olive oil, garlic, onion, leeks and sea water. It then evolved to its present form with the inclusion of many more different rock fish and flavourings, and in particular the special garlic mayonnaise called rouille.

Some rouille sauces can be very fiery, depending on the strength of the cayenne. And the blending of the hot broth with the sauce helps to thicken and bind it.

Sadly, it is difficult to reproduce this delicious dish exactly, away from the Mediterranean, mainly because the local fish are unobtainable, but the recipe here is an excellent alternative.

To be really tasty, Bouillabaisse must combine a wide variety of fish, each kind adding its own particular flavour. So 3 kg (6 lb) fish is the smallest amount to use satisfactorily. The choice of fish is wide, the most popular being conger eel, sea bass (sea perch), whiting, red and grey mullet, John Dory, turbot, hake and sea bream, together with shellfish like crab, lobster, jumbo prawns or crayfish.

Bourride is another famous Mediterranean soup dish, but the classic recipe doesn't confine its choice of fish to rock sea fish as Bouillabaisse does. Often fatty fish, like sardines, are included and indeed in its earliest form, Bourride was a sardine soup bound with ailloli, another kind of garlic mayonnaise.

13 Ladle some of the hot broth over the pieces of fish **14** Pour the remaining broth into a hot soup tureen **15** Serve the platter of fish and shellfish separately from the rouille sauce, broth and croutes

Bouillabaisse – Fish Soup Provençale

3 kg (6 lb) salt water fish (use a variety of 6 or more kinds)
8-10 Dublin Bay prawns, fresh or frozen
few fish bones for the stock
1 kg (2 lb) very ripe tomatoes
500 g (good 1 lb) onions
1 carrot
1 bulb garlic
4 large leeks
2 bulbs fennel
¼ litre (8 fl oz) (1 cup) olive oil
1 bouquet garni
good pinch saffron
salt and pepper
1 large crusty loaf

For the rouille:
5 cloves garlic
salt
1 egg yolk
pinch cayenne pepper
pinch saffron
400 ml (¾ pint) (scant 2 cups) olive oil

1 Remove the skin and bones from the fish and wash them well. Roughly chop up the fish bones and wash them.

2 Cut the fish into pieces, making the slices from the more tender and delicate fish larger than the others. Wash them again. Clean the Dublin Bay prawns.

3 Peel, wash and dry the vegetables. Skin, deseed and chop the tomatoes. Peel the onions, carrot and garlic cloves; slice 1 onion and the carrot, then chop the remaining onions finely as well as a few cloves of garlic. Wash, dry and chop the parsley finely. Wash the leeks well, trim them and the fennel, then cut into fine matchsticks.

4 Heat 30-45 ml (2-3 tablespoons) of oil in a large pan. Fry the sliced vegetables and chopped garlic in it on a very low heat for 2-3 minutes without letting them colour, then add the chopped up fish bones. Cover liberally with cold water and add the bouquet garni. Bring to the boil, then simmer for 20 minutes on a low heat. Skim the fish stock as

necessary.

5 Peel 4 or 5 cloves of garlic and crush them.

6 Heat 50 ml (3 tablespoons) of oil in a large heavy pan. Add the chopped onions, fennel and leeks and fry gently for 3 or 4 minutes without letting them colour. Then take them off the heat and sprinkle with the saffron. Mix well. Add the tomatoes and garlic and mix again.

7 Add the fish with the Dublin Bay prawns. Mix in carefully and leave to stand for about 30 minutes.

8 When the fish stock is cooked, pour it through a conical strainer and leave it to cool.

9 Pour the stock over the fish and other ingredients. If the liquid doesn't completely cover them add water to do so. Add salt and pepper, bring to the boil on a high heat and simmer for 15 minutes. Check and adjust the seasoning halfway through the cooking.

10 During this time, prepare the rouille. Peel the garlic, chop it up very finely and put it in a mortar with an egg yolk, cayenne pepper, saffron and salt. Pound it well, then little by little incorporate the olive oil by trickling it in as when making mayonnaise, continuously stirring with the pestle instead of a wooden spoon. Then put the mixture in a sauce-boat.

11 Cut the bread into slices and place on a baking (cookie) sheet. Sprinkle with the rest of the olive oil and bake in a hot oven or toast under the grill (broiler). Peel the rest of the garlic cloves. When the croûtes are ready rub them generously with the garlic. Heat a soup tureen.

12 Carefully put the fish and the prawns onto a large serving dish, pour over them a ladle of stock and keep hot in the oven or under the grill (broiler). Place the toasted croûtes in the hot soup tureen. Strain the stock into it. Serve at once with the rouille.

Serves 6-8

Bourride
(Fish Soup with Garlic Mayonnaise)

2 onions
2 firm, ripe tomatoes
4 cloves garlic
grated rind 1 orange
1½ litres (2½ pints) (5 cups) water
good bunch fresh thyme, fennel
  and bay leaves (imported)
salt and pepper
pinch saffron
50 ml (2 fl oz) (⅓ cup) olive oil
300 ml (½ pint) (1¼ cups) dry white
  wine
1½ kg (3 lb) mixed sea fish (hake,
  conger eel, whiting, red mullet,
  plaice (flounder), cod, red
  gurnet)

300 ml (½ pint) (1 cup) quantity
  aioli sauce (see right)
2 egg yolks
toasted croûtes of bread

1 Peel and chop the onions. Wash and chop the tomatoes. Peel and chop the garlic. Wash and dry the herbs. Bring the water to the boil.

2 Put the onions, tomatoes, garlic, grated orange rind and herbs in a large, heavy-based saucepan. Season with salt and pepper and add the saffron.

3 Stir the olive oil, followed by the white wine, into the onion mixture, then mix in the boiling water. Bring the pan back to the boil.

4 Clean and wash the fish, and cut into chunks if very large. Add them to the pan of boiling broth and cook for 10 minutes. Then lift the fish out of the pan, using a draining spoon, and keep hot.

5 Strain the fish broth through a fine sieve (strainer); either rub through the vegetables at the same time or purée in a blender and return to the broth; reheat. Heat a soup tureen.

6 Beat the egg yolks and blend with half the ailloli in a bowl. Gradually add a ladleful of the boiling broth and blend together; return this mixture to the pan of soup, stir in and reheat gently but do not boil.

7 Put the toasted croûtes of bread in the bottom of a hot soup tureen and pour in the soup. Serve at once, with the dish of fish separately, and accompanied by the rest of the ailloli in a sauce-boat.

Serves 6

Aioli (Garlic) Mayonnaise

6 garlic cloves
¼ litre (8 fl oz) (1 cup) olive oil
2 egg yolks
salt and pepper
½ lemon

1 Peel the cloves of garlic, put them in a mortar and pestle and pound, while gradually adding about 15 ml (1 tablespoon) of the oil, until they are reduced to a paste.

2 Add the egg yolks to the garlic paste in the mortar and mix well with a wooden spoon. Then add the remaining oil, little by little, stirring continuously at the same time. Add salt and pepper to taste.

3 When the mayonnaise has thickened, squeeze the juice from the lemon, strain and stir into the mayonnaise. Cover and chill until required.

Makes about 300 ml (½ pint) (1¼ cups)

Bourride

Appetizers

These can be either a single ingredient or two, simply served, like Parma ham with figs or melon, or several combined together, like Seafood Hors d'oeuvre or Stuffed Artichokes. Ideally, appetizers should stimulate the appetite, not dull it, so choose ingredients that contrast well in flavour, texture and colour, and only serve small portions

Cold Appetizers

Tomatoes Stuffed with Cream and Herbs

4 large, round firm tomatoes
bunch mixed fresh herbs
  (chervil, tarragon, chives, etc.)
2 shallots
1 clove garlic
90 ml (6 tablespoons) double
  (heavy) cream
salt and pepper
few lettuce leaves

1 Scoop out the tomatoes (see opposite page). Wash, dry and chop the herbs finely. Peel and chop the shallots and garlic.

2 Rinse and dry the tomato shells. Whip the cream until fairly stiff, then fold in the herbs, shallots, garlic, salt and pepper. Fill the tomatoes with this mixture and put a lid on each one. Chill until ready to serve.

3 Wash and dry the lettuce leaves, then arrange on a serving dish. Arrange the stuffed tomatoes on the dish and serve.

Serves 4

Swedish Herring Rissoles

3 medium potatoes
2 onions
25 g (1 oz) (2 tablespoons) butter
3 fresh herrings (ask the fishmonger to skin and fillet them)
salt and pepper
nutmeg
225 g (½ lb) (1 cup)
  redcurrant jelly
150 ml (4 fl oz) (½ cup) oil

1 Wash the potatoes without peeling them, and cook them in salted boiling water. Peel and finely chop the onions.

2 Melt the butter in a pan, and cook the onions, without letting them colour too much, for 7 or 8 minutes. Put them on one side and leave to cool.

Stuffed Tomatoes with Cream and Herbs are simple to prepare and make a light, refreshing start to any meal

3 When the potatoes are cooked, cool them in cold water, then peel them and mash them to a purée.

4 Put the herring fillets through the mincer (grinder). Add the onions, potatoes, a little salt, pepper and a little grated nutmeg. Mix well together, then shape into round flat rissoles.

5 Put the redcurrant jelly and 150 ml (¼ pint) (⅝ cup) water in a saucepan and heat slowly.

6 Heat the oil in a frying pan (skillet). When it is hot, cook the rissoles for about 10 minutes, turning them over once or twice.

7 Heat a serving dish and a sauce-boat.

8 Arrange the rissoles on the dish. Pour the hot redcurrant jelly sauce into the sauce-boat and serve very hot.

Serves 4

Tip: The mixture of sweet and savoury is typical of Scandinavian cookery. Ascertain the tastes of guests before serving this recipe or miss out the sauce.

Herring in Sherry Pickle

2 salted herrings, filleted and
  skinned
90 ml (6 tablespoons) (⅓ cup)
  sherry
60 ml (4 tablespoons) (¼ cup)
  water
45 ml (3 tablespoons) wine
  vinegar
1.25 ml (¼ teaspoon) allspice
2 onions, thinly sliced into rings
chopped fresh dill

1 Cover the herrings with cold water and leave to soak for 24 hours. Drain, rinse and dry. Place in a non-metallic bowl.

2 Combine the sherry, water, vinegar and allspice. Pour over the herrings. Cover with plastic film and refrigerate for 24 hours.

3 Serve garnished with the onion rings and dill.

Serves 4

Look 'n Cook Scooping out Tomatoes

1 and **2** Cut out tomato stalk end, then cut a slice from the other end to give a flat base; use as a lid
3 Using a melon baller or teaspoon, scoop out seeds and core, leaving sides and base intact
4 Sprinkle insides with salt to draw out moisture, turn upside down, drain, dry and then stuff

Seafood Hors d'oeuvre

1 litre (1¾ pints) (approx 5 cups)
   cockles
pinch sea salt
1 onion
bay leaf
bouquet garni
1 litre (1¾ pints) (approx 5 cups)
   mussels
1 can crab
1 small can tomato concentrate
   (paste)
15 ml (1 tablespoon) brandy
200 ml (7 fl oz) (scant 1 cup) double (whipping or heavy) cream
salt and pepper
½ kg (1 lb), fresh or frozen prawns
small bunch parsley

1 Put the cockles into a basin with water and a pinch of sea salt.

2 Peel the onion and cut in slices.

3 Prepare the cooking liquid (court bouillon): in a large saucepan put 300 ml (½ pint) (1¼ cups) water, the onion, the bay leaf and the bouquet garni; simmer for 20 minutes.

4 Scrape the mussels and wash them in several changes of water. Clean and rinse the cockles. Put the shellfish in the court bouillon and cook gently, stirring now and then, until they open. Discard any which do not open.

5 When the mussels and cockles are fully open, lift them out of the saucepan with a skimming ladle. Shell them and put in a dish.

6 Put the liquid through a strainer lined with a fine cloth and set it aside.

7 Open the can of crab, drain it, remove any cartilage and quickly flake the flesh.

8 Open the can of tomato concentrate (paste). Pour the contents into a bowl. Stir in the brandy, then pour in the cream, stirring constantly, as though thickening mayonnaise. Then add 75 ml (5 tablespoons) of the reserved seafood liquid and mix. Add a little salt and a generous sprinkling of pepper. The sauce should now be well seasoned and very smooth.

9 Divide the mussels, cockles, flaked crab and peeled prawns among 8 individual serving dishes and pour sauce over each.

10 Wash, dry and chop the parsley. Sprinkle some on top of each dish.

11 Refrigerate and serve chilled.

Serves 8

Crunchy Salad Starter

1 small tight white cabbage
coarse salt
salt and pepper
100 g (¼ lb) (⅔ packed cup)
   sultanas (seedless white
   raisins)
½ head celery
2 apples
juice ½ lemon
¼ lb walnuts
5 ml (1 teaspoon) made mustard
15 ml (1 tablespoon) vinegar
45 ml (3 tablespoons) oil
100 g (¼ lb) (1 generous cup)
   shelled chopped walnuts

1 Trim the cabbage, pulling off any withered leaves, the hard stalk and side leaves. Wash the remainder. Dry and shred them finely with a large kitchen knife. Sprinkle with coarse salt and leave for about 30 minutes to draw out excess moisture.

2 Soak the sultanas (seedless white raisins) in warm water for 10 minutes.

3 Clean the celery. Wash, dry and shred it. Peel and core the apples, then dice, sprinkle with lemon juice.

4 Drain the shredded cabbage, dry it on absorbent paper and put into a salad bowl with the celery. Mix well.

5 Make a dressing by blending together the mustard, vinegar and oil, season with salt and pepper and stir well. Pour this over the cabbage and celery and mix well but do not crush the ingredients.

6 Drain and dry the sultanas (seedless white raisins) and add them to the bowl, together with the nuts and diced apple. Stir again and serve immediately.

Serves 6

Ham Logs

6 thick slices very lean ham
1½ small celery heart
2 shallots
handful parsley
small bunch chives
juice ½ lemon
3 portions Demi-sel cheese
5 ml (1 teaspoon) strong mustard
salt
5 ml (1 teaspoon) paprika
pinch cayenne pepper
100 g (¼ lb) chopped walnuts

1 Cut 2 of the slices of ham into fine strips.

2 Clean the celery and chop it as finely as possible. Peel and finely chop the shallots. Wash, dry and chop the parsley and chives.

3 Mash the cheese and beat in the parsley, chives, shallots 15 ml (1 tablespoon) lemon juice, the mustard, salt, paprika and cayenne pepper.

4 Stir in the chopped ham, celery and nuts. Beat well until the mixture is very smooth and creamy. Spread this mixture on the four remaining ham slices and roll these up to form 'logs'. Serve chilled, on a bed of lettuce and decorated with sliced tomatoes and a few sprigs of parsley.

Serves 4

Seafood Hors d'oeuvre is a delicious medley of shellfish, brandy and cream

Artichoke Hearts with Cottage Cheese

300 g (11 oz) (2 cups) cottage
  cheese
4 large globe artichokes
large bunch chives, chervil and
  parsley, mixed
salt and pepper
pinch cayenne pepper
few lettuce leaves

For the Blanching Mixture:
juice 3 lemons
15 g (1 tablespoon) flour
1½ litres (2¾ pints) (7 cups) water

1 Put the cottage cheese in a cloth-lined sieve (strainer) and leave to drain completely.

2 Prepare the artichoke hearts and blanch (see pages 58-59). Cook them for 40 minutes in the blanching mixture, or till tender, then drain and cool.

3 Wash the herbs; dry them well and chop finely. Tip them into a bowl. Add the cottage cheese, salt and pepper, and cayenne, and mix well with a fork; then whisk (beat) vigorously.

4 Wash and dry the lettuce leaves. Arrange them on a serving dish. Lay the artichoke hearts on the lettuce and pile a pyramid of the cheese mixture on each one. Serve chilled.

Serves 4

Apple Hors d'oeuvre

1 lemon
1 small celery heart
1 small cucumber
few lettuce leaves
3 tomatoes
few sprigs chives and chervil
150 ml (6 fl oz) (¾ cup) double
  (whipping or heavy) cream
2.5 ml (½ teaspoon) paprika
salt and pepper
3 eating apples
12 radishes

1 Squeeze the lemon and reserve the juice. Wash the celery and chop it into fine strips.

2 Peel the cucumber, split it in half lengthways and remove the seeds. Sprinkle both halves with salt, to remove the excess moisture.

3 Wash and dry the lettuce leaves. Wash and dry the tomatoes and then quarter them. Wash the chives and the chervil; dry and chop them.

4 In a bowl beat together the cream, lemon juice and paprika, and season with salt and pepper.

5 Rinse and dry the cucumber and cut it into small cubes. Peel and core the apples and dice them.

6 Put the cucumber, apples, celery and tomatoes into a dish. Pour the cream sauce over and stir it in

7 Wash and scrape the radishes. Cut them into flower shapes.

8 Line the sides and bottom of a salad bowl with the lettuce leaves. Arrange the salad in the centre. Sprinkle with the chopped chives and chervil, and decorate with the radishes. Serve chilled.

Serves 6

Apple Hors d'oeuvre is a refreshing starter which sharpens the taste buds

Look 'n Cook Preparation of Artichoke Hearts

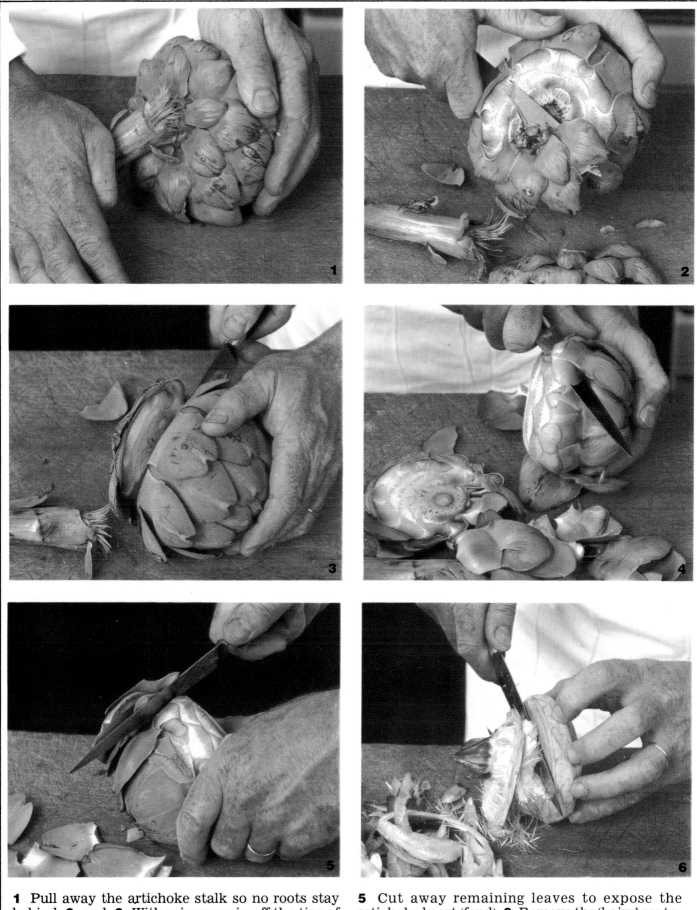

1 Pull away the artichoke stalk so no roots stay behind **2** and **3** With scissors snip off the tips of the leaves, then cut round and level the base **4** and

5 Cut away remaining leaves to expose the artichoke heart (fond) **6** Remove the 'hairy' centre (choke) **7** Trim round the heart to neaten **8** and

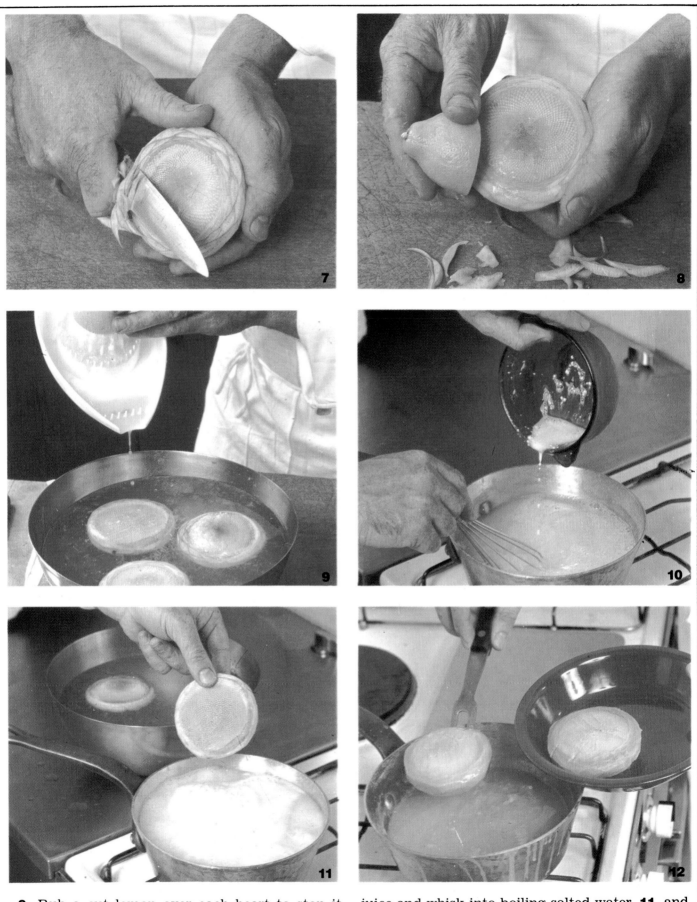

9 Rub a cut lemon over each heart to stop it blackening; place in cold water with some of the lemon juice 10 Mix flour with remaining lemon juice and whisk into boiling salted water 11 and 12 Cook the artichoke hearts till tender, then drain and chill them until needed

Anchovy and Garlic Stuffed Eggs make an attractive egg starter

Oyster Cocktails

2 dozen fresh oysters
2 small sticks celery, taken from
  the heart
60 ml (4 tablespoons) tomato
  ketchup (catsup)
75 ml (2½ fl oz) (⅓ cup) gin
15 ml (1 tablespoon) cream
5 ml (1 teaspoon) lemon juice
salt and pepper
pinch cayenne pepper
bunch chervil
5 ml (1 teaspoon) paprika

1 Open the oysters with an oys-ter knife and scrape them from the shells. Drain them, keeping the juice. Strain the juice through muslin (cheesecloth) and put the oysters in a bowl.

2 Wash and dry the celery sticks. Chop them finely and add to the oysters.

3 Stir into the oyster liquor the tomato ketchup (catsup), gin cream and lemon juice and beat for a moment. Taste and adjust the seasoning. Then add a pinch of cayenne pepper.

4 Pour this sauce over the oys-ters and celery and mix gently. Spoon the oyster cocktail into 4 glasses or small bowls.

5 Wash, dry and chop the cher-vil. Sprinkle the chopped chervil over the cocktails together with some paprika. Chill the glasses or bowls in the refrigerator for 1 hour and serve very cold.

Serves 4

Anchovy and Garlic Stuffed Eggs

4 eggs
4 large cloves garlic
40 g (1½ oz) (3 tablespoons) butter
salt and pepper
8 olives
8 anchovy fillets
few lettuce leaves
chopped parsley
4 small tomatoes

1 Put the eggs in a pan of cold water and bring to the boil. Peel the garlic cloves and add to the boiling water. Remove them after 7 minutes, drain and then pound in a mortar.

2 When the water has been boil-ing for 10 minutes, take out the eggs, cool them in cold water and shell. Cut the shelled hard-boiled eggs in half lengthways. Leave them to cool.

3 Put the butter in a bowl and work it to a very soft paste with a wooden spoon.

4 Carefully remove the yolks from the eggs, without damaging the whites. Mash and sieve the yolks, and add them to the soft-ened butter. Then add the garlic purée and stir well until smooth. Season.

5 Pile this paste back into the half egg whites. Decorate each with an olive with an anchovy fillet wrapped around it.

6 Arrange the lettuce leaves on a serving platter, place the stuffed eggs on top and sprinkle with the finely-chopped parsley. Slice the tomatoes in half horizontally and use the halves to garnish the platter. Refrigerate and serve cold.

Serves 4

Mussels in Spicy Sauce

100 g (4 oz) (1 cup) canned or
  bottled mussels, drained
30 ml (2 tablespoons)
  mayonnaise
10 ml (2 teaspoons) mustard
5 ml (1 teaspoon) sherry
2.5 ml (½ teaspoon) lemon juice
70 g (2 oz) bottled or
  canned pimientoes

1 Put the mussels in the serving dish.

2 To the mayonnaise add the mustard, sherry and lemon juice and stir carefully until blended. Cut the pimientoes into strips and stir into the sauce.

3 Spoon this sauce over the mussels.

Serves 2

Tip: This is a tasty way of serving mussels when fresh ones are not in season.
  If using fresh, reserve a few shells for decoration.

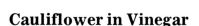

Cauliflower in Vinegar

1 medium cauliflower
salt
225 ml (8 fl oz) (1 cup) vinegar
225 ml (8 fl oz) (1 cup) water
1 clove garlic, cut in half
4 g (2 teaspoons) dried basil
45 ml (3 tablespoons) oil
15 ml (1 tablespoon) lime or
  lemon juice
2 g (1 teaspoon) chopped
  parsley
2 g (1 teaspoon) chopped chives
freshly ground black pepper

1 Wash and trim the cauliflower and divide into florets or sprigs. Add to boiling salted water and cook for 10-15 minutes. Drain.

2 Bring the vinegar, water, garlic and basil to the boil and pour over the cauliflower. Leave until cold, then chill.

3 Mix the oil, lime or lemon juice, parsley, chives, salt and black pepper to make a smooth dressing. Drain the cauliflower, pour on the dressing and serve at once.

Serves 6

Red Peppers and Mushrooms

200 g (¼ lb) button mushrooms
salt and pepper
2 lemons
75 ml (5 tablespoons) olive oil
6 large red peppers
small bunch chervil

1 Clean the mushrooms. Cut the ends off the stalks. Wash the mushrooms quickly but do not leave them under water longer than necessary. Slice them thinly and season with salt and pepper.

2 Squeeze 1 of the lemons and sprinkle 30 ml (2 tablespoons) of the juice and 30 ml (2 tablespoons) olive oil over the mushrooms. Leave them to marinate.

3 Wash and dry the peppers. Grill (broil) them under a high heat (the skin should swell and darken) or hold over a flame on a skewer. Then rinse them under cold water and peel them. The darkened outer skin should come off very easily, exposing the soft red flesh underneath.

4 Cut the peppers in half and remove the seeds. Cut the flesh in strips. Season with salt and pepper, and sprinkle over the rest of the lemon juice and oil.

5 Wash the other lemon and quarter it. Wash, dry and chop the chervil.

6 Mix the peppers and mush-

rooms together in a deep dish. Garnish with the lemon quarters and sprinkle chervil over the top. Chill 1 hour before serving.

Serves 6

Red Herrings with Sauerkraut

6 herring fillets (smoked and
  salted)
45 ml (3 tablespoons) oil
2 dessert apples
450 g (1 lb) (6 cups packed) raw
  sauerkraut
2 mild onions
1 lemon
30 ml (2 tablespoons) double
  (heavy) cream
1 carton plain yogurt
pepper
bunch parsley

1 Cut the herring fillets into small pieces. Put them on a deep plate and pour the oil over them.

2 Peel, core and dice the apples.

3 Wash the sauerkraut in fresh water. Drain it thoroughly, squeezing with the hands to extract all the water. Put it into a cloth, dry it well then separate the shreds.

4 Peel the onions. Cut them into rounds, then separate into rings. Squeeze the juice from the lemon.

5 Mix the lemon juice with the cream and yogurt. Add pepper to taste and blend all these ingredients together.

6 Mix the sauerkraut and the diced apple, pour on the lemon-flavoured yogurt and stir gently.

7 Wash, dry and chop the parsley.

8 Arrange the sauerkraut and apple salad round the edge of a serving dish.

9 Drain the herring fillets and place them in the centre of the dish. Cover them with the onion rings. Sprinkle with chopped parsley and serve very cold.

Serves 6

Tuna Fish with Aubergines (Eggplant) in Sweet-sour Sauce

 ★ ♨♨♨

In Sicily this dish is a speciality and is called Caponata; some versions omit the tuna fish.

3 aubergines (eggplants)
1 head young celery
1 litre (1¾ pints) (4½ cups) water
6 canned anchovies, drained
5 large ripe firm tomatoes
1 large onion
1 bunch parsley
100 ml (4 fl oz) (½ cup) oil
salt and pepper
few sprigs thyme
1 bay leaf, imported
40 g (1½ oz) (1½ tablespoons) sugar
10 ml (2 teaspoons) vinegar
100 g (¼ lb) (1 cup) small black
   olives, stoned (pitted) if large
50 g (2 oz) capers
350 g (¾ lb) (1½ cups) canned
   tuna fish

1 Peel the aubergines (egg plants). Cut them into cubes, sprinkle with salt to draw out the excess moisture and any bitterness and leave for about 30 minutes. Wash and trim the celery, and slice thinly.

2 Bring the water to the boil, add salt and put in the celery; simmer for about 8 minutes, then drain and plunge into a pan of cold water; drain again and set aside.

3 Wash the anchovies to remove the excess salt. Separate the fillets and rinse again thoroughly in water. Cut them into small pieces.

4 Skin the tomatoes; quarter them, remove the seeds and chop the flesh. Peel and thinly slice the onion. Wash, dry and chop the parsley.

5 Heat 30 ml (2 tablespoons) oil in a saucepan. When hot, add the onion and cook gently until soft but not browned. Add the tomatoes, season with salt and pepper, add the thyme and bay leaf and cook over a very low heat until the mixture is a soft pulp. Remove the thyme and bay leaf and rub the mixture through a conical sieve (strainer).

6 Put the tomato purée in a pan, add the sugar and cook until thickened and lightly browned. Then add the vinegar and cook for a further 3-4 minutes.

7 Meanwhile, drain and dry the aubergine (eggplant) pieces. Heat the rest of the oil in a saucepan, put in the aubergine (eggplant) and cook briskly until lightly browned. Drain off the oil.

8 Remove the pan of tomato sauce from the heat and stir into the aubergines (eggplants), together with the celery, anchovies, black olives and capers. Correct the seasoning – this dish should be fairly spicy – and mix together.

9 Set the mixture aside to cool, then chill in the refrigerator overnight. Turn the mixture into a salad bowl. Break the tuna fish into regular bite-sized pieces and arrange over the top. Chill and serve.
Serves 6

Tuna fish and aubergines (eggplant) in a piquant sauce, a deliciously refreshing dish for a hot summer's day

Smoked Fish Starter

1 tight white cabbage heart
  (small)
2 marinated herrings
2.5 ml (½ teaspoon) cumin seed
90 ml (6 tablespoons) double
  (heavy) cream
3 smoked sprats (sardines)
2 lemons
2 apples
12 thin slices wholemeal bread
50 g (2 oz) (4 tablespoons) butter
75 g (scant ⅛ lb) thin slices
  smoked salmon
6 thin slices smoked eel
coarse salt and pepper

1 Trim, wash and dry the cabbage and shred it finely with a
large sharp kitchen knife. Put the
shredded cabbage into a bowl,
sprinkle lightly with salt and
leave to stand while continuing
with the preparation.

2 Drain the marinated herrings
and fillet them. Put the fillets
in a blender or through a mincer
(grinder) to make a purée. Add to
this half the cumin and 30 ml
(2 tablespoons) cream.

3 Wash the smoked sprats.

4 Squeeze 1 lemon and reserve
juice. Wash and dry the second
lemon and cut it in thin rounds,
then each round in half.

5 Peel the apples and cut them
in quarters, remove the cores and
pips and dice the flesh.

6 Butter 9 slices of wholemeal
bread and cut them diagonally to
make 18 triangles. Arrange the
slices of smoked eel on 6 of these
triangles, and the slices of
smoked salmon on the others.
Pipe round a border of mayonnaise if liked.

7 Butter the remainder of the
slices of bread with the herring
purée, and cut them into
triangles. Place 1 sprat fillet on
each of the triangles, and a semi-
circle of lemon on each slice.

8 Drain and dry the cabbage.
Add to it the diced apple and the
rest of the cumin. Sprinkle with
lemon juice and pepper and mix
gently.

9 Arrange the cabbage in a heap
in the centre of a serving dish,
and pour over the rest of the
cream. Arrange the various fish-
covered triangles of bread round
the edge of the dish and serve
cold.
Serves 6

*An eye-catching appetizer,
choose several kinds of smoked
fish for colour and flavour
contrast*

Vegetables à la Grecque

3 globe artichoke hearts
1 small cauliflower
1 lemon
225 g (½ lb) mushrooms
3 carrots
2 bulbs fennel
3 turnips
2 leeks
3 cloves garlic
225 g (½ lb) green olives
¼ litre (8 fl oz) (1 cup) oil
15 ml (1 tablespoon) tomato
   concentrate (paste)
5 ml (1 teaspoon) coriander seeds
100 ml (4 fl oz) (½ cup) wine
   vinegar
salt and pepper

1 Peel and wash all the vegetables. Break the cauliflower into florets. Squeeze the juice of the lemon.

2 Put the artichoke hearts, the cauliflower florets, the mushrooms (whole small ones, cut in half if large) into water. Add the lemon juice to prevent the vegetables discolouring.

3 Slice the carrots, fennel, turnips and leeks. Peel and crush the garlic. Stone (pit) the olives and wash in cold water.

4 Heat the oil in a pan. When it is hot, add the leeks, then all the other vegetables, stirring all the time to prevent them sticking.

5 Add the crushed garlic, the tomato concentrate (paste), the coriander, the vinegar, the water, salt and pepper.

6 Leave to cook for 30 minutes, stirring from time to time. The vegetables should stay firm. When cooked, leave to cool.

Serves 8-10

Artichokes à la Grecque

4 globe artichokes
2 lemons
225 g (½ lb) canned tomatoes,
   drained
6 shallots
100 ml (4 fl oz) (½ cup) oil
6 coriander seeds
1 bouquet garni
100 ml (4 fl oz) (½ cup) dry white
   wine
salt and pepper

1 Prepare the artichoke hearts (see page 58). Cut 1 lemon in half. Rub the artichoke hearts with one half. Squeeze the other half, pouring the juice into a bowl. Fill the bowl with water.

2 Cut the hearts into 4 or 6 pieces. Remove all the hairs with a serrated-edge knife. Dip the artichokes into the lemon water.

3 Put the artichokes into a saucepan. Add the lemon water. Bring to the boil and boil for 1 minute. Chop the tomatoes roughly. Peel the baby onions and squeeze the last lemon.

4 Warm the oil in a sauté pan. Drain the artichokes and put them into the pan. Add the tomatoes, the onions, the coriander seeds, the bouquet garni, the lemon juice and the white wine. Add seasoning, cover and cook on a low heat for 30 minutes.

5 When the cooking is finished, remove the bouquet garni, tip the artichoke pieces into an hors d'oeuvre dish. Leave to cool, then put the dish in the refrigerator.

Serves 4

Vegetables à la Grecque — mixed vegetables served cold in this way make a delicious starter

Look'n Cook Artichoke Hearts à la Grecque

1 Cut the hearts into pieces and put into lemon water **2** Cut away the hairy part **3** Put the hearts into a pan, strain the lemon water over them and boil for 1 minute **4** The ingredients **5** Put all the ingredients into a sauté pan and cook gently **6** The finished dish. Keep in the refrigerator until needed.

Crayfish with Avocados

1kg (2lb) crayfish
sea salt
1 bouquet garni
1 small cucumber
2 avocados
30ml (2 tablespoons) gin
2.5ml (½ teaspoon) Tabasco sauce
salt and pepper
300ml (½ pint) (1¼ cups)
  mayonnaise,
  home-made or bottled
pinch cayenne pepper
2.5ml (½ teaspoon) paprika

1 Wash and drain the crayfish.

2 Boil water in a large saucepan with a handful or sea salt and the bouquet garni. Drop the crayfish into the boiling water and cook for about 10 minutes.

3 Drain the crayfish and leave to cool.

4 Peel the cucumber and split in two lengthwise. Take out the seeds with a small spoon. Grate the flesh of the cucumber, put it into a bowl and leave to drain without salting it.

5 Cut the avocados into halves, remove the stone (pit), and, with a melon baller, scoop the flesh into balls.

6 When the crayfish are cold, remove the meat from the tails.

7 Put the avocado balls and the crayfish tails into a glass serving bowl. Pour over the gin and Tabasco sauce. Season with a little salt and pepper and mix well. Leave to marinate for about 20 minutes.

8 Lay a piece of muslin (cheesecloth) over a colander. Pour in the cucumber pulp, and press down well to extract as much water as possible. Blend this pulp into the mayonnaise, folding it in gently. Then season with cayenne.

9 Pour the cucumber mayonnaise over the crayfish and avocado, mixing well. Sprinkle with paprika and serve very cold.

Serves 4

Crab and Avocado Cocktail

4 eggs
225g (½lb) (1 cup) crabmeat
1 tablespoon (15ml) tomato
  concentrate (paste)
300ml (½ pint) (1¼ cups)
  mayonnaise, home-made or
  bottled
salt and pepper
3 avocados
paprika

1 Put 6 small glass dishes into the refrigerator.

2 Cook the eggs in boiling water for 10 minutes. Cool them in cold water and then shell them.

3 Flake the crabmeat, removing the cartilage. Add the tomato concentrate (paste) to the mayonnaise. Pass the hard-boiled eggs through a food mill or chop them.

4 Mix together the crabmeat, chopped eggs and the mayonnaise in a bowl. Season.

5 Cut the avocados in half, take out the stones (pits), cut the flesh into large cubes and place them in the chilled dishes. Cover with the crab mixture and sprinkle with paprika. Chill until ready to serve.

Serves 6

Peaches Filled with Crab — a mixture of fruit and fish gives an interesting light first course

Tomatoes Stuffed with Anchovies and Rice

6 firm tomatoes
salt
125g (¼lb) (¾ cup) long-grain rice
24 canned anchovy fillets
24 black olives
1 small head fennel
2 shallots
chopped parsley
1 green pepper
2.5ml (½ teaspoon) Pernod
  (optional)
juice of ½ lemon
300ml (½ pint) (1¼ cups) mayonnaise, home-made or bottled

1 Scoop out the tomatoes. Wash the rice under running cold water until the water is clear.

2 Bring to the boil a pan of salted water, twice the volume of the rice (i.e. 300ml (½ pint) (1¼ cups). Add the rice, simmer for about 12 minutes or until tender, then drain and leave until cold.

3 Put aside 6 anchovy fillets and 6 olives. Chop the rest of the anchovies. Stone (pit) the olives and cut into quarters.

4 Trim the fennel, wash, dry and chop. Peel and chop the shallots. Wash, dry and chop the parsley.

Wash and dry the pepper; cut it in half, remove the seeds and white membrane and chop finely.

5 Add the pastis, if used, and the lemon juice to the mayonaise. Add the cooked rice, chopped anchovies, olives, shallots, fennel, pepper and the parsley to the mayonnaise. Fold carefully together.

6 Rince and dry the tomatoes. Fill with the rice salad and make a dome on top. Top with an olive and a rolled anchovy fillet. Arrange the stuffed tomatoes on a serving dish and refrigerate for 1 hour before serving.

Serves 6

Peaches Filled with Crab

5 large peaches
100 g (¼ lb) canned crabmeat
100 ml (4 fl oz) (½ cup) double (heavy) cream
1.25 ml (¼ teaspoon) lemon juice
10 ml (2 teaspoons) brandy
8 lettuce leaves
large pinch paprika
salt and pepper

1 Peel the peaches: halve them and remove the stones (pits).

2 Drain the crab, and mash the crabmeat together with 1 of the peaches in a basin.

3 Add the cream, lemon juice, brandy, paprika, salt and pepper, and blend all the ingredients together well.

4 Wash the lettuce leaves, and dry them on absorbent paper. Make a bed of the leaves on a flat serving dish, and place a peach half on each of the leaves. Fill each peach half with the crab mixture.

5 Chill the dish for at least 1 hour before serving.

Serves 4

Tomatoes Stuffed with Anchovies and Rice — this simple dish goes down well at buffet parties

Look 'n Cook Fish Terrine

Prepare the fish and make the panada (see page 77).
1 Cook the panada until smooth and thick **2**
Sauté the mushrooms, add the shallots and fry until soft. Remove **3** Add the cubed fish, cook until golden, then remove **4** Pour in the wine and boil, stirring in all the sediment **5** and **6** Put back the

fish, mushrooms and shallots and stir in the parsley **7** and **8** Blend the fish fillets with 2 egg whites **9** Add the panada, blend and turn into a bowl **10** Stir in the whipped (beaten) cream **11** and **12** Fold in the fish and mushroom mixture, spoon into a greased terrine and cook.

Fish Terrine

80 g (3½ oz) (⅓ cup) butter or
  margarine
about 1½ kg firm white fish
  (e.g. pike, haddock, cod)
3 eggs
90 g (3¾ oz) (9 tablespoons) flour
salt and pepper
200 ml (6 fl oz) (¾ cup) milk
200 g (7 oz) (3½ cups) button
  mushrooms
2 shallots
100 ml (4 fl oz) (½ cup) dry
  white wine
2 g (½ tablespoon) chopped
  parsley
400 ml (¾ pint) (2 cups) double
  (heavy) cream

1 Take the fat out of the refrigerator to soften.

2 Fillet and skin the fish. Put the fillets in a basin, cover, and put them in the refrigerator. Trim away the flesh from the stomach and cut into tiny dice.

3 Work 40 g (1½ oz) (3 tablespoons) of the fat in a bowl to soften. Separate the eggs, and whip (beat) in the egg yolks and flour to make a stiff paste (panada); add salt and pepper.

4 Bring the milk to the boil in a saucepan, pour onto the panada, little by little, whisking all the time, then turn the mixture into a heavy pan. Cook over a low heat, stirring with a wooden spoon all the time, until the mixture comes away cleanly from the sides of the pan. Lightly grease a plate, put the panada on it, cool, then chill in the refrigerator.

5 Peel and wipe the mushrooms. Slice them and sauté in 20 g (¾ oz) (1¼ tablespoons) fat. Peel and finely chop the shallots; and add them to the sauté pan. Cook very gently for about 3 minutes; season with salt and pepper, then turn the mixture into a bowl.

6 Put the sauté pan back on a moderate heat; put in the diced fish and cook till golden-brown, then turn the fish into the bowl. Place the sauté pan on a high heat, tip in the wine and boil for 2 minutes, stirring and scraping across the bottom of the pan to incorporate all the drippings. Reduce (evaporate) to half the quantity, then return the contents of the bowl to the sauté pan.

Sprinkle with chopped parsley, add salt and pepper; blend together well and spoon back into the bowl.

7 Season the fish fillets with salt and pepper. Put them in a blender with 2 egg whites and the panada; blend until smooth.

8 Beat (whip) the cream until stiff, then stir into the fish mixture and blend again. Turn the mixture into a casserole or bowl. Stir in the mushrooms, shallots and fish.

9 Preheat the oven to 170°C, 325°F, gas 3. Lightly grease the terrine with 20 g (¾ oz) (1½ tablespoons) fat; spoon in the mixture and press down well. Cover and seal the terrine, then cook in a bain marie in the oven for about 1½ hours.

10 Cool, then chill until ready to serve.

Serves 10-12

Fish terrine — slicing the terrine into individual portions for serving

All about herbs and their uses

Mint *This is a popular herb which is used as a flavouring for boiled new potatoes and peas and as a garnish for fruit and iced drinks. It is probably best known for its use in mint sauce or jelly to accompany roast lamb.*

Sorrel *The leaves of this herb have a pungent acid flavour and the young ones are used in salads. The older plant can be cooked in the same way as spinach and is used to flavour sauces and soups. Sorrel is also known as dock.*

Thyme *The excellent flavour of thyme means that it is used extensively in the kitchen and is one of the basic ingredients of a bouquet garni. The leaves contain an oil called thymol which aids the digestion of fatty foods. Thyme can be used with cheese dishes, shellfish and poultry stuffing and as a garnish for vegetables.*

Rosemary *The leaves are used both fresh and dried and go well with beef, salmon, duck, boiled ham and pork. Rosemary can also be used with sweet dishes such as jellies (jellos), fruit salads and biscuits.*

Marjoram *There are three types of marjoram, sweet marjoram being* the one most often used for flavouring. It can be added to soups, stews, cheese and egg dishes, and salads and blends well with other herbs such as thyme.

Fennel *This herb is related to dill but is sweeter and more aromatic. The digestive properties of fennel make it a good accompaniment for oily fish dishes, and it is also used to flavour soups, sauces, salads, cakes and pastry.*

Sage *This is a slightly bitter herb which, because of its strong flavour, should be used carefully. Sage is probably best known for its use with onion in poultry stuffings, but it also gives a good flavour to peas and beans. Chopped fresh leaves can be added to salads, pickles and cheese, and the dried leaves to casseroles and sausagemeat.*

Bay leaves *These have a strong spicy flavour which goes well with game, meat, fish, poultry, salads, sauces and vegetables. Bay leaves are a basic ingredient of a bouquet garni and can be added to the milk used for custards, moulds, and milk puddings and to the stock for boiling fish. Their flavour becomes stronger if they are crushed or dried.*

Chives *Chive is a member of the leek and onion family and, as would be expected, the flavour is reminiscent of onion. The thin, tubular stalks are a bright green colour and so look very attractive chopped into short lengths and sprinkled over soups or mixed into pale dishes such as potato salad and cream cheese.*

Dill *Dill leaves are blue-green and feathery in appearance and their flavour is similar to aniseed and caraway. They can be chopped and added to salads, green vegetables, soups and stews, but because their flavour soon disappears when they are cooked, they should be added to hot dishes just before serving. Dill adds flavour to pickles and is particularly suited to use with fish dishes.*

Basil *The large, heart-shaped leaves of basil have a peppery flavour and can be used in combination with other herbs such as rosemary, sage and oregano. The flavour develops with cooking so basil should be used carefully. This herb is particularly effective with vegetables which have little flavour and with chicken, egg and rice dishes.*

Mint   Sorrel   Thyme   Rosemary   Marjoram

Fennel   Lemon sage   Bay leaves

Chives   Sage   Dill   Basil

All about Salads

An exotic salad with cheese and fruit

All about Salads

In the next three issues we give you lots of new ideas for salads. Salads need not only be a mixture of lettuce and tomatoes which are served as an accompaniment to cold meat; they can also be served as hors d'oeuvres or as main meals in themselves. The term 'salad' is now used to encompass a wide range of dishes and foods. Salads can be made with herbs, plants, raw or cooked vegetables, eggs, cheese, meat, fish, fruits, nuts, pasta or rice. The list is seemingly endless.

With the emphasis on healthy, raw and wholefoods and the present trend towards a more natural way of eating, salads are becoming ever more popular and original. They are also ideal if you are slimming or diet-conscious, as usually they contain very little carbohydrate or fat and are rich in vitamins and roughage.

Salad Dressings

A perfect salad should be crisp, cool and served in a delicious dressing. Never toss a salad in an acid dressing too long before serving it – it will go soggy. Always toss it at the last moment. The French are masters of the salad dressing. They use only the best olive oil and wine vinegars. A few useful tips to remember when making a French dressing are:

1 Use the best oil if possible – *eg* olive, walnut or ground-nut oil
2 Never use malt vinegar – it will give your salad a bitter flavour.
3 If you want to use mustard in your dressing, add a wine-flavoured type.

There are four types of dressings: the classical French dressing; mayonnaise; creamy white sauce; and blue cheese dressing. Of course, there are many variations on these. Try adding tomato concentrate (paste), lemon juice, chutneys, herbs and spices, curry powder or Tabasco to mayonnaise for an unusual flavour. French dressings can be more tasty and tangy if you mix in some chopped onions or capers.

Salad Hors d'Oeuvres

Salads are delicious for hors d'oeuvres or appetizers before a main course. They make a light and refreshing start to a meal. Opposite are some ideas for salad starters which will whet your appetite for what is to come. Try them as appetizers or serve them as canapés at a buffet or party. They are all quickly and easily prepared, and can be made in advance and refrigerated until you wish to serve them. The key below will help you to identify them.

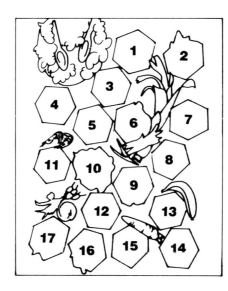

1 Black olives, sliced tomato, halved green grapes and nuts surrounded by orange segments (sections) and thinly sliced cucumber, then topped with onion rings.

2 Alternate slices of tomato and hard-boiled egg on a bed of chicory leaves garnished with black and green olives.

3 Chopped beetroot (beet) with spring onions (scallions) on deseeded tomato slices arranged like the petals of a flower.

4 Tomato slices and onion rings in a classic French dressing, sprinkled with chopped chives.

5 Sliced tomato, cucumber, hard-boiled eggs and black olives, with onion rings and anchovy strips on a bed of lettuce leaves.

6 Sliced blanched courgettes (zucchini) and sliced tomatoes on a bed of lettuce leaves, generously sprinkled with chopped chives.

7 Deseeded segments of tomato with pineapple chunks in an oily dressing to which pineapple juice is added.

8 Lobster chunks in a spicy mayonnaise with sliced bananas and tiny onions, garnished with a sprig of fresh watercress.

9 Hard-boiled eggs, split and filled with chopped red pepper and prawns in sour cream. Then sprinkled with finely grated cheese on a bed of cress.

10 Prawns, tomato wedges and black olives heaped on a bed of crisp lettuce leaves.

11 A hollowed-out tomato stuffed with cream cheese, celery seeds and chives surrounded by an attractive border of cress.

12 Chunks of canned meat with cooked rice, mixed with chopped red and green peppers, onion and hard-boiled eggs.

13 Overlapping thinly sliced tomatoes, dressed with natural yogurt and chopped chives with a cucumber border, and a slice of cucumber in the centre.

14 Sliced tomatoes, prawns and bean sprouts surrounded by sliced apples which have been sprinkled with lemon juice.

15 Sliced tomatoes and raw mushrooms on a bed of lettuce leaves, sprinkled with chopped chives in a French dressing.

16 Half an avocado pear on a plain lettuce leaf, filled with chopped ham, onions and red pepper in a vinaigrette dressing.

17 Sliced tomatoes, garnished with Cheddar cheese cubes on a bed of flower-shaped chicory leaves.

Ham and Egg Salad

1 apple
100 g (¼ lb) ham cut into 5 mm
  (¼ in) cubes
100 g (¼ lb) boiled new potatoes,
  cut into 5 mm (¼ in) cubes
15 ml (1 tablespoon) chopped
  chives or shallots
150 ml (¼ pint) (⅝ cup) mayonnaise
4 lettuce leaves
4 hard-boiled eggs
5 ml (1 teaspoon) chopped
  parsley

1 Peel and core the apple. Dice it
finely. Combine with the ham,
potatoes and chives or shallots.
Pour over the mayonnaise,
reserving a little for later, and toss.

2 Wash, dry and shred the lettuce. Place a quarter of the lettuce
in the bottom of each of 4 glasses.
Top with the ham and potato
mixture.

3 Cut each egg into 8 wedges and
arrange them like the spokes of a
wheel on each serving. Dot the
yolks with a little mayonnaise
and sprinkle with the chopped
parsley.

Serves 4

Avocado Starter

2 avocados
1 grapefruit
8 lettuce leaves

For the Dressing:
150 ml (¼ pint) (⅝ cup) mayonnaise
15 ml (1 tablespoon) tomato
  ketchup (catsup)
2-3 drops Worcestershire sauce
dash Tabasco (optional)
juice half lemon

1 Prepare the dressing by combining the mayonnaise, tomato
ketchup (catsup), Worcestershire
sauce, and Tabasco if desired.
Add the lemon juice.

2 Peel and stone (seed) the

avocados and cut them into small
pieces.

3 Peel the grapefruit, remove
the white skin, and divide into
segments (sections). Cut each
segment (section) into 4 and
combine with the avocado.

4 Wash and dry the lettuce.
Place one leaf at the bottom of
each of 4 glasses. Shred the
remaining leaves and place equal
amounts in the glasses. Pour in
the avocado mixture.

5 Chill for 1 hour before serving.

Serves 4

*Ham and Egg Salad is easy to
make and attractively
served in glasses, garnished
with parsley and eggs*

Prawn Starter

2 oranges
8 walnuts, shelled
2 apples, cored
1 stick celery
100 g (¼ lb) (¾ cup) cooked, peeled
  prawns
½ lettuce
4 slices lemon

Prawn Starter combines juicy apples and oranges with nuts, prawns and vegetables in a glass, garnished with lemon

1 Peel the oranges, remove the white skin and divide into segments (sections). Roughly chop the walnuts and apples and dice the celery. Combine these ingredients in a bowl with the prawns.

2 Wash and drain the lettuce. Shred it finely and place equal portions in 4 glasses. Pour in the mixture. Chill for 1 hour and garnish with a slice of lemon.

Serves 4

Prawn Salad

450 g (1 lb) (3 cups) cooked, peeled prawns
225 g (½ lb) (2½ cups) sliced mushrooms
2 medium tomatoes, each cut into 8
225 g (½ lb) canned asparagus tips, drained
100 g (¼ lb) (1 cup) cooked peas
30 ml (2 tablespoons) oil
5 ml (1 teaspoon) white wine vinegar
2.5 ml (½ teaspoon) salt

Avocado Starter makes a fruity and refreshing start to any meal, and it can easily be prepared the previous day

1.25 ml (¼ teaspoon) pickled dill weed
2 hard-boiled eggs

1 Put the prawns, mushrooms, tomatoes, asparagus and peas into a salad bowl.

2 Mix the oil, wine vinegar, salt and dill together and pour over the salad. Cut each egg into 8 pieces and use as garnish.

Serves 4

Green Olive Salad

12 green stuffed olives, chopped
3 sticks celery, chopped
1 onion, finely chopped
3 apples, cored and chopped
60 ml (2 fl oz) (4 tablespoons)
  mayonnaise
60 ml (2 fl oz) (4 tablespoons)
  yogurt
15 ml (1 tablespoon) horseradish
15 ml (1 tablespoon) apple purée
5 ml (1 teaspoon) honey
5 ml (1 teaspoon) chopped spring
  onions (scallions)
225 g (½ lb) (2 cups) cooked
  potatoes
6 radishes
few sprigs parsley

1 Make an olive paste by combining the olives with ⅓ of the
celery, the onion, half one apple
and 15 ml (1 tablespoon) of the
mayonnaise. Chill.

2 Mix the yogurt, the rest of the
mayonnaise, horseradish, apple
purée, honey, and spring onions
(scallions).

3 Season and mix with the
remaining celery, potatoes and
apples.

4 Serve the salad on lettuce
leaves and place the olive paste in
the middle, garnished with cut
radishes and parsley.

Serves 4

Tuna Olive Salad with Garlic Toast

1 aubergine (eggplant), peeled
  and cubed
salt and pepper
30 ml (1 fl oz) (2 tablespoons) oil
45 ml (1½ fl oz) (3 tablespoons)
  olive oil
15 ml (1 tablespoon) vinegar
1 clove garlic, crushed
2.5 ml (½ teaspoon) mustard
225 g (½ lb) canned tuna
2 sticks celery, chopped
8 black olives
stick French bread

For the Garlic Butter:
50 g (2 oz) (4 tablespoons) butter
1 clove garlic, crushed

1 Sprinkle the aubergine (eggplant) with salt and leave for
½ hour. Wash and drain, then fry
quickly in the oil. Cool.

2 Preheat the oven to 190°C,
375°F, gas 5.

3 Mix the olive oil, vinegar,
garlic, mustard, salt and pepper,
and pour over the tuna, celery and
aubergine (eggplant) in a bowl.
Garnish with black olives. Chill.

4 Slice the bread and toast each
piece.

5 Mix the butter with the garlic
and brush each piece. Heat in the
oven for about 10 minutes. Until
all the butter is soaked up.

6 Serve the hot garlic toast with
the chilled tuna mixture.

Serves 4

Tuna Olive Salad with Garlic Toast (right) and Green Olive Salad (left) are unusual ways of serving olives

Californian Avocado Salad with Olives

few lettuce leaves
3 grapefruit
3 avocados, peeled
225 (½ lb) cooked prawns
juice 1 lemon
30 ml (1 fl oz) (2 tablespoons)
  brandy
pinch cayenne pepper
dash Tabasco
15 ml (1 tablespoon) tomato
  ketchup (catsup)
6 stuffed green olives, sliced
1 lemon, sliced

For the Mayonnaise:
1 egg yolk
5 ml (1 teaspoon) made mustard
15 ml (1 tablespoon) white wine
  vinegar
salt and pepper
225 ml (8 fl oz) (1 cup) oil

1 Wash and dry the lettuce leaves.

2 Prepare the mayonnaise. Make sure that the egg yolk is free of all traces of white and place it in a bowl. Add the mustard, a few drops of the vinegar, salt and pepper. Add the oil, a drop at a time at first, stirring continually in the same direction. When the mayonnaise thickens, pour in the oil in a thin trickle. Lastly, stir in the rest of the vinegar. Put in a cool place.

3 Cut the grapefuit into halves. Using a grapefruit knife, remove the thin skin separating the segments (sections). Scoop out the flesh and place it in a bowl.

4 Halve the avocados and remove the stones (seeds). Dice the flesh. Mix this with the grapefruit pieces. Peel half the prawns and add them to the mixture.

Californian Avocado Salad with Olives looks delicate but tastes a million dollars — it is soaked in Tabasco and brandy

Sprinkle the lemon juice and brandy over the top. Season. Add the cayenne pepper, Tabasco and tomato ketchup (catsup). Carefully fold the mayonnaise into this mixture.

5 Line the base of a shallow serving dish with the lettuce leaves. Spoon the salad into the middle. Garnish with the lemon and the sliced green olives. Chill. Serve surrounded with the remaining prawns.

Serves 6

Egg and Pepper Salad

2 green peppers
1 red pepper
2 large onions, sliced
3 hard-boiled eggs
6 stuffed green olives

For the Dressing:
15 ml (1 tablespoon) vinegar
30 ml (1 fl oz) (2 tablespoons) oil
2.5 ml (½ teaspoon) made mustard
salt and pepper

For the Mayonnaise:
50 ml (2 fl oz) (¼ cup) mayonnaise
45 ml (1½ fl oz) (3 tablespoons) double (heavy) cream
5 ml (1 teaspoon) vinegar
15 ml (1 tablespoon) tomato concentrate (paste)
10 ml (2 teaspoons) paprika
pinch salt

1 Deseed the peppers and cut them into thickish rings. Place them in salted boiling water and simmer for one minute. Refresh in cold water, drain and dry.

2 Combine all the dressing ingredients and mix well. Toss the vegetables in the dressing.

3 Halve the eggs and place them on top. Garnish with the olives.

4 Whisk together the mayonnaise ingredients and serve with the salad.

Serves 4

Insalata Marinara is tangy and tastes of the sea with chunks of herring, olives and egg in a classic dressing

Insalata Marinara

225 g (½ lb) French (snap) beans
¼ cucumber
3 tomatoes, skinned and quartered
1 small onion, finely chopped
225 g (½ lb) smoked herrings, or
225 g (½ lb) (1 cup) canned salmon, well drained
1 hard-boiled egg
50 g (2 oz) stuffed green olives
5 ml (1 teaspoon) chopped parsley

For the Dressing:
45 ml (1½ fl oz) (3 tablespoons) oil
22 ml (1 fl oz) (1½ tablespoons) vinegar
salt and pepper
2.5 ml (½ teaspoon) French mustard
2.5 ml (½ teaspoon) castor sugar
1 clove garlic, crushed

1 Boil the French (snap) beans for 8 minutes in salted water. Drain, refresh in cold water and allow to cool.

2 Cut the cucumber into slices 1 cm (½ in) thick, and quarter.

3 Prepare the dressing. Place the oil, vinegar, seasoning and French mustard in a bowl, and whisk together. Add the sugar and crushed garlic and stir well.

4 Place the tomatoes, cucumber, beans and onion in a salad bowl. Pour the dressing over the vegetables and mix thoroughly. Cut the herrings into cubes approximately 2.5 cm (1 in) in size. If you use salmon, flake it roughly. Add the fish to the vegetables and turn carefully.

5 Shell and quarter the egg. Arrange the pieces on top of the salad with the olives. Chill and serve garnished with the chopped parsley.

Serves 4

Ratatouille Salads

Ratatouille means a mixture of vegetables in French. The basic ingredients, aubergines (eggplants) and courgettes (zucchini) are members of the marrow family, but tomatoes, onions and peppers are also traditionally included. For a variation you may add celery, fennel or sliced mushrooms.

It may be served as a hot dish or a cold salad, either on its own or with an assortment of cold meats or fish. Below, we provide a recipe for basic ratatouille. It can be garnished in any number of tasty ways. Try sprinkling it with sliced black olives or gherkins. For a complete meal, blend in cooked green noodles and serve with a crisp green salad. Ratatouille also makes a delicious appetizer when served cold on a hot summer's day.

Ratatouille

2 courgettes (zucchini)
2 aubergines (eggplants)
salt and pepper
2 green peppers
1 red pepper
100 ml (4 fl oz) (½ cup) oil
2 medium onions, chopped
2 cloves garlic, chopped
4 tomatoes, skinned, deseeded and chopped
pinch thyme
1 bay leaf
2.5 ml (½ teaspoon) sugar (optional)
25 g (1 oz) (4 tablespoons) flour
15 ml (1 tablespoon) vinegar
juice ½ lemon
2.5 ml (½ teaspoon) basil

Ratatouille is a sautéed dish of vegetables from Provence which can be served hot or cold as a starter or salad

1 Cut the courgettes (zucchini) and aubergines (eggplants) into slices, 1.5 cm (¾ in) thick. Sprinkle with salt and leave for 30 minutes. Wash, drain and dry.

2 Split the peppers lengthways. Remove the seeds and cut in thin slices.

3 Heat ½ of the oil in a large pan and sauté the onions for 3 minutes or until tender. Do not allow them to brown.

4 Add the peppers, courgettes (zucchini) and garlic to the pan. Cook for 2 minutes, then add the tomatoes, thyme, bay leaf and sugar (optional). Season and cook for a further 6 minutes.

5 In a separate pan, heat the remaining oil. Coat the aubergine (eggplant) slices in flour. Shake off any excess. If the slices are large, halve or quarter them so that they are equivalent to the courgettes (zucchini) in diameter. Fry for ½ minute on each side or until golden. Remove and drain well.

6 Combine all the vegetables in a casserole dish. Add the vinegar and lemon juice, and mix well. Chill and serve sprinkled with chopped basil.

Serves 6

Ratatouille with Tuna

225 g (½ lb) (1 cup) canned tuna
juice ½ lemon
950 g (2 lb) ratatouille

1 Place the tuna fish in the centre of a shallow serving dish.

2 Pour over the lemon juice and surround the tuna with the ratatouille. Alternatively, you can flake the fish and blend it with the ratatouille.

Serves 6

Ratatouille with Tuna brings a taste of the Mediterranean to your dinner table – try it as a main meal with green salad

Ratatouille Flan

2 eggs, beaten
300 ml (½ pint) (1¼ cups) milk
100 g (¼ lb) (1 cup + 2 tablespoons) flour
pinch salt
50 ml (2 fl oz) (¼ cup) oil
225 g (½ lb) (2 cups) ratatouille
¼ cucumber, thinly sliced

1 Preheat the oven to 200°C, 400°F, gas 6.

2 Make the batter: beat together the eggs and milk. Beat in the flour and salt, then rest it for a few minutes.

3 Place the oil in a shallow oven-proof dish and put in the oven for about 5 minutes. When the oil is hot, pour half the batter into the dish and cook for 20 minutes.

4 Remove from the oven and add

Ratatouille Flan is really a type of Yorkshire pudding filled with ratatouille layers and served with a crisp salad

the layer of ratatouille and cover with the remaining batter. Reduce the temperature to 190°C, 375°F, gas 5. Bake the dish for 20 minutes until risen and golden-brown. Turn out on to a plate, decorate the top with overlapping cucumber slices and serve with salad.

Serves 4-6

Portofino Fish Salad

50 ml (2 fl oz) (¼ cup) oil
½ onion, chopped
1 clove garlic, crushed
225 g (½ lb) bream, mullet or mackerel fillets, cut in small cubes
2 courgettes (zucchini), sliced
½ red pepper, deseeded and thinly sliced
4 new potatoes, cooked and sliced
salt and pepper
pinch rosemary
pinch basil
juice ½ lemon
300 ml (½ pint) (1¼ cups) thin tomato sauce

1 Heat the oil in a frying pan (skillet). Fry the onion and garlic for 2-3 minutes until tender, but still crisp.

2 Add the fish and stir-fry for 2 minutes, then add the courgettes (zucchini), sliced pepper and potatoes. Season with the salt and pepper and herbs.

3 Fry for 5 minutes, stirring occasionally. Then sprinkle on the lemon juice and arrange on a serving dish. Serve hot or cold with a tomato sauce and salad.

Serves 4

Tip: This dish is a variation on the usual ratatouille. To make it go further, you can add chopped tomatoes and sautéed auber-gines (eggplants). The veget-ables should be crisp and firm.

Portofino Fish Salad makes a change from the more traditional ratatouille with its sautéed fish and potatoes

Prawn Puffs

450 g (1 lb) puff pastry, fresh or
 frozen and thawed
175 g (6 oz) (1¼ cups) peeled,
 cooked prawns
175 g (6 oz) (1 cup) flaked, cooked
 white fish
75 ml (3 fl oz) (⅜ cup) white sauce
1 clove garlic, crushed
pinch chopped parsley
salt and pepper
pinch paprika
oil for deep frying

1 Roll out the pastry, 3 mm (⅛ in)
thick and cut out some circles,
12.5 cm (5 in) in diameter.

2 Mix the prawns and fish into
the white sauce. Stir in the
crushed garlic, parsley and seasoning.

3 Place a spoonful of this mixture in the centre of each pastry
circle. Wet the edges with water
and fold over, sealing the edges

4 Heat the oil to 190°C, 375°F, and
deep-fry the prawn puffs for
4 minutes until golden-brown.

Serves 4-6

Fruity Avocados

2 oranges
1 grapefruit
6 lettuce leaves
3 avocados, halved and stoned
 (pitted)
juice 1 lemon

For the Dressing:
30 ml (1 fl oz) (2 tablespoons)
 yogurt
15 ml (1 tablespoon) oil
15 ml (1 tablespoon) lemon juice

1 Peel the oranges and the
grapefruit and divide into segments (sections). Then remove
the skin from each segment (section).

2 Arrange the lettuce leaves and
avocados on a serving dish.

3 Sprinkle the avocados with
lemon juice.

4 Fill the avocados with the
orange and grapefruit.

5 Mix together the dressing
ingredients and serve separately
or top each avocado with a spoonful of the dressing .

Serves 6

Taramasalata

175 g (6 oz) smoked cod's roe
100 ml (4 fl oz) (½ cup) oil
75 ml (3 fl oz) (⅜ cup) double
 (heavy) cream
50 g (2 oz) (1 cup) fresh
 breadcrumbs
1 clove garlic, crushed
juice 1 lemon
salt and pepper
pinch paprika

1 In a bowl, blend the cod's roe
with the oil until it is smooth.

2 Blend in the cream, then the
breadcrumbs and garlic.

3 Lastly add the lemon juice and
season to taste.

4 Pile the taramasalata up in a
dish and pull a fork around the
sides to achieve a 'petalled' effect.
Sprinkle with paprika and serve
with hot pitta bread.

Serves 6

Tip: For a slightly different
flavour, you can blend in some
cream cheese or sesame oil.

*Prawn Puffs, Taramasalata and
Fruity Avocados, served
with hot pitta bread, all make a
tasty Greek start to a meal*

Prawn and Asparagus Salad

1 lettuce
100 g (¼ lb) (½ cup) long grain rice
100 ml (4 fl oz) (½ cup) mayonnaise
salt and pepper
pinch paprika
1 lemon
15 ml (1 tablespoon) dry sherry
225 g (½ lb) (1½ cups) shelled prawns
225 g (½ lb) (1 cup) canned asparagus
1 red pepper, cut in thin strips
15 ml (1 tablespoon) chopped parsley

1 Wash and drain the lettuce. Arrange the leaves on a serving dish.

2 Cook the rice in boiling salted water until tender. Drain and refresh under a running cold tap.

3 In a bowl, mix the mayonnaise with the salt and pepper and paprika. Cut the lemon in half and squeeze the juice of one half into the mayonnaise. Put the other half aside for the garnish.

4 Mix in the sherry, the rice and half of the prawns.

Prawn and Asparagus Salad is the ideal choice for a sophisticated dinner party or a cold summer buffet

5 Pile the mixture on top of the lettuce leaves in the centre of the dish. Arrange the remaining prawns on top.

6 Arrange the asparagus in bundles around the edge to form a border with wedges of lemon in between. Place a thin strip of red pepper around the middle of each asparagus bundle.

7 Sprinkle the prawns with the chopped parsley and serve.

Serves 4

Riviera Melon Salad

1 cantaloup melon
1 lettuce
30 ml (2 tablespoons) oil
1 small onion, chopped
5 ml (1 teaspoon) curry powder
150 ml (¼ pint) (⅝ cup) mayonnaise

5 ml (1 teaspoon) tomato ketchup (catsup)
juice ½ lemon
100 g (¼ lb) (¾ cup) peeled prawns
100 g (¼ lb) (⅝ cup) crab meat
salt and pepper
4 whole prawns
1 lemon, cut in wedges

1 Cut the melon in two, remove the seeds and rind and slice the flesh thinly.

2 Wash, dry and separate the lettuce leaves. Arrange them on a large, flat dish and decorate the border with the melon slices. Chill in the refrigerator.

3 Heat the oil and sauté the onion gently until soft – do not let it brown. Stir in the curry powder and cook for 30 seconds. Then allow to cool

4 Blend together the onion and mayonnaise in a bowl. Add the tomato ketchup (catsup) and lemon juice. Then stir in the prawns and crab meat. Season to taste with salt and pepper.

5 Place a spoonful of the mixture on each lettuce leaf and garnish with the whole prawns and lemon wedges. Chill for 30 minutes before serving.

Serves 4

'Daisy' Hors d'Oeuvre

1 kg (2 lb) firm potatoes,
  unpeeled
100 ml (4 fl oz) (½ cup) white wine
800 g (1¾ lb) white fish
450 g (1 lb) (4 cups) cooked peas
4 hard-boiled eggs, halved
  lengthways
few lettuce leaves
4 gherkins, quartered
  lengthways
1 red chilli, sliced

For the Court Bouillon:
1½ litres (2½ pints) (6½ cups) water
225 ml (8 fl oz) (1 cup) white wine
salt and pepper
bouquet garni
1 onion studded with a clove

For the Sauce:
100 ml (4 fl oz) (½ cup) oil
45 ml (1½ fl oz) (3 tablespoons)
  vinegar
pinch each chopped parsley and
  chives
4 shallots, chopped
2 cloves garlic, peeled and
  chopped

1 Put the ingredients for the court bouillon in a pan, bring to the boil and boil gently for 30 minutes. Allow to cool.

2 Meanwhile, cook the unpeeled potatoes in boiling salted water. Drain, peel and dice them.

3 Pour the second measure of wine into a small pan. Bring to the boil, pour it over the diced potatoes while they are still warm and stir. Leave to cool.

4 When the court bouillon is cool, add the fish to it and bring to the boil. Simmer over a gentle heat for about 15 minutes. Leave to cool.

5 In a large bowl, mix the cooled potatoes and peas.

6 Prepare the sauce: in another bowl, mix the oil, vinegar, chopped herbs, salt and pepper, shallots and garlic. Beat the sauce lightly, pour it over the potatoes, stir and leave to soak.

7 Remove the yolks from the eggs and set aside. Cut the whites in half lengthways again. Rub the yolks through a sieve and form it into a neat round.

8 Drain the fish, remove the bones and skin and flake it.

9 Cover a large round plate with the lettuce leaves and pile the potato and pea mixture in the centre. Arrange the fish pieces on the top.

10 On the very top, place the round of egg yolk, to make the centre of the 'daisy', and arrange the lengths of egg white around it, to make the petals of the flower.

11 Decorate the base of the mound with the gherkin slices and the edge of the dish with the chopped chilli. Serve chilled.

Serves 8

Tips: A court bouillon is a classic preparation used to cook both small pieces of fish and whole fish. Small pieces should be added to a hot bouillon, but if you are using the whole fish, allow the liquid to cool before adding it to the fish.

Once cooked, the fish can be allowed to cool in the court bouillon and, when completely cold, stored in the refrigerator to be reheated the next day.

You can vary the flavour of the court bouillon by adding carrots, celery, or fennel and by using herbs such as mint.

Spanish Salad

½ lettuce
4 tomatoes, skinned, quartered
  and deseeded
16 canned anchovy fillets,
  drained
100 g (¼ lb) (¾ cup) peeled cooked
  prawns
8 stuffed green olives, halved
2 hard-boiled eggs, sliced
For the Dressing:
90 ml (3 fl oz) (6 tablespoons) oil
30 ml (1 fl oz) (2 tablespoons)
  lemon juice
salt and pepper
pinch dry mustard
pinch sugar

1 Wash the lettuce, drain well and tear into small pieces.

2 Place the lettuce in a salad bowl and add the tomatoes, anchovies, prawns and olives.

3 Mix the ingredients for the dressing together and pour it over the salad. Toss well.

4 Decorate the salad with the sliced hard-boiled eggs.

Serves 4

Scampi (Prawn) Tartlets

225 g (½ lb) shortcrust (pie crust)
100 g (¼ lb) (1 cup) diced cooked
  potato
50 g (2 oz) (½ cup) cooked peas
50 g (2 oz) (½ cup) diced cooked
  carrot
150 ml (¼ pint) (⅝ cup) mayonnaise
salt and pepper
8 frozen cooked scampi or king
  prawns, thawed
8 black olives, halved
1 gherkin, sliced
1 hard-boiled egg, sliced

1 Preheat the oven to 200°C, 400°F, gas 6. Roll out the shortcrust (pie crust) to 3 mm (⅛ in) thick. Cut 4 rounds, 10 cm (4 in) in diameter and use them to line 4 greased tartlet (muffin) pans. Prick evenly with a fork and bake them blind in the preheated oven for 12-15 minutes. Allow to cool.

2 Combine the potato, peas, carrot and mayonnaise in a bowl and check the seasoning. Place the mixture in the cooled tartlets and top each with 2 scampi or king prawns and a few halved olives.

3 Decorate the edge of each tartlet with the slices of gherkin. Top each slice of egg with an olive half and arrange the slices around the serving dish.

Serves 4

Scampi (Prawn) Tartlets are delicious little shells filled with shellfish, carrot and peas in a mayonnaise sauce.

Exotic Salads

As exotic vegetables and fruits become more widely available, there is a growing tendency to use them in salads. Citrus fruits such as oranges, lemons and limes, and the more unusual avocados, papaws, pineapples and mangoes are now often mixed with salad vegetables and nuts or cheese in a delicious dressing or flavoured mayonnaise.

Hawaiian Salad

1 lettuce
8 radishes
100 g (¼ lb) (⅔ cup) diced ham
100 g (¼ lb) (¾ cup) diced fresh
  pineapple
1 stick celery, chopped
½ small cucumber, thinly sliced
few sprigs parsley

For the Dressing:
50 ml (2 fl oz) (¼ cup) pineapple
  juice
30 ml (1 fl oz) (2 tablespoons)
  lemon juice
15 ml (1 tablespoon) sugar
50 ml (2 fl oz) (¼ cup) oil
pinch salt
pinch paprika

1 Wash the lettuce and radishes. Separate the lettuce leaves and arrange on a serving dish. Slice downwards through each radish to make a star-shape on top. Place them in iced water until they open out into flowers.

2 Mix together the dressing ingredients and toss the ham, pineapple and celery in the dressing. Pile on top of the lettuce leaves and decorate with cucumber slices, radishes and parsley.

Serves 4

Hawaiian Salad combines the fresh, sharp taste of pineapple with ham and celery in a tangy lemon dressing

Avocado and Cervelas Salad

1 avocado pear, stoned (pitted),
  peeled and thinly sliced
100 g (¼ lb) (⅔ cup) diced cervelas
  or ham sausage
100 g (¼ lb) (1 cup) diced Gruyère
  cheese
2 sticks celery, thinly sliced
100 g (¼ lb) (1 cup) chopped
  walnuts
225 ml (8 fl oz) (1 cup) mayonnaise
15 ml (1 tablespoon) lemon juice
30 ml (1 fl oz) (2 tablespoons)
  apple purée
salt and pepper
15 ml (tablespoon) chopped
  chives
pinch paprika

1 In a bowl, mix together the sliced avocado, cervelas, Gruyère cheese, celery and walnuts. Mix in the mayonnaise, lemon juice and apple purée. Make sure that all the ingredients are coated with the mayonnaise mixture.

2 Season with the salt and pepper.

3 Transfer the salad to a serving

dish and sprinkle with the chopped chives and paprika. Or, alternatively, you can serve it in individual bowls as an appetizer.

Serves 4

Ham and Pineapple Salad

100 g (¼ lb) (⅔ cup) diced ham
100 g (¼ lb) (1 cup) diced cooked potatoes
100 g (¼ lb) (1 cup) diced Gruyère cheese

Ham and Pineapple Salad, mixed with grapes and Gruyere in a fruity mayonnaise, tastes as delicious as it looks

100 g (¼ lb) seedless green grapes, skinned
100 g (¼ lb) (½ cup) canned pineapple chunks
200 ml (6 fl oz) (¾ cup) mayonnaise
30 ml (1 fl oz) (2 tablespoons) pineapple juice
salt and pepper
30 ml (1 fl oz) (2 tablespoons) sour cream
15 g (½ oz) (3 tablespoons) chopped parsley

1 Combine together the ham,

cooked potatoes, Gruyère, grapes and pineapple chunks in a bowl.

2 Mix in the mayonnaise and pineapple juice so that all the ingredients are well coated. Season with the salt and pepper and stir in the sour cream.

3 Serve in an attractive dish, sprinkled with the chopped parsley.

Serves 4

Tip: As a delicious variation on this salad, why not try adding some sliced bananas or cashew nuts? You can give it a more spicy flavour by mixing in a pinch of curry powder.

Look'n Cook American-style Cranberry Salad

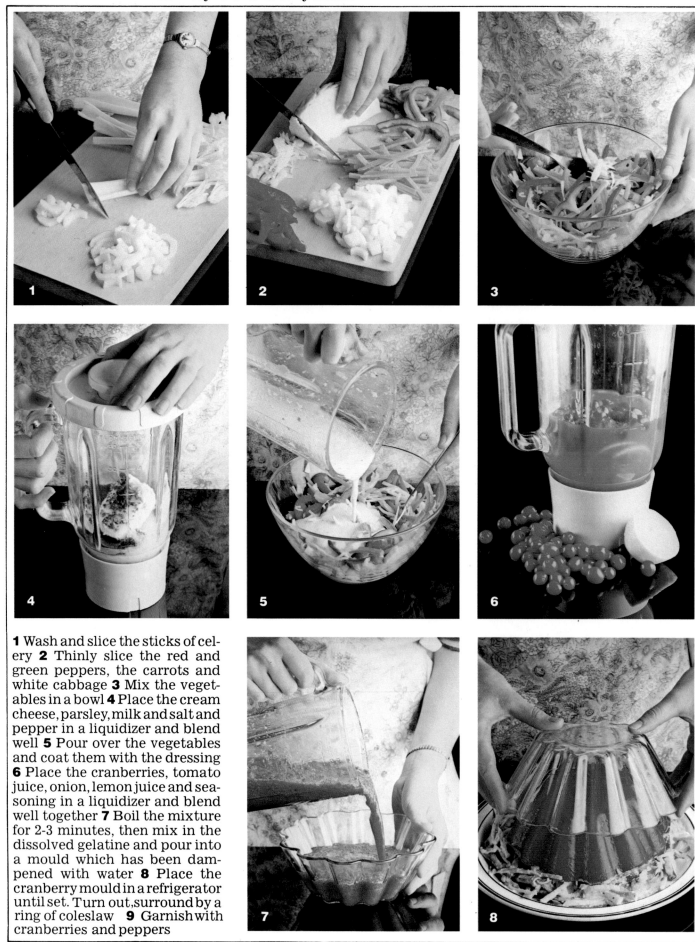

1 Wash and slice the sticks of celery 2 Thinly slice the red and green peppers, the carrots and white cabbage 3 Mix the vegetables in a bowl 4 Place the cream cheese, parsley, milk and salt and pepper in a liquidizer and blend well 5 Pour over the vegetables and coat them with the dressing 6 Place the cranberries, tomato juice, onion, lemon juice and seasoning in a liquidizer and blend well together 7 Boil the mixture for 2-3 minutes, then mix in the dissolved gelatine and pour into a mould which has been dampened with water 8 Place the cranberry mould in a refrigerator until set. Turn out, surround by a ring of coleslaw 9 Garnish with cranberries and peppers

American-style Cranberry Salad

225 g (½ lb) (2 cups) cranberries
300 ml (½ pint) (1¼ cups) tomato juice
juice ½ lemon
5 ml (1 teaspoon) grated onion (optional)
salt and pepper
pinch cinnamon
25 g (1 oz) (4 tablespoons) powdered gelatine
50 g (2 oz) (¼ cup) castor sugar
75 ml (3 fl oz) (⅜ cup) warm water

For the Coleslaw:
2 sticks celery, thinly sliced
½ green pepper, deseeded and sliced
½ red pepper, deseeded and sliced
1 carrot, cut in thin strips
225 g (½ lb) (3 cups) shredded white cabbage

For the Dressing:
175 g (6 oz) (1 cup) cream cheese
sprig parsley
75 ml (3 fl oz) (⅜ cup) milk or single (light) cream
salt and pepper

For the Garnish:
2 rings green pepper
50 g (2 oz) (½ cup) cranberries

1 Make the coleslaw by mixing all the sliced and shredded vegetables together in a bowl.

2 Make the dressing. Place the cream cheese, parsley, milk or cream and seasoning in a liquidizer and blend well. If you do not have a liquidizer, you can strain them through a sieve.

3 Toss the coleslaw vegetables in the dressing until they are well covered and put aside.

4 Place the cranberries, tomato and lemon juice, grated onion, salt, pepper and cinnamon in a liquidizer and blend well.

5 Pour the cranberry mixture into a saucepan and bring to the boil. Boil for 2-3 minutes, then remove from the heat.

6 Mix together the gelatine and sugar and dissolve in the warm water. Stir into the cranberry mixture.

7 Dampen a fluted 550 ml (1 pint) (2½ cups) mould with a little water. Then pour the cranberry mixture into the mould and refrigerate for at least 2 hours until firm and set.

8 Arrange the coleslaw around a serving plate and unmould the cranberry salad into the centre.

9 Garnish the top with the rings of green pepper and a few cranberries. Sprinkle the surrounding salad with more of the cranberries. Serve with a salad.

Serves 4-6

Tip: If you do not have a liquidizer, do not despair – you can still make this delicious recipe. Just rub the ingredients through a nylon sieve. Push them through the sieve using a wooden spoon. The resulting purée will be just as smooth.

Egg and Melon Salad

1 small cabbage
1 firm, ripe papaw or canteloup
1 orange
2 carrots, grated
salt and pepper
4 hard-boiled eggs
few sprigs watercress
few leaves chicory
8 radishes

For the Dressing:
5 ml (1 teaspoon) flour
15 g (½ oz) (1 tablespoon) sugar
salt and pepper
2.5 ml (½ teaspoon) mustard powder
1 large egg
30 ml (1 fl oz) (2 tablespoons) vinegar
30 ml (1 fl oz) (2 tablespoons) water
5 ml (1 teaspoon) butter

1 Prepare the dressing first. Combine the flour, sugar, seasoning and mustard powder in a heavy based saucepan. Beat the egg and mix it in to form a smooth paste. Add the vinegar, water and butter and stir over a low heat until the sauce begins to thicken.

Remove from the heat, stir thoroughly and strain if any lumps still remain. Cool in the refrigerator.

2 Chop the cabbage very finely. Cube the papaw or canteloup. Peel the orange and cut the segments into pieces. Combine these ingredients with the grated carrot in a mixing bowl. Season.

3 Pour over the cooled dressing and spoon the salad mixture onto a large salad dish.

4 Slice the hard-boiled eggs and arrange them with the watercress and chicory leaves around the salad. Garnish with the radishes cut in a floral pattern and serve.

Serves 4

Salad Ramatuelle

1 lettuce
225 g (½ lb) (1 cup) canned bamboo shoots
1 red pepper
450 g (1 lb) (6 cups) cooked long grain rice
50 g (2 oz) (½ cup) flaked almonds
45 ml (1½ fl oz) (3 tablespoons) mayonnaise
5 ml (1 teaspoon) made mustard
5 ml (1 teaspoon) capers
225 g (½ lb) cooked chicken meat, cut into strips

1 Wash and dry the lettuce leaves, and tear them into pieces. Drain the bamboo shoots and finely dice the red pepper.

2 Mix the rice and almonds in a salad bowl. Blend the mayonnaise, mustard and capers and add to the rice mixture. Refrigerate for 1 hour to cool.

3 Just before serving add the lettuce, bamboo shoots, red pepper and chicken. Toss and serve.

*Serves 6-8 as a starter
3-4 as a main course*

Egg and Melon Salad makes an unusual and attractive appetizer—you can substitute papaws for an exotic change

91

Chinese Leaves Salad

225 g (½ lb) Chinese leaves or cos lettuce
1 red pepper, deseeded
1 green pepper, deseeded
1 avocado
1 onion, sliced in rings
1 hard-boiled egg
1 stick celery, diced

For the Dressing:
30 ml (1 fl oz) (2 tablespoons) oil
juice ½ lemon
salt and pepper

1 Wash and dry the Chinese leaves or lettuce. Tear into pieces. Slice the peppers into rings. Peel the avocado and remove the stone (seed). Quarter lengthways and slice into segments.

2 Combine the dressing ingredients and mix well.

3 Place the Chinese leaves or lettuce in the bottom of a salad bowl. Add the peppers and onion in alternate layers, then the avocado and finally the egg. Place the celery on the very top. Chill and serve with the dressing.

Serves 3

Orange and Cabbage Slaw

¾ kg (1½ lb) cabbage
3 oranges
rind 1 orange, grated
juice ½ orange

For the Dressing:
150 ml (¼ pint) (⅝ cup) single (light) cream
15 ml (1 tablespoon) cornflour (cornstarch)
45 ml (1½ fl oz) (3 tablespoons) cold water
2.5 ml (½ teaspoon) sugar
juice ½ lemon
5 ml (1 teaspoon) vinegar
15 ml (1 tablespoon) oil

Chineses Leaves Salad makes a welcome change from the ordinary lettuce – Chinese leaves are crisp like cabbage

1 Make the dressing. Boil the cream. Mix the cornflour (cornstarch) and water to a smooth paste. Add to the cream and simmer for 30 seconds. Remove from the heat and stir in the sugar, lemon juice and vinegar. Slowly add the oil and stir. Strain if necessary to remove any lumps.

2 Shred the cabbage and place in a salad bowl. Break 2 of the oranges into segments (sections), remove any white skin, and dice.

3 Sprinkle the orange rind over the cabbage. Toss well. Add the orange juice, diced orange and dressing a few minutes before serving. Toss and garnish with segments (sections) of the remaining orange.

Serves 6

Cheese Salads

Cheese has always been a favourite accompaniment for salads. Its mild but tangy flavour and smooth texture is an excellent complement to crisp, juicy salad vegetables. Mellow, firm English, Dutch and Swiss cheeses can be diced, or cut in strips, to hold their own with crunchy salads. Blue cheeses bring extra flavour to salads and salad dressings. Cream cheese forms an ideal base for mixed salads, or mild dressings that go as well with fruit as with vegetables.

Blue Cheese Salad

1 large lettuce
3 large tomatoes
45 ml (2 fl oz) (3 tablespoons) olive oil
15 ml (1 tablespoon) white wine vinegar
salt and pepper
100 g (¼ lb) firm blue cheese – Danish Blue, Auvergne Blue, or Stilton

1 Wash the lettuce thoroughly, separating the leaves and discarding any damaged ones.

2 Wash the tomatoes and cut them into 1 cm (⅜ in) slices.

3 In a bowl or jug, blend the olive oil, vinegar, and a pinch of salt and freshly ground black pepper to taste.

4 Cut the cheese into 2 cm (¾ in) cubes, and mix them into the salad dressing.

5 Arrange the lettuce and tomato in a salad bowl and pour the cheese dressing over them, tossing the salad lightly so that all the pieces are covered in dressing. Serve with crisp French bread.

Serves 4

Blue Cheese Salad – vinegar, oil and firm blue cheese mixed together and poured over a lettuce and tomato salad

Blue Cheese Salad Dressing

50 g (2 oz) blue cheese – Danish Blue, Roquefort, or Stilton
300 ml (½ pint) (1¼ cups) mayonnaise
50 ml (2 fl oz) (¼ cup) double (heavy) cream
5 g (1 tablespoon) chopped fresh parsley and sage
1 clove garlic, crushed
salt and pepper

1 Crumble the blue cheese into small pieces, and stir them into the mayonnaise and the cream.

2 Add the chopped herbs, garlic and salt and pepper to taste. Place all ingredients in an electric blender and beat until smooth.

3 Serve the Blue Cheese Salad Dressing with a crisp green salad or a potato salad. It may also be poured over hot baked potatoes.

Makes 450 ml (¾ pint) (1⅞ cups)

Tagliatelle Salad

100 g (¼ lb) (1 cup) green
 tagliatelle noodles
1 bunch radishes
4 large tomatoes
12 spring onions (scallions)
50 g (2 oz) Gruyère cheese
½ red pepper, deseeded and diced
30 ml (2 tablespoons) olive oil
15 ml (1 tablespoon) lemon juice
5 ml (1 teaspoon) each chopped
 fresh parsley, chives and basil
pinch garlic salt
salt and pepper

1 Boil the tagliatelle noodles in salted water until just tender. Rinse them in cold water, drain and leave to cool.

2 Clean the radishes and remove the leaves from all but 6 (for decoration). Clean and quarter the tomatoes. Wash the spring onions (scallions) and discard the green leaves.

3 Cut the Gruyère cheese into 2 cm (¾ in) cubes. Mix the cold noodles, radishes, spring onions (scallions) and red pepper.

4 Blend the oil, lemon juice, herbs, garlic salt, and salt and pepper to taste. Pour the dressing over the salad, tossing to ensure that all the ingredients are evenly coated.

5 Arrange the tomato quarters around the salad, decorate with the leafy radishes, and serve.

Serves 4

Dutch Salad

100 g (¼ lb) Edam or Gouda
 cheese
6 crisp white cabbage leaves
6 crisp red cabbage leaves
2 large carrots
½ green pepper, deseeded
30 ml (2 tablespoons) oil
15 ml (1 tablespoon) vinegar
15 ml (1 tablespoon) chopped
 celery leaves
5 ml (1 teaspoon) cumin seeds
salt and pepper

1 Remove any rind from the cheese and cut it into matchstick strips about ½ cm (¼ in) thick and 4 cm (1½ in) long.

2 Cut the white and red cabbage leaves, carrots and green pepper into strips of a similar size.

3 Blend together the oil, vinegar, chopped celery leaves, cumin seeds, and salt and pepper to taste. Mix all the ingredients together in a wooden salad bowl and serve with boiled ham or cold meats.

Serves 4

Tagliatelle Salad contains pasta, cheese and lots of salad vegetables and so makes a colourful and filling meal

Salade des Fromages

100 g (¼ lb) Cheddar cheese
100 g (¼ lb) Gruyère cheese
225 g (½ lb) ham
4 gherkins
1 lettuce

For the Dressing:
45 ml (1½ fl oz) (3 tablespoons) oil
juice 1 lemon
15 ml (1 tablespoon) single (light)
  cream
5 ml (1 teaspoon) made mustard
salt and pepper
15 ml (1 tablespoon) chopped
  fresh chives
25 g (1 oz) (3 tablespoons) grated
  Parmesan cheese

1 Cut the Cheddar cheese and the Gruyére cheese into dice about 2 cm (¾ in) across. Cut the ham into cubes of a similar size. Slice the gherkins. Wash the lettuce and discard any damaged leaves.

2 Blend all the ingredients for the dressing to form a smooth liquid.

3 Arrange the lettuce leaves in a large salad bowl. Toss the cheese and ham in the salad dressing until well coated. Serve the cheese salad and lettuce separately, or place the cheese salad in the middle of the lettuce.

Serves 4-6

Avocado Creams

2 large ripe avocados
225 g (½ lb) (1⅓ cups) cottage or
  cream cheese
30 ml (1 fl oz) (2 tablespoons)
  mayonnaise
15 ml (1 tablespoon) vinaigrette
juice 1 lemon
salt and pepper
15 ml (1 tablespoon) chopped
  fresh chives

1 Cut the avocados in half. Discard the stones (seeds) Scoop out the flesh, keeping the shells.

2 Place the avocado flesh in an

electric blender with the rest of the ingredients except the chopped chives. Blend until a smooth, thick mixture is formed.

3 Divide the avocado mixture between the four avocado shells. Top each one with a sprinkling of chopped chives. Chill before serving as an hors d'oeuvre.

Serves 4

Pacific Cheese Salad

2 grapefruit
100 g (¼ lb) Dutch or Swiss cheese
12 pearl onions, pickled
12 cocktail cherries
30 ml (1 fl oz) (2 tablespoons) oil
15 ml (1 tablespoon) lemon juice
salt and pepper
6 fresh mint leaves, chopped
1 lettuce, shredded

1 Cut the grapefruit in halves and remove the flesh, keeping the skins. Remove pith and dice the flesh.

2 Dice the cheese. Mix together the grapefruit, cheese, pickled pearl onions and cocktail cherries.

3 Make a dressing of the oil and lemon juice, seasoned to taste with salt and pepper and blended with the chopped mint.

4 Toss the salad and the dressing together. Divide the salad between the four grapefuit halves. Set each half on a bed of shredded lettuce and serve immediately.

Serves 4

Mandarin Cream Cheese Salad

1 large bunch watercress
450 g (1 lb) (2⅔ cups) cottage
  cheese
225 g (½ lb) (1 cup) canned
  mandarin orange segments
  (sections)
pinch paprika

1 Wash the watercress thoroughly and discard any thick stalks. Arrange a bed of watercress on each of 4 salad dishes.

2 Using a scoop or a soup ladle, place an evenly circular mound of cottage cheese in the middle of each bed of watercress.

3 Drain the juice from the mandarin segments (sections) and arrange them in a rosette pattern round each mound of cottage cheese. Dust the cottage cheese with a little paprika, and serve.

Serves 4

Cottage Cheese and Peach Salad

225 g (½ lb) (1⅓ cups) cottage
  cheese
50 ml (2 fl oz) (¼ cup) sour cream
salt and pepper
50 g (2 oz) (⅓ cup) raisins
75 g (3 oz) (½ cup) chopped canned
  pineapple
15 ml (1 tablespoon) lemon juice
1 lettuce
4 fresh or canned peach halves
2 carrots, washed and grated

1 Blend together the cottage cheese and the sour cream and season. Stir in the raisins, pineapple, and lemon juice.

2 Wash the lettuce and arrange several leaves on each serving plate. Cut a small slice off the round side of each peach half so that it will stand hollow side upright.

3 Place a peach half in the middle of each serving plate, on the lettuce leaves, and scoop ¼ of the cottage cheese mixture into each peach half.

4 Sprinkle each salad with some grated carrot. Serve immediately.

Serves 4

Fruits de Mer Salad

1 lettuce
225 g (½ lb) cooked white fish
100 g (¼ lb) (½ cup) crabmeat
100 g (¼ lb) (½ cup) crayfish
   meat or a similar amount of
   other shellfish
150 ml (¼ pint) (⅝ cup) mayonnaise
15 ml (1 tablespoon) apple purée
5 ml (1 teaspoon) Worcestershire
   sauce
salt and pepper
12 whole cooked prawns

1 Separate the leaves of the lettuce and wash quickly. Drain well, and line a salad bowl.

2 Dice the white fish, crab and crayfish, or other shellfish, and place on top of the lettuce.

3 Mix the mayonnaise with the

Fruits de Mer Salad is an infinitely variable dish which you can alter according to the fish that are available

apple purée and Worcestershire sauce. Season.

4 Spoon over the shellfish.

5 Decorate the bowl by arranging the prawns to curve over the sides.

Serves 4

Avocado and Crab Salad

1 lettuce
2 avocados
225 g (½ lb) (1 cup) crabmeat
2 eating apples
150 ml (¼ pint) (⅝ cup) mayonnaise
5 ml (1 teaspoon) tomato ketchup
   (catsup)
pinch paprika
juice ½ lemon
6 celery leaves

1 Separate the leaves of the lettuce and wash briefly. Drain.

2 Remove the skins of the

avocados and cut into segments. Cut the crabmeat into chunks. Peel and dice the apples.

3 Mix the mayonnaise with the tomato ketchup (catsup), paprika and lemon juice. Toss the salad in the dressing.

4 To serve, line a bowl with the lettuce leaves, garnish with celery leaves and place the salad in the middle.

Serves 4

Quick fish Salad

Try combining some cooked mussels with cold boiled potatoes cut in slices. Toss in mayonnaise and arrange on a bed of lettuce leaves. Arrange some slices of cooked white mushrooms on top. To add colour, decorate with radishes or slices of tomatoes.

---

*For that special dinner party,
Avocado and Crab Salad –
a deliciously delicate mixture
with tomato mayonnaise*

Chicken Salads

The use of chicken as an ingredient in a mixed salad is often overlooked. The following recipes show just how tasty this delicate meat can be, blended with various dressings and combined with different salad vegetables.

Chicken Salad New York

1 avocado
100 g (¼ lb) white grapes
1 cos lettuce
1 Webb's or iceberg lettuce
2 sticks celery, diced
175 g (6 oz) (1 cup) thin strips
  ham, 4 cm (1½ in) long
175 g (6 oz) (1 cup) thin strips
  cooked chicken, 4 cm (1½ in) long
40 g (1½ oz) Swiss cheese, cut into
  thin strips

For the Dressing:
75 ml (2½ fl oz) (⅓ cup) oil
30 ml (1 fl oz) (2 tablespoons)
  vinegar
30 ml (1 fl oz) (2 tablespoons)
  tomato ketchup (catsup)
10 ml (2 teaspoons) grated onion
5 ml (1 teaspoon) prepared
  mustard
2.5 ml (½ teaspoon) salt
1.25 ml (¼ teaspoon) sugar
dash Tabasco (chilli) sauce

1 Prepare the dressing. Place all the ingredients in a screw top jar or any watertight container. Cover and shake well. Chill.

2 Peel and halve the avocado. Remove the stone (seed), quarter and slice. Halve the grapes and remove the pips.

3 Wash the lettuce leaves and dry. Tear them into bite-size pieces. Place them in a salad bowl and toss.

4 Arrange the celery, ham, chicken, cheese, avocado and grapes on top of the lettuce.

5 Just before serving toss the salad with the chilled dressing.

Serves 8

Chicken and Cranberry Salad

225 g (½ lb) (1 cup) cranberry jelly
100 ml (4 fl oz) (½ cup) sour cream
100 g (¼ lb) (⅔ cup) cream cheese,
  softened
2 sticks celery, diced
50 g (2 oz) (½ cup) chopped
  walnuts
1 green pepper, deseeded and
  finely chopped
225 g (½ lb) (1⅓ cups) diced
  cooked chicken
350 g (¾ lb) (1½ cups) canned
  pineapple pieces, drained

1 Spread the cranberry jelly 1 cm (½ in) thick over the base of a freezing tray. Freeze the jelly for 1 hour or until it has set solid.

2 Blend the sour cream with the cheese. Stir in the celery, walnuts and pepper. Finally fold in the chicken and pineapple pieces, and season to taste. Chill.

3 Cut the frozen cranberry jelly into small cubes and sprinkle them over the salad before serving.

Serves 4

Chicken Tapenade

225 g (½ lb) (1⅓ cups) diced cooked
  chicken
1 lettuce
100 g (¼ lb) anchovy fillets
8 stuffed green olives

For the Dressing:
2 egg yolks
5 ml (1 teaspoon) made mustard
salt and pepper
150 ml (¼ pint) (⅝ cup) olive oil
juice ½ lemon
30 ml (1 fl oz) (2 tablespoons)
  double (heavy) cream

1 small onion, chopped
5 ml (1 teaspoon) capers,
  chopped

1 First, prepare the dressing. Whisk together the egg yolks (make sure there is no white remaining on the yolk), mustard, salt and pepper in a bowl. Slowly blend in the oil a little at a time until you have a thick creamy mixture of even consistency. Stir in the lemon juice and cream and finally the chopped onion and capers.

2 Toss the diced chicken in the dressing and chill for 30 minutes.

3 Break up the lettuce and wash and dry the leaves. Use as many leaves as necessary to line the base and sides of a salad bowl.

4 Spoon in the chicken and mayonnaise mixture. Decorate with the anchovy fillets by lining them criss-cross over the top of the salad and garnish with the olives. Serve.

Serves 4

Peppers Stuffed with Chicken

2 red peppers, deseeded
salt and pepper
30 ml (1 fl oz) (2 tablespoons)
  plain yogurt
30 ml (1 fl oz) (2 tablespoons)
  canned corn kernels
225 g (½ lb) (1⅓ cups) diced cooked
  chicken
few sprigs parsley

1 Halve the peppers and boil them for 5 minutes in salted water. Refresh, dry and allow them to cool.

2 Blend the yogurt with the corn and chicken. Season and spoon into the pepper halves. Garnish with the parsley and serve.

Serves 4

Chicken Tapenade – the chicken is mixed with a creamy dressing and garnished with anchovies and stuffed olives

Mayonnaise Chicken Salad

150 ml (¼ pint) (⅝ cup) chicken
  stock
30 ml (2 tablespoons) powdered
  gelatine
300 ml (½ pint) (1¼ cups)
  mayonnaise
500 g (1 lb) (2⅔ cups) diced cooked
  chicken meat
few lettuce leaves
75 g (3 oz) cooked ox tongue, cut
  in strips
75 g (3 oz) cooked ham, cut in
  strips
50 g (2 oz) canned anchovy fillets,
  drained
4 olives, sliced
1 avocado
juice 1 lemon

1 Place the chicken stock in a pan and bring just to the boil. Remove from the heat, add the gelatine and stir until dissolved. Leave to cool.

2 When the gelatine mixture is cool, blend in the mayonnaise. In a bowl, mix the chicken meat with ¾ of the mayonnaise.

3 Arrange the lettuce leaves in a glass salad bowl and place the chicken and mayonnaise mixture on top. Pour the rest of the mayonnaise over the top and smooth the surface with the blade of a knife.

4 Make a lattice pattern on the mayonnaise with the strips of tongue and ham and with the anchovy fillets. Place olive slices in the spaces of the lattice. Chill.

5 Just before serving, peel and slice the avocado and sprinkle the slices with the lemon juice. Arrange the avocado around the edge of the salad and serve immediately.

Serves 8

Tip: The mayonnaise can be varied by adding a fruit purée, which will taste delicious with cooked meat. Apple would be ideal – for each 225 ml (8 fl oz) (1 cup) of mayonnaise, add 60 ml (4 tablespoons) of the fruit purée. You could also use crushed pineapple, or a purée of blackcurrants or cooked plums. For a lower-calorie meal, the mayonnaise could be replaced by low-fat yogurt, to which you could again add a fruit purée.

Chicken and Orange Salad

100 g (¼ lb) (½ cup) long grain rice
1 small onion, chopped
salt and pepper
225 g (½ lb) (1⅓ cups) diced cooked
  chicken
2 sticks celery, diced
½ green pepper, chopped
4 stuffed olives, chopped
100 ml (4 fl oz) (½ cup) mayonnaise
2 oranges
few lettuce leaves

1 Cook the rice in boiling salted water until tender. Drain and, while still hot, mix with the onion and seasoning. Leave to cool.

2 Add the chicken, celery, pepper, olives and mayonnaise and toss lightly. Peel the oranges, split them into segments (sections) and cut half into small pieces.

3 Add the orange pieces to the salad and mix well. Chill thoroughly.

4 To serve, place the salad on a bed of lettuce and garnish with the rest of the orange segments (sections).

Serves 4

Chicken Noodle Salad

225 g (½ lb) cooked chicken meat,
  cut in 1 cm (½ in) cubes
1 small onion, finely chopped
15 ml (1 tablespoon) chopped
  pimento
3 olives, chopped
75 g (3 oz) (¾ cup) walnuts,
  chopped
15 ml (1 tablespoon) chopped
  parsley
juice half lemon
5 ml (1 teaspoon) Worcestershire
  sauce
salt and pepper
100 g (¼ lb) noodles
100 ml (4 fl oz) (½ cup) mayonnaise

1 Combine the chicken, onion, pimento, olives, walnuts, parsley, lemon juice, Worcestershire sauce and seasoning.

2 Cook the noodles in boiling salted water, drain and rinse in cold water.

3 Combine the chicken mixture and the cooked noodles, add the mayonnaise and toss lightly until all the ingredients are well mixed. Chill and serve.

Serves 4

Chicken and Peach Salad

8 fresh or canned peach halves,
  sliced
4 cold roast chicken breasts,
  skinned and diced
few lettuce leaves
5 ml (1 teaspoon) chopped
  parsley

For the Mustard Dressing:
150 ml (¼ pint) (⅝ cup) mayonnaise
2 peach halves, chopped
juice 1 lemon
5 ml (1 teaspoon) made mustard

1 Mix the sliced peaches and diced chicken in a bowl.

2 Make the dressing: blend the mayonnaise with the chopped peaches, lemon juice and mustard. Toss the chicken mixture in the dressing.

3 Chill the salad for 30 minutes.

4 When ready to serve, arrange the salad in the centre of a serving dish on a bed of lettuce leaves. Decorate the top of the salad with the chopped parsley.

Serves 4

Chicken and Peach Salad is a delicious combination of flavours which is topped with a tangy mustard dressing

Ham Espagnole Salad

225 g (½ lb) ham
1 onion
4 tomatoes
1 green pepper
30 ml (1 fl oz) (2 tablespoons) oil
15 ml (1 tablespoon) vinegar
2 cloves garlic, crushed
salt and pepper

1 Cut the ham into strips.

2 Slice the onions into rings.

3 Cut the tomatoes in quarters, and the pepper in rings, discarding the seeds.

4 Make a dressing by mixing the oil and vinegar. Add the crushed garlic and season with salt and pepper.

5 Toss the onions, tomatoes, and peppers and ham in the dressing and arrange in a bowl.

6 Serve the new potatoes, tossed in butter, and sprinkled with parsley.

Serves 4

Caesar Salad

1 large crisp lettuce
225 g (½ lb) rashers (slices) streaky bacon
25 g (1 oz) (2 tablespoons) butter
15 ml (1 tablespoon) oil
2 slices bread, diced
1 raw egg
6 anchovy fillets
25 g (1 oz) (3 tablespoons) grated Parmesan cheese

For the Dressing:
60 ml (2½ fl oz) (4 tablespoons) oil
30 ml (1 fl oz) (2 tablespoons) vinegar
salt and pepper
5 ml (1 teaspoon) mild mustard
2 cloves garlic, crushed
30 ml (2 tablespoons) finely chopped parsley

1 Wash the lettuce leaves and shred them. Place in a bowl.

2 Cut the bacon into strips and

Ham Espagnole Salad makes an ideal start to a meal or it can be served with potatoes as a main meal in itself

fry them in the butter and oil until crisp. Remove from the pan. Add the diced bread and fry until crisp.

3 Mix the lettuce, bacon, and croûtons lightly together in the salad bowl. Break the raw egg over the salad and stir it in.

4 Combine the ingredients for the dressing and toss the salad. Top it with the anchovy fillets and sprinkle over the grated Parmesan cheese. Serve with meat.

Serves 4

Chicken and Melon Salad

1 medium-sized melon
225 g (½ lb) cooked chicken, or white meat
1 green pepper
50 g (2 oz) (½ cup) walnuts
50 ml (2 fl oz) (¼ cup) mayonnaise
1 lettuce, washed and separated
15 ml (1 tablespoon) chopped parsley

1 Cut the melon in half, and remove the seeds. Scoop out the flesh with a melon baller, or a teaspoon. Place in a bowl.

2 Dice the chicken.

3 Finely chop the green pepper and walnuts.

4 Place all the ingredients in the bowl. Add the mayonnaise and mix well.

5 Line a shallow dish with lettuce leaves, and place the salad in the middle. Sprinkle with chopped parsley.

Serves 4

Aubergine (Eggplant) Ham Salad

1 large aubergine (eggplant)
pinch salt

2 red peppers
2 pickled cucumbers
50 ml (2 fl oz) (¼ cup) vinegar
salt and pepper
50 g (2 oz) (½ cup) flour
50 ml (2 fl oz) (¼ cup) oil
½ lettuce, washed and separated
225 g (½ lb) (1⅓ cups) chopped ham
15 ml (1 tablespoon) chopped dill

1 Cut the aubergine (eggplant) into 'chips'. Sprinkle with salt and leave for ½ hour.

2 Dice the peppers and cucumbers and put in a bowl with the vinegar and seasoning.

3 Dry the aubergine (eggplant) 'chips' and roll in flour. Fry in hot oil for 2-3 minutes until crisp. Add to the salad. Leave to cool for a few hours.

4 Serve on a bed of lettuce leaves, with the chopped ham arranged on top. Sprinkle with the dill.

Serves 4

Melon Balls and Tongue Salad

1 medium-sized melon
1 large grapefruit
225 g (½ lb) tongue
30 ml (1 fl oz) (2 tablespoons) oil
15 ml (1 tablespoon) vinegar
salt and pepper
pinch paprika

1 Cut the melon in half, and remove the seeds. Scoop out the flesh with a melon baller and place in a bowl.

2 Cut the grapefruit into segments (sections).

3 Cut the tongue into thin strips.

4 Make the dressing by mixing the oil, vinegar, salt and pepper, and toss the melon grapefruit and tongue in it.

5 Place in a bowl and sprinkle with the paprika. Chill until served.

Serves 4

Chicken and Melon Salad and Melon Ball and Tongue Salad are two tempting salads you can make with melons

Avocado, Egg and Ham Salad

8 hard-boiled eggs
1 avocado
30 ml (1 fl oz) (2 tablespoons) yogurt
2.5 ml (½ teaspoon) grated lemon rind
salt and pepper
dash chilli sauce
1 lettuce, washed and separated
5 tomatoes, halved
225 g (½ lb) (1⅓ cups) chopped ham
2 sticks celery, chopped
4 sprigs parsley

1 Cut the eggs in half lengthways and remove the yolks. Mash the yolks thoroughly.

2 Remove the skin and stone (seed) from the avocado, mash the flesh and mix with the egg yolks, yogurt, lemon rind, salt, pepper and chilli sauce.

3 Put this mixture into an icing (decorator's) bag and pipe into the egg whites.

4 Line a shallow dish with the lettuce leaves, and arrange the halved tomatoes, chopped ham and celery on top. Place the eggs on this mixture, and decorate with the sprigs of parsley.

Serves 4

Meat and Corn Salad

100 g (¼ lb) cooked ham
100 g (¼ lb) tongue
1 small red pepper
1 small green pepper
3 spring onions (scallions)
100 g (¼ lb) (1 cup) corn kernels
salt and pepper
150 ml (¼ pint) (⅝ cup) mayonnaise
few sprigs parsley

1 Cut the ham and tongue into 1 cm (½ in) cubes.

2 Deseed the red and green peppers and dice the flesh. Mix them with the meats in a salad bowl.

3 Slice the spring onions (scallions) thinly, including some of the green parts.

4 Mix all the ingredients together in a salad bowl, season, and stir in the mayonnaise until everything is coated. Decorate with the sprigs of parsley.

Serves 4

Farmhouse Salad

1 small red cabbage
salt and pepper
225 g (½ lb) belly pork
60 ml (2¼ fl oz) (4 tablespoons) oil
15 ml (1 tablespoon) vinegar
5 ml (1 teaspoon) mustard
50 g (2 oz) (½ cup) walnuts

1 Cut the cabbage into thin slices. Dust with salt and leave in a bowl for 1 hour. Rinse thoroughly and drain.

2 Meanwhile, cut the pork belly into thin strips. Heat half the oil and fry the pork pieces until golden brown. Drain and allow to cool.

3 Mix together the rest of the oil, vinegar and mustard, and season to taste. Add the dressing to the pork and cabbage and toss the salad to blend it well. Fold in the walnuts just before serving.

Serves 4

Turkey and Cranberry Salad

350 g (¾ lb) (2 cups) cooked turkey
100 g (¼ lb) (½ cup) seedless grapes
15 ml (1 tablespoon) lemon juice
3 sticks celery
2 hard-boiled eggs
150 ml (¼ pint) (⅝ cup) mayonnaise
150 ml (¼ pint) (⅝ cup) cranberry
  sauce
salt and pepper
pinch basil
25 g (1 oz) (¼ cup) toasted split
  almonds

1 Dice the turkey meat and mix it with the grapes and lemon juice.

2 Clean and chop the celery. Chop the hard-boiled eggs. Add both to the meat and grapes.

3 Blend together the mayonnaise, cranberry sauce, salt and pepper, and basil. Fold the dressing into the meat mixture. Mix in the nuts and serve.

Serves 6

Carmen Salad

100 g (¼ lb) (½ cup) rice
100 g (¼ lb) (½ cup) peas
2 red peppers
225 g (½ lb) cooked
  chicken
3 sprigs fresh tarragon
45 ml (2 fl oz) (3 tablespoons)
  olive oil
15 ml (1 tablespoon) vinegar
15 ml (1 tablespoon) lemon juice
5 ml (1 teaspoon) mild mustard
salt and pepper

1 Boil the rice in salted water until just tender. Rinse, drain, and allow to cool.

2 Boil the green peas in a little water until tender. Drain.

3 Holding each red pepper on a fork, turn it over a flame to blister the fine skin. Scrape off the skin. Split the pepper, remove the seeds and dice the flesh.

4 Cut the chicken into small chunks. Finely chop the tarragon. Mix the rest of the ingredients to make the dressing.

5 Place the rice, peas, red pepper and chicken in a salad bowl. Toss in the chopped tarragon and dressing. Serve at once.

Serves 4

Lentil and Salami Salad with Artichoke Hearts

225 g (½ lb) (1⅓ cups) brown lentils
2 red peppers
225 g (½ lb) salami
6 canned artichoke hearts
60 ml (2¼ fl oz) (4 tablespoons) oil
30 ml (1 fl oz) (2 tablespoons)
  wine vinegar
5 ml (1 teaspoon) mild mustard
salt and pepper
30 ml (2 tablespoons)
  chopped fresh parsley and
  chervil

1 Boil the lentils (without any salt in the water) for about 1 hour or until they are tender but not mushy. Drain and allow to cool.

2 Meanwhile deseed the red pepper and cut it into thick strips. Boil the pieces for about 10 minutes until they are soft. Drain and allow to cool.

3 Cut the salami sausage into thin slices. Drain the artichoke hearts. Beat together the oil, vinegar, mustard, salt and pepper to make a dressing.

4 Mix together the lentils and red pepper and toss them lightly in the dressing. Arrange on a large serving dish. Place the artichoke hearts in a row down the middle, and the salami slices around the sides. Sprinkle the whole dish with the chopped fresh herbs.

Serves 6

Salami and Lentil Salad with Artichoke Hearts makes a delicious starter and is easy to prepare well in advance

Asparagus Ham Rolls

1 kg (2 lb) fresh asparagus
25 g (1 oz) (2 tablespoons) butter
salt and pepper
15 ml (1 tablespoon) chopped
 parsley
2 hard-boiled eggs
6 slices ham
30 ml (2 tablespoons) Parmesan
 cheese

1 Cook the asparagus spears for 20 minutes or until tender in boiling salted water. When they are cooked remove the white ends. Toss the spears in half the butter seasoned with salt and pepper and allow them to cool.

2 Finely dice the hard-boiled eggs. In a bowl combine the eggs, remaining butter and the chopped parsley. Knead these ingredients together until you have a fine crumble.

3 Lay out the slices of ham and sprinkle each with the Parmesan cheese.

4 Divide the asparagus spears into 7 equal bundles. Reserve one for later and place each of the others on a slice of ham.

5 Roll the ham around the asparagus and place them, join downwards, on a serving dish. Sprinkle over the egg mixture and decorate the dish with the remaining spears. Serve with a crisp green salad and a vinaigrette dressing.

Serves 6

Tip: A delicious alternative to the ham in this recipe is smoked ham (Parma or Prosciutto).

Asparagus Ham Rolls make an appetizing and luxurious start to a special dinner or a delicious party snack

Orange Duck Salad

1 lettuce
3 spring onions (scallions)
225 g (½ lb) (1⅓ cups) diced cooked
 duck
1 green pepper, deseeded and
 chopped
1 stick celery, chopped
2.5 ml (½ teaspoon) finely
 chopped mint
3 oranges

For the Dressing:
50 ml (2 fl oz) (¼ cup) oil
15 ml (1 tablespoon) vinegar
15 ml (1 tablespoon) orange juice
salt and pepper

1 Remove the heart from the lettuce. Wash and dry both the leaves and the heart. Finely dice the lettuce heart and the spring onions (scallions).

2 Prepare the dressing. Combine

the oil, vinegar and orange juice in a watertight container. Season and shake well.

3 Place the duck meat in a bowl. Add the diced lettuce heart, spring onions (scallions), green pepper and celery to the mixture. Pour over the dressing and toss. Stir in the finely chopped mint and leave for 1 hour.

4 Grate the rind of 2 of the oranges and stir it into the salad mixture.

5 Peel the oranges and remove any excess white skin. Break them into segments (sections). Cut the segments (sections) in half and add to the bowl. Chill.

6 Line a salad bowl with the lettuce leaves and spoon in the chilled salad mixture. Serve.

Serves 6

Sweet 'n Sour Turkey Salad

1 lettuce
1 red pepper
6 radishes
100 g (¼ lb) rice, cooked
15 ml (1 tablespoon) chopped spring onions (scallions)
5 ml (1 teaspoon) green peppercorns
100 g (¼ lb) (⅝ cup) diced turkey

For the Dressing:
50 g (2 oz) canned pineapple pieces, drained
45 ml (2 fl oz) (3 tablespoons) oil
15 ml (1 tablespoon) vinegar
2.5 ml (½ teaspoon) Worcestershire sauce
pinch curry powder
salt and pepper

1 Wash and dry the lettuce and break it into small pieces. Deseed and finely dice the red pepper. Chop the radishes into small pieces.

2 Prepare the dressing. Chop the pineapple pieces and combine them with the oil, vinegar, Worcestershire sauce, curry powder, salt and pepper. Blend

thoroughly or shake well in a watertight container. Chill.

3 Place the rice in a salad bowl. Add the lettuce pieces, red pepper, radishes, spring onions (scallions), peppercorns and toss. Finally add the turkey meat and pour over the chilled dressing. Toss thoroughly and serve.

Serves 4

Tip: You may substitute any leftover chicken or pork for the turkey in this recipe. For those who like a spicy dressing with more bite, try substituting half the pineapple pieces with 30 ml (1 fl oz) (2 tablespoons) of chopped mango chutney.

Pork and Prawn Salad Cantonese

175 g (6 oz) (1 cup) diced pork, cooked
175 g (6 oz) canned bamboo shoots, drained
1 carrot, cooked
175 g (6 oz) bean shoots
175 g (6 oz) cooked prawns, peeled

Sweet 'n Sour Turkey Salad is an oriental dish which uses up turkey and cold rice leftovers in a tasty way

For the Dressing:
5 ml (1 teaspoon) chopped fresh ginger
1 clove garlic, chopped
75 ml (3 fl oz) (⅓ cup) pineapple juice
50 ml (2 fl oz) (¼ cup) oil
juice ½ lemon
2.5 ml (½ teaspoon) soya sauce
salt and pepper

1 Prepare the dressing first. Pound together the ginger and garlic, until they are thoroughly mashed. Combine the pineapple juice, oil, lemon juice, soya sauce, seasoning and the garlic and ginger paste in a bowl. Whisk quickly until all the ingredients are well blended. Strain through a sieve if necessary and chill.

2 Cut the pork into fine strips 5 cm (2 in) long. Do the same with the bamboo shoots and carrot.

3 Wash and drain the bean shoots.

4 Combine the pork, prawns, bamboo shoots, carrot and bean shoots in a salad bowl. Pour over the dressing, toss and serve.

Serves 4-6

Aspic Salads

Nothing looks as cool or attractive on a summer evening as a brilliantly clear, chilled aspic salad. The great advantage of a salad prepared in this way is that you can use virtually any leftovers from the fridge and mould them into a tempting and delicious dish. The best aspics are those made from reduced chicken beef or veal stocks, but you can use stock cubes or canned consommés. Nowadays you can purchase aspic crystals in a packet. Below we give recipes using crystals and a basic stock for the quick and easy preparation of an aspic.

Prawn Aspic

550 ml (1 pint) (2½ cups) water
1 chicken stock cube
5 tarragon leaves
2 celery leaves
25 g (1 oz) (¼ cup) gelatine
salt and pepper
juice 1 lemon
1 carrot
1 turnip
50 g (2 oz) beans
50 g (2 oz) (½ cup) peas
2 hard-boiled eggs
6 lettuce leaves
3 tomatoes
1 radish, sliced
225 g (½ lb) peeled cooked prawns
8 black olives

Prawn Aspic – a beautifully colourful dish which is decorated with tomatoes, olives, lettuce and hard-boiled eggs

1 Bring the water to the boil. Crumble the stock cube into the water and simmer for 5 minutes. Add 3 of the tarragon leaves and both the celery leaves and boil for 1 minute. Dissolve the gelatine and add it to the stock. Season with the salt and pour in the lemon juice. Simmer for 5 minutes, strain and allow to cool. Do not refrigerate.

2 Meanwhile, peel and dice the carrot and turnip into small cubes. Finely slice the beans. Boil these vegetables and the peas separately in salted water until they are tender.

3 Cut 1 egg into wedges and slice the other. Wash and dry the lettuce leaves and slice the tomatoes.

4 Prepare a 1.2 litre (2 pint) (5 cup) mould by rinsing it in cold water. Place the mould in a bowl of crushed ice.

5 Pour in ½ the aspic jelly and swirl the mould in one direction in

the ice until the inside is covered with a thin skin of jelly. When it is set, dip the slices of egg into the remaining aspic and stick them to the side of the mould. Do the same with the sliced radish and a few tarragon leaves, but when you stick them to the mould arrange them around the egg slices to form a floral design.

6 Place the boiled vegetables in a bowl, add the prawns, season and toss together. Pour the remaining aspic jelly (it should still be liquid) into the bowl and stir until it is mixed through the vegetables and prawns. Pour this mixture into the mould. Allow the aspic to set either on the ice or in the fridge.

7 Arrange the lettuce leaves on a serving dish. Turn the set aspic on to the bed of lettuce and surround it with the sliced tomatoes, quartered hard-boiled egg and olives before serving.

Serves 6

Tip: For a slightly different flavour you can add other ingredients to this dish. Other seafoods such as minced clams, chopped lobster and tuna fish all blend well with the prawns.

Vegetables in Aspic makes an impressive and attractive salad for a summer lunch or a dish for a buffet party

Vegetables in Aspic

100 g (¼ lb) carrots, peeled
2 large parsnips, peeled
50 g (2 oz) French (snap) beans
75 g (3 oz) peas
1 packet aspic jelly crystals
salt and pepper
75 g (3 oz) canned asparagus tips, drained

1 Dice 1 of the carrots. Cut the remaining carrots and parsnips into small cubes. Cut the French beans into diamond shapes.

2 Boil the carrots, parsnips, beans and peas in salted water, until tender. Drain. Keep the vegetables separate for the moment and allow to cool.

3 Prepare a 900 ml (1½ pint) (3⅝ cup) mould by rinsing it in cold water. Place the mould in a bowl of crushed ice.

4 Follow the instructions on the packet of aspic jelly and make 300

ml (½ pint) (1¼ cups) aspic. Check the seasoning.

5 Pour ½ the aspic into the mould and immediately start to swirl the bowl in the ice in the same direction all the time. Keep swirling until the aspic coats the inside of the mould and begins to set.

6 Take the carrot slices and asparagus tips and dip them in the remaining aspic. Line the top of the mould with alternate slices of carrot and asparagus.

7 Combine the remaining vegetables in a bowl and gently toss. Check the seasoning. Spoon the vegetables into the mould. Pour over the remaining aspic until the mould is full. Chill until it is set hard.

8 Turn the aspic salad out onto a plate and serve immediately.

Serves 6

Tip: All sorts of other vegetables can be used in this dish. Choose colourful vegetables such as peppers, beetroot (beet) or tomato. Also, you can change the flavour of the jelly by adding wine, dry sherry or port or even a liqueur. Always use a dry wine or sherry in a savoury aspic mould.

Eggs in Aspic

15 g (½ oz) (2 tablespoons) aspic
  crystals
50 ml (2 fl oz) (¼ cup) sherry
300 ml (½ pint) (1¼ cups) water
4 hard-boiled eggs
4 tomatoes
5 ml (1 teaspoon) chopped
  parsley
100 g (¼ lb) thin slices ham
sprig rosemary

1 Soak the aspic crystals in the
sherry. Bring the water to the boil,
then dissolve the aspic in the boiling hot water, and simmer until
the liquid clears.

2 When the aspic mixture is cool,
but still liquid, place 15 ml (1 tablespoon) in the bottoms of 6 oval
150 ml (¼ pint) (⅝ cup) moulds.
Allow the jelly to set.

3 Split the hard-boiled eggs and
chop the yolk and white of one of
the eggs.

4 Skin, deseed and chop one of
the tomatoes.

5 Sprinkle a little chopped
parsley, egg yolk and white, and
tomato into each mould. Cut the
ham into 6 strips, 5 cm (2 in) wide.
Line each mould with a strip of
ham and place a halved egg inside
each.

6 Top up the moulds with aspic
and pour the remaining aspic into
a square mould.

7 Leave in a refrigerator for 2
hours until firm and set. Turn out
the aspic eggs on to an attractive
serving dish and garnish with the
remaining quartered tomatoes
and the sprig of rosemary.

8 Cut the aspic in the square dish
or mould into small cubes and use
as a garnish.

Serves 6

Tip: This dish is ideal for summer
parties and buffets. You can decorate the tops of the eggs with
chopped herbs, ham or onion as
well as eggs and tomatoes. Or, if
you feel really extravagant, how
about chopped truffles, the most
luxurious food of all?

Lamb in Mint Jelly Mould

275 g (10 oz) (1⅔ cups) diced
  leftover cold lamb
15 g (½ oz) (1 tablespoon) butter
100 g (¼ lb) (1 cup) diced, cooked
  potatoes
salt and pepper
150 ml (¼ pint) (⅝ cup) meat stock
15 ml (1 tablespoon) chopped
  mint
15 ml (1 tablespoon) sugar
15 ml (1 tablespoon) vinegar

---

*Eggs in Aspic are surrounded
by ham, decorated with
tomatoes and encased in aspic
jelly, topped with parsley*

15 g (½ oz) (2 tablespoons)
  powdered gelatine
50 ml (2 fl oz) (¼ cup) water
4 tomatoes, quartered
1 cos lettuce, shredded

1 Heat the butter in a frying pan
(skillet) and sauté the diced lamb
for about 5 minutes. Add the
potatoes and toss gently, then
remove from the pan and season
with salt and pepper.

2 Bring the stock to the boil – it
should be clear and transparent.

3 Mix together the mint, sugar
and vinegar and add to the boiling stock. Remove from the heat.

4 Blend the powdered gelatine
with the cold water and then stir
this mixture into the hot stock.
Add the meat and potatoes, then

pour into a 22.5 cm (9 in) ring mould (tube pan).

5 Cool a little, then allow to set for 2 hours in the refrigerator.

6 When set and firm, turn the mint jelly mould out on to a dish and decorate the centre with quartered tomatoes. Arrange the shredded cos lettuce around the sides of the mould, then serve.

Serves 4

Tip: This dish is an original and tasty way of using up leftover roast lamb from the Sunday joint which is bound to become a firm favourite with your family. Instead of using fresh mint and making the mint sauce, you can use one of the bottled commercial varieties. It is especially nice if served with a crisp green salad and sautéed potatoes.

Lobster in Aspic

one 1 kg (2 lb) lobster, live or
  cooked
1 litre (1¾ pints) (4¼ cups) court
  bouillon (fish stock)
4 eggs, separated

*Lamb in Mint Jelly Mould is
a tasty, attractive way
of using up leftover lamb in
aspic with a cold salad*

12 leaves gelatine, or 50 g (2 oz)
  (½ cup) powdered gelatine
100 ml (4 fl oz) (½ cup) water
100 g (¼ lb) (½ cup) minced whiting
  or any white fish
15 ml (1 tablespoon) chopped
  tarragon
7 tomatoes
few tarragon leaves
1 truffle, sliced (optional)
225 g (½ lb) (2 cups) diced carrots
225 g (½ lb) (2 cups) diced turnips
100 g (¼ lb) (1 cup) peas
small bunch chives
100 ml (4 fl oz) (½ cup) mayonnaise
salt and pepper
few lettuce leaves

1 If the lobster is alive, plunge it into boiling water or the court bouillon (it will die instantly). Cook it for 15 minutes, then leave to cool in the court bouillon until completely cold.

2 Poach two of the egg whites in a pan or in a bain-marie in the oven.

3 Soak the gelatine in the cold water and stir well. Place in a bowl with the minced whiting, chopped tarragon and uncooked egg whites. Mix briskly, then strain in the warm court bouillon.

4 Mix well, then pour into a saucepan and bring to the boil, stirring constantly. Simmer for 15 minutes until the mixture has coagulated on top.

5 When cooked, pour this jelly through some damp muslin (cheesecloth) into a bowl and cool.

6 Place a 1 litre (1¾ pints) (4¼ cups) aspic, or charlotte, mould into a large bowl, containing plenty of crushed ice.

7 Add some of the jelly to the mould and coat the bottom and edges, turning the bowl all the time over the ice.

8 With a knife, remove the skin of 1 tomato and cut into decorative diamond shapes. Do the same with the poached egg whites.

9 Scald the tarragon leaves. Arrange the egg white, tomato, a few slices of truffle and the tarragon around the inside of the mould in a pattern and fix in place with another layer of jelly. Leave to set.

10 Shell the lobster, remove the soft skin from the tail and cut the meat into even rounds. You can also use the meat in the claws.

11 Arrange the meat in the mould with the remaining sliced truffle, then cover with a layer of jelly and leave to set. Repeat the layers of lobster and jelly until the mould is full. Place in the refrigerator for 2 hours until set.

12 Meanwhile, cook the carrots, turnips and peas in salted water until cooked.

13 Place them in a bowl with the chives and mayonnaise and mix well.

14 Slice off the tops of the remaining tomatoes and scoop out the pulp. Fill the tomato shells with the mayonnaise mixture.

15 When the aspic mould is set, turn it out on to a serving dish. Wrap a hot cloth around the mould for a few minutes first.

16 Decorate with lettuce and surround with the tomatoes.

Serves 6

Look'n Cook Lobster in Aspic

1 All the ingredients **2** Cook the lobster in a court bouillon of water, carrots, onions with herbs and seasoning. Chop the carrot, and onions and put them in a pot with the turbot trimmings. Cover with cold water and simmer **3** Separate the eggs, reserving the yolks. Put the whites in a small dish and poach in a bain marie **4** Chop the whiting fillets, and tarragon. Add the leaf gelatine, egg whites and water.

Mix well **5** Add the fish stock through a strainer
6 Put the mixture into a large saucepan, bring to the
boil and simmer **7** Pour the jelly through a damp
cloth. Cool **8** Chill the metal mould in a bowl of ice.

Put a little aspic in it and swirl round to coat the
mould **9** Cut the truffle, egg white and tomato into
decorative shapes **10** Arrange in the metal mould
11 Fix in place with more aspic **12** Shell the lobster

13 Cut the lobster into even pieces **14** Arrange the pieces of the lobster in the mould, alternating with rounds of truffles **15** Carefully spoon in a little aspic to fix the pieces and allow to set **16** Pour over another layer of aspic and allow to set. Continue with layers of lobster and truffles stuck down with a little aspic, followed by a layer of aspic until all the ingredients are used. Put the mould in the refrigerator to set **17** Finely dice the carrots, turnips and chives. Cook the vegetables with the peas for a few minutes, until tender, in boiling salted water. Drain and cool **18** Scoop out the insides of the tomatoes. Discard the seeds and mix the vegetables with the tomato pulp and the mayonnaise, then season. Stuff the tomatoes **19** To unmould the lobster in aspic, either wrap a hot cloth round the mould for a few seconds, or dip the mould in hot water briefly. Turn over on a serving dish, hold the mould and dish firmly and shake the dish once sharply **20** Arrange the stuffed tomatoes alternately with lettuce leaves round the lobster in aspic

Vegetarian Salads

In this section, we give you recipes for delicous, nourishing salads without meat. Although they contain no meat, many have a high protein content derived from nuts, eggs, cheese, lentils, wheat or beans. Do not make the mistake of regarding all vegetarian food as 'rabbit food' – it's not. Just try some of these exciting recipes – at least one of them is bound to become a firm family favourite.

Tabbouleh

550 ml (1 pint) (2½ cups) water
225 g (½ lb) crushed wheat
1 onion, chopped
juice 1 lemon
50 ml (2 fl oz) (¼ cup) olive oil
salt and pepper
15 ml (1 tablespoon) chopped
   parsley
15 ml (1 tablespoon) chopped
   mint
4 tomatoes, cut in wedges

1 Bring the water to the boil and soak the crushed wheat in it for about 5 minutes, then drain.

2 Blend together the chopped onion, lemon juice and olive oil. Five minutes before serving the Tabbouleh, season the dressing and stir it into the crushed wheat.

3 Sprinkle with the chopped parsley and mint and arrange the tomato wedges on top. Serve as an appetizer.

Serves 4

Tip: This is a Lebanese salad which can be served as a starter or an accompaniment to kebabs or grilled (broiled) lamb. The texture should be crunchy but soft. For a slightly different flavour, you can mix some crushed garlic into the dressing. *Never* add the dressing until 5 minutes before serving or the wheat will become soggy.

Tabbouleh, on the left, is shown with its classic accompaniment, fattoush, which is an onion and tomato salad

Curried Spaghetti Salad

150 g (5 oz) cooked spaghetti
3 sticks celery, chopped
100 g (¼ lb) (1¼ cups) sliced raw
   mushrooms
15 ml (1 tablespoon) chopped
   onion
1 lettuce

For the Mayonnaise:
75 ml (3 fl oz) (⅜ cup) mayonnaise
salt and pepper
good pinch curry powder
10 ml (2 teaspoons) mango
   chutney
5 ml (1 teaspoon) lemon juice
15 ml (1 tablespoon) chopped
   parsley

1 Mix together the cooked cold spaghetti, celery, mushrooms and onion in a bowl.

2 Prepare the mayonnaise. Mix the mayonnaise, seasoning, curry powder and chutney together in a bowl. Stir in the lemon juice and chopped parsley.

3 Toss the spaghetti mixture in the mayonnaise so that it is evenly coated.

4 Wash and drain the lettuce. Arrange the separated leaves around a serving dish and pile the spaghetti in the centre.

Serves 4

Tip: You can use different types of pasta in this salad. Try substituting cooked pasta shells and shapes or macaroni for the spaghetti. A more Italian way to serve this salad is to make a vinaigrette-type dressing with oil, vinegar, garlic and fresh tomato juice. Mix in some tomato ketchup (catsup), curry powder, mango chutney and sugar. Then toss the spaghetti in this dressing, and serve garnished with chopped herbs such as basil or parsley and sliced red and green peppers. This is a good way of using up cold leftover pasta, and it is also economical.

Mushroom Salad Provençale

450 g (1 lb) (5 cups) button
  mushrooms
2 cloves garlic, crushed
juice and grated rind 1 lemon
30 ml (1 fl oz) (2 tablespoons) oil
15 ml (1 tablespoon) yogurt
salt and pepper
15 ml (1 tablespoon) chopped
  parsley

1 Wash and drain the mushrooms. Wipe them dry, then trim the ends from the stalks. Slice the mushrooms thinly and place in a bowl with the garlic.

2 Next make the dressing. Mix the lemon juice and rind, and oil. Stir in the yogurt, salt and pepper.

3 Five minutes before serving, toss the mushrooms in the salad dressing. Sprinkle with the chopped parsley and serve.

Serves 4

Mushroom Salad Provençale will brighten up a summer lunch with its fresh tangy taste of lemons, garlic and yogurt

Leek Salad

8 small leeks
5 ml (1 teaspoon) made mustard
salt and pepper
50 ml (2 fl oz) (¼ cup) oil
15 ml (1 tablespoon) wine
  vinegar
15 ml (1 tablespoon) single (light)
  cream
10 ml (2 teaspoons) chopped
  parsley

1 Trim the green ends of the leeks. Split each leek from the centre of the white up into the stem, keeping the leek intact and whole. Wash the leeks thoroughly under running cold water until they are completely clean.

2 Make the leeks into a bundle and tie it securely around the centre with string.

3 Fill a saucepan with water, bring to the boil and stand the bundle of leeks in the boiling water. Boil for 5 minutes, then drain and refresh the leeks in ice-cold water. This will restore the vivid green colour. Drain again and remove the string.

4 In a bowl, prepare the dressing. Mix together the mustard, salt, pepper and oil. Stir in the vinegar and finally the cream.

5 When the leeks are completely cold, arrange them in a flat serving dish and pour the dressing over the top. Sprinkle them with the chopped parsley, then serve.

Serves 4

Tip: This salad is delicious when served with a new potatoes and watercress salad. If you wish to increase the nutritious content and add some protein, sprinkle in a few chopped nuts or quartered hard-boiled eggs. Other vegetables such as celery, asparagus and fennel can also be cooked.

Slimmers' Salads

A balanced salad makes the perfect meal for a slimmer. It should be eaten with or include protein in the form of meat, eggs, cheese or fish with an interesting combination of salad and root vegetables and fruit. A little salad dressing will make it delicious to eat, and add very little in the way of calories.

Eat a light but sensible breakfast of a boiled egg, salads and fruit at lunchtime, and make sure you have a light protein meal in the evening, and you will lose weight gradually.

Eat your meals slowly, savour your food, and include plenty of green vegetables. By the time you have munched your way through plenty of lettuce or cabbage you will feel that you have eaten enough, and will not be tempted to take a second helping. Cut the sugar and starch right down, but balance the rest of your diet and you will feel well, healthy and full of vitality. Aim for slimness, which is compatible with perfect health, and not emaciation. Don't be tempted to slim beyond what is sensible for your build and metabolism, as this will make you feel exhausted and drained of energy. You may become thin, but you won't be beautiful.

Greek Onion Salad

8 large onions
225 g (½ lb) (1⅓ cups) finely chopped ham
1 pickled cucumber, diced
30 ml (2 tablespoons) corn kernels
salt and pepper
100 ml (4 fl oz) (½ cup) white wine
100 ml (4 fl oz) (½ cup) water
juice 1 lemon
150 ml (¼ pint) (⅝ cup) single (light) cream
5 ml (1 teaspoon) French mustard
15 ml (1 tablespoon) chopped parsley

1 Remove the outside yellow skin from the onions, but leave them whole. Place them close together in one layer in a large pan and just cover with water. Bring to the boil and cook for 10 minutes.

2 Scoop out the inside of each onion. Chop and blend with the chopped ham and diced pickled cucumber. Add the corn kernels and season. Refill the onion cases.

3 Preheat the oven to 190°C, 375°F, gas 5.

4 Place the onions in a shallow ovenproof dish. Pour over the white wine mixed with the water, half the lemon juice and 30 ml (2 tablespoons) cream. Bake in the oven for 20 minutes until cooked, but still firm. Cool in the liquid.

5 Make the sauce with the rest of the cream, lemon juice and mustard.

6 When ready to serve, lift the onions on to a dish, pour a little of the sauce over, and serve the remainder separately. Sprinkle the onions with chopped parsley. Serve with a rice salad.

Serves 4

Cauliflower and Cottage Cheese Salad

1 cauliflower
50 ml (2 fl oz) (¼ cup) oil
30 ml (1 fl oz) (2 tablespoons) vinegar
5 ml (1 teaspoon) chopped basil
salt and pepper
275 g (10 oz) (1⅓ cups) cottage cheese
15 ml (1 tablespoon) chopped chives
½ lettuce
4 tomatoes

1 Wash and trim the cauliflower and divide into sprigs. Boil in salted water until just tender for about 5 minutes. Drain.

2 While hot, pour over a dressing made of the oil, vinegar, basil and salt and pepper. Cool, spooning the liquid over the cauliflower from time to time.

3 Mix the cottage cheese with the chopped chives.

4 When ready to serve, line a shallow dish with the lettuce leaves, arrange the cold cauliflower salad in a circle, and put the cottage cheese in the middle. Decorate with the tomatoes, cut in slices.

Serves 4

Avocado and Chinese Leaves Salad

1 head of Chinese leaves, or 1 lettuce
1 avocado
1 grapefruit
225 g (½ lb) (2 cups) carrots, cut in strips
sprigs of watercress for garnish
15 ml (1 tablespoon) boiled rice (optional)

1 Wash the Chinese leaves, or lettuce. Drain well and arrange in a bowl.

2 Remove the peel and stone (seed) from the avocado and cut into chunks.

3 Peel the grapefruit and cut into segments (sections).

4 Arrange the avocado, grapefruit and strips of carrots on the Chinese leaves. Decorate with the watercress, and sprinkle the rice (optional) on top. Serve with a bowl of low calorie salad dressing.

Serves 4

Avocado and Chinese Leaves Salad is an exotic medley of rice, fruit and salad vegetables with a mayonnaise

119

Salad Antibes

½ lettuce
50 g (2 oz) cooked French (snap)
  beans
1 small onion, sliced
½ green pepper, sliced
½ red pepper, sliced
1 tomato, quartered
1 hard-boiled egg, quartered
8 black olives

For the Low Calorie Dressing:
75 ml (2½ fl oz) (⅓ cup) lemon juice
150 ml (5 fl oz) (⅝ cup) water
5 ml (1 teaspoon) sugar
1.25 ml (¼ teaspoon) salt

1 Combine the dressing ingredients and mix well. Chill.

2 Wash and dry the lettuce. Tear the leaves into pieces and place in a bowl. Cut the beans into pieces 5 cm (2 in) long.

3 Add the beans, onion and peppers. Toss in the dressing and decorate with the tomato, egg and black olives.

Serves 2

Cucumber and Yogurt Salad

1 large or 2 small cucumbers,
  peeled and sliced
½ onion, finely chopped
225 ml (½ lb) (8 fl oz) plain low-fat
  yogurt
2.5 ml (½ teaspoon) salt
freshly ground (milled) black
  pepper
45 ml (1½ fl oz) (3 tablespoons)
  finely chopped fresh mint or
  2.5 ml (½ teaspoon) dried mint
15 ml (1 tablespoon) finely
  chopped fresh basil or 2.5 ml
  (½ teaspoon) dried basil

1 Place the cucumber and onion in a bowl. Add the yogurt, salt and pepper and mix well. Chill.

2 Just before serving sprinkle with the mint and basil.

Serves 4

---

*Salade Antibes has the colour
and exotic flavour of the
French Riviera with its olives,
peppers and crispy lettuce*

Low Calorie Thousand Islands Dressing

200 ml (6 fl oz) (¾ cup) tarragon
  vinegar
300 ml (½ pint) (1¼ cups)
  condensed tomato soup
1 clove garlic, crushed
pinch cayenne pepper
30 ml (2 tablespoons) chopped
  dill pickle
30 ml (2 tablespoons) finely
  chopped celery
30 ml (2 tablespoons) finely
  chopped parsley
15 ml (1 tablespoon)
  Worcestershire sauce
5 ml (1 teaspoon) paprika
5 ml (1 teaspoon) made mustard

1 Combine all the ingredients in a screw top jar or watertight container and shake well. Store in the fridge.

Makes 575 ml (1 pint) (2½ cups)

Papaw Citrus Salad

1 papaw
1 orange
1 grapefruit
½ lettuce
12 olives
1 dill pickle
225 ml (8 fl oz) (1 cup) plain
  yogurt
salt

1 Slice the papaw. Peel the orange and grapefruit and separate the segments (sections). Arrange the papaw and fruit on the lettuce leaves. Garnish with the olives and dill pickle.

2 Season the yogurt with a little salt and pour over the salad.

Serves 4

Savoury Sauces

An imaginative sauce can transform a simple dish into something special. Once you've mastered the principal base sauces — béchamel and velouté for white sauces, espagnole for brown sauces, and hollandaise for emulsified sauces — you have the key to countless variations

Basis of a Sauce

The principal elements in a sauce are stock, seasonings and other flavourings, fat and thickening agents. To make a good sauce you must first make a good stock – strongly flavoured and concentrated. Never rush a stock – cook it for a long time at simmering point (88°C, 180°F) to draw out the essential juices and flavour from the meat bones. And leave well alone, except to top up with fresh cold water, so it stays clear.

Both white and brown stocks are used in sauces, together with concentrated extracts like meat gravies, essences and stock cubes. With the base white or brown sauce made, you can then think about the countless variations possible, for base sauces are rarely used without adjustment.

These base sauces (sometimes referred to as 'mother' sauces) are the white béchamel and velouté, and brown espagnole: recipes for all three appear on the following pages. You can save time by making a quantity of very thick base sauce which can be kept, covered, in a bowl in the refrigerator. Then you can take a spoonful of cold sauce and enrich a gravy or stock in no time at all. And for variations you simply thin down the base sauce with about 300ml ($\frac{1}{2}$ pint) ($\frac{5}{8}$ cup) of stock or other liquid, depending on the type of sauce required.

To make a smooth sauce, quite a lot of the fat used (at least 4%) must remain in the sauce. If too much fat is used, however, fatty globules will rise to the surface and spoil both flavour and appearance. You can only skim them off in the event of this happening.

There are various ways to thicken and bind a sauce. Egg yolk, starch (any kind of flour) and sometimes blood are the main binding agents used: simply blend the egg yolk or starch with a little of the cold liquid to form a smooth paste, then whisk in a little of the hot liquid, pour back into the pan of liquid, and heat to just below boiling point, stirring all the time, until the sauce is thick and smooth. If the thickening agent only were added direct to the hot sauce or boiled, the mixture would curdle and look unappetizing.

Arrowroot and cornflour (cornstarch) give better results than ordinary flour in semi- and thick gravies, fruit and sweet-sour sauces. To use, blend the starch with 4 times the amount of cold liquid, then at the last minute stir into the boiling liquid and boil until the sauce clears and thickens. Use at once.

Emulsified sauces like hollandaise, and its variations such as Béarnaise and mousseline sauces, undergo a different thickening process. Air is beaten (whipped) into egg yolks, sometimes over heat, so they increase their volume and thicken. In the case of mayonnaise, the thickening is brought about by the combining of egg yolks, oil and vinegar or lemon.

The addition of starch, a white sauce or a gelatinous mixture helps to bind an emulsified sauce together, making separation less likely and the sauce more resistant to heat or refrigeration.

If a sauce has to stand for a while before serving, keep in a bain-marie (double saucepan) or basin over a pan of hot water so there's no risk of burning or loss of texture and flavour; then place a little butter or margarine on top and cover with greaseproof (waxed) paper to prevent a skin forming.

And if you want to give a sauce a fillip, any fortified wine (port, Madeira, sherry) can be added at the last moment in the ratio of 50ml (2fl oz) ($\frac{1}{4}$ cup) per $\frac{1}{2}$ litre (1 pint) ($2\frac{1}{2}$ cups).

If making a béchamel with milk or water instead of stock to serve as a plain white sauce, season with salt, pepper and nutmeg, together with a bouquet garni of 1 bay leaf, celery and thyme, and strain before use. If the béchamel is to serve with fish, add the juice of 1 lemon at the last moment.

Thickening Sauces
There are three basic methods of thickening a sauce – by means of a roux, a liaison, and a purée.

Roux
A roux is a paste of flour cooked in fat which can be used to thicken liquids to various consistencies, according to their intended use. The degree to which the roux is cooked determines the flavour and final colour of the sauce, and the three stages of cooking a roux are known as white, blond and brown.

White roux: equal quantities of butter or margarine and flour are cooked gently together in a pan for about 2 minutes or until the mixture has the appearance of wet sand. It should not be coloured. This type of roux is used mainly for thickening béchamel sauces and for any white soups.

Blond roux: the ratio of fat to flour is the same as for a white roux, but the two are cooked together for a slightly longer time until a light-brown, nutty colour is obtained. This roux is used for velouté sauces, tomato sauce and soups.

Brown roux: the ratio of fat to flour is increased – the amount of fat is $1\frac{1}{4}$ times that of the flour – and the two are cooked together for a longer time – about 10-12 minutes or until well browned. The fat used is usually dripping, pure vegetable fat or lard. Since the time taken to brown the roux is so long, the heat beneath the pan must be very low indeed so that the mixture does not burn and so become bitter.

In order to shorten this cooking time and to produce the distinctive baked flavour of a brown sauce, the flour can first be toasted in the oven: place it on a baking sheet and cook at 180°C, 350°F, gas 4 for about 12 minutes or until golden in colour. The flour can then be used as for the other kinds of roux and need only be cooked with the fat for about 3-4 minutes.

After the flour and fat have been cooked, the liquid is added by one of two methods. In the first, the cooked roux is taken off the heat and the cold liquid is added gradually, stirring all the time with a wooden spoon, until a smooth sauce is obtained. The pan is then returned to the heat and the sauce heated until thick. Or, you can remove the roux from the heat after cooking, allow it to cool and then add the hot liquid to it beating all the time. The sauce is returned to the heat and cooked until thick. Finally, the sauce can be whisked quickly at the end in order to make sure it is smooth.

Liaison

The two basic liaisons are egg yolks and blood; these are ingredients which, when heated gently, coagulate and therefore thicken the sauce into which they have been incorporated. The coagulant is placed in a bowl and blended with a spoonful of cold liquid.

A larger quantity (usually about a cupful) of the warm sauce is then added to the coagulant and the mixture is returned to the main sauce and heated gently until thick. To add the egg yolk or the blood directly to the sauce would only result in a too rapid coagulation and a curdled sauce. Coagulation occurs at about 80°C, 180°F, and so it is important that the sauce is heated gently – preferably in a bain marie or in a bowl over a deep pan of boiling water.

Purée

Another method of thickening a sauce, which reflects new trends in modern cookery, is to add meat, or vegetable purées; these are simply made by working in a blender with a little liquid or the food's own cooking juices. In this way, starchy elements can be reduced to a minimum, making purée thickening ideal for weightwatchers and slimmers in general.

Stuffed Fennel in Mornay Sauce

25 g (1 oz) (4 tablespoons) flour
50 g (2 oz) (4 tablespoons) butter
2 litres (4 pints) boiling water
30 ml (2 tablespoons) white vinegar
20 g (¾ oz) (1½ tablespoons) salt
4 large fennel bulbs
50 g (2 oz) (1 cup) fresh breadcrumbs
30 ml (2 tablespoons) single (light) cream
2 slices cooked ham
150 g (5 oz) smoked bacon
few sprigs parsley
1 clove garlic, peeled and chopped
50 g (2 oz) (½ cup) grated cheese

For the Sauce:
25 g (1 oz) (4 tablespoons) flour
25 g (1 oz) (2 tablespoons) butter or margarine
300 ml (½ pint) (1¼ cups) milk
25 g (1 oz) (2 tablespoons) tomato concentrate (paste)
pinch nutmeg
salt and pepper

1 In a pan, blend the flour with 25 g (1 oz) (2 tablespoons) of the butter to form a paste and then pour over the boiling water, whisking all the time. Add the vinegar and the salt and bring this mixture to the boil. This forms a white stock in which to

Stuffed fennel in mornay sauce, baked in a hot oven till brown and bubbling. Any vegetable can be cooked in this way

cook the fennel bulbs.

2 Clean the fennel bulbs and cut away the hard bases but leave them whole. Place the bulbs in the stock and bring to the boil. Simmer for 30 minutes.

3 Place the breadcrumbs in a bowl with the cream and mix well. Chop the ham and bacon; wash, dry and chop the parsley. Add the chopped meats and parsley, the garlic and the egg to the breadcrumbs and mix well.

4 Preheat the oven to 200°C, 400°F, gas 6. Drain the fennel. Cut the bulbs in half, fill each half with stuffing and then put the two halves together again. Place the stuffed fennel bulbs in an ovenproof dish.

5 Make the white roux (see page 196) using the flour, butter or margarine and milk. Add the tomato concentrate (paste) and nutmeg and season to taste.

6 Coat the fennel bulbs with the sauce and sprinkle them with the grated cheese. Cut the remaining butter into small pieces and dot these over the top. Place the fennel in the preheated oven and bake for 35-40 minutes.

Serves 4

Béchamel Sauce

Béchamel Sauce

The quantity below makes a panada *or thick paste-like mixture which can be stored, covered, in a refrigerator for up to 1 week. For a flowing or pouring sauce, add up to 450 ml ($\frac{3}{4}$ pint) (2 cups) liquid – 300 ml ($\frac{1}{2}$ pint) (1$\frac{1}{4}$ cups) is usually sufficient; reheat gently, stirring all the time, until smooth.*

1 small onion, studded with 2 cloves
500 ml (1 pint) (2$\frac{1}{2}$ cups) milk
50 g (2 oz) (4 tablespoons) butter or margarine, or mixture of both
50 g (2 oz) (good $\frac{1}{2}$ cup) plain flour
salt and pepper
pinch nutmeg
pinch thyme

1 Place the onion in a saucepan with the milk. Bring it gently to the boil, then remove the pan from the heat and allow to cool. Cover with a lid and leave the milk to infuse and absorb the flavour of the onion.

2 Melt the fat in a pan and stir in the flour. Cook the roux over a low heat, without letting it colour, for about 1 minute, stirring with a wooden spoon. Gradually pour in the milk, stirring continuously until a smooth sauce forms.

3 Add the onion and simmer the sauce for 5 minutes. Remove the onion and add salt, pepper, the nutmeg and thyme.

Makes 500 ml (1 pint) (2$\frac{1}{2}$ cups)

Consistency of Sauces
A useful formula to remember is that the proportion of fat and flour to liquid is 5 percent for a pouring consistency and 10 percent for a coating sauce; that is, 25 g (1 oz) fat and 25 g (1 oz) flour to 500 ml (1 pint) (2$\frac{1}{2}$ cups) liquid and 50 g (2 oz) fat and 50 g (2 oz) flour to 500 ml (1 pint) (2$\frac{1}{2}$ cups) liquid, respectively.
The liquid used can be milk, cream, stock or water, according to the recipe.

Variations

Anchovy Sauce
1 To 300 ml ($\frac{1}{2}$ pint) (1$\frac{1}{4}$ cups) of basic béchamel sauce, add 50 g (2 oz) drained and chopped canned anchovy fillets, 25 g (1 oz) (2 tablespoons) unsalted (fresh) butter, 5 ml (1 teaspoon) tomato concentrate (paste) and, for colour, a pinch of paprika.

2 Thin down the sauce to the required consistency with 300 ml ($\frac{1}{2}$ pint) (1$\frac{1}{4}$ cups) stock (use fish stock for fish, and chicken or white stock for meat dishes). Check the seasoning.

Serve with eggs, celery or fish.

Asparagus Sauce
1 To 300 ml ($\frac{1}{2}$ pint) (1$\frac{1}{4}$ cups) of basic béchamel sauce, add 50 g (2 oz) cooked asparagus, blended with 300 ml ($\frac{1}{2}$ pint) (1$\frac{1}{4}$ cups) of the water in which the asparagus was cooked.

2 After the sauce is cooked, remove the pan from the heat and add 50 ml (2 fl oz) (4 tablespoons) soured cream or natural yogurt to give the sauce a piquant flavour. Check the seasoning.

Serve with chicken, veal or salmon dishes.

Butter Sauce
1 Use the basic béchamel sauce recipe, but replace the milk with water and use butter only. For extra flavour, a chicken stock cube can be crumbled into the sauce.

Serve with vegetables and potatoes.

Carrot Sauce
1 To 300 ml ($\frac{1}{2}$ pint) (1$\frac{1}{4}$ cups) of basic béchamel sauce, add a purée of 50 g (2 oz) cooked carrots, liquidized with 150 ml ($\frac{1}{4}$ pint) ($\frac{5}{8}$ cup) of their cooking water.

2 Add 50 ml (2 fl oz) ($\frac{1}{4}$ cup) soured or single (light) cream and reheat. Flavour the sauce with a pinch of paprika, 2.5 ml ($\frac{1}{2}$ teaspoon) liquid honey and 30 ml (2 tablespoons) lemon juice. Check the seasoning.

Serve with boiled beef, chicken or white fish.

Cheese Sauce
1 To 300 ml ($\frac{1}{2}$ pint) (1$\frac{1}{4}$ cups) of basic béchamel sauce, add 300 ml ($\frac{1}{2}$ pint) (1$\frac{1}{4}$ cups) milk and 50 g (2 oz) ($\frac{1}{2}$ cup) grated cheese (such as Cheddar, Gruyère, Edam or Emmenthal). If the sauce is to be used for vegetables, such as cauliflower, asparagus, leek, onion, celery and cabbage, use less milk and make up the liquid content with some of the water in which the vegetables have been cooked. Check the seasoning.

Serve with meat, vegetable, fish and pasta dishes.

Cream Sauce
1 To 300 ml ($\frac{1}{2}$ pint) (1$\frac{1}{4}$ cups) of basic béchamel sauce, add 300 ml ($\frac{1}{2}$ pint) (1$\frac{1}{4}$ cups) single (light) cream. Blend, bring to the boil and boil for 5 minutes.

2 Add the strained juice of $\frac{1}{2}$ lemon and season, with salt and pepper to taste.

Serve with fish, egg and vegetable dishes.

Divine Sauce
1 Boil 150 g (5 oz) (2$\frac{1}{2}$ cups) button mushrooms in the strained juice of 1 lemon and 150 ml ($\frac{1}{4}$ pint) ($\frac{5}{8}$ cup) dry sherry for 2 minutes. Pour this mixture into 300 ml ($\frac{1}{2}$ pint) (1$\frac{1}{4}$ cups) of basic béchamel sauce.

2 Finally, add 75 ml (2$\frac{1}{2}$ fl oz) ($\frac{1}{3}$ cup) double (heavy) or single (light) cream, a pinch of paprika and 15 ml (1 tablespoon) tomato ketchup (catsup) or tomato concentrate (paste). Boil for 8 minutes and season with salt and pepper to taste.

Serve with chicken quenelles.

Look'n Cook Béchamel Sauce

1 Ingredients for béchamel sauce: butter, flour, milk, nutmeg, and 1 onion studded with cloves **2** Heat the butter gently in a pan until melted **3** Draw the pan off the heat and add the flour to make a roux **4** Return to the heat and cook the roux until it bubbles and has the appearance of wet sand. Stir all the time with a wooden spoon **5** Draw the pan off the heat again and blend in the milk **6** The sauce is heated again for a few minutes, then seasoned and poured into a sauce-boat to serve

Egg Sauce

1 Place 2 egg yolks and 150 ml (¼ pint) (⅝ cup) single (light) cream in a bowl and mix together with a spoon. Gradually add 300 ml (½ pint) (1¼ cups) of basic béchamel sauce and return this mixture to the rest of the sauce.

2 Bring to the boil and boil for 5 minutes. Finally, add the strained juice of ½ lemon and season with salt and pepper to taste.

Serve with fish, poultry and vegetables.

Mushroom Sauce

1 Slice 150 g (5 oz) (2½ cups) white button mushrooms. Boil them in the strained juice of ½ lemon and 150 ml (¼ pint) (⅝ cup) stock for 3 minutes. Pour this mixture into 300 ml (½ pint) (1¼ cups) of basic béchamel sauce.

2 Season and stir in 75 ml (2½ fl oz) (⅓ cup) single (light) cream.

Serve with chicken, noodles, fish and vegetable dishes.

Mustard Sauce

1 To 300 ml (½ pint) (1¼ cups) of the butter sauce, add, with the pan off the heat, 15 ml (1 tablespoon) of made English mustard (vary the amount according to taste).

2 Thin down the sauce to the required consistency with 300 ml (½ pint) (1¼ cups) chicken or white stock and season with salt and pepper to taste.

Serve with oily fish, pork or grilled duck.

Parsley Sauce

1 To 300 ml (½ pint) (1¼ cups) of basic béchamel sauce, add either 5 g (1 tablespoon) freshly chopped parsley (never use dried parsley for this sauce) or 25 g (1 oz) savoury butter (see page 224).

2 Thin down the sauce to the required consistency with 300 ml (½ pint) (1¼ cups) chicken or white stock and season with salt and pepper to taste.

Serve with fish, white meat, calf's head and tongue.

Soubise Sauce

1 To 300 ml (½ pint) (1¼ cups) of basic béchamel sauce, add 100 g (¼ lb) cooked onion, liquidized with 200 ml (6 fl oz) (¾ cup) cold milk and blend. If liked, flavour with a pinch of sage.

2 Add 100 ml (4 fl oz) (½ cup) single (light) cream and boil for 5 minutes. Season with salt and pepper to taste.

Serve with roast or boiled mutton or veal.

Condiments for Sauces

Clearly, one of the most important steps in making sauces is achieving the correct balance of seasoning. The basic ingredient of seasoning is salt.

Salt

Two types of salt are used: grey or sea salt, and rock salt which is used to season clear soups or sauces. Table salt is used at the last moment to adjust seasoning. Spice salt is a mixture of salt and spice.

You can make your own spice salt by mixing 100 g (¼ lb) salt with 20 g (¾ oz) mixed spice and 10 g (⅜ oz) white pepper. Keep the mixture in an airtight container. Salt is used in the ratio of 10 g (⅜ oz) salt to 1 litre (1¾ pints) liquid or 1 kg (2 lb) solid weight.

Four-spice Mixture

A four-spice mixture can be made by mixing together 75 g (3 oz) Jamaican spice (all-spice), 15 g (½ oz) nutmeg, 15 g (½ oz) ground (powdered) clove, 15 g (½ oz) cinnamon and 15 g (½ oz) salt. Again, keep the mixture in an airtight container.

Four-herb Mixture

Mix together 10 g (⅔ oz) of each of the following, in ground (powdered) form: bay leaf, thyme, rosemary and marjoram. Add 10 g (⅔ oz) salt and keep the mixture in an airtight container.

Chilli Paste for Curry Sauce

Mix the following ingredients together and combine in a liquidizer: 15 g (½ oz) fresh green chillies, 15 g (½ oz) peeled fresh ginger root, 15 g (½ oz) fresh peeled garlic, 15 g (½ oz) chopped onion, 50 ml (2 fl oz) (¼ cup) olive or nut oil, 15 ml (½ fl oz) (1 tablespoon) lemon juice, 50 ml (2 fl oz) (¼ cup) water.

Spice for Curry

Blend the following ingredients together and mix them with chilli paste: 2 g (½ teaspoon) ground (powdered) coriander, 2 g (½ teaspoon) paprika, 2 g (½ teaspoon) ground (powdered) cumin seeds, 2 g (½ teaspoon) ground (powdered) cloves), 3 g (½ teaspoon) tumeric, 10 g (⅓ oz) cornflour (cornstarch) or arrowroot, 5 g (1 teaspoon) mustard, and 2 g (½ teaspoon) ground (powdered) cardamom seeds.

Brussels Sprouts in Curry Sauce

salt
1 kg (2 lb) brussels sprouts
15 g (½ oz) (1 tablespoon) butter
15 g (½ oz) (2 tablespoons) flour
10 ml (2 teaspoons) curry powder
300 ml (½ pint) (1¼ cups) milk
pepper

1 Bring a saucepan of salted water to the boil.

2 Meanwhile, prepare and wash the sprouts. Mark a cross in the end of the stalks.

3 Tip the sprouts into the boiling water and simmer for 8-10 minutes or until tender.

4 Meanwhile, make a white sauce. Melt the butter in a small pan, stir in the flour and curry powder and cook gently, stirring with a wooden spoon, for 1 minute. Take the pan off the heat and blend in the milk. Return the pan to the heat, bring to the boil and boil for a few minutes, stirring all the time. Keep the sauce hot.

5 When the sprouts are almost cooked, strain off 100 ml (4 fl oz) (½ cup) of the cooking liquid. Add this to the sauce and stir well. Taste and correct the seasoning.

6 Drain the sprouts well and tip them into a heated serving dish. Coat with the curry sauce. Serve hot.

Serves 4

Veal Scallopini à la Antonia

50 g (2 oz) (4 tablespoons) butter
700 g (1½ lb) escalopes of veal
  (veal scallopini)
5 g (1 teaspoon) salt
freshly ground (milled) black
  pepper
2 spring onions (scallions),
  thinly sliced
3 tomatoes, skinned, seeded and
  cut into strips
175 g (6 oz) (1½ cups) thinly sliced
  mushrooms
150 ml (¼ pint) (⅝ cup) chicken
  stock
2.5 ml (½ teaspoon) dried oregano
150 ml (¼ pint) (⅝ cup) béchamel
  sauce (see page 196)

pinch nutmeg
5 g (1 tablespoon) chopped
  parsley

1 Heat the butter in a large frying pan (skillet) and fry the escalopes of veal quickly on both sides over a high heat. Remove the meat from the pan, season with salt and pepper, and keep warm.

2 Add the sliced onions to the pan and fry gently for 2 minutes then add the tomatoes and mushrooms and cook for a further 4-5 minutes. Add the stock and oregano, bring to the boil and boil for 5 minutes.

3 Add the béchamel sauce and boil again for 8 minutes to reduce (evaporate) the liquid by half.

4 Check the seasoning and add the nutmeg. Return the veal to the pan and coat it with the sauce until well heated.

5 Transfer the meat and sauce to a warmed serving dish and sprinkle with the chopped parsley. Serve with boiled rice and a crisp green salad.

Serves 6

Tip: Instead of using chicken stock, you can add an equal quantity of white wine. Also, the béchamel sauce can be replaced by the same amount of single (light) cream or a mixture of cream and sauce.

Brussels sprouts in curry sauce. This creamy béchamel-based sauce turns sprouts into something rather special

Velouté Sauce

Basic Velouté Sauce

The quantity below makes a panada *or thick paste-like mixture which can be stored, covered, in a refrigerator for up to 1 week. For a flowing or pouring sauce, add up to 450 ml (¾ pint) (2 cups) liquid – 300 ml (½ pint) (1¼ cups) is usually sufficient; reheat gently, stirring all the time, until smooth.*

**50 g (2 oz) (4 tablespoons)
  margarine or melted chicken fat
50 g (2 oz) (good ½ cup) plain flour
½ litre (17½ fl oz) (2¼ cups) chicken
  stock or use household stock,
  with 2 chicken stock cubes**

1 Melt the fat in a heavy pan and cook the flour to a roux blond for 2 minutes or until it looks like wet sand but has a nutty colour and flavour.

2 Gradually pour in the cold stock or, alternatively, cool the roux and gradually stir in the boiling stock.

3 Whisk the sauce for a few seconds for smoothness and then simmer for 30 minutes, removing any skin or scum as it rises.

Makes about ½ litre (1 pint) (2½ cups)

Conil Cucumber Sauce

**225 g (½ lb) cucumber
1 red pepper
1 medium onion
30 ml (2 tablespoons) white
  vinegar
salt and pepper
pinch grated nutmeg**

**juice and rind 1 lemon
½ litre (1 pint) (2½ cups)
  velouté sauce
2 egg yolks
100 ml (4 fl oz) (½ cup) single
  (light) cream
5 g (1 tablespoon) chopped chives
  and parsley**

1 Peel and deseed the cucumber, and dice the pulp neatly. Place in a large mixing bowl. Deseed the pepper and chop. Peel and chop the onion, and add with the chopped pepper, the vinegar and the lemon rind and juice to the cucumber, season

2 Place the velouté sauce in a saucepan and bring to the boil.

3 Blend the egg yolks and cream in a bowl. Then gradually stir in a little of the sauce, return this mixture to the rest of the sauce, stirring all the time, and simmer for 5 minutes. Add the cucumber mixture and simmer for a further 10 minutes. Season and sprinkle in the herbs.

*Serve with boiled meats
Makes ½ litre (1 pint) (2½ cups)*

Curry Sauce

1 Melt 25 g (1 oz) margarine in a saucepan, then stir in 5 g (1 teaspoon) curry powder and 15 g (1 tablespoon) desiccated coconut. Cook without letting it colour for 1 minute, then gradually pour in 300 ml (½ pint) (1¼ cups) basic velouté sauce.

2 Thin down with 300 ml (½ pint) (1¼ cups) chicken or white stock. Finally add the strained juice of ½ lemon. Season with salt to taste. The colour of the finished sauce should be a very delicate pale yellow.

Serve with eggs, vegetables and chicken.

German Sauce

1 To 300 ml (½ pint) (1¼ cups) of basic velouté sauce, add 2 sliced white button mushrooms, juice of ½ lemon, 1 bouquet garni and 2 sticks celery. Thin down with up to 450 ml (¾ pint) (2 cups) stock to the required pouring consistency.

2 Place 2 egg yolks and 150 ml (¼ pint) (⅝ cup) of cold stock in a bowl. Stir well and pour in 150 ml (¼ pint) (⅝ cup) of the velouté sauce. Then pour back into the rest of the sauce, while whisking all the time. Simmer for 5 minutes, then remove the bouquet garni.

Serve with fricassée of chicken or veal.

Avocado Sauce

1 Liquidize or work through a sieve (strainer) the flesh of 2 ripe avocados, together with the juice of 1 lemon, 15 ml (1 tablespoon) lime cordial and 25 ml (1 fl oz) (2 tablespoons) chicken or white stock. Blend the resulting purée with 300 ml (½ pint) (1¼ cups) basic suprême sauce.

2 Thin down the sauce with 150 ml (¼ pint) (⅝ cup) chicken or white stock and 75 ml (2½ fl oz) (⅓ cup) dry sherry; season with salt and pepper to taste.

Serve with shrimps (prawns), chicken, veal, and pork chops.

Mornay Sauce

1 Place 2 egg yolks and 150 ml (¼ pint) (⅝ cup) of single (light) cream in a bowl. Stir well and dilute with 150 ml (¼ pint) (⅝ cup) of cold suprême sauce, adding 50 g (2 oz) (⅓ cup) of grated Parmesan or Cheddar cheese.

2 Pour the mixture into 450 ml (¾ pint) (2 cups) of suprême sauce and thin down to the required consistency with 150 ml (¼ pint) (⅝ cup) of milk.

Serve with fish, vegetables, eggs, pastas, veal and chicken.

Suprême Sauce

1 Use the same ingredients as for German Sauce but omit the egg yolks; add 300 ml (½ pint) (1¼ cups) double (heavy) cream with the stock.

2 Boil the sauce for 20 minutes, then season with salt and pepper to taste. The sauce should have an extra creamy consistency.

Serve as a base for Chaudfroid Sauce (see recipe page 213) with chicken dishes, and to blend with fillings for vol-au-vents or with vegetables.

Hot Mushroom Mousse with Cream Sauce

1 kg (2 lb) very fresh, white
  button mushrooms
125 g (6 oz) (¾ cup) butter or
  margarine
1 lemon, halved
4 shallots or 1 medium onion,
  finely chopped
1 small clove garlic, peeled and
  crushed
350 g (¾ lb) (1½ cups) cooked ham,
  minced (ground)
10 g (2 tablespoons) finely
  chopped parsley
100 g (¼ lb) (2 cups) fine
  breadcrumbs
60 ml (4 tablespoons) single
  (light) cream
salt and pepper
pinch nutmeg
30 ml (2 tablespoons) brandy

For the Sauce:
40 g (1½ oz) (3 tablespoons) butter
  or margarine
20 g (¾ oz) (3 tablespoons) flour
15 ml (1 tablespoon) tomato
  concentrate (paste)
150 ml (¼ pint) (⅝ cup) single
  (light) cream

1 Reserve 12-15 of the best mushrooms and set them aside for the garnish; finely chop the rest.

2 Melt 50 g (2 oz) (¼ cup) fat in a sauté pan. Add the chopped mushrooms, the strained juice from the 2 lemon halves, and the chopped shallots or onion, and sauté over a high heat until the mixture is completely dry – about 5 minutes.

3 Stir in the crushed garlic, minced (ground) ham, 5 g (1 tablespoon) chopped parsley, breadcrumbs, cream, salt and pepper, nutmeg and brandy and cook over a moderate heat for 5 minutes, stirring from time to time.

4 Separate 2 of the eggs and stir the yolks, together with the 2 whole eggs, lightly beaten, into the mushroom mixture during the last 2 minutes of cooking. Take the pan off the heat and check the seasoning; leave to cool.

5 Preheat the oven to 180°C, 350°F, gas 4.

6 In a clean dry bowl whip the 2 egg whites until stiff. Using a metal spoon or spatula, cut and fold the egg whites into the cooled mushroom mixture. Do not beat or the air trapped in the egg whites will be forced out.

7 Well grease a 1 kg (2 lb) capacity charlotte tin (mould) or basin; turn the mousse mixture into it. Stand the tin (mould) or basin in a roasting pan, filled with enough hot water to come two-thirds of the way up the pan, and cook in the preheated oven for 45 minutes. After 30 minutes, increase the oven temperature to 200°C, 400°F, gas 6.

8 Meanwhile prepare the sauce. Melt 50 g (2 oz) (4 tablespoons) fat in a small saucepan. Add the flour and stir to make a roux, but do not let it brown. Stir in the tomato concentrate (paste) and then the cream. Bring to the boil, boil for 5 minutes, stirring continuously, until smooth and creamy. Check the seasoning.

9 Heat the remaining fat in a pan and toss the reserved mushrooms in it until lightly browned.

10 When cooked, turn out the mousse onto a hot serving dish. Pour over the hot sauce, garnish with the whole mushrooms and sprinkle with the remaining chopped parsley. Serve at once.

Serves 4

Tip: Alternatively, fill the mushroom mixture into individual dishes (use ramekins or dariole moulds) and cook in the oven as for a large mousse, for the same length of time: then turn out and serve as individual mousses.

To turn out a hot mixture: slide a knife round inside the mould or basin to free the mixture cleanly, then invert, with a plate over the top, tap sharply once or twice and the mixture will slide out cleanly.

Hot mushroom mousse with cream sauce is a stunning yet economical dish to make

Look'n Cook Chicken with Chaudfroid Sauce

1 Ingredients for chicken chaudfroid: chicken with giblets, bouquet garni, onion, celery and carrot. Place the ingredients in a pan with the water and cook gently until the chicken is tender **2** Melt the margarine, stir in the flour and cook the roux until sandy in texture. Add the stock **3** Draw the pan off the heat and stir in the cream. Add seasoning **4** Add half the aspic (gelatine) to the sauce, stir until dissolved, then season and simmer for 15 minutes **5** Pour the sauce through a sieve (strainer) to remove any

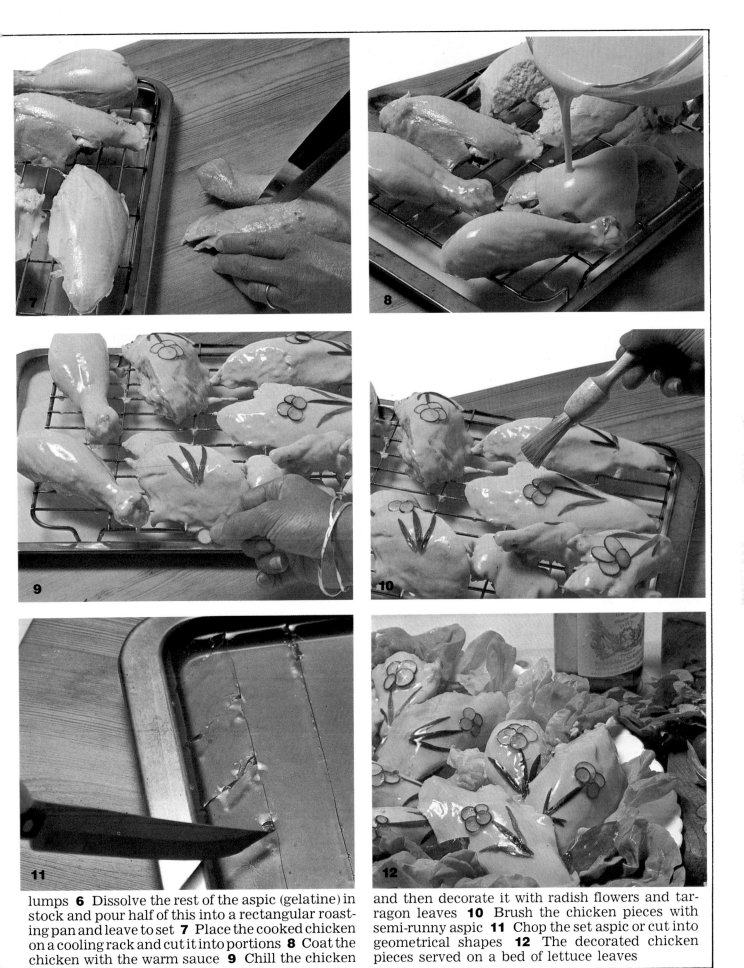

lumps **6** Dissolve the rest of the aspic (gelatine) in stock and pour half of this into a rectangular roasting pan and leave to set **7** Place the cooked chicken on a cooling rack and cut it into portions **8** Coat the chicken with the warm sauce **9** Chill the chicken and then decorate it with radish flowers and tarragon leaves **10** Brush the chicken pieces with semi-runny aspic **11** Chop the set aspic or cut into geometrical shapes **12** The decorated chicken pieces served on a bed of lettuce leaves

Poached Eggs with Braised Chicory in Suprême Sauce

100 g (¼ lb) (½ cup) butter or margarine
450 g (1 lb) chicory (Belgian endive), washed, trimmed and cut into 2-3 cm (¾-1¼ in) pieces
salt and pepper
5 g (1 teaspoon) sugar
4 eggs
1 litre (1¾ pints) (4½ cups) water
30 ml (2 tablespoons) white vinegar
4 slices bread, 4-5 cm (1½-2 in) thick
225 ml (½ pint) (⅝ cup) suprême sauce

1 Melt 40 g (1½ oz) (3 tablespoons) fat in a sauté pan. Add the chicory (endive), cover and braise over a low heat for 7-8 minutes or until tender. Then season with salt and pepper to taste, add the sugar and leave to cook further, uncovered, until the chicory (endive) breaks down to a purée.

2 While the chicory (endive) is cooking, soft-poach the eggs in the water, to which the vinegar has been added. Bring the water to the boil, then lower the heat until just below simmering point.

3 Break 1 egg into a cup; lower the lip of the cup close to the surface of the water and slide the egg carefully into the water; then spoon the white up and over the yolk and cook for 3 minutes. Lift out the egg with a slotted spoon, trim the white neatly, then slide the egg into a bowl of warm water. Repeat the poaching process with the remaining eggs.

4 Hollow out the centre of each piece of bread, but without cutting all the way through. Spread inside and out with the remaining butter and toast until golden.

5 Fill the toast 'nests' with hot chicory (endive) purée and top with a drained egg. Arrange on a serving dish, cover with hot suprême sauce and serve.
Serves 4

Tip: Shelled hard-boiled eggs can be substituted for soft-poached eggs if preferred.

Chicken with Chaudfroid Sauce

2 small or 1 large roasting chicken, with giblets
2 litres (3½ pints) (8 cups) water
1 leek, sliced
1 carrot, sliced
2 sticks celery, sliced
1 bouquet garni
salt and pepper
sprig tarragon

For the Chaudfroid Sauce:
50 g (2 oz) (4 tablespoons) butter or margarine
50 g (2 oz) (good ½ cup) flour
300 ml (½ pint) (1¼ cups) single (light) cream
50 g (2 oz) powdered aspic (savoury gelatine)
pinch nutmeg
100 ml (4 fl oz) (½ cup) dark sherry

1 Wash the chicken and the giblets to remove all traces of blood. Place the chicken in a large saucepan (side by side if using 2 birds). Cover level with water.

2 Parboil the giblets (without the liver) in a pan of salted water for 5 minutes. Refresh in cold

Poached eggs in suprême sauce – a stylish way to dress up soft-poached eggs

water, drain and add to the chicken.

3 Add the sliced leek, carrot and celery to the chicken, together with the bouquet garni. Season with salt and pepper and bring the liquid to the boil gently. Simmer for 45 minutes. Remove the pan from the heat and cool the chicken in the liquid until both are completely cold. Take out the chicken and chill in a refrigerator for at least 4 hours.

4 Reboil the pan of giblets, vegetables and liquor for 1 hour to concentrate the flavour, then strain and reserve the liquor.

5 To make the chaudfroid sauce: melt the fat in a saucepan, stir in the flour and cook the roux for 2 minutes until it has a sandy texture. Gradually stir in 300 ml (½ pint) (1¼ cups) of the reserved liquor, whisking gently to form a smooth velouté sauce. Pour in the cream and season to taste.

6 Dissolve half of the aspic powder (gelatine) in the hot sauce, stirring all the time. Season with salt, white pepper and nutmeg. Simmer for 15 minutes, then strain through a conical fine sieve (strainer).

7 To make the aspic (savoury gelatine): pour 400 ml (¾ pint) (1¾ cups) of the rest of the reserved liquor into a saucepan with 100 ml (4 fl oz) (½ cup) dark sherry and a sprig of tarragon. Boil for 2 minutes, then remove the tarragon. Refresh the tarragon in cold water and drain. Place all the leaves in a dish. Meanwhile, dissolve the rest of the aspic (savoury gelatine) in the tarragon stock, simmer for 5 minutes and set aside until cold.

8 To decorate the chicken: place the chicken(s) on a cooling rack

over a deep tray. Carve into 4 portions, and skin them. Discard unwanted bones and be sure to cut the knuckle bones from the legs.

9 Coat each piece of chicken with warm chaudfroid sauce (if it is too stiff, thin it down with a little stock). Chill the chicken in the refrigerator for 20 minutes to set the sauce, then decorate each piece with 2 tarragon leaves.

10 Glaze the chicken with a little semi-runny aspic (gelatine), leave to firm, then carefully lift onto a serving dish, using 2 spatulas. Decorate with lettuce leaves, cucumber slices, tomatoes and slices of green pepper.

11 Pour the rest of the aspic (gelatine) into an oblong tray 3 cm (1½ in) deep and allow to set. When firm, cut the aspic jelly (jello) with

a knife into geometrical shapes or dice, or chopped; turn out onto dampened greaseproof (waxed) paper and cut with a pastry (cookie) cutter into small half-moon shapes. Place the aspic jelly (jello) shapes round the dish.

Serves 4-8

Tip: If you use a boiling fowl or capons for this dish, the breast can be sliced into thin escalopes after cooking and each slice coated with chaudfroid sauce. Instead of tarragon, you could substitute 3-4 drained, canned asparagus tips: place them on top of each chicken piece, securing them in position with a little semi-runny aspic jelly (jello).

Chicken with chaudfroid sauce – an eye-catching dish to serve for a cold buffet

Brown Sauces

Basic Brown Sauce

75 g (3 oz) (good ¾ cup) plain flour
100 g (¼ lb) (½ cup) beef dripping
   (shortening)
2 medium carrots, coarsely
   sliced
2 medium onions, coarsely sliced
2 sticks celery and trimmings,
   coarsely sliced
100 g (¼ lb) streaky bacon rashers
   (slices), chopped
1 bouquet garni
1 clove garlic
50 g (2 oz) tomato concentrate
   (paste)
1 litre (1¾ pints) (5 cups) brown
   stock or other liquid (see
   method)
salt and pepper
pinch mace

1 Brown the flour on a baking
(cookie) sheet for 15 minutes at
200°C, 400°F, gas 6; do not brown it
too much. Remove. Heat half of
the dripping (shortening) in a
heavy-bottomed pan and stir in
the baked flour. Cook the roux for
3 minutes to a sandy texture.
Cool.

2 In another pan heat the
remaining dripping (shortening)
and brown the vegetables and
bacon for 8 minutes, keeping the
lid on the pan throughout. Add
the bouquet garni, garlic and the
tomato concentrate (paste).
Drain off the surplus fat. Pour in
the brown stock, bring to the boil
for 1 hour. This reduces (evaporates) the stock and concentrates
its flavour; skim from time to
time.

3 Stir the cold roux into the boiling stock, then stir with a whisk to
avoid lumps. Simmer for another
hour, skimming from time to time,

until the sauce is clear (a chef
would simmer this sauce for as
long as 4 hours, but this is not
necessary for home cooking).

4 Strain the sauce and season
with salt, pepper and mace. Thin
down with 300 ml (½ pint) (1¼ cups)
of brown stock, or beer, wine, cider
or fruit juice if preferred, and boil
for another 30 minutes, adjusting
the seasoning at the last moment.

Makes ½ litre (1 pint) (2½ cups)

Conil Brown Sauce

50 g (2 oz) (4 tablespoons)
   margarine or fat
50 g (2 oz) (¼ cup) onions, chopped
   or diced
50 g (2 oz) (½ cup) carrots, chopped
   or diced
50 g (2 oz) (½ cup) celery, chopped
   or diced
50 g (2 oz) leeks, chopped or diced
50 g (2 oz) (good ½ cup) plain flour
50 g (2 oz) (4 tablespoons) tomato
   concentrate (paste)
3 beef stock cubes or 25 g (1 oz)
   beef extract
1 litre (1¾ pints) (5 cups) water
1 bouquet garni
1 sprig fresh mint
1 clove garlic
salt and pepper
pinch mace

1 Heat the fat in a heavy-
bottomed pan, add the vegetables, cover, and sweat until soft.
Then remove the lid and brown a
little.

2 Stir in the flour to absorb the
fat and cook the roux for
2 minutes. Stir in the tomato concentrate (paste) and cook a
further minute.

3 Crumble the stock cubes in the
water and add to the pan,
together with the bouquet garni,
mint and garlic.

4 Stir the sauce a little and boil
for 30 minutes. Strain, then
simmer for 15 minutes. Season
with salt, pepper and mace.
Diluted with a thin stock, this
makes a quick, thick gravy.

Makes ½ litre (1 pint) (2½ cups)

Demi-glace Madeira Sauce

1 Thin down ½ litre (1 pint)
(2½ cups) basic brown sauce with
150 ml (¼ pint) (⅝ cup) brown stock
and 150 ml (¼ pint) (⅝ cup) Madeira,
stirring in 5 ml (1 teaspoon) beef
extract.

2 Boil the sauce for 15 minutes to
reduce (evaporate) by one-third,
to give a thinner, glossier and
more aromatic mixture than the
basic brown sauce.

Serve with meat, poultry and
game.

*Makes about 1 litre (1½ pints)
(4 cups)*

Demi-glace Sherry Sauce

1 Use the same ingredients as for
demi-glace Madeira sauce but
substitute medium sherry for
Madeira and flavour with a sprig
of mint and sage.

Serve with meat, poultry and
game.

*Makes about 1 litre (1½ pints)
(4 cups)*

Bordelaise Sauce

50 g (2 oz) (¼ cup) sweet onions or
   shallots, finely chopped
6 black peppercorns, crushed
1 sprig thyme
1 bay leaf, imported
150 ml (¼ pint) (⅝ cup) red wine
   (claret)
½ litre (1 pint) (2½ cups)
   demi-glace Madeira or sherry
   sauce

1 Place onion in a saucepan with
peppercorn, thyme, bay leaf and
wine. Boil for 5 minutes, then add
demi-glace sauce.

2 Boil a further 30 minutes and
pass through a fine conical sieve
(strainer). Serve with Steak Bordelaise.

Makes ½ litre (1 pint) (2½ cups)

Tip: This sauce can also include
diced or sliced poached beef marrow, but this does tend to make
the sauce richer and greasy.

Burgundy Sauce

150 g (5 oz) button mushrooms
50 g (2 oz) (4 tablespoons)
  margarine
150 g (5 oz) button onions, peeled
½ litre (1 pint) (2½ cups) bordelaise
  sauce, substituting a good red
  Burgundy wine for claret
salt and pepper
15 ml (1 tablespoon) brandy

1 To prepare the garnish: wash mushrooms and remove stalks (these can be used to make a mushroom-flavoured stock). Heat the fat, put in the onions and brown for 4 minutes. Drain off the fat.

2 Pour in the bordelaise sauce and boil for 10 minutes until the onions are almost soft. Strain the sauce.

3 Reheat the sauce and add the mushroom caps. Boil for 3 minutes. Check the seasoning, adding salt and pepper to flavour, then pour in the brandy. Serve with chicken (as in coq au vin), veal and beef dishes.

Makes ½ litre (1 pint) (2½ cups)

Chasseur Sauce

25 g (1 oz) (2 tablespoons) butter
  mixed with 25 ml (1 fl oz) (⅛ cup)
  oil
50 g (2 oz) (½ cup) shallots or
  onions, peeled and chopped
50 g (2 oz) (⅝ cup) white
  mushrooms, trimmed and
  sliced (stalks optional)
150 ml (¼ pint) (⅝ cup) dry white
  wine
½ litre (1 pint) (2½ cups)
  demi-glace or plain brown
  sauce
150 g (5 oz) (½ cup) fresh tomatoes,
  skinned, deseeded and coarsely
  chopped
salt and pepper
15 ml (1 tablespoon) chopped
  parsley and tarragon leaves

1 Heat the fat in a sauté pan and sweat the shallots for 2 minutes

without colouring them. Add the mushrooms and cook a further minute.

2 Strain off the fat and pour in the wine. Reduce (evaporate) the sauce by boiling hard for 4 minutes, then stir in the demi-glace sauce and tomatoes and simmer for 15 minutes. Season with salt and pepper.

3 Add the chopped parsley and tarragon before serving.

Serve with veal escalopes or chops, lamb noisettes and sautéed chicken.

Makes about ½ litre (1 pint) (2½ cups)

Basquaise Sauce

1 Cut in halves 1 red and 1 green pepper, deseed and shred finely.

2 Scald and drain the peppers, then add to ½ litre (1 pint) (2½ cups) chasseur sauce and simmer for 10 minutes. Season with salt, pepper and garlic salt.

Serve with chicken, veal and pork chops.

Makes about ½ litre (1 pint) (2½ cups)

Devilled Sauce (Sauce Diable)

50 g (2 oz) (½ cup) shallots or sweet
  onions, peeled and finely
  chopped
150 ml (¼ pint) (⅝ cup) dry white
  wine
25 ml (1 fl oz) (⅛ cup) wine vinegar
6 white peppercorns, crushed
1 dried chilli
½ litre (1 pint) (2½ cups)
  demi-glace or plain brown
  sauce
salt and pepper

1 Boil the shallots in a saucepan with the wine, vinegar, peppercorns and chilli until reduced (evaporated) by half.

2 Stir in the demi-glace or brown sauce and simmer for 15 minutes. Season with salt and pepper, then

strain through a fine sieve (strainer).
Serve with grilled chicken legs, grilled gammon steaks or fish.

Makes ½ litre (1 pint) (2½ cups)

Poivrade Sauce

25 ml (1 fl oz) (⅛ cup) oil
50 g (2 oz) (½ cup) onions, peeled
  and diced
50 g (2 oz) (½ cup) carrots, peeled
  and diced
50 g (2 oz) (½ cup) celery, peeled
  and diced
150 ml (¼ pint) (⅝ cup) dry white or
  red wine
50 ml (2 fl oz) (¼ cup) wine vinegar
3 peppercorns, crushed
1 bouquet garni
½ litre (1 pint) (2½ cups)
  demi-glace or plain brown
  sauce
salt and pepper
ground (powdered) mace or
  nutmeg

1 Heat the oil in a heavy-bottomed saucepan and sauté the vegetables until soft, keeping the lid on the pan throughout. Drain off the fat and add the wine, vinegar, peppercorns and bouquet garni.

2 Reduce (evaporate) the liquid by half by boiling hard for 8 minutes, then stir in the demi-glace sauce. Simmer for 30 minutes and season with salt, pepper, and ground (powdered) mace or nutmeg to taste. Strain into a sauce-boat.

Serve with game such as hare or venison.

Makes ½ litre (1 pint) (2½ cups)

Reform Sauce

1 Cut into very thin, short strips 50 g (2 oz) of each of the following: hard-boiled (hard-cooked) egg white, gherkins (dill pickles) and beetroot (beet), mushrooms, truffles and salted cooked tongue.

2 Add to ½ litre (1 pint) (2½ cups) poivrade sauce.

Serve with lamb cutlets and chops.

Makes ½ litre (1 pint) (2½ cups)

Sharp Sauces

Piquant Sauce

50 g (2 oz) (¼ cup) onions or
  shallots, peeled and chopped
50 ml (2 fl oz) (¼ cup) malt, wine or
  cider, vinegar
½ litre (1 pint) (2½ cups)
  demi-glace or plain brown
  sauce
50 g (2 oz) gherkins (dill pickles),
  chopped
15 g (½ oz) pickled capers
5 g (1 tablespoon) chopped
  parsley and tarragon leaves,
  mixed
salt and pepper

1 Boil the onions in the vinegar
for 4 minutes to reduce (evaporate) the liquid by half, then stir in
the sauce and simmer for 15
minutes.

2 Add the gherkins (dill pickles),
capers, parsley and tarragon, and
season with salt and pepper to
taste.

Serve with made-up cooked meat
dishes, boiled beef, gammon and
pork.

*Makes about ½ litre (1 pint)
(2½ cups)*

Robert Sauce

Use the same ingredients as for
piquant sauce but omit the gherkins (dill pickles) and capers; at
the last moment, draw the pan off
the heat and mix in 5 g (1 teaspoon) made English mustard to
prevent curdling.

Serve with grilled pork chops,
grilled leg of duck, and any other
fatty meat.

*Makes about ½ litre (1 pint)
(2½ cups)*

Tomato Sauces

Tomato Sauce

25 ml (1 fl oz) (⅛ cup) oil
25 g (1 oz) (2 tablespoons)
  margarine
50 g (2 oz) celery, peeled and diced
50 g (2 oz) (½ cup) carrots, peeled
  and diced
50 g (2 oz) (¼ cup) onions, peeled
  and diced
50 g (2 oz) (⅓ cup) unsmoked bacon
  trimmings and bones, diced
25 g (1 oz) (4 tablespoons) plain
  flour
75 g (3 oz) (6 tablespoons) tomato
  concentrate (paste)
1 litre (1¾ pints) (5 cups) white
  stock (or 3 chicken stock cubes
  dissolved in water)
1 bouquet garni
1 sprig mint
salt and pepper
pinch paprika
15 g (½ oz) (½ tablespoon) sugar

1 Heat the oil and margarine in a
large saucepan and fry the vegetables and bacon trimmings for
15 minutes.

2 Add the flour, cook for a further
5 minutes, then stir in the tomato
concentrate (paste); cook for
5 more minutes.

3 Stir in the stock, add the bouquet garni and mint, and bring to
the boil. Simmer for 1 hour.

4 Season with salt, pepper, paprika and sugar, then strain
through a fine conical sieve
(strainer).

Serve with pasta, eggs or hamburgers, and also vegetables
including beans.

*Makes about 900 ml (1½ pints)
(4½ cups)*

Roman Sauce

25 ml (1 fl oz) (⅛ cup) oil
50 g (2 oz) (⅝ cup) white
  mushrooms, chopped
25 g (1 oz) (¼ cup) shallots or
  onions, peeled and chopped
50 g (2 oz) (½ cup) ham, chopped
150 g (5 oz) (½ cup) fresh tomatoes,
  skinned, deseeded and chopped
1 clove garlic, peeled, chopped
25 g (1 oz) (2 tablespoons) tomato
  concentrate (paste)
½ litre (1 pint) (2½ cups)
  demi-glace, tomato sauce
salt and pepper
5 g (1 tablespoon) chopped
  parsley, mint, tarragon

1 Heat the oil in a pan and sweat
the vegetables for 5 minutes.
Then add the ham, tomatoes
and garlic and cook for another 10
minutes.

2 Stir in the tomato concentrate
(paste) and sauce and simmer for
10 minutes. Then season with salt
and pepper and add the parsley,
mint and tarragon.

Serve with escalopes, steaks,
and cauliflower.

*Makes about ½ litre (1 pint)
(2½ cups)*

Portuguese Sauce

1 To 600 ml (1 pint) (2½ cups) basic
tomato sauce, add 150 g (5 oz)
(½ cup) of skinned, seeded
and chopped tomatoes, and 2
chopped cloves of garlic.

2 Bring the sauce back to the
boil for 10 minutes. Season to
taste with salt and pepper.

Serve with meat, eggs and fish.

Makes 600 ml (1 pint) (2½ cups)

Neapolitan Sauce

1 To 300 ml (½ pint) (1¼ cups) basic
tomato sauce, add 225 g (½ lb) of
fresh, skinned, seeded and
chopped tomatoes.

2 Season with salt and pepper
and reboil for 5 minutes. Add mint
or oregano to flavour.

Serve with meat fish, eggs and
pasta.

Makes 600 ml (1 pint) (2½ cups)

Barbecue Sauces

American Barbecue Sauce

25 g (1 oz) (2 tablespoons) butter
25 ml (1 fl oz) (1½ tablespoons) oil
1 medium onion, chopped
75 ml (2½ fl oz) (⅓ cup) malt vinegar
75 ml (2½ fl oz) (⅓ cup) soya sauce
1 clove garlic, peeled and
  crushed
5 ml (1 teaspoon) allspice
5 ml (1 teaspoon) salt
good pinch pepper
good pinch cayenne pepper
15 ml (½ oz) (1 tablespoon) tomato
  concentrate (paste)
25 g (1 oz) (1½ tablespoons) honey
25 g (1 oz) (1 tablespoon) sugar
350 ml (12 fl oz) (1½ cups)
  pineapple juice

1 Heat the butter and oil together in a pan, add the onion and cook gently until the onion is soft and tender but not brown. Add the rest of the ingredients and bring to the boil. Boil for 10 minutes.

2 Draw the pan off the heat, cover with a lid and leave to cool. When cold, strain the sauce and store it in a screw-topped jar. Use to marinade steaks or any meat for grilling; soak them for 15 to 20 minutes in the sauce before cooking.

Makes about ½ litre (1 pint) (2½ cups)

To Prepare Chillies

Fresh Chillies: soak in cold salted water for 1 hour to help temper their hot flavour, then drain. Cut in half and discard stem, seeds and pith. Avoid handling chillies as much as possible as their pungent oils can burn and irritate your skin.
Canned Chillies: rinse under cold running water, then drain. Use as required.

Dried Chillies: wash in cold water, cut away stem, seeds and core if necessary. Put in a basin, add 10 ml (2 teaspoons) vinegar and pour over about 1¾ litres (3 pints) (6 cups) for every 225 g (½ lb) (1 cup) dried chillies. Leave for 30-40 minutes, then drain.

Mexican Barbecue Sauce

3 red peppers, skinned (see
  below) and chopped
3 small fresh green chillies,
  deseeded and chopped
salt
6 cloves garlic, peeled
300 ml (½ pint) (1¼ cups) olive oil
6 onions, peeled and finely
  chopped
1½ kg (3 lb) ripe tomatoes,
  skinned, deseeded and diced
50 g (2 oz) (3 tablespoons) (¼ cup)
  sugar
45 ml (3 tablespoons) vinegar
1 bouquet garni
5 g (¼ oz) saffron

1 Put the chopped pepper and chilli in a mortar, together with a pinch of salt and the garlic.

2 Pound these ingredients, adding some of the oil drop by drop. When it has acquired a very smooth, paste-like consistency, set aside.

3 Heat 15 ml (1 tablespoon) olive oil in a frying pan (skillet). Add the onions and cook until they are golden-brown.

4 When the onions are a deep golden-brown, sprinkle them with the sugar. Leave to caramelize, watching that the sugar does not burn. Remove from the heat, add the vinegar and diced tomatoes.

5 Add the bouquet garni to the mixture, cook over a low heat for about 20 minutes, stirring frequently with a wooden spoon, to make a thick tomato mixture.

6 Remove the bouquet garni from the tomato mixture and rub through a sieve (strainer), or work in a blender to a purée. Put the chilli paste in the blender at the same time if liked.

7 Tip the mixture into a small saucepan and add the saffron and the chilli paste, if not already included. Cook for 2 minutes, beating with a whisk. Remove the pan from the heat and leave to cool.

8 Just before serving, incorporate the rest of the oil, little by little (as for mayonnaise), while beating the sauce with a whisk. Serve cold or chilled with grilled meat or fish.

Makes about 300 ml (½ pint) (⅝ cup)

Honolulu Sauce

300 ml (½ pint) (1¼ cups) pineapple
  juice
100 g (¼ lb) canned pineapple
  cubes, drained
300 ml (½ pint) (1¼ cups) thickened
  gravy
5 g (1 teaspoon) made mustard,
  or to taste
25 g (1 oz) finely chopped red
  pepper

For the chilli paste:
10 g (¼ oz) fresh green chillies,
  deseeded and chopped
10 g (¼ oz) fresh ginger root,
  peeled
10 g (¼ oz) clove garlic, peeled
75 g (3 oz) (⅓ cup) finely chopped
  onion
75 ml (2½ fl oz) (⅓ cup) wine
  vinegar
50 g (2 oz) (¼ cup) sugar
15 g (½ oz) salt
75 ml (2½ fl oz) (⅓ cup) lemon juice
pinch turmeric

1 Put all the chilli paste ingredients, together with 30 ml (2 tablespoons) pineapple juice, in a blender and work till smooth.

2 Blend in the remaining pineapple juice, add the salt and transfer the mixture to a saucepan. Bring to the boil and boil for 20 minutes. Stir in the mustard and pineapple cubes, heat through and serve at once, with the chopped red pepper sprinkled over. Serve with grilled pork, ham and gammon or roast duck or goose.

Makes about 300 ml (½ pint) (1¼ cups)

Steak Chasseur

75 g (3 oz) ($\frac{3}{8}$ cup) butter
4 sirloin steaks, round-cut and
  each weighing about 225 g ($\frac{1}{2}$ lb)
sprigs watercress
5 g (1 tablespoon) finely chopped
  parsley and tarragon leaves

For the Chasseur Sauce:
100 g ($\frac{1}{4}$ lb) (1$\frac{1}{4}$ cups) mushrooms,
  wiped and chopped
25 g (1 oz) ($\frac{1}{4}$ cup) shallots or
  onions, peeled and finely
  chopped
100 g ($\frac{1}{4}$ lb) ($\frac{5}{8}$ cup) dry white wine
300 ml ($\frac{1}{2}$ pint) (1$\frac{1}{4}$ cups)
  demi-glace sauce
15 ml (1 tablespoon) tomato
  concentrate (paste)
salt and pepper

1 To make the chasseur sauce:
heat 25 g (1 oz) (2 tablespoons)
butter in a sauté pan. Add the
mushrooms and shallots and
soften but do not let them colour.
Stir in the wine and cook, uncovered, until the liquid has evaporated to half its quantity.

2 Stir in the demi-glace sauce
and tomato concentrate (paste)

and simmer the sauce for about 5
minutes to mellow the flavours.
Check the seasoning.

3 Heat 50 g (2 oz) (4 tablespoons)
of the butter or oil in a frying pan
(skillet). When hot, sauté. the
steaks for about 5-8 minutes on
each side, according to how rare
you like your steak. Season with
salt and pepper to taste, then take
out the steaks and arrange on a
hot serving platter. Pour the
sauce over the steaks, garnish
with the watercress and sprinkle
with the parsley and tarragon.

Serves 4

Beef and Pork Dumplings in Tomato Sauce

1 medium onion, peeled and
  coarsely chopped
1 medium carrot, peeled and
  coarsely chopped
2 sticks celery, peeled and
  coarsely chopped
2 cloves garlic

75 ml (2$\frac{1}{2}$ fl oz) ($\frac{1}{3}$ cup) oil
450 g (1 lb) (2 cups) lean minced
  (ground) beef (from shin or
  skirt)
250 g (9 oz) (1 cup) pork
  sausagemeat
1 egg, beaten
100 g ($\frac{1}{4}$ lb) ($\frac{1}{2}$ cup) fresh white
  breadcrumbs
salt and black pepper
pinch oregano, basil or mint
pinch each paprika, ground
  (powdered) ginger and mace
5 g (1 tablespoon) freshly
  chopped parsley
225 g ($\frac{1}{2}$ lb) spaghetti
400 ml ($\frac{3}{4}$ pint) (1$\frac{3}{4}$ cups) tomato
  sauce

1 Pass all the vegetables twice
through a mincer (grinder) or
work in a blender. Heat the oil in a
saucepan and sauté the vegetables, with the lid on, for 5
minutes to concentrate the
flavour.

2 Remove the mixture from the
heat and place in a large bowl
with the minced beef and

*Beef and Pork Dumplings in
Tomato Sauce. Serve with
spaghetti instead of potatoes for
a dish with a difference*

sausagemeat. Combine well and bind the mixture with the egg and breadcrumbs. Season with salt, pepper, oregano, paprika, ginger, mace and chopped parsley.

3 Preheat the oven to 180°C, 350°F, gas 4.

4 Divide the mixture and roll into small balls, about 25 g (1 oz) in size, on a work surface sprinkled with flour for easier handling.

5 Grease a roasting pan and place the dumplings on it at regular intervals. Bake for 30 minutes in the preheated oven.

6 Meanwhile cook the spaghetti in a large pan of boiling water for 10-12 minutes or until just tender. Drain and turn into a hot serving dish; dot with a knob of butter.

7 Remove the dumplings when cooked and place on the spaghetti. The tomato sauce can either be poured over the dumplings or served separately, together with grated Parmesan, Gruyère or Cheddar cheese.

Serves 6

Chaudfroid Sauce

1 To every 600 ml (1 pint) (2½ cups) sauce – this can be béchamel, velouté, suprême, brown or tomato – add 25 g (1 oz) aspic powder (savoury gelatine). Dissolve the aspic (gelatine) in a little of the hot sauce, then add to the rest of the sauce and bring to the boil; boil for 2-3 minutes. Cool a little, then strain through a conical sieve (strainer) before use.

2 While still warm, pour the chaudfroid sauce over the cold cooked pieces of fish or meat to coat. Allow to cool and firm, then glaze with a little semi-liquid aspic (gelatine) and leave to set. Use for cold dishes and salads (see recipe for Chicken with Chaudfroid Sauce on page 204).

Makes 1 litre (1¾ pints) (4½ cups)

Tip: Always make sure any food to be coated with chaudfroid sauce or mayonnaise is completely dry or the sauce will slide off.

Emulsified Sauces

Hollandaise and Béarnaise sauces and their derivations are made in smaller quantities than other sauces, because they must not be left standing for very long at room temperature. Like fresh cream they are susceptible to bacterial spoilage. Unfortunately, they cannot be refrigerated in the basic form because the butter hardens and so solidifies the sauce.

Use only fresh eggs and good quality unsalted (fresh) butter. Serve the sauces within 2 hours of making and always try to make them at the last possible moment. And of course, all equipment – whisks, bowls, etc – should be spotlessly clean.

Basic Hollandaise Sauce

4 egg yolks
60 ml (4 tablespoons) cold water
15 ml (1 tablespoon) white vinegar
225 (½ lb) (1 cup) butter, melted
juice 1 lemon
salt and white pepper
pinch cayenne

1 Whip the egg yolks, water and vinegar together in a stainless steel bowl (a metal bowl is the best conductor of heat).

2 Place the bowl over a deep pan of boiling water, making sure that the bottom of the bowl does not touch the water – egg yolks coagulate at 60°C, 140°F, a temperature which is lower than that of boiling water. Beat lightly until the eggs are cooked to the consistency of a custard

sauce. Mix well, stirring up from the bottom of the bowl and scraping down any sauce that adheres to the sides.

3 Remove the bowl from the heat. Stir for another 5 minutes while gradually pouring in the melted butter, and whisking all the time to obtain a thick emulsion.

4 Add the juice of the lemon and season to taste. This sauce should be served immediately, and will not keep for longer than 2 or 3 hours.

Makes about 300 ml (½ pint) (⅝ cup)

Béarnaise Sauce

15 ml (1 tablespoon) chopped shallots
pinch chopped tarragon
6 finely crushed white peppercorns
45 ml (3 tablespoons) wine vinegar (preferably tarragon vinegar)
300 ml (½ pint) (1¼ cups) basic hollandaise sauce
pinch chopped parsley

1 Place the shallots, half the tarragon, and the vinegar in a small pan. Bring to the boil and boil briskly until the vinegar has almost evaporated. Remove the pan from the heat.

2 Add the mixture to the hollandaise sauce and then strain the sauce through muslin (cheesecloth) into a bowl. Add the rest of the tarragon and the chopped parsley and mix.

Serve with grilled meat or fish steaks.

Makes 300 ml (½ pint) (1¼ cups)

Mock Hollandaise

1 To 300 ml (½ pint) (1¼ cups) basic hollandaise sauce, add 300 ml (½ pint) (1¼ cups) velouté or white sauce. Check the seasoning.

Serve with eggs, vegetables and fish.

Mousseline sauce

1 Whip 300 ml (½ pint) (1¼ cups) cream.

2 Add the cream to 300 ml (½ pint) (1¼ cups) hollandaise sauce.

Serve with eggs, vegetables and fish.

Paloise Sauce

1 To 300 ml (½ pint) (1¼ cups) hollandaise sauce, add 5g (1 tablespoon) finely chopped blanched mint.

Serve with eggs, vegetables and fish.

Conil Sauce

1 In a pan mix 10g (2 tablespoons) of mixed chopped parsley, tarragon, chervil and mint, 30ml (2 tablespoons) dry vermouth, 5ml (1 teaspoon) tomato concentrate (paste) and 1 peeled clove garlic. Bring to the boil and simmer for 1 minute.

2 Rub the mixture through a sieve (strainer) or work in a blender and add the purée to 300ml (½ pint) (1¼ cups) basic hollandaise sauce.

Serve with grilled steaks and beef kebabs.

Rosalie Sauce

1 To 300 ml (½ pint) (1¼ cups) Conil sauce, add 150ml (¼ pint) (⅝ cup) velouté or white sauce.

2 Fold in 150ml (¼ pint) (⅝ cup) whipped double (heavy) cream.

Serve with grilled veal chops, salmon steaks and grilled chicken.

Sophia Loren

1 To 300 ml (½ pint) (1¼ cups) basic hollandaise sauce, add 5ml (1 teaspoon) anchovy essence, a pinch of garlic salt, 30ml (2 tablespoons) cream and a pinch of curry powder.

Serve with fish.

Vino Sauce

1 To 300 ml (½ pint) (1¼ cups) basic hollandaise sauce, add 5g (1 tablespoon) mixed chopped herbs and 15ml (1 tablespoon) sweet or dry sherry.

Serve with eggs, grilled fish, meat and vegetables.

Maltese Sauce

1 To 300 ml (½ pint) (1¼ cups) basic hollandaise sauce, add the strained juice of 1 blood orange.

Serve with cold roast duck, oily fish.

Choron Sauce

1 To 300 ml (½ pint) (1¼ cups) basic hollandaise sauce, add 15ml (1 tablespoon) tomato ketchup (catsup) and 5ml (1 teaspoon) tarragon vinegar.

Serve with grilled fish, meat and poultry.

Quantities
All the sauces on this page make 300 ml (½ pint) (1¼ cups).

Asparagus with Mousseline Sauce

2 kg (4 lb) (approx 50 spears) green asparagus
sea salt

For the Mousseline Sauce:
175 g (6 oz) (¾ cup) butter
3 eggs
15 ml (1 tablespoon) double (heavy) cream
small sprig chervil
juice 1 lemon
salt and pepper

1 Prepare the asparagus.

2 Boil a large pan of salted water. Tie the asparagus in bundles and place them carefully in the boiling water. Cover and cook for 12-20 minutes. The cooking time depends on the freshness and thickness of the asparagus. Test to see if it is cooked by pricking the green part with the point of a knife.

3 Once the asparagus is cooked, lift it out, and rinse in cold water.

4 To prepare the Mousseline Sauce: put the butter into a small saucepan, let it melt gently, then turn off the heat. Let it rest for several minutes. Skim it with a small spoon to take off the particles which have risen to the top. Carefully pour the melted butter into a basin, leaving only the milk-like liquid in the bottom of the saucepan.

5 Break and separate the eggs. Put the yolks into a bain-marie or a bowl placed over a pan of boiling water. Add 25ml (1½ tablespoons) of water and beat until the mixture becomes thick and comes away from the bottom of the pan.

6 Add the melted butter to this egg yolk-water mixture (sabayon) beating continuously. Take the sauce off the heat.

7 Pour the cream into a bowl and beat it until it has doubled in volume. Add it to the warm sauce off the heat, mixing carefully with a wooden spoon.

8 Wash and dry the chervil and chop finely. Add the lemon juice and the chervil to the sauce with salt and pepper. Mix carefully and keep warm in the bain-marie.

9 Heat some water and put the asparagus in it for 2-3 minutes to reheat.

10 Put a folded napkin on a heated serving dish. Warm a sauce-boat.

11 Strain the asparagus, remove the string and put the spears into the folded napkin (this will absorb any liquid). Pour the sauce into the sauce-boat and serve.

Serves 4

Tips: Keep the cooking juice of the asparagus to make a soup.

The asparagus and Mousseline Sauce can be liquidized together to make a Rich Asparagus Purée Sauce.

Look'n Cook Mousseline Sauce

1 Clarify the butter by melting it slowly. Let it rest then skim to remove any scum from the surface. Pour the butter into a receptacle very slowly so that the milk-like mixture can be left in the saucepan **2** Break the eggs separating the yolks from the whites. Put the yolks into a saucepan. Place it in a bain-marie (or over hot water) and add water **3** Keep whisking the mixture over the heat until it thickens and the bottom can be seen during the whisking **4** Add the clarified butter to this mixture in a slow steady stream from a ladle and keep whisking all the time **5** Prepare the whisked cream: put the cream into a small bowl, whisking until it has doubled in volume and has a light consistency **6** Add the whisked cream to the hot sauce off the heat. Mix the cream and the sauce together very carefully

Look'n Cook Hollandaise, Béarnaise and White Butter Sauces

1 To make hollandaise sauce: melt the butter in a deep, heavy-based saucepan over a gentle heat, or use a bain marie. Skim off the froth which forms **2** Break the eggs and separate the whites from the yolks. Put the yolks in a metal bowl with the cold water and the vinegar **3** Place the bowl over a deep pan of boiling water, making sure that the bowl does not actually touch the water. Beat the mixture lightly until thick and creamy **4** Remove the bowl of sauce from the heat and continue stirring while gradually adding the melted butter in a thin stream. Add the lemon juice and seasoning **5** To make béarnaise sauce, place the chopped shallots, crushed peppercorns, half the tarragon and the vinegar in a small pan and boil briskly until the vinegar has almost evaporated **6** Make hollandaise sauce and add the melted butter to it (see steps 1-4). Then add the chopped shallots, tarragon and peppercorn mixture **7** Strain the sauce through fine muslin (cheesecloth) over a bowl or through a conical sieve

142

(strainer) **8** Sprinkle in the rest of the tarragon, stir and check the seasoning **9** To make white butter sauce (recipe on page 224), sweat the chopped shallots in butter until soft, then add the water, wine vinegar and salt and pepper. Cut the rest of the butter into small pieces **10** Add the butter gradually, whisking all the time to form an emulsion **11** Adjust the seasoning **12** Pour into a sauce-boat

Brown Butter Sauce

50 g (2 oz) (4 tablespoons) butter
5 ml (1 teaspoon) brown vinegar
5 g (1 tablespoon) chopped
  parsley

1 Heat the butter in a frying pan (skillet) until it begins to colour.

2 Add the vinegar and the chopped parsley and mix. Pour the sauce immediately over the chosen dish.

Serve with plainly cooked fish

Tip: Stir in 5 g (1 tablespoon) drained capers, if liked, just before serving.

White Butter Sauce

50 g (2 oz) (4 tablespoons)
  clarified butter
75 g (3 oz) (¾ cup) chopped shallots
50 ml (2 fl oz) (¼ cup) fish stock
50 ml (2 fl oz) (¼ cup) dry white
  wine
50 ml (2 fl oz) (¼ cup) spirit vinegar
pinch white pepper
pinch salt
200 g (7 oz) (¾ cup + 2 tablespoons)
  fresh creamy butter, softened

1 Put the clarified butter in a pan, add the chopped shallots and fry gently until the shallots are soft.

2 Add the rest of the ingredients, except the butter, and cook for 5 minutes more until reduced (evaporated) to a syrupy consistency. Draw off the heat and allow to cool.

3 Cut the softened butter into small pieces. When the shallot mixture is cold, add the butter, a piece at a time, whisking continuously to form an emulsion. Serve immediately.

Serve with plainly cooked fish
Makes about 150 ml (¼ pint) (⅝ cup)

Basic Sauces Mixtures

Before you can make some sauces, different kinds of mixtures must be assembled and prepared so you save time later on and the cooking can proceed smoothly.

Mushroom Duxelles

25 ml (1 fl oz) (⅛ cup) oil
25 g (1 oz) clarified butter
100 g (¼ lb) (½ cup) finely chopped
  onion
25 g (1 oz) finely chopped shallot
450 g (1 lb) finely chopped
  mushrooms or mushroom
  peelings and stalks
salt and pepper to taste
10 g (2 tablespoons) finely
  chopped parsley

1 Heat the oil and butter in a pan. Add the onions and shallots, cover, and cook them gently until soft but not coloured (this is called 'sweating').

2 Add the mushrooms and cook gently again, uncovered, until all the moisture has evaporated.

3 When dry, season the mixture with salt and pepper, stir in the parsley, then turn into a bowl and cover with greaseproof (waxed) paper until required.

Add to sauces, white or brown; liquidize for use in soup, or sprinkle over fish gratin dishes.

Green Herbs

1 Wash and drain sprigs of fresh chervil, parsley or tarragon. Dry well in a cloth or on absorbent paper.

2 For chopped herbs: take off the leaves and chop them finely or coarsely (called *concassé* in French). Dry again on absorbent paper.

3 For whole leaves: take off the stems, put in a pan of boiling consommé or stock to scald, then drain and dry on absorbent paper. If the leaves are too large, tear them with your fingers; *chiffonnade* is the French term for this shredding or tearing process.

Use for decoration on cold dishes.

Flavoured Butters

Flavoured Butters

As their name suggests, flavoured, or compound, butters consist of softened butter blended with the chosen flavouring. Many butters are served as garnishes, toppings for grilled and fried meats and fish, while others are added to sauces to enhance their flavour and colour.

You may find it more convenient to make up larger quantities of butters than those below, using 225 g (½ lb) (1 cup) butter for example, and all the other ingredients increased accordingly. Shape the finished butter into a sausage shape, wrap in foil and then store in the refrigerator or freezer until required.

Colbert Butter

100 g (¼ lb) (½ cup creamy butter,
  softened
5 g (1 tablespoon) chopped
  tarragon
10 g (2 tablespoons) chopped
  parsley
15 ml (1 tablespoon) lemon juice
15 g (½ oz) meat glaze

Mix all the ingredients into the butter and blend well.

Use with shellfish or grilled (broiled) fish or meat, or add to fish sauces

Variation: When all the ingredients are blended, gradually beat in 50 ml (2 fl oz) (¼ cup) olive oil.
Use with snails or scallops

Mâitre d'Hotel Butter

As for Colbert butter but omit the meat glaze and tarragon.

Kneaded Butter (Beurre Manié)

Cream 50 g (2 oz) (4 tablespoons) butter with 30 g (1 oz) (4 tablespoons) sieved flour.

Use for thickening sauces, stocks and stews

Shallot Butter

25 g (1 oz) (¼ cup) chopped shallots
50 ml (2 fl oz) (¼ cup) red wine
15 g (½ oz) meat glaze
150 g (5 oz) (⅝ cup) butter
15 g (3 tablespoons) chopped
  parsley
15 ml (1 tablespoon) lemon juice
pinch salt
pinch pepper

1 Put the shallots in a pan with the red wine and boil together until the shallots are soft. Add the meat glaze and allow the mixture to cool.

2 Blend in the butter, parsley and lemon juice and season to taste.

Use with steaks or in sauces for grilled (broiled) meat

Herb Butter

100 g (¼ lb) (½ cup) butter, softened
2 sprigs tarragon
2 sprigs parsley
15 ml (1 tablespoon) lemon juice
  or to taste
salt and pepper

1 Cream the butter in a bowl.

2 Chop the tarragon and parsley finely and mix into the butter. Add the lemon juice and the salt and pepper to taste.

Serve with grilled (broiled) meat or fish

Meunière Butter

100 g (¼ lb) (½ cup) butter
15 ml (1 tablespoon) lemon juice

1 Put the butter in a pan and heat until the froth which forms dies down and the butter is lightly browned.

2 When the butter is clear, add the lemon juice.

Serve poured over fried food which has been sprinkled with chopped parsley

Mayonnaise Butter

1 egg yolk
2.5 ml (½ teaspoon) dry mustard
salt and pepper
¼ litre (9 fl oz) (1⅛ cup) oil
10 ml (2 teaspoons) vinegar or
  lemon juice)
50 g (2 oz) (¼ cup) butter,
  softened

1 Place the egg yolk in a bowl with the mustard and salt and pepper. Gradually mix in the oil, whisking (beating) the whole time, until the mixture thickens and all the oil is incorporated. Stir in the vinegar or lemon juice.

2 Cream the butter in a bowl. Mix into the mayonnaise and season again to taste.

Use to decorate canapés, hors-d'oeuvre and open sandwiches

Tip: If using a blender to make the mayonnaise, use the whole egg.

Bercy or Bordelaise Butter

15 g (½ oz) (⅛ cup) shallots, chopped
150 ml (¼ pint) (⅝ cup) dry white
  wine
100 g (¼ lb) (½ cup) softened butter
pinch salt and white pepper
15 ml (1 tablespoon) lemon juice

5 g (1 tablespoon) chopped
  parsley

1 Put the chopped shallots in a pan, add the white wine and bring to the boil. Boil for 5 minutes and then allow to cool.

2 When the shallot mixture is cold, blend it with the butter, adding the rest of the ingredients as well. Cream well.

Use to garnish Steak Bordelaise or for blending into Bordelaise Sauce.

Garlic Butter

2-8 cloves garlic
100 g (¼ lb) (½ cup) butter, softened
salt and pepper to taste

1 Pound the cloves of garlic to a smooth paste either by using a garlic press or a pestle and mortar, or by firmly crushing the peeled cloves, sprinkled liberally with salt, with the flat blade of a knife until a pulp is obtained.

2 Cream the butter in a bowl, then mix it with the garlic and season to taste with salt and pepper.

Serve with grilled (broiled) fish, steaks, hamburgers, lamb chops, boiled or baked (jacket) potatoes, canapés and sandwiches

Clarified Butter

Melt a quantity of butter in a bowl stood over a pan of hot water. Allow to cool, then put in the refrigerator to firm; turn out and scrape off the solids which have collected on the bottom of the cake of butter. The butter is then ready for use.

Tip: Thick solids coagulate to form caseins which caramelize during cooking and impart a bitter flavour to mixtures when heated at too high a temperature.

Cooking with Eggs

Eggs, which are one of the most nutritious foods available to man, are both versatile in and vital to cooking. They can be cooked in numerous ways for serving hot or cold as main course dishes, savouries and appetizers; as preserves, desserts and in drinks, and used also as a garnish, a binding agent and for aeration

Fish and Pasta Florentine

This is a very spectacular dinner party appetizer, especially if served in individual, shell-shaped, ovenproof dishes. Or serve as a "special" supper treat.

175 g (6 oz) pasta shapes or short-cut macaroni (or 1 can macaroni cheese)
3 hard-boiled (hard-cooked) eggs
450 ml (¾ pint) (1¾ cups) white sauce, or 150 ml (¼ pint) (⅝ cup) if using canned pasta
175 g (6 oz) cooked smoked haddock, flaked
50 g (2 oz) peeled prawns
salt and pepper
packet frozen chopped spinach, thawed
50 g (2 oz) (½ cup) grated cheese
few unpeeled prawns, fresh or frozen and thawed (optional)

1 Cook the pasta shapes in boiling salted water until just tender. Drain.

2 Mix the pasta with the hard-boiled (hard-cooked) eggs, white sauce, smoked haddock and peeled prawns. Season to taste.

3 Spoon half the mixture into an ovenproof dish. Top with the spinach and then the remaining pasta and fish mixture. Sprinkle with the grated cheese.

4 Bake at 190°C, 375°F, gas 5, for 30 minutes. Serve hot, cut into wedges and garnished with the unpeeled prawns.

Serves 4-6

Tip: If using dehydrated savoury cheese pasta, make up the pasta according to the directions on the packet and use only 300 ml (½ pint) (1¼ cups) white sauce.

Fish and pasta Florentine – chopped hard-boiled (hard-cooked) eggs, smoked haddock, prawns and pasta shells mixed in a rich white sauce and served on a bed of spinach

Boiled Eggs

Time Table for Boiling Eggs	Large	Standard	Medium
Eggs immersed in boiling water and gently simmered	3½ mins	3½ mins	3 mins
Eggs put into cold water, brought to the boil and gently simmered (uncovered)	3 mins after water has boiled	2¾ mins after water has boiled	2½ mins after water has boiled
Eggs placed in boiling water, covered and drawn off the heat to prevent further boiling	8/9 mins	8/9 mins	7/8 mins (depending on temperature of eggs)
For eggs with hard-boiled (hard-cooked) whites and soft yolks	7 mins	7 mins in simmering water	6 mins
For true hard-boiled (hard-cooked) eggs	12 mins	11 mins in simmering water	10 mins

Eggs are never literally boiled: high temperatures toughen protein, and since the white of an egg is almost entirely protein, it will be spoiled if it is cooked at a very high temperature. An egg white coagulates at 60-62°C, 140-143°F, and the yolk at 65°C, 149°F; therefore the temperature of boiling water (100°C, 212°F) is more than adequate to cook an egg. Also, if you use too high a temperature, the eggs will knock against each other in the bubbling water and the shells may crack. Cooking eggs without actually boiling them should also prevent them discolouring when they are exposed to the air.

Hard-boiled (Hard-cooked) Eggs in Onion Sauce

4 small bridge rolls
75 g (3 oz) sliced onions
150 ml (¼ pint) (⅝ cup) béchamel sauce
pinch salt and white pepper
4 hard-boiled (hard-cooked) eggs
10 g (2 tablespoons) chopped parsley
35 g (1¼ oz) (good ¼ cup) grated cheese

1 Split the rolls. Remove the white crumb section.

2 Blanch the onions for 5 minutes, rinse in fresh water, then reboil in cold water till tender. Add to the béchamel sauce, reheat and season.

3 Dice the egg and blend with the sauce. Mix in the chopped parsley. Fill each roll half neatly. Sprinkle with grated cheese and glaze.

Serves 4

Hard-boiled (Hard-cooked) Egg Bellevue

6 eggs
1 small lettuce
3 slices cooked ham
sprigs parsley, chervil and chives
few tarragon leaves
¼ litre (8 fl oz) (1 cup) mayonnaise
20 hazelnuts, shelled
1 cup peeled, cooked, deveined shrimp (prawns)
1 lemon
2 tomatoes
few olives
salt and pepper

1 Hard-boil (hard-cook) the eggs for 10 minutes. Drain, cool and remove the shells.

2 Wash and drain the lettuce leaves without breaking up the heart. Arrange 6 good leaves round a serving dish.

3 Cut the slices of ham in half and put half a slice on each lettuce leaf. Cover each with a cooked egg.

4 Wash the parsley, chervil, chives and tarragon under running water. Dry them and chop finely. Add them to the mayonnaise and mix well.

5 Coarsely crush the hazelnuts, and add them too, together with one-third of the peeled shrimps (prawns). Mix carefully.

6 Coat the eggs with this sauce, and top with the remainder of the shrimps (prawns).

7 Decorate the centre of the dish with a few unpeeled shrimps (prawns) or cut the lemon and tomatoes into rounds and use them to decorate the edge of the dish. Place the little lettuce heart in the centre and scatter with olives. Keep cool until ready to serve.

Serves 6

Eggs should never be placed in boiling water immediately after being removed from the refrigerator since the sudden change in temperature may cause the shells to crack. Allow eggs to stand at room temperature for an hour before cooking. If the shell has cracked, prick small holes in the wider end of the shell, and this should prevent the contents oozing out while the eggs is cooking.

Eggs Bellevue – a spectacular dish for a cold buffet. Hard-boiled (hard-cooked) eggs are coated with mustard mayonnaise and garnished with shrimps (prawns)

Look 'n Cook Poached Eggs in Aspic (Gelatine)

1 Add the vinegar (preferably distilled vinegar) to the boiling water 2 When the mixture is simmering, slip in the eggs one by one, taking care to put each in in a single movement from the level of the water's surface 3 Check that they are cooked by pressing gently with a finger 4 Drain the eggs and immerse in cold water 5 Still in the cold water, trim the eggs 6 Prepare a sachet of aspic jelly, according to the instructions on the packet 7 Strain the made jelly 8 Put the moulds on crushed ice or in ice water and pour a spoonful of jelly into each 9 Prepare and cut out the ingredients used for

decoration: eg, truffle, tomato, ham, hard-boiled egg white **10** Decorate the bottom of each mould and put in the eggs **11** Fill the moulds with jelly and leave to set in the refrigerator **12** Unmould on to lettuce leaves. Keep cold until served

Poached Eggs

Poached Eggs

1 Fill a sauté pan with hot water, adding 25 g (1 oz) wine vinegar and 10 g (⅜ oz) salt per 1 litre (1¾ pints) (4½ cups) water. Use a large, shallow pan or deep tray for preference.

2 Bring to the boil and add the eggs (up to 8 at a time): break them into a saucer one at a time, then slip them into the sauté pan.

3 Simmer the eggs for 3-3½ minutes, turning them over smartly when they begin to set, to wrap the white around the yolks.

4 Drain and refresh in cold water. Trim the excess white and keep in cold water until required. To reheat, plunge in hot salted water and simmer for 1 minute.

In general, eggs for luncheons are served, hot or cold, as the first course.

Poached Eggs in Tomato Aspic (Gelatine)

1 onion
50 g (2 oz) (¼ cup) butter
700 g (1½ lb) very ripe tomatoes
salt and pepper
sprig thyme
45 ml (3 tablespoons) white vinegar to each litre (1¾ pints) (4½ cups) water
8 eggs
½ litre (1 pint) (2½ cups) commercially-made aspic jelly (gelatine)
few sprigs fresh tarragon

1 Put 8 ramekins or individual moulds into the refrigerator. Peel and chop the onion. Melt the butter in a small saucepan. When it is barely hot, put in the onion. Cover and cook slowly until the onion is soft.

2 Bring a small pan of water to the boil. Plunge the tomatoes in for a few seconds, then drain, skin, remove the seeds (pips) and chop the flesh coarsely. Add this to the onion. Season with salt and pepper, and add a sprig of thyme. Cover the pan and cook gently for 20 minutes.

3 Prepare the poached eggs. Partly fill a large saucepan with water and add the vinegar, then bring to the boil. Break the eggs into separate cups; fill a bowl with cold water. When the pan of water reaches boiling point, slide the eggs in, putting the rim of each cup to the surface of the water. Simmer for 3 minutes.

4 After 3 minutes cooking, carefully remove the eggs with a slotted spoon (skimmer). Check that they are cooked by pressing lightly with a finger. Plunge them into the cold water. Remove the white threads formed during cooking and trim them to an even, regular shape. Leave in the cold water.

5 Prepare the aspic (gelatine) as instructed on the packet, then pass through a fine sieve and leave to get cold.

6 When the tomatoes are cooked, rub them through a sieve or purée in a blender. Put the resultant purée back into the saucepan and reduce (evaporate) over a brisk heat, stirring with a wooden spoon. When the tomato mixture becomes sticky, take the pan off the heat. Add half the aspic jelly (gelatine), stir vigorously and stand the saucepan in cold water.

7 Put crushed ice or ice water in a large container. Take the ramekins or moulds out of the refrigerator and put them on ice or in the ice water. Put a spoonful of aspic jelly (gelatine) in each.

8 Wash and dry the tarragon and remove the leaves. Decorate the bottoms of the ramekins with the leaves.

9 Dry the eggs with a cloth or absorbent paper and put them on a cooling rack. When the tomato sauce has nearly set, pour it over the eggs in repeated layers so as to coat them well. Let the sauce attach itself well.

10 Put 1 tomato-covered egg into each of the ramekins of moulds. Pour in the rest of the tomato jelly (gelatine) carefully, filling them completely. Put them in the refrigerator for several hours to set completely.

11 Unmould the eggs onto a serving dish and serve cold.

Serves 4

Tip: It is essential to dry the poached eggs completely or the tomato aspic (gelatine) will slip off.

Egg Tips

1 If eggs are too cold, they will crack on being boiled in the shell.

2 When cracking eggs, break them one by one into a cup before tipping them into a bowl. This way, if one is bad, the others will not be spoilt by it.

3 Eggs may be kept at normal room temperature or in a cool larder. Or, they can be stored in a refrigerator, where there is often a special rack provided to protect them from breakage, but make sure they are not near the ice box. When possible, remove eggs from a refrigerator about 1 hour before use, to allow them to return to room temperature. This makes them easier to whisk and helps to prevent them cracking when they are boiled. Any dirty eggs should be wiped clean with a damp cloth before use.

4 Egg whites are used as clarifying agents, for instance in making broth. The protein in the egg white coagulates and gathers the suspended particles, so cleaning the liquid.

Eggs Hussar

6 tomatoes
salt and pepper
30 ml (2 tablespoons) oil
3 onions
25 g (1 oz) (2 tablespoons) butter
225 g (½ lb) cooked ham (hock)
bunch parsley
1 litre (1¾ pints) (4½ cups) water
30 ml (2 tablespoons) white
　vinegar
6 eggs

For the sauce:
100 g (¼ lb) streaky bacon
1 large onion
1 carrot
50 g (2 oz) (4 tablespoons) butter
sprig thyme
½ bay leaf
15 g (2 tablespoons) flour
300 ml (½ pint) (1¼ cups) brown
　stock
15 ml (1 tablespoon) tomato
　concentrate (paste)
100 ml (4 fl oz) (½ cup) Madeira

1 Cut a slice from the end opposite to the stalk of the tomatoes and scoop out the inside with a small spoon. Salt them to draw out excess moisture and turn upside down on a plate to drain until needed, then dry with absorbent paper. Preheat the oven to 190°C, 375°F, gas 5.

2 To make the sauce: derind and dice the bacon. Peel and finely chop the onion. Peel and dice the carrot. In a sauté pan heat the butter for the sauce. Add the bacon, chopped onion, carrot, thyme and bay leaf. Cook gently until the onion is golden, stirring with a wooden spoon. Then sprinkle with flour and let the mixture brown. Gradually add the stock (bouillon) to the mixture, mix well and simmer gently for 20 minutes.

3 Put the tomatoes in an oven-proof dish, baste them with the oil, then place in the oven and cook for 20 minutes. Meanwhile, peel the remaining onions and slice them into rings. Heat the remaining butter in a pan and fry the onion rings until golden.

4 Dice the ham (hock). Wash, dry and chop the parsley.

5 Add the vinegar to the pan of water, bring to the boil and poach the eggs. Keep hot in a bowl of warm water.

6 When the sauce is cooked, strain through a fine conical sieve (strainer), add the tomato concentrate (paste) the Madeira and the diced ham (hock). Adjust the seasoning and heat through thoroughly.

7 Take the tomatoes out of the oven and arrange them on a hot serving dish. Put a poached egg in each tomato, topped with the onion rings. Pour the sauce and the diced ham into the centre of the dish. Sprinkle with parsley and serve immediately.

Serves 6

Poached Eggs with Spinach

1 kg (2 lb) spinach
salt
1 litre (1¾ pints) (4½ cups) water
45 ml (3 tablespoons) white
　vinegar
4 eggs
40 g (3 tablespoons) (1½ oz)
　margarine
2 slices bread
40 g (1½ oz) (3 tablespoons) butter

1 Wash and trim the spinach and remove the tough stems. Wash it carefully and drain.

2 Put it into a saucepan with the water clinging to the leaves. Cook over a gentle heat to begin with, increasing the heat as moisture runs from the spinach. Heat until cooked, about 10 minutes. Add salt to taste.

3 When the spinach is cooked, drain it, cool, pressing out all surplus water with the hands, then keep hot.

4 Heat the water in a large pan and add the vinegar. Break an egg into a cup and as soon as the water boils, slide in the eggs, putting the rim of the cup to the surface of the water. Simmer for 3 minutes.

5 Partly fill a bowl with warm water. When the eggs have been cooking for 4 minutes, lift them out with a draining spoon (skimmer). Check that they are cooked by pressing lightly with a finger, and plunge them into the warm water. Carefully cut off the white threads which will have formed during cooking.

6 Heat the margarine in a frying pan (skillet). Trim the crusts off the bread and cut the slices across diagonally to make triangles. Put them in the hot margarine and fry until golden.

7 Heat a serving dish. Add the butter to the spinach. Mix well together and place in the serving dish. Make 4 hollows in the spinach.

8 Dry the eggs with a cloth or absorbent paper. Put them in the hollows in the spinach. Insert the croûtons cornerwise in the spinach, so that they stand up. Serve hot.

Serves 4

Storage of eggs. They require a clean, cool storage place that is not too dry. A refrigerator with a temperature range of 2-4°C, 35.5-39°F, is ideal, and not only for eggs but for cream, too.

Keep eggs away from any pungent smells, such as of cheese, fish or any other strong-smelling food, while in storage because they will absorb any odour, through the porous shell.

Egg Cutlets

2 eggs, separated
150 ml (¼ pint) (⅝ cup) béchamel
  sauce
pinch salt and pepper
pinch nutmeg
4 hard-boiled (hard-cooked) eggs
35 g (1¼ oz) (5 tablespoons) diced
  mushrooms
50 g (2 oz) (4 tablespoons)
  clarified butter
flour for dusting
25 g (1 oz) (¼ cup) chopped
  (minced) nuts
100 g (¼ lb) (2 cups) dry
  breadcrumbs
300 ml (½ pint) (1¼ cup) tomato
  sauce
sprig parsley

1 Blend the egg yolks with the cold béchamel sauce. Reheat gently without boiling. Season.

2 Dice the hard-boiled (hard-cooked) eggs. Lightly whip the egg whites.

3 Cook the mushrooms gently in clarified butter for 1 minute only.

4 Blend the mushroom mixture with the sauce, divide into 4 portions, and shape into ovals or cutlet form. Dust with flour, then dip in the beaten egg whites, then the nut and crumb mixtures to cover. Shake off any excess crumbs.

5 Deep-fry the cutlets for 4 minutes till golden. Drain on absorbent paper, then serve with a rich tomato sauce. Dish up and garnish with parsley.

Serves 4

Variations

Cromesquis Egg Fritters

1 Use the same ingredients as for Egg Cutlets (see recipe above), but add 15 g (½ oz) diced truffles if liked. Shape the mixture into small, flat rounds.

2 Roll in sieved (strained) flour, then dip in batter. Deep-fry till golden, then drain on absorbent paper.

3 Garnish the fritters with a sprig of parsley and serve with tomato sauce.

154

Coddled Eggs

Eggs in cocotte are served on a special shallow dish which resembles a small soufflé dish. The cocotte dish is placed on a plate lined with a napkin. Eggs cooked in small cocotte moulds are said to be "coddled."

1 Grease each cocotte dish with 15 g (½ oz) (1 tablespoon) softened butter or margarine.

2 Crack an egg into a saucer and add to the cocotte dish.

3 Place the cocotte dish in a shallow tray or pan which is half-filled with hot water.

4 Cover with a lid and bring to the boil. Remove the lid and simmer for 2½-3 minutes until the egg white is set.

5 Cover with a little double (heavy) cream and serve.

Tip: Do not season with salt.

Variations

Bergère
1 Grease a cocotte dish and add 25 g (1 oz) (2 tablespoons) cooked, minced (ground) lamb blended with some Chasseur sauce.

2 Crack an egg into a saucer and pour in on top of the mixture. Cook as outlined above.

3 Coat with chasseur sauce.

Bordelaise
1 Place a slice of poached beef bone marrow inside a greased cocotte dish.

2 Add an egg and cook as above.

3 Coat with bordelaise sauce.

Capucine
1 Add a purée of cooked mushrooms and cream sauce to a greased cocotte dish.

2 Add an egg and cook as above.

3 Coat with cream sauce.

Diane
1 Grease a cocotte dish and add 25 g (1 oz) minced (ground) cooked game mixed with poivrade sauce.

2 Add an egg and cook as above.

3 Coat with poivrade sauce and top with a slice of truffle.

Diplomate
1 Place a small piece of foie gras inside a greased cocotte dish.

2 Add an egg and cook as above.

3 Pour over Madeira sauce.

Maryland
1 Place 25 g (1 oz) creamed sweetcorn in a greased cocotte dish.

2 Add an egg and cook as above.

3 Coat with a cream sauce and decorate with cooked red peppers.

Soubise
1 Grease a cocotte dish and add 25 g (1 oz) cooked onion purée.

2 Add an egg and cook as above.

3 Coat with soubise sauce and decorate with a slice of truffle or a strip of cooked red pepper.

Valentine
1 Place 25 g (1 oz) chopped tomato pulp inside a greased cocotte dish.

2 Add an egg and cook as above.

3 Coat with espagnole sauce.

> **Egg Tip**
> A good egg pâté can be made by chopping hard-boiled (hard-cooked) eggs, mixing them with a little mayonnaise and cooked mushroom purée, and then blending whipped cream into the mixture. Serve chilled.

Savoury Quiche
(Basic Recipe)

2 eggs
300 ml ($\frac{1}{2}$ pint) (1$\frac{1}{4}$ cups) milk
pinch salt
pinch nutmeg

1 Beat the eggs for 5 minutes, then blend into the milk. Preheat the oven to 200°C, 400°F, gas 6.

2 Season with salt and nutmeg, then strain and pour into the prepared flan case until about two-thirds full. Bake in the preheated oven for 20 minutes, then reduce the oven temperature to 180°C, 350°F, gas 4 for the remaining 20-25 minutes baking time. Overall cooking time should be about 45 minutes. Serve hot or cold.

Makes enough to fill 20 cm (8 in) diameter flan case

Variations

Bacon Quiche
Sprinkle over flan base 100 g ($\frac{1}{4}$ lb) fried bacon rashers (slices), derinded and cut up. Pour over custard and bake as basic recipe.

Onion and Cheese Quiche
Sprinkle over flan base 50 g (2 oz) ($\frac{1}{2}$ cup) grated cheese, then top with a layer of fried sliced onions. Pour over custard and bake as basic recipe.

Tip: To thicken and enrich basic savoury custard, add 150 ml ($\frac{1}{4}$ pint) ($\frac{5}{8}$ cup) thick béchamel sauce to basic custard.

Quiche Lorraine

3 thin rashers (slices streaky unsmoked bacon, derinded
25 g (1 oz) (4 tablespoons) butter, melted
1 x 20 cm (8 in) unbaked flan case (pie shell), 4 cm (1$\frac{1}{2}$ in) deep
100 g ($\frac{1}{4}$ lb) (1 cup) grated hard cheese
3 eggs, beaten
200 ml (7 fl oz) ($\frac{7}{8}$ cup) single (light) cream
50 ml (2 fl oz) ($\frac{1}{4}$ cup) milk

Quiche Lorraine – the classic French savoury custard flan

pinch salt and white pepper
pinch grated nutmeg
pinch cayenne pepper, optional

1 Scald the bacon and refresh, then cut into small pieces.

2 Set the oven at 190°C, 375°F, gas 5.

3 Brush melted butter over the bottom of the flan case (pie shell), then place on a greased baking (cookie) sheet. Sprinkle grated cheese over the pastry, then layer with the bacon pieces.

4 In a bowl blend the beaten eggs, cream, milk and the seasonings. Pour half the custard only into the flan case (pie shell). Bake in the preheated oven for 20 minutes, then remove and add the rest of the custard and bake for another 20 minutes longer. Serve hot or cold.

Makes 6 – 8 portions

Tip: Quiche Lorraine lends itself to countless variations: the cheese or bacon can be omitted, or instead of bacon use salt beef or garlic sausage.

155

Look 'n Cook Flat Omelette

1 Peel the onions and chop finely. Cut the red and green peppers into halves, remove the seeds, wash and chop. Scald, peel, deseed and finely chop the tomatoes **2** Add the chopped onions to hot, but not smoking oil, and cook until soft but not col-oured **3** Add the peppers and cook over a moderate heat until soft **4** Add the chopped tomatoes with salt and pepper and cook uncovered, to evaporate some of the water from the vegetables. Remove from the heat **5** Break the eggs and beat

with salt and pepper. Add a pinch of mixed herbs and the mixed vegetables and beat again, with a fork **6** Put a frying pan (skillet) with 30 ml (2 tablespoons) of oil over a good heat. Pour in the prepared egg and vegetable mixture and stir in all directions to prevent it sticking **7** When the underside is cooked, turn like a pancake and cook the second side **8** When the second side is cooked, slide the omelette onto a heated serving dish. On no account leave it in the hot pan or it will over cook and dry

Omelettes

The term 'omelette' is derived from the latin 'ova mellita', which, in the days of the Roman empire, consisted of a mixture of eggs and honey beaten together and baked.

Preparing the pan

Unless you have a non-stick omelette pan, it is best to prepare the pan you are going to use so that your omelettes are perfect every time. First of all, rub round the inside with coarse salt. Then cover the bottom of the pan with oil and heat it on the cooker for about 5 minutes or until the oil is hot. Tip away the oil. The pan is now ready to use.

Mushroom Omelette

½ lemon
300 g (scant ¾ lb) mushrooms
90 g (3½ oz) (⅓ cup + 1 tablespoon) butter
8 eggs
30 ml (2 tablespoons) cream
salt and pepper
small bunch parsley

1 Squeeze the half lemon.

2 Clean the mushrooms: cut off the base of the stalks and wash the mushrooms rapidly (do not let them soak). Slice them into thin strips. Sprinkle the lemon juice over them.

3 Melt 25 g (1 oz) (2 tablespoons) butter into a frying pan (skillet) and when it begins to turn golden put in the mushrooms. Cook until the juices have boiled away and the mushrooms are golden brown.

4 Cut about 25 g (1 oz) (2 tablespoons) butter into small pieces.

5 Break the eggs into a bowl. Add the pieces of butter, the cream, salt and pepper. Beat with a fork. When the eggs are frothy, stop beating.

6 Warm a serving dish. Wash and chop the parsley.

7 Melt the rest of the butter in the frying pan (skillet) and when it begins to turn golden pour in the egg mixture. Make the omelette.

8 When the omelette is done, i.e. set but still soft, tip 3 spoonsful of mushrooms over it. Fold it into half and slide it onto the serving dish.

9 Pile the rest of the mushrooms onto the dish around the omelette and sprinkle chopped parsley on top.

Serves 4

Mushroom omelette makes an excellent family meal accompanied by fried potatoes and salad

Spanish Omelette with Spiced Sausage

3 onions
2 peppers
450 g (1 lb) tomatoes
2 cloves garlic
100 ml (4 fl oz) (1 cup) oil
1 bouquet garni
salt and pepper
200 g (7 oz) chorizo
  (Spanish sausage)
150 ml (¼ pint) (⅔ cup) white stock
8 eggs

1 Peel the onions. Mince (grind) one and shred the other two. Wash and dry the peppers, and cut them in halves. Remove the pips and cut into thin strips. Skin and chop the tomatoes, discarding the seeds. Peel and crush the garlic.

2 To make the tomato puree: heat 25 ml (1 fl oz) of the oil in a small sauté pan. Add the minced (ground) onion. Cook until golden-brown, then add the tomatoes, the bouquet garni, and half of the crushed garlic. Season with salt and pepper. Cover and cook for 15 minutes over a slow heat.

3 In the meantime, cut the chorizo or other sliced sausage into thin slices.

4 Heat 50 ml (2 fl oz) oil in a frying pan (skillet). Add the chorizo, cook gently, then drain and keep warm.

5 Cook the shredded onions in the same oil until they are golden-brown. Add the peppers and cook until soft. Season with salt and pepper.

6 When the peppers begin to brown, add the rest of the garlic. Cook for another 5 minutes then remove from the heat and keep hot with the chorizo.

7 Pour the tomato purée through a fine strainer. Return to a low heat and thin with the stock. Adjust the seasoning and leave to cook over the low heat.

8 Break the eggs into a mixing bowl. Season with salt and pepper. Beat gently with a fork until frothy.

9 Heat the rest of the oil in a frying pan (skillet). When it is hot, pour in the beaten eggs, and mix, scraping the bottom of the pan with a fork. Before the eggs start to solidify add the onions, the pepper and the chorizo, stirring all the time.

10 When the omelette is cooked, place it on a warmed serving dish. Serve hot with the tomato sauce in a sauce-boat.

Serves 4

Rolled Omelettes

25 g (1 oz) (2¼ tablespoons) flour
3 beaten eggs
75 ml (2½ fl oz) (⅓ cup) milk
25 g (1 oz) (2 tablespoons) butter
pinch of chopped parsley or
  mixed herbs
pinch of salt and pepper

1 Sieve the flour and add the beaten eggs and milk. Season with salt and pepper and strain.

2 Add a pinch of chopped parsley or mixed herbs for flavouring.

3 Melt the butter in an omelette pan (skillet) and, when it is foaming, add the egg mixture. Stir it through and when it is cooked on one side, toss it over like a pancake and cook until golden-brown.

4 Remove the omelette from the pan (skillet) and spread with a filling. Roll up and serve.

Cheshire-Style

1 Sprinkle 50 g (2 oz) (½ cup) grated Cheshire cheese onto the cooked omelette. Add a few drops of Worcestershire sauce.

2 Place under a hot grill (broiler) to melt the cheese.

3 Roll up and serve.

Rolled Herb Omelette

bunch of fresh mixed herbs
  (chives, chervil, tarragon etc.)
6 eggs
salt and pepper
5 ml (1 tablespoon) oil
25 g (1 oz) (2 tablespoons) butter

1 Pick over the mixed herbs. Wash and dry them, then chop finely.

2 Break the eggs into a bowl. Add salt and pepper. Beat with a fork until the eggs are blended but not frothy.

3 Add the chopped herbs and mix in with the fork.

4 Melt the oil and butter together in a frying pan (skillet) until foaming and hot, then pour in the eggs. Stir, in all directions, with a wooden spoon or the back of a fork to prevent the cooked eggs from sticking to the pan.

5 When the omelette is cooked, but the eggs are still creamy, roll it up by tilting the pan and assisting the rolling with the wooden spoon or fork. Slide the rolled omelette to the edge of the pan.

6 Bring a heated serving dish to the edge of the pan. Lift the opposite side of the pan to turn out the omelette.

7 Serve immediately.

Serves 4

Tips: Always heat the serving dish and, if possible, the plates. Omelettes should be served either very hot or cold.

If intending to serve an omelette cold, cook it more thoroughly. It should be quite set and no longer creamy.

Cold omelettes make excellent picnic fare. They can also be served as a sandwich filling either whole in a French loaf or sliced and packed into rolls.

Look'n Cook Mayonnaise

1 The ingredients needed to make the four mayonnaise variations – tartare sauce, garlic mayonnaise, remoulade mayonnaise tomato ketchup (catsup): olive oil, groundnut oil, vinegar, mustard, white pepper, salt, egg, tomato ketchup (catsup), capers, lemon, garlic, chives, tarragon and parsley **2** Break the egg, separating the white from the yolk. Place the yolk in a deep mixing bowl **3** Add the mustard to the egg yolk **4** Make the mayonnaise by stirring in the groundnut oil. Add only a little of the oil at a time, beating continuously with a wooden spoon. Alternatively, you can use a hand whisk or an electric mixer for the blending operation **5** When the mayonnaise is of a firm consistency, add freshly ground white pepper **6** Add salt **7, 8** and **9** Then add either vinegar, or lemon, or tomato ketchup (catsup) according to the type of mayonnaise you wish to make **10** If making a tartare sauce, chop the chives, tarragon and parsley **11** Mix the chopped herbs into the stiff mayonnaise **12** Finally, add the capers to this mixture **13** For garlic mayonnaise, use olive

Look'n Cook Mayonnaise

13

14

15

16

17

18

19

20

21

oil instead of groundnut oil **14** Chop the cloves of garlic finely **15** Mix the chopped garlic into the stiff mayonnaise **16** To make the rémoulade: hard-boil (hard-cook) the eggs, allow them to cool, then remove the shells. Cut the cold eggs into halves **17** Remove the egg yolks and place them in a bowl **18** Mash them with a fork **19** Add the mustard **20** Make the rémoulade with groundnut oil. Decorate the finished rémoulade with a little chopped yolk and white of egg **21** To rescue a curdled mayonnaise, mix an egg yolk with some mustard in a bowl, then pour in, one after the other in very small quantities the 'turned' mayonnaise and a little oil. Keep stirring until the mayonnaise has returned to the correct consistency **22** The finished mayonnaise variations on show: (left to right): tomato ketchup (catsup) mayonnaise, garlic mayonnaise, rémoulade and tartare sauce (front)

22

Mayonnaise

Mayonnaise (Basic Recipe)

1 egg
5 ml (1 teaspoon) mustard
¼ litre (8 fl oz) (1 cup) groundnut oil
salt
freshly ground white pepper
5 ml (1 teaspoon) vinegar

1 Break the egg, separating the white from the yolk.

2 Put the yolk into a small deep bowl with the mustard.

3 Pour in the oil little by little, stirring continuously with a wooden spoon, whisk or electric whisk.

4 When the mayonnaise is stiff, add salt and pepper. Add the vinegar. Cover and put in a cool place until you wish to serve it.

Makes ¼ litre (8 fl oz) (1 cup)

Tips: If the egg yolks are very pale, a little natural egg colouring or a pinch of tumeric powder will enhance the final colour of the mayonnaise. A few drops of tabasco can be added to give the mayonnaise a little more bite.

A extra egg yolk can be added which will help to make the sauce a little thicker.

Variations

Lemon Mayonnaise

1 Prepare the mayonnaise as shown in the basic recipe. Replace the vinegar with the juice of ½ a lemon. You can also peel a fresh lemon, cut the flesh into small cubes and add this to the mayonnaise at the time of serving.

Lemon Cream Mayonnaise

1 Prepare ¼ litre (8 fl oz) (1 cup) of the basic mayonnaise, reducing the mustard to 2.5 ml (½ teaspoon). Add the juice of 1 lemon. Put the mayonnaise in a cool place.

2 Pour 100 ml (4 fl oz) (½ cup) double (heavy) cream in a deep bowl, and put this into another deep bowl filled with crushed ice.

3 Whip (beat) the cream until it forms peaks.

4 Fold into the mayonnaise without delay so that you have a frothy mixture. Pour this sauce into a sauce-boat.

Tip: The whipped cream can be replaced by a stiffly beaten white of egg.

Variations

Antiboise Mayonnaise

1 Chop 2 drained canned anchovy fillets.

2 Mix the anchovy fillets with 5 ml (1 teaspoon) anchovy essence, a pinch of garlic salt and a pinch of chopped tarragon.

3 Add this mixture to ¼ litre (8 fl oz) (1 cup) of the basic mayonnaise.

Andalusia Mayonnaise

1 Purée 25 g (1 oz) red peppers with a pinch of garlic salt.

2 Add the purée to ¼ litre (8 fl oz) (1 cup) of the basic mayonnaise and garnish with 25 g (1 oz) chopped peppers.

Madrilène Mayonnaise

1 Chop 25 g (1 oz) ham and add a pinch of garlic salt and 5 g (1 teaspoon) tomato concentrate (paste).

2 Blend this mixture into ¼ litre (8 fl oz) (1 cup) of the basic mayonnaise.

Britannia Mayonnaise

1 Place 2 g (1 teaspoon) freshly chopped mint in a pan and add 5 g (1 teaspoon) sugar. Add 15 ml (1 tablespoon) wine vinegar and simmer the mint for 10 minutes.

2 Add the mint and vinegar to ¼ litre (8 fl oz) (1 cup) of the basic mayonnaise and stir in a drop of green edible food colouring to make the mayonnaise a pale green colour.

Santa Lucia Mayonnaise

1 Mix together 25 g (1 oz) grated horseradish, 40 g (1½ oz) (¾ cup) fresh white breadcrumbs, 40 g (1½ oz) desiccated coconut, 40 ml (1½ fl oz) (2½ tablespoons) lime juice, 5 g (1 teaspoon) sugar and a pinch of cayenne pepper.

2 Blend these ingredients into ¼ litre (8 fl oz) (1 cup) of the basic mayonnaise.

3 Just before serving, whip (beat) 85 ml (3 fl oz) (⅜ cup) double (heavy) cream and fold it into the mayonnaise.

Herb Mayonnaise (Sauce Verte)

1 To ¼ litre (8 fl oz) (1 cup) of the basic mayonnaise, add 25 g (1 oz) spinach purée and 5 g (1 tablespoon) of mixed chopped fresh herbs, such as parsley, cress, tarragon and chives.

Tartare Sauce

1 Prepare ¼ litre (8 fl oz) (1 cup) of the basic mayonnaise. Wash, dry and chop a small bunch of chives, tarragon and parsley. Mix the chopped herbs and some capers with the mayonnaise.

Tomato Ketchup (Catsup) Mayonnaise

1 To ¼ litre (8 fl oz) (1 cup) of the basic mayonnaise, add 45 ml (3 tablespoons) tomato ketchup (catsup) or 15 ml (1 tablespoon) of tomato concentrate (paste) and a generous quantity of pepper.

Rescuing a Curdled Mayonnaise

Break an egg, separating the white from the yolk. Put the yolk with a little made mustard into a deep bowl. Add oil and the curdled mayonnaise alternately, little by little, stirring continuously with a whisk.

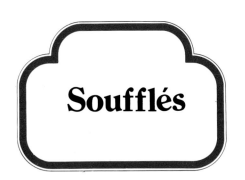

Soufflés

Salmon Soufflé

50 g (2 oz) (4 tablespoons)
  clarified butter
50 g (2 oz) (⅓ cup) grated
  Parmesan cheese
4 peeled prawns
150 ml (¼ pint) (½ cup) thick
  béchamel sauce
4 egg yolks
125 g (¼ lb) canned salmon, skin
  and bones removed
pinch salt and white pepper
3 egg whites
juice 1 lemon
grated Parmesan cheese

1 Preheat the oven to 200°C,
400°F, gas 6. Grease 4 individual
soufflé dishes with clarified butter. Sprinkle the insides with
grated Parmesan cheese. Place 1
peeled prawn in each dish.

2 Warm up the béchamel with 2
egg yolks and the dry fish paste.
Season to taste, then remove from
the heat and add the remaining 2
egg yolks and the lemon juice.

3 In a large bowl, beat the egg
whites to a soft meringue, making
sure the whisk and bowl are clean
and that no specks of yolk are left
in the whites.

4 Fold the egg whites lightly into
the fish mixture, then fill the prepared dishes to the top. Level off
with a palette knife or spatula.
Pass the tip of your thumb all
round the inside edge to form a
hollow ring.

5 Place the dishes in a roasting
pan and bake in the middle of the
preheated oven for 15-18 minutes

6 Remove the soufflés from the
oven, sprinkle the tops with
Parmesan cheese and serve.

Serves 4

Cheese and Tomato Soufflé

2 large ripe tomatoes, skinned,
  de-seeded and diced
4 eggs, separated
100 g (¼ lb) (1 cup) grated cheese
15 ml (1 tablespoon) single (light)
  cream
salt and pepper
pinch grated nutmeg

For the Béchamel Sauce:
50 g (2 oz) (4 tablespoons) butter
50 g (2 oz) (4 tablespoons) flour
300 ml (½ pint) (1¼ cups) infused
  milk

1 Prepare the béchamel sauce
(see page 260).

2 Preheat the oven to 220°C,
425°F, gas 7. Grease a 1.4 litre (2½
pint) (6 cup) capacity soufflé dish.

3 Put the egg whites into a large
bowl. Take the sauce off the heat
and beat in the egg yolks, grated
cheese, diced tomatoes, cream,
salt and pepper to taste and
nutmeg.

4 Beat the egg whites until they
stand in stiff peaks, then, using a
metal spoon, carefully cut and
fold them into the sauce until well
combined. Quickly pour into the
prepared dish and run the tip of
your thumb round the rim, 5mm
(¼ in) deep in the mixture so that
it rises evenly. Cook in the oven
for 25 minutes or until risen and
golden. Serve immediately.

Serves 6

---

*Salmon Soufflé — a delicious
starter to any meal. Bake the
mixture in smaller moulds to
serve as individual souffles*

1 Butter the inside of a soufflé dish **2** Sprinkle evenly with Parmesan cheese (or any finely grated cheese) **3** Melt the butter in a saucepan without allowing it to brown **4** Add the flour and mix with a wooden spoon to form a roux. Remove from the heat and allow the mixture to cool a little, then add the milk, all at once **5** Return the pan to the heat and let the sauce thicken, stirring all the time until smooth. This takes about 10-15 minutes. Grate a little nutmeg into the sauce and season with salt and pepper. Remove the saucepan from the heat **6** Add the egg yolks to the sauce and mix well **7** Add the grated cheese and allow it to melt into the sauce, stirring all the time with a wooden spoon **8** Beat the egg whites with a pinch of salt until they are stiff **9** Fold the egg whites gently into the cheese sauce with a metal spoon **10** Pour the mixture into the buttered soufflé dish and smooth over the top. Place in an oven 220°C, 425°F, gas 7 and cook for 25 minutes. Then higher the temperature to 240°C, 475°F, gas 9 and cook for a further 5 minutes **11** Remove from the oven and serve immediately. The soufflé should be well-risen and should stand for at least 15 minutes after baking without collapsing

Cheese Soufflé

50 g (2 oz) (¼ cup) butter or
  margarine
40 g (1½ oz) (6 tablespoons) flour
300 ml (½ pint) (1¼ cups) milk
pinch grated nutmeg
salt and pepper
100 g (¼ lb) (1 cup) grated cheese
4 or 5 eggs, depending on size,
  separated

1 Make a thick béchamel sauce: Melt 40g (1½oz) (3 tablespoons) butter or margarine in a saucepan without allowing it to brown. Add the flour and stir briskly with a wooden spoon so that the butter and flour are mixed to form a roux. Remove pan from heat and let the mixture cool a little. Then add the milk all at once. Return the pan to the heat. Let the sauce thicken for 10-15 minutes, stirring continuously until smooth. Add the nutmeg. Salt lightly and pepper generously.

2 Add the grated cheese to the sauce and let it melt whilst stirring it with a whisk or wooden spoon. It is now a mornay sauce.

3 Taking the saucepan off the heat, add the egg yolks to the sauce and mix well.

4 Preheat the oven to 220°C, 425°F, gas 7. Butter a soufflé dish (about 18 cm [7 in] diameter and 10 cm [4 in] deep) with the remaining butter.

5 Add a pinch of salt to the egg whites. Beat them in a large bowl until they are stiff.

6 Using a metal spoon or spatula, fold the whites into the mornay sauce very carefully.

7 Pour the mixture into the buttered soufflé dish and smooth over the top, making sure it is level. Then run the tip of your thumb around the inside of the dish, about 5 mm (¼ in) deep in the mixture. This helps the soufflé to rise evenly. Put into the oven. Cook for 25 minutes then, without opening the oven door, turn the temperature up to 240°C, 475°F, gas 9. Remove the soufflé from the oven after it has been in for 30 minutes.

Serves 4

Soufflé Omelettes

When preparing a soufflé omelette, the egg whites are beaten separately to provide maximum expansion of the mixture and to make the finished dish as light as possible.

(Basic recipe)
4 eggs
15 g (½ oz) (1 tablespoon) flour
pinch of salt and pepper
25 g (1 oz) (2 tablespoons) butter

1 Crack the eggs, separating the egg whites from the yolks.

2 Add the flour to the yolks and blend. Season with a pinch of pepper.

3 Beat the egg whites until they stand in stiff peaks. Add a pinch of salt.

4 Gradually fold the yolk mixture into the beaten egg whites.

5 Melt the butter in an omelette pan (skillet) and pour in the egg mixture. Cook for a few minutes until the bottom of the omelette is set and golden-brown.

6 Place the pan in a preheated oven of 190°C, 375°F, gas 5 and cook for 2-4 minutes.

7 Remove and fold the omelette over like a book. Bake for another 3 minutes.

8 Turn out onto a buttered dish and serve.

Tip: Various sweet (and even savoury) fillings can be added to this omelette before it is folded. The favourites are jam and fruit fillings.

Variations:

Devonshire

1 Prepare the basic omelette mixture but add 25 g (1 oz) grated Cheddar cheese and 20 ml (1¼ fl oz) sherry to the yolks.

2 Cook as above and sprinkle with more grated cheese.

3 Place under a grill (broiler) until the cheese begins to bubble and turn brown.

Pancakes

Pancakes with Soufflé Stuffing

½ litre (1 pint) (2½ cups) pancake
  batter
375 ml (16 fl oz) (2 cups) béchamel
  sauce
4 eggs, separated
50 g (2 oz) Gruyère
  cheese, diced

1 Preheat the oven to 200°C, 400°F, gas 6. Heat a greased pancake pan and add enough batter to cover the bottom. Cook the pancake on both sides and repeat until the batter is used up, storing the pancakes in a flat pile as they are cooked.

2 Make the soufflé stuffing: blend the béchamel sauce with the egg yolks and the diced cheese. Whisk (beat) the egg whites in a clean bowl until stiff and then fold them gently into the cheese mixture.

3 Place a little of the filling on each pancake and then fold it over to enclose the mixture completely. Place the filled pancakes on a greased ovenproof dish and place them in the oven for 12 minutes to cook the filling.

Makes 16

1 Prepare the batter **2** Make the pancakes **3** Prepare the filling: mix the béchamel sauce, egg yolks and diced Gruyère cheese **4** Whisk (beat) the egg whites until stiff and then fold them gently into the cheese mixture **5** Place a little of the filling on each pancake, fold over to enclose the mixture completely **6** Arrange the filled pancakes on a greased oven-proof dish and bake in the oven

Look'n Cook Soufflé Pancakes

Cheese Savouries

Emmenthal Potato Pancake

1 kg (2 lb) baked, jacket potatoes
salt and pepper
50 g (2 oz) (4 tablespoons) butter
60 ml (2 fl oz) (6 tablespoons) oil
150 g (5 oz) (1 cup) Emmenthal
  cheese, grated

1 When the baked, jacket potatoes are cool, cut each into two and scoop out the pulp and mash coarsely. Season with salt and pepper.

2 Heat the butter and the oil in a frying pan (skillet), 22.5 cm (9 in) in diameter. Stir in 100 g (¼ lb) of the grated cheese. Spread evenly across the pan. When the potato pancake is golden-brown underneath, turn and cook the other side.

3 Sprinkle with the remaining grated cheese and place under a hot grill (broiler) until the cheese melts and bubbles. Cut the pancake into 4 and serve with grilled meat or salad.

Serves 4

Corn Gnocchi Mamaliga

1 litre (1¾ pints) (4½ cups) water
pinch salt
400 g (14 oz) (2⅓ cups) fine
  cornmeal
pinch ground nutmeg
50 g (2 oz) (4 tablespoons) butter
25 g (1 oz) (3 tablespoons) grated
  Parmesan cheese
pinch garlic salt

1 Pour the water into a large saucepan, add the salt and bring to the boil.

2 Stir in the cornmeal with a wooden spoon and reboil. Add the garlic salt and nutmeg and cook for 15 minutes over a low heat, stirring constantly, until the mixture thickens to a pouring consistency.

3 Butter a gratin dish (using half the butter) and pour in the mixture. Leave until it is completely cold and set. Preheat the oven to 220°C, 425°F, gas 7.

4 Remove and cut into small squares and replace, overlapping, in the buttered gratin dish.

5 Dot with the remaining butter and sprinkle with the grated cheese.

6 Place in the preheated oven for 10 minutes to brown. Serve as an entree or with a meat dish.

Swiss Cheese Fritters

2 eggs
pepper to taste
50 g (2 oz) (1 cup) fine dry
  breadcrumbs
deep fat fryer
350 g (¾ lb) Gruyère cheese

1 Break the eggs into a bowl. Add pepper and beat with a fork.

2 Tip the breadcrumbs into a deep plate. Heat the fat bath.

3 Cut the rind off the Gruyère cheese. Cut the cheese into small sticks about 1cm (½ in) thick.

4 Beat the eggs again. Dip the small sticks of Gruyère cheese into the beaten egg, making sure they are well coated. Roll them in the breadcrumbs, shaking them to get rid of the excess. Heat the deep fat fryer and when hot, add the fritters.

5 Drain the fritters on absorbent paper as soon as they are golden. Cover the serving dish with a white napkin and arrange the fritters on top. Serve piping hot.

Serves 4

Avocado Grill

100 g (¼ lb) bacon
4 soft rolls
1 large avocado
10 ml (2 teaspoons) made
  mustard
175 g (6 oz) (1½ cups) grated
  Cheddar or Cheshire cheese
1 tomato, sliced
8 olives (black or green)

1 Cut the bacon into strips and fry until crisp. Keep hot.

2 Split each roll lengthways into two and toast and butter.

3 Remove the stone (seed) from the avocado, peel and slice the fruit thinly.

4 Place the avocado slices on the toasted rolls and spread lightly with mustard.

5 Sprinkle with grated cheese, making sure that the avocado is well-covered.

6 Place under a hot grill (broiler) until the cheese melts and bubbles.

7 Decorate with the bacon strips and thin, twisted slices of avocado. Garnish with sliced tomatoes and olives.

Serves 8

Puffed Cheese Fritters

¼ litre (scant ½ pint) (1 cup) water
large pinch salt
pinch pepper
65 g (2½ oz) (¼ cup + 1 tablespoon)
  butter
125 g (¼ lb) (1 cup) flour
oil for deep frying
5 eggs (or 6 if they are small)
75 g (3 oz) (¾ cup) grated Cheddar
  or Parmesan cheese

1 Make the choux pastry: measure out the water. Pour it into a saucepan and add the salt and the pepper.

2 Cut the butter into large pieces and add to the saucepan.

Sift the flour onto a large sheet of paper.

3 Put the saucepan containing the water, salt, pepper and butter over a high heat and boil it. Watch it carefully as the liquid rises up like milk.

4 Heat the deep fat fryer.

5 Take the saucepan off the stove and add the flour all at once.

6 Put the saucepan back on the stove and stir briskly with a wooden spoon to dry out the paste. It should come away from the sides of the saucepan. Take the pan off the heat.

7 Break 1 egg into a cup. Add it to the paste and beat it in very well. Do the same with the other eggs. The pastry should be soft but not liquid.

8 Add the grated cheese to the mixture.

9 When the fat is hot (but not smoking) add small spoonfuls of

Avocado Grill — soft rolls covered with slices of avocado and topped with mustard, cheese and crispy bacon strips

pastry, a few at a time.

10 When the fritters are nicely golden (this takes about 3 minutes), take them out of the fat and drain them on absorbent paper.

11 Serve the fritters piping hot.

Serves 6

171

Look'n Cook Puffed Cheese Fritters

1 The ingredients: butter, flour, eggs, grated cheese, salt, water and oil. Weigh the butter and the flour **2** Measure the water and pour it into a saucepan **3** Cut up the butter Fritto pieces. Put these into the saucepan **4** Bring the mixture to the boil (be careful, it rises up like milk). Heat the deep fryer **5** Sift the flour **6** Take the saucepan off the heat and add the flour all at once **7** Stir briskly with a wooden spoon to blend it well and so that the mixture comes away from the side of the

pan and curls round the spoon **8** Break an egg. Add it to the mixture off the heat. Blend it in well. Add the other eggs, one by one, in the same way **9** Add the cheese and mix well. Add pepper and stir again **10** Using 2 small spoons, drop small quantities of the mixture at a time into the hot fat. The fritters should not touch each other **11** Leave them to fry. They turn themselves when one side is done **12** Lift the basket out of the pan and drain the fritters on absorbent paper

Look 'n Cook Cheese Fondue

1 All the ingredients you will need to make the fondue 2 Grate the Emmenthal and Gruyère cheeses finely 3 Rub around the inside of the fondue dish (or a flameproof casserole) with a clove of garlic 4 Heat the white wine in a saucepan until it is warmed through and pour into the fondue dish over a low heat 5 Add the grated cheese gradually, stirring constantly with a wooden spoon until the mixture thickens 6 Add the Kirsch and season with salt and freshly ground pepper. Add the cornflour (cornstarch) and bring to the boil, stirring all the time. Serve immediately with French bread

Cheese Fondue

Cheese Fondue

300 g (11 oz) (2¾ cups) grated
  Emmenthal cheese
300 g (11 oz) (2¾ cups) grated
  Gruyère cheese
1 clove garlic
300 ml (10 fl oz) (1¼ cups) dry
white wine
1 tablespoon (1½ tablespoons)
  Kirsch
pinch salt
freshly ground (milled
  black pepper
15 g (½ oz) (1½ tablespoons)
  cornflour (cornstarch)
1 crusty French loaf

1 Rub around the inside of a fondue dish, or flameproof casserole,
with a clove of garlic.

2 Pour the white wine into a
saucepan and warm through over
a low heat. Pour into the fondue
dish.

3 Place the fondue dish over a
low heat or spirit-heater and
gradually add the grated cheese,
stirring constantly with a wooden
spoon.

4 When it thickens, add the
Kirsch and freshly ground
pepper. Season to taste.

5 Add the cornflour (cornstarch)
and bring to the boil, stirring
constantly.

6 Serve hot by dipping cubes of
French bread, on long handled
forks, into the fondue.

Serves 4

Tip: Fondues are great fun to
serve instead of a dip when guests
come for a meal, or at a party.
They are traditionally eaten in
Switzerland on high days and
holidays. Use long-handled forks
or skewers for spearing the cubes
of bread.

*Cheese Fondue — an
increasingly popular dish for
entertaining friends, which
involves very little preparation
time*

Cheese and Pastry

Cheese Straws

225 g (½ lb) puff pastry,
  home-made or frozen and
  thawed
50 g (2 oz) (⅓ cup) grated
  Parmesan
50 g (2 oz) (½ cup) grated
  Leicester or other hard cheese
pinch cayenne
pinch paprika

1 Roll out the pastry to a rectangle about 3 mm (⅛ in) thick. Sprinkle over grated cheese to which the paprika and cayenne has been added. Fold in two and roll out again to the same thickness.

2 Set the oven at 200°C, 400°F, gas 6.

3 Roll out the pastry to the width of your baking (cookie) sheet. Cut it into strips 1 cm (½ in) wide. Place on a board and twist with both hands, then place on a greased baking (cookie) sheet.

4 Bake in the pre-set oven for 8 minutes or until golden.

5 Cut the strips in regular lengths of 10 cm (4 in). Heap 12 per portion.

Makes about 32 straws

Tip: It is usual to bake some of the pastry in 5 cm (2 in) rings into which bundles of cheese straws can be inserted (see photo below). Serve them on a plate lined with a d'oyley, if liked.

Savoury Cheese and Spinach Puffs

450 g (1 lb) frozen puff pastry
150 g (5 oz) (1½ cups) spinach
100 g (¼ lb) sorrel
25 g (1 oz) (2 tablespoons) butter
200 g (7 oz) (1¼ cups) well-drained
  cottage or cream cheese
25 g (1 oz) (¼ cup) Gruyère cheese,
  grated
pinch grated nutmeg
salt and pepper
1 whole egg plus 2 yolks

1 Thaw the frozen pastry for 1 hour at room temperature.

2 Pick over the spinach and the sorrel. Wash and dry and chop coarsely.

3 Melt the butter without browning in a heavy sauté pan. Add the chopped spinach and sorrel. Cook for 7 minutes over a low heat, stirring with a wooden spoon, then remove the pan from the heat.

4 Sieve the cottage or cream cheese into a bowl. Add the cooked spinach and sorrel, the grated Gruyère cheese, nutmeg, salt and pepper to taste. Mix well.

5 Add the whole egg and 1 yolk to this mixture. Work with a wooden spoon until the mixture is smooth and firm. Preheat the oven to 230°C, 450°F, gas 8.

6 Divide the pastry dough into two. Roll out each piece to a rectangle about 10 x 18 cm (4 x 7 in).

7 Grease a baking (cookie) sheet and place 1 rectangle on it. Spread with the filling to within 1 cm (½ in) of the pastry edge. Top with the remaining pastry rectangle and score the surface with a knife to give 10-12 portions. Pinch the edges to seal.

8 Beat the remaining egg yolk with 15 ml (1 tablespoon) water. Brush the top of the rectangle with this egg glaze.

9 Put the baking (cookie) sheet into the oven and bake until the pastry is golden-brown and well-risen (about 30 minutes). Take out and cut the pastry into portions with a sharp knife. Serve immediately.

Makes 6

Tip: If fresh sorrel is not available, substitute the same quantity of spinach.

Cheese Straws. Wrapped round sausages and cut into rounds or straw shapes shown here are several ways of serving a basic cheese pastry

Look 'n Cook Vatrouchka

1

2

3

4

5

1 The ingredients: flour, butter (softened at room temperature), sugar, cottage or cream cheese, eggs, candied fruits, vanilla, brandy, salt **2** Make the pastry: break the eggs separating the whites from the yolks. Keep the whites that are not needed to one side **3** Whisk together the yolks, the white and the sugar **4** Add the softened butter. Stir with the whisk until the mixture is smooth **5** Tip in the flour and mix in. Roll the pastry into a ball and leave it to rest in a cool place **6** Flour the pastry board. Roll out the pastry adding flour as necessary **7** Cover the baking tray (cookie sheet) with greaseproof (wax) paper. Put a flan ring on top of it. Roll out the pastry and place this in the ring **8** Line the ring making sure the pastry is pushed into the bottom and sides **9** Roll the excess pastry off the edges with the thumbs or a rolling pin. Prick the bottom of the pastry with a fork. Line with foil and bake 'blind' **10** Prepare the filling: whisk together eggs and sugar, add the brandy and stir

Cheesecakes

Russian Cheesecake Vatrouchka

For the Pastry:
3 egg yolks
1 egg white
225 g (½ lb) (1 cup) caster sugar
125 g (¼ lb) (½ cup) butter, softened
375 g (13 oz) (3¼ cups) sifted plain flour

For the Filling:
200 g (½ lb) mixed candied fruits (glacé cherries, angelica and pineapple) soaked in 50 ml (2 fl oz) (¼ cup) brandy
450 g (1 lb) (2 cups) cream cheese
225 g (½ lb) (1 cup) caster sugar
5 drops each vanilla, orange and lemon essences
2 whole eggs plus 2 yolks
20 ml (1½ tablespoons) brandy
5 ml (1 teaspoon) mixed spice
4 egg whites

1 whole egg, beaten
25 g (1 oz) (¼ cup) icing (confectioner's) sugar for dusting

◄ 11 Add the vanilla, stir again 12 Add the cottage or cream cheese and stir 13 Add the candied fruit. Mix it all together 14 Take the filling on a wooden spoon and fill the bottom of the tart. Smooth the surface with a metal spoon 15 Roll out the off-cuts of pastry into long even strips. Make a criss-cross pattern on top of the tart and brush the whole surface with beaten egg. Put the cheesecake in the oven 16 When cooked, dredge with icing sugar (confectioner's sugar) and serve

1 Grease a baking sheet (cookie sheet) and cover with a sheet of grease proof (waxed) paper. Grease a 25 cm (10 in) in diameter flan ring and place it on the baking (cookie) sheet.

2 Place 3 egg yolks and 1 egg white (reserving the unwanted egg whites at this stage to use in the filling) in a pastry bowl. Whisk in the sugar for 4 minutes until white and fluffy.

3 Blend the soft butter into the egg mixture and whisk again for 3 minutes until the mixture is smooth.

4 Mix in the sifted flour and, with your hand, knead to a firm dough. Roll into a ball and place in the refrigerator for 1 hour.

5 Dust the pastry board and a rolling pin with flour and roll out the sweet pastry dough to a thickness of ½ cm (¼ in) and 28 cm (11 in) in diameter. Wrap it round the rolling pin for easy handling and unroll over the pastry flan ring. Press the pastry down well around the inside of the ring with your fingers and cut surplus pastry with a knife. Spread a piece of paper inside. Fill with dry cooking beans and bake blind for 15 minutes at 200°C, 400°F, gas 6. Cool, and discard beans.

6 Roll all the pastry left over into a ball to be used later for the criss-cross pattern design.

7 Place 4 egg whites in a clean basin and beat until the mixture forms stiff peaks when lifted with a whisk. Add only 100 g (4 oz) (¼ cup) of caster sugar, a little at a time, and whisk until the mixture is stiff. Blend in the cream cheese.

8 Place 2 whole eggs and 2 egg yolks in another bowl and flavour with the mixed spices, brandy and vanilla, lemon and orange essences. Beat the mixture for 2 minutes.

9 Fold in the cream cheese mixture.

10 Add the candied fruits and chill.

11 Spread the cheese mixture

thickly into the baked pastry shell.

12 Roll the left over pastry thinly on a floured board and cut into thin strips, 3 mm wide (14 strips in all). Place the strips across the top in a criss-cross pattern. Brush the pastry strips with eggwash and bake the cheesecake on the middle shelf for 35/40 minutes at 190°C, 375°F, gas 5, until golden-brown.

13 Cool for 15 minutes, dust with icing sugar (confectioner's sugar) and serve.

Serves 8-10

Variation

For a simpler cheesecake which is quicker to prepare, try this cold version:

1 Blend together 100 g (¼ lb) cream cheese with the juice and grated rind of 1 lemon.

2 Blend 50 g (2 oz) (¼ cup) sugar and 25 g (1 oz) gelatine and dissolve in 150 ml (¼ pt) (⅝ cup) of hot water.

3 Pour into the cream cheese mixture and blend well.

4 When cool, stir in 150 ml (¼ pint) (⅝ cup) whipped double (heavy) cream.

5 Mix 225 g (½ lb) of crushed biscuits with 100 g (¼ lb) (½ cup) of melted butter and press down in a greased and lined loose-bottomed flan tin.

6 Fill with the cheese mixture and chill in the refrigerator.

Buying and Storing Cheese
Cheese must be enjoyed fresh, so try to buy it from a specialist shop. Only buy as much as you need. Fresh and soft cheeses should preferably be eaten on the day they are bought, or kept under refrigeration for a few days at most. Hard cheeses last longer but they, too, should be kept under refrigeration at about 4-10°C (40-50°F), wrapped loosely in polythene, aluminium foil or greaseproof (waxed) paper. Take the cheese out of the refrigerator at least 1 hour before serving.

All about Garden Vegetables

Vegetables have been an integral part of our diets since the beginning of time. In early days, poor people relied on root vegetables to eke out a starvation diet. Every labourer who had access to a plot of land grew what he could: carrots, onions, radishes, parsnips, and other root vegetables in addition to herbs grown for medicinal purposes.

Plants brought back from the 'new world' to Europe enriched the scope for creating more imaginative dishes. It is difficult to think of a time when there were no potatoes, tomatoes, corn cobs or sweet peppers. Even the rich, who ate more meat and fish in a month than any peasant saw in a lifetime, were not immune to the lure of vegetables.

Varieties of vegetables have been bred and brought to near perfection – not least because market gardening has been a profitable industry in Europe since the seventeenth century, and in America and Australasia as soon as trade was established. French cooks have always had a reputation for cooking vegetables well, and often serve them as a separate course. The English, however, are infamous for boiling vegetables until no hint of flavour is left, then demanding that they be eaten up 'because they are good for you'. The reputation is largely undeserved; cooks like Mrs Hannah Glasse, whose book was published in 1747, had excellent recipes for asparagus, broad beans, cucumbers and a 'fricassey of mushrooms'.

We now have access to fresh vegetables all the year round – and good frozen or canned brands. We have become aware of their importance in creating a balanced, healthy diet. Through their alkalis, they help neutralize acids produced by proteins.

A diet rich in animal fats is currently thought to contribute to the high rate of heart disease endemic in the western world, and thus the substitution of vegetables and vegetable oils is recommended by many doctors. Vegetables, in addition to their dietary value, lend complementary flavours to other foods and, with their different colours and textures, can make a meal look as good as it tastes.

Vegetables can be defined according to the way they grow:
Roots and tubers are cultivated in the earth. Potatoes, carrots, turnips, celeriac, beetroot, Jerusalem artichokes and swedes are all in this family. They all have a high carbohydrate value and contain vitamin C.
Fruits include tomatoes, aubergines (eggplants) and peppers, all high in vitamins A, B, C and E and abundant in minerals.
Leaves Lettuce, cabbage, spinach and chicory are just a few. They are rich in vitamin C, iron and calcium.
Legumes Peas, beans and lentils are full of protein and carbohydrates, plus vitamin B complex and iron. Soya beans are now widely accepted as a protein-substitute for meat.
Bulbs include onions and garlic.
Shoots Chives, leeks, celery, asparagus are all shoots.
Flowers Cauliflower and broccoli are in this category.
Fungi Mushrooms and truffles are edible fungi.

As a general rule, buy vegetables of medium size, when they will have developed their flavour and still be tender.

To cook vegetables, clean them well, scrubbing if appropriate. If they can be eaten in their skins, do not peel them because much of their nutrient value lies close to the skin. If you must peel them, do so thinly.

Avoid overcooking vegetables – if possible, steam them. If they are to be boiled or simmered, use very little water, and after cooking add the water to your stock pot. (Try cooking green vegetables in a stock made with ½ a chicken or vegetable stock cube, water and a little butter.)

To keep the colour of green vegetables, before cooking them blanch for 1 minute in a pan of boiling salted water, then plunge them immediately into cold water. *Never* use bicarbonate of soda (baking soda).

Root Vegetables

Carrot Casserole with Mushrooms in Sherry

450 g (1 lb) (8 cups) button
  mushrooms
50 g (2 oz) (4 tablespoons) butter
1 small onion, chopped
1 kg (2 lb) (8 cups) small carrots,
  sliced
15 g (½ oz) (1 tablespoon) tomato
  concentrate (paste)
350 ml (12 fl oz) (1½ cups) water
1 chicken stock cube
150 ml (¼ pint) (⅝ cup) sherry
salt and pepper
pinch each mace and oregano
5 g (1 tablespoon) chives and
  parsley, chopped

1 Wash the mushrooms and trim the ends of the stalks.

2 Heat the butter and gently sauté the onion for 4 minutes without browning it.

3 Add to the onion, the carrots, tomato concentrate (paste) and water. Bring to the boil and boil for 30 minutes.

4 Crumble the stock cube into the mixture and add the sherry, seasoning, spices and mushrooms. Simmer for 10 minutes.

5 Place in a serving dish and sprinkle with the chopped chives and parsley.

Serves 4

Tips: The mushroom stalks can be trimmed from the raw mushrooms and used for making stuffing (chop them and blend with meat or breadcrumbs), or puréed for mushroom soup.

Carrot Casserole with Mushrooms in Sherry is a delicious accompaniment for roast pork or lamb

Look 'n Cook Chopping Vegetables

Paysanne
1 Slice the leeks into fine strips widthways **2** Cut the carrots, turnips and potatoes into thin slices, then into small, irregular-shaped cubes. Use in soups which will not be strained – such as minestrone

Jardinière
3 Cut the peeled carrots into large pieces **4** Cut the turnips into thick, even slices **5** Cut the vegetables again into smallish sticks about 2 cm (¾ in) long. Use with meat and fish dishes

Macédoine
6 Cut the carrots in slices lengthways **7** Cut them again into thinner strips **8** Chop the carrots into even-sized cubes **9** Cut the turnips in the same way. Use a macédoine of vegetables hot or cold, in vegetable dishes and in salads with peas and green beans

Brunoise
10 Cut the carrots into very thin slices using a grater or a very sharp knife **11** Cut them into thin sticks and then into tiny cubes. Use in soup-making

Julienne
12 Slice carrots and turnips into thin slices **13** Use a sharp knife to cut them into very thin strips lengthways **14** Cut the white part of the leek into thin strips

Mirepoix
15 Roughly chop some carrots, a stick of celery, a few parsley stems, a little thyme and a bay leaf. Use a mirepoix to flavour stocks and stews **16** The six classic ways of chopping vegetables displayed

Braised Sliced Carrots

450 g (1 lb) (4 cups) old carrots,
   peeled and sliced
50 g (2 oz) (4 tablespoons) butter
1 onion, chopped
500 ml (1 pint) (2½ cups) water
salt and pepper
pinch sugar
pinch bicarbonate of soda

1 Place the carrots in a pan with the butter and onion and sauté gently for 5 minutes with the lid on.

2 Pour in the water and add the seasoning, sugar and bicarbonate of soda. Bring to the boil and simmer gently, uncovered, for about 35 minutes or until the carrots are tender and the liquid has almost evaporated.

Serves 4

Tip: A rasher (slice) of bacon cooked with the carrots gives them a delicious meaty flavour.

In France, this dish is cooked in Vichy water because it contains the natural minerals which enrich and tenderize the carrots.

The bicarbonate of soda can be omitted if the carrots are young and fresh.

Baked Turnip au Gratin

50 g (2 oz) (4 tablespoons) butter
450 g (1 lb) (3 cups) peeled and
   sliced small white turnips
1 onion, chopped
225 g (½ lb) (2 cups) chopped
   mushrooms
1 clove garlic, chopped
150 ml (¼ pint) (⅝ cup) natural
   yogurt
salt and pepper
25 g (1 oz) (½ cup) fresh white
   breadcrumbs

1 Preheat the oven to 200°C, 400°F, gas 6.

2 Heat the butter in a frying pan (skillet), add the turnips, onion, mushrooms and garlic and fry gently for 4 minutes.

3 Stir in the yogurt and seasoning. Transfer the mixture to a small shallow ovenproof dish and sprinkle over the breadcrumbs. Bake in the preheated oven for 15 minutes.

Serves 4

Baked Parsnips with Radishes in Cream Sauce

6 large parsnips, peeled and cut
   in strips
50 g (2 oz) (4 tablespoons) butter
   or margarine
25 g (1 oz) (4 tablespoons) flour
500 ml (1 pint) (2½ cups) milk
salt and pepper
60 ml (2¼ fl oz) (4 tablespoons)
   single (light) cream
2 egg yolks
juice 1 lemon

For the Garnish:
6 radishes, diced
5 g (1 tablespoon) chopped
   parsley and chervil
5 g (1 tablespoon) chopped
   chives

1 Preheat the oven to 180°C, 350°F, gas 4. Boil the parsnips in salted water for 15 minutes. Drain.

2 Heat the fat in a pan and sauté the parsnips for 5 minutes then transfer them to a shallow ovenproof dish.

3 Add the flour to the fat left in the pan and cook for 1 minute. Blend in the milk to produce a smooth white sauce. Simmer the sauce for 10 minutes and season with salt and pepper.

4 Remove the pan from the heat and beat in the cream and egg yolks. Pour the sauce over the parsnips and bake in the preheated oven for 15 minutes.

5 Remove the dish from the oven and sprinkle the lemon juice over the parsnips. Garnish with the radishes and herbs and serve.

Serves 6

Tip: Enrich the flavour of this dish by including a little garlic, and for a touch of colour, add 2 tomatoes, skinned, deseeded and chopped.

Braised Parsnips with Chopped Eggs and Tomatoes

450 g (1 lb) (4 cups) peeled and
   sliced parsnips
50 g (2 oz) (4 tablespoons) butter
1 medium onion, chopped
1 clove garlic, chopped
2 tomatoes, skinned, deseeded
   and chopped
salt and pepper
2 hard-boiled (hard-cooked)
   eggs, chopped
5 g (1 tablespoon) chopped
   parsley

1 Preheat the oven to 200°C, 400°F, gas 6. Boil the parsnips in salted water for 15 minutes only. Drain.

2 In a sauté pan, heat the butter and fry the onion and garlic for 4 minutes until tender but not coloured. Add the tomatoes, parsnips and seasoning.

3 Transfer the mixture to a shallow ovenproof dish and bake in the preheated oven for 20 minutes. Serve sprinkled with the chopped egg and parsley.

Serves 4

Tip: For a more nutritious dish, add 125 g (5 oz) (1 cup) to the chopped eggs, and sprinkle with a little grated cheese.

Baked Parsnips with Radishes in Cream Sauce – an attractive and easy dish to prepare

Look 'n Cook Shaping Carrots and Turnips

1 Thinly peel, then wash and dry the carrots and turnips **2** Cut the carrots into even pieces about 4-5 cm (1½-2 in) long **3** Split each piece into four (or according to the thickness of the carrot) **4** With a very sharp knife cut away the hard part in the middle of the carrot and pare off angles or sharp edges so that the pieces (shown in the bowl on the right) are smooth and neat **5** Trim the turnips so that every side is smooth **6** Cut the turnips into quarters as for the carrots and pare away angles. If all the pieces of vegetable are an identical size and shape they look most professional and attractive when they are served

Glazed Carrots with Grapes

450 g (1 lb) small carrots
225 ml (8 fl oz) (1 cup) water
50 g (2 oz) (4 tablespoons)
    butter
25 g (1 oz) (1½ tablespoons)
    sugar or honey
salt and pepper
225 (½ lb) black or white
    grapes, or both, deseeded

1 Peel, wash and trim the carrots and cut them in quarters.

2 Put them in the water with the butter, sugar or honey, salt and pepper and bring to the boil. Boil until the liquid has almost evaporated and the carrots look glossy and tender.

3 Scald the grapes, dipping them quickly in boiling water, and serve with the carrots.

Serves 4

Jerusalem Artichokes with Carrots and Rice

450 g (1 lb) (3 cups) Jerusalem
    artichokes, peeled and sliced
juice and rind 1 lemon
150 g (5 oz) (1½ cups) sliced
    carrots
150 g (5 oz) (1¼ cups) sliced
    onion
90 ml (3 fl oz) (⅜ cup) oil
75 g (3 oz) (⅜ cup) rice
900 ml (1½ pints) (3¾ cups)
    water
7 g (⅓ oz) (1 teaspoon) sugar
5 g (1 tablespoon) each chopped
    parsley and chopped mint

1 Soak the sliced artichoke in the lemon juice.

2 Fry the carrots and onion in the oil in a covered pan over a low heat for 9 minutes until they are soft.

3 Add the rice and water and bring to the boil. Boil for 20 minutes.

4 Add the artichokes, lemon rind and sugar and cook for 5 more minutes.

5 Season and serve sprinkled with the chopped parsley and mint.

Serves 4

Sweet and Sour Beetroot (Beet) with Orange Sauce

8 small beetroots (beets)
1 grapefruit
1 orange
300 ml (½ pint) (1¼ cups) water
1 chicken stock cube
salt and pepper
50 g (2 oz) (2 tablespoons) sugar
30 ml (2 tablespoons) vinegar
pinch ground (powdered) ginger
15 g (½ oz) (1½ tablespoons)
    arrowroot mixed with 75 ml
    (2½ fl oz) (⅓ cup) water

1 Preheat the oven to 200°C, 400°F, gas 6. Wash the beetroots (beets). Bake them in their skins for 30 to 35 minutes.

2 Peel the grapefruit and orange, removing all the pith and white skin and reserving the peel. Cut the fruit into segments (sections).

3 Cut a little of the orange rind into very narrow strips, put them in a pan, cover with water and boil for 8 minutes, then drain.

4 Peel the beetroots (beets) and put them in a saucepan with the water, the stock cube, seasoning, sugar, vinegar and ground (powdered) ginger and boil for 5 minutes.

5 Add the thickening of arrowroot and water and boil for a further 3 minutes.

6 When the mixture is cold, serve it in a shallow dish garnished with orange and grapefruit segments (sections).

Serves 4

Glazed Carrots with Black Grapes is the ideal dish to serve with roast meat at a dinner party

The Marrow Family

Stuffed Cucumber Alphonso

1 whole cucumber
salt and pepper
25 g (1 oz) (2 tablespoons) butter
75 g (3 oz) (¾ cup) grated Cheddar
  cheese

For the Rice Stuffing:
50 ml (2 fl oz) (¼ cup) oil
1 onion, chopped
4 mushrooms, chopped
50 g (2 oz) (½ cup) pecan nuts,
  chopped
125 g (5 oz) (⅝ cup) long grain rice
1 clove garlic, peeled and
  crushed
300 ml (½ pint) (1¼ cups) water
1 chicken stock cube
pinch ground (powdered) mace
25 g (1 oz) (2 tablespoons) butter

1 Peel the cucumber and cut into two, lengthways. Scoop out the seeds and cut each side into 2 pieces. Season.

2 Butter a shallow, ovenproof dish and place the cucumber pieces on the dish.

3 Preheat the oven to 200°C, 400°F, gas 6.

4 Prepare the rice stuffing. Heat the oil in a pan and sauté the onions, without colouring, for 4 minutes. Add the mushrooms and pecan nuts, then stir in the rice. Simmer for 2 minutes.

5 Add the garlic and water, then crumble in the stock cube. Cover the pan and boil gently for 15 minutes. Season with salt and pepper and mace, then add the butter. The rice should have absorbed all the liquid.

6 Pile the rice stuffing into the cucumber pieces and sprinkle with the grated cheese. Bake in the oven for 20 minutes.

Serves 4

Aubergines (Eggplants) au Gratin

1 kg (2 lb) aubergines (eggplants)
50 g (2 oz) (¼ cup) salt
2 kg (4 lb) tomatoes
75 ml (5 tablespoons) oil
salt and pepper
2 cloves garlic
1 bunch parsley
oil for deep frying
50 g (2 oz) (½ cup) grated Gruyère
  cheese

1 Peel the aubergines (eggplants). Cut into slices about 1 cm (½ in) thick. Sprinkle with salt and leave for 20 minutes, wash and dry.

2 Meanwhile, skin the tomatoes and cut into halves. Remove the seeds and chop up the pulp.

3 Heat 60 ml (4 tablespoons) of the oil in a frying pan (skillet). Add the tomatoes. Cook gently for 15 minutes, mashing from time to time with a fork. Season with salt and pepper to taste.

4 Peel and chop the garlic. Wash and chop the parsley. Add the garlic and parsley to the tomato sauce.

5 Heat the deep fat fryer to 185°C, 360°F.

6 Lower the aubergine (eggplant) slices into the hot oil and fry until they are golden-brown. Remove from the oil and drain

7 Preheat the oven to 220°C, 425°F, gas 7.

8 Arrange the slices of aubergine (eggplant) and the tomato sauce in alternate layers in an attractive ovenproof dish, finishing with a layer of tomato sauce. Sprinkle with the Gruyère cheese and trickle the remaining 15 ml (1 tablespoon) of oil on to the top. Brown in the oven for about 10 minutes.

Serves 6

Stuffed Courgettes (Zucchini) with Sausagemeat

4 large firm courgettes
  (zucchini)
sprig parsley
100 g (¼ lb) (½ cup) butter
15 ml (1 tablespoon) milk
75 g (3 oz) (1½ cups) fresh
  breadcrumbs
5 g (1 teaspoon) chopped chives
pinch dried thyme
150 g (5 oz) (½ cup +
  2 tablespoons) sausagemeat

1 Wash and dry the courgettes (zucchini). Cut them in half lengthways and scoop out the insides. Chop the parsley.

2 Using 20 g (¾ oz) (1½ tablespoons) of the butter, grease an ovenproof dish. Arrange the halved courgettes (zucchini) in the dish.

3 Put the milk, 25 g (1 oz) (½ cup) breadcrumbs and 50 g (2 oz) (¼ cup) of the butter in a small pan. Add the parsley, chives and thyme and cook for a few minutes, stirring.

4 Preheat the oven to 220°C, 425°F, gas 7.

5 Remove the pan from the heat and thoroughly mix in the sausagemeat. Fill the courgette (zucchini) shells with stuffing.

6 Sprinkle the remaining fresh breadcrumbs over the courgette (zucchini) halves. Cut the remaining butter into small pieces and dot over the top.

7 Put the dish towards the top of the oven and bake for 25 minutes or until the topping is golden and the courgettes (zucchini) are tender.

Serves 4

Stuffed Cucumber Alphonso – hollowed out cucumbers stuffed with rice and mushrooms, and topped with melted cheese

Beef Casserole with Aubergines (Eggplants) and Chick Peas

¼ kg (½ lb) (1 cup) canned chick
  peas, or half that quantity of
  dried chick peas
1 kg (2 lb) braising or stewing
  beef, eg chuck steak
50 ml (2 fl oz) (¼ cup) oil
5 g (1 teaspoon) paprika
4 cloves garlic, peeled and
  crushed
2 chopped onions
25 g (1 oz) (2 tablespoons) tomato
  concentrate (paste)
1½ litres (2½ pints) (6 cups) water
4 medium aubergines
  (eggplants)
salt and pepper
oil for deep frying

1 If using dried chick peas, soak
them overnight in water.

2 Cut the steak into 4 cm (1½ in)
chunks. Heat a little oil in a large
pan, and brown the meat and the
paprika for 5-10 minutes, stirring
occasionally.

3 Strain off excess oil. Add the
strained chick peas, garlic,
onions, tomato concentrate
(paste) and water. Bring to the
boil, cover and simmer gently for
2-2½ hours.

4 Meanwhile slice the aubergines (eggplants), place on a dish
or wooden board and sprinkle liberally with salt. Leave for 30
minutes, then rinse and dry the
slices.

5 Heat the oil in a deep fat fryer to
185°C, 360°F . Deep fry the aubergine (eggplant) slices until
golden-brown. Drain on absorbent paper.

6 Add the aubergine (eggplant)
slices to the beef casserole, and
season to taste with salt and
pepper. Simmer for another 30
minutes. Serve immediately in a
heated serving dish.

Serves 6

Tip: Like many other dishes
originating in North Africa and
the Middle East, this casserole
should contain plenty of richly-

flavoured liquid which may be
eaten with a spoon, like a soup.

Ratatouille

2 large aubergines (eggplants),
  about 350 g (12 oz)
4 medium courgettes (zucchini)
50 g (2 oz) (good ½ cup) flour
  seasoned with salt
oil for deep frying
50 ml (2 fl oz) (¼ cup) cooking oil
1 onion, chopped
1 clove garlic, chopped
2 green peppers, split, deseeded,
  and cut in strips
4 tomatoes, skinned, deseeded
  and chopped
25 g (1 oz) (2 tablespoons) tomato
  concentrate (paste)
1 sprig mint leaves
pinch oregano or basil
salt and pepper

1 Peel the aubergines (eggplants) and cut slantwise in 1 cm
(½ in) slices. Slice the courgettes
(zucchini) slantwise. Put the
aubergine (eggplant) and
courgette (zucchini) slices on a
dish or board, sprinkle with salt
and let them stand for 30 minutes.

2 Rinse, drain and dry the slices.
Dredge in the seasoned flour.
Heat the deep fryer to 190°C, 375°F
and fry the aubergine (eggplant)
and courgette (zucchini) slices for
1 minute.

3 Drain and dry the fried slices
and place in a casserole dish.

4 In a sauté pan, heat the oil. Fry
the onion gently for 2 minutes.
Add the garlic and green pepper,
and fry for 2 minutes, stirring frequently.

5 Preheat the oven to 180°C,
350°F, gas 4.

6 Add the chopped tomatoes,
tomato concentrate (paste), mint,
oregano or basil, and a pinch of
salt and pepper to taste. Cover
and simmer gently for 10 minutes.

7 Pour this mixture over the
aubergines (eggplants) and
courgettes (zucchini) in the cas-

serole dish. Mix them together
lightly and bake in the oven for
20-30 minutes. Serve hot or cold.

Serves 6

Aubergine (Eggplant) and Mushroom Quiche

1 large aubergine (eggplant),
  about 275 g (10 oz)
175 g (6 oz) frozen shortcrust
  pastry, thawed
2 eggs
300 ml (½ pint) (1¼ cups) milk
75 g (3 oz) (¾ cup) grated cheese
salt and pepper
100 g (¼ lb) small mushrooms
  (or 2 tomatoes, sliced)

1 Preheat the oven to 200°C,
400°F, gas 6.

2 Bake the aubergine (eggplant)
in its skin for 20 minutes.

3 Meanwhile roll out the pastry
and use it to line an 18 cm (7 in) flan
case. Cover pastry with foil or
greaseproof (waxed) paper, scatter in dried beans or bread crusts
to weight the pastry down, and
bake in the same oven for 15
minutes. Remove the paper and
beans or crusts. Reduce the
oven temperature to 180°C,
350°F, gas 4.

4 Scoop the pulp out of the
baked aubergine (eggplant) skin,
crush or liquidize to a purée, and
spoon into the pastry shell.

5 Beat the eggs lightly and mix
in the milk. Add the grated
cheese, salt and pepper. Pour the
mixture into the pastry shell.
Arrange the mushrooms (or
tomatoes) on top.

6 Bake for 30 minutes, until the
top is golden-brown. Serve hot or
cold.

Serves 4

*Aubergine (Eggplant) and
Mushroom Quiche is easy
to prepare and makes a
tasty supper snack or
buffet dish*

Peppers & Tomatoes

Vegetable Casserole with Caraway Scones

50 ml (2 fl oz) (¼ cup) oil
1 onion, chopped
1 green pepper, deseeded and cut in strips
1 red pepper, deseeded and cut in strips
1 carrot, sliced
salt and pepper
150 ml (¼ pint) (⅝ cup) dry white wine
150 ml (¼ pint) (⅝ cup) water
15 ml (1 tablespoon) soya sauce

For the Caraway Scones:
225 g (½ lb) (2¼ cups) plain flour
5 g (1 teaspoon) baking powder
50 g (2 oz) (4 tablespoons) margarine
7 g (¼ oz) (1½ teaspoons) caraway seeds
150 ml (¼ pint) (⅝ cup) milk

1 Heat the oil in a pan, add the onion and cook for 5 minutes until soft. Add the peppers and carrots, stir well and season.

2 Add the wine, water and soya sauce, mix and cook, covered, for 20 minutes or until the carrots are tender. Check the seasoning.

3 Place the mixture in a shallow dish and keep warm.

4 Make the caraway scones: preheat the oven to 200°C, 400°F, gas 6.

5 Sift the flour and baking powder into a bowl, add a pinch of salt and rub in the margarine. Add the caraway seeds and enough milk to make a stiff dough. Roll out the dough to 5 mm (¼ in) thickness and cut into rounds.

6 Place the rounds on a greased baking (cookie) sheet and brush the tops with a little cold milk. Bake in the preheated oven for 15 minutes.

7 Arrange the cooked scones around the vegetable casserole and serve.

Serves 4

Vegetable Casserole with Caraway Scones – an economical casserole with a delicious scone topping

Vegetable Curry

450 g (1 lb) new potatoes, peeled
500 ml (1 pint) (2½ cups) water
50 g (2 oz) (4 tablespoons) margarine
50 ml (2 fl oz) (¼ cup) oil
2 onions, chopped
25 g (1 oz) (2 tablespoons) curry powder
pinch paprika
1 red pepper, deseeded and diced
1 green pepper, deseeded and diced
4 courgettes (zuccini), sliced
4 tomatoes, quartered
1 clove garlic, crushed
5 g (1 tablespoon) desiccated coconut
15 g (½ oz) (2 tablespoons) flour
1 chicken stock cube
15 g (½ oz) (1 tablespoon) tomato concentrate (paste)
50 g (2 oz) (⅓ cup) sultanas
salt and pepper

1 Put the potatoes and water in a pan, add a little salt, and boil for 20 minutes. Strain the liquid into a bowl and reserve.

2 Heat the margarine and oil together in a pan, add the onion and cook for 5 minutes until brown.

3 Add the curry powder and paprika and cook for 2 minutes. Add the peppers, courgettes (zucchini), tomatoes, garlic coconut, flour, stock cube, tomato concentrate (paste) and sultanas and cook gently for 10 minutes. Add the potatoes and cook for a further 10 minutes to heat the potatoes through. Check the seasoning and serve the curry with boiled rice and salted peanuts.

Serves 6

Stuffed Peppers with Pine Kernels

75 ml (5 tablespoons) oil
2 onions, chopped

Vegetable Curry is a delicious mixture of tomatoes, peppers, potatoes and courgettes (zucchini) in a curry sauce

2 tomatoes, skinned, deseeded and chopped
150 g (5 oz) (⅔ cup) long grain rice
5 g (1 tablespoon) chopped parsley
15 g (½ oz) (1 tablespoon) raisins
15 g (½ oz) (1 tablespoon) pine kernels
¾ litre (1¼ pints) (3 cups) boiling water
salt and pepper
4 large green or red peppers
15 g (½ oz) (3 tablespoons) dried white breadcrumbs

1 Heat 45 ml (3 tablespoons) of the oil in a saucepan. Fry the onions until softened. Add the tomato pulp and leave to cook over a low heat.

2 Add the rice, parsley, raisins and pine kernels to the tomato mixture and stir well. Cook, stirring, for 2 minutes. Pour in the boiling water and add salt and pepper to taste. Cover the saucepan and simmer for 15 minutes over a low heat. All the water should be absorbed.

3 Preheat the oven to 220°C, 425°F, gas 7.

4 Wash and dry the peppers. Cut out a little lid at the stalk end. Remove the white pith and seeds through the hole. Salt and pepper the insides.

5 Fill the peppers with the rice mixture. Place them in a baking dish. Replace the lids. Sprinkle the peppers with breadcrumbs and then with the rest of the oil. Put the dish in the oven and cook for 15 minutes. Serve hot or cold.

Serves 4

French Beans Old Style

50 g (2 oz) (4 tablespoons) butter
100 g (¼ lb) unsmoked rashers
  (slices) bacon, cut into strips
12 button (pearl) onions, peeled
12 young carrots, peeled
1 kg (2 lb) French beans, washed
600 ml (1 pint) (2½ cups) water
1 bouquet garni
salt and pepper
pinch sugar
1 chicken stock cube
50 ml (2 fl oz) (¼ cup) single (light)
  cream

1 Heat the butter in a pan and sauté the bacon for 2 minutes. Add the onions and lightly brown them. Add the carrots and simmer for 3 minutes.

2 Add the French beans and cover with the water. Bring to the boil and crumble in a stock cube. Add the bouquet garni, salt, pepper and sugar. Cook for 20 minutes until the vegetables are tender and the liquid has almost evaporated. Remove the bouquet garni.

3 Stir in the cream, check the seasoning and serve.

Serves 4

Tip: If you boil the French beans separately in salted water and add them to the other ingredients at the last minute, they will retain their green colouring. However, although this method improves the appearance of the dish there may be a loss of flavour in the beans.

French Bean Fritters

1 kg (2 lb) French beans
50 g (2 oz) (good ½ cup) seasoned
  flour
2 eggs, beaten
oil for deep frying
pinch salt

1 Top, tail and wash the beans. Boil in salted water for 12 minutes and drain.

2 Dredge the beans in seasoned flour and then dip in beaten egg.

3 Heat the deep fat fryer to 190°C, 375°F. Fry the beans until golden-brown.

4 Drain on absorbent paper, sprinkle with salt and serve.

Serves 6

French Beans with Ham, Mushrooms and Tomatoes

1 kg (2 lb) French beans
50 g (2 oz) (4 tablespoons) butter
100 g (¼ lb) ham, cut into strips
100 g (¼ lb) (1¼ cups) mushrooms,
  sliced
4 tomatoes, skinned, deseeded
  and chopped
salt and pepper
pinch garlic salt

1 Top and tail and wash the beans. Boil them in salted water for 20 minutes and drain.

2 Heat the butter in a sauté pan. Sauté the ham and mushrooms for 5 minutes. Add the beans and tomatoes, salt, pepper and garlic salt.

3 Simmer for 6 minutes, stirring occasionally and then serve.

Serves 6

Peas Westminster

2 mint leaves
25 g (1 oz) (2 tablespoons) brown
  sugar
450 g (1 lb) (4 cups) peas
50 g (2 oz) (4 tablespoons) butter
salt and pepper

1 Chop the mint leaves and mix

them with the brown sugar.

2 Add the peas to boiling salted water and parboil for 5 minutes. Refresh in cold water. Drain.

3 Heat the butter in a pan, add the peas, chopped mint and seasoning and toss for a few minutes until heated through. Serve.

Serves 4

Petits Pois à la Sevigné

50 g (2 oz) (4 tablespoons) butter
150 g (5 oz) (1¼ cups) button (pearl)
  onions
150 g (5 oz) (2½ cups) button
  mushrooms
450 g (1 lb) (4 cups) small peas
salt and pepper
pinch caraway seeds
15 g (½ oz) (1½ teaspoons) sugar
100 ml (4 fl oz) (½ cup) dry white
  wine
50 ml (2 fl oz) (¼ cup) single (light)
  cream

1 Heat the butter in a pan, add the onions and cook, covered, for 5 minutes without browning. Add the mushrooms and cook for 1 minute more.

2 Add the peas to boiling salted water and parboil for 5 minutes. Drain and add to the onions. Season and add the caraway seeds, sugar and wine. Boil gently for 8 minutes, then stir in the cream. Boil for 4 minutes. Serve, decorated with fried croutons.

Serves 4

Peas Bonne Femme

100 g (¼ lb) (½ cup) button (pearl)
  onions
450 g (1 lb) (4 cups) peas
100 g (¼ lb) lean rashers (slices)

bacon, cut into thin strips
300 ml (½ pint) (1¼ cups) water
1 chicken stock cube
1 bouquet garni
salt and pepper
25 g (1 oz) (2 tablespoons) butter
25 g (1 oz) (4 tablespoons) flour

1 Parboil the button (pearl) onions for 5 minutes and drain.

2 Place the peas, onions and bacon in a pan, cover with water and sprinkle in the stock cube. Add the bouquet garni, season with salt and pepper and cook for 20 minutes with the lid on.

3 Cream together the butter and flour and add to the peas, a little at a time. Stir over a low heat until the sauce thickens.

Remove the bouquet garni and serve.

Serves 6

Petits Pois à la Française

450 g (1 lb) (4 cups) small peas
225 g (½ lb) (2 cups) button (pearl) onions, peeled
50 g (2 oz) (½ cup) shredded lettuce leaves
salt and pepper
15 g (½ oz) (1½ teaspoons) sugar
300 ml (½ pint) (1¼ cups) water or stock

French Beans Old Style – beans, French onions, baby carrots and bacon served in a creamy sauce

15 g (½ oz) (2 tablespoons) flour
25 g (1oz) (2 tablespoons) butter

1 Place the peas in a pan, add the onions, lettuce, salt, pepper and sugar. Add the water or stock and cook gently for 10-15 minutes. Strain, reserving the liquid. Keep the peas warm.

2 Pour the liquid into a pan. Blend the flour and butter together and add this mixture to the liquid. Cook until thickened and add to the peas. Mix well and serve.

Serves 4

Cabbage & Spinach

Bubble and Squeak (Colcannon)

½ medium cabbage
40 g (1½ oz) (3 tablespoons) butter
  or bacon fat
1 small onion, finely chopped
leftover mashed potato
  equal to the amount of
  cabbage

1 Bring a saucepan of water to the boil.

2 Remove the core and any damaged leaves from the cabbage. Shred the cabbage.

3 Put the cabbage into the water and cook for 6-7 minutes. Drain well.

4 Heat the butter or bacon fat in a large frying pan (skillet). Fry the onion gently until softened. Add the cabbage and stir over a low heat for 2 minutes.

5 Fold in the mashed potato until it is completely mixed with the cabbage. Press the mixture lightly into the frying pan (skillet) to form a large pancake (crêpe).

6 Cook for 5 minutes or until the underside is lightly browned. Turn and brown on the other side for 5 minutes. Serve very hot.

Serves 4

Tip: The easiest way to turn Bubble and Squeak is to put a plate over it and invert the pan and the plate together so it falls out onto the plate with the browned side uppermost. Then slide it back into the pan.

This is an excellent way of using up leftover cooked cabbage and mashed potatoes.

Spring Green Cabbage and Celery Royal

900 g (2 lb) spring green cabbage
50 g (2 oz) (4 tablespoons) butter
4 celery sticks, sliced
salt and pepper
pinch nutmeg
100 g (¼ lb) (⅔ cup) salted peanuts

1 Discard the core of the cabbage and slice the leaves. Boil the cabbage in salted water for 10 minutes. Drain.

2 Heat the butter in a pan, add the cabbage and celery and cook for 5 minutes. Season with salt, pepper and nutmeg. Serve sprinkled with the salted peanuts.

Serves 4

Tip: To make this into a main dish, add 100 g (¼ lb) (⅔ cup) ham, cut in strips, to the cooked cabbage and cook for a few minutes until the ham is heated through.

Spinach with Walnuts and Anchovies

900 g (2 lb) frozen leaf spinach,
  thawed
4 canned anchovy fillets,
  drained
100 g (¼ lb) (½ cup) butter
100 g (¼ lb) (1 cup) shelled walnuts
salt and pepper
pinch mace
50 g (2 oz) (⅛ cup) grated
  Parmesan cheese

1 Squeeze any moisture from the spinach and chop. Chop the anchovy fillets.

2 Heat the butter in a pan, add the spinach and cook, covered, for 10 minutes. Add the walnuts. Season with salt, pepper and mace and simmer for a further 5 minutes.

3 Transfer the mixture to a shallow dish, sprinkle with the cheese

and brown under the grill (broiler) for 3-4 minutes.

Serves 4

Tip: Adding nuts to vegetables increases the protein content of the dish. Any nuts can be used such as pecan nuts, peanuts, almonds and hazel nuts.

Sprouts and Swede with Chestnuts

450 g (1 lb) swede, peeled and cut
  in cubes
450 g (1 lb) (6 cups) brussels
  sprouts, trimmed
350 g (¾ lb) (3 cups) chestnuts,
  canned or fresh and skinned
100 g (¼ lb) (½ cup) butter
1 onion, chopped
1 small red pepper, deseeded and
  chopped
2 sticks celery, diced
salt and pepper
pinch grated nutmeg

1 Boil the swede, sprouts, and chestnuts separately in salted water for 5 minutes, 8 minutes and 10 minutes respectively. Drain.

2 Heat the butter in a pan, add the onion and cook for 4 minutes without browning. Add the swede, sprouts, chestnuts, pepper and celery, cover and simmer gently for 8 minutes. Season with salt, pepper and nutmeg and serve.

Serves 6

Tip: To give the sprouts a good colour, refresh them in iced water after they have been boiled and drained.

Cabbage is not the boring vegetable which many people imagine it to be. It can, in fact, be used in a wide range of delicious, easily prepared dishes. Featured opposite are Spicy Red Cabbage with Sausages, Stuffed Cabbage Leaves and Cabbage Coleslaw with Scotch Eggs

Stuffed Cabbage Provençale

1 kg (2 lb) cabbage
25 g (1 oz) ($\frac{1}{2}$ cup) fresh
  breadcrumbs
$\frac{1}{4}$ litre (8 fl oz) (1 cup) milk
225 g ($\frac{1}{2}$ lb) salt pork, blanched
  and finely chopped
100 g ($\frac{1}{4}$ lb) lean belly pork, finely
  chopped
100 g ($\frac{1}{4}$ lb) lean veal, finely
  chopped
2 medium onions, chopped
2 cloves garlic, peeled and
  crushed
2 sprigs parsley, chopped
30 ml (2 tablespoons) oil
1 egg yolk
25 g (1 oz) (2 tablespoons) tomato
  concentrate (paste)
25 g (1 oz) (2 tablespoons) butter

For the Tomato Sauce:
30 ml (2 tablespoons) oil
675 g (1$\frac{1}{2}$ lb) tomatoes, skinned,
  deseeded and chopped
1 onion, chopped
2 cloves garlic, peeled and
  crushed
1 carrot, sliced
pinch dried thyme
1 bay leaf, imported
5 g (1 tablespoon) chopped
  parsley
salt and pepper

1 Remove the outer cabbage leaves and cut into wide strips. Keep the heart intact.

2 Add the cabbage strips to a pan of boiling water and simmer for 10 minutes. Drain and dry.

3 Prepare the sauce. Heat the oil and add the tomatoes, onion, garlic, carrot, thyme, bay leaf and parsley. Season and cook gently, stirring occasionally, for 5 minutes. Increase the heat and cook until the liquid has evaporated.

4 Strain and set aside.

5 Soak the breadcrumbs in the milk. Finely chop the cabbage heart and mix with the salt pork, belly pork, veal, onions, garlic and parsley and season to taste.

6 Heat the oil in a frying pan. Fry the mixture for a few minutes, remove from the heat.

7 Add the egg yolk and the tomato concentrate (paste) and mix well.

8 Divide the stuffing between the cabbage strips and roll up to make small parcels. Tie with string.

9 Heat the butter in a pan and fry the cabbage parcels until golden-brown.

10 Coat with the tomato sauce, cover and simmer for 20 minutes.

Stuffed Cabbage Provençale – cabbage parcels with a meaty stuffing served in a piquant, tomato sauce

11 Arrange on a serving dish.

Serves 4

Cabbage and Bacon Hotpot

1 kg (2 lb) unsmoked gammon
  joint
450 g (1 lb) lean, salted belly pork
1$\frac{1}{2}$ litres (2$\frac{1}{2}$ pints) (6 cups) water
1 kg (2 lb) cabbage, washed and
  quartered
4 celery sticks, halved
4 leeks, cleaned and halved
3 onions, peeled and studded
  with cloves
4 carrots, peeled and quartered
4 small turnips, quartered
1 bouquet garni
3 cloves garlic, peeled and
  crushed
salt and pepper
2 beef stock cubes
450 g ($\frac{1}{2}$ lb) beef sausages

1 Soak the gammon and belly pork in water overnight and drain.

2 Cover the meat with the water and bring to the boil, then simmer for 1$\frac{1}{2}$ hours, removing the surface scum.

3 Add the cabbage, celery, leeks, onions, carrots, turnips, bouquet garni and garlic. Season and crumble in the stock cubes. Bring to the boil, then simmer for 20 minutes until tender.

4 Meanwhile, grill (broil) the beef sausages for 20 minutes, slice thickly and keep warm.

5 Add the cabbage to the hotpot and cook for a further 15 minutes. Strain off the liquid and place the vegetables on a serving dish.

6 Remove the cooked meat and cut into thick slices. Arrange the meat and sausages on top of the vegetables and serve.

Serves 8

Cabbage and Bacon Hotpot is a hearty meal of vegetables, gammon and sausages for all the family

Cauliflower & Broccoli

Broccoli with Red Pepper

1 kg (2 lb) broccoli
2 sticks celery
50 g (2 oz) (¼ cup) butter
1 small red pepper, deseeded and
  chopped
30 ml (2 tablespoons) lemon juice
salt and black pepper

1 Wash and trim the broccoli, discarding any slightly wilted leaves. Drain. Bring a pan of salted water to the boil. Put in the broccoli and simmer for 10-15 minutes or until tender.

2 Meanwhile, wash, drain and chop the celery. Melt the butter in a small pan. Cook for 1 minute.

3 Add the chopped pepper to the celery with the lemon juice, salt and pepper.

4 Drain the broccoli very well. Put into a heated serving dish. Pour the contents of the small pan over the broccoli and serve.

Serves 4

Broccoli Siciliana

450 g (1 lb) broccoli
1 onion, chopped
50 ml (2 fl oz) (¼ cup) oil
2 anchovy fillets, diced
150 ml (¼ pint) (⅝ cup) white wine
salt and pepper
4 black olives, stoned (pitted)

1 Preheat the oven to 180°C, 350°F, gas 4. Wash the broccoli and trim surplus stalks.

2 Boil the broccoli in salted water for 10 minutes, then drain. Place in a casserole.

3 Gently fry the onion in the oil without browning and when it is tender, add the anchovies and cook for a further 2 minutes.

4 Pour the onion mixture over the broccoli. Cover with white wine and season to taste.

5 Bake, with the lid on, for 20 minutes.

6 Garnish with the olives.

Serves 4

Cauliflower Cheese with Potatoes

1 small cauliflower
4 large potatoes, peeled and
  sliced
75 g (3 oz) (6 tablespoons) butter
40 g (1½ oz) (6 tablespoons) flour
350 ml (12 fl oz) (1½ cups) milk
pinch grated nutmeg
salt and pepper
100 g (¼ lb) (1 cup) grated cheese

1 Bring a pan of salted water to the boil.

2 Clean the cauliflower, break it into small florets and wash them. Put the potatoes into the boiling water. Cook for 10 minutes, then add the cauliflower. Continue to cook until the cauliflower is just tender but still firm.

3 Meanwhile, make a white sauce with 40 g (1½ oz) (3 tablespoons) of the butter, the flour, milk, a pinch of nutmeg and salt and pepper to taste. Add half the cheese and stir well until it is melted. Keep hot.

4 Drain the potatoes and cauliflower. Keep hot.

5 Use half of the remaining butter to grease a flameproof dish. Heat the grill (broiler).

6 Spread the drained potatoes and cauliflower evenly over the buttered dish and cover with the cheese sauce.

7 Sprinkle the remaining grated cheese over the top. Cut the rest of the butter into small pieces and dot over the top. Put the dish under the grill (broiler) and brown.

Serves 4-5

Hungarian Style Cauliflower

1 medium cauliflower

For the Sauce:
50 ml (2 fl oz) (¼ cup) oil
1 medium onion, sliced
10 g (1 tablespoon) paprika
450 g (1 lb) boiled salted beef, cut
  into strips
25 g (1 oz) (2 tablespoons) tomato
  concentrate (paste)
4 tomatoes, skinned, deseeded
  and chopped
1 red pepper, deseeded and cut
  into strips
15 g (½ oz) (1½ tablespoons)
  cornflour (cornstarch)
100 ml (4 fl oz) (½ cup) sour cream
salt and pepper
5 g (1 tablespoon) chopped
  parsley

1 Remove the leaves, wash the cauliflower and boil for 20 minutes in just enough salted water to cover. Reserve ½ pint of the cauliflower water. Keep the cauliflower hot.

2 Meanwhile, heat the oil and fry the onion gently without browning. Add the paprika, the boiled salted beef, the tomato concentrate (paste), the tomatoes and red pepper strips and cook for 4 minutes. Stir in the reserved cauliflower stock and boil for 8 minutes. Mix the cornflour (cornstarch) with the cream and stir into the sauce and boil for 3 minutes until it thickens. Season.

3 Sprinkle the cauliflower with chopped parsley and serve the sauce separately.

Serves 4

*Hungarian Style Cauliflower –
Cauliflower served with strips of
red pepper and beef in a paprika
flavoured sauce*

Stem Vegetables

Hungarian Asparagus with Yogurt

1 kg (2 lb) (about 28 spears) asparagus
100 g (¼ lb) (1 cup) very dry bread
75 g (3 oz) (6 tablespoons) butter
2 cartons plain yogurt
100 ml (4 fl oz) (½ cup) single (light) cream
5 g (1 teaspoon) paprika
salt and pepper

1 Bring a pan of salted water to the boil.

2 Peel the asparagus and tie in bundles. Plunge them in the boiling water, tips uppermost, and simmer for 20 minutes.

3 In the meantime, cut off and discard the crust of the dry bread and make into very fine crumbs in a blender or with a rolling pin.

4 Melt the butter in a sauté pan. When it begins to brown, add the breadcrumbs and cook till golden brown, stirring with a wooden spoon.

5 Preheat the oven to 220°C, 425°F, gas 7.

6 Sprinkle about half the breadcrumbs in the bottom of an ovenproof dish.

7 Drain the bundles of asparagus, untie the strings and arrange in the dish. Beat the yogurt, the cream and the paprika together and salt lightly but season liberally with pepper. Pour over the asparagus and cover with the rest of the breadcrumbs.

8 Brown in the oven for 10-12 minutes.

9 Remove from the oven and serve very hot in the same dish.

Serves 4

Asparagus with Cheese and Ham Sauce

1½ kg (3 lb) very tender asparagus spears
6 eggs
50 g (2 oz) (½ cup) Gruyère cheese, grated
20 g (¾ oz) (1½ tablespoons) butter

Hungarian Asparagus with Yogurt – the asparagus spears are baked in yogurt, topped with breadcrumbs and seasoned with paprika

For the Sauce:
3 slices cooked ham
50 g (2 oz) (¼ cup) butter
50 g (2 oz) (½ cup) flour
¼ litre (8 fl oz) (1 cup) milk
60 ml (2 fl oz) (4 tablespoons) single (light) cream
salt and pepper
pinch grated nutmeg

1 Bring a saucepan of salted water to the boil.

2 Scrape the asparagus spears, or peel them if necessary. Trim them all to the same length and tie into several bundles to make it easier to remove them from the water. Put them into the boiling water, keeping the tips above the water level, cook for 10-15 minutes or until tender.

3 Meanwhile, hard-boil (hardcook) the eggs. Drain the eggs and cool in cold water. Remove the shells and slice the eggs.

4 Chop the ham for the sauce roughly.

5 Make a white sauce with the butter, flour, milk and ¼ litre (8 fl oz) (1 cup) of the cooking liquid from the asparagus.

6 Stir in the cream and season with salt, pepper and a pinch of grated nutmeg.

7 Mix in the chopped ham.

8 Spread a few spoonfuls of the sauce on the bottom of a rectangular or oval ovenproof dish.

9 Preheat the oven to 220°C, 425°F, gas 7.

10 Drain the asparagus and untie the strings. Arrange a layer of asparagus in the ovenproof dish. Cover with slices of egg and then with a few spoonfuls of sauce. Repeat until all the ingredients are used up.

11 Sprinkle the top of the dish with the grated Gruyère cheese.

12 Melt the 20 g (¾ oz) (1½ tablespoons) butter and pour over the cheese. Cook in the oven until the cheese is beginning to brown (about 10 minutes).

13 Serve very hot in the same dish.

Serves 6

Asparagus au Gratin

1 kg (2 lb) thick asparagus spears
4 tomatoes
50 g (2 oz) (½ cup) grated cheese
5 g (1 tablespoon) chopped
  parsley
salt and pepper
50 g (2 oz) (4 tablespoons) butter

1 Wash the asparagus. Trim any tough parts from the thick end of the stalks, and scrape the stems lightly with a potato peeler. Tie in bundles of about 8 stalks, and boil for 15 minutes in salted water.

2 Preheat the oven to 200°C, 400°F, gas 6.

3 Drain the asparagus and arrange the spears in rows in a lightly greased, ovenproof dish.

4 Slice the tomatoes, and lay the slices in overlapping rows between the asparagus heads. Sprinkle with the grated cheese and chopped parsley. Season with the salt and pepper, and bake in the oven for 10 minutes. Melt the butter and pour over the dish before serving.

Serves 4

Tip: The inedible, tough ends of asparagus stalks, together with the cooking water, can be used to make a delicious soup. Just blend with an equal quantity of white sauce and a little chopped ham. Liquidize the mixture to a purée and season to taste.

Asparagus au Gratin – the asparagus is baked in the oven with sliced tomatoes and grated cheese

Braised Onions with Sultanas (Raisins)

½ kg (1 lb) small onions, all about the same size
300 ml (½ pint) (1¼ cups) water
225 ml (8 fl oz) (1 cup) white wine vinegar
45 ml (3 tablespoons) olive oil
4 tomatoes, skinned
salt and freshly ground (milled) pepper

50 g (2 oz) (⅓ cup) sultanas (raisins)
1 bouquet garni
2 pinches sugar

1 Peel the onions, without cutting off the root ends. Put the onions into a pan with the water and vinegar. Stir in the olive oil. Bring to the boil and simmer gently.

Braised Onions with Sultanas (Raisins) – the onions are braised in a tangy tomato and vinegar sauce

2 Slice the tomatoes thinly. Add to the onions with a pinch of salt and pepper.

3 Add the sultanas (raisins), bouquet garni and sugar.

4 Return to the boil. Reduce the heat. Cover and cook slowly for about 30 minutes, stirring occasionally.

5 Remove from the heat and leave to cool. Chill for at least 2 hours.

6 Before serving, remove the bouquet garni.

Serves 4

Braised Onions in Vermouth

60 very small onions
juice 4 lemons
50 ml (2 fl oz) (¼ cup) dry vermouth
30 ml (2 tablespoons) olive oil
25 g (1 oz) (2 tablespoons) tomato concentrate (paste)
30 coriander seeds
1 g (½ teaspoon) fennel seeds
1 g (½ teaspoon) dried (powdered) rosemary
pinch sugar
salt and pepper

1 Peel the onions, without cutting off the root ends.

2 Put the lemon juice into a saucepan with the vermouth, olive oil and tomato concentrate (paste). Stir well.

3 Bring the vermouth mixture to the boil. Add the coriander seeds, fennel, rosemary, sugar and season with salt and pepper.

4 Reduce the heat and cook for a further 3 minutes. Add the onions, cover and simmer for about 25 minutes or until very tender.

5 Arrange the onions in a serving dish. Pour over a little of the liquid in which they were cooked.

6 Leave to cool completely, then chill in the refrigerator. Serve very cold.

Serves 6

Stuffed Onions

6 large Spanish onions
**225 g (½ lb) (1 cup) pork
  sausagemeat**
1 egg
50 ml (2 fl oz) (¼ cup) milk
**5 g (1 tablespoon) chopped
  parsley**
salt and pepper
50 g (2 oz) (1 cup) breadcrumbs
100 ml (4 fl oz) (½ cup) oil

1 Peel the onions. Cut off one third at their tips ends, leaving the two thirds of the stem end. Boil them in salted water for 15 minutes, then drain.

2 Preheat the oven to 180°C, 350°F, gas 4.

3 Squeeze out the centre of each onion, leaving the outer layers to form a case. Chop the squeezed-out onion, put it in a bowl and blend well with the sausagemeat, egg, milk and parsley.

4 Fill each onion case with the sausagemeat mixture. Place the onions in a shallow dish, sprinkle with breadcrumbs and pour a little oil over each.

5 Bake in the oven for 45 minutes. Serve with a tomato sauce.

Serves 6

Tip: Sweet and Sour Onions make an excellent accompaniment to boiled beef or gammon. Cook peeled button (pearl) onions in a mixture of water, vinegar and sugar in the proportions of 2:1:1,

Onions in Cream Sauce

sea salt
18 medium onions
75 g (3 oz) (6 tablespoons) butter
25 g (1 oz) (1 tablespoon) sugar
**100 ml (4 fl oz) (½ cup) dry white
  wine**
**200 ml (7 fl oz) (⅞ cup) double
  (heavy) cream**

**salt and freshly ground (milled)
  pepper**
pinch ground (powdered) ginger
few sprigs chervil, chopped

1 Bring a large pan of water to the boil. Add a handful of sea salt.

2 Peel the onions, without cutting off the root end. Drop them into the boiling water and simmer until they begin to soften. Drain.

3 Melt the butter in a heavy-based saucepan. Add the onions. Sprinkle them with the sugar and let them caramelize, turning gently with a wooden spoon without breaking them.

4 When the onions are well and evenly browned, pour them into a heated serving dish and keep hot.

Stuffed Onions are filled with sausagemeat and parsley, topped with breadcrumbs and baked until crispy

5 Pour the wine into the saucepan. Stir quickly to mix with the caramelized juices. Stir in the cream and let the sauce thicken over a low heat, stirring constantly.

6 Season to taste with salt and pepper and the ground (powdered) ginger. Pour this sauce over the onions.

7 Sprinkle the onions with the chopped chervil and serve very hot.

Serves 6

Leeks in Tomato Sauce

900 g (2 lb) small leeks, washed
  and trimmed
225 g (½ lb) sliced carrots
300 ml (½ pint) (1¼ cups) water
salt

For the Sauce:
50 ml (2 fl oz) (¼ cup) oil
225 g (½ lb) (1 cup) chopped onions
50 g (2 oz) (4 tablespoons) tomato
  concentrate (paste)
15 g (½ oz) (1½ tablespoons)
  arrowroot
150 ml (¼ pint) (⅝ cup) water
salt and pepper
pinch sugar
pinch grated nutmeg
pinch dried basil or oregano

1 Boil the leeks and carrots in
the water, adding salt to taste, for
15 minutes. Drain, keep warm and
reserve cooking liquor.

2 To make the sauce: heat the
oil in a frying pan (skillet) and
sauté the chopped onions until
they are soft but not brown (about
10 minutes).

3 Add the tomato concentrate
(paste) and the liquor in which the
leeks were cooked. Bring to the
boil and simmer for 10 minutes.

4 Blend the arrowroot with the
water and stir into the sauce.
Cook for a further 5 minutes, then
add seasonings to taste. Pour
over the leeks and carrots and
serve.

Serves 4

Braised Fennel

1 bulb fennel, about 450 g (1 lb),
  trimmed and quartered
1 carrot, chopped
1 onion, chopped
75 g (3 oz) (⅜ cup) bacon fat or
  75 ml (3 fl oz) (⅜ cup) oil
1 chicken stock cube dissolved
  in 450 ml (16 fl oz) (2 cups) water
salt and pepper

For the Sauce:
25 g (1 oz) (2 tablespoons) butter
25 g (1 oz) (4 tablespoons) flour
25 g (1 oz) (2 tablespoons) tomato
  concentrate (paste)

1 Preheat the oven to 180°C,
350°F, gas 4.

2 Parboil the fennel in salted
water for 5 minutes. Refresh.

3 Lightly fry the carrot and
onion in the bacon fat or oil in a
frying pan (skillet). Add the
drained fennel, pour over the
chicken stock and transfer to an
ovenproof dish. Braise, covered,
for 1 hour in the oven.

4 To make the sauce, prepare a
roux with the butter and flour and
stir in the tomato concentrate
(paste). Pour over the braising
liquor (strained). Bring to the boil
and season to taste. Simmer for 15
minutes and pour over the fennel.

Serves 4

---

*Celery and Onion Casserole –
onions, bacon and celery in a
tomato sauce make a delicious
snack or accompaniment for
meat*

Celery and Onion Casserole

50 ml (2 fl oz) (¼ cup) oil
225 g (½ lb) (1⅓ cups) diced bacon
225 g (½ lb) button (pearl) onions,
  peeled
1 head of celery, about 900 g (2 lb),
  trimmed into 10 cm (4 in) pieces
15 g (½ oz) (1 tablespoon) tomato
  concentrate (paste)
½ chicken stock cubes dissolved
  in 450 ml (¾ pint) (2 cups) water
bouquet garni
salt and pepper

1 Preheat the oven to 180°C,
350°F, gas 4.

2 Heat the oil in a frying pan
(skillet), add the bacon and sauté
for 4 minutes. Remove and add
the peeled onions, then the celery.
Cook for 5 minutes.

3 Stir in the tomato concentrate
(paste) and pour over the chicken
stock; add bouquet garni. Season,
replace the bacon, and transfer to
an ovenproof dish. Cover and
cook in the oven for 35 minutes.

Serves 4

Spanish Artichokes

6 large artichokes
100 g (¼ lb) (¾ cup) long grain rice
2 peppers
1 onion
3 tomatoes
275 g (10 oz) smoked streaky
  bacon
2 cloves garlic
bunch parsley
75 ml (5 tablespoons) olive oil
pinch saffron
salt and pepper
½ lemon

1 Trim the artichokes by cutting the stalk and leaves 3 cm (1¼ in) from the base. (Use a serrated knife or scissors for the leaves.) Wash and drain them.

2 Boil salted water in a large saucepan. Put in the artichokes and boil for 15 minutes.

3 Meanwhile, wash the rice until the water is quite clear.

4 Put the rice in twice its volume of boiling salted water, and simmer for 12 minutes.

5 Drain the rice, rinse it under cold running water, then drain once more.

6 Wash and dry the peppers. Split them in two and remove the seeds and white fibre. Dice the flesh. Peel and chop the onion. Peel the tomatoes, cut them in quarters, remove the seeds, then dice them also. Dice the bacon finely. Peel and chop the garlic cloves. Wash, dry and chop the parsley.

7 Heat 30 ml (2 tablespoons) olive oil in a sauté pan. Put in the diced bacon, onion and peppers, and fry.

8 When they are golden-brown, add the diced tomatoes, garlic, parsley, saffron and rice. Season with salt and pepper. Stir for 3 or 4 minutes over a moderate heat.

9 Drain the artichokes, and put them in cold water, then drain and dry. Pull the outside leaves apart and, with a small spoon, remove the hairy centres (chokes) and little leaves. Fill the

artichokes with the rice mixture.

10 Heat the rest of the oil in a sauté pan. Put in the artichokes, cover and leave to finish cooking on a low heat for 40 minutes.

11 Squeeze the half lemon. Heat a serving dish.

12 Half-way through the cooking, add the lemon juice and 45 ml (3 tablespoons) hot water to the artichokes.

13 Arrange the artichokes on a serving dish and serve very hot.

Serves 6

Artichoke Hearts with Herbs

4 globe artichokes
½ lemon
large bunch chives, parsley and
  tarragon, mixed
40 g (1½ oz) (3 tablespoons) butter
salt and pepper

Trimmed and prepared artichoke in boiling water

For the blanching mixture:
2½ lemons
1½ litres (2¾ pints) (3⅜ pints) water
15 g (1 tablespoon) flour

1 Prepare the artichokes to give you 4 hearts, then rub each heart all over with a ½ lemon. Prepare the blanching mixture with the lemons, water and flour and cook the hearts in the boiling liquid for 40 minutes or until tender. Drain them, rinse under cold water and cool.

2 Wash the bunch of herbs, dry and chop finely.

3 Melt the butter in a frying pan (skillet). Cut the hearts into pieces and sauté them until they are golden-brown, then add the chopped herbs. Add a little pepper, mixing with the wooden spoon.

4 Warm a vegetable dish. Put in the artichoke hearts and serve hot.

Serves 4

Artichokes Stuffed with Vegetables

8 medium globe artichokes
1 lemon
4 onions
4 carrots
100 g (¼ lb) streaky bacon
200 g (7 oz) mushrooms
small bunch parsley
15 ml (1 tablespoon) oil
sprig sage
100 ml (4 fl oz) (½ cup) dry white
   wine
pinch of dried thyme
salt and pepper

1 Break off the artichoke stems and rub each base with lemon. Also cut off the large leaves in a circle. Wash the artichokes under running water. Cook in boiling salted water for 25-30 minutes and then drain and keep hot.

2 Meanwhile, peel the onions and chop them roughly. Peel the carrots and cut them into matchsticks. Cut the bacon into small pieces. Prepare the mushrooms and cut into slices. Wash, dry and chop the parsley.

3 Fry the bacon and onions in the oil until the onions brown. Add the mushrooms, carrots, chopped parsley and sage. Let them brown also. Add the white wine and sprinkle in the thyme. Cover and simmer for about 20 minutes. Drain them and keep them hot.

4 Cut off the tops of the artichoke leaves and scoop out the choke. Stuff the artichokes with the bacon and vegetables.

Serves 8

Artichokes Stuffed with Vegetables — the shapely artichokes lend themselves to holding a variety of hot or cold fillings

All about Potatoes

Potatoes are part of the solanum family, which also includes tomatoes, aubergines (egg plants) – and deadly nightshade! Potatoes are an energy food – one of the cheapest we have.

Although low in protein (3.8 per cent), they are rich in carbohydrates, and contain vitamins B and C and iron (however, much of the vitamin C is lost in cooking). They provide an excellent food

for a growing child. If a protein food such as eggs, cheese, fish or meat is included, potatoes make an invaluable aid towards a balanced diet. (Fish and chips, a dish that has overtaken roast beef as ▶

Potato and Leek Soup

the archetypal British meal, is an example: full of nourishing goodness.)

Buy potatoes carefully – do not use them if their skins are green, if they are sprouting or suffering from frost damage. Store potatoes away from light – the cause of the inedible green patches – in an airy but not too cold place. At too low a temperature the potatoes can spoil and possibly freeze which will give them a bitter taste.

It follows that the potatoes you put in your home freezer should either be cooked or partly-cooked and wrapped (chips are best frozen partly-cooked). Commercial freezing is a different process.

Peeled potatoes should be kept in cold water or they will discolour. If peeled and left overnight in cold water, put them in the refrigerator, because they will ferment at room temperature.

Potatoes to be used for baking, for creamed or puréed dishes and for potato pancakes must be floury when they are cooked. King Edwards, Majestics, the Dutch varieties, Idahos and Burbanks are all good examples of floury potatoes which lend themselves to this form of cooking. Eat baked potatoes in their skins – this is where most of the vitamins, minerals and protein lie. Eat them with butter and Cheddar cheese, with blue cheese and soured cream, with freshly chopped chives or dill, and a generous sprinkling of salt and pepper. New potatoes boiled in their skins are delicious eaten hot with butter, salt, fresh mint or parsley – or as a potato salad, with mayonnaise or a vinaigrette dressing. Waxy, close-textured potatoes hold their shape after cooking; choose them to make chips, French fries, and the splendid sauté and gratin dishes you will find in this issue.

Throughout the centuries, botanists have been working towards perfecting the potato and eliminating the diseases to which it is prone. As a result, we now enjoy a wide range of varieties, with subtly different flavours and textures.

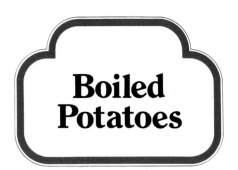

Boiled Potatoes

Potato and Leek Soup

225 g (½ lb) potatoes
225 g (½ lb) leeks
50 g (2 oz) (4 tablespoons) butter
15 ml (1 tablespoon) oil
300 ml (½ pint) (1¼ cups) water
150 ml (¼ pint) (⅝ cup) single (light) cream
150 ml (¼ pint) (⅝ cup) milk
salt and pepper
pinch nutmeg
5 g (1 tablespoon) chopped parsley

1 Peel the potatoes. Slice and cut them into 2 cm (1 in) strips.

2 Wash the leeks and trim off any wilted looking leaves. Cut the leeks across in thin slices.

3 Heat the butter and oil in a saucepan and sweat the leeks for 2 minutes without browning them.

4 Add the potato strips, stir and cook for 2 minutes.

5 Add the water and boil for 12 minutes.

6 Stir in the cream and milk and reheat, then season to taste. Serve in a soup tureen, sprinkled with chopped parsley.

Serves 4

Tip: This soup can be liquidized, chilled and served cold with a sprinkling of chopped basil.

The Fisherman's Potato Hotpot

In many parts of the world the fisherman's diet has often been maintained with a fish and potato hotpot. Potatoes and onions are boiled for 10 minutes

then white fish steaks added and cooked like hotpot, covered with a lid, for another 12 minutes. In just over 20 minutes a potato dish enriched with fish has been cooked.

In Brittany this dish is called a *cotriade*. On occasion, cider, wine or lemon juice is added with herbs to give the dish its characteristic distinction.

Potatoes Smitana

675 g (1½ lb) new potatoes

For the Smitana Sauce:
25 ml (1 fl oz) (⅛ cup) oil
25 g (1 oz) (2 tablespoons) butter
1 medium onion, chopped
300 ml (½ pint) (1¼ cups) single (light) cream
salt and pepper
juice 1 lemon
5 g (1 tablespoon) chopped parsley

1 Peel or scrape the potatoes.

2 Cook them in boiling salted water for 20 minutes.

3 Heat the oil and butter in a small saucepan. Gently sauté the onion for 2 minutes without colouring it.

4 Add the cream and season with salt and pepper. Boil for 5 minutes.

5 Remove from the heat and add the lemon juice.

6 Place the potatoes in a shallow dish, pour the sauce over them and sprinkle with chopped parsley.

Serves 4

Tip: When available, use sour cream for this sauce and omit the lemon juice.

Roast Potatoes au Gratin, Anna Potatoes and Potatoes Savoyarde — some delicious potato dishes

Potato and Onion Cakes

550 g (1¼ lb) potatoes
sea salt
75 g (3 oz) (6 tablespoons) butter
2 medium onions, chopped
salt and pepper
1 egg
mixed spice
50 g (2 oz) (good ½ cup) flour
tomato slices and parsley

1 Scrub the potatoes. Put them into a saucepan, cover with cold water and add a handful of sea salt. Bring to the boil and simmer for 30 minutes.

2 Meanwhile, melt 25 g (1 oz) (2 tablespoons) of the butter in a frying pan (skillet). Add the onions and fry gently until they are soft and brown. Season well with salt and pepper.

3 When the potatoes are cooked, drain and peel them. Pass them through a food mill or sieve (strainer) to make a purée.

4 Put the potato purée into a saucepan. Break the egg into the centre, and stir over a low heat until reheated and well mixed. Season generously with salt and pepper and with mixed spice

5 Carefully stir the onions into the potato purée. Divide into 4 small heaps and flatten each into the shape of a small round. Coat on both sides with the flour.

6 Melt the rest of the butter in a frying pan (skillet). Put the cakes into the pan and fry until browned on both sides.

Potato and Onion Cakes — the potatoes are first mashed, then moulded into flat cakes and shallow-fried

7 Drain the cakes on absorbent paper. Arrange on a heated serving dish garnished with tomato slices and parsley.

Serves 4

Flavourings
To preserve all their flavour, boil and serve potatoes hot in their jackets. Potatoes which are to be sautéed or used in salads should be boiled in their jackets, cooled, drained, peeled while they are warm and left covered in the refrigerator overnight so that they can be shaped without breaking.

The main flavouring for boiled potatoes is fresh butter, added at the last minute so that the heat of the potatoes melts it. Or add a few fresh mint leaves or freshly-chopped parsley 5 minutes before they finish cooking.

Potato Casseroles

Lamb Navarin with New Potatoes

550 g (1¼ lb) stewing lamb
salt and pepper
25 g (1 oz) (2 tablespoons) butter
  or margarine
100 g (¼ lb) (1 cup) diced carrots
100 g (¼ lb) (½ cup) diced onion
25 g (1 oz) (4 tablespoons) flour
15 g (½ oz) (1 tablespoon) tomato
  concentrate (paste)
1 clove garlic
900 ml (1½ pints) (3¾ cups) beef
  stock
1 bouquet garni
450 g (1 lb) new potatoes
5 g (1 tablespoon) chopped
  parsley

1 Preheat the oven to 180°C, 350°F, gas 4. Trim the meat into even-sized pieces and season.

2 Heat the fat in an ovenproof casserole, add the meat and fry for 5 minutes. Add the chopped carrot and onion and cook for a further 3 minutes.

3 Drain off the surplus fat, add the flour and mix. Cook for 5 minutes until browned.

4 Add the tomato concentrate (paste) and garlic and then stir in the stock and seasoning. Add the bouquet garni, bring to the boil, skim, and cover with a lid. Cook in the preheated oven for 1½ hours.

5 Meanwhile, parboil the new potatoes in salted water for 10 minutes.

6 After 1½ hours, remove the casserole from the oven and add the potatoes. Return to the oven and cook for a further ½ hour or until the meat and potatoes are tender.

7 Arrange the meat and vegetables on a warmed serving dish, correct the seasoning of the liquid and pour over. Sprinkle with the chopped parsley.

Serves 4

Lamb Navarin with New Potatoes is a tasty casserole of lamb, carrots and potatoes in a beefy sauce

Look'n Cook Potato and Sauerkraut Hotpot

1 The ingredients: sauerkraut, frankfurters, meat, potatoes, bouquet garni, onions, garlic, wine, fat, peppercorns, juniper berries, carrots, bay leaves, cloves, seasoning **2** Wash the sauerkraut and then dry thoroughly, squeezing between the hands to remove excess moisture **3** Spread out the sauerkraut **4** Melt the goose fat, chicken fat or margarine in a pan and pour over the sauerkraut.

Mix well **5** Transfer half of the sauerkraut to an ovenproof dish and add the carrots and the onions studded with cloves **6** Tie the garlic, peppercorns and juniper berries in a small piece of muslin (cheesecloth) and add the bag to the sauerkraut with the bouquet garni, bay leaves and seasoning **7** Cover with the rest of the sauerkraut **8** Add the gin, if used, and the water and wine

9 Cover with foil and bake the preheated oven for 20 minutes **10** Remove the foil and place the meat on top of the sauerkraut. Bring to the boil, cover and simmer for 1¼ hours **11** Lift out the meat; transfer to the oven to keep warm **12** Add the potatoes, cover again and simmer for 20 minutes or until the potatoes are cooked and the liquid has almost evaporated **13** Add the frankfur-

14

15

16

ters to a pan of boiling water and simmer for 8 minutes to warm through. Drain **14** When the potatoes are cooked, discard the carrots, bouquet garni, onions and muslin (cheesecloth) bag. Pile the sauerkraut on a serving dish **15** Remove the meat from the oven and cut into neat slices **16** Arrange the meat slices round the sauerkraut with the frankfurters and potatoes

Potato and Sauerkraut Hotpot

1 kg (2 lb) canned sauerkraut
100 g (¼ lb) canned goose fat,
  chicken fat or margarine
6 black peppercorns
1 clove garlic, crushed
6 juniper berries or 30 ml
  (2 tablespoons) gin
4 carrots
2 onions, studded with 4 cloves
1 bouquet garni
2 bay leaves, imported
salt and pepper
300 ml (½ pint) (1¼ cups) dry white
  wine
600 ml (1 pint) (2½ cups) water
450 g (1 lb) piece unsmoked
  gammon or bacon
1 knuckle gammon, 675 g (1½ lb)
900 g (2 lb) peeled potatoes
6 frankfurters

1 Preheat the oven to 200°C, 400°F, gas 6. Wash the sauerkraut and then drain, pressing well to remove moisture.

2 Place the dried sauerkraut in a dish. Warm the fat in a pan and mix it with the sauerkraut.

3 Tie the peppercorns, garlic and juniper berries in a small piece of muslin (cheesecloth). Transfer half of the sauerkraut to an ovenproof dish and add the muslin (cheesecloth) bag, carrots, onions, bouquet garni, bay leaves and seasoning. Cover with the rest of the sauerkraut. Pour in the gin, if used, and the wine and water. Cover the dish with foil and bake for 20 minutes.

4 Remove the foil and add the meat. Bring to the boil, cover and simmer for 1¼ hours.

5 Lift out the meat and add the potatoes. Cover again and cook for 20 minutes or until they are cooked and the liquid has almost evaporated. Meanwhile, keep the meat warm in the oven.

6 Add the frankfurters to a pan of boiling water and simmer for 8 minutes until warmed through. Drain.

7 Discard the muslin (cheesecloth) bag, carrots, bouquet garni and onions. Place the sauerkraut on a serving dish. Cut the meat into neat slices and arrange them round the pile of sauerkraut with the frankfurters and potatoes.

Serves 6

Tip: To save time, the meat can be cooked beforehand. Simply boil it in water for 1½ hours and then reheat by covering with cold water, bringing it to the boil and simmering for 20 minutes. If too salty, soak the meat in cold water overnight.

Farmhouse Potato and Chicken Casserole

50 g (2 oz) (6 tablespoons)
  cornflour (cornstarch)
salt and pepper
4 chicken joints
50 g (2 oz) (4 tablespoons) butter
  or margarine
25 ml (1 fl oz) (⅛ cup) oil
900 g (2 lb) potatoes, peeled and
  quartered
4 rashers (slices) streaky bacon,
  derinded and cut in strips
50 g (2 oz) (½ cup) mushrooms,
  quartered
6 spring onions (scallions)
150 ml (¼ pint) (⅝ cup) chicken
  stock
5 g (1 tablespoon) chopped chives

1 Preheat the oven to 190°C, 375 °F, gas 5. Season the cornflour (cornstarch) and use it to coat the chicken joints.

2 Heat the fat and oil in a pan, and fry the chicken joints until golden.

3 Remove the chicken from the pan and place in an ovenproof casserole with the potatoes.

4 Add the bacon, mushrooms and onions to the pan and fry until golden. Add to the casserole. Pour the stock into the pan and bring to the boil, stirring. Pour the stock into the casserole. Cover the dish and bake in the preheated oven for

1 hour or until the chicken is tender.

5 Check the seasoning of the sauce and sprinkle the finished dish with the chopped chives.

Serves 4

Old Country Potato Hotpot

450 g (1 lb) potatoes
1 onion
50 g (2 oz) leek, white part only
50 g (2 oz) celery
1 chicken breast
1 rasher (slice) unsmoked bacon,
  derinded
25 g (1 oz) (2 tablespoons) butter
50 ml (2 fl oz) (¼ cup) oil
2 chicken stock cubes
1 litre (1¾ pints) (4½ cups) water
salt and pepper
juice ½ lemon
150 ml (¼ pint) (⅝ cup) single (light)
  cream
5 g (1 tablespoon) chopped
  parsley and chervil

1 Cut the potatoes, onion, leek and celery into thin strips, 5 cm (2 in) by 5 mm (¼ in).

2 Skin the chicken breast and remove the bone. Cut the chicken meat and bacon into strips of the same size.

3 Heat the butter and oil in a pan, add the vegetable and meat strips and cook, covered, for 5 minutes.

4 Crumble the stock cubes into the water and add to the pan. Bring to the boil and simmer for 20 minutes.

5 Add seasoning and lemon juice. Stir in the cream and boil for 2 minutes more. Serve, sprinkled with the chopped herbs.

Serves 4

Farmhouse Potato and Chicken Casserole — an economical family casserole of chicken, potatoes and mushrooms

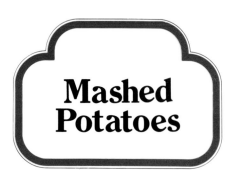

Mashed Potatoes

For perfect mashed potato every time, drain the cooked potatoes thoroughly before mashing them. Return them to the pan and place over a low heat, uncovered, for 3-4 minutes to evaporate the last drops of moisture.

Curried Shepherds Pie

450 g (1 lb) potatoes
salt and pepper
25-50 g (1-2 oz) (2-4 tablespoons) margarine
a little milk
5 g (¼ oz) (¾ tablespoon) cornflour (cornstarch)
150 ml (¼ pint) (⅝ cup) beef stock

40 g (1½ oz) (3 tablespoons) butter or margarine
100 g (¼ lb) (½ cup) onion, finely chopped
450 g (1 lb) (2 cups) minced (ground) cooked lamb or mutton
15 g (½ oz) (1 tablespoon) curry powder

1 Cook the potatoes in boiling salted water until just tender. Mash with a fork or masher, adding margarine and milk to give a smooth consistency. Season to taste.

2 Preheat the oven to 200°C, 400°F, gas 6. To the cornflour (cornstarch) add 60 ml (5 tablespoons) water and stir to give a smooth paste. Bring the stock to the boil, add the cornflour (cornstarch) and continue cooking until thickened.

3 Heat the fat in a pan, add the chopped onion and cook for 5 minutes without colouring. Add the minced (ground) meat and

Curried Shepherds Pie—curried minced lamb with a crisp potato topping is a variation on the traditional Shepherds Pie

seasoning. Stir in the curry powder and add sufficient thickened stock to bind. Bring to the boil and simmer for 10-15 minutes.

4 Transfer the meat to a pie dish and arrange the potato on top. Make swirls on the top of the potato with a fork and place in the preheated oven for 10 minutes to brown.

Serves 4

Tip: Cooked beef can also be used in this dish. When using cooked meat, care must be taken to heat the meat thoroughly.

Coconut Potato Cake

450 g (1 lb) potatoes, unpeeled
3 egg yolks
5 ml (1 teaspoon) lemon juice
15 g (½ oz) (1 tablespoon) butter or margarine
50 ml (2 fl oz) (¼ cup) milk
salt
15 g (½ oz) (1 tablespoon) grated cheese
25 g (1 oz) (5 tablespoons) desiccated coconut

For the Garnish:
slices bacon or sausage
strips red pepper
few stuffed olives

1 Preheat the oven to 180°C, 350°F, gas 4. Boil the potatoes in their skins until cooked. Drain.

2 Beat the egg yolks with the lemon juice. Grease a 20 cm (8 in) pie dish with the fat. Peel the potatoes, mash and mix with the egg yolks, milk and salt. Beat for 1 minute.

3 Turn the potato into the pie dish, level the top and sprinkle with the cheese and coconut. Bake in the oven for 15-20 minutes until browned on top.

4 Turn the cake onto a warm dish and garnish with the meat slices, pepper strips and olives. Cut in slices to serve.

Serves 4

Look'n Cook Duchesse Potatoes

1 Peel and quarter some large potatoes. Place in cold salted water, bring to the boil and cook until just tender. Drain and place in a hot oven to dry **2** Pass the potatoes through a vegetable mill **3** and **4** For every 1 kg (2 lb) potatoes, mix in 50 g (2 oz) (4 tablespoons) butter, 2 egg yolks, salt and pepper and grated nutmeg to taste. If liked, colour some of the potato with tomato concentrate (paste) and a pinch of paprika **5** Spoon the potato into a piping (decorator's) bag fitted with a large star nozzle **6** and **7** Use the duchesse potato mixture to pipe attractive borders round a serving dish or round the edge of scallop shells **8** Alternatively, pipe different shapes, such as swirls, cones and nests, on to a greased baking (cookie) sheet. To make the nest, pipe a flat round for the base and then build up the sides, round and round **9** and **10** For better colour, brush with beaten egg. Place the sheet in the oven to dry out the potato and brown the tops

223

Duchesse Potatoes

900 g (2 lb) floury, old potatoes,
  peeled
2 egg yolks, beaten
50 g (2 oz) ($\frac{1}{4}$ cup) butter
salt and pepper
pinch grated nutmeg
1 egg, beaten

1 Preheat the oven to 200°C,
400°F, gas 6.

2 Boil the potatoes in salted
water. When soft but not mushy,
drain. Return to the pan, and
shake gently over medium heat
to dry thoroughly.

*Duchesse Potatoes with Almonds
— duchesse potato nests filled
with chicken in a sherry sauce
and topped with flaked almonds*

2 Mash, and blend in the egg
yolks and butter. Season and add
a pinch of nutmeg.

3 Pass the potatoes through a
sieve (strainer).

4 Lightly oil a baking tray
(cookie sheet). Fill a piping
(decorator's) bag with the potato
mixture and fit a star-shaped
nozzle. Pipe the mixture onto the
tray (sheet), forming small cones.
Bake in the oven for 15 minutes.

5 Take out and brush the cones
with the beaten egg. Return to the
oven for 4-5 minutes to brown.
Serve immediately.

Serves 6

Tip: Pipe duchesse potatoes in a
variety of different shapes and
sizes. Tiny rosettes, topped with
grated cheese or chopped nuts,
are delicious with cocktails.

Use your favourite vol-au-vent
filling with duchesse potato
nests. Any kind of creamy,
savoury mixture of meat, fish or
vegetables is suitable.

Duchesse Potatoes with Almonds

450 g (1 lb) duchesse potato
  mixture
1 beaten egg
25 g (1 oz) (2 tablespoons) melted
  butter

For the Filling:
75 ml (2$\frac{1}{2}$ fl oz) ($\frac{1}{3}$ cup) medium
  sherry
225 g ($\frac{1}{2}$ lb) (1$\frac{1}{3}$ cups) diced, cooked
  turkey or chicken

300 ml (½ pint) (1¼ cups) white
  sauce
1 egg yolk
50 ml (2 fl oz) (¼ cup) double
  (heavy) cream
salt and pepper
pinch grated nutmeg
50 g (2 oz) (⅜ cup) flaked almonds,
  toasted

1 Preheat the oven at 180°C,
350°F, gas 4.

2 Fill a piping (decorator's) bag
with the duchesse potato mixture
and fit it with a star-shaped
nozzle. Pipe the mixture neatly
onto a greased baking tray
(cookie sheet) to make six nest
shapes.

3 Dry in the oven for 10 minutes,
then brush the potato nests with
the beaten egg. Return to the
oven for 4-5 minutes. Take out
and keep warm.

4 Next make the filling. Pour the
sherry into a saucepan, add the
turkey or chicken and bring to the
boil. Stir in the white sauce and
reduce heat to simmering. Take
off the heat, blend in the egg yolk
and cream and season with salt
and pepper and grated nutmeg.
Return to the heat, stirring all the
time.

5 Fill each potato nest with the
sauce and sprinkle over the
flaked almonds. Brush the potato
with the melted butter and return
to the oven for 4-5 minutes. Serve
immediately.

Serves 6

*Duchesse Potato and Prawn
Scallops — the scallop shells are
filled with prawn and tomato
sauce and surrounded with
piped duchesse potato*

Duchesse Potato and Prawn Scallops

4 scallop shells
225 g (½ lb) duchesse potato
  mixture
1 beaten egg
25 g (1 oz) (2 tablespoons) melted
  butter

For the Filling:
25 ml (1 fl oz) (⅛ cup) oil
25 g (1 oz) (2 tablespoons) butter
1 onion, finely chopped
15 g (½ oz) (1 tablespoon) flour
4 tomatoes, peeled, deseeded and
  chopped
15 g (½ oz) (1 tablespoon) tomato
  concentrate (paste)
150 ml (¼ pint) (⅝ cup) water
½ chicken stock cube
15 ml (1 tablespoon) anchovy
  essence
juice ½ lemon
salt and pepper
225 g (½ lb) (1½ cups) peeled
  prawns

1 Preheat the oven to 180°C,
350°F, gas 4.

2 Using a piping (decorator's)
bag with a star-shaped nozzle,
pipe the edges of the scallop shells
with the duchesse potato mix-

*Duchesse Potatoes can be piped
into decorative pyramids, glazed
with beaten egg and browned in
a hot oven*

ture. Place them on a baking tray
(cookie sheet) and dry in the oven
for 10 minutes. Remove and brush
the potato with the beaten egg.

3 Now make the filling. Heat the
oil and the butter in a frying pan
(skillet), and gently fry the
chopped onion until it is soft
but not brown – about 5 minutes.
Stir in the flour and cook for
2 minutes more.

4 Add the chopped tomatoes
and the tomato concentrate
(paste). Pour over the water and
add the crumbled ½ stock cube.
Bring to the boil, then simmer for
5 minutes.

5 Flavour the sauce with the
anchovy essence, lemon juice and
salt and pepper to taste. Add the
peeled prawns, bring to the boil
again, then cook gently for a
further 5-6 minutes.

6 Increase the heat of the oven to
200°C, 400°F, gas 6.

7 Fill each scallop shell with the
prawn and tomato sauce inside
the border of piped potato. Place
them on the baking tray (cookie
sheet) and bake for 8 minutes,
until the potato is golden-brown.
Take out, brush the potato with
melted butter and serve immediately.

Serves 4

Baked & Jacket Potatoes

Potatoes are delicious, peeled and baked in a sauce in the oven, or baked in their jackets. Always eat the skin – it contains essential minerals and vitamin C. Baking potatoes in their jackets retains all the goodness which can be lost by boiling or frying.

Always wash and scrub the potatoes well and make a cross-shaped incision in each potato before baking. If you prefer your potatoes soft-skinned, wrap each potato in aluminium foil. Baking the potato with a thin, metal skewer inserted through the centre, ensures that the heat is conducted right through the potato.

Potato Feast

Potatoes can make a main meal or an excellent party dish if baked in their jackets and served with a variety of toppings, fillings and sauces. Here are some ideas for you to try out. They are sufficient to stuff or top 10 medium-sized potatoes.

Sour Cream and Chives Topping

5 g (1 tablespoon) chopped chives
150 ml (¼ pint) (⅝ cup) sour cream or plain yogurt
salt and pepper

Potato Feast — serve jacket potatoes as a party dish, with a variety of tasty fillings and toppings

1 Blend together the chives and sour cream. Season with salt and pepper.

2 Top each baked potato with a swirl of sour cream mixture or serve separately.

Bacon and Onion Topping

100 g (¼ lb) rashers (slices) bacon
25 g (1 oz) (2 tablespoons) bacon fat
100 g (¼ lb) (½ cup) onions, chopped

1 Cut the bacon into thin strips.

2 Heat the bacon fat in a frying pan (skillet) and sauté the bacon for 3 minutes. Remove and keep warm.

3 Add the onions to the pan (skillet) and sauté until soft and light brown. Drain off the fat and mix with the bacon.

4 Serve in a separate bowl or as a topping for baked potatoes. Alternatively, you can mix the bacon mixture with scooped out potato pulp and butter and replace inside the potato skin.

Tomato Fondue

30 ml (1 fl oz) (2 tablespoons) oil
1 small onion, chopped
1 clove garlic, peeled and chopped
4 tomatoes, skinned, deseeded and chopped
150 ml (¼ pint) (⅝ cup) mayonnaise
salt and pepper

1 Heat the oil in a frying pan (skillet), add the chopped onions and sauté until soft. Add the garlic and tomatoes and simmer for 4 minutes. Cool and strain.

2 Blend this tomato mixture with the mayonnaise and season. Top each potato with the mixture or serve in a separate dish.

Baked Potatoes au Gratin

4 medium-sized potatoes

For the Filling:
50 g (2 oz) (4 tablespoons) butter
50 g (2 oz) (¼ cup) chopped ham
5 g (1 tablespoon) chopped chives
salt
freshly ground (milled) black pepper
100 g (¼ lb) (1 cup) grated Cheddar cheese
few sprigs parsley

1 Preheat the oven to 200°C, 400°F, gas 6.

2 Wash and scrub the potatoes. Prick the skins and place on a baking tray (cookie sheet). Bake in the oven for about 1 hour.

3 Cut the cooked potatoes lengthways and scoop out the

Baked Potatoes au Gratin are filled with ham and chopped chives and topped with melted Cheddar cheese

pulp. Place the potato pulp in a basin and mix with the butter, chopped ham and chives until it is soft and well blended. Season with salt and freshly ground (milled) pepper.

4 Place the potato mixture back inside the potato skins and sprinkle with the grated cheese.

5 Place under a hot grill (broiler) until the cheese is bubbling and golden-brown. Top each potato with a sprig of parsley.

Serves 4

Tip: If you sprinkle a layer of coarse salt between the potatoes and the baking tray (cookie sheet) it will prevent the potato skins from burning.

Potatoes Gratin Dauphinois

1 kg (2 lb) potatoes
1 clove garlic, peeled and
  crushed
100 g (¼ lb) (½ cup) butter,
  softened
2 eggs
½ litre (1 pint) (2½ cups) milk
200 ml (6 fl oz) (¾ cup) single
  (light) cream
salt and pepper
grated nutmeg
100 g (¼ lb) (1 cup) grated
  Gruyère cheese

1 Preheat the oven to 200°C, 400°F, gas 6.

2 Peel the potatoes, place in a pan of salted water and bring to the boil. Boil for 1 minute, then cool and thinly slice.

3 Rub the garlic around the inside of an ovenproof dish. Use 50 g (2 oz) (¼ cup) butter to grease the dish.

4 Break the eggs into a bowl, add the milk, cream, salt and pepper and nutmeg and beat. Stir in 75 g (3 oz) (¾ cup) of the grated cheese.

5 Cover the bottom of the greased dish with a layer of potato slices. Cover with a little of the cream and cheese mixture. Continue with alternate layers of potato and cheese until they are used up. Sprinkle the top with the remainder of the grated cheese and dot with butter.

6 Bake in the oven for 45 minutes. Cover with foil if it becomes too brown. Serve with roast meat or grilled steak.

Serves 4

Tip: For delicious variations, try adding layers of sautéed, sliced mushrooms and chopped onions. Never use raw potatoes in this dish – very often they will cause the milk to curdle. Parboiling the potatoes first or thickening the milk with cornflour (cornstarch) will prevent this.

228

Jacket Potatoes Stuffed with Prawns

8 medium-sized potatoes
50 g (2 oz) (4 tablespoons) butter
150 ml (¼ pint) (⅝ cup) plain
  yogurt
15 ml (1 tablespoon) tomato
  ketchup
225 g (½ lb) (1½ cups) peeled
  prawns
5 g (1 tablespoon) chopped chives
salt and pepper
5 g (1 tablespoon) paprika

1 Preheat the oven to 200°C, 400°F, gas 6.

2 Wash and scrub the potatoes and bake in the oven for about 1 hour.

3 Make a criss-cross on the top of each potato with a knife.

Jacket Potatoes Stuffed with Prawns make an excellent party dish or supper snack

Remove most of the pulp and mix it in a bowl with the butter, yogurt, tomato ketchup, prawns and chives. Season with salt and pepper.

4 Place the mixture inside the potato skins and warm through in the oven. Sprinkle with paprika and serve.

Serves 4

Tip: A more sophisticated way to serve jacket potatoes is to scoop out the potato pulp and mix with beaten egg, butter and single (light) cream. Sieve or liquidize the mixture to a purée. Fill the potato skin with prawns, mushrooms or chicken in a sauce, and pipe the puréed potato mixture around the edge. Brush with beaten egg and grill (broil) until golden-brown.

Roast Potatoes

Roast Potatoes

900 g (2 lb) potatoes, about 75 g (3 oz) each
100 g (¾ lb) (1½ cups) beef dripping
salt
50 g (2 oz) (¼ cup) butter

1 Preheat the oven to 200°C, 400°F, gas 6.

2 Peel the potatoes and cut each in half lengthways. Soak in a pan of cold, salted water.

3 Place the dripping in a shallow, oven proof dish. Melt the dripping on top of the stove.

4 Dry the potatoes and place them in the dish. Season with salt and roast in the oven for 25 minutes, basting.

5 Drain off the dripping into a jug. Add the butter to the potatoes and roast for 5 minutes.

Serves 4

Honeyed Roast Potatoes

900 g (2 lb) new potatoes
salt
75 ml (3 fl oz) (⅜ cup) oil
75 g (3 oz) (⅓ cup) butter, melted
50 g (2 oz) (¼ cup) honey

1 Preheat the oven to 200°C, 400°F, gas 6.

2 Place the potatoes in a pan of cold, salted water. Bring to the boil, then drain immediately.

3 Place the oil and 25 g (1 oz) (2 tablespoons) of the butter in a shallow, oven-proof dish.

4 Season the potatoes with salt, and place them in the dish. Roast in the oven for 20 minutes.

5 Mix the remaining butter with the honey. Use it to baste the potatoes while they roast.

Serves 4

Traditional Sunday joint with roast potatoes

Roast potatoes must be crisp and golden-brown on the outside, floury inside. Roast separately, or with a joint of meat and always baste during cooking. Large potatoes (about 125 g, 4½ oz) may be browned for a few minutes in beef dripping, then, after the dripping has been poured away, roasted in beef stock and meat glaze for 45 minutes until they are glazed, soft and brown. Other root vegetables such as parsnips, Jerusalem artichokes, carrots and sweet potatoes can be also roasted.

Sautéed Potatoes

Potatoes are excellent sautéed – that is, cooked in a frying pan (skillet) over a high heat with the pan shaken so that the food literally jumps. (*Sauter* means 'to jump' in French.) A mixture of oil and clarified butter makes an ideal cooking medium, and the potatoes may be raw or boiled and sliced. If you use raw potatoes, make sure that they are thoroughly dried on absorbent kitchen paper before they are cooked, and use a frying pan (skillet) with a lid. This speeds up the cooking and allows you to toss them in the fat more easily. When the potatoes are nearly cooked, try adding sliced onions, tomato pulp, chopped garlic or herbs.

Pan Sautéed Potatoes with Chicken and Mushrooms in Sour Cream

25 ml (1 fl oz) (⅛ cup) oil
450 g (1 lb) potatoes, boiled and sliced
salt and pepper

For the Filling:
25 g (1 oz) (⅛ cup) butter
1 onion, chopped
100 g (¼ lb) (1 cup) mushrooms, sliced
225 g (½ lb) (1⅓ cups) diced, cooked chicken
100 ml (4 fl oz) (½ cup) sour cream
25 ml (1 fl oz) (⅛ cup) medium sherry
pinch paprika

1 Heat the oil in a frying pan (skillet). Sauté the potatoes until they are golden brown. Season, remove from the pan and keep hot.

2 In the same pan (skillet), melt the butter and fry the chopped onion gently for 4 minutes. Stir in the mushrooms and diced chicken, and cook for 4 minutes.

3 Pour in the cream and the sherry, bring to the boil, and cook for a further 5 minutes.

4 Surround the mixture with the overlapping sautéed potatoes, sprinkle on the paprika and serve immediately, using the pan as the serving dish.

Serves 4

Pan Sautéed Potato with Chicken and Mushrooms in Sour Cream — the creamy sauce is surrounded by overlapping sautéed potatoes and served straight from the pan

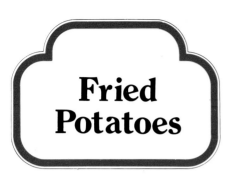

Fried Potatoes

Crispy Pan-fried Potatoes with Bacon

50 ml (2 fl oz) (¼ cup) oil
50 g (2 oz) (4 tablespoons) bacon fat or butter
4 slices (rashers) bacon, cut into strips
1 onion, chopped
50 g (2 oz) (¾ cup) button mushrooms, sliced
450 g (1 lb) cold boiled potatoes, sliced
salt and pepper

1 Heat the oil and fat in a frying pan (skillet) and fry the bacon until crisp (about 2 minutes). Remove from the pan and keep warm.

2 In the same pan, fry the chopped onions and mushrooms for 2-3 minutes. Remove from the pan and keep warm.

3 Add the potatoes to the pan and sauté (with the lid on), turning them several times until they are golden-brown.

4 Return the bacon, mushrooms and onions to the pan and season with the salt and pepper. Heat through. Serve immediately as a snack with sausages or hamburgers.

Serves 4

French Fried Potatoes

6 medium potatoes
deep fat bath
salt

1 Peel the potatoes, slice them lengthwise and then cut into strips. Put into a bowl of iced water for 10 minutes, then drain and dry well on absorbent paper.

2 Heat the fat to 190°C, 375°F.

Put a handful of potato slices into the frying basket (if used) and lower carefully into the fat. Fry for about 8 minutes (the potatoes should not brown at this stage). Drain on absorbent paper.

3 Continue to fry in this way until all the potatoes are partially cooked, then increase the heat to 200°C, 400°F. Add all the potatoes and fry until they are crisp and golden-brown (about 3 minutes).

4 Drain on absorbent paper, sprinkle with salt and serve at once.

Serves 4

Tip: Do not cover the potatoes with absorbent paper or the steam will not be able to escape and the potatoes will lose their crispness.
After the first stage in cooking, the chips may be left for a while and the second frying process carried out just before serving.

Crispy Pan-fried Potatoes with Bacon is a quick and easy-to-prepare meal for all the family

Mushroom Stuffed Potato Pancakes (Crêpes)

450 g (1 lb) (2⅔ cups) potatoes, peeled and grated
2 eggs, beaten
salt and pepper
1 onion, chopped or grated
100 g (¼ lb) (1 cup + 2 tablespoons) flour, sifted
2 g (1 teaspoon) baking powder
75 ml (3 fl oz) (⅜ cup) milk
150 ml (¼ pint) (⅝ cup) oil
1 tomato, quartered

For the Filling:
25 ml (1 fl oz) (⅛ cup) oil
25 g (1 oz) (2 tablespoons) butter
450 g (1 lb) (5 cups) mushrooms, sliced
50 g (2 oz) (1 cup) fresh breadcrumbs
5 g (1 tablespoon) chopped parsley
salt and pepper
50 ml (2 fl oz) (¼ cup) double (heavy) cream

1 Place the grated potatoes in a clean tea towel and gently squeeze out the moisture, then place in a bowl.

2 Blend in the beaten eggs, seasoning and chopped or grated onion. Add the flour and baking powder. Gradually add the milk, beating all the time, to form a thick batter.

3 Heat 30 ml (2 tablespoons) oil in a frying pan (skillet). Drop in 2 or 3 spoonfuls of the mixture. When it is cooked underneath, turn the pancake (crêpe) over and cook the other side. Remove

Mushroom Stuffed Potato Pancakes (Crêpes) are pancakes with a difference — they are made with fried potato, not batter

and keep warm. Repeat until all the mixture is used up (it should make 4 pancakes [crêpes]).

4 Meanwhile, make the filling. Heat the oil and butter in a frying pan (skillet) and shallow-fry the mushrooms for 4 minutes until soft. Mix in the breadcrumbs, chopped parsley and seasoning. Then stir in the cream. Gently heat the filling through.

5 Place some mushroom filling in each pancake (crêpe), fold over and serve. Garnish with tomato quarters.

Serves 4

Look 'n Cook Potato Dauphine

1 Place the potatoes in salted water, bring to the boil and simmer until cooked **2** Sieve the potatoes, or mash until there are no lumps **3** Prepare the choux pastry: put the water, butter, salt and grated nutmeg in a pan and bring to a rolling boil **4** Sieve the flour **5** When the water is boiling, remove the pan from the heat and tip in the flour, all at once, and beat **6** Return the pan to the heat and

stir until the mixture no longer sticks to the pan or wooden spoon **7** Away from the heat, beat in the eggs, one by one. The paste should be soft but not runny **8** Stir in the mashed potato **9** Add the

Gruyère cheese (optional) **10** and **11** Heat the deep fryer and, using a spoon or a piping bag, add pieces of the potato/choux paste mixture and cook until golden-brown **12** Pile in a bowl and serve

Potatoes Dauphine

450 g (1 lb) potatoes
1 egg yolk
25 g (1 oz) (2 tablespoons) butter
salt and pepper
oil for deep frying

For the Choux Paste:
150 ml (¼ pint) (⅝ cup) water
50 g (2 oz) (4 tablespoons) butter
pinch salt
pinch grated nutmeg
100 g (¼ lb) (1 cup + 2 tablespoons)
  plain flour, sieved
2 eggs

1 Wash, peel and slice the potatoes. Boil in salted water for 15 minutes, then drain.

2 Mash the potatoes finely or pass through a sieve. Blend in a bowl with the egg yolk, butter and seasoning.

3 Make the choux paste. Place the water, butter, salt and nutmeg in a saucepan and bring to a rolling boil. Remove the pan from the heat and tip in the flour, all at once. Beat until the mixture is thick and smooth and no longer sticks to the pan. Beat in the eggs, one by one, and continue beating until the mixture is smooth and soft, but not runny.

4 Mix the choux paste with the mashed potato mixture.

5 Heat the deep fryer to 180°C, 350°F. Shape small, oval pieces of the dauphine mixture with a spoon and add, a few at a time, to the hot oil. Alternatively, use a piping bag to pipe the mixture into small cylindrical-shaped pieces.

6 Fry until golden-brown. Drain on absorbent paper and serve immediately.

Serves 4

Tip: For a delicious alternative to Potatoes Dauphine, try Potatoes Lorette. Just add some grated Gruyère cheese to the choux paste/potato mixture before frying.

Fried Potato Allumettes

1 kg (2 lb) potatoes
oil for deep frying

For the Garnish:
4 tomatoes, peeled
10-15 anchovy fillets
5 g (1 tablespoon) chopped
  parsley

Potatoes Dauphine are choux paste and mashed potato fingers, deep-fried until crisp and golden-brown

1 Peel, wash and slice the potatoes. Cut into strips 5 cm (2 in) long by 3 mm (⅛ in) thick. Wash and dry on absorbent kitchen paper.

2 Heat the deep fryer to 190°C, 375°F. Fry the potato chips until golden-brown. Drain and arrange on a serving dish.

3 Meanwhile, cut the peeled tomatoes into halves and arrange around the potato allumettes. Garnish with the anchovy fillets and sprinkle with the chopped parsley.

Serves 4

Ham and Potato Scones

450 g (1 lb) cooked, mashed
  potatoes
50 g (2 oz) (½ cup) mushrooms,
  finely chopped
50 g (2 oz) (⅜ cup) ham, chopped
1 onion, finely chopped
75 g (3 oz) (good ¾ cup) flour
25 g (1 oz) (2 tablespoons) butter
1 egg, beaten
salt and pepper
100 ml (4 fl oz) (½ cup) oil

1 Mix together the mashed potato, mushrooms, ham and onion in a bowl. Add the flour, butter and beaten egg and stir until the mixture is smooth and well blended. Season with salt and pepper.

2 Place the mixture on a floured surface and roll it out like a large sausage until it is 7 cm (3 in) in diameter. Cut into about 10 slices.

3 Heat the oil in a frying pan (skillet), add the potato scones and fry on both sides until golden-brown (about 3-4 minutes).

4 Serve the potato scones with a coleslaw salad.

Serves 4

Look'n Cook Potato Croquettes

1 Boil the potatoes in salted water 2 Dry the cooked potatoes on a baking tray (cookie sheet) in the oven 3 Grate or mince (grind) the potatoes finely 4 Melt some butter in a saucepan and blend with the potato mixture 5 When the pulp is very hot, add the egg yolks in a continuous stream, stirring all the time 6 Oil a plate, cover with the potato mixture and leave to cool 7 and 8 Flour

your hands and, when it is cool, roll out the mixture into a long sausage shape **9** Cut the mixture at regular intervals **10** Dredge the croquettes in flour, then dip in seasoned, beaten egg

11 Roll the croquettes in breadcrumbs. Press with a knife so that the breadcrumbs stick to the croquettes **12** Place in a frying basket and cook in hot oil until well-browned. Serve immediately

Potato Croquettes

1 kg (2 lb) potatoes
salt and pepper
3 eggs
50 g (2 oz) (4 tablespoons) butter
25 g (1 oz) (4 tablespoons) flour
5 ml (1 teaspoon) oil
oil for deep frying
100 g (¼ lb) (2 cups) fresh
  breadcrumbs

1 Preheat the oven to 200°C, 400°F, gas 6. Peel the potatoes and cut them into even-sized pieces. Boil them in salted water for 20 minutes.

2 Drain the potatoes, place on a baking tray (cookie sheet) in the oven to dry until the outsides become a little floury (about 10 minutes).

3 Separate 2 of the eggs.

4 Sieve (strain) the potatoes into a pan and mix them with the butter over a low heat. Increase the heat and continue to stir until hot.

5 Stirring all the while, slowly add the two egg yolks to the potato. Season with salt and pepper.

6 Spread the mixture on an oiled plate to cool.

7 Flour your hands and the working surface, take a handful of potato mixture, form it into a ball, then roll the ball under your hands into a long thin sausage shape, about 2 cm (1 in) in diameter.

8 With a warm knife cut the potato roll into short lengths.

9 Heat the oil to 190°C, 375°F, ready to deep fry the croquettes.

10 For the glaze, beat the whole egg with the egg whites, salt and pepper and a little oil. Spread the breadcrumbs on the working surface.

11 Dip the croquettes in the beaten egg then roll them gently in the breadcrumbs, pressing on the crumbs with a palette knife.

12 Dip the frying basket in the hot oil before adding the croquettes, then fry the croquettes briskly for about a minute until they are golden-brown.

Makes about 16

Tips: The success of frying cro-quettes depends on the quality and condition of the fat used, whether animal or vegetable. Vegetable fats usually contain no moisture and can thus be heated to higher temperatures than animal fats. Also, they go rancid less quickly – all fats exposed to the air tend to become rancid in time. Therefore, frying oil should always be stored in an airtight container. The temperature used when frying depends on the size of the portion to be fried – the smaller the portion, the hotter the fat. Remember that when cold potato is added to fat, the temperature of the fat is automatically lowered.

Fried potatoes, clockwise from top: potato croquettes, crisps, fried potato and onion balls, potatoes dauphine, croquettes, slices, allumettes and, in the centre, matchstick potatoes

All about Beef

Roast Rib of Beef

Beef has always enjoyed a sumptuous reputation – it became famous as the 'roast beef of Olde England' and was even knighted by King Henry VIII, after which the two hindquarters, including the legs, rump, sirloin and wing ribs, were always referred to as *Baronne de Boeuf*.

Beef is very nutritious and a good source of energy. It is rich in protein, vitamin B and iron. The price of beef varies with the cut. The most expensive are usually the most tender and can be quickroasted, fried or grilled (broiled). Tougher cheaper cuts require slower cooking methods to soften them but are just as nutritious.

Beef is extremely versatile and can be prepared and cooked in so many ways. You can roast, fry, grill (broil), casserole, pot-roast, stew, boil, braise, stuff, smoke or salt it. It can be minced (ground) and made into hamburgers, or baked *en croûte* in a pastry case. Of course, the method of cooking you use will depend on the cut and quality of the beef and how much you can afford to spend.

Choosing Beef
When choosing beef, always take the colour and texture into account. The lean flesh should be light rosy or cherry red in colour, whereas the fat should be a creamy yellow. The lean meat should be marbled with fat – this is always a sign of good quality, tender meat. There should be a minimum of gristle. The texture will determine the tenderness of the meat – the most tender cuts such as sirloin spring back when touched.

Cuts of Beef
Different cuts will require different methods of cooking. Always be sure that you choose the right one. Cuts vary from one country to another, and even between areas and districts. The British, American and Australian cuts which you can use are often different. Many cuts such as rib, chuck, leg, skirt, blade, shin, silverside and brisket are very similar indeed, if not the same. The main differences lie in the cutting and terminology used, especially

with steaks. The American equivalent of British fillet steak is tenderloin. As well as sirloin steak, they also have T-bone, Porterhouse, pin bone, and Club or Delmonico (rib eye) steaks. All these steaks are now becoming popular in Britain and also in Australia.

Storing Beef
Store raw meat loosely wrapped, in a cool place or refrigerator. Beef will keep in a refrigerator for 2-3 days. The most economical way to buy beef is in bulk if you have a freezer. The recommended storage time in a freezer is 8 months. Always thaw out frozen meat either in the refrigerator or at room temperature slowly. Never immerse in hot water to speed the process up. Once thawed, you should never refreeze the beef.

Seasoning Beef
Always season beef before cooking, especially roasting or grilling (broiling), with salt and freshly ground (milled) black pepper. For additional flavour you can season the beef with herbs or spices. Try rubbing the joint with garlic, onion, herbs or spices before cooking, or insert a clove of garlic or a small piece of onion into the meat itself.

Improving the Texture and Flavour of Beef
One way to improve the texture and flavour of cheaper cuts of meat is to marinate them for several hours. Try using wine, beer or cider or an acidic mixture of fruit juices and vinegar. You can tenderize a tough steak or joint with a ready made tenderizer which most supermarkets sell. These tenderizing powders are usually prepared from extract of figs, pawpaws and pineapple – the fresh juice of these fruits works equally well.

Larding Beef
You can lard tough, cheaper cuts of meat with a larding needle to tenderize them. Just push a larding needle through the meat with the grain, thread with fat and pull back through. This is explained in the step-by-step photo guide to larding on page 606. Introducing the fat into the flesh will make the meat more moist and lubricate it during cooking.

Steaks

The most popular and well-known steak cuts are – in usual order of costliness – fillet, sirloin, rib, and rump. Being very expensive, fillet is graded into several different cuts.

An average beef fillet is 45-50 cm (18-20 in) in length and tapers in width from 10 cm (4 in) to 2.5 cm (1 in). A whole fillet weighs from 3-4½ kg (6-9 lbs) untrimmed, and when prepared for cooking, a fillet will weigh on average 1¾-2 kg (3½-4 lb).

The Châteaubriand is taken from the head of the fillet. A piece 10 cm (4 in) is cut off, weighing from 350 g to 500 g (12-16 oz). It is wrapped round with a cloth, and flattened until it is 5 cm (2 in) thick, widening to double its original size at 20 cm (8 in) in diameter. When cooked it is served in slices, and is always for two.

The Coeur de Filet or Medaillon steak is cut 2½ cm (1 in) thick, and weighs 250 g (½ lb). It is cut from the heart of the fillet, and is also flattened to a diameter of 7.5 cm (3 in). The fillet steak is cut from the middle of the fillet, 6.5 cm (2½ in) thick, about 10 cm (4 in) in diameter, and weighs 200 g (7 oz).

Sirloin steaks are tender and flavoursome. Entrecôte means 'between the ribs' but the term now includes any sirloin steak. Porterhouse is another cut of the sirloin. Rib steaks are a luxury, large and tasty. The famous T-bone steak cut includes part of the fillet and sirloin. Rump steak is often hung to mature, producing a fine flavour. The tenderest cut of rump steak is a point steak.

The Tournedos is also cut from the middle of the fillet. It is tied in a scalded rasher of bacon before cooking. It is cut 4 cm (1½ in) thick, 7.5 cm (3 in) in diameter, and weighs 150 g (5 oz). Filet Mignon is cut from the thin end in a triangular shape, and weighs 100 g (¼ lb). This end of the fillet is also used for Strognoff where the steak is cut into strips 2.5 cm × 5 mm (1 × ¼ in), or raw for Steak Tartare.

The cooking times will vary with the method used and the type and thickness of steak, but in general 2 minutes cooking (1 minute each side) produces a rare steak, 4 minutes a medium steak, and 8-12 minutes a well-done one. Grilling (broiling) is suitable for the best types of steak, while cheaper cuts may be fried very quickly.

Apollo Steaks

30 ml (2 tablespoons) oil
4 sirloin or rump steaks

For the Sauce:
1 lamb's kidney, skinned, cored and sliced
25 g (1 oz) (2 tablespoons) butter or margarine
1 large onion, sliced
2 tomatoes, skinned, deseeded and chopped
1 green pepper, deseeded and chopped

Juicy Apollo Steaks are dressed with a richly flavoured sauce of kidneys, green pepper, tomato and onion

150 ml (¼ pint) (⅝ cup) red wine
150 ml (¼ pint) (⅝ cup) beef stock
salt and pepper
pinch oregano

1 Fry the sauce ingredients, except the wine, stock and seasonings, in a saucepan for 5 minutes until they are tender. Add the wine and stock, and season with salt, pepper and a pinch of oregano. Bring to the boil and simmer for 5 minutes to thicken.

2 Heat the oil in a frying pan (skillet) and fry the steaks for 2-8 minutes or according to taste. Pour the sauce over them and serve immediately. Serve with buttered new potatoes and a green or mixed salad.

Serves 4

Steak au Poivre Vert

4 sirloin steaks, 1 cm ($\frac{1}{2}$ in) thick
50 ml (2 fl oz) ($\frac{1}{4}$ cup) oil
pinch salt
50 g (2 oz) (4 tablespoons) butter
45 ml (3 tablespoons) brandy
100 ml (4 fl oz) ($\frac{1}{2}$ cup) dry sherry
  or dry Madeira wine
1 medium onion, chopped
25 g (1 oz) (2 tablespoons) green
  peppercorns, canned
30 ml (2 tablespoons) soya sauce
5 ml (1 teaspoon) vinegar
150 ml ($\frac{1}{4}$ pint) ($\frac{5}{8}$ cup) single
  (light) cream
pinch paprika
5 g (1 tablespoon) chopped fresh
  parsley

1 Trim the steaks of any excess fat and sinew. Brush with a little oil and season very lightly with salt.

2 Heat the rest of the oil and but-ter in a frying pan (skillet) and quickly fry the steaks on both sides to sear the flesh, for about 2 minutes. Pour in the brandy and set it alight. Almost immediately pour in the sherry or Madeira to put out the brandy flames. Remove the steaks and keep them warm while cooking the sauce.

3 To the mixture in the pan add the onion, peppercorns, soya sauce, and vinegar. Boil for 4 minutes. Add the cream and paprika and boil briskly for another minute.

4 Return the steaks to the sauce to reheat for a minute on each side. Serve immediately, garnished with the chopped parsley.

Serves 4

*Steak au Poivre Vert has
the real taste
of luxury, with brandy to flame,
wine, and mildly spicy
green peppercorns*

Tips: Green peppercorns are the fresh berries of the spice more commonly used in its dried form as black or white ground (powdered) pepper. They are usually only available in canned form, and have a mild and aromatic flavour.

The given cooking times for the sirloin steak are designed for a rare-cooked steak of 1 cm ($\frac{1}{2}$ in) thick. Thicker steaks should be fried for twice the given length of time, or beaten with a rolling pin or meat mallet to the given thickness. For a medium-cooked steak, fry for 4 minutes. For a well-cooked steak, cover the pan (skillet) while frying for 4 or 5 minutes.

Entrecôte Bordelaise

4 sirloin steaks, about 3 cm (1$\frac{1}{2}$ in)
  thick
30 ml (2 tablespoons) oil
salt and pepper
5 g (1 tablespoon) chopped fresh
  parsley

For the Bordelaise Sauce:
4 shallots or 1 onion, chopped
200 ml (6 fl oz) ($\frac{3}{4}$ cup) good red
  wine
bouquet garni
45 ml (3 tablespoons) meat juice
200 ml (6 fl oz) ($\frac{3}{4}$ cup) beef stock
15 g ($\frac{1}{2}$ oz) (1 tablespoon) tomato
  concentrate (paste)
15 g ($\frac{1}{2}$ oz) (1 tablespoon) beef fat
15 g ($\frac{1}{2}$ oz) (2 tablespoons) flour

1 Brush the steaks with the oil and grill (broil) them for 8-12 minutes according to taste, turning once. Reserve the meat juices and keep the steaks warm.

2 To make the sauce, boil the shallot or onion in the wine, with the bouquet garni, for 5 minutes. Stir in the meat juice, beef stock and tomato concentrate (paste).

3 Make a roux by melting the beef fat and cooking the flour in it for 2 minutes. Remove from the heat and gradually stir in the wine and stock mixture to form a

smooth sauce. Simmer very gently for 20 minutes.

4 Season the steaks lightly with salt and generously with freshly ground (milled) black pepper. Pour the sauce over them and garnish with chopped parsley. Serve immediately.

Serves 4

Steak Manzanilla

2 rump steaks, about 225 g
  (½ lb) each
30 ml (2 tablespoons) oil
salt and pepper
2 slices Cheddar cheese,
  ½ cm (¼ in) thick
pinch paprika
4 anchovy fillets
2 stuffed green olives, sliced

1 Brush the steaks with oil and season with a little salt and plenty of freshly ground (milled) black pepper. Grill (broil) the steaks under high heat for 3-4 minutes on each side according to taste.

2 Place a slice of cheese on each steak, sprinkle with paprika and grill (broil) until the cheese is melted and just starting to brown.

3 Place the steaks on a warmed serving dish. Decorate each steak with a cross of anchovy fillets, and slices of stuffed olive. Serve immediately.

Serves 2

Steak à l'Orange

4 sirloin steaks, 2 cm (¾ in) thick
24 black peppercorns, crushed
rind 1 orange, cut in matchstick
  strips
15 ml (1 tablespoon) oil
150 ml (¼ pint) (⅝ cup) dry sherry
4 fresh mint leaves

150 ml (¼ pint) (⅝ cup) single (light) cream

For the Marinade:
juice 2 oranges
2 cloves garlic, peeled and
  crushed
5 g (1 teaspoon) fresh root ginger,
  finely chopped
30 ml (2 tablespoons) soya sauce
50 ml (2 fl oz) (¼ cup) oil
30 ml (2 tablespoons) cider
  vinegar

1 Trim the steaks and rub the crushed black peppercorns into them.

2 Thoroughly blend the orange juice, garlic, ginger, soya sauce, oil, and vinegar to make a marinade. Soak the steaks in it for 20 minutes and then remove

Steak Manzanilla is an unusual idea featuring cheese and anchovies, which would also suit cheaper steak cuts

them, reserving the marinade.

3 Meanwhile boil the orange rind for 8 minutes. Drain and rinse the strips in cold water and add them to the leftover marinade.

4 Fry the steaks in the oil until done to taste. Remove and keep warm. Pour the marinade into the pan and boil for 4 minutes to reduce. Add the sherry and mint leaves and boil for 3 minutes; then stir in the cream and boil 3 more minutes. Pour the sauce over the steaks and serve at once.

Serves 4

Sirloin with Peppercorns and Garlic

**four 350 g (¾ lb) sirloin steaks,
  2.5 cm (1 in) thick
12 black peppercorns
4 cloves garlic, thinly sliced
75 ml (2½ fl oz) (⅓ cup) oil
salt**

1 Trim the fat from the steaks. Crush the peppercorns, using a rolling pin, and then sprinkle over both sides of the steaks, pressing well into the meat.

2 Make several slits in the surface of the steaks and insert the slices of garlic into the slits. Brush the steaks with oil and then cook them under a grill, over a charcoal fire, or in a frying pan (skillet). Cook for 2 minutes on both sides for underdone meat, 4 minutes for medium or 8 minutes for well-done.

3 Season with salt and serve with watercress, French fries and a pat of garlic butter.

Serves 4

Rump Steak Royal

**1 kg (2 lb) rump steak in 1 piece
salt
5 g (1 teaspoon) crushed
  peppercorns
45 ml (3 tablespoons) oil
2 cloves garlic, peeled and
  chopped**

*Sirloin with Peppercorns
and Garlic — try this
deliciously different way
of serving your steaks*

**50 g (2 oz) (4 tablespoons) peanut
  butter
150 ml (¼ pint) (⅝ cup) medium
  vermouth**

1 Season the steak with salt and peppercorns.

2 Heat the oil in a frying pan (skillet) and shallow fry the steak. Cook for 6 minutes on either side for underdone meat, 12 minutes for medium, 14 minutes for well-done.

3 Remove the steak from the pan and keep warm on a dish.

4 Mix the garlic and peanut butter and put in the frying pan (skillet). Add the vermouth, stir and boil for 4 minutes. Pour over the steak.

5 Serve the whole steak and cut into 3 or 4 portions in front of the guests. Serve with a lettuce and orange salad.

Serves 3-4

Tournedos with Anchovy Butter

6 rashers (slices) streaky bacon
  (scalded)
6 tournedos steaks, 150 g (5 oz)
  each 4 cm (1½ in) thick
salt and freshly ground (milled)
  pepper
oil for frying steaks
6 green olives
6 anchovy fillets
25 ml (2 tablespoons) tomato
  ketchup (catsup)

For the Anchovy Butter:
100 g (¼ lb) (½ cup) butter
5 g (1 tablespoon) chopped
  parsley
juice ½ lemon
4 anchovy fillets, finely chopped

For the Croutons:
6 slices bread
25 g (1 oz) (2 tablespoons) butter
25 ml (1 fl oz) (⅛ cup) oil

1 Prepare the anchovy butter by creaming the butter with the parsley, lemon juice and anchovy fillets to form a paste. Roll the paste into a cylinder, wrap in greaseproof (parchment) paper, and chill for 1 hour.

2 Make the croutons by cutting six bread circles using a plain cutter of 6.5 cm (2½ in). Put the butter and oil in a frying pan (skillet) and fry the bread on both sides until golden. Place the croutons on a dish and keep warm.

3 Tie a rasher of streaky bacon round each steak and season. Heat some oil in the frying pan (skillet) and fry the steaks for 4-10 minutes, depending on whether you want the steaks rare, medium or well-done. If

Tournedos with Anchovy Butter combines succulent steak with piquant anchovies, topped by green olives

preferred, brush the steaks with oil, and grill (broil). Remove the bacon. Place on the croutons.

4 When ready to serve, cut slices off the roll of anchovy butter and place one on each steak. Place a green olive on each, surrounded by an anchovy fillet, and trickle a little tomato ketchup (catsup) round as decoration. Serve at once with Pommes Allumettes (thin chips) as illustrated.

Serves 6

Steak Mignonette

4 slices of 150 g (5 oz) fillet steak,
  cut from the thin end
1 medium onion
25 g (1 oz) (2 tablespoons) butter

4 mushrooms
150 ml ($\frac{1}{4}$ pint) ($\frac{5}{8}$ cup) port
25 g (1 oz) (2 tablespoons) tomato
 concentrate (paste)
pinch thyme
pinch cinnamon
75 ml (2$\frac{1}{2}$ fl oz) ($\frac{1}{3}$ cup) whipping
 cream
salt and pepper
25 ml (1 fl oz) ($\frac{1}{8}$ cup) oil
8 stuffed olives, sliced ·

1 Flatten the steaks to 12.5 × 5 cm (5 × 2$\frac{1}{2}$ in).

2 Chop the onion and fry gently in the butter for 4 minutes until tender without colouring. Chop the mushrooms and add, and cook for 1 minute. Then add the port, tomato concentrate (paste), thyme and cinnamon. Boil for 5 minutes. Stir in the cream, season and put aside. Keep warm.

3 Heat the oil in a frying pan (skillet). Quickly cook the steaks for 1 minute on each side.

4 Put in a dish, pour half of the sauce over the steaks and sprinkle with the sliced stuffed olives. Serve the remainder of the sauce separately. Serve garnished with braised chicory (endive).

Serves 4

Brandy Steak with Mandarin Rice

175 g (6 oz) ($\frac{3}{4}$ cup) long grain rice
salt and pepper
25 g (1oz) (2 tablespoons) butter
300 g (11 oz) canned mandarin
 oranges
4 fillet steaks, 150 g (5 oz) each,
 4 cm (1$\frac{1}{2}$ in) thick
4 rashers (slices) streaky bacon
 (scalded)
25 g (1 oz) (2 tablespoons) butter
30 ml (2 tablespoons) oil
60 ml (4 tablespoons) brandy
100 ml (4 fl oz) ($\frac{1}{2}$ cup) single
 (light) cream

Brandy Steak with Mandarin Rice, tender tournedos are flamed in brandy and flavoured with mandarin oranges

1 Wash the rice and cook in salted boiling water for 20 minutes. Drain, and stir in the butter. Season and keep warm.

2 Meanwhile, heat the mandarin oranges in their syrup and drain. Keep the juice. Add the oranges to the rice. Keep warm.

3 Season the steaks, and tie a rasher (slice) of bacon around each. Heat the butter and oil in a frying pan, and shallow fry the steaks for 2-3 minutes on each side, if you like them rare. Cook for longer if you prefer. If you want the steaks well done, put a lid on.

4 Pour the brandy into the frying pan and flame the steaks. Remove the steaks, discard the bacon, and put them on a dish and keep warm.

5 Pour the cream into the frying pan, and mix with the meat juices, and boil for 2 minutes to make a smooth sauce. Remove from the heat, add 15 ml (1 tablespoon) of the mandarin juice and pour over the steaks. Serve at once with the mandarin rice, and a green salad.

Serves 4

Marengo Meatballs

1 large slice white bread
30 ml (2 tablespoons) milk
675 g (1½ lb) (3 cups) lean minced (ground) beef
1 egg yolk
1 onion, finely chopped
pinch salt and pepper
15 g (½ oz) (1 tablespoon) flour
50 g (2 oz) (4 tablespoons) butter
75 ml (3 fl oz) (⅜ cup) dry white wine
4 large tomatoes, skinned, deseeded and chopped
pinch sugar
350 g (¾ lb) (1½ cups) long grain rice
30 ml (2 tablespoons) single (light) cream
5 g (1 tablespoon) chopped parsley,

1 Soak the bread in the milk for 5 minutes. Squeeze out, remove excess liquid and crumble into breadcrumbs.

2 In a mixing bowl, combine the beef, egg yolk, onion, salt and pepper and breadcrumbs. Divide into 6 and roll into flattened balls. Dust with the flour.

3 Heat the butter in a frying pan (skillet) and fry the meatballs for 10 minutes, turning them once. Pour on the wine, then add the tomatoes and a pinch of sugar. Bring to the boil, then reduce the heat and simmer for 25 minutes.

4 Meanwhile, place the rice in a pan of slightly salted water. Bring to the boil and cook for 15 minutes or until the rice is just tender. Drain. Heat the cream in a small pan and pour over the rice. Sprinkle with the parsley and arrange in the centre of a serving dish surrounded by the meat balls and sauce.

Serves 6

Marengo Meatballs use cheap minced (ground) beef with creamy rice for a nourishing and economical meal

Mushroom Burgers

25 g (1 oz) (2 tablespoons) butter
30 ml (2 tablespoons) oil
2 onions, finely chopped
225 g (½ lb) (2 cups) finely chopped mushrooms,
good pinch mixed herbs
1 clove garlic, peeled and crushed
675 g (1½ lb) (3 cups) lean minced (ground) beef
pinch salt and pepper
15 g (½ oz) (2 tablespoons) flour

1 Heat the butter and 15 ml (1 tablespoon) oil in a frying pan (skillet). Gently fry the onions and the mushrooms for 5 minutes. Add the mixed herbs and the crushed garlic clove and cook for a further minute. Allow to cool.

2 In a bowl, combine the beef with the onion and mushroom mixture. Season. Divide into 8 balls, then flatten slightly. Dust with the flour.

3 Heat the rest of the oil in the pan and fry the mushroom burgers slowly for 4-6 minutes each side.

Serves 4

Tip: To make a quick, tasty sauce, take the burgers out of the pan when they are cooked and keep hot. Pour away the oil and add 100 ml (4 fl oz) (½ cup) sherry, wine or fruit juice to the pan. Boil rapidly until the sauce is reduced by half and pour it over the burgers.

Mushroom Burgers are tasty and easy to make. Serve them with a big mixed salad and French fried potatoes

Meatballs with Courgettes (Zucchini)

50 g (2 oz) ($\frac{1}{3}$ cup) chick peas,
  cooked or canned and drained
450 g (1 lb) (2 cups) lean minced
  (ground) beef
1 clove garlic, peeled and
  crushed
50 g (2 oz) (1 cup) fresh
  breadcrumbs
50 g (2 oz) ($\frac{1}{3}$ cup) hazelnuts, finely
  chopped
1 egg, beaten
1 small green chilli pepper,
  finely chopped
5 g (1 tablespoon) chopped
  parsley
pinch cumin
salt and pepper
15 g ($\frac{1}{2}$ oz) (2 tablespoons) flour
60 ml (2 fl oz) ($\frac{1}{4}$ cup) oil

For the Sauce:
30 ml (2 tablespoons) oil
1 onion, chopped
1 clove garlic, peeled and
  crushed

*Meatballs with Courgettes
(Zucchini) includes other unusual
vegetables — chick peas,
hot chilli pepper and hazelnuts*

4 courgettes (zucchini), sliced
4 tomatoes, skinned, deseeded
  and chopped
150 g (5 oz) (1$\frac{1}{4}$ cups) peas, fresh or
  frozen
300 ml ($\frac{1}{2}$ pint) (1$\frac{1}{4}$ cups) water
1 chicken stock cube
5 g (1 tablespoon) mixed mint
  and parsley, chopped

1 Preheat the oven to 200°C,
400°F, gas 6.

2 Mash the chick peas with a
fork. Place them in a mixing bowl,
and add the beef, garlic, breadcrumbs, hazelnuts, beaten egg
and chilli pepper. Blend together
well and add the parsley, cumin,
salt and pepper. Shape into 8
slightly flattened balls and dust
with the flour.

3 Heat the oil in a frying pan
(skillet) and fry the meatballs for
6-8 minutes. Drain and keep hot.

4 To make the sauce, pour away
the oil in which the meatballs
were cooked and wipe the pan
clean. Heat 30 ml (2 tablespoons)
oil and gently fry the onion for 4
minutes, until soft but not brown.
Add the garlic, courgettes (zucchini), tomatoes and peas. Pour
on the water and crumble in the
stock cube. Bring to the boil, add
the parsley and mint and season
to taste. Transfer to a casserole,
add the meatballs, and place in
the oven for 20 minutes.

Serves 4

Tips: Try using equal quantities
of minced (ground) pork and beef
for a good texture as well as a
delicious flavour.

For economy, replace 150 g
(5 oz) (good $\frac{1}{2}$ cup) minced (ground)
meat with 65 g (2$\frac{1}{2}$ oz) texturized
vegetable protein.

Meatballs can be braised in the
oven or deep fried and any kind of
cereal binder can be used, such as
matzo meal, oats, cooked rice or
rusk.

Steak Tartare

Steak Tartare is the name given to a delicious, unusual and highly digestible dish of raw steak.

You should use fillet steak – preferably the thin, tail end – but you can use sirloin or rib, both of which are very tender. Make sure the meat is absolutely fresh: locally killed beef is best. Allow 150 g (5 oz) (good ½ cup) meat for a generous portion per person, and make sure it is passed through a mincer (grinder) twice.

600 g (1¼ lb) (2½ cups) minced (ground) fillet steak
salt and freshly ground (milled) black pepper
100 g (¼ lb) (½ cup) shallots, finely chopped
10 g (2 tablespoons) chopped parsley
8 anchovy fillets, chopped
15 g (1 tablespoon) capers
15 g (1 tablespoon) gherkins (dill pickles), chopped
15 g (1 tablespoon) pearl onions
150 ml (¼ pint) (⅝ cup) vinaigrette sauce
150 ml (¼ pint) (⅝ cup) mayonnaise
4 eggs

1 Season the minced (ground) steak with salt and freshly ground (milled) black pepper. Divide it into 4 portions and shape each into a ball. Place each in the centre of a dinner plate, flatten slightly and make a small cavity in the centre.

Steak Tartare is a classic dish in which diners garnish raw fillet steak according to their individual tastes

2 Either surround each portion with, or serve separately, the shallots, parsley, anchovy fillets, capers, gherkins (dill pickles) and pearl onions. Serve a bowl each of vinaigrette sauce and mayonnaise.

3 Carefully break each egg and separate the white from the yolk. Leave the yolk in half the shell and place in the centre of each steak.

4 Allow your guests to help themselves to the various garnishes and sauces.

Serves 4

Tip: Serve Tartare with a crisp salad. Try lettuce and chicory (Belgian endive), or potato or orange and watercress or Waldorf Salad, which combines celery, crisp eating apples and walnuts.

251

Roast Beef

There are two methods of roasting beef. The old-fashioned method roasts the meat at a high temperature. This sears the outside of the joint and keeps the meat juices inside. The moisture acts as a heat conductor and so the joint stays moist and juicy long after cooking. Lovers of underdone beef also claim that it has more flavour this way. An alternative is to start the cooking on a high temperature and sear the joint for 20 minutes, then lower the temperature for the remainder of the cooking time.

The second method which is commonly used in America roasts the meat at a low temperature. This way, the meat is cooked throughout and it is difficult to obtain an underdone, juicy, red joint. You will probably find it best to sear your joint first, then lower the temperature.

Basic rules for Roasting

There are some basic rules for roasting and, if you follow them, you should always have good results. They are:

1 Always season the joint lightly with salt and freshly ground (milled) pepper.

2 Always handle the meat very gently and never pierce it with a knife or skewer. It is important that the meat juices should stay intact.

3 Always smother your meat with plenty of fat – a mixture of butter and lard is best. Use 25 g (1 oz) fat for every 450 g (1 lb) meat. Baste the meat frequently with the fat during cooking.

4 If you can, stand the joint on a rack or grille or trivet above a roasting pan to catch the juices. An alternative is to place the joint on a bed of root vegetables (carrots, celery and onions) or meat bones. The vegetable and meat juices can be used as a base for the gravy.

5 Always use a meat thermometer if you like your meat well-done. It is essential to obtain good results. Insert it into the meat but take care that it does not touch the bone.

6 Always preheat the oven before roasting to 220°C, 425°F, gas 7. Cook the meat on the middle shelf and sear it at the high temperature. Then, if you like your beef underdone, continue cooking it at this temperature. If you prefer well-done beef, lower the temperature to 190°C, 375°F, gas 5.

Serving Roast Beef

The traditional way to serve roast beef is with roast potatoes, Yorkshire puddings and horseradish sauce and mustard. You can make a delicious gravy from the meat juices and vegetable water. Rest the joint for 15 minutes before carving – keep it warm in the bottom of the oven – and garnish with sprigs of watercress.

Suitable Cuts of Meat

Sirloin, wing rib or loin, forerib and middlerib are all suitable for roasting. If these are too expensive, try topside or round which are cheaper and slightly tougher cuts.

Roasting Times

Sirloin, rib and the better cuts of beef should be seared for 20 minutes in a hot oven. Then, if you like your meat underdone, roast it a further 10 minutes for every 450 g (1 lb). For well cooked meat, allow 15-20 minutes per 450 g (1 lb). Topside and the cheaper cuts need 20 minutes also.

Yorkshire Pudding

2 eggs
150 g (5 oz) (1¼ cups) plain flour, sifted
300 ml (½ pint) (1¼ cups) water, or milk and water mixed
pinch salt

1 Beat the eggs well together, then stir in the flour. Add the liquid and beat for 3 to 4 minutes to obtain a smooth batter. Season with the salt and leave the batter to rest for 1 hour.

2 If your oven is not already hot, preheat it to 190°C, 375°F, gas 5.

3 Place a teaspoonful of the meat fat and juices in the bottom of each patty tin (muffin pan) and heat in the oven for 5 minutes. Then half-fill them with batter and bake for 15-20 minutes until well-risen and golden.

Makes 6-8

Horseradish Sauce

75 g (3 oz) fresh horseradish root, peeled and washed
45 ml (3 tablespoons) wine vinegar
salt and pepper
pinch sugar
300 ml (½ pint) (1¼ cups) milk
75 g (3 oz) (1½ cups) fresh white breadcrumbs

1 Grate the horseradish and soak in the wine vinegar for 1 hour. Season with the salt and pepper and sugar.

2 Heat the milk in a saucepan and bring to the boil. Stir in the breadcrumbs and leave them to soak for 10 minutes. Blend in the horseradish mixture and serve the sauce with roast beef.

Makes about 300 ml (½ pint) (1¼ cups)

Tip: For a change, try making horseradish sauce in the Hungarian way. Just mix the horseradish and vinegar mixture into 300 ml (½ pint) (1¼ cups) white sauce.

Roast Rib of Beef, served with Yorkshire Pudding and Horseradish Sauce, is a meal fit for an English king

CHEF'S CHOICE

The main characteristic of this dish is that the meat is cooked wrapped in pastry. Originally a bread dough was used, but over the years this has changed and a brioche dough or puff pastry is now used.

The basic method is that the meat is first browned in hot fat to seal in the juices and, when cold, is wrapped in pastry and baked.

The most famous version of this dish is Beef Wellington, created in honour of the Duke of Wellington after his victory over Napoleon at the Battle of Waterloo. For this the finest meat was chosen – a fillet of beef.

The French decided to commemorate the loser, and created Beef Napoleon. In this dish, the sealed fillet was spread with foie gras (goose liver) and rolled in chopped truffles, and then wrapped in brioche pastry and baked.

We show you a plain version leaving you to choose your own flavoured paste. Here is a suggestion, which will add a touch of distinction – spread the sealed meat with liver paté mixed with freshly chopped mushrooms, before wrapping it up in the brioche dough.

In each part of the world the finest quality meat is chosen for this dish. In England we call it a fillet, in the USA a tenderloin, and in Australia an eye fillet.

Boeuf en Brioche

1 kg 225 g (2½ lb) piece of fillet
  steak wrapped in fat
salt and pepper
75 ml (3 fl oz) (⅜ cup) oil
1 egg, beaten

For the Brioche Dough:
6 75 g (1½ lb) (6¾ cups) strong bread
  flour
15 g (½ oz) (2 teaspoons) salt
15 g (½ oz) fresh yeast
150 ml (¼ pint) (⅝ cup) warm water
4 eggs
175 g (6 oz) (¾ cup) soft margarine
  or butter

1 Sift the flour and salt on to a board. Put ¼ of the flour to one side, making two circles.

2 Crumble the yeast into the warm water, and place in the small circle. Mix in the flour, put in a bowl, sprinkle with more flour and put in a warm place for 30 minutes.

3 Break the eggs into the well of the larger circle and mix in the flour to a soft dough, using your fingertips. Beat with an up and down yo-yo-like motion for 6-7 minutes until the dough is firmer and no longer sticks to your fingers.

4 Mix the yeast dough with the egg dough and give the mixture a thorough beating.

5 Mix in the soft fat in small pieces. Put the dough in a basin, cover with a cloth and allow to prove and rise for 45 minutes.

6 Preheat the oven to 220°C, 425°F, gas 7.

7 Meanwhile, season the fillet. Heat the oil in a frying pan (skillet) and seal the meat all over for 5 minutes with the lid on. Transfer the meat and oil to a roasting pan and roast in the oven for 15-35 minutes. Cool. Remove the fat.

8 Grease a baking (cookie) sheet.

9 When the meat is cold, knead the dough for 5 minutes. Roll out to 5 mm (¼ in) thick. Place the meat in the middle and brush with beaten egg. (Add flavoured pastes at this stage if you wish.) Brush the dough with beaten egg and fold over the meat, making a large overlap. Turn the joint over so that the join is underneath. Trim off both ends and shape into a loaf.

10 Roll out the trimmings and cut into thin strips. Brush the loaf with beaten egg, arrange the strips and brush again. Place on the greased baking (cookie) sheet.

11 Preheat the oven to 220°C, 425°F, gas 7.

12 Allow the loaf to prove for 25 minutes so that the brioche dough may rise. Prick in two or three places.

13 Bake on the middle shelf of the oven for 15 minutes, then reduce the temperature to 190°C, 375°F, gas 5 for another 20 minutes. Watch the pastry so that it does not burn.

14 Remove from the oven and rest for 10 minutes before carving. Cut in 2.5 cm (1 in) slices. Serve with a brown sauce flavoured with Madeira or sherry.

Serves 8

Tip: The success of this dish depends on cooking the fillet steak at the beginning for the right amount of time to rare; medium or well-done. When the dough is wrapped round, no further heat will penetrate the meat and only the pastry (pie crust) will be cooked.

Variation

If you wish to make the classic Beef Wellington, spread the prepared fillet with the following mixture. Chop 225 g (½ lb) mushrooms and 1 onion, and mix with 50 g (2 oz) (⅓ cup) of diced ham. Put in a frying pan (skillet) with 25 g (1 oz) (½ cup) breadcrumbs and sauté for 5 minutes in 25 ml (1 fl oz) of oil. Then add 100 g (¼ lb) (½ cup) of minced (ground) chicken livers and stir. When the mixture has cooled, add 50 g (2 oz) (4 tablespoons) butter and a beaten egg, seasoning and 2 g (1 teaspoon) of chopped fresh parsley.

You will see that the meat shrinks slightly during the baking, and the pastry expands, leaving a gap between. If you use a flavoured spread like this, the gap is filled, and the dish enhanced by the extra flavours that you have added.

Boeuf en Brioche combines simplicity with excellence — a delicious fillet of beef, cooked in light pastry

1 Make two circles of sifted flour. Mix the yeast with water, pour into the smaller circle and mix with the flour **2** Put the yeast mixture into a small bowl in a warm place to rise. Break the eggs into the larger circle **3** Gradually mix the flour to a soft dough using the fingertips **4** Beat with an up and down, yo-yo like motion for 5-6 minutes until the dough no longer sticks to your fingers **5** Mix in the soft fat in small pieces. Cover with a cloth and leave to prove for 45 minutes **6** Heat the oil in a frying pan (skillet) and

add the seasoned fillet **7** Brown all over for 5 minutes to seal the juices, with a lid on. Roast in the oven for 15 minutes at 220°C, 425°F, gas 7, and then cool **8** Roll out the dough 5mm (¼ in) thick **9** Place the cold fillet in the centre and brush with beaten egg. (Add flavoured pastes at this stage if you wish). **10** Brush the dough with beaten egg and fold over the fillet **11** Fold over the other half making a large overlap, and turn over so that the join is underneath **12** Trim off each end, sealing the fillet inside

13 Form into a loaf shape **14** Roll out the trimmings and cut into strips. Brush the loaf with beaten egg **15** Arrange the strips decoratively **16** Brush them with beaten egg and place on a baking (cookie) sheet and prove for 25 minutes. Prick in two or three places **17** Bake for 15 minutes at 220°C, 425°F, gas 7, and for 20 minutes at 190°C, 375°F, gas 5. Watch the pastry so that it does not burn. Remove from the oven and rest for 10 minutes **18** Carve in 2.5 cm (1 in) slices and serve hot

Beef Italienne

675 g (1½ lb) piece fillet steak
4 strips bacon fat
75 ml (3 fl oz) (⅜ cup) oil
1 carrot, 1 onion and 2 celery
  sticks, sliced

For the Gravy:
150 ml (¼ pint) (⅝ cup) white wine
225 ml (8 fl oz) (1 cup) water
1 stock cube
bouquet garni
5 g (1 teaspoon) cornflour
  (cornstarch)

1 Prepare the fillet by removing the tough skin carefully with a knife to avoid damaging the meat. Lay the bacon fat along the fillet and secure with string, tied at intervals of 2.5 cm (1 in).

2 Preheat the oven to 200°C, 400°F, gas 6.

3 Heat the oil in a frying pan (skillet) and brown the meat all over for 8 minutes to seal.

4 Transfer the meat to a roasting pan and add the carrot, onion and celery.

5 Roast for 40 minutes. Remove from the oven, discard the bacon fat, string, and vegetables. Place on a serving dish and keep hot.

6 To the juices in the roasting pan, add the wine, 150 ml (¼ pint) (⅝ cup) water, stock cube, and bouquet garni and simmer for 15 minutes. Thicken with cornflour (cornstarch) mixed with the remaining water. Boil for 3 minutes, season and strain.

Serves 6

Beef Italienne could be the star turn at a special dinner — superb fillet beef, flamboyantly garnished

Tip: As the photograph shows, the Beef Italienne may be garnished in several ways.

With small strips of fresh noodle paste deep fried until crisp and golden and arranged in heaps around the dish.

With globe artichokes, boiled in water and lemon juice, after the outside leaves and hairy choke have been removed. The artichokes may be filled with a duxelles of ham, mushrooms, onion and breadcrumbs, sautéed for 5 minutes.

The dish may be decorated with a few button mushrooms, which have been scribed with the point of a knife blade, and then blanched in water with lemon juice or wine.

The garnishes should be prepared before the fillet is cooked.

Look 'n Cook Preparing and Garnishing Rib of Beef

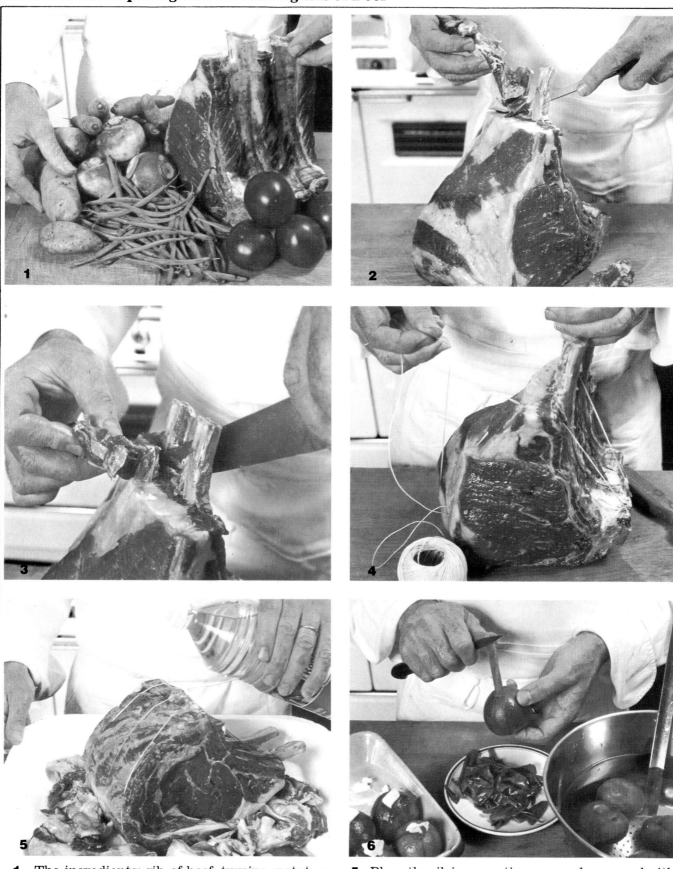

1 The ingredients: rib of beef, turnips, potatoes, carrots, green beans and tomatoes **2** and **3** Trim the rib for roasting. Expose the ends of the bones and remove the fat and trimmings. Reserve for use later **4** Tie the rib with trussing string to keep its shape

5 Place the rib in a roasting pan and surround with the trimmings, which will provide the gravy. Season lightly and pour on a little oil **6** Scald and skin the tomatoes. Place them in a greased ovenproof dish and dot with butter **7** Peel the carrots, turnips and

potatoes and trim them to a uniform size **8** Put each vegetable into a separate pan. Pour on enough water to cover and add a little butter and a pinch each salt and sugar. Cover, and put on to boil **9, 10** and **11** When the vegetables are tender, reduce the water in which they were cooked and glaze them with the sugar and butter. Brown the potatoes in a sauté pan with a little more butter **12** The finished dish: roast rib of beef, surrounded by vegetables, ready to carve and serve

Look 'n Cook Carving Rib of Beef

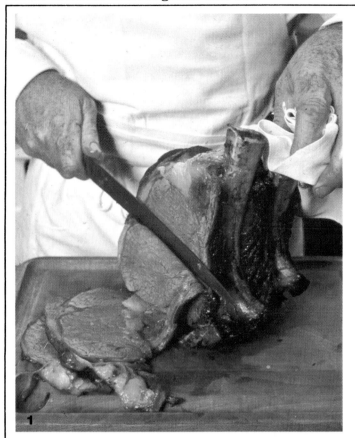

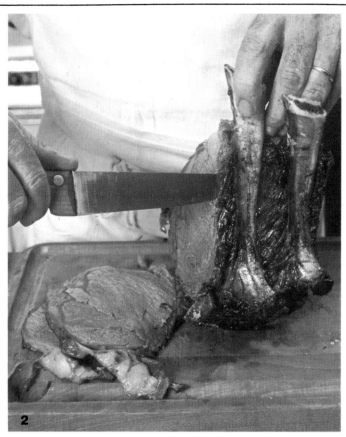

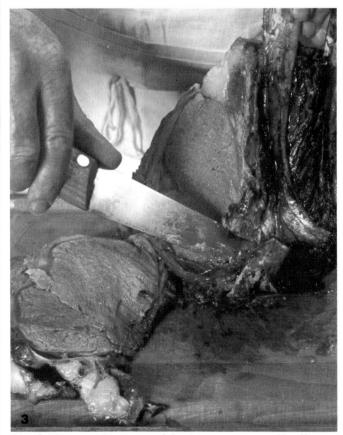

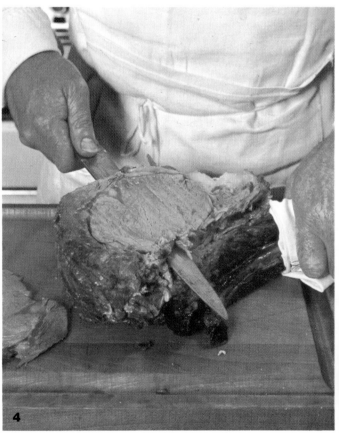

Beef ribs can be carved in two ways, vertically or horizontally **1** To carve vertically, hold the ribs upright on their base and cut regular slices until the knife meets the first bone **2** Start to remove the first bone by sliding the blade of the knife down between the bone and the meat **3** Complete the removal **4** To carve horizontally, place the ribs flat and slice from the thickest part of the joint **5** Continue until

262

5

6

7

8

the knife reaches the narrow part and then the first bone. Cut out the bone by running the blade of the knife right around **6** Bend the bone back to separate it from the meat **7** Put the slices on the serving dish. Surround them with the vegetables such as those illustrated here **8** The completed dish with the sauce-boat of gravy, peas, carrots, potatoes and tomatoes

Braised Beef

Braised meat is first seared in hot fat to seal in the juices, and then barely covered with a water-based liquid and cooked gently until tender. For additional flavour, the meat can be soaked in a marinade before it is cooked; the marinade liquid should always include vinegar, wine or fruit juice for the best flavour.

Beef Olives with Ham

4 thin slices braising steak, 150 g (5 oz) each, from leg or shoulder
4 thin slices cooked ham
1 small onion, chopped
1 clove garlic, chopped
few sage leaves, chopped
10 g (2 tablespoons) chopped parsley
salt and pepper
110 g (4¼ oz) (8½ tablespoons) butter

Beef Olives with Ham uses less expensive beef dressed up with a garnish of button mushrooms and onions

100 ml (4 fl oz) (½ cup) oil
1 onion, coarsely chopped
1 carrot, coarsely chopped
7 g (1 tablespoon) flour
150 ml (¼ pint) (⅝ cup) red wine
300 ml (½ pint) (1¼ cups) brown stock
10 g (1 tablespoon) capers
150 g (5 oz) (⅝ cup) long grain rice
225 g (½ lb) (2 cups) button (pearl) onions
225 g (½ lb) (4 cups) button mushrooms

1 Preheat the oven to 180°C, 350°F, gas 4.

2 Beat the steaks until very thin. Place a slice of ham on each steak. Mix together the chopped onion garlic, sage and half the parsley and divide the mixture between the steaks. Sprinkle with salt and pepper.

3 Roll up the steaks tightly and secure with string or wooden cocktail sticks (toothpicks).

4 Heat 35 g (1¼ oz) (2½ table-spoons) of the butter and half the oil together in a pan, add the meat and fry briskly for 5 minutes.

5 Transfer the meat to a casserole dish. Add the chopped vegetables to the pan, and fry gently, covered, for about 8 minutes or until soft. Sprinkle in the flour and cook for 1-2 minutes or until brown. Stir in the wine and stock and bring to the boil. Pour the contents of the pan over the meat, add the capers and season to taste. Cover the dish and cook in the oven for 1¼ hours.

6 Meanwhile, prepare the garnish. Boil the rice in salted water for 18 minutes, drain and blend in 50 g (2 oz) (4 tablespoons) of the butter and salt and pepper. Heat the rest of the oil and butter in a pan and sauté the onions for 3 minutes until brown. Add the mushrooms and cook for 1 minute more. Cover the vegetables with water and boil for 6 minutes. Drain.

7 When the meat is cooked, arrange the rice on a warmed serving dish, place the meat on top and garnish with the mushrooms and onions and the rest of the parsley.

Serves 4

Braised Beef Home-style

1 kg (2 lb) braising beef from leg, in 1 piece
1 onion, finely sliced
1 clove garlic, peeled and quartered
1 bouquet garni
50 ml (2 fl oz) (¼ cup) brandy
300 ml (½ pint) (1¼ cups) dry white wine
100 g (¼ lb) (½ cup) butter
2 onions, chopped
200 ml (7 fl oz) (⅞ cup) stock
pinch mixed spice
salt and pepper
450 g (1 lb) carrots, sliced
450 g (1 lb) French beans

Braised Beef Home-Style provides a hearty mixture of lean beef and vegetables to satisfy a hungry family

1 Place the meat in a bowl, and add the sliced onion, garlic, bouquet garni, brandy and two-thirds of the wine. Leave to marinate for 3 hours.

2 Drain the meat, reserving the marinade, and dry. Melt half the butter in a flameproof casserole, add the meat and fry briskly until browned all over. Add the chopped onion and fry until golden-brown. Strain the reserved marinade and add it to the pan with the stock, mixed spice and salt and pepper to taste.

Cover and cook gently for 2 hours.

3 Melt the remaining butter in a separate pan, add the carrots and fry gently until browned. Add just enough water to cover, then cook gently until the carrots are tender. Cook the beans in salted water until tender, then drain.

4 When the meat is cooked, add the vegetables to the casserole, cover and cook for a further 15 minutes.

5 Drain the meat and carve into neat slices. Arrange on a warmed serving dish and surround with the vegetables and gravy. Serve hot with roast potatoes.

Serves 6

13

14

15

16

1 The ingredients **2** and **3** Push the larding needle through the beef, thread the strip of fat through the needle and draw back through the meat **4** and **5** Add to the beef the vegetables, garlic, bouquet garni, peppercorns, brandy and wine. Soak for 2 hours **6** Strain, reserving the liquid **7** Brown the beef and remove **8** Fry the vegetables and herbs **9** Return the beef to the pan with the calves' feet, reserved liquid and stock **10** Bring to the boil, remove any scum and place in the oven. Glaze the onions and carrots **11** After 1½ hours, transfer the beef to another casserole. Dice the meat from the calves' feet and add **12** Add the glazed carrots and onions **13** Strain over ¾ of the gravy and complete the cooking **14** Reduce (evaporate) the rest of the gravy and use to glaze the cooked beef **15** and **16** Serve the beef with the vegetables and the juices left in the casserole

Boeuf à la Mode

450 g (1 lb) belly pork fat
salt and pepper
10 g (2 tablespoons) chopped
  parsley
2 kg (4 lb) braising beef
600 ml (1 pint) (2½ cups) red wine
1 bouquet garni
675 g (1½ lb) carrots
1 shallot, sliced
2 large onions, sliced
2 cloves garlic, crushed
6 peppercorns
50 ml (2 fl oz) (¼ cup) brandy
100 ml (4 fl oz) (½ cup) oil
2 calves' feet, cut in half
1 litre (1¾ pints) (4½ cups) beef
  stock
100 g (¼ lb) (½ cup) butter
10 g (1 teaspoon) sugar
12 button (pearl) onions
25 g (1 oz) (3 tablespoons)
  cornflour (cornstarch) mixed
  with 150 ml (¼ pint) (⅝ cup) water
  (optional)

1 Cut the pork fat into strips, 1 cm (½ in) thick. Season and sprinkle over the parsley. Lard the beef at regular intervals with the strips (see pages 606-607).

2 Place the meat in an earthenware dish with the wine and bouquet garni. Cut half the carrots in slices across and add them to the dish with the shallot, onions, garlic, peppercorns and brandy. Leave in the refrigerator for 2 hours, turning from time to time.

3 Preheat the oven to 180°C, 350°F, gas 4. Strain the meat and vegetables, reserving the liquid. Heat the oil in an ovenproof casserole, add the beef and cook quickly for 10 minutes until browned. Lift out the meat and fry the strained vegetables and bouquet garni for 5 minutes.

4 Return the beef to the pan, add the calves' feet and pour in the reserved liquid and the beef stock. Season and bring to the boil. Remove any scum, cover the dish and cook in the oven for 2-2½ hours.

5 Heat half the butter in a pan, add the rest of the carrots, the sugar and enough water to cover.

Cook until the liquid has evaporated. In a separate pan, heat the rest of the butter, add the onions and enough water to cover and cook for 8 minutes.

6 After the meat has been cooking for 1½ hours, remove from the oven and transfer the beef to another casserole. Dice the meat of the calves' feet and discard the bones. Add the diced meat to the beef with the glazed carrots and onions. Strain the gravy and add about three-quarters to the beef. Cover again and return to the oven for the rest of the cooking time.

7 Boil the rest of the gravy for 5 minutes to reduce (evaporate) it. Season.

As a variation on Boeuf à la Mode, beef topside may be braised in stout (dark beer) instead of wine. This gives it a darker colour and a rich malty flavour. It may be served cold in its gravy which forms a jelly

8 Place the cooked meat on a serving dish and coat with the reduced (evaporated) gravy. Return to the oven for a few minutes to glaze.

9 Surround the meat with the vegetables, coat with the gravy and serve hot. The gravy can be thickened with cornflour (cornstarch) if liked.

Serves 8

All about Beef Stews and Casseroles
Daube of Beef in Red Wine

Beef Stews

Stews and casseroles provide the best methods of cooking tougher cuts of beef. They all involve slow cooking at a low heat with a measured volume of liquid: (that is, one cup meat to one cup liquid) although you can use a pressure cooker. You can use a covered pan on the stove and simmer at 85°C, 180°F, but for best results, cook in a casserole in an oven preheated to 180°C, 350°F, gas 4.

The cooking liquor should be slightly acid, to help tenderize the meat. Include a little wine, cider, beer, tomato concentrate (paste) or fruit juice. The meat can be marinated first, and the marinade included in the cooking liquor. For a better flavour, fry the meat quickly in fat to brown it and seal in the juices. Root vegetables and onions which are added for flavour should be lightly fried, too, before you add stock and any aromatic herbs you may wish to include. Flour for thickening can be added when the meat is browned, or as a roux stirred into the cooking liquor when the stew is nearly done. A stew cooked with pulses or beans makes a meal in itself.

Cuts suitable for stewing come from muscular areas, such as leg and shoulder. Buttock steak, silverside, flank, skirt, clod and chuck steak are all good and economical. Beef offal (variety meats) lend themselves to slow cooking. Oxtail provides a rich stew and ox kidney and liver, which tend to be strongly flavoured, are often cooked with stewing beef or bacon.

Stews have the great merit of being suitable for cooking in advance, for reheating or freezing. Many casseroles improve with reheating because their sauce continues its work of tenderizing even as it cools.

Beef from Burgundy

100 ml (4 fl oz) (½ cup) oil
1 kg (2 lb) silverside, cut into
  2.5 cm (1 in) cubes
1 carrot, thinly sliced
1 large onion, thinly sliced
25 g (1 oz) (4 tablespoons) flour
500 ml (1 pint) (2½ cups) dry red
  wine
salt and pepper
2 cloves garlic, peeled and
  crushed
1 bouquet garni
100 g (¼ lb) (1 cup) small (pearl)
  onions, peeled
15 g (½ oz) (1 tablespoon) sugar
50 g (2 oz) (¼ cup) butter
100 g (¼ lb) streaky bacon rashers
  (slices), cut in strips
100 g (¼ lb) (1 cup) mushrooms,
  chopped

1 Heat three-quarters of the oil in a stewpan, put the pieces of beef into it and brown over a high heat. Remove the meat, then pour out any remaining oil and add the slices of carrot and onion. Let them brown lightly, then add the flour and cook it, stirring constantly with a wooden spoon.

2 Mix in all the wine. Bring it to the boil and allow at least a third of it to evaporate on a high heat. Return the meat to the pan and add enough cold water to cover it. Add salt, pepper, the garlic and the bouquet garni. Cover and cook gently for 2½ hours.

3 Put the small (pearl) onions in a pan with the sugar, the butter and enough water to cover. Cover and cook until the water has evaporated. When a golden caramel mixture remains, roll the small onions in it and put to one side.

4 Heat the rest of the oil in a pan and lightly fry the bacon. Drain and reserve. Fry the mushrooms in the same oil and reserve.

5 When the stew is cooked, sieve (strain) the sauce, then return it to the pan. Add the small (pearl) onions, bacon and mushrooms and cook for a further 10 minutes.

Serves 6

Czardaz Beef with Caraway Rice

30 ml (1 fl oz) (2 tablespoons) oil
1 kg (2 lb) stewing beef, cut into
  2.5 cm (1 in) cubes
3 sticks celery, chopped
1 large onion, sliced
150 ml (¼ pint) (⅝ cup) water
½ beef stock cube
450 g (1 lb) (2⅔ cups) canned
  pineapple cubes, with juice
5 g (1 tablespoon) chopped
  parsley
good pinch sugar
15 g (½ oz) (1 tablespoon) tomato
  concentrate (paste)
few drops Worcestershire sauce
salt and pepper
350 g (¾ lb) (1½ cups) long grain
  rice
25 g (1 oz) (2 tablespoons) butter
10 g (2 teaspoons) caraway seeds

1 Preheat the oven to 180°C, 350°F, gas 4.

2 Heat the oil in a frying pan (skillet). Brown the meat in it, remove and place in a casserole. Add the celery and the onion to the oil and fry for 3 minutes, then add to the casserole.

3 Pour the water into a pan, bring to the boil and crumble in the stock cube. Drain the pineapple and add the juice to the stock with the parsley, sugar, tomato concentrate (paste), Worcestershire sauce and salt and pepper to taste. Pour over the meat in the casserole, cover, and Cook for 1½ hours, adding more stock if necessary.

4 15 minutes before the end of cooking, add the pineapple.

5 To cook the rice, first place it in a sieve (strainer) and wash it thoroughly under cold running water. Remove any discoloured grains. Place it in a large pan of boiling, slightly salted water. Boil for 12 minutes or until the rice is tender. Drain and return to the pan to dry. Gently stir in the butter and the caraway seeds.

Serves 6

Czardas Beef with Caraway Rice is a fruity casserole with a Russian flavour which will delight your family and friends

Austrian Beef Casserole with Horseradish Sauce

1 kg (2 lb) stewing beef
50 ml (2 fl oz) (¼ cup) oil
6 small onions
1½ litres (3 pints) (7½ cups) water
3 beef stock cubes
bouquet garni
6 leeks

For the Horseradish Sauce:
150 ml (¼ pint) (⅝ cup) water
25 ml (1 fl oz) (⅛ cup) white vinegar
150 g (6 oz) horseradish, scraped
150 g (6 oz) cooking (green) apples, peeled and cored
25 g (1 oz) (½ cup) fresh white breadcrumbs
50 ml (2 fl oz) (¼ cup) single (light) cream

1 Cut the meat into 4 mm (1½ in) cubes.

2 Heat the oil in a heavy pan and brown the meat, covered with a lid, for 8 minutes. Stir often.

3 Slice the onions and add to the meat, and brown for 3 minutes.

4 Cover with the water mixed with the beef cubes and bouquet garni.

5 Wash the leeks, split into four, tie in a bundle and put with the meat.

6 Bring to the boil, and remove the scum as it rises with a spoon. Simmer for 2-2½ hours until the meat is tender.

7 Meanwhile, put the water and vinegar in a bowl and grate the horseradish and apple into it. Soak for 1 hour. Drain the liquid off, and mix the breadcrumbs and cream into the mixture. Place in a bowl.

8 When the meat is cooked, the broth may be strained off and served separately as soup. Remove the leeks, discard the string, and place on top of the meat.

Serves 6

Beef Nicoise is a casserole from the Mediterranean, cooked in wine and garnished with tomatoes and black olives

Tip: In Central Europe the broth would be served with liver dumplings.

Beef Niçoise

1 kg (2 lb) stewing beef
100 g (¼ lb) streaky bacon
50 ml (2 fl oz) (¼ cup) oil
4 onions, sliced
2 cloves garlic, peeled and crushed
bouquet garni
25 g (1 oz) (4 tablespoons) flour
300 ml (½ pint) (1¼ cups) wine
300 ml (½ pint) (1¼ cups) water
1 beef stock cube
25 g (1 oz) (2 tablespoons) tomato concentrate (paste)
6 tomatoes, skinned, deseeded and chopped
salt and pepper
5 g (1 tablespoon) chopped parsley
6 black olives

1 Cut the meat into 2.5 cm (1 in) cubes and the bacon into small cubes, 5 mm (¼ in), or, if in rashers (slices), into strips.

2 Heat the oil in a thick pan. Brown the beef and bacon for 8 minutes, covered with a lid. Stir often.

3 Add the onion, garlic and bouquet garni, cook for 4 minutes. Sprinkle on the flour, cook for 1 minute.

4 Add the wine, water, stock cube, tomato concentrate (paste) and chopped tomatoes. Season. Bring to the boil and simmer for 1½-2 hours until the meat is tender. Or cook in the oven with a lid on at 180°C, 350°F, gas 4 for the same time.

5 When ready to serve, add the chopped parsley and olives.

Serves 6

Austrian Beef Casserole with Horseradish Sauce is a tasty, way of serving beef with leeks and a creamy sauce

Look'n Cook Daube of Beef with Red Wine

1 The ingredients **2** Cut the belly of pork and white belly pork fat into strips. Put the belly pork fat in a dish, sprinkle with brandy and chopped parsley and chill **3** Cut the meat into cubes, and thread each piece with a strip of fat **4** Place the ingredients in a bowl, and add the mushrooms **5** Pour over the red wine, oil and brandy. Season and marinate for 2 hours. Remove the meat and belly of pork and dry.

Put some oil in the casserole and brown the meat
6 Add the vegetables and brown. Add the marinade
and water **7** Bring to the boil and cook in the oven for
2½ hours at 180°C, 350°F, gas 4 **8** When the meat is
tender, remove the fat with a ladle, and remove the
bouquet garni and pork rind **9** Place the meat on a
serving dish and pour the sauce over. Sprinkle with
the parsley and serve with new potatoes

Daube of Beef with Red Wine

225 g (½ lb) belly of pork
225 g (½ lb) white belly pork fat (optional)
50 ml (2 fl oz) (¼ cup) brandy or port
5 g (1 tablespoon) chopped parsley
2 kg (4 lb) topside of beef
3 large carrots, chopped
3 large onions, chopped
3 large tomatoes, chopped
3 cloves garlic, crushed
8 mushrooms
225 g (½ lb) pork rind (optional)
½ bottle red wine
100 ml (4 fl oz) (½ cup) oil
salt
12 peppercorns, crushed
pinch mixed spice
300 ml (½ pint) (1¼ cup) water
bouquet garni
7 g (1 tablespoon) cornflour (cornstarch), optional

1 Cut the lean belly of pork into strips, and scald by plunging in boiling water for 1 minute. Cool.

2 Cut the white belly pork fat (if used) into strips 5 cm x 5 mm (2 x ¼ in), sprinkle with a few drops of brandy and a pinch of parsley. Chill for ½ hour.

3 Cut the meat into 4 cm (1½ in) cubes. If using the pork fat, take a larding needle, and thread each piece with a strip of fat.

4 Place the belly of pork and the meat in a bowl with the carrots, onions and tomatoes, garlic, mushrooms and pork rind (if used).

5 Pour on the wine, brandy and half of the oil. Add salt, the peppercorns and the mixed spice and marinate for 2 hours. Remove the meat and dry on absorbent paper.

6 Preheat the oven to 180°C, 350°F, gas 4.

7 Put the remainder of the oil in a thick pan, add the meat and belly of pork and brown for 5 minutes. Add the vegetables and brown for 3 minutes. Add the marinade, water, and bouquet garni and bring to the boil. Put in the oven with a lid on and cook for 2½ hours, or until the meat is tender.

8 When cooked, remove the fat from the surface carefully with a ladle. Remove the bouquet garni and pork rind (if used).

9 If you wish, thicken the daube with the cornflour (cornstarch) mixed with 100 ml (4 fl oz) (½ cup) water and cook for 2 minutes, stirring gently.

10 Place the meat on a serving dish, pour over the sauce and sprinkle with the remainder of the chopped parsley. Serve with new potatoes.

Serves 8

Steak Romanov

450 g (1 lb) fillet (cut from the thin end)
50 ml (2 fl oz) (¼ cup) oil
1 medium onion, or 3 shallots, chopped
7 g (1 tablespoon) paprika
25 g (1 oz) (2 tablespoons) tomato concentrate (paste)
150 ml (¼ pint) (⅝ cup) water
150 ml (¼ pint) (⅝ cup) whipping cream
15 ml (1 tablespoon) vodka
salt and pepper

1 Remove the skin and fat from the fillet and cut the meat into cubes 2 cm (¾ in) thick.

2 Heat the oil in a frying pan (skillet). Brown the meat for 4 minutes, stirring constantly. Remove from the pan.

3 In the same pan, fry the onions gently for 2 minutes without colouring.

4 Sprinkle on the paprika and add the tomato concentrate (paste) and cook for 2 minutes, stirring.

5 Add the water and boil for 5 minutes. Beat the cream until stiff, add to the pan and boil for 2 minutes.

6 Reheat the meat in the sauce for 3 minutes. Remove from the heat.

7 Just before serving, add the vodka and check the seasoning. Serve with boiled rice.

Serves 4

Variation

This recipe for Steak Romanov is given as an illustration of a style of cooking steak in a frying pan (skillet) in front of the guests. Because it is cooked in only a few minutes, fillet steak must be used so that the meat is both cooked and tender.

The Russians tend to use sour cream, rather than the fresh cream we have used, and they call it Sauce Smitane. If you wish to try this, you can buy sour cream, or make your own by adding a few drops of lemon juice to the fresh cream.

To make Sauce Smitane, gently fry some chopped onions in butter. Add wine and reduce (evaporate). Pour in the sour cream and boil for a few moments. Strain through a sieve and add lemon juice. Try this sauce with beef, or with chicken, veal or lamb.

Another Russian variation on Steak Romanov would be to use caraway seeds instead of paprika, and to add a little kummel, which is a liqueur flavoured with caraway seeds.

The classic dish of Beef Strogonoff is another variation of a dish to be cooked in public. For this the fillet is cut in thin strips and cooked with mushrooms and sour cream. The dish was created by the head chef of the Count Strogonoff in the 1880s in Russia. The dish was almost unknown in Europe, until the great mass of Russian emigrants came to France after the Russian Revolution. The dish then became very popular in the big hotels of the French Riviera in the 1920s and gradually spread through Europe as the head waiters of famous restaurants enjoyed the drama of preparing this dish, flaming in brandy, before honoured customers. Brandy is the traditional spirit used, although other spirits may be added. In our section on wine and spirits which will follow in a later issue, we shall explain Strogonoff in detail.

Look'n Cook Steak Romanov

1 Cut the fillet into cubes **2** Heat the oil in a frying pan (skillet) and brown the meat, stirring constantly **3** Remove the meat from the pan **4** Fry the chopped onions gently, sprinkle on the paprika and add the tomato concentrate (paste) and stir. Cook for 2 minutes. Add the water **5** Add the cream, stir and boil **6** Reheat the meat in the sauce. Remove from the heat, add the vodka and season

Country Beef and Olive Casserole

675 g (1½ lb) stewing beef
30 ml (2 tablespoons) oil
3 carrots, sliced
2 small onions, quartered
1 stick celery, sliced
1 clove garlic, peeled and
   crushed
25 g (1 oz) (4 tablespoons) flour
300 ml (½ pint) (1¼ cups) water
150 ml (¼ pint) (⅝ cup) sherry
450 g (1 lb) (1¾ cups) canned
   tomatoes
1 beef stock cube
1 bay leaf, imported
few sprigs parsley
salt and pepper
6 stuffed green olives, sliced

1 Cut the beef into 4 cm (1½ in) cubes.

2 Preheat the oven to 180°C, 350°F, gas 4.

3 Heat the oil in a saucepan and fry the meat until browned. Remove from the pan.

4 Add the carrots, onions, celery and garlic to the pan. Fry over a low heat for 5 minutes.

5 Stir in the flour and cook gently for a few minutes, then add the water, sherry and canned tomatoes. Crumble in the stock cube and stir well. Add the bay leaf and parsley and season with salt and pepper.

6 Bring to the boil, stirring all the time until it thickens. Transfer to an ovenproof dish, cover with a lid and cook in the oven for 2½ hours. Remove the bay leaf and parsley. Stir in the olives and serve with French beans and boiled potatoes.

Serves 4

Country Beef and Olive Casserole has a distinctive Spanish flavour with its tomatoes and stuffed olives

Sweet and Sour Beef

4 beef sausages
30 ml (2 tablespoons) oil
1 onion, chopped
225 g (½ lb) (1⅓ cups) diced, boiled
   beef

For the Sauce:
300 ml (½ pint) (1¼ cups) water
½ cucumber, cut into chunks
2 sticks celery, sliced
1 carrot, cut into thin strips
50 ml (2 fl oz) (¼ cup) soya sauce
1 beef stock cube
1 clove garlic, peeled and
   chopped
10 g (1 tablespoon) fresh ginger,
   peeled and chopped
25 g (1 oz) (1½ tablespoons) honey
30 ml (2 tablespoons) vinegar
15 g (½ oz) (1½ tablespoons)
   cornflour (cornstarch)
salt and pepper

1 Grill (broil) or fry the sausages. Cool and cut in thick slices.

2 Heat the oil and fry the onion until soft, then add the beef and sausages. Fry for 5 minutes.

3 Bring the water to the boil, and cook the cucumber, celery and carrot for 5 minutes so that they are still crisp.

4 Add the soya sauce and crumble in the stock cube. Add the garlic, ginger, honey and vinegar and stir well. Mix the cornflour (cornstarch) with a little water and stir into the sauce. Boil for 3 minutes until it thickens, stirring all the time. Stir in the sausage, beef and onion mixture and simmer for 10 minutes.

5 Arrange on a serving dish, surrounded by boiled rice.

Serves 4

Tip: For a sweeter and more colourful sauce, try adding strips of red pepper, pineapple chunks and tangerine segments (sections) to the sauce before serving.

Sweet and Sour Beef Curried Meat Balls and Beef Farmhouse Pie are three supper dishes, for cold evenings

Look'n Cook Beef Goulash

1 The ingredients 2 Peel the onions and slice them finely 3 Cut the meat into 3 cm (1in) cubes 4 Fry the onion in the oil for 4 minutes until pale brown 5 Add the cubed meat, reduce the heat and cook gently for 8 minutes, stirring from time to time 6 While the meat is cooking, remove the seeds from the pepper and cut the flesh into shreds. Skin, deseed and chop the tomatoes 7 Add the paprika,

cumin, garlic, seasoning and marjoram to the pan and cook for 1 minute **8** Add the tomatoes and pepper and cook for another 10 minutes **9** Stir in the wine and water and crumble in the beef stock cubes.

Cook gently for 1½ hours **10** Boil the potatoes **11** Thicken the goulash and add the lemon juice to the cream **12** Serve the goulash with the sour cream and the potatoes

Beef Goulash

75 ml (2½ fl oz) (⅜ cup) oil
3 medium onions, thinly
  sliced
675 g (1½ lb) stewing beef,
  eg chuck steak, cut in
  3 cm (1 in) cubes
15 g (½ oz) (1 tablespoon) paprika
good pinch cumin
2 cloves garlic, crushed
salt and pepper
pinch marjoram
3 tomatoes, skinned, deseeded
  and chopped
1 green pepper, shredded
150 ml (¼ pint) (⅝ cup) red wine
1 litre (1¾ pints) (4½ cups) water
2 beef stock cubes
675 g (1½ lb) potatoes, peeled
25 g (1 oz) (3 tablespoons)
  cornflour (cornstarch)
juice half lemon
150 ml (¼ pint) (⅝ cup) single
  (light) cream

1 Heat the oil in a pan and fry the onion for 4 minutes until pale brown. Add the meat, reduce the heat and cook gently for 8 minutes, stirring from time to time.

2 Add the paprika, cumin, garlic, seasoning and marjoram and cook for 1 minute more. Add the tomatoes and pepper and simmer for another 10 minutes. Stir in the wine and water and crumble in the stock cubes. Cook gently for 1½ hours.

3 Towards the end of the cooking time, boil the potatoes in salted water for 18 minutes.

4 When ready to serve, dissolve the cornflour (cornstarch) in 150ml (¼ pint) (⅝ cup) water, stir into the meat and cook for 2-3 minutes until thickened.

5 Add the lemon juice to the cream. Serve the goulash with the sour cream and the boiled potatoes.

Serves 6

Tip: Shell pasta or rice can be served with this dish in place of the boiled potatoes, if preferred.

Beef Casseroles

Hungarian Meatballs Casserole

450 g (1 lb) (2 cups) minced
  (ground) beef
25 g (1 oz) (½ cup) breadcrumbs
1 egg
salt and pepper
5 g (1 tablespoon) chopped
  parsley
50 g (2 oz) (good ½ cup) flour
50 ml (2 fl oz) (¼ cup) oil
3 large onions, sliced
25 g (1 oz) (2 tablespoons) paprika
50 g (2 oz) (4 tablespoons) tomato
  concentrate (paste)
15 g (½ oz) (2 tablespoons) flour
1 stock cube
300 ml (½ pint) (1¼ cups) boiling
  water
pinch caraway seeds (optional)
450 g (1 lb) potatoes, sliced

1 Mix the minced (ground) meat, breadcrumbs, egg, salt and pepper, and parsley in a bowl. Make 12 meatballs and dust with the flour.

2 Preheat the oven to 190°C, 375°F, gas 5.

3 Heat most of the oil in a frying pan (skillet), brown the meatballs and place in a casserole.

4 To make the sauce, slice the onions, and brown in the rest of the oil. Add the paprika and tomato concentrate (paste) and cook for 2 minutes. Sprinkle on the flour. Stir; cook for 1 minute.

5 Add the stock cube mixed with the boiling water. Season and add the caraway seeds.

6 Pour the sauce over the meatballs. Arrange slices of potato round the dish and bake for 45 minutes.

Serves 4

Hellenic Casserole

½ kg (1 lb) aubergines (eggplants),
  sliced
50 ml (2 fl oz) (¼ cup) oil
2 large onions, thinly sliced
1 clove garlic, crushed
450 g (1 lb) (2 cups) minced
  (ground) beef
25 g (1 oz) (2 tablespoons) tomato
  concentrate (paste)
salt and pepper
300 ml (½ pint) (1¼ cups) boiling
  water
1 stock cube
450 g (1 lb) tomatoes, sliced
450 g (1 lb) boiled potatoes, sliced
2 eggs
150 ml (¼ pint) (⅝ cup) single (light)
  cream
50 g (2 oz) (½ cup) grated cheese
25 g (1 oz) (3 tablespoons) grated
  Parmesan cheese

1 Sprinkle the aubergines (eggplants), with salt and leave for ½ hour. Wash off the bitter juices and dry.

2 Heat the oil in a frying pan (skillet) and cook the aubergine (eggplant) slices for ½ minute on each side. Remove from the pan.

3 Preheat the oven to 180°C, 350°F, gas 4.

4 Fry the onions and garlic until golden-brown. Add the minced (ground) meat and brown, stirring. Add the tomato concentrate (paste) and cook for 2 minutes. Season. Add the boiling water mixed with the stock cube. Simmer for 10 minutes.

5 Arrange the aubergines (eggplants), meat and onions, sliced tomatoes and sliced potatoes, in layers in a casserole and bake for 35 minutes.

6 Beat the eggs with the cream and stir in the cheese. Pour on to the casserole and return to the oven for 20 minutes until the topping is golden-brown.

Serves 4

The centre of our table shows, from top to bottom: Hungarian Meatballs Casserole, Steak and Kidney Pudding, Hellenic Casserole

Quick Chicken and Beef Casserole

300 ml (½ pint) (1¼ cups) white sauce
50 ml (2 fl oz) (¼ cup) dry sherry
salt and pepper
100 g (¼ lb) (⅔ cup) cooked beef, cut into strips
1 gherkin (dill pickle), sliced
100 g (¼ lb) (⅔ cup) cooked chicken, diced
50 g (2 oz) (⅔ cup) sliced mushrooms
100 g (¼ lb) (⅔ cup) ham, cut into strips
50 g (2 oz) (½ cup) flaked almonds

1 Heat the white sauce and stir in the sherry and season with salt and pepper.

2 Preheat the oven to 180°C, 350°F, gas 4.

3 Place the beef and gherkin (dill pickle) in the bottom of an oven-proof dish. Pour in half of the white sauce. Put a layer of chicken, mushrooms and 75 g (3 oz) (½ cup) of the ham on top. Pour over the remaining white sauce and sprinkle with the almonds and ham strips.

4 Place in the oven and warm through for 15 minutes.

Serves 4

Tip: This casserole is especially quick to make and all sorts of leftover meat could be used such as pork or turkey or even veal. For extra body, mix in some canned butter beans.

Mexican Hotpot

25 ml (1 fl oz) (⅛ cup) oil
1 large onion, chopped
1 green pepper, deseeded and chopped
1 red pepper, deseeded and chopped
450 g (1 lb) minced (ground) beef
pinch paprika
pinch chilli powder
25 g (1 oz) (4 tablespoons) flour

25 g (1 oz) (2 tablespoons) tomato concentrate (paste)
400 ml (¾ pint) (1¾ cups) water
1 beef stock cube
bouquet garni
salt and pepper
225 g (½ lb) (1 cup) canned kidney beans, drained

1 Heat the oil in a saucepan and fry the onion until soft. Add the green and red peppers and cook for 1 minute. Add the minced (ground) beef and brown for 5 minutes, stirring occasionally.

2 Stir in the paprika, chilli powder and flour and cook for 2 minutes. Add the tomato concentrate (paste) and water, and crumble in the stock cube. Bring to the boil, stirring all the time, then add the bouquet garni, lower the heat and cook gently on top of the stove for 30 minutes.

3 Season with salt and pepper to taste and add the drained kidney beans. Continue cooking for another 5 minutes until the kidney beans are heated through, then serve with plain boiled rice.

Serves 4

Tip: If you like really hot spicy food, try increasing the amount of chilli powder and adding some corn kernels for a more authentic South American flavour.

Beef Cobbler

50 ml (2 fl oz) (¼ cup) oil
675 g (1½ lb) stewing steak, cubed
1 onion, chopped
1 carrot, chopped
25 g (1 oz) (4 tablespoons) flour
25 g (1 oz) (2 tablespoons) tomato concentrate (paste)
300 ml (½ pint) (1¼ cups) water
300 ml (½ pint) (1¼ cups) beer
1 beef stock cube
1 clove garlic, peeled and crushed
pinch rosemary
salt and pepper
15 ml (1 tablespoon) milk
5 g (1 tablespoon) chopped parsley

For the Cobbler Topping:
175 g (6 oz) (1½ cups) self-raising flour
pinch salt
2 sticks celery, finely chopped
10 g (2 tablespoons) chopped parsley
40 g (1½ oz) (3 tablespoons) butter or margarine
100 ml (4 fl oz) (½ cup) milk

1 Heat the oil in a pan and brown the stewing steak for 5 minutes. Add the onion and carrot and cook for 2-3 more minutes until soft. Stir in the flour and cook for a further minute.

2 Preheat the oven to 180°C, 350°F, gas 4.

3 Add the tomato concentrate (paste), water and beer and crumble in the stock cube. Add the garlic and rosemary and bring to the boil.

4 Transfer to an ovenproof casserole dish and place in the oven for 1½ hours.

5 Meanwhile, make the cobbler topping. Mix together the flour, salt, celery and parsley in a bowl. Rub in the fat until the mixture resembles fine breadcrumbs. Add the milk, a little at a time, and mix together well to make a soft dough.

6 Knead the dough lightly on a floured worktop and roll out 2 cm (¾ in) thick. Using a 7 cm (3 in) cutter, cut out as many circles as you can. Then, using a 1 cm (½ in) cutter, cut a hole in the centre of each dough circle.

7 Increase the oven temperature to 220°C, 425°F, gas 7. Remove the casserole and season to taste. Arrange the scone rings, overlapping each other, around the top and brush with milk.

8 Bake for a further 20 minutes until the topping is golden-brown. Garnish with chopped parsley.

Serves 4

Mexican Hotpot, Beef Cobbler and Quick Chicken and Beef Casserole are all deliciously different ideas for casseroling beef

Beef Hotpots

Hot pot Parisienne

225 g (½ lb) butter beans or lima
  beans
675 g (1½ lb) stewing beef, cut into
  2½ cm (1 in) cubes
50 ml (2 fl oz) (¼ cup) oil
2 onions, chopped
1 clove garlic, crushed
15 g (½ oz) (2 tablespoons) flour
15 g (½ oz) (1 tablespoon) tomato
  concentrate (paste)
300 ml (½ pint) (1¼ cups) water
150 ml (¼ pint) (⅝ cup) white wine

bouquet garni
sprig rosemary
salt and pepper
2 courgettes (zucchini), sliced
4 tomatoes, quartered

1 If using dried beans, soak them overnight in water, then bring to boil and simmer until tender. Rinse and drain.

2 Preheat oven to 180°C, 350°F, gas 4. Brown the meat in the oil for 5 minutes in a saucepan. Add the onion and garlic and cook for 2 minutes. Sprinkle in the flour and cook for 2 minutes to brown it. Stir in the tomato concentrate (paste) and then pour in the water and wine. Season with the bouquet garni, rosemary, salt and pepper. Bring it to the boil and simmer for 10 minutes.

*Hotpot Parisienne makes
a colourful and economical dish
for a dinner party —
serve with boiled or savoury rice*

3 Transfer the mixture to an earthenware pot. Add the beans, cover, and bake in the oven for 1½-2 hours.

4 Remove the hotpot from the oven, add the courgettes (zucchini) and tomatoes, and return to the oven for 15 minutes. Check seasoning, and serve hot.

Serves 6

Beef in Cider Hotpot

40 g (1½ oz) (3 tablespoons) butter
675 g (1½ lb) beef topside, cut into
  thin slices
1 large onion, sliced
2 large carrots, peeled and sliced
2 turnips, peeled and diced
40 g (1½ oz) (6 tablespoons) flour
450 ml (¾ pint) (2 cups) dry cider,
  or 300 ml (½ pint) (1¼ cups) apple
  juice with 150 ml (¼ pint) (⅝ cup)
  water and 15 ml (1 tablespoon)
  vinegar
salt and pepper
1 beef stock cube, crumbled
450 g (1 lb) (3 cups) potatoes,
  peeled and thinly sliced
75 g (3 oz) (¾ cup) grated cheese

1 Preheat oven to 180°C, 350°F, gas 4. Melt the butter and fry the beef slices for 5 minutes. Remove. Add the onion, carrots and turnips to the pan and fry gently for 10 minutes. Stir in the flour for 1 minute. Remove from heat and pour in the cider or apple juice. Bring to the boil, then add seasoning and the stock cube. Cook for 5 minutes.

2 Pour into an earthenware pot and arrange the potato slices on top. Cover and cook in the oven for 1½-2 hours. Increase the oven temperature to 200°C, 400°F, gas 6. Sprinkle the grated cheese on top and bake for 15-20 minutes uncovered until the cheese is golden-brown. Serve.

Serves 4

*Beef in Cider Hotpot is a delicious
variation on the
traditional hotpot — the beef is
cooked in cider
and topped with cheese*

Beef Fondues

Sukiyaki

225 g (½ lb) (1 cup) rice
salt
225 g (½ lb) (3 cups) finely
　shredded white cabbage
1 large leek, cleaned and sliced
　slantways
225 g (½ lb) canned water
　chestnuts
2 large carrots, thinly sliced
100 g (¼ lb) radishes, sliced
4 unbroken egg yolks

450 g (1 lb) fillet beef, cut in 3 mm
(⅛ in) slices, about 5 cm (2 in)
long

For the Stock:
600 ml (1 pint) (2½ cups) water
2 beef stock cubes
50 ml (2 fl oz) (¼ cup) soya sauce
150 ml (¼ pint) (⅝ cup) dry sherry

1 Boil the rice in salted water until just tender. Rinse and drain. Prepare the vegetables and arrange in a wide dish.

2 At the table, serve each diner with a bowl of rice and a side dish containing an unbroken egg yolk. Bring the water to the boil in the fondue pot. Crumble in the stock cubes and stir to dissolve. Pour in the soya sauce and sherry, bring back to the boil and keep just under boiling point.

3 Place pieces of each vegetable in the stock, and a piece of meat for each diner in the middle. Diners may remove the meat when it is cooked to their individual taste – a couple of minutes should be enough. Serve the vegetables, also cooked to taste, on the rice, and dip the pieces of meat in the egg yolk before eating. Replenish the stock with vegetables and meat as required.

Serves 4

Sukiyaki is a traditional Japanese dish — the guests cook their own meat and help themselves to dips and vegetables

Beef Fondue with Dips

300 ml (½ pint) (1¼ cups)
　mayonnaise
5 g (1 teaspoon) curry powder or
　15 ml (1 tablespoon) curry sauce
1 clove garlic, crushed
5 g (1 tablespoon) chopped fresh
　parsley and chives
750 ml (1¼ pints) (3 cups) water
2 beef stock cubes
150 ml (¼ pint) (⅝ cup) dry sherry
bouquet garni
2 fresh mint leaves
salt and pepper
450 g (1 lb) fillet beef, diced

1 Divide the mayonnaise between 2 dishes. Into one, mix the curry powder or sauce to make a curry dip. Into the other stir the garlic, parsley and chives to make a garlic herb dip.

2 At the table, boil the water, add the stock cubes, sherry, bouquet garni, mint leaves, and season to taste. Keep just below boiling point. Diners take a piece of meat on a fondue fork and leave it in the stock 2-5 minutes until cooked to taste. Dip the meat into one of the dips before eating.

Serves 4

Tip: Other fondue sauces include horseradish, tomato, mustard or tartare.

Beef Fondue with Dips is fun to eat — diners boil meat at the table and flavour it with dips and sauces

Economy Beef

Texturized soya protein has proved of great help to cooks to stretch meat further and hence economize, especially with beef. It reduces the need for starchy additives like potato and has the same nutritional value as meat. Its neutral taste absorbs the flavour of whatever it is cooked with. To increase its flavour, fry at the same time as the beef.

Curried Beef and Golden Rice

225 g (½ lb) (1 cup) long-grain rice
good pinch turmeric
225 g (½ lb) basic economy beef
1 carrot, diced
15 g (½ oz) (1 tablespoon) curry powder
5 g (1 teaspoon) desiccated coconut
25 g (1 oz) (2 tablespoons) sultanas (seedless white raisins)
1 apple, peeled, cored and diced

1 Boil the rice in plenty of salted water to which a good pinch of turmeric has been added. Simmer until tender, rinse and drain. Keep warm.

2 Make the basic economy beef, according to the recipe, but add the diced carrot to the onion before frying, and stir in the curry powder when browning the meat. Stir in the coconut, sultanas (white raisins) and apple after adding the soya protein.

3 Arrange the rice around the edge of a large dish, and pour the curry into the middle. Serve hot.

Serves 4

Basic Economy Beef

1 large onion, chopped
25 g (1 oz) (2 tablespoons) fat
450 g (1 lb) (2 cups) minced (ground) beef
25 g (1 oz) (4 tablespoons) flour
25 g (1 oz) (2 tablespoons) tomato concentrate (paste)
300 ml (½ pint) (1¼ cups) water
1 beef stock cube
salt, pepper, pinch mace
100 g (¼ lb) (½ cup) reconstituted texturized soya protein

1 Fry the onion gently in the fat until soft. Stir in the beef and flour and cook until browned. Add the tomato concentrate (paste) and continue to cook for 2 minutes.

2 Pour in the water, in which the stock cube has been dissolved, and season with salt, pepper and a pinch of mace. Add the soya protein. Simmer for ½ hour, stirring from time to time.

Makes 675 g (1½ lb)
Serves 4

Beef and Vegetable Vol-au-vent

one 15 cm (6 in) vol-au-vent shell
225 g (½ lb) basic economy beef
50 g (2 oz) (½ cup) frozen peas
2 courgettes (zucchini), peeled and sliced

1 Preheat the oven to 220°C, 425°F, gas 7. Bake the vol-au-vent shell for 20-25 minutes or until golden-brown. Keep warm.

2 Meanwhile prepare the basic economy beef, according to the recipe. While it is cooking, add the peas to boiling, salted water. Bring back to the boil, add the courgettes (zucchini) and cook them together for 4 minutes.

3 When the beef is cooked, stir in the peas and courgettes (zucchini) and pour the mixture into the vol-au-vent case. Serve immediately.

Serves 4

Stuffed Pancakes (Crêpes)

225 g (½ lb) basic economy beef
½ green pepper, diced
100 g (¼ lb) (1 cup) corn kernels
5 g (1 teaspoon) chilli powder
300 ml (½ pint) (1¼ cups) batter
100 g (¼ lb) (1 cup) grated cheese

1 Make the basic economy beef as in the recipe, but add the diced green pepper to the onion before frying, and add the corn kernels and chilli powder with the soya protein.

2 Meanwhile make 4 pancakes (crêpes) from the batter. Preheat the oven to 200°C, 400°F, gas 6. When the beef is cooked, spoon ¼ of the mixture into the middle of each pancake (crêpe) and roll them up. Arrange the rolls in a greased shallow dish and sprinkle the grated cheese over them. Bake for 20 minutes until the cheese is melted and golden. Serve immediately.

Serves 4

Beef Brunchies

225 g (½ lb) basic economy beef
50 g (2 oz) (3 tablespoons) sweet pickle or mango chutney
2 hard-boiled (hard-cooked) eggs, chopped
4 slices toasted bread
50 g (2 oz) (½ cup) grated cheese

1 Make the basic economy beef as in the recipe. When cooked, stir in the sweet pickle or chutney and the chopped eggs.

2 Make the toast and spoon ¼ of the beef mixture on to each slice. Sprinkle the grated cheese over them and serve.

Serves 4

Reading clockwise: Stuffed Pancakes (Crêpes), Beef and Vegetable Vol-au-vent, Beef Brunchies and Curried Beef and Golden Rice

Beef Espana

450 g (1 lb) boiled beef

For the Sauce:
30 ml (1 fl oz) (2 tablespoons) oil
1 medium onion, chopped
15 g (½ oz) (2 tablespoons) flour
25 g (1 oz) (2 tablespoons) tomato
  concentrate (paste)
1 clove garlic, peeled and
  crushed
300 ml (½ pint) (1¼ cups) water
1 beef stock cube
60 ml (2 fl oz) (¼ cup) medium
  sherry
salt and pepper
12 green olives, stuffed
sprig rosemary

1 Preheat the oven to 200°C, 400°F, gas 6.

2 Slice the boiled beef thickly and place in an ovenproof dish.

3 To make the sauce, heat the oil in a frying pan (skillet) and fry the onion lightly for 5 minutes, until tender and slightly brown. Stir in the flour and cook for 1 minute more. Stir in the tomato concentrate (paste) and garlic and pour on the water. Crumble in the stock cube and bring to the boil. Add the sherry and simmer for 15 minutes. Pass the sauce through a sieve (strainer).

4 Season to taste. Scatter the olives over the beef, pour on the sauce and place the dish in the oven for 20 minutes. Garnish with a sprig of rosemary and serve hot.

Serves 4

Tip: You can replace the olives by gherkins (dill pickles) or capers.

Spanish Pie

**675 g (1½ lb) stewing beef, cut in
  1.5 cm (¾ in) cubes**
25 g (1 oz) (4 tablespoons) flour
5 g (1 teaspoon) salt
good pinch pepper

Beef Espana is a quick and easy way of using up boiled beef in a sherry flavoured sauce with olives

---

40 g (1½ oz) (3 tablespoons) lard or
  shortening
2 large onions, finely sliced
2 sticks celery, sliced
150 ml (¼ pint) (⅔ cup) water
½ beef stock cube
225 g (½ lb) (¾ cup) tomatoes,
  skinned, deseeded and
  chopped
15 g (½ oz) (1 tablespoon) tomato
  concentrate (paste)
20 green olives, stuffed
350 g (¾ lb) puff pastry dough
1 egg, beaten

1 Preheat the oven to 170°C, 325°F, gas 3.

2 Coat the beef cubes with the flour, seasoned with salt and pepper. Heat the fat in a frying pan (skillet) and quickly brown the meat in it. Remove and place in a casserole. Fry the onion and celery in the fat for 3 minutes, then add to the meat. Boil the water in a pan and crumble in the ½ stock cube. Pour into the casserole and stir in the tomatoes and tomato concentrate (paste). Cover and cook for 2 hours or until the meat is tender. Take out of the oven, add the olives and check the seasoning. Turn into a 1.4 litre (2½ pint) pie dish. Leave to cool.

3 Turn the oven heat up to 220°C, 425°F, gas 7.

4 Roll out the puff pastry dough to a thickness of 3 mm (⅛ in) on a floured board. Place over the pie dish, trim, and seal the edges. Brush with the beaten egg. Make 2 small slits in the centre of the pie and bake for 45 minutes.

Serves 6

All about Veal
Veal in Vermouth and Tuna Sauce

Veal is the meat of the young milk-fed calf of up to 3 months in age, although animals of up to 1 year may be sold as veal.

Dutch veal is considered the best and the meat is very popular in Italy, Northern France and in Holland.

Veal is at its best from May to September. When choosing veal, the flesh should be pale pink, moist, firm and smell pleasant. The fat should be white and slightly pinkish. The connective tissue should be gelatinous (which will disappear during cooking) but not hard or bubbly. If very white meat is desired for a fricassée, or blanquette, the veal may be soaked in salted water to remove the blood, and even bleached with a little lemon juice in the water.

The joints of veal are similar to beef, with shin, cushion (topside), under-cushion (silverside and thick flank) and thick rump being cut from the leg. Shin is used for stews and the famous dish of Osso Buco. The cushions and thick rump are used for roasts, braising or escalopes. Rump and loin can also be roasted, braised or made into escalopes. Best rib and middle rib are used grilled (broiled) or sautéed. Shoulder and breast can be used for roasts or stews, and neck for piemeat or stews. Use top rib for sautées or braising and shank for stock and Osso Buco.

The liver and kidneys are renowned for their high quality. Calf's head and feet may be boiled and served with a sharp vinaigrette sauce.

Veal is an expensive meat and is probably best known for the world-famous Wiener Schnitzel. To make a Wiener Schnitzel escalope, only 75 g (3 oz) of meat is used. It is flattened out and cooked very briefly in a mixture of oil and butter.

The meat has very little fat and tends to be rather bland and lacking in flavour. For this reason, interesting sauces are often made to go with veal, and pot roasting on a bed of vegetables, or braising, is a better, more tasty way to cook veal than a simple roast.

Veal Joints

Veal in Vermouth and Tuna Sauce

1 kg (2 lb) boned rolled leg of veal
25 g (1 oz) (2 tablespoons) butter
25 ml (1 fl oz) ($\frac{1}{8}$ cup) oil
300 ml ($\frac{1}{2}$ pint) ($1\frac{1}{4}$ cups) water

For the Marinade:
$\frac{1}{2}$ litre ($17\frac{1}{2}$ fl oz) ($2\frac{1}{4}$ cups) dry vermouth
30 ml (1 fl oz) (2 tablespoons) vinegar
1 large onion, sliced
1 large carrot, sliced
2 cloves garlic, peeled and chopped
salt and pepper
pinch basil

For the Sauce:
150 g (5 oz) tuna fish
4 anchovy fillets
3 egg yolks
yolks of 2 hard-boiled eggs
juice 1 lemon
15 ml (1 tablespoon) olive oil
7 ml ($\frac{1}{2}$ tablespoon) wine vinegar
salt and pepper
1 pickled cucumber, sliced
25 g (1 oz) (2 tablespoons) capers

1 Mix the marinade ingredients and leave the veal to marinate for 2 hours. Remove the meat and dry with absorbent paper.

2 Put the butter and oil in a saucepan and brown the meat. Add the marinade and water, bring to the boil and simmer for 1 hour. Allow to cool in the marinade. If convenient, this part may be done the day before.

3 Remove the meat, and wipe it.

4 Strain the marinade and reduce (evaporate) by fast boiling until 300 ml ($\frac{1}{2}$ pint) ($1\frac{1}{4}$ cups) remains. Cool.

5 Make the sauce by mixing the tuna fish, anchovy fillets, egg

yolks, hard-boiled egg yolks, lemon juice, olive oil and vinegar. Add the marinade and blend to a smooth, thick sauce, in a liquidizer if possible. Season with salt and pepper, and add the pickled cucumber and capers.

6 Cut the veal in thin slices, arrange on a dish, and pour on the sauce. Serve with a rice salad.
Serves 6-8

Veal Vesuvio

15 g ($\frac{1}{2}$ oz) (1 tablespoon) butter
15 g ($\frac{1}{2}$ oz) (2 tablespoons) flour
150 ml ($\frac{1}{4}$ pint) ($\frac{5}{8}$ cup) stock
300 ml ($\frac{1}{2}$ pint) ($1\frac{1}{4}$ cups) milk
pinch salt, nutmeg, pepper
juice 1 lemon
50 g (2 oz) (4 tablespoons) corn kernels
1 kg (2 lb) boned rolled breast of veal
175 g (6 oz) slices ham
few sprigs watercress
salt and pepper
50 ml (2 fl oz) ($\frac{1}{4}$ cup) oil
300 ml ($\frac{1}{2}$ pint) ($1\frac{1}{4}$ cup) water

1 To make the sauce, make a roux and add the stock. Boil for 10 minutes, add the milk, seasoning and lemon juice. Simmer for 5 minutes. Add the corn kernels.

2 Preheat the oven to 200°C, 400°F, gas 6.

3 Unroll the meat, spread with the ham slices, reserving one for decoration, and watercress leaves. Spread with half of the sauce and season. Roll the meat and tie with string. Season and brush with oil.

4 Roast the meat for 1 hour. Add 300 ml ($\frac{1}{2}$ pint) ($1\frac{1}{4}$ cups) water to the pan, and cook for $\frac{1}{2}$ hour, basting with the liquid. When cooked, place the meat on a dish.

5 Reheat the remaining sauce and pour over the meat. Decorate with the slice of ham and sprigs of watercress.
Serves 6-8

Veal Vesuvio is a real test for your culinary skills, but the end result makes it all very worthwhile

Veal with Lemon Sauce

1 kg (2 lb) veal loin, chump end or
  rolled, boned shoulder
50 ml (2 fl oz) (¼ cup) oil
2 onions, 2 carrots, 2 sticks
  celery, diced
2 lemons
300 ml (½ pint) (1¼ cups) stock
pinch thyme
1 bay leaf, imported
salt and pepper
60 ml (4 tablespoons) sherry
5 g (1 teaspoon) cornflour
  (cornstarch)
50 ml (2 fl oz) (¼ cup) water
pinch caraway seeds

1 Preheat the oven to 190°C,
375°F, gas 5.

2 Brown the veal in the oil in a
flameproof casserole, then
remove the veal.

3 Put the diced onions, carrots
and celery in the casserole, and
place the meat on top.

4 Add the finely chopped rind of
one lemon.

5 Pour the stock, the juice of the
2 lemons, thyme and bay leaf on
to the meat and season. Cover
and cook in the oven for 1½ hours.

6 Remove the meat and keep
warm.

7 Strain off the liquid and reduce
(evaporate) it by fast boiling to
300 ml (½ pint) (1¼ cups). Add the
sherry and boil for 5 minutes. Mix
the cornflour (cornstarch) and
water and use to thicken the
sauce.

8 To serve, carve the meat in
slices, arrange on a dish with saffron flavoured rice and sprinkle

---

*Veal with Lemon Sauce is served
with savoury saffron
rice and makes an extra special
roast meal*

the veal with caraway seeds.
Serve the sauce separately.

Serves 8

Creole Veal with Avocados

50 ml (2 fl oz) (¼ cup) oil
1½ kg (3 lb) loin of veal, boned
2 onions, sliced
2 carrots, sliced
50 g (2 oz) (4 tablespoons) butter
50 g (2 oz) (½ cup) flour
225 ml (8 fl oz) (1 cup) milk
275 ml (9 fl oz) (1⅛ cup) single
  (light) cream
4 avocado pears
150 ml (5 oz) (⅝ cup) rum
juice 2 lemons
cayenne pepper, salt and pepper
450 g (1 lb) puff pastry
1 beaten egg

1 Preheat the oven to 190°C, 375°F, gas 5.

2 Heat the oil in a casserole and brown the meat for 10 minutes and remove.

3 Gently fry the onions and carrots and place the meat on top. Cover and cook for 1½ hours. Cool.

4 Make 1 pint of thick white sauce using the butter, flour, milk and cream but reserving 30 ml (2 tablespoons) of cream. Cool and add 1 mashed up avocado pear and flavour with rum, half the lemon juice, cayenne pepper, salt and pepper.

5 When the meat and sauce are cold, roll out the pastry 5 mm (¼ in) thick.

6 Preheat the oven to 200°C, 400°F, gas 6.

7 Slice the meat in 1 cm (½ in) slices and sandwich some sauce between. Press together in the shape of the joint and place on the pastry. Brush the pastry with beaten egg, and wrap round the meat. Turn over, and trim the ends. Brush with beaten egg. Decorate with leaves cut from pastry trimmings, and brush with egg. Rest for 20 minutes, and bake for 25 minutes.

Veal en Croûte, in its succulent pastry case, is an impressive dish to serve at dinner parties

8 Meanwhile, thin the remainder of the sauce with the remainder of the lemon juice and cream.

9 Just before serving, garnish the joint with slices of avocado pears. Serve cold with the sauce.

Serves 8

Veal en Croûte

675 g (1½ lb) loin of veal
50 ml (2 fl oz) (¼ cup) oil
salt and pepper

To make the Flavoured Paste:
175 g (6 oz) (¾ cup) calves' liver
1 large onion
175 g (6 oz) (1½ cups) mushrooms
1 egg
50 g (2 oz) (1 cup) breadcrumbs
1 clove garlic, chopped
5 g (1 tablespoon) parsley
salt and pepper
450 g (1 lb) puff pastry
1 beaten egg

1 Preheat the oven to 200°C, 400°F, gas 6.

2 Brush the loin of veal with oil. Season with salt and pepper and place in a roasting tin (pan). Roast for 1 hour. Cool.

3 To make the flavoured paste, remove the skin from the raw calves' liver and mince (grind). Chop the onion and mushrooms finely, and mix with the egg, breadcrumbs, garlic, parsley and seasoning. Mix with the liver to a smooth paste.

4 When the meat is cold, roll the pastry to an oblong 5 mm (¼ in) thick. Place the veal in the middle and brush with beaten egg. Spread the paste thickly over it. Brush the pastry with beaten egg. Wrap round the meat with a wide overlap. Turn over so that the join is underneath, and trim off the ends, making a loaf shape.

5 Place on a greased tray, and brush the outside with beaten egg. Roll out the trimmings to make leaves and place on top for decoration, brushing again with beaten egg. Rest for 20 minutes.

6 Bake for 25 minutes. Serve hot or cold.

Serves 6

Braised Veal in Mushroom Sauce

one 1¼ kg (2½ lb) boned and rolled
  veal joint (leg or shoulder)
75 g (3 oz) (6 tablespoons) butter
2 shallots, chopped
2 onions, chopped
1 sprig thyme
1 bay leaf, imported
salt and pepper
400 ml (¾ pint) (1¾ cups) cider
225 g (½ lb) mushrooms, chopped
1 egg yolk
100 ml (4 fl oz) (½ cup) single
  (light) cream
10 g (2 tablespoons) chopped
  parsley

1 Fry the veal gently in 50 g (2 oz)
(¼ cup) of the butter until browned
on all sides. Lift out. Fry the shallots and onions in the same fat
until softened.

2 Return the veal to the pan and
add the thyme, bay leaf, salt and
pepper to taste and the cider.
Bring to the boil, cover and cook
over a low heat for 1½ hours.

3 Fry the mushrooms in the rest
of the butter for 3-4 minutes.

4 When the veal has cooked for 1½
hours, add the mushrooms to the
pan and continue cooking for a
further 10 minutes.

5 Drain the veal and place on a
serving dish. Keep warm. Discard
the thyme and bay leaf.

6 Beat the egg yolk with the
cream. Beat into the cooking
liquid and cook gently until
thickened. Cover the meat with
this sauce, sprinkle with the
parsley and serve hot.

Serves 6

Roast Veal Steaks Parisienne

1 kg (2 lb) loin of veal, cut in
  6 steaks
salt and pepper
100 g (¼ lb) (½ cup) butter
300 ml (½ pint) (1¼ cups) dry white
  wine
800 g (1¾ lb) potatoes, cut into
  balls
225 g (½ lb) small onions
100 ml (4 fl oz) (½ cup) single
  (light) cream
2 slices cooked ham, diced
225 g (½ lb) cooked mushrooms,
  diced
6 cooked artichoke bottoms
sprig parsley, chopped

1 Preheat the oven to 200°C,
400°F, gas 6. Season the veal
steaks and spread them with half
of the butter. Cook in the oven for
½ hour, turning once to brown both
sides. During the cooking, use the
wine to baste the meat.

2 Meanwhile, fry the potato balls
and onions, covered, in the rest of
the butter for 10 minutes. Drain
and keep hot.

3 When the meat is cooked, drain
the gravy into a pan and bring to
the boil. Add the cream and boil
for 5 minutes. Season.

4 Place the steaks on an ovenproof dish and pour a little of the
sauce over. Mix the ham and
mushrooms and pile on top of the
artichoke bottoms. Arrange
these around the meat and place
in the oven for 12 minutes to heat
through.

5 Decorate the dish with the
potato and onions and sprinkle
with the parsley. Serve the rest of
the sauce separately.

Serves 6

Shoulder of Veal in Vermouth

one 1½ kg (3 lb) boned shoulder of
  veal
60 ml (4 tablespoons) brandy
salt and pepper
60 ml (4 tablespoons) milk
100 g (¼ lb) (2 cups) fresh
  breadcrumbs
150 g (5 oz) (⅝ cup) cream cheese
100 g (¼ lb) (1 cup) finely chopped
  mushrooms
225 g (½ lb) (1⅓ cups) chopped
  cooked ham
5 g (1 tablespoon) chopped
  parsley
1 large clove garlic, chopped
2 onions, chopped
1 egg
20 g (¾ oz) (1½ tablespoons) butter
30 ml (2 tablespoons) oil
300 ml (½ pint) (1¼ cups) dry white
  vermouth
150 ml (¼ pint) (⅝ cup) single
  (light) cream

1 Place the veal in a dish, spoon
over the brandy and season with
salt and pepper. Leave to soak,
turning once.

2 Pour the milk over the breadcrumbs. Let it soak in, then
squeeze the bread dry.

3 Put the cream cheese, mushrooms, ham, breadcrumbs,
parsley, garlic and onions in a
bowl. Add the egg and season
with salt and pepper. Mix
thoroughly.

4 Spread this stuffing thinly over
the inside of the veal. Roll up and
tie securely with kitchen string.

5 Heat the butter and oil in a
large pan. Add the meat and
brown on all sides. Add the vermouth, cover and leave to cook
over a low heat for about 1½ hours.

6 Place the meat on a heated
serving dish and keep hot.

7 Add the cream to the pan. Mix
quickly with a wooden spoon over
a brisk heat. Correct the seasoning, pour the sauce into a sauce-
boat and serve with the veal.

Serves 7-8

For Extra Flavour
The delicate flavour of veal
can be enhanced by cooking it
with aromatic vegetables
such as carrots, celery and
onions, and with fragrant
herbs including basil, rosemary and marjoram. To add
flavour to the gravy to be
served with veal joints, you
can use veal stock, but try also
incorporating dry white wine,
sherry or even vermouth for a
really impressive sauce.

---

*Roast Veal Steaks Parisienne
are garnished with
artichoke hearts topped with
ham and mushrooms*

Escalopes and Steaks

Veal escalopes (scallops), which come from the leg of the calf, are considered particularly choice cuts since they contain no fat or gristle. They are cut about 5 mm (¼ in) thick and are then usually beaten with a mallet or rolling pin until very thin.

Scaloppines and escalopes (scallops) are similar cuts of veal but differ in the way in which they are cut from the main joint: scaloppines are cut against the grain of the meat whereas escalopes (scallops) are cut with it.

We have included in this section one recipe which uses veal loin steaks. The loin is a prime cut and so the steaks can be very expensive; pork loin steaks would make a suitable alternative, but the cooking time should be lengthened to ensure that the meat is cooked through.

Veal Steaks with Jerusalem Artichokes

50 ml (2 fl oz) (¼ cup) oil
50 g (2 oz) (4 tablespoons) butter
six 225 g (½ lb) veal loin steaks,
  1 cm (½ in) thick

For the Sauce:
1 onion, chopped
bouquet garni
150 ml (¼ pint) (⅝ cup) dry
  vermouth
1 stock cube
150 ml (¼ pint) (⅝ cup) water
juice ½ lemon
15 g (½ oz) (1½ tablespoons)
  cornflour (cornstarch)

For the Garnish:
50 g (2 oz) (4 tablespoons) butter
1 kg (2 lb) Jerusalem artichokes,
  cut in halves
1 onion, chopped

1 Heat the oil and butter in a pan, add the veal steaks and fry for 12-14 minutes over a low heat and covered with a lid. Turn the steaks over once or twice during the cooking time. Remove the steaks and keep them warm.

2 Make the sauce. Using the fat left from cooking the meat, fry the onion for 5 minutes and then remove surplus fat. Add the bouquet garni and vermouth and boil for 8 minutes.

3 Dissolve the stock cube in the water, add the stock to the pan and boil for 4 minutes more. Season to taste and add the lemon juice.

4 Mix the cornflour (cornstarch) with 90 ml (4 fl oz) (6 tablespoons) water and add to the sauce. Boil for 1 minute until thickened. Strain the sauce and pour a little of the sauce over the veal.

5 For the garnish, heat the butter in a pan and sauté the Jerusalem artichokes for 6 minutes, covered with a lid. Add the chopped onion and cook for 2 minutes more. Drain off the fat, add 100 ml (4 fl oz) (½ cup) of the sauce and simmer for 5 minutes. Season.

6 Serve the veal steaks with the garnish and pour the rest of the sauce into a sauce-boat.

Serves 6

Wiener Schnitzel

4 veal escalopes (scallops)
40 g (1½ oz) (6 tablespoons) plain
  flour, seasoned
1 egg, beaten
50 g (2 oz) (¾ cup) fine dried
  breadcrumbs
50 g (2 oz) (¼ cup) butter
4 slices lemon

1 Place the veal escalopes (scallops) between 2 sheets of dampened greaseproof (parchment) paper and beat with a mallet or rolling pin until very thin, 3 mm (⅛ in).

2 Coat the veal with the seasoned flour, then dip in the beaten egg and the breadcrumbs until thoroughly coated.

3 Melt the butter in a large frying pan (skillet). Add the veal and fry over a moderate heat until golden-brown on both sides, turning once during cooking.

4 Transfer the veal to a warmed serving dish and serve immediately, garnished with the lemon slices. Serve with new potatoes tossed in parsley and a green salad.

Serves 4

Veal Escalopes (Scallops) in Marsala

4 veal escalopes (scallops)
50 g (2 oz) (4 tablespoons) butter
100 ml (4 fl oz) (½ cup) Marsala
200 ml (6 fl oz) (¾ cup) gravy or
  thickened stock
pinch cayenne pepper

1 Place the veal escalopes (scallops) between 2 sheets of dampened greaseproof (parchment) paper and beat with a mallet or rolling pin until they are 3 mm (⅛ in) thick.

2 Heat the butter in a frying pan (skillet) and fry the escalopes until well browned. Transfer them to a warmed serving dish and keep hot.

3 Add the Marsala to the fat in the pan and boil for 5 minutes, stirring well. Add the gravy or stock and cayenne, mix well and pour the sauce over the veal.

Serves 4

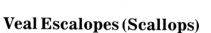

Veal Escalopes (Scallops) Milanese

1 bunch asparagus
4 veal escalopes (scallops)

300

50 g (2 oz) (¼ cup) butter
5 ml (1 teaspoon) arrowroot
60 ml (4 tablespoons) white port
45 ml (2 fl oz) (3 tablespoons) single (light) cream
sprig tarragon, finely chopped
pinch paprika
salt and pepper

Veal Steaks with Jerusalem Artichokes is a dish that shows how well veal combines with less familiar vegetables

1 Cook the asparagus in boiling salted water for 15-20 minutes.

2 Meanwhile, place the veal escalopes (scallops) between 2 sheets of dampened greaseproof (parchment) paper and beat with a mallet or rolling pin until very thin. Heat the butter in a frying pan (skillet) and fry the escalopes over a low heat for 5-8 minutes on each side or until cooked through.

3 Mix the arrowroot and the port. Drain the escalopes (scallops) and arrange them on a heated serving dish. Keep hot.

4 Pour the cream into the frying pan (skillet) and stir well to mix with the pan juices. Add the tar-ragon. Boil for 2 minutes, then add the arrowroot mixed with the port. Simmer, stirring, until thickened. Add the paprika and the salt and pepper to taste.

5 Drain the asparagus and arrange round the escalopes (scallops). Pour the sauce over the top and serve very hot.

Serves 4

Tip: The asparagus must be very carefully drained to ensure that no extra water is added to the sauce – otherwise it will become diluted.

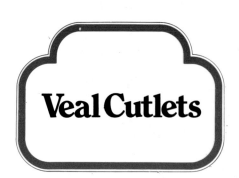

Veal Cutlets

Veal cutlets can either be grilled (broiled) or fried. It is important to differentiate between cutlets and chops – many people confuse the two. Cutlets are taken from the best rib part of the animal; chops from the loin. Cutlets usually weigh about 275 g (10 oz) and are 1 cm (½ in) thick. Frying is the best method of cooking them. Season the cutlets with salt and pepper, dredge with flour and brown the cutlet on both sides. Then fry gently, covered with a lid, for 15 minutes. Use clarified butter or oil and butter mixed for the best results and flavour. When the cutlets are cooked, drain off the butter, remove the cutlets and pour a little white wine, sherry or Madeira into the pan. Add some demi-glace sauce and boil for 5 minutes. Serve with the cutlets.

Veal Cutlets Provençale

4 tomatoes
salt and pepper
45 ml (3 tablespoons) olive oil
four 225 g (½ lb) veal cutlets
50 g (2 oz) (½ cup) flour
100 g (¼ lb) (½ cup) butter
50 g (2 oz) (⅜ cup) green olives, stoned (pitted) and blanched
1 clove garlic, peeled and crushed
1 bunch parsley, chopped

1 Preheat the oven to 190°C, 375°F, gas 5.

2 Wash the tomatoes and place them in an ovenproof dish. Sprinkle with salt and pepper and pour in the oil. Place in the oven for about 10 minutes.

3 Tenderize the cutlets by beating with a mallet or rolling pin. Season with salt and pepper and dredge with flour.

4 Melt half of the butter in a frying pan (skillet) and fry the cutlets for about 5 minutes on each side until browned and cooked.

5 Arrange the cutlets in a dish, place the olives and baked tomatoes around the edges. Keep warm.

6 Melt the rest of the butter in a pan and fry the garlic and parsley for a minute, stirring all the time. Pour this butter mixture over the cutlets and serve at once.

Serves 4

Veal Cutlets with Mushrooms

100 g (¼ lb) (½ cup) butter
350 g (¾ lb) (3¾ cups) sliced mushrooms
salt and pepper
four 225 g (½ lb) veal cutlets
30 ml (2 tablespoons) brandy
100 ml (4 fl oz) (½ cup) single (light) cream
5 g (1 tablespoon) chopped parsley

1 Melt the butter in a frying pan (skillet). Add the sliced mushrooms and salt and pepper and fry until tender. Remove from the pan and keep warm.

2 Season the cutlets with salt and pepper and place in the pan. Fry gently until browned on both sides and cooked through.

3 Warm the brandy and pour it over the cutlets. Set alight and, when the flames die down, transfer the cutlets to a heated serving dish and keep warm.

4 Add the cream to the pan and boil for 2 minutes to thicken, stirring all the time. Taste the sauce and correct the seasoning.

5 Arrange the mushrooms around the veal cutlets. Pour the sauce over the cutlets and sprinkle with the chopped parsley. Serve very hot with sautéed potatoes.

Serves 4

Tip: Veal cutlets are delicious when dredged with flour and fried and served on a bed of French beans, as shown in the picture. Pour the butter and meat juices over the veal and sprinkle with chopped parsley. This makes a very quick and easy meal to prepare.

Veal Cutlets Portuguese

six 225 g (½ lb) veal cutlets
salt and pepper
50 g (2 oz) (½ cup) flour
50 ml (2 fl oz) (¼ cup) oil
1 onion, sliced
1 red pepper, deseeded and sliced
2 tomatoes, skinned, deseeded and chopped
2 cloves garlic, peeled and chopped
pinch rosemary
50 g (2 oz) (½ cup) corn kernels
150 ml (¼ pint) (⅝ cup) dry sherry
150 ml (¼ pint) (⅝ cup) water
1 chicken stock cube
salt and pepper
pinch paprika

1 Sprinkle the cutlets with salt and pepper and dredge with flour. Heat the oil in a frying pan (skillet) and fry the cutlets for 5 minutes on each side until browned. Transfer the cutlets to a shallow ovenproof dish and keep warm.

2 Preheat the oven to 190°C, 375°F, gas 5.

3 Fry the onion in the same pan for 5 minutes until soft. Add the sliced pepper and fry for a further 2 minutes. Add the tomatoes, garlic, rosemary and corn kernels and stir well. Pour in the sherry and water and sprinkle in the stock cube. Season with salt and pepper and paprika, and boil for 5 minutes.

4 Pour the sauce over the veal and braise gently in the oven for 35 minutes, covered with a lid. Serve with plain boiled rice.

Serves 6

Veal Cutlets Bonne Femme

four 225 g (½ lb) veal cutlets
salt and pepper
50 g (2 oz) (½ cup) flour
100 g (¼ lb) (½ cup) clarified butter
  or butter and oil mixed
225 g (½ lb) (1½ cups) boiled, cold
  potatoes, thinly sliced
100 g (¼ lb) (1 cup) button onions
100 ml (4 fl oz) (½ cup) sherry
150 ml (¼ pint) (⅝ cup) demi-glace
  sauce
5 g (1 tablespoon) chopped
  parsley

*Veal cutlets look as good as
they taste if served with
a colourful vegetable, such as
these tender green beans*

1 Sprinkle the veal cutlets with
the salt and pepper and dredge
with flour.

2 Preheat the oven to 200°C,
400°F, gas 4.

3 Heat the butter in a frying
pan (skillet) and gently fry the
cutlets on both sides for a few
minutes.

4 Place the cutlets on an
ovenproof dish in the oven to
continue cooking.

5 Fry the potatoes in the same
pan until golden-brown, remove
and keep warm. Then fry the
onions for 2 minutes. Transfer
the onions to a saucepan of
water and boil until soft.

6 Drain off the butter and pour
the sherry into the pan. Add the
demi-glace sauce and bring to
the boil, stirring all the time.

7 Arrange the cutlets on a
serving dish, surrounded by the
fried potatoes and onions. Cover
with the sauce and sprinkle with
chopped parsley.

Serves 4

Stuffed Veal

These dishes use escalopes (scallops) in a different way by stuffing them with interesting fills, rolling them up into little parcels, and then gently braising them. The long slow cooking means that it is not necessary to use expensive cuts and the escalopes (scallops) can be cut from any part.

Veal Paupiettes

150 g (5 oz) lean pork or veal trimmings
1 egg
300 ml (½ pint) (1¼ cups) whipping cream
4 veal escalopes (scallops), 175 g (6 oz) each
salt, pepper and nutmeg
25 g (1 oz) (2 tablespoons) butter
200 ml (6 fl oz) (¾ cup) white wine

1 Chop and mince the pork or veal trimmings. Put in a bowl, add the egg and mix well. Stir in 50 ml (2 fl oz) (¼ cup) of the cream and chill to make a firm paste.

2 On a wet board, beat the escalopes (scallops) to make them very thin. Season with salt, pepper and nutmeg.

3 Spread the stuffing on the escalopes (scallops), roll up and tie with string.

4 Heat the butter and brown the paupiettes all over.

5 Add the rest of the cream and the white wine and stir carefully. Bring to the boil and simmer the paupiettes for 1 hour.

6 Remove the paupiettes. Discard the string and keep hot.

7 Reduce (evaporate) the sauce to 300 ml (½ pint) (1¼ cups) by fast boiling, and pour over the paupiettes.

Serves 4

Hungarian Veal Paupiettes

100 g (¼ lb) (½ cup) sausagemeat
100 g (¼ lb) (½ cup) ham, minced
1 egg
salt and pepper
6 escalopes (scallops), 100 g (¼ lb) each
50 g (2 oz) (½ cup) flour
50 ml (2 fl oz) (¼ cup) oil
450 g (1 lb) carrots
100 g (¼ lb) streaky bacon rashers (slices)
50 g (2 oz) (4 tablespoons) margarine
200 ml (6 fl oz) (¾ cup) white wine
225 g (½ lb) button (pearl) onions
300 ml (½ pint) (1¼ cups) stock
5 g (1 tablespoon) chopped parsley

1 Blend the sausagemeat, minced ham, egg and seasoning to a smooth paste. Chill.

2 On a wet board, flatten the escalopes (scallops) by beating to make them thin. Spread the filling on each escalope (scallop). Roll up and tie with string, and dip in flour.

3 Heat half of the oil in a pan and brown the paupiettes for 4 minutes, covered with a lid. Remove and put in a casserole.

4 Slice the carrots. Cut the bacon into strips.

5 Heat the margarine and rest of the oil and fry the bacon for 1 minute, then add the carrots. Sauté for 3 minutes, then add the bacon and carrots to the veal.

6 Add the white wine and bring to the boil. Cover the dish and simmer for 1 hour.

7 Meanwhile, boil the button (pearl) onions in stock for 2 minutes.

8 Remove the paupiettes, discard the string.

9 Reduce (evaporate) the sauce by fast boiling to 300 ml (½ pint) (1¼ cups).

10 Serve the paupiettes surrounded by the bacon, carrots and onions. Pour over the sauce. Sprinkle with parsley.

Serves 6

Veal with Olives

2 large onions chopped
50 g (2 oz) (¼ cup) butter
100 g (¼ lb) (⅔ cup) calves' liver
100 g (¼ lb) (⅔ cup) streaky bacon
100 g (¼ lb) (1 cup) olives, stoned (pitted)
100 g (¼ lb) veal trimmings
50 g (2 oz) (1 cup) breadcrumbs
1 egg
salt and pepper
6 veal escalopes (scallops), 175 g (6 oz) each
1 carrot, chopped
15 ml (1 tablespoon) flour
100 ml (4 fl oz) (½ cup) white wine
225 ml (8 fl oz) (1 cup) stock
25 g (1 oz) (2 tablespoons) tomato concentrate (paste)
bouquet garni

1 Fry one chopped onion in 25 g (1 oz) (2 tablespoons) of the butter and brown lightly. Put in a bowl. Briefly fry the calves' liver to brown and remove.

2 Mince the bacon, one third of the olives, veal trimmings and liver, and add to the onions. Add the breadcrumbs and egg.

3 On a wet board, beat the escalopes (scallops) to make them thin. Spread with the stuffing. Roll up and tie with string.

4 Brown the paupiettes all over in the remainder of the butter. Remove and put in a casserole.

5 Fry the other chopped onion and carrot and brown. Stir in the flour and brown. Add the white wine, stock and tomato concentrate (paste). Add the bouquet garni, salt and pepper.

6 Pour over the paupiettes and cook for 1 hour. Add the remainder of the olives 10 minutes before the end.

7 Remove the paupiettes. Discard the string, and arrange on a dish. Reduce (evaporate) the sauce to 300 ml (½ pint) (1¼ cups) and pour over.

Serves 6

Hungarian Veal Paupiettes, stuffed with sausagemeat, would win plenty of compliments from guests at the dinner table

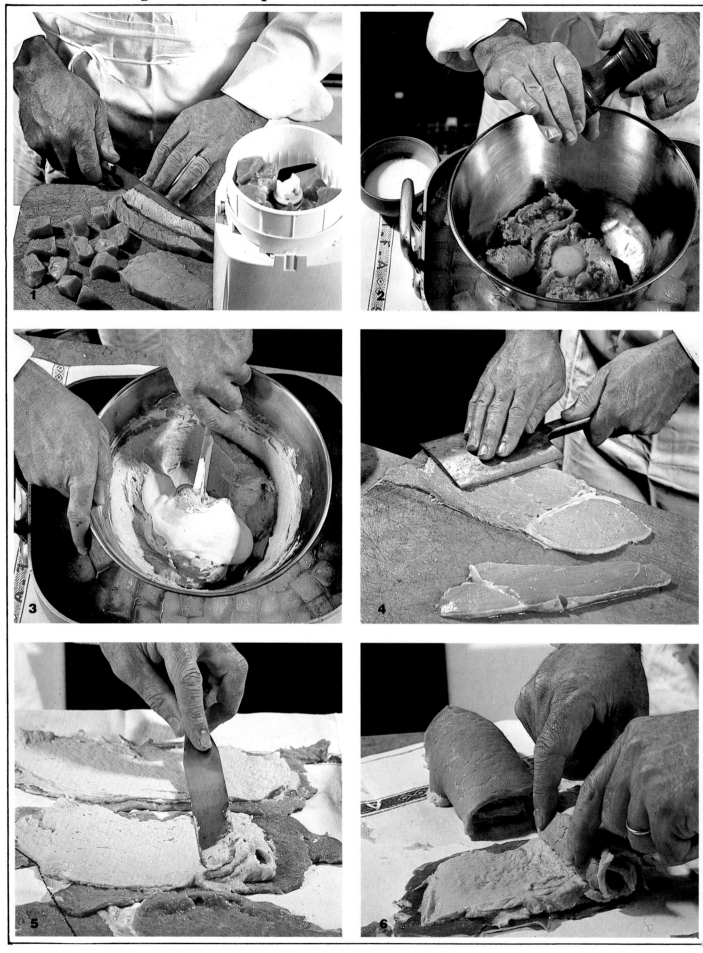

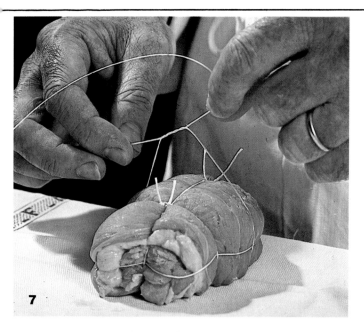

1 Chop the lean pork or veal trimmings to be used for the stuffing and put through a mincer (grinder) **2** Place in a bowl and keep cool over ice cubes or chill in a refrigerator when made. Add 1 egg and season with salt and freshly ground (milled) pepper **3** Add the cream gradually and stir to make a smooth firm paste and chill until used **4** On a wet board, beat the escalopes (scallops) until they are very thin **5** Place on a cloth to dry and then spread the chilled stuffing carefully on each escalope (scallop) **6** Roll up tightly **7** Tie up securely with string into neat parcels **8** Heat a mixture of butter and oil and brown the paupiettes all over, covered with a lid **9** Add the cream and white wine. Stir carefully, season and add a bouquet garni, bring to the boil and simmer for 1 hour **10** When the paupiettes are tender, remove from the pan. Carefully remove all the string and arrange on a dish. Reduce the sauce by fast boiling to 300 ml ($\frac{1}{2}$ pint) ($1\frac{1}{4}$ cups) and check the seasoning and pour over the paupiettes and serve hot

Veal Stews

Blanquette de Veau

900 g (2 lb) stewing veal from
  neck or shoulder
salt and pepper
2 large carrots
1 large leek
1 stick celery
2 cloves garlic
bouquet garni
1 onion studded with 2 cloves
100 g (¼ lb) (½ cup) butter
50 g (2 oz) (½ cup) flour
450 g (1 lb) small onions
450 g (1 lb) button mushrooms
juice ½ lemon
2 egg yolks
150 ml (¼ pint) (⅝ cup) double
  (heavy) cream
pinch nutmeg

1 Cut the veal into 3½ cm (1½ in)
cubes. Place in a saucepan,
cover with cold water and bring
to the boil. Drain and rinse in
cold water, removing any scum.
Return the meat to the pan,
cover with water, season with
salt and pepper. Bring to the
boil, then simmer.

2 Slice the carrots in 4 lengthways, trim and clean the leek,
chop the celery and garlic. Add
these vegetables, with the bouquet garni and the onion
studded with 2 cloves, to the
meat. Cover and simmer gently
for 1¼ hours.

3 Make a roux with half of the
butter, and the flour. Cook for 2
minutes and leave to cool.

4 Fry the small onions in half of
the remaining butter. Blanch
the mushrooms in the other half
of the butter, the lemon juice
and 30 ml (2 tablespoons) water,
until tender. The liquor may be
added to the stew.

5 Take the meat from the pan

and keep warm. Remove the
vegetables and strain the sauce.
Pour some of the liquid on to the
roux and blend to produce a
thin, smooth sauce. Bring to the
boil, adjust seasoning.

6 In another bowl beat together
the egg yolks and cream with a
pinch of nutmeg. Stir in 100 ml
(4 fl oz) (½ cup) of the sauce. Pour
this liaison into the stew sauce,
stirring briskly with a sauce
whisk to a thick, smooth sauce.

7 Return meat, mushrooms
and small onions to a pan and
pour the sauce over them
through a sieve. Reheat without
bringing to the boil. Arrange the
meat and vegetables in a heated
serving dish, pour the sauce over
them, and serve hot.

Serves 8

Veal Fricassée

2 onions, chopped
675 g (1½ lb) stewing veal cut in
  3 cm (1¼ in) cubes
150 ml (¼ pint) (⅝ cup) white wine
1 bay leaf, imported
pinch thyme
salt and pepper
25 g (1 oz) (¼ cup) flour
25 g (1 oz) (2 tablespoons) butter
30 ml (2 tablespoons) milk
100 g (¼ lb) button mushrooms

1 Preheat oven to 170°C, 325°F,
gas 3. Place the veal, onions,
wine, herbs, and seasoning to
taste in a casserole, cover and
cook in the oven for about 1¼
hours or until the meat is tender.
Remove the meat, strain liquid.

2 Make a roux of the flour and
butter and cook for 2 minutes.
Remove from the heat, add the
milk to make a smooth paste,
and stir in the cooking liquid to
make up 300 ml (½ pint) (1¼ cups)
of smooth sauce.

3 Pour the sauce over the veal
in the casserole, add the mushrooms, and return to the oven for
20 minutes. Serve hot.

Serves 4

Mediterranean Veal Stew

675 g (1½ lb) shoulder veal cut
  into 3 cm (1¼ in) cubes
3 onions, chopped
45 ml (3 tablespoons) oil
25 g (1 oz) (¼ cup) flour
juice 1 lemon
300 ml (½ pint) (1¼ cups) white
  meat stock
2 cloves garlic, peeled and
  chopped
450 g (1 lb) tomatoes, skinned,
  deseeded and chopped
2 green peppers, deseeded and
  sliced
225 g (½ lb) (2 cups) garden peas
salt and pepper
100 g (¼ lb) (⅔ cup) stoned (pitted)
  green olives
100 ml (4 fl oz) (½ cup) single
  (light) cream

1 Fry the meat and onions in
the oil until lightly browned.
Add the flour and stir while
cooking for 2 minutes.

2 Stir in the lemon juice, stock,
garlic, tomatoes, green peppers,
garden peas and seasoning to
taste. Bring to the boil, cover
and simmer gently for 25
minutes.

3 Dip the olives into boiling
water for 1 minute, drain and
chop them roughly. Add them to
the pan and continue to cook for
15 minutes.

4 Remove the meat and vegetables and transfer them to a
heated serving dish. Add the
cream to the pan and boil, stirring constantly, for 5 minutes to
thicken. Pour the sauce over the
meat and serve at once.

Serves 4

Serbian Veal with Yogurt

2 green peppers, deseeded and
  diced
30 ml (2 tablespoons) oil
675 g (1½ lb) shoulder veal
2 large onions, quartered

1 Cut a juicy lemon in two and squeeze the juice out **2** Put the butter into a thick-bottomed saucepan. Break it into pieces with a wooden spoon. Pour in the lemon juice. Heat to melt the butter, stirring and not allowing the mixture to brown **3** Add the turned mushroom heads and the water. Simmer gently without a lid **4** When the mushrooms are tender, remove them from the pan

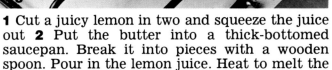

50 g (2 oz) (¼ cup) lard
  (shortening)
salt and pepper
225 ml (8 fl oz) (1 cup) white meat
  stock
7 g (¼ oz) (1 tablespoon) paprika
4 large tomatoes, peeled,
  deseeded and chopped
300 ml (½ pint) (2 cups) yogurt

1 Fry the diced green peppers in the oil for 10-15 minutes over low heat.

2 Cut the meat into ½ cm (¼ in) slices. In a saucepan, fry the veal and onions in the lard (shortening) until lightly browned. Season with salt and pepper, pour in the stock, add the paprika and bring to the boil. Cover and simmer for 20 minutes.

3 Add the tomatoes to the green peppers and cook for 10 minutes over low heat, stirring constantly.

4 Remove the veal and onion from the saucepan, leaving the liquid, and place in a warmed serving dish. Strain the green pepper and tomato, arrange them around the meat, and pour any remaining liquid from them into the meat liquor.

5 Stir the yogurt into the liquor over heat, and beat for 2 minutes with a whisk. Pour over the veal.

Serves 4

Look'n Cook Blanquette de Veau

1 Place veal in a saucepan, cover with cold water and bring to the boil **2** Drain and rinse in cold water. Return veal to pan, cover with water and season. Bring to the boil **3** Slice carrots, trim and clean leek, prepare onion, bouquet garni, celery, garlic. Add vegetables to meat and simmer 1¼ hours **4** Make a roux from the butter and flour. Cook 2 minutes and let cool **5** Fry the small onions in butter **6** Poach the mushrooms in butter, water and lemon juice until soft. Add the liquor to the stew **7** Remove

meat from pan and reserve. Discard vegetables. Strain cooking liquor through a sieve **8** Pour part of the liquor on the roux. Bring to the boil, stirring, and add more liquor if needed to make a smooth thin sauce **9** Mix cream and egg yolks with some of the sauce. Add to the sauce, beating to thicken **10** Combine meat, mushrooms and onions and pour the sauce over them through a sieve. Reheat without boiling **11** and **12** Place meat mixture in a dish, pour over the sauce and serve hot

Veal Marengo

900 g (2 lb) stewing veal (from the
  shoulder)
50 ml (2 fl oz) (¼ cup) oil
50 g (2 oz) (4 tablespoons) butter
2 large onions, finely chopped
50 g (2 oz) (½ cup) flour
300 ml (½ pint) (1¼ cups) white
  wine
4 tomatoes, skinned, deseeded
  and chopped
2 cloves garlic, crushed
bouquet garni
salt and pepper
450 g (1 lb) spring onions
  (scallions)
15 g (½ oz) (1 tablespoon) butter
15 g (½ oz) (1 tablespoon) sugar
225 g (½ lb) (3 cups) button
  mushrooms
4 slices white bread
5 g (1 tablespoon) chopped
  parsley

1 Cut the veal into 3 cm (1¼ in)
cubes. Brown it quickly in half the
oil and butter, mixed. Add the
chopped onions and cook them
gently with the meat until soft.
Dust with flour and cook until it
just browns.

2 Add the white wine and stir to
absorb any juices which are stuck
on to the pan. Mix in the
tomatoes, garlic and bouquet
garni, cover with water, and
season with salt and pepper.
Bring to the boil, cover the pan
and simmer over low heat for 1-1¼
hours.

3 Peel the spring onion (scallion)
bulbs, cutting away the green
leaves, and sauté them to light
golden in the butter and sugar.

4 Quarter the mushrooms and
fry them gently in the other half of
the oil and butter mixture.

5 Cut the bread into heart-
shaped croûtons, and fry them
until crisp and golden-brown in
the rest of the oil and butter.

6 Add the spring onions (scallions) and mushrooms to the
meat and simmer for 5 minutes
more. Chop the parsley and dip
the pointed end of each croûton in
the meat sauce and then in the

parsley. Serve in a deep, heated
dish, garnished with the
croûtons.

Serves 8

Veal Knuckle Riviera with Noodles

600 g (1½ lb) veal knuckle sawn
  into 5 cm (2 in) thick pieces
175 g (6 oz) veal kidney, sliced
50 ml (2 fl oz) (¼ cup) oil
1 large onion, chopped
3 carrots, scraped and sliced
2 stalks celery, sliced
150 ml (¼ pint) (⅝ cup) white wine
150 ml (¼ pint) (⅝ cup) white meat
  stock
1 clove garlic, crushed
225 g (½ lb) (2 cups) noodles
50 g (2 oz) (4 tablespoons) butter
50 g (2 oz) (⅓ cup) grated
  Parmesan cheese
salt and pepper
50 ml (2 fl oz) (¼ cup) single (light)
  cream
large pinch paprika
parsley to garnish

1 Brown the veal knuckle and
kidney in the oil for 8 minutes,
turning the knuckle pieces once.
Add the vegetables, cover and
simmer very gently for 10
minutes.

2 Pour in the wine and stock, add
the garlic and season to taste.
Simmer for 1½-2 hours.

3 Boil the noodles in salted
water for 8-10 minutes until tender. Drain them and stir in the
butter, Parmesan cheese, and a
pinch of salt and pepper.

4 Stir the cream and paprika
into the meat mixture. Bring
back to boil and remove from
heat.

5 Arrange the noodles around a
heated serving dish and fill the
centre with the meat and sauce.
Garnish with sprigs of parsley,
and serve at once.

Serves 4

Pancakes Corsican Style

2 eggs
100 g (¼ lb) (1⅛ cups) flour
300 ml (½ pint) (1¼ cups) milk
50 g (2 oz) (¼ cup) butter
1 large onion, chopped
50 g (2 oz) (½ cup) diced
  mushrooms
125 g (5 oz) (¾ cup) minced
  (ground) cooked veal
pinch curry powder
1 clove garlic, chopped
15 g (½ oz) (1 tablespoon) tomato
  concentrate (paste)
7 g (¼ oz) (1 tablespoon) flour
salt and pepper
pinch oregano

For the Sauce:
1 egg yolk
5 ml (1 teaspoon) made mustard
300 ml (½ pint) (1¼ cups) white
  sauce
50 g (2 oz) (½ cup) grated cheese
pinch paprika

1 Combine the eggs, flour and
milk into a smooth batter and
make 6 pancakes, about 15 cm
(6 in) wide.

2 Melt the butter and fry the
chopped onion for 5 minutes until
soft. Add the mushrooms and fry
for 1 minute. Blend in the minced
(ground) veal, curry powder,
garlic, tomato concentrate
(paste), flour, salt and pepper to
taste, and oregano. Cook gently
for 8 minutes, and leave to cool.

3 Divide the mixture between
the pancakes. Roll up each pancake and place them in a shallow
ovenproof dish.

4 Blend the egg yolk and mustard and mix in the white sauce.
Stir in ¾ of the grated cheese, and
season with salt, pepper and a
pinch of paprika. Pour the sauce
over the pancakes, sprinkle over
the rest of the cheese, and place
dish under grill (broiler) until
browned. Serve hot.

Serves 3

*Veal Knuckle Riviera with
Noodles (left), and Pancakes
Corsican Style (right)
are two tasty ideas for lunch*

1 The main ingredients: veal, bread, tomatoes, onions, mushrooms, herbs and garlic **2** Cut the veal into cubes and brown quickly in oil and butter **3** Cook the chopped onions gently with the meat **4** Dust with flour and cook gently to brown **5** Add the white wine and stir to absorb any juices stuck to the pan. Add tomatoes, garlic, bouquet garni and hot water to cover, and season. Bring to boil, cover and simmer for 1-1¼ hours **6** Peel the spring onion (scallion) bulbs and brown in butter and sugar **7** Clean the mushrooms, quarter and sauté them in butter **8** Cut the bread into heart-shaped croûtons. Fry to golden-brown **9** Add the mushrooms and spring onions (scallions) to the meat and simmer for 5 minutes. Chop the parsley **10** Serve in a deep, heated serving dish. Dip the point of each croûton in the sauce and then in the chopped parsley. Arrange the croûtons round the dish. Serve very hot

Osso Buco with Artichoke Hearts

15 g (½ oz) (2 tablespoons) flour
salt and pepper
 8 slices knuckle of veal,
   2.5 cm (1 in) thick
25 g (1 oz) (2 tablespoons) butter
1 large onion, sliced
2 cloves garlic, peeled and
   crushed
2 carrots, sliced
2 sticks celery, finely chopped
200 ml (6 fl oz) (¾ cup) dry white
   wine
4 large tomatoes, skinned,
   deseeded and chopped
15 g (½ oz) (1 tablespoon) tomato
   concentrate (paste)
1 bay leaf, imported
pinch dried rosemary
8 canned artichoke hearts
   (optional)
juice and grated peel 1 lemon
5 g (1 tablespoon) chopped parsley

1 Season the flour with salt and pepper. Dredge the veal in it. Heat the butter in a frying pan (skillet) and brown the veal. Take out and place in a heavy-bottomed pan.

2 Lightly fry the onion, garlic, carrots and celery in the oil, then add to the meat.

3 Pour the wine over the meat and vegetables. Bring to the boil, then lower heat to simmering. Stir in the tomatoes, tomato concentrate (paste), bay leaf and rosemary. Season to taste. Cover and leave to simmer for 1 hour or until the meat is tender.

4 Add the drained artichoke hearts and the juice and grated rind of the lemon. Cook for 10 minutes more. Immediately before serving, sprinkle on the chopped parsley. Serve with plain boiled potatoes, rice or noodles and a crisp green salad.

Serves 4

Tips: This dish can also be made using veal knuckles 5 cm (2 in) thick. Allow one per portion and cook for 1½ hours.

The marrow inside the knuckle is delicious: eat it with the stew.

Knuckle of Veal Paysanne

20 pearl onions
20 small carrots
salt and pepper
1½ kg (3 lb) knuckle of veal cut in
   5 cm (2 in) pieces
25 g (1 oz) (4 tablespoons) flour
25 g (1 oz) (2 tablespoons) butter
350 ml (12 fl oz) (1½ cups) water
1 chicken stock cube
bouquet garni
20 small new potatoes
450 g (1 lb) (4 cups) green peas,
   fresh or frozen

1 Carefully peel the onions, leaving them whole. Peel and trim the carrots.

2 Season the veal and dredge in the flour. Heat the butter in a frying pan (skillet) and brown the meat in it. Transfer to a heavy-bottomed stewing pan. Sauté the onions and carrots in the butter for 1 minute, then add to the meat.

3 Pour on the water, crumble in the stock cube and bring to the boil. Reduce heat at once, add the bouquet garni and check seasoning. Cover and simmer gently for 30 minutes.

4 Peel the new potatoes and add them to the pan with the peas. Add more stock, if necessary, so the vegetables are just covered. Replace the lid on the pan and simmer again for 45 minutes–1 hour, until the meat is tender.

Serves 6

Veal Hotpot

675 g (1½ lb) shin (leg) of veal
100 g (¼ lb) bacon
2 medium potatoes
1 medium carrot
1 large onion
1 green or red pepper
1 clove garlic
4 tomatoes

salt and pepper
15 g (½ oz) (2 tablespoons) flour
30 ml (1 fl oz) (2 tablespoons) oil
15 g (½ oz) (1 tablespoon) tomato
   concentrate (paste)
bouquet garni
pinch paprika
600 ml (1 pint) (2½ cups) water
1 chicken stock cube

1 Preheat the oven to 180°C, 350°F, gas 4.

2 Cut the veal and the bacon into 5 cm (2 in) cubes. Peel and quarter the potatoes and carrot. Slice the onion and deseed the pepper, cutting it into 5 cm (2 in) strips. Peel and crush the garlic. Skin, deseed and quarter the tomatoes.

3 Season the veal and dredge in the flour. Heat the oil in a frying pan (skillet) and fry the meat until browned. Remove and place in a casserole. Lightly fry the bacon, onion and pepper. Add the garlic, potatoes and carrot and fry for 2 minutes more. Transfer to the casserole.

4 Stir in the tomatoes, tomato concentrate (paste), the bouquet garni and the paprika. Bring the water to the boil in a pan, crumble in the stock cube, and pour over the meat. Cover tightly and place in the oven for about 1 hour or until the veal is tender.

Serves 4-5

Using Knuckle of Bacon
Dishes which use knuckle or shin of veal can be made more interesting by using half the quantity of veal and making up the difference with knuckle of bacon. This joint has a higher proportion of meat to bone for the same weight and so will work out more economical. Bacon and veal combine well together, the bacon adding a considerable amount of flavour while the veal supplies the gelatinous ingredient necessary for a good gravy.

Osso Buco is a traditional veal stew from Italy, usually garnished with parsley, lemon and garlic

Cold Veal

Cold Veal Galantine

one 225 g (½ lb) aubergine
  (eggplant)
450 g (1 lb) (2 cups) minced
  stewing veal
225 g (½ lb) (1 cup) minced pork
50 g (2 oz) (¼ cup) minced bacon
1 onion, chopped
50 g (2 oz) (1 cup) fresh
  breadcrumbs
5 g (1 tablespoon) chopped
  parsley
salt and pepper
pinch curry powder
pinch garlic salt
1 egg, beaten
6 slices cucumber
3 radishes, sliced

1 Preheat the oven to 200°C,
400°F, gas 6.

2 Bake the aubergine (eggplant)
in its skin for 15 minutes. Cut in
two and scoop out the pulp. Mix in
a bowl with the meat, onion,
breadcrumbs and parsley, salt
and pepper, curry powder and
garlic salt. Blend in the beaten
egg.

3 Place the meat mixture in a
greased, oblong bread tin. Stand
the tin on a baking tray (cookie
sheet) half-filled with water and
bake for 1½ hours. Cool and turn
out on to a dish. Garnish with the
cucumber and radishes.

Serves 6

Veal Roulade

six 100 g (¼ lb) veal escalopes
salt and pepper
25 g (1 oz) (4 tablespoons) flour
50 ml (2 fl oz) (¼ cup) oil

For the Stuffing:
150 g (5 oz) (1 cup) diced liver ·
1 onion, chopped
25 g (1 oz) (4 tablespoons) flour
1 egg, beaten
12 asparagus tips, canned or
  frozen

For the Chaudfroid Sauce:
300 ml (½ pint) (1¼ cups) white
  sauce
150 ml (¼ pint) (⅝ cup) chicken
  stock
10 g (2 teaspoons) ground
  gelatine

1 Beat each escalope thinly with
a mallet or rolling pin. Season and
dredge with flour.

2 Heat the oil in a frying pan
(skillet) and fry the escalopes
for 5 minutes each side. Then cool.

3 Fry the diced liver in the same
pan for 4 minutes, add the onion
and cook for a further 4 minutes.
Stir in the flour and cook for
1 minute.

4 Mince (grind) the stuffing mixture finely – twice if necessary –
and blend with the beaten egg.

5 Spread this liver stuffing over
each escalope, roll up tightly and
wrap in foil. Chill overnight, then
unwrap and place on a rack.

6 Heat the white sauce. Heat the
stock and add the gelatine.
Simmer for 2 minutes. Blend half
of the jelly stock with the white
sauce and put the remainder
aside for glazing and allow to cool.

7 Coat each stuffed veal roll
evenly with the chaudfroid sauce.
Leave to cool and set. Then brush
with the aspic jelly. Decorate each
roll with two asparagus tips and
serve.

Serves 6

*Cold Veal Galantine makes a
tasty summer lunch;
it is also ideal for picnics
and buffet parties*

Poultry

All kinds of chicken and fowl, turkeys, ducks, geese, and guinea fowl are classed as poultry. They are available fresh or frozen (and sometimes smoked), either whole or as separate joints, so ensuring a good all-year-round supply. Most poultry is sold oven-ready — drawn, plucked and trussed — but should you have to prepare a freshly-killed bird yourself, there are full Step-by-step photo guides are on the following pages

Poultry Tips

Hanging and Storing. Freshly-killed poultry is usually plucked before hanging but should not be drawn (cleaned); hang a bird, by its feet and protected from flies, for 2-3 days in a cool place.

Plucking and Singeing. Feathers are most easily removed while a bird is still warm. Spread out a large cloth or paper and pluck into this: hold the bird firmly, then take a few feathers at a time – too many can cause the skin to tear – and tug them sharply towards the head, in the opposite direction to which they lie. Large wing feathers may need plucking singly with pliers. Singe off single hairs or down by holding the bird over a naked flame, while turning it quickly.

For details of trussing and preparing giblets, feet and wings, see following pages.

Frozen Poultry. Frozen birds are usually sold trussed and ready for stuffing; the giblets are wrapped in polythene inside the body cavity, so remove them before cooking. All frozen poultry must be thawed completely before cooking; otherwise the inside will be partially cooked only when the outside is done, thus running the risk of leaving possible food-poisoning bacteria active. This is especially important when cooking large turkeys.

As a general rule, thaw frozen birds 5 hours per 450g (1lb) in a fridge or in a cool place, or follow the instructions on the wrapper.

Some frozen turkeys are self- or deep-basting, meaning they are impregnated with a fat to keep them moist during cooking.

Carving Poultry. As soon as the bird is cooked, let it stand for about 15 minutes to allow the juices to settle; this makes carving easier.

Sit the bird on a non-slip surface, with the neck end and breast diagonally towards you. With the flat of the knife firmly against the breast, lever the leg outwards to reveal the thigh joint; cut through with the knife. Separate the drumstick from the thigh by cutting through its joint. Steady the wing with the fork, then cut through the joint, taking a little breast meat at the same time. Ease the wing away from the body and sever it completely. Repeat both processes for the other leg and wing.

Carve thin slices of breast meat, parallel with the breastbone, including stuffing if used.

ROASTING TABLE FOR POULTRY

Type of bird (unstuffed)	Weight and Servings	Average Time and Oven temperature
CHICKENS		
Poussin 6-8 weeks old	450g-1kg (1-2lb) *Serves 1-2*	40-50 mins at 190°C, 375°F, gas 5
Broiler or Spring 10-12 weeks old	1¼-1¾kg (2½-3½lb) *Serves 3-4*	50-60 mins at 190°C, 375°F, gas 5
Roaster	1½-3kg (3-6lb) *Serves 4-6*	20 mins per kg (lb) plus extra 20 mins at 200°C, 400°F, gas 6
Capon Young neutered cockerel especially fattened	4-5kg (8-10lb) *Serves 6-10*	25 mins per kg (lb) plus extra 25 mins at 170°C, 325°F, gas 3
TURKEYS	up to 5kg (10lb) *Serves 8-12*	slow roast 20 mins per kg (lb) plus extra 20 mins at 170°C, 325°F, gas 3
	5-7kg (10-14lb) *Serves 12-16*	slow roast 18 mins per kg (lb) plus extra 18 mins at 170°C, 325°F, gas 3
	over 7kg (14lb) *Serves 16-25*	slow roast 15 mins per kg (lb) plus extra 20 mins at 170°C, 325°F, gas 3
		Fast roast all turkey weights at 230°C, 450°F, gas 8, allowing 2¾ hours, 3 hours, and 3¾ hours overall respectively
DUCKS including Duckling 2-3 months old	1½-3kg (3-6lb) *Serves 2-4*	25 mins per kg (lb) at 200°C, 400°F, gas 6
GEESE	3-6kg (6-12lb) *Serves 4-10*	Slow roast 30 mins per kg (lb) at 180°C, 350°F, gas 4 Fast roast 15 mins per kg (lb) at 200°C, 400°F, gas 6
GUINEA FOWL	900g-1½kg (2-3lb) *Serves 2-3*	45-60 mins at 200°C, 400°F, gas 6

NB: For stuffed birds, weigh before stuffing and increase overall roasting time by 15-45 minutes, according to weight of bird

Chicken Roast & Braised

Roast Chicken with Almonds

50 g (2 oz) ($\frac{1}{3}$ cup) currants
1$\frac{1}{2}$ kg (2$\frac{1}{2}$-3 lb) chicken, oven-ready
salt and pepper
sprig of thyme
100 g ($\frac{1}{4}$ lb) ($\frac{1}{2}$ cup) butter
45 ml (3 tablespoons) water
200 g (7 oz) (1$\frac{1}{3}$ cups) long grain
  rice
about 300 ml ($\frac{1}{2}$ pint) (1$\frac{1}{4}$ cups)
  chicken stock (bouillon) –
  about the equivalent to 1$\frac{1}{2}$ times
  the volume of the rice
50 g (2 oz) ($\frac{1}{3}$ cup) shelled almonds
25 g (1 oz) (1 tablespoon) pine
  kernels

1 Wash the currants and leave them to soak in a bowl of tepid water. Preheat the oven to 200°C, 400°F, gas 6.

2 Cut open the gizzard and remove the stone-filled pouch. Remove the spleen from the liver, being careful not to let it split open, and discard. Cut away any greenish parts which may be sticking to the liver and which would give a bitter taste. Wash and dry the chicken and giblets.

3 Season the inside of the chicken with salt and pepper. Put in the sprig of thyme, 25 g (1 oz) (2 tablespoons) of butter and the liver. Rub over the chicken a further 25 g (1 oz) (2 tablespoons) butter. Season the outside. Place the bird in a roasting pan. Pour the water into the pan, put it in the oven and let it cook for 1 hour. Baste the bird from time to time and turn it around so it cooks evenly.

4 Thirty minutes before the chicken is ready, measure the rice. Boil the stock (bouillon), adding all the prepared giblets. Melt the remaining butter in a stewpan. Add the dry rice and cook over moderate heat. Stir with a wooden spoon until the grains become transparent. Pour in the boiling stock (bouillon), cover the pan and simmer until all the liquid is absorbed.

5 Place the almonds in a non-stick frying pan (skillet) and heat, stirring frequently until they are golden-brown.

6 Warm a serving dish and sauceboat. Drain the currants.

7 When the rice is cooked, tip it onto the serving dish. Add the currants and pine kernels and mix them carefully into the rice. Spread the browned almonds on top.

8 Drain the chicken and place it on top of the rice.

9 Pour 2-3 tablespoons of hot water into the roasting pan. Stir vigorously with a spoon to dissolve all the meat juices. Pour the liquid into the sauceboat and serve hot.
Serves 4

Roast Chicken with Almonds — served on a bed of almonds, pine kernels and raisins

Chicken in Wine with Mushrooms

1½ kg (3½ lb) chicken, oven-ready
75 g (3 oz) (⅓ cup) butter
1 clove garlic
2 onions
sprig thyme
1 bay leaf, imported
¼ litre (8 fl oz) (1 cup) dry white wine
salt and pepper
250 g (good ½ lb) mushrooms, wiped and trimmed
juice 1 lemon
12 g (about ½ oz) canned truffle, drained (optional)
300 ml (½ pint) (1¼ cups) single (light) cream

1 Brown the chicken in 50 g (2 oz) (4 tablespoons) butter. Peel and chop the garlic and the onions. Put the chicken, together with the garlic and onions, in a large pan with the sprig of thyme, bay leaf and the white wine. Season with salt and pepper, cover and cook gently for about 1 hour.

2 About 20 minutes before the end of the cooking time, heat the remaining butter in a pan, add the strained lemon juice and heat, stirring continuously, without letting the mixture colour. Add the mushrooms, then enough cold water just to cover them. Reduce (evaporate) the liquid to about half its quantity, with the lid off the pan. As soon as the mushrooms are tender, take them off the heat.

3 Cut the truffle, if used, in strips. Remove the chicken from the pan and place on a hot serving dish. Discard the bay leaf and thyme.

4 Reduce (evaporate) the cooking juices a little, then stir in the cream. Pour the sauce over the chicken. Decorate the dish with the strips of truffle, if used, and arrange the drained mushrooms all round.

Serves 6

Scandinavian Roast Chicken

Traditionally, the chicken is wrapped up with pine needles and the parcel is left for 24 hours for the flavour to infuse. However, some needles may be poisonous.

24 juniper berries
1½ kg (3 lb) chicken, oven-ready
2.5 ml (½ teaspoon) salt
pepper
4 shallots
40 g (1½ oz) (3 tablespoons) butter

1 Pound the juniper berries in a mortar or work in a blender and put aside half until the following day.

2 Insert a little of the remaining crushed juniper berries in the chicken and rub the outside with the rest. Season with salt and pepper.

3 Preheat the oven to 200°C, 400°F, gas 6.

4 Peel the shallots and chop them coarsely.

5 Heat the butter in a frying pan (skillet). As soon as it stops frothing, add the shallots and brown them.

6 Add the reserved crushed juniper berries. Cook the mixture gently for 1 minute over a low heat, stirring all the time.

7 Pour half the juniper- and shallot-flavoured butter into a roasting pan. Place the chicken on top, and baste with the rest of the butter. Put the chicken into the oven and cook for 45-60 minutes, turning and basting the chicken from time to time.

8 Serve very hot straight from the oven.

Serves 4

Tip: Scandinavians serve this dish with potatoes baked in ashes and then basted with cream.

Chicken with Mustard

1½ kg (3 lb) chicken, oven-ready
200 ml (7 fl oz) (⅞ cup) oil
salt and pepper
1 egg
25 ml (1½ tablespoons) French (Dijon-style) mustard
50 g (2 oz) (1 cup) dry white breadcrumbs
30 ml (2 tablespoons) white vinegar
5 ml (1 teaspoon) capers, drained and chopped
Small bunch parsley, finely chopped

1 Preheat the oven to 170°C, 325°F, gas 3.

2 Put the chicken in a roasting pan. Baste it with 30 ml (2 tablespoons) of oil. Season it with salt and pepper. Cook for 30 minutes in the oven.

3 Boil some water in a small saucepan. Hard-boil the egg for 10 minutes. Put it into cold water. Shell it. Halve it. Remove the yolk and place the yolk in a bowl. (Use the white for other purposes.)

4 When the chicken has been cooking for 30 minutes, take it out of the oven. Spread 15 ml (1 tablespoon) of the mustard over the bird. Sprinkle the breadcrumbs over it. Put it back into the roasting pan and cook for a further 15 minutes.

5 Add the rest of the mustard to the egg yolk. Blend in the vinegar. Add the rest of the oil a little at a time, stirring continuously with a wooden spoon. Add the chopped capers and parsley to the sauce. Add salt and pepper to taste and mix again.

6 Warm a serving dish and a sauceboat. Place the chicken on it. Pour the sauce into a sauceboat and serve very hot.

Serves 4

Scandinavian Roast Chicken, with juniper berries, a deliciously different way with chicken

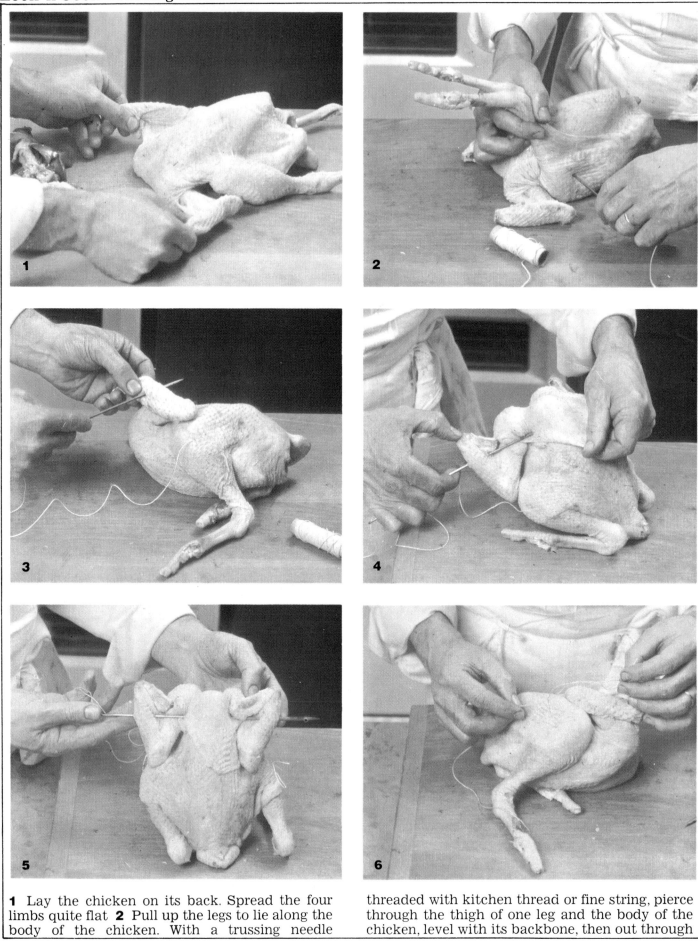

1 Lay the chicken on its back. Spread the four limbs quite flat **2** Pull up the clegs to lie along the body of the chicken. With a trussing needle threaded with kitchen thread or fine string, pierce through the thigh of one leg and the body of the chicken, level with its backbone, then out through

7

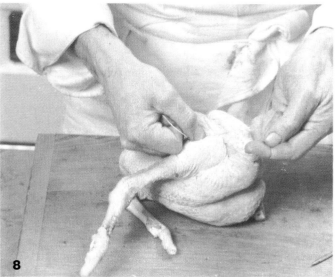

8

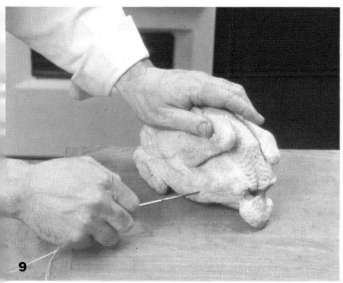

9

10

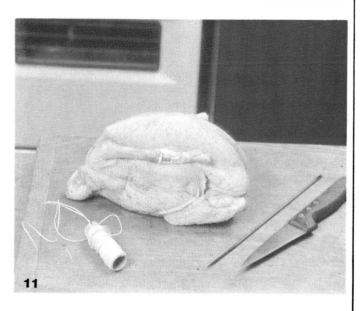

11

he other thigh. Pull out the needle and pull through
he thread **3** Place the chicken breast-down. Pierce
hrough one wing with the needle **4** Pull the flap of
kin from the neck over the back of the chicken and
ass the needle through it and the body and out
hrough the other side **5** Pass the needle through
he second wing and pull the thread through **6**
Vith one hand, hold the end of the thread which is
oming out of the leg and with the other hand hold
he thread coming out of the wing **7** Pull these two
nds tightly **8** Tie them together with a double
not without relaxing the tension. This will secure
he wings firmly in position **9** Hold the legs
gainst the sides of the chicken. Pass the needle
hrough its rear from one side to the other, keeping
s close as possible to the backbone; pull the thread
hrough without letting the needle become
nthreaded **10** Still holding the legs in position,
ass the needle again through the chicken from one
de to the other, but this time over the drumstick
nd under the breastbone so that the legs are sec-
red with thread. Pull tightly and tie again with a

double knot **11** How the trussed chicken should
look – neat and tidy – together with the essential
trussing needle, thread and knife

Spit-roast Chicken with Tarragon Stuffing

1¼ kg (2½ lb) chicken, oven-ready
  and including its liver
bunch tarragon
40 g (1½ oz) (3 tablespoons) butter
salt and pepper

1 Wash and dry the tarragon. Strip off the leaves and chop them. Put them into a bowl with half of the butter and the chicken liver. Work the mixture with a fork until it has a paste-like consistency. Add salt and pepper. Put the mixture into the chicken.

2 Truss the chicken (instructions on pages 102-103).

3 Soften the rest of the butter in a bowl with a wooden spoon. Season the outside of the chicken with salt and pepper and coat it with the softened butter.

4 Heat the rôtisserie unit (spit roaster) or grill (broiler).

5 Pierce the chicken from the head to the rump with the skewer or kebab stick. Place it in position on the rôtisserie (spit roaster) or under the hot grill (broiler) and cook for about 50 minutes, basting occasionally, above a dish or drip tray. If using a grill (broiler), turn and baste the bird from time to time so it cooks evenly.

6 Warm a serving dish and a sauceboat. When the chicken is cooked remove the skewer or kebab stick. Cut and pull out the trussing thread. Place the chicken on the dish.

7 Pour 30 ml (2 tablespoons) of hot water into the drip tray. Stir vigorously with a wooden spoon to dissolve all the meat juices and pour the liquid into the sauceboat. Serve this dish with watercress and creamed potatoes.

Serves 4

326

Spanish Chicken with Red Peppers

1 onion
3 red peppers
250 g (10 oz) (1¼ cups) long grain
  rice
125 g (5 oz) (⅝ cup) butter
30 ml (2 tablespoons) olive oil
150 g (5 oz) (scant 1 cup) diced
  chorizo (Spanish red pepper
  sausage)
small bouquet garni
1½ kg (3 lb) chicken, oven-ready
100 g (¼ lb) (1 cup) cooked petits
  pois (tiny young peas)
salt and pepper
75 ml (2½ fl oz) (⅓ cup) glass dry
  white wine
300 ml (½ pint) (1¼ cups) stock
  (bouillon)
15-30 ml (1-2 tablespoons) single
  (light) cream, optional

1 Preheat the oven to 190°C, 375°F, gas 5.

2 Peel the onion and chop it finely. Cut the red peppers in half and remove the seeds (pips) and white membranes; dice the flesh. Use a cup or bowl to measure the volume of the rice and then put 1½ times its volume in water in a pan and add salt. Set aside.

3 Melt 40 g (1½ oz) (3 tablespoons) butter in a frying pan (skillet) over a medium heat. Add 15 ml (1 tablespoon) olive oil and when the butter is hot, add the onion and the diced peppers. Fry them together for 2 minutes, then stir in the chorizo and brown for 1 minute.

4 When this mixture is ready, add the dry rice. Mix together so that the rice absorbs the flavour from the fried ingredients. Transfer to a casserole, then pour the prepared salted water over the rice mixture. Add the bouquet garni and bring to the boil.

5 Cover with the lid, put into the oven and leave for 18 minutes.

6 When the rice is cooked add 40 g (1½ oz) (3 tablespoons) butter and mix well with a fork until it is all melted. Stir in the cooked petits pois (tiny young peas), mixing gently.

7 Remove one-quarter of the prepared rice and spread it out on a plate to cool. This will be the stuffing for the chicken. Put the rest of the rice, covered with foil, to one side and reheat in the oven about 30 minutes before the final cooking.

8 Stuff the chicken with the cooled rice. Then truss the bird (see pages 102-103).

9 Heat 15 ml (1 tablespoon) olive oil and the remaining butter in a stewpan.

10 Rub salt into the chicken and place the bird in the stewpan over a low heat until it is browned all over (this takes about 15-20 minutes).

11 When the chicken is golden-brown, pour in the white wine, then the stock (bouillon). Season with pepper, cover and finish cooking over a gentle heat for 50 minutes. Reheat the rice.

12 Warm a large, preferably round, serving dish and a sauceboat.

13 When the chicken is done, lift it out of the cooking juices. Snip and remove the trussing string and set the chicken aside but keep it warm.

14 Boil the cooking juices rapidly until the quantity is reduced (evaporated) by half. Check the seasoning, then strain the sauce through a conical sieve or fine strainer into the sauceboat. Stir in the cream, if liked. Keep warm.

15 Arrange the hot rice mixture in a ring round the edge of the serving dish. Place the stuffed chicken in the centre and give it an attractive, bright glaze by spooning a little of the sauce over it. Serve very hot.

Serves 4

Tip: If you cannot buy chorizo sausage use a boiling sausage instead such as capanos, knackwurst or frankfurters, together with a good pinch of cayenne pepper and 2.5 ml (½ teaspoon) paprika.

Spicy Roast Chicken with Peanuts

5 ml (1 teaspoon) paprika
pinch cayenne pepper
pinch ground (powdered)
  ginger
salt and pepper
45 ml (3 tablespoons) oil
350 g (¾ lb) (3 generous cups)
  shelled peanuts
1½ kg (3½ lb) chicken, oven-ready
100 g (¼ lb) (½ cup) butter
few slices dry white bread
30 ml (2 tablespoons) light rum

1 In a small bowl put the paprika, cayenne pepper, ginger and salt. Add the oil and beat together well.

2 Put 50 g (2 oz) (½ cup) peanuts through a small mill or work in a blender. Add the resulting powder to the oil and spice mixture. Preheat the oven to 200°C, 400°F, gas 6.

3 Wash, drain and wipe the chicken and season the inside with salt and pepper and truss (pages 102-103). Coat the bird all over with the spicy oil and nut mixture, place it in a roasting pan and put in the oven to cook.

4 Put another 50 g (2 oz) (¼ cup) peanuts through the small mill or work in a blender and mix this powder into half of the butter. Add a little salt.

5 Toast the slices of dry bread and spread them with the prepared peanut butter mixture.

6 Put the remaining butter in a

*Spicy Chicken with Peanuts —
chicken coated with a delicious
mixture of pepper, ginger and
ground peanuts*

small frying pan (skillet) and when it is just golden add the rest of the peanuts. Fry them.

7 Put the toast on a baking (cookie) sheet in the top of the oven and cook briefly, or until the peanut butter topping is browned and bubbling.

8 When the chicken is done, pour over the rum and set it alight.

9 Arrange the chicken on a hot serving dish and sprinkle over the fried peanuts. Arrange the baked peanut bread slices round the chicken and serve at once.

Serves 6

Chicken Stuffed with Ham

2 kg (4 lb) chicken
50 g (2 oz) bacon fat
30 ml (2 tablespoons) olive oil

For the stuffing:
125 g (good ¼ lb) bacon, slightly
  salted
1 onion
2 shallots
small bunch parsley
125 g (good ¼ lb) lean veal
2 cloves garlic
pinch mixed spice
1.25 ml (¼ teaspoon) dried
  (powdered) thyme
pinch ground (crushed) bay leaf
100 g (¼ lb) (1 cup) dry white
  breadcrumbs
45 ml (3 tablespoons) milk
1 egg
salt and pepper
2-4 slices cooked ham (gammon)

For the garnish:
1 kg (2 lb) green peppers
1 kg (2 lb) tomatoes
2 onions
2 cloves garlic
few sprigs parsley

1 Wash, drain and wipe the chicken. Prepare the giblets (see pages 126-127) and reserve the zard, first removing stone-filled pouch, and liver. Wash and dry the chicken.

2 Make the stuffing. Dice the bacon. Heat some water in a saucepan and as soon as it is boiling, put in the bacon pieces and blanch them for about 5 minutes. Drain them, cool them in cold water, and dry them.

3 Peel the onion and cut in quarters. Peel the shallots. Wash and dry the parsley.

4 Work in a blender or through a mincer (grinder) the following stuffing ingredients: the bacon, lean veal, chicken gizzard and liver, the onion, shallots and parsley.

5 Peel and finely chop the cloves of garlic. Add them to the rest of the stuffing ingredients, together with the mixed spice, thyme and bay leaf.

6 Rub the dry breadcrumbs through a sieve. Moisten them with the milk and then squeeze out any excess liquid.

7 Add the whole egg to the breadcrumbs and mix well. Fold into the stuffing ingredients. Season with salt and pepper to taste and mix well to obtain an even consistency.

8 Wrap the stuffing in the slices of ham, and slide them into the chicken. Sew up the opening with a trussing needle and thread so that the stuffing does not escape.

9 Cut the bacon fat into small pieces. Heat the oil in a large flameproof casserole. Add the diced bacon fat and melt over a low heat. Put the chicken into the casserole and brown it over a moderate heat, so that it is sealed on all sides. Cover the pan and leave the chicken to cook for about 45 minutes.

10 Meanwhile, prepare the garnish. Wash and dry the peppers. Cut them in half, remove the membranes and take out the seeds. Cut them into strips. Skin the tomatoes by placing in a bowl of boiling water, let stand for 1-2 minutes, then drain and skin; take out the seeds and dice the pulp. Peel the onions and cut them in quarters. Peel and crush the garlic. Wash, dry and chop the parsley.

11 When the chicken has cooked for about 45 minutes, add the onions, green peppers and garlic. Season with salt and pepper to taste and fry for 15 minutes.

12 Then mix in the tomatoes and chopped parsley. Cover and finish the cooking (about 15 minutes).

Chicken Stuffed with Ham — a tasty stuffing made with bacon, veal, spices and herbs

13 Heat a serving dish.

14 Arrange the chicken on the hot dish, surround it with the garnish and serve very hot.

Serves 6

Chicken stuffed with Raisins

150 g (5 oz) (1 cup) seedless raisins
(100 ml) (½ cup) dry sherry
1 large onion
350 g (12 oz) (2¼ cups) long grain
   rice
45 ml (3 tablespoons) oil
100 g (4 oz) (¾ cup) flaked
   almonds
pinch ginger
pinch powdered saffron
1.25 ml (¼ teaspoon)
   chilli powder
pinch mixed spice
salt and pepper
2 kg (4 lb) chicken, oven-ready
75 g (3 oz) (⅓ cup) butter
   or margarine

1 Wash the raisins and soak them for 30 minutes in the dry sherry.

2 Peel and chop the onion. Measure the amount of rice and boil twice its volume of water.

3 Heat the oil in a stewpan. Add the flaked almonds and chopped onion and fry them until golden.

4 Add the rice to the onion and almond mixture and fry, stirring constantly with a wooden spoon, until the grains of rice are opaque. Pour in the boiling water, cover the pan and cook over a very low heat for about 18 minutes.

5 Mix the spices in a bowl – ginger, saffron, chilli and mixed spice. Add a little salt and pepper. When the rice is cooked, mix in the spices and raisins. Preheat the oven to 200°C, 400°F, gas 6.

6 Fill the inside of the chicken with part of the prepared rice and keep the rest hot in either a bain

marie, or a warm oven.

7 Sew up the opening in the chicken so that the stuffing does not leak out.

8 Melt the fat in a roasting tin, add the chicken and roast for about 1½ hours, or until cooked. Baste the bird occasionally during roasting.

9 Put the cooked chicken on a flat serving dish, surrounded by the rice which has been kept hot. Serve hot.

Serves 6

Chicken with Cider

2 kg (4 lb) chicken
1¼ kg (2½ lb) cooking (green)
   apples
100 g (¼ lb) (1 cup) walnuts,
   shelled
10 g (2 tablespoons) parsley,
   chopped
50 g (2 oz) bacon
1 small onion
75 g (3 oz) (1½ cups) fresh white
   breadcrumbs
1 egg
2.5 ml (½ teaspoon) ground
   (powdered) cinnamon or ginger
15 g (1 tablespoon) dark brown
   sugar
100 g (¼ lb) (½ cup) butter or
   margarine
2-3 shallots
sprig fresh thyme
2 cloves
salt and pepper
½ bottle dry cider
150 ml (¼ pint) (⅝ cup) single
   (light) cream

1 Preheat the oven to 190°C, 375°F, gas 5.

2 Peel, core and quarter the apples. Place them in a bowl of lightly salted water to prevent browning.

3 Roughly chop the shelled walnuts.

4 Remove the rind from the bacon and chop it finely. Peel and dice the onion. Melt 25 g (1 oz) of

the fat in a frying pan, and fry the bacon and onion gently until they are softened.

5 Rinse two-thirds of the apples to remove the salty water. Shred (grate) the apples into a bowl, add the bacon, onions, walnuts, parsley, breadcrumbs, beaten egg, half of the cinnamon, seasoning and half of the sugar. Mix well. Stuff the chicken with this mixture, and sew it up with a trussing needle, to prevent the stuffing coming out during cooking.

6 Put the chicken in the roasting tin and spread it with half of the fat. Put into the oven and roast for about one and three-quarter hours, or until the chicken is cooked. 15 minutes before the end of cooking, rinse the remaining apple quarters and place them in the roasting pan around the chicken. Pour over the cider, and baste both the chicken and apples with the cider.

7 Meanwhile, peel and chop the shallots finely. Heat the rest of the fat in a large pan. Add the chopped shallots and fry for 5-6 minutes on a low heat, then add the cloves, pepper and remaining sugar. Stir in the cream, and heat gently for 5 minutes.

8 When the chicken is cooked, remove it from the roasting pan with the apples. Skim off any excess fat from the pan juices, then gradually pour the juices into the sauce.

9 Serve the chicken on a warmed plate surrounded by the apple quarters, with the sauce poured over it.

10 When the chicken is cooked, add the cream and shake the pan to mix the sauce well. Taste and adjust the seasoning with salt and pepper and a pinch of ground (powdered) cinnamon or ginger.

11 Transfer the chicken to a hot serving dish, or carve and arrange the pieces on a hot serving dish, surrounded by the apple quarters and the sauce. Serve immediately.

Serves 6

Look 'n Cook Glazed Onions

1 Peel the small (pearl) onions carefully, leaving all the layers joined at the root end. Cut off the stem down to the onion. Wash the onions in clear water **2** Put the onions into a small thick-bottomed saucepan, and add just enough cold water to cover the onions **3** Add a large lump of butter and bring to the boil **4** Add the finely powdered sugar **5** Heat until all the liquid has been absorbed. The simmering heat should be just enough to make all the water evaporate and not enough to make the onions fall to pieces **6** When all the liquid has been absorbed and the caramel becomes golden brown, shake the saucepan round in a circle so that the onions roll about and become coated in the glaze

Roast Chicken with Caramelized Onions

1½ kg (3 lb) chicken, oven-ready
sprig thyme
sprig rosemary
salt and pepper
15 ml (1 tablespoon) oil
150 g (5 oz) (⅔ cup) butter
125 g (¼ lb) smoked bacon
750 g (1¾ lb) potatoes, peeled and
  diced
20 button or small (pearl)
  onions
10 ml (2 teaspoons) sugar
225 g (½ lb) tiny button
  mushrooms
bunch parsley

1 Preheat the oven to 220°C, 425°F, gas 7. Prepare the giblets (see pages 126-127). Rinse the herbs and place them inside the chicken, season with salt and pepper and truss the bird (see pages 102-103).

2 Place the chicken on its side in a roasting pan. Coat it well with the oil. Spread 25 g (1 oz) (2 tablespoons) butter on top. Season with salt and pepper. Put the roasting pan into the oven. After 15 minutes turn the chicken on to its other side, basting with the cooking juices (if necessary add a spoonful of boiling water). Fifteen minutes later, turn the chicken onto its back again and leave it until it is completely cooked, basting often (about 25 minutes).

3 Meanwhile, take the bacon and cut it into thin strips. Heat 25 g (1 oz) (2 tablespoons) of butter in a frying pan (skillet) and fry the pieces of bacon in it. Put them to one side of the pan and keep the fat.

4 Fry the diced potato in the fat left in the frying pan (skillet).

5 Peel the onions, being careful to keep them whole. Place them in a pan large enough for them to cover bottom but not sit on top of each other. Add 50 g (2 oz) (4 tablespoons) butter, a pinch of salt, the sugar and enough water to cover half the depth of the onions. Cover the pan with foil and bring to the boil. The onions are cooked when the water has

completely evaporated and the sugar has caramelized. Only cook them long enough to soften but still stay whole. Roll them in the caramelized juices to glaze them.

6 Cut off the ends of the mushroom stalks. Wash the mushrooms quickly and wipe dry. In a second frying pan (skillet) fry them in the rest of the butter over a high heat. When all the natural moisture from the mushrooms has evaporated, transfer them to the pan of fried bacon and potatoes. Wash the parsley, dry and chop it.

7 When the chicken is cooked take it out of the roasting pan and keep it warm in the oven on a

serving dish. Heat the roasting pan and skim off the fat from the cooking juices; deglaze the juices by stirring in a little boiling water. Leave this gravy to simmer for 2 minutes.

8 Reheat the pan (skillet) of bacon, potatoes and mushrooms as well as the pan of caramelized onions. Pour the gravy into the sauceboat. Spoon the vegetable garnish around the chicken. Sprinkle over the parsley and serve immediately.

Serves 6

Roast Chicken with Caramelized Onions, also garnished with bacon rolls, sauté potatoes and mushrooms

Roast Chicken with Blue Cheese Stuffing

40 g (1½ oz) Roquefort or other blue cheese
2 Baby Bel cheeses
75 g (3 oz) (⅓ cup) butter
1½ kg (3 lb) chicken, oven-ready
sprig thyme
salt and pepper
15 ml (1 tablespoon) single (light) cream

1 Preheat the oven to 200°C, 400°F, gas 6. Blend the cheeses with 25 g (1 oz) (2 tablespoons) butter. Stuff the inside of the chicken with this mixture. Add a sprig of thyme.

2 Truss the chicken, see page 102. Grease a roasting pan with half the rest of the butter. Season the outside of the chicken with salt and pepper.

3 Place the chicken in the greased roasting pan. Put a few knobs of butter on the chicken. Place the pan in the oven and cook the chicken for 50 minutes.

4 Skim off the fat from the juices in the roasting pan and then stir in the cream. Place the chicken on a warmed serving dish. Pour the sauce in a sauceboat and serve with the chicken.

Serves 4

Chicken Cooked in Salt

1½ kg (3 lb) chicken, oven-ready
25 g (1 oz) canned truffle (optional)
5 ml (1 teaspoon) brandy
pepper
5 kg (10 lb) rock salt

1 Preheat the oven to 240-250°C, 475°F, gas 9.

2 Drain the truffle but save the juice. Cut it into round slices. Make small notches under the skin of the chicken and put the slices of truffle into them.

3 Pepper the interior of the bird. Pour the juice from the truffle and the brandy into it.

4 Spread out 2 kg (4 lb) of rock salt on bottom of an ovenproof dish (pan), and place the chicken on it. Cover with the rest of the salt. Do *not* put a lid on the pot. Put it in the oven and cook for 1½ hours without opening the door.

5 Warm a serving dish.

6 When it is cooked, take the chicken out of the pot. Break the crust of salt with a hammer and cut up the bird. Arrange the pieces on the hot dish and serve immediately.

Serves 4

Tip: The oven should be extremely hot when the chicken is put in so that the salt will firm up properly.

If the stewing pot is covered while cooking, the humidity from the chicken will not be able to escape and the salt will melt and will penetrate the flesh.

Break up the lumps of salt and use again for the same dish.

Roast Chicken with Pineapple

1½ kg (3 lb) chicken, oven-ready
salt and pepper
1 lemon, cut in half
2 oranges
100 ml (4 fl oz) (½ cup) light rum
50 g (2 oz) (¼ cup) butter, melted
10 ml (2 teaspoons) sugar
1 small pineapple

1 Season inside the chicken with salt and pepper. Rub 1 lemon half over the skin so that it absorbs the juice; reserve the lemon. Squeeze the juice from the remaining half lemon and set aside.

2 Peel 1 orange. Remove the membranes between the segments (sections) so that the flesh alone remains. Chop this coarsely. Sprinkle 30 ml (2 tablespoons) rum and 15 ml (1 tablespoon) lemon juice over the orange pieces. Fill the chicken with the prepared orange pieces and leave the chicken in the refrigerator until the next day, so the flavours can mature.

3 An hour and a quarter before the time to serve the chicken, put it in the roasting pan in an oven preheated to 220°C, 425°F, gas 7. (The oven should be hotter than is usually needed to roast a chicken, because of its cold stuffing). After 20 minutes, sprinkle salt and pepper over the outside of the chicken and pour the melted butter over it. Replace the bird in the oven.

4 Squeeze the reserved lemon half. Put the juice into a small saucepan with the sugar. Heat, stirring, until it is a fairly dark-coloured caramel.

5 Top and tail the pineapple, then cut away the prickly skin. Slice it, and cut away or stamp out the fibrous core with a pastry (cookie) cutter. Collect any juice that runs out and add it to the lemon caramel.

6 Pour this lemon sauce and the remaining rum alternately over the chicken. Ten minutes before serving, put the pineapple slices in the roasting pan to heat through.

7 Remove the chicken from the oven and cut up into joints. Arrange them on a hot serving dish, surrounded by pineapple slices. Add the cooking juices from the pan and the juice squeezed from the other orange to the sauce. Correct the seasoning and pour into a sauceboat. Serve with either rice or potato straws.

Tip: An alternative presentation is to put the rice on a serving dish and place the whole chicken in the centre, with the pineapple slices surrounding it. For added colour heat a few glacé (candied) cherries with the pineapple slices, then place them in the centre of some of the pineapple rings and around the chicken.

Serves 6

Chicken Portions

Chicken with Caramelized Apples

4 chicken pieces
3 onions
45 ml (3 tablespoons) oil
salt and pepper
5 ml (1 teaspoon) paprika
2.5 ml (½ teaspoon) ground
  (powdered) ginger
5 ml (1 teaspoon) ground
  (powdered) coriander seeds
pinch ground (powdered)
  saffron
½ litre (1 pint) (2½ cups) water
1 kg (2 lb) firm dessert apples
50 g (2 oz) (¼ cup) butter

1 Lightly fry the peeled and sliced onions in oil. Add the chicken joints and brown.

2 Season the chicken with the salt, pepper, paprika, ginger, coriander and saffron. Pour in the water and simmer for 30 min.

3 Meanwhile, wash and dry the apples. Cut them in half without peeling, and core them. Heat the butter in a frying pan (skillet). Add the apple halves and brown them over a brisk heat.

4 Preheat the oven to 180°C, 350°F, gas 4.

5 After the chicken has simmered for 30 minutes, place the pieces in an ovenproof dish. Add the caramelized apple halves. Pour over the cooking juices from the pan. Cover the dish with foil and pierce a few holes in it. Place the dish in the oven and let the chicken cook for 30 minutes more. Serve at once.

Serves 4

Chicken with Green Peppers and Paprika Rice

225 g (½ lb) bacon, sliced
50 g (2 oz) (¼ cup) butter
1¼ kg (2½ lb) oven-ready chicken,
  cut up into serving pieces
1.25 ml (¼ teaspoon) salt
freshly ground (milled) black
  pepper
1 large onion, peeled and
  chopped
5 ml (1 teaspoon) flour
225 ml (8 fl oz) (1 cup) wine, red or
  white
1 bay leaf, imported
500 ml (1 pint) (2½ cups) chicken
  stock (bouillon)
3 green peppers, halved, cored
  and deseeded
5 ml (1 teaspoon) paprika
225 g (½ lb) (1 cup) long grain rice

1 Preheat the oven to 180°C, 350°F, gas 4. Gently fry the bacon in a deep frying pan (skillet) or stewpan. When the fat has run from the bacon, remove it and pour all but 15 ml (1 tablespoon) of the fat from the pan. Put half the butter in the pan, add the chicken pieces and brown them evenly on all sides. Remove the pieces and season them with salt and pepper.

2 Fry half the onion in the same fat for 3 minutes or until soft. Stir in the flour and cook the roux slowly for a few minutes; then stir in the wine and the bay leaf. Cook over a high heat to reduce (evaporate) the wine to about 100 ml (4 fl oz) (½ cup). Add 100 ml (4 fl oz) (½ cup) of the stock (bouillon) and bring to the boil.

3 Put the chicken pieces, bacon and any juices left in the pan in a casserole, cover with a lid and cook in the oven for 50 minutes or until the chicken is tender.

4 Heat the remaining butter in a pan and add the green peppers cut into 2.5 cm (1 in) squares and the remaining onion. Fry over a moderate heat for 5 minutes, then stir in the paprika and the rice. Stir over a moderate heat for 3 minutes, then add the remaining chicken stock (bouillon), boiling; cover and simmer for 20 minutes. Discard the bay leaf.

5 Serve the chicken from the casserole, with the rice served separately.

Serves 4

Chicken Waterzoi

2 large carrots
8 leeks
4 stalks celery
50 g (2 oz) (¼ cup) butter
salt and pepper
bunch parsley
2 kg (4 lb) chicken, oven-ready
1½ litres (1¼ pints) (3 cups) chicken
  stock (bouillon)
3 egg yolks
200 ml (7 fl oz) (7⅞ cup)
  double (heavy) cream
juice of 1 lemon

1 Peel the carrots; trim and clean the leeks and celery. Wash them, dry and chop finely. Heat the butter in a stewpan, add the prepared vegetables and leave to soften over a low heat for about 15 minutes. Season lightly. Wash the parsley, dry, chop and add three-quarters of it to the pan of vegetables.

2 Cut the chicken in pieces (see pages 112-113 . Put half the vegetables into a casserole. Cover with the chicken pieces and then with the remaining vegetables. Place over a low heat for 10 minutes, then gradually pour in the chicken stock. Cover and cook slowly for at least 50 minutes or until the chicken pieces are very tender.

3 Place the pieces of chicken on a heated serving dish. Beat the egg yolks with the cream and the juice of the lemon. Pour this liaison into the casserole whilst stirring with a wooden spoon. Heat for a few minutes, stirring continuously, but do not allow to boil. Pour the thickened vegetable soup into a hot tureen and sprinkle with the remaining chopped parsley.

4 Serve some of the soup in wide soup bowls, topping each one with a piece of chicken.

Serves 6

Look'n Cook Jointing an Uncooked Chicken

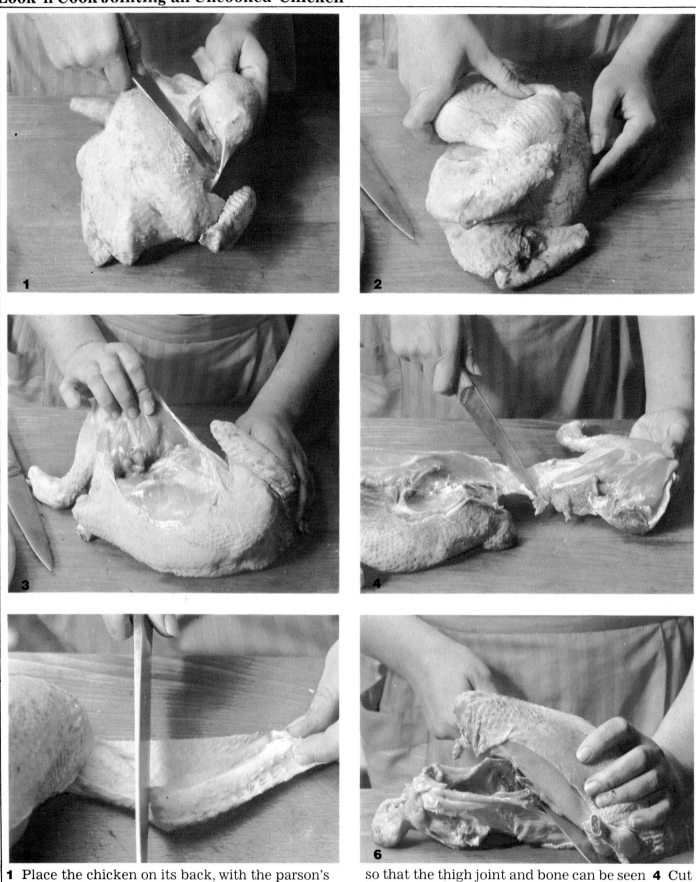

1 Place the chicken on its back, with the parson's nose towards you. Lift one leg and pull it away from the body of the chicken. Cut the skin between the body and the leg **2** Pull the joint out of place by swinging the leg from right to left **3** Pull up the leg so that the thigh joint and bone can be seen **4** Cut through the ball and socket joint and detach each leg **5** Cut off the wings at the centre of the joints **6** Cut through the carcass parallel to the breast **7** Detach it by carving carefully along next to the

backbone **8** Cut the two sides of the breast (the fillets or suprêmes) in two along the breastbone, which in a young chicken, will be quite pliable and split easily **9** Carefully pull away the rib cage **10** Cut off the ends of each drumstick **11** Using a sharp knife, cut out the large bones from the legs. Insert the knife into the leg and, keeping the blade as close to the bone as possible, cut all round the bone which can then be pulled away **12** The 6 chicken joints are now ready to use

Chicken in the Pot

2 kg (4 lb) boiling fowl, oven-
  ready and with a few extra
  giblets (necks, wings, bones and
  gizzards)
bouquet garni
sea salt
450 g (1 lb) carrots
450 g (1 lb) turnips
3 leeks
1 head (bunch) celery
450 g (1 lb) potatoes
6 slices wholemeal bread
200 g (7 oz) (1¾ cups) grated
  Gruyère cheese

1 Cut up the chicken into 10 pieces (see page 112). Put them into a large stewpan. Add the giblets. Cover with cold water and bring to the boil. Drain the chicken meat and rinse under cold water. Put back into the pan with about 4 litres (7 pints) (9 cups) cold water. Add the bouquet garni and a handful of sea salt and boil up again, skimming now and then.

2 Peel the carrots and the turnips. Wash them. Cut up both vegetables into equal-sized dice.

3 Carefully trim and wash the leeks and the celery. Cut them into 2 or 3 pieces. Tie them together in bundles with string.

4 After the chicken has been cooking for 45 minutes, add the carrots, turnips and bundles of leeks and celery. Leave to cook for about 1 hour (the time will depend on the age and size of fowl). Check if the bird is done by piercing the thigh with the point of a knife or trussing needle; the flesh should no longer feel firm.

5 Peel the potatoes. Wash them and cut them up into pieces the same size as the carrots and turnips. Put them into a saucepan. Cover with cold water. Add a little sea salt and cook for about 20-25 minutes or until tender.

6 Preheat the oven to 190°C, 375°F, gas 5. Cut the slices of bread in half. Put them on a rack in the oven to allow them to dry.

7 Put the grated cheese into a small bowl. Put the bread on a plate. Warm a deep serving dish.

8 Just before serving, drain the chicken pieces. Put them into the warm dish. Arrange the carrots and turnips all round them. Remove the string from the leeks and celery. Drain the potatoes. Put the rest of the vegetables on the plate. Sprinkle with a little stock (bouillon) from the pot and serve piping hot with the baked bread and Gruyère cheese.

Serves 6

An impressive party dish, Devilled Chicken with Coconut combines a mixture of spices with fresh coconut

Devilled Chicken with Coconut

2 kg (4 lb) chicken, oven-ready
8 peppercorns
2 cloves
2.5 ml (½ teaspoon) ground
  (powdered) ginger
2.5 ml (½ teaspoon) ground
  (powdered) cinnamon
salt and pepper
3 onions
1 fresh coconut (full of milk)
300 ml (½ pint) (1¼ cups) water
100 ml (¼ pint) (½ cup) oil
25 g (1 oz) (2 tablespoons) butter
pinch cayenne pepper

1 Cut up the chicken into pieces.

2 Crush the peppercorns with the cloves, ginger and cinnamon. Add salt and mix well.

3 Sprinkle this spicy mixture over the chicken pieces, turning them so that they are well impregnated.

4 Peel and finely chop the onions.

5 Pierce one of the coconut 'eyes' and drain off the milk; reserve. Cut open the coconut, scoop out the flesh and grate finely.

6 Boil the water in a small saucepan, add half of the grated coconut and then simmer for 5 or 6 minutes.

7 Take the saucepan off the heat and leave the coconut to infuse whilst keeping hot.

8 Heat the oil in a pan, add the chopped onions and chicken pieces, and brown over a low heat; then continue to cook for 35 minutes, stirring frequently. At the end of this time the chicken pieces should be evenly browned.

9 Strain the water in which the coconut has been infusing through muslin (cheesecloth), squeezing well. Mix this coconut milk with the milk taken from the coconut.

10 Heat a serving dish.

11 Drain the chicken pieces and arrange them on the dish. Keep hot.

12 Pour the coconut milk into the pan and boil gently until reduced (evaporated) by half.

13 Meanwhile, heat the butter in a small pan. When it starts to go a deep yellow, add the rest of the grated coconut and brown over a low heat, whilst stirring with a wooden spoon.

14 Salt and pepper the coconut milk sauce, season with a pinch of cayenne pepper and pour over the chicken.

15 Sprinkle the chicken pieces with the browned coconut and serve hot.

Serves 6

Pan-fried Chicken with Pasta

2-2½ kg (4-5 lb) chicken, oven-ready
salt and pepper
15 g (½ oz) (2 tablespoons) flour
50 g (2 oz) (¼ cup) butter
30 ml (2 tablespoons) oil
400 g (14 oz) fresh pasta (ribbon noodles, spaghetti, macaroni, etc)
250 g (good ½ lb) mushrooms
3 shallots
100 ml (4 fl oz) (½ cup) brandy
100 ml (4 fl oz) (½ cup) dry white wine
225 g (½ lb) canned tomatoes
sprig tarragon, chopped
100 ml (4 fl oz) (½ cup) chicken stock
125 g (good ¼ lb) bacon
125 g (good ¼ lb) diced ham (gammon)

1 Cut up the chicken into pieces (see page 112). Season the pieces with salt and pepper. Roll them in the flour. Put them in a pan with half the butter and all the oil and cook them for 20 minutes until brown and tender. Take out and keep hot.

2 Put the fresh pasta into a large saucepan of salted, boiling water. Let the pasta cook for about 20 minutes or until just tender (time will depend on the shape and thickness of the pasta).

3 Trim and wash the mushrooms. Fry them in the same pan used to brown the chicken pieces.

4 Peel and chop the shallots. Add them to the mushrooms and let them soften for 1 minute. Pour in the brandy. Heat it and then flame it (set it alight). Add the white wine. Stir. Add the tomatoes, tarragon and stock. Let it reduce (evaporate) by one-third over a brisk heat.

5 Brown the bacon in the rest of the butter. Add the ham (gammon) and heat.

6 Drain the pasta and put into a deep serving dish or vegetable

dish. Mix in the bacon and the ham (gammon). Arrange the chicken on a separate serving dish and cover it with the sauce. Serve at once.

Serves 4

Portuguese Chicken Stew with Fried Eggs

1½ kg (3½ lb) oven-ready chicken, cut up into pieces
100 g (¼ lb) (½ cup) butter
100 ml (4 fl oz) (½ cup) dry white wine
2 small onions, peeled and finely chopped
5 ml (1 teaspoon) salt
freshly ground (milled) black pepper
1 chicken liver
4 eggs

1 Put into a pan the chicken pieces, half the butter, the wine, chopped onions, salt and pepper. Cover and simmer over a low heat for about 45 minutes or until the chicken is tender. Remove the chicken from the pan and keep it warm.

2 Rub the chicken liver through a sieve into the cooking liquid. Heat and stir without boiling. Return the chicken pieces to the pan to reheat. Then arrange on a heated serving dish.

3 Fry the eggs in the remaining butter and serve them with the chicken pieces. Serve the sauce in a sauceboat. Serve boiled rice separately.

Tip: Instead of the chicken liver the chicken can be flavoured with 30 ml (2 tablespoons) tomato concentrate (paste) and thickened with a little cornflour (cornstarch) or with a liaison of 2 egg yolks mixed with 30 ml (2 tablespoons) double (heavy) cream. Do not let the sauce boil if egg yolks are used or else they will curdle and the sauce will separate.

Serves 4

Chicken Suprêmes with Spinach

1 kg (2 lb) (2 cups) cooked spinach
salt and pepper
1 shallot
15 ml (1 tablespoon) oil
150 g (5 oz) (⅝ cup) butter
4 chicken breasts (or duck or
 turkey breasts – see Tip)
65 g (2½ oz) (7 tablespoons) flour
700 ml (1¼ pints) (3 cups) milk
2 egg yolks
100 g (¼ lb) (1 cup) grated Gruyère
 cheese

1 Cut out the tough stalks and discard any wilted spinach leaves. Wash the spinach thoroughly in several changes of water.

2 Put the undrained spinach straight into a pan, add salt, cover with a lid and cook slowly for about 10 minutes or until cooked (there's sufficient water on the leaves to cook them). Then rinse under cold water, drain well and squeeze out all the moisture with the hands. Peel and chop the shallot.

3 Heat the oil and 25 g (1 oz) (2 tablespoons) butter in a stewpan. When the fat is very hot, place the chicken breasts in the pan and fry them over a medium heat until they are just golden but not brown. Season with salt and pepper. Continue to cook slowly until they are cooked, turn them after 10 minutes and then add the chopped shallot.

4 Slowly melt 65 g (2¼ oz) (5 tablespoons) butter in a saucepan. Add the flour and stir and cook for 2 minutes but do not let the roux brown. Then remove the pan from the heat, pour in the milk and blend until smooth, add the salt and pepper, return the pan to the heat, bring to the boil and cook for 5 minutes.

5 Chop the spinach roughly. Preheat the oven to 220°C, 425°F, gas 7.

6 Heat the rest of the butter in a saucepan. When it is just liquid add the spinach. Stir well and season with salt and pepper to taste. Heat the spinach through, then tip into an oven-to-table dish. Place the chicken suprêmes on top and, leaving the door open, place the dish in the oven to keep it warm.

7 Pour the sauce into the pan in which the chicken suprêmes were cooked. Boil for 2 minutes, stirring vigorously to dissolve any juices that are stuck to the bottom of the pan. Beat in the egg yolks and the Gruyère cheese. Coat the chicken with this sauce.

8 Bake in the top of the hot oven for about 10-15 minutes or until browned. Serve straight from the oven.

Tips: If using frozen, chopped spinach put it into a sieve to thaw, if time permits. Then squeeze the moisture out and heat gently as given in the method above. Or put the frozen spinach into a pan over a low heat until thawed.

Cooked chicken breasts, or thick slices from the cooked breasts of duck or turkey can be used. In that case in step 3, fry lightly until the meat is heated through.

Serves 4

Chicken with Paprika Sauce

50 g (2 oz) (½ cup) flour
100 ml (4 fl oz) (½ cup) milk
1 kg (2 lb) oven-ready chicken,
 cut in half
salt and pepper
75 g (3 oz) (6 tablespoons) butter
oil for frying

For the sauce:
2 onions
50 g (2 oz) (¼ cup) butter
30 ml (2 tablespoons) flour
salt
5 ml (1 teaspoon) paprika
300 ml (½ pint) (1¼ cups) double
 (heavy) cream or cream and
 milk, mixed

1 Put the flour in a deep plate or dish. Pour the milk into a bowl and dip the 2 halves of chicken in it. Drain them well, then season with salt and pepper and roll them in the flour.

2 Heat the butter with some oil in a frying pan (skillet). Use enough oil to have a depth of about 5 mm (¼ in). Brown the chicken halves on both sides. Reduce the heat under the pan and continue to fry the chicken for about 45 minutes or until tender, depending upon size.

3 Meanwhile prepare the sauce. Peel the onions and cut them into thin slices. Heat the butter in a pan and soften the onions over a gentle heat without browning. Add the flour, salt and paprika to taste and stir with a wooden spoon over a low heat. Mix in the cream or cream and milk mixture and continue to mix until the sauce is smooth and thick. Keep hot in a double saucepan or a bain marie.

4 When the chicken halves are cooked, drain them on absorbent paper and put on a heated dish. Pour the sauce into a sauceboat. Serve them both very hot.

Serves 4

Chicken Suprêmes with Mushrooms

4 chicken breasts, with wing
 bones attached
salt and pepper
pinch ground (powdered) thyme
2 slices cooked ham (gammon)
85 g (3½ oz) (1 cup) flour
50 g (2 oz) (¼ cup) butter
50 ml (2 fl oz) (¼ cup) Madeira

For the sauce:
100 g (¼ lb) (streaky) bacon
 (lightly salted)
1 onion
1 carrot
1 small stick (stalk) celery
225 g (½ lb) mushrooms
50 g (2 oz) (¼ cup) butter
15 ml (1 tablespoon) flour

cocktail sticks. Dip the stuffed suprêmes into the flour and shake off any excess.

3 Heat the butter in a stewpan, add the suprêmes and fry them over a moderate heat for 25 minutes, turning them several times.

4 Meanwhile make the sauce. Wash, dry and finely dice the bacon. Peel and chop the onion. Peel, wash, dry and finely dice the carrot. Wash, dry and thinly slice the celery. Trim the mushroom stalks. Wash, and slice the mushrooms.

5 Heat the butter for the sauce in a pan. Add the mushrooms, cook for 10 minutes, then drain and keep hot.

6 In the same butter, fry the bacon, onion, carrot and celery, stirring them with a wooden spoon.

7 When these sauce ingredients are golden-brown, add the flour and cook until nut-coloured. Then stir in the chicken stock and half the Madeira. Add the bouquet garni, tomato concentrate (paste) and meat juice, with salt and pepper to taste, and continue to cook slowly for 20 minutes.

8 Heat a serving dish.

9 Arrange the chicken suprêmes on the hot serving dish, first taking out the cocktail sticks. Pile the mushrooms in the centre of the dish and keep hot.

10 Pour the remaining Madeira into the pan used for cooking the chicken suprêmes and boil for 2 minutes, scraping up the juices on the bottom of the pan.

11 Strain the sauce through a conical strainer, pressing it down well, into a pan. Return it to the stove, add the cooking juices scraped from the pan and boil the sauce for 2 minutes.

12 Wash, dry and finely chop the parsley.

13 Pour the sauce over the chicken suprêmes, sprinkle with chopped parsley and serve immediately.

Serves 4

300 ml (½ pint) (1¼ cups) stock
100 ml (4 fl oz) (½ cup) Madeira
1 bouquet garni
15 ml (1 tablespoon) tomato
    concentrate (paste)
30 ml (2 tablespoons) meat glaze
bunch parsley

1 Cut off and discard the end of the wings. Remove the skin from the wings, cut the flesh on the inside and take out the bone. Continue the slit the length of

Chicken Suprêmes with Mushrooms — chicken breasts stuffed with ham and cooked in a mushroom and Madeira sauce

the breast, and open out the 'suprêmes.' Season inside and out with salt and pepper and sprinkle lightly with thyme.

2 Cut the slices of ham (gammon) in half and slide them into the chicken suprêmes. Fold together and secure with wooden

Chicken with Quinces

3 onions
75 ml (5 tablespoons) oil
1.5-2 kg (3-4 lb) oven-ready
  chicken, cut up into pieces
salt and pepper
5 ml (1 teaspoon) paprika
5 ml (1 teaspoon) ground
  (powdered) ginger
pinch ground (powdered)
  saffron
bunch coriander leaves or 5 ml
  (1 teaspoon) ground
  (powdered) coriander
  seeds
½ litre (1 pint) (2½ cups) water
1 kg (2 lb) quinces or apples if
  preferred
50 g (2 oz) (¼ cup) butter

1 Peel the onions and cut them into rounds.

2 Put the oil into a large pan and brown the chicken pieces and then the sliced onions.

3 Season with salt, pepper, paprika, ginger and saffron. Add the washed coriander leaves or ground (powdered) coriander seeds, then the water and cook with the lid off for 30 minutes.

4 Meanwhile halve the quinces or apples, leaving the skins on but removing the core and pips.

5 Put the butter in a frying pan (skillet) and brown the quince or apple pieces over a brisk heat. Take them off the heat when they are lightly caramelized.

6 Preheat the oven to 180°C, 350°F, gas 4.

7 Arrange the quinces or apples and chicken pieces in an oven-proof dish, and pour the cooking liquid from the chicken over them. Cover with foil, pierced with several holes.

8 Put the dish into the oven and cook for 30 minutes. Serve the chicken in its cooking dish.

Serves 4-5

Southern Fried Chicken

Southern Fried Chicken—pieces of chicken dipped in batter and fried until tender

75 g (3 oz) (good ¾ cup) flour
1.25 ml (¼ teaspoon) salt
225 ml (8 fl oz) (1 cup) milk
1 egg
30 ml (2 tablespoons)
  vegetable oil
1½ kg (3 lb) frying chicken, cut
  into serving pieces
oil for frying

1 Mix the flour, salt, milk, egg and oil in a bowl and beat with a wire whisk to obtain a smooth batter. Dip the chicken pieces in the batter and, immediately after coating, fry in hot oil 190°C, 375°F, for about 30 minutes, or until the chicken is almost tender.

2 Remove the chicken from the fat and drain on paper towels. Increase the heat under the oil to 200°C, 400°F, and fry the chicken for a further 5 minutes until the batter is crisp and golden.

Tip: Serve the chicken in a wicker basket with French fried potatoes and corn bread, or with a salad. For variety trickle a little liquid honey over the chicken just before serving.

Serves 6

Chicken in Piquant Sauce

1¼kg (2½lb) chicken, oven-ready
100 ml (4 fl oz) (½ cup) vinegar
1 lemon
1 bay leaf
sprig thyme
1 clove garlic
salt and pepper to taste
25 g (1 oz) (4 tablespoons) flour
30 ml (2 tablespoons) oil
25 g (1 oz) (2 tablespoons) butter
1 onion
2 shallots
30 ml (2 tablespoons) brandy
200 ml (7 fl oz) (⅞ cup) red wine
4 tomatoes
30 ml (2 tablespoons) chopped
  parsley

For the kneaded butter:
15 g (½ oz) (1 tablespoon) butter
15 g (½ oz) (1 tablespoon) flour

1 Cut up the chicken into pieces (see page 112). Put pieces into a plastic bag.

2 Put the vinegar into a bowl. Squeeze the juice from the lemon and add to the vinegar, together with the bay leaf and sprig of thyme. Peel and crush the garlic. Add with the salt and pepper. Mix all together and tip into the bag of chicken pieces.

3 Seal the bag and then turn it over and over until all the pieces are well coated. Leave the chicken in a cool place to marinate for 3 hours, turning the bag from time to time.

4 Then drain and pat dry the chicken pieces with absorbent paper. Roll them in the flour. Heat the oil and butter together in a pan, put in the chicken pieces and brown them for about 20 minutes. Remove them and keep warm.

5 Peel the onion and shallots. Chop finely and put into the pan in which the chicken was cooked. Allow to soften for 1-2 minutes, then pour in the brandy, heat a little and flame (set alight).

6 Pour in the red wine. Skin, chop and add the tomatoes. Add the chopped parsley. Boil quickly for 10 minutes to reduce (evaporate) and concentrate the sauce.

7 Mix the butter and flour together with a fork or by hand to make the kneaded butter. Remove the sauce from the heat and cool for 1-2 minutes. Using a whisk, beat in the kneaded butter bit by bit to thicken the sauce. When all has been incorporated let the sauce boil and thicken for 5 minutes.

8 Coat the chicken pieces with the sauce and serve very hot.

Serves 4

Coq au Vin

Coq au vin is a traditional French dish: chicken pieces are cooked in a rich red wine sauce with onions, carrots and mushrooms. The chicken is first sealed all over in a frying pan and for a luxury touch a little brandy can be poured in at this stage and then flamed.

This dish is relatively inexpensive to make, but if a fairly good quality wine is used, the taste will be so much better. And if left overnight and then reheated the next day, the flavours of coq au vin are greatly enhanced.

100 g (¼ lb) lean salt pork or bacon
  rashers (slices)
2 small carrots
18 button (pearl) onions
2 tomatoes
6 chicken portions
salt and pepper
30 ml (2 tablespoons) brandy
20 g (¾ oz) (1½ tablespoons) flour
750 ml (1¼ pints) (3 cups) red wine
5 g (1 tablespoon) freshly
  chopped parsley
2.5 ml (½ teaspoon) dried thyme
1 bay leaf, imported
225 g (½ lb) (4 cups) button
  mushrooms

1 Cut the pork or bacon into thin strips. Peel and slice the carrots. Peel the onions. Skin and chop the tomatoes, discarding the seeds.

2 Put the pork or bacon in a flameproof casserole and fry gently to brown the meat. Add the carrots and onions and fry gently for 5 minutes, turning frequently. Remove from the pan with a slotted spoon and set aside.

3 Add the chicken to the pan and fry until golden on both sides. Sprinkle with salt and pepper to taste. Warm the brandy, pour over the chicken, then set alight.

4 Add the tomatoes and cook for a few minutes, then return the pork and vegetables to the pan. Sprinkle with the flour, then fry for a further few minutes, stirring constantly.

5 Add the remaining ingredients except the mushrooms and bring to the boil, stirring constantly. Cover and simmer for 30 minutes.

6 Wipe the mushrooms, trim the stalks and slice or quarter them if large. Add to the casserole and continue cooking a further 15 minutes or until the chicken is tender.

7 Remove the bay leaf, taste and adjust the seasoning then serve hot straight from the casserole.

Serves 6

Look'n Cook Chicken and Ham Quenelles (continued)

1 Ingredients for quenelles **2** Mince (grind) meats **3** Make the panada **4** Blend egg whites, lemon juice and cream; mix in the meat; refrigerate. Combine the cold panada with the chicken and ham mixture and refrigerate **5** Using 2 tablespoons scoop out the mixture a little at a time and mould into 50g (2oz) ovals; dip the spoons into warm water each time to prevent the mixture from sticking. Grease a flameproof dish and place the quenelles in it **6** Decorate each quenelle with a small piece of truffle, if liked **7** Make the roux for the Divine Sauce **8** Strain the chicken stock **9** Add tomato concentrate (paste) to the roux, then gradually stir in the stock and cold milk until you have a smooth sauce; simmer for 5 minutes. Cook the mushrooms for the garnish in the sherry and lemon juice, then strain the liquor into the white sauce; season with salt and pepper, and mace or nutmeg. Boil for 5 minutes, then stir in the single (light) cream and boil again for 3 minutes **10** Pour the remaining chicken stock over the quenelles, bring to the boil, then finish the cooking in the oven for 3 minutes **11** Drain and transfer the quenelles to a serving dish **12** Sieve (strain) the sauce, check the seasoning and pour over the quenelles **13** Finish cooking the quenelles in a hot oven for about 10 minutes, then serve at once

Gratin of Chicken and Ham Quenelles with Divine Sauce

Quenelle is derived from an old French word meaning rabbit because originally quenelles were made with rabbit meat, but any kind of fish or meat may be used. The mixture is then shaped into oval or thin cigars before poaching. In the recipe below, the choux paste used to bind the chicken and ham forcemeat is called a panada.

1½ kg (3 lb) roasting chicken, oven-ready
100 g (¼ lb) lean gammon or raw ham, unsmoked
2 egg whites
juice and grated rind ½ lemon
150 ml (¼ pint) (⅝ cup) double (heavy) cream
15 g (½ oz) canned truffle, optional
1 litre (1½ pints) (about 4 cups) chicken stock, made with the carcass (for the sauce and poaching quenelles)

For the Choux Paste:
50 g (2 oz) (4 tablespoons) butter or margarine
50 g (2 oz) (6 tablespoons) flour
150 ml (¼ pint) (⅝ cup) cold milk
2 egg yolks

For the Divine Sauce:
25 g (1 oz) (2 tablespoons) butter or margarine
25 g (1 oz) (4 tablespoons) flour
15 g (½ oz) tomato concentrate (paste)
150 ml (¼ pint) (⅝ cup) chicken stock (reserved from overall quantity)
150 ml (¼ pint) (⅝ cup) cold milk
150 ml (¼ pint) (⅝ cup) dry sherry
juice ½ lemon
salt and pepper
pinch mace or nutmeg
150 ml (¼ pint) (⅝ cup) single (light) cream

For the Garnish:
150 g (5 oz) white button mushrooms, optional
finely chopped parsley and tarragon, mixed (optional)

1 First make the quenelles forcemeat. Remove the chicken skin, then remove the flesh from the bones, scraping them clean. Set aside the flesh, and use the skin and cartilaginous parts for making the stock.

2 Cut the gammon or ham in small cubes; mince (grind) the chicken flesh and ham together in a Moulinex or with a hand machine.

3 In a mixing bowl blend together the egg whites, lemon juice and rind, then gently blend in 150 ml (¼ pint) (⅝ cup) double (heavy) cream. Blend in the chicken and ham, then refrigerate the mixture while preparing the choux paste for binding it.

4 Prepare the choux paste: melt the fat in a pan and stir in the flour. Allow to cook without colouring for 2 minutes until the roux looks like wet sand, then gradually pour in the cold milk, stirring gently to form a smooth paste. The paste will form itself into a dough and come cleanly away from the sides of the pan. When it no longer sticks to the pan, remove from the heat and cool; then blend in the 2 egg yolks. Allow the mixture to cool completely in the refrigerator, then combine with the raw chicken and ham mixture, beating it to a smooth paste. Refrigerate again for 15 minutes.

5 Using a tablespoon, scoop out the mixture a little at a time, and mould into 50 g (2 oz) ovals, using another tablespoon in reverse to give the quenelles an egg-shape. Dip the spoons each time in warm water to prevent the mixture from sticking. Grease a deep flameproof dish and place the quenelles in it, one at a time.

6 Cut the truffle, if used, into thin slices, then into little rounds with a tiny pastry (cookie) cutter for decoration. Put a small truffle round on top of each quenelle, then store in the refrigerator for 20 minutes to harden the quenelles while you prepare the sauce.

7 To make the Divine Sauce: melt the fat in a pan and add the flour. Cook the roux gently to a sandy texture, without colouring, for 1 minute. Add the tomato concentrate (paste), gradually stir in the 150 ml (¼ pint) (⅝ cup) stock, followed by the cold milk until you have a smooth sauce; simmer for 5 minutes.

8 Wash and slice the button mushrooms for the garnish, or leave them whole, minus the stalks, if very tiny. Boil them in the sherry and lemon juice for 4 minutes. Strain the liquor into the white sauce, season with salt and pepper and a pinch of mace or nutmeg. Boil for 5 minutes, add the single (light) cream, give it a stir and boil again for 3 minutes longer.

9 Preheat the oven to 180°C, 350°F, gas 4. Pour the rest of the chicken stock over the quenelles; bring to the boil gently, then finish the cooking in the preheated oven for 3 minutes, covering the dish with buttered greaseproof (waxed) paper; grease an ovenproof serving dish.

10 Drain the quenelles carefully with a perforated spoon and put them on the greased dish; increase the oven temperature to 200°C, 400°F, gas 6. Pour the cream sauce through a conical sieve (strainer) and check the seasoning. Surround the serving dish with the button mushrooms, if used.

11 Pour the sauce over the quenelles; finish cooking in the hot oven for about 10 minutes. Serve at once, with the mushroom garnish, and sprinkled with the chopped parsley and tarragon mixture, if liked.

Serves 8

Grilled Chicken

Grilled (Broiled) Chicken with Onion

1.5 kg (3 lb) chicken, oven-ready
30 ml (2 tablespoons) oil
salt and pepper
40 g (1½ oz) (2½ tablespoons) butter
  or margarine
2 onions
8 small tomatoes
15 ml (1 tablespoon) strong made
  mustard
15 ml (1 tablespoon) double
  (heavy) cream or top of milk
150 g (5 oz) (2½ cups) stale, white
  breadcrumbs
½ carton cress or watercress

1 Cut up the chicken (see pages 112-113).

2 Heat the grill (broiler). Preheat the oven to 200°C, 400°F, gas 6.

3 Baste the chicken with half of the oil. Season with salt and pepper. Place it under the grill (broiler), skin side up, and grill (broil) it on both sides, turning it a quarter of a turn every 2 minutes. Total time is about 8 minutes each side.

4 Place the chicken in an oven-proof dish and cook in the oven for 30 minutes.

5 Peel and grate the onions. Melt the fat in a frying pan (skillet). Add the grated onion and cook over a low heat until soft, with the consistency of a purée.

6 Wash and dry the tomatoes; slice them in half, and cover them in the rest of the oil. Put them on a roasting pan, add salt and pepper, and put them in the oven to cook.

7 Tip the onion purée into a bowl. Add the mustard and cream or top of the milk. Mix them well. Put the breadcrumbs on a large plate.

8 When the chicken has been cooking for 30 minutes, drain it. Cover it with the onion and mustard mixture. Then coat both sides with the breadcrumbs, pressing them on well. Put it back in the roasting pan and baste it with the cooking juices. Let it cook for another 10 minutes.

9 Cut the cress if used. Wash and drain the cress or watercress. Warm a serving dish.

10 When the chicken is cooked, put it on the serving dish. Place the baked tomatoes and cress round it. Pour the juices from the dish over the chicken and serve hot.

Serves 4

Grilled (Broiled) Chicken with Mustard

1½ kg (3 lb) frying chicken, cut
  into serving pieces
65 g (2¼ oz) (5 tablespoons) butter
10 ml (2 tablespoons) mild
  mustard
5 ml (1 teaspoon) Worcestershire
  sauce
5 ml (1 teaspoon) chopped
  rosemary
30 ml (2 tablespoons) finely
  chopped parsley
2.5 ml (½ teaspoon) salt
freshly ground black pepper

1 Preheat the oven to 200°C, 400°F, gas 6. Put the chicken pieces into a buttered fireproof dish and dot with 25 g (1 oz) (2 tablespoons) butter. Bake in the oven for 20 minutes.

2 Mix the remaining butter with the rest of the ingredients. Brush half the mixture over the chicken pieces and grill (broil) for 12 minutes. Turn the chicken over, brush with the remaining butter mixture, and grill (broil) for a further 12-15 minutes or until the chicken is tender.

3 Serve with a green salad.
Serves 4

Provençal Split Chicken

1.5 kg (3 lb) chicken, oven-ready
3 shallots
2 cloves garlic
3 lemons
15 ml (1 tablespoon) crushed
  thyme and rosemary
75 ml (5 tablespoons) oil
salt and pepper
small bunch watercress

1 Cut up the chicken (see pages 112-113).

2 Peel the shallots and the garlic. Chop them finely. Squeeze 2 of the lemons and pour the juice into a bowl; add the shallots and garlic, the thyme and rosemary and the oil. Add salt and pepper. Beat the marinade with a fork.

3 Place the prepared chicken flat in a deep dish. Pour over the marinade and let the bird marinate for 3 hours in a cool place.

4 Heat the grill (broiler). Drain the chicken and reserve the marinade. Place the bird in the grill (broiler) pan, skin side down. Put it under the grill (broiler) and grill (broil) it under a high heat. Turn the bird after about 15 minutes. Baste it with the marinade and let it cook for a further 15 minutes.

5 Warm a serving dish. Place the well-browned chicken on it, spoon over the cooking juices and serve very hot, garnished with lemon quarters and small bunches of watercress.

Serves 4

> **Spatchcock**
> The French phrase for this method of preparing a chicken is *en crapaudine*: the split bird has its legs and wings tucked in to resemble a flattened toad – *crapaud* being the French word for a toad.

346

Chicken Stews

Rumanian Chicken Stew

1½ kg (3 lb) chicken pieces
5 ml (1 teaspoon) salt
black pepper
1.25 ml (¼ teaspoon) dried
  marjoram
2.5 ml (½ teaspoon) paprika
50 g (2 oz) (4 tablespoons) butter
  or margarine
30 ml (2 tablespoons) oil
2 onions
2 carrots
1 leek
450 g (1 lb) canned butter beans
100 ml (4 fl oz) (½ cup) stock
5 ml (1 teaspoon) lemon juice

1 Dry the chicken pieces and rub them with the salt, pepper, marjoram and paprika mixed together.

2 Heat half the fat and the oil in a frying pan (skillet). Fry the chicken pieces for about 10 minutes, turning them as necessary to brown all over. Peel the onions and cut into rings. Peel the carrots and slice them. Trim off the green part and wash the leek well to remove soil, then cut it into rings. Drain the beans.

3 Heat the remaining fat in a clean pan. Add the onion slices and fry until they are golden-brown. Add the carrots, leek and beans and cook over a low heat for 15 minutes. Add the chicken pieces and the stock. Cover the pan with its lid. Simmer for 1 hour or until tender.

4 Taste for seasoning and adjust if necessary. Add the lemon juice and serve at once.

Serves 4-6

Chicken Fricassée with Walnuts

3 shallots
75 g (3 oz) (¾ cup) shelled walnuts
1½ kg (3 lb) chicken, oven-ready
75 g (3 oz) (6 tablespoons) butter
  or margarine
25 g (1 oz) (2 tablespoons) flour
15 ml (1 tablespoon) paprika
100 ml (4 fl oz) (½ cup) dry white
  wine
½ litre (1 pint) (2½ cups) stock
salt and pepper
15 ml (1 tablespoon) tomato
  concentrate (paste)

1 Peel the shallots and chop them finely. Chop the walnuts.

2 Cut up the chicken into serving pieces (see pages 112-113).

3 Heat the fat in a sauté pan and when hot, brown the pieces of chicken, 2 or 3 at a time. Then add the shallots and leave them to brown. Sprinkle with the flour and the paprika. Stir and cook for 2 minutes.

4 Add the white wine and stock together with the salt and pepper. Add the tomato concentrate (paste) and the walnuts. Blend well together, bring to the boil, then cover the pan, reduce the heat, and simmer for 40 minutes.

5 Heat a serving dish.

6 Taste and adjust the seasoning. Pour the fricassée into the serving dish and serve hot.

Serves 4

Rumanian Chicken Stew – a homely chicken and vegetable stew

Fricassée of Chicken with Paprika

1.2 kg (2½ lb) chicken, oven-ready
salt and pepper
3 medium onions
45 ml (3 tablespoons) lard
5 ml (1 teaspoon) paprika
5 ml (1 teaspoon) caraway seeds
250 ml (8 fl oz) (1 cup) chicken
  stock
300 ml (½ pint) (1¼ cups) fresh
  tomato sauce (see below)
8 medium potatoes
150 g (5 fl oz) (generous ½ cup)
  natural yogurt
15 ml (1 tablespoon)
  double (heavy) cream
7 g (1 tablespoon) flour

1 Cut the chicken into 8 pieces (see pages 112-113) and season.

2 Peel the onions and cut into thin slices.

3 Heat the lard in a sauté pan. Add the sliced onions and the chicken pieces. Cook until golden-brown, stirring often, and until the chicken is done (about 15 minutes).

4 When the chicken and onions are brown, sprinkle them with the paprika. Add the caraway seeds and stir for 1 minute with a wooden spoon to incorporate them.

5 Add the stock and the tomato sauce. Season with salt and pepper and cook over a low heat for 1 hour.

6 Peel and wash the potatoes. Steam or boil them.

7 Heat a deep serving dish.

8 Drain the pieces of chicken, arrange them on the serving dish and surround with the cooked potatoes.

9 Mix together the yogurt, the cream and the flour and pour into the sauce. Blend over a low heat, without boiling, stirring with a wooden spoon until the sauce thickens (3-4 minutes).

10 Pour the sauce over the chicken pieces and serve hot.

Serves 4

Poached Chicken

Chicken Mousse

2 chicken joints
300 ml (½ pint) (1¼ cups) chicken
  stock
150 ml (¼ pint) (⅝ cup) creamy milk
1 bayleaf, imported
few peppercorns
2-3 slices onion
2 hard-boiled (hard-cooked) eggs

For the béchamel sauce:
7 g (¼ oz) (½ tablespoon) butter
7 g (¼ oz) (1 tablespoon) flour
salt and pepper
7 g (¼ oz) powdered gelatin
bunch watercress
1 medium onion
150 ml (¼ pint) (⅝ cup) double
  (heavy) cream
few sprigs parsley

1 Put the chicken joints in a pan and add enough chicken stock to cover. Bring to the boil, then reduce the heat and poach, with the lid on, until the chicken is tender – about 30 minutes for legs, 25 minutes for breast meat. Drain, reserving 150 ml (¼ pint) (⅝ cup) of the stock. Put the milk in a pan, together with the bayleaf, peppercorns and slices of onion and heat just to boiling point; take off the heat and set aside to infuse for about 10 minutes. Strain, reserving the milk.

2 Slice the hard-boiled (hard-cooked) eggs and place them in the bottom of a lightly oiled 20 cm (8 in) ring mould.

3 Make the béchamel sauce: melt the fat in a pan, stir in the flour to make a roux and cook for 1 minute, stirring all the time. Take the pan off the heat and blend in half the reserved milk. Stir in the rest of the milk until smooth. Return the pan to the heat and cook until the sauce thickens, stirring continuously.

Add salt and pepper to taste and leave to cool.

4 In a pan, dissolve the gelatin in a little of the reserved chicken stock and leave for about 5 minutes or until spongy. Then heat gently until the gelatin is completely dissolved, stirring all the time. Take the pan off the heat and cool slightly.

5 Wash and chop half the watercress; peel and slice the onion; stiffly whip the cream.

6 Remove the meat from the chicken joints; put in a blender and work with the rest of the chicken stock to a smooth purée. Add this mixture to the cooled béchamel sauce.

7 When the gelatin is on the point of setting but still liquid, stir it into the sauce (it is important to blend in the gelatin so it sets evenly and without jellied [gelled] lumps). Cut and fold in the cream and chopped watercress as lightly as possible. Check the seasoning, then pour the mousse into the mould and place it in the refrigerator to set.

8 When firm, place your chosen serving dish on top of the mould, invert, tap sharply on the bottom and the mousse should slide out without damage. Garnish the centre with the remaining watercress, the onion slices and parsley. Serve chilled.

Serves 4

Fresh Tomato Sauce
Peel and chop 1 carrot and 1 onion; fry in 25 g (1 oz) (2 tablespoons) fat for 5 minutes. Stir in 15 g (½ oz) (2 tablespoons) flour, then add 450 g (1 lb) skinned and chopped tomatoes, 300 ml (½ pint) (1¼ cups) stock, 1 bay leaf, 5 g (½ teaspoon) sugar, salt and pepper to taste. Bring to the boil, cover and simmer 45 minutes; sieve, reheat and check seasoning. Use as required.

Makes about 400 ml (¾ pint) (2 cups)

Chicken Mousse and Chicken with Orange Sauce – two mouth-watering dishes to make using poached chicken joints

Chicken with Orange Sauce

4 chicken joints
1 bay leaf, imported
few peppercorns
1 litre (2 pints) (5 cups) chicken
  stock or water
few sprigs watercress

For the orange sauce:
25 g (1 oz) (3 tablespoons) butter
  or margarine
25 g (1 oz) (4 tablespoons) flour
½ litre (1 pint) (2½ cups) cooking
  liquid (see recipe)
juice and grated rind 2 oranges
15 ml (1 tablespoon) medium
  sherry
salt and pepper

1 Put the chicken joints, bay leaf and peppercorns in a pan and add enough chicken stock or water to cover. Bring to the boil, reduce the heat and poach, with the lid on, for 30-45 minutes or until the chicken is tender. Strain, reserving ½ litre (1 pint) (2½ cups) of the cooking liquid. Keep the chicken hot.

2 To make the sauce: melt the fat in a small pan, stir in the flour to make a roux and cook gently for 1 minute, stirring all the time. Take the pan off the heat and blend in half the reserved cooking liquid. Stir in the rest of the liquid until smooth and return the pan to the heat. Cook the sauce until it thickens, stirring continuously. Add the juice and grated rind of the oranges, the sherry and salt and pepper to taste.

3 Place the chicken joints on a warmed serving dish, pour over the sauce and garnish with watercress sprigs and segments of the oranges.

Serves 4

Cold Chicken Tonnato is a delicious standby for hot weather eating. This version is derived from the classic Italian recipe, Veal in Tuna Fish Sauce (Vitello Tonnato)

Chicken Tonnato

1 onion
1 stalk celery
4 whole chicken breasts, skinned
  and boned
½ litre (1 pint) (2½ cups) chicken
  stock
salt and pepper
pinch thyme
few parsley stalks
½ bay leaf, imported
150 ml (¼ pint) (⅝ cup) white wine
  (optional)

For the sauce:
210 g (7½ oz) (1 cup) canned tuna
  fish
6 canned flat anchovy fillets
2 tomatoes
400 ml (¾ pint) (2 cups)
  mayonnaise
30 ml (2 tablespoons) lemon juice
45 g (3 tablespoons) capers

For the garnish:
few anchovy fillets
few capers
crisp lettuce leaves

1 Peel and halve the onion. Wash well and halve the celery.

2 Place the chicken breasts, chicken stock, onion, celery, seasoning, herbs, wine and enough water to cover in a large pan and bring to the boil. Simmer very gently for 20-30 minutes, depending on the size of the chicken breasts, until tender and cooked.

3 Remove the chicken breasts from the pan with a draining spoon and leave to cool.

4 To make the sauce: drain the tuna fish and anchovy fillets. Wash and thinly slice the tomatoes. In a blender, work the mayonnaise, tuna fish, anchovy fillets, lemon juice and capers until smooth and well combined.

5 Place the cooled chicken breasts on a serving dish and spoon the sauce over them to cover. Garnish with more anchovy fillets and capers and arrange tomato slices round them. Serve on a bed of crisp lettuce leaves and any remaining sauce.

Serves 4

Chicken Cutlets with Mushrooms and Almonds

125 g ($\frac{1}{4}$ lb) ($\frac{1}{2}$ cup) butter
  or margarine
120 g ($\frac{1}{4}$ lb) (1 cup + 2 tablespoons)
  flour
300 ml ($\frac{1}{2}$ pint) ($1\frac{1}{4}$ cups) chicken
  stock (in which the chicken
  was poached)
350 g ($\frac{3}{4}$ lb) (6 cups) mushrooms
white flesh only from 1.2 kg
  ($2\frac{1}{2}$ lb) chicken, poached in
  stock
150 g (5 oz) cooked ham
3 eggs
250 ml (8 fl oz) (1 cup) double
  (heavy) cream
30 ml (2 tablespoons) finely
  ground almonds
30 ml (2 tablespoons) brandy
salt and pepper
5 ml (1 teaspoon) paprika
pinch mixed spice
75 g (3 oz) (1 cup) dried white
  breadcrumbs
100 g ($\frac{1}{4}$ lb) ($\frac{3}{4}$ cup) flaked almonds
50 ml (3 tablespoons) white port

1 Melt one-third of the fat in a small pan, add 60 g ($2\frac{1}{4}$ oz) (good $\frac{1}{2}$ cup + 1 tablespoon) flour, and stir over a low heat to make a white roux.

2 Mix the roux with the stock and cook for 10 minutes on a very low heat, stirring frequently with a wooden spoon.

3 During this time, trim the bottom of the mushroom stalks, wash the mushrooms briefly, dry and coarsely chop one-third of them. Slice the rest finely.

4 Heat 15 ml (1 tablespoon) fat, add the chopped mushrooms, and fry until all the liquid from them has evaporated.

5 Dice the white chicken flesh and chop the cooked ham.

6 Break 1 egg into a bowl and beat in half the cream and the ground almonds.

7 Take the pan of sauce off the heat and stir in the egg and cream liquid, the chopped mushrooms, chopped ham, diced chicken and the brandy. Season with salt, pepper, pap-

rika and mixed spice.

8 Return the pan to a low heat for 3 minutes, mixing well with a wooden spoon.

9 Lightly butter a large dish, pour in this mixture to a depth of about 3 cm ($1\frac{1}{4}$ in) and leave to cool and set completely.

10 Heat 25 g (1 oz) (2 tablespoons) fat in a small pan and fry the sliced mushrooms.

11 Preheat the oven to 200°C, 400°F, gas 6.

12 Cut the cold meat mixture into four and shape each piece into an oval cake about 2 cm ($\frac{3}{4}$ in) thick. Curve one of the sides and make it thinner at one end so as to make the cakes into the shape of a cutlet.

13 Break the remaining eggs into a bowl and beat well together.

14 Dip the "cutlets" into the rest of the flour, then in the beaten egg, and coat them with the breadcrumbs.

15 Heat the rest of the fat in a frying pan (skillet), add the egg and breadcrumbed cutlets and brown on each side over not too brisk a heat.

16 Put the flaked almonds to brown in the hot oven, then switch off the heat but leave the door closed.

17 Heat a serving dish.

18 Drain the cutlets on absorbent paper and arrange them on the hot serving dish.

19 Put the cutlets into the still hot oven, but with the door open.

20 Stir the port into the fat left over from cooking the cutlets, scraping the bottom of the pan with a wooden spoon, and cook for 2 minutes on a brisk heat. Add the rest of the cream, season with salt and pepper, and stir on a brisk heat until the mixture thickens.

21 Take the serving dish from the oven, surround the cutlets with the sliced mushrooms and coat with the sauce. Sprinkle with flaked almonds and serve very hot.
Serves 4

Chicken Sautés

Sautéed Chicken in Cream Sauce

1.2 kg ($2\frac{1}{2}$ lb) chicken pieces
salt and pepper
30 ml (2 tablespoons) oil
25 g (1 oz) (2 tablespoons) butter
225 g ($\frac{1}{2}$ lb) (4 cups) button
  mushrooms
3 shallots
100 ml (4 fl oz) ($\frac{1}{2}$ cup) dry
  white wine
200 ml (7 fl oz) ($\frac{7}{8}$ cup) double
  (heavy) cream

1 Season the chicken pieces.

2 Heat the oil and fat in a sauté pan over a high heat. Seal the pieces of chicken in the fat for about 15-20 minutes, without letting them brown. Turn the pieces and let them cook over a low heat for 15 minutes, without a lid.

3 Meanwhile, trim, wash, dry and slice the mushrooms. Peel the shallots and grate them.

4 Heat a serving dish. Remove the chicken pieces from the pan. Arrange them on the serving dish and keep them warm.

5 Put the mushrooms into the pan. Fry them for 5 minutes but don't let them brown. Then add the shallots and let them soften for 2 minutes over a low heat. Add the white wine. Stir in all the cooking juices at the bottom of the pan and let the liquid reduce (evaporate) by about half over a high heat.

6 Add the cream. Stir vigorously and let the mixture reduce (evaporate) by about half its quantity over a high heat. Taste the sauce and adjust the seasoning. Coat the chicken with the sauce and serve hot.
Serves 4

1 The ingredients required for this dish **2** Season each piece of chicken with salt and pepper **3** Heat a mixture of oil and butter in a pan. Brown the chicken pieces lightly on the outer, skin-covered sides **4** Turn the chicken pieces over and leave them to cook over a low heat, without a lid **5** Wash and slice the mushrooms. Grate the shallots **6** Take the chicken pieces out of the pan and arrange them on a warmed serving dish. Add the mushrooms to the fat in which the chicken pieces have been cooking and fry them, without letting them brown **7** Add the grated shallots and let them soften, without browning them **8** Add the white wine and heat until the juice reduces (evaporates) **9** Add the cream and stir. Let the mixture reduce (evaporate) again to half its volume **10** Adjust the seasoning, if necessary, by adding salt and pepper, and stir again **11** Coat the chicken pieces with the sauce

Sautéed Chicken in Rich Cream Sauce

1½ kg (3 lb) chicken, oven-ready
salt and pepper
30 ml (2 tablespoons) oil
50 g (2 oz) (¼ cup) butter
350 g (¾ lb) (6 cups) mushrooms
3 shallots
100 ml (4 fl oz) (½ cup) dry
  white wine
1 egg yolk
juice ½ lemon
pinch ground (powdered)
  nutmeg
20 g (¾ oz) (3 tablespoons) flour
300 ml (½ pint) (1¼ cups) double
  (heavy) cream
75 g (3 oz) (¾ cup) grated cheese

1 Cut up the chicken (see pages 112-113). Season with salt and pepper.

2 Pour the oil in a frying pan (skillet). Add half the butter and heat. When hot put in the chicken pieces and sauté for about 10 minutes on each side.

3 Meanwhile, trim the mushroom stalks. Wash the mushrooms quickly, dry and slice them. Peel and chop the shallots.

4 Remove the chicken pieces from the frying pan (skillet) after 10 minutes or so and keep them warm. Add the mushrooms to the same frying pan (skillet) and fry them for 5 minutes. Then add the shallots and soften over a low heat for 2 minutes.

5 Pour in the white wine and stir, scraping the bottom of the pan to dissolve the cooking juices; then reduce (evaporate) the liquid to about half its quantity over a high heat.

6 Preheat the oven to 220°C, 425°F, gas 7.

7 Put the egg yolk into a cup. Mix it with the lemon juice and nutmeg. Using a fork work the rest of the butter thoroughly with the flour on a plate.

8 Add the kneaded butter to the sauce bit by bit, whisking vigorously. Boil it for 1 minute, then add the egg and lemon mixture, still whisking the mixture, and without letting it boil. Stir in the cream.

9 Arrange the chicken pieces in a heated ovenproof serving dish. Coat them with the cream sauce. Sprinkle with the grated cheese and put the dish in the oven to brown. When golden and bubbling on top, serve the chicken at once.

Serves 4

Sautéed Chicken with Grape Juice

1.2 kg (2½ lb) chicken, oven-ready
salt and pepper
30 ml (2 tablespoons) chicken
  (poultry) fat
2 shallots
few tarragon leaves
12 mushrooms
100 g (¼ lb) rashers (slices)
  smoked bacon
few sprigs parsley
2 cloves garlic
70 ml (2 fl oz) (¼ cup) natural grape
  juice
30 ml (2 tablespoons) double
  (heavy) cream

1 Cut up the chicken (see pages 112-113) and season with salt and pepper

2 Heat the poultry fat in a stew-pan and when it is hot put in the chicken pieces, skin side down, and cook over a slow heat for about 15 minutes; then turn and cook for 15 minutes more.

3 Peel and chop the shallots. Wash the tarragon leaves, dry and chop them finely. Trim, wash, dry and chop the mushrooms. Cut the bacon into thin strips.

4 Wash and dry the parsley. Peel the garlic. Chop the parsley and garlic together. When the chicken is cooked arrange it on a dish and sprinkle with the parsley and garlic. Keep warm.

5 Put the shallots, tarragon, mushrooms and bacon into the pan in which the chicken was cooked. Cook slowly for about 10 minutes, then add the grape juice and cook for a further 10 minutes. Then add the cream, bring to the boil and reduce (evaporate) to about half its volume.

6 Pour the sauce over the chicken and serve very hot.

Serves 4

Sautéed Chicken in Rich Cream Sauce

Sautéed Chicken in Avocado Sauce

1½ kg (3 lb) chicken, oven-ready
salt and pepper
2.5 ml (½ teaspoon) ground
  (powdered) ginger
30 ml (2 tablespoons) oil
75 g (3 oz) (⅓ cup) butter
  or margarine
4 avocados (1 very ripe)
3 shallots
225 g (½ lb) (4 cups) mushrooms
pinch cayenne pepper
100 ml (4 fl oz) (½ cup) dry
  white wine
200 ml (7 fl oz) (¾ cup)
  double (heavy) cream

1 Cut up the chicken (see pages 112-113). Season the pieces with salt, pepper and ginger.

2 Heat the oil and half the fat in a pan. Seal the chicken pieces, skin side down, in hot fat for about 10 minutes without letting them brown. Turn over the pieces and let them cook over a low heat for another 10 minutes, without a lid.

3 Halve the avocados and remove the stones (seeds). Put the very ripe one on one side. Scoop out small balls, using a potato or melon baller, from the flesh of the other three. Rub any flesh remaining from these, together with the very ripe avocado flesh, through a fine mesh sieve (strainer). Peel and finely chop the shallots. Wash, dry and slice the mushrooms.

4 Melt the rest of the fat in a frying pan (skillet). Add the avocado balls and season them with salt, pepper and cayenne pepper. Let the balls brown over a low heat, shaking the frying pan (skillet) gently so as not to crush them.

5 Remove the chicken pieces from the pan when cooked, arrange them on a heated oven-proof serving dish and keep hot in a warm oven, with the heat turned off.

6 Put the chopped shallots and the sliced mushrooms in the pan and let them soften. Add the

white wine and let it reduce (evaporate) over a high heat. Stir in the cream and the avocado purée.

7 Arrange the avocado balls round the chicken. Cover with the sauce and serve hot.

Serves 4

Spiced Chicken with Tomato Sauce

4 boneless chicken portions
salt and pepper
2 pinches ground (powdered)
  ginger
75 ml (5 tablespoons) (⅓ cup) rum
1 large onion
100 ml (4 fl oz) (½ cup) oil
5 ml (1 teaspoon) curry powder
pinch cayenne pepper
200 ml (7 fl oz) (⅞ cup) stock
75 g (3 oz) (½ cup) seedless raisins
300 g (11 oz) (1⅓ cups) long grain
  rice
5 thin rashers (slices) bacon
  (smoked if available)
5 bananas
2 hard-boiled (hard-cooked) eggs

For the spicy tomato sauce:
2 shallots
30 ml (2 tablespoons) oil
60 ml (4 tablespoons) (¼ cup)
  tomato concentrate (paste)
200 ml (7 fl oz) (⅞ cup) stock
salt and pepper
ground (powdered) ginger, to
  taste
15 ml (1 tablespoon) honey
30 ml (2 tablespoons) white
  vinegar
1 bouquet garni

1 Place the chicken flat on a cloth, skin side down, then sprinkle with salt, pepper, a pinch of ginger and 15 ml (1 tablespoon) rum.

2 Roll up the joints as tightly as possible and tie securely with kitchen thread. Rub the remaining ginger into the exposed skin.

3 Peel the onion and chop finely.

4 Heat half the oil in a pan. Add the chicken and fry until

browned on all sides. Add the onion and fry until golden, stirring constantly.

5 Stir in the curry powder, cayenne and stock. Cover and cook gently for 30 minutes.

6 Meanwhile, put the raisins in a bowl, stir in the remaining rum, then leave to soak.

7 Prepare the tomato sauce: peel and chop the shallots. Heat the oil in a pan, add the shallots and fry gently till golden-brown. Stir in the tomato concentrate (paste) and stock, then season to taste with salt, pepper and ginger. Mix the honey with the vinegar, then stir into the pan and add the bouquet garni. Cook gently for 10 minutes.

8 While the sauce is cooking, rinse the rice, and cook it in boiling salted water. When cooked, drain and keep warm.

9 When the chicken is cooked, remove from the pan with a slotted spoon, discard the thread and keep the chicken hot. Boil the cooking liquid until reduced by half, then add to the tomato sauce. Taste and adjust seasoning, then remove the bouquet garni.

10 Drain the raisins and reserve the rum, stir the raisins into the sauce. Return the chicken to the pan, pour over the reserved rum, heat through, then set alight.

11 Heat the remaining oil in a separate frying pan (skillet), add the bacon and fry until crisp and brown. Remove from the pan with a slotted spoon and keep hot.

12 Peel the bananas, add to the pan and fry until lightly coloured on all sides.

13 Put the rice on a warmed serving platter, then arrange the bacon and bananas on top.

14 Chop the eggs finely. Arrange the chicken pieces over the bacon and bananas, then sprinkle with the egg.

15 Serve immediately with the tomato sauce separate.

Serves 4

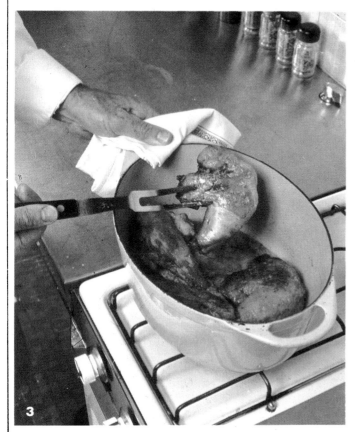

1 Season the chicken pieces with salt and pepper. Roll them in flour **2** Heat a mixture of oil and butter in a deep pan. Put in the chicken, skin side down, and brown for about 10 minutes **3** Turn the pieces and brown on the other side for another 10 minutes or so **4** Meanwhile, trim and wash the mushrooms, dry and slice them. Peel and finely chop the shallots. Remove the chicken from the pan

and fry the mushrooms in the same fat **5** Add the shallots and let them soften for 1 minute over a low heat **6** Add the brandy and flame, then stir in the white wine **7** Add the chopped tomatoes and tarragon, and the veal or chicken stock. Reduce (evaporate) over a high heat, uncovered **8** Adjust the seasoning. Place the chicken on a hot serving dish and cover with the sauce

Sautéed Chicken with Mushrooms

1¼ kg (2½ lb) chicken pieces
salt and pepper
100 g (¼ lb) (1 cup) flour
30 ml (2 tablespoons) oil
30 g (1 oz) (2 tablespoons) butter
  or margarine
225 g (½ lb) (4 cups) mushrooms
3 shallots
100 ml (4 fl oz) (½ cup)
  brandy
100 ml (4 fl oz) (½ cup)
  dry white wine
225 g (8 oz) canned tomatoes,
  drained
sprig tarragon
¼ litre (8 fl oz) (1 cup)
  chicken stock

1 Season the pieces of chicken and roll them in the flour.

2 Put the oil and fat into a sauté pan; over a high heat brown the chicken for about 10 minutes, then turn and brown on the other side for another 10 minutes.

3 While the chicken is cooking, trim the mushroom stalks. Wash, dry and slice the mushrooms. Peel and finely chop the shallots.

4 Take the pieces of chicken out of the pan as they are cooked: the quicker-cooking wings first, then the legs, etc. The wings shouldn't take longer than 15 minutes, the legs about 20 minutes. Keep them warm. Add the mushrooms to the pan and fry quickly. Add the shallots, reduce the heat and soften them for 1 minute.

5 Pour in the brandy and flame (set fire to it). Add the wine and stir to dissolve the meat juices.

6 Chop the drained tomatoes roughly and add them to the pan. Chop the tarragon. Add the tarragon and the stock. Let the mixture reduce (evaporate) over a high heat, uncovered, for 10 minutes.

7 Warm a serving dish. Arrange the pieces of chicken on it. Taste and adjust the seasoning of the sauce. Cover the chicken with the sauce and serve hot.

Serves 4

Turkey Roasts and Stews

All kinds of turkey products – both cooked and uncooked, are available to cooks today, thus offering plenty of scope for inventive dishes as well as for evergreen favourites.

Uncooked Turkey
Whole turkeys (fresh or frozen) can reach giant proportions but for most of us a mini bird of between 3-4 kg (6-8 lb), oven-ready, is a popular choice. Just right for family gatherings or picnics, when value for money is often an important consideration.

Apart from whole birds, turkey can be also be bought as:

Portions: breasts, drumsticks, thighs (some already boned and stuffed), wings (either whole or the tips only), and chops (similar to noisettes of lamb).
Turkey roasts: these are boned and rolled white and red meat roasts, wrapped in pork fat and deep frozen – thaw and cook as for ordinary roasts.
Assorted packs of minced and chunked meat, giblets and livers are also available. These are ideal for making stews, casseroles, soups and stocks, or for pâtés and risotto.

Cooked Turkey Products
For lazy cooks, there is a choice of various cooked boneless turkey rolls: some are already sliced, others can be cured or smoked. All will give plenty of lean meat with no wastage. Some convenience foods may also be cooked.

Convenience foods
There are a whole host of these turkey products – uncooked, ready-cooked, and others requiring nothing more than heating through, or deep frying. Choose from turkey meat loaves and pâtés, burgers, crispy fries, fingers, croquettes and sausages.

Stuffing a Turkey
If stuffing a turkey for roasting, allow about 450 g (1 lb) stuffing for the neck end of a bird weighing up to 7 kg (14 lb) – double the quantity for larger birds – and allow about 450-900 g (1-2 lb) for the body cavity, according to the size of the bird. Vary the flavours if using two stuffings: chestnut or veal forcemeat, say, for the neck end and sausagemeat for the body cavity.

Roasting a Turkey
There are many theories on the best way to roast a turkey, but whichever way you choose, make sure the breast is amply covered with softened fat (butter, margarine or dripping) to keep it moist and tender during cooking. For extra flavour lay rashers (slices) of bacon on top as well.

Cover the bird with several thicknesses of greased paper or foil to prevent the flesh drying out and toughening, but remove the coverings for the last 30-40 minutes so the bird can crisp and brown, and be basted with its cooking juices.

Wrap foil round the leg ends so they don't burn during roasting, then dress them with paper turkey frills for serving at the table.

Roast Turkey with Chipolatas (Link Sausages)

450 g (1 lb) fresh chestnuts
4 large potatoes
3½-4 kg (7-8 lb) turkey
salt and pepper
60 ml (2¼ fl oz) (¼ cup) oil
100 g (¼ lb) (½ cup) butter or
  margarine

3 large onions
450 g (1 lb) carrots
100 ml (4 fl oz) (½ cup) dry white wine
10 g (2 teaspoons) sugar
350 g (¾ lb) button (pearl) onions
350 g (¾ lb) lean bacon rashers (slices)
450 g (1 lb) chipolatas (link sausages)
100 ml (4 fl oz) (½ cup) chicken stock

1 Preheat the oven to 200°C, 400°F, gas 6.

2 Peel the chestnuts and cook until tender (see opposite).

3 Peel the potatoes.

4 Stuff the turkey with the potatoes, truss securely with kitchen thread (see pages 102-103), then sprinkle salt and pepper all over the bird. Put the turkey in a roasting pan, pour over half the oil, then dot with half the fat. Roast in the preheated oven until golden brown.

5 Meanwhile, peel the large onions and 2 carrots and slice finely. Place them around the turkey, continue roasting until the vegetables are browned, then add the wine. Continue roasting for about 1½ hours or until the turkey is tender, basting frequently. Cover with foil if the skin becomes too brown during cooking.

6 Meanwhile, peel and dice the remaining carrots. Put in a pan with enough water just to cover, then add salt, half the sugar and 25 g (1 oz) (2 tablespoons) fat. Cover with foil and cook over high heat until the carrots are tender and have absorbed all the liquid. Do not allow the carrots to become brown.

7 Peel the small onions, then caramelize them with water and the remaining sugar and fat as for the carrots.

8 Cut the bacon into neat strips and blanch in boiling water for 3 minutes. Drain, rinse under cold running water, then drain again.

9 Slice the chipolatas (link sausages) into 3 cm (1¼ in) lengths.

10 Heat the remaining oil in a frying pan (skillet), add the bacon and fry until brown. Add the chipolatas (link sausages) and fry until brown, then drain off any excess fat. Add the caramelized carrots and onions and stir well to mix. Drain the chestnuts and add to the pan to heat through. Transfer the mixture to an ovenproof dish and keep hot in the oven.

11 To test if the turkey is cooked, prick the thickest part of the thigh: the juices should run clear. Remove the trussing thread from the turkey, and take out the potatoes. Put the turkey on a warmed serving platter and keep hot.

12 Transfer the roasting pan to the top of the stove and skim off the fat from the cooking juices. Add the stock, then boil until the liquid is reduced (evaporated) by a quarter. Taste and adjust the seasoning, then pour through a fine sieve (strainer) into a sauce boat.

13 Arrange the chipolata (link sausage) and vegetable garnish around the turkey and serve hot with the sauce separate.

Serves 8

> **Cooking Fresh Chestnuts**
> Slit the brown outer skin and put the chestnuts into cold water. Bring to the boil and cook for 5 minutes, then drain and remove the outer and inner skins. Return the chestnuts to the pan, cover with stock and simmer for about 30 minutes or until tender.

Roast Turkey with Chipolatas (Link Sausages) – garnished with chestnuts, sausages, carrots, onions and bacon strips

Turkey Roast with Fruit Sauce

25 g (1 oz) (2 tablespoons) butter
   or margarine
2¾ kg (5½ lb) white turkey roast
1 red pepper
1 small green pepper
1 onion
225 g (8 oz) canned mandarin
   oranges in juice
225 g (8 oz) canned sweetcorn

For the sauce:
5 g (2 teaspoons) cornflour
   (cornstarch)
reserved juice from mandarin
   oranges
reserved juice from canned
   sweetcorn
15 ml (1 tablespoon) vinegar
4 g (1 teaspoon) sugar
5 ml (1 teaspoon) Worcestershire
   sauce
15-30 ml (1-2 tablespoons) sherry

1 Preheat the oven to 190°C,
375°F, gas 5. Spread the fat over
the turkey roast then wrap it in
foil to make a parcel. Place in a
roasting pan and roast for 1½
hours.

2 Wash, deseed and core the
peppers; peel and chop the
onion. Drain the mandarins and
corn, reserving the juices. Mix the
mandarins, corn, peppers and
onion together.

3 To make the sauce: mix the
cornflour with a little water to
make a smooth paste. Blend the
juice from the mandarins and
corn with the vinegar, sugar, Worcestershire sauce, sherry and
cornflour and heat until thickened, stirring well. Add the fruit
and vegetables.

4 Remove the turkey roast from
the oven and unwrap the foil.
Pour a little of the sauce all over
and round the turkey and cover
again with the foil.

5 Replace the turkey in the oven
and cook for a further 1-1½ hours
or until the turkey is tender and
cooked through.

6 Unwrap the turkey and place
it on a serving dish surrounded
by its fruity sauce and serve the
rest of the sauce separately.

Serves 6-8

Turkey en Croûte with Ratatouille

25 g (1 oz) (2 tablespoons) butter
   or margarine
2¾ kg (5½ lb) white turkey roast
1 lb shortcrust pastry,
   home-made or frozen and
   thawed

For the stuffing:
1 medium onion
75 g (3 oz) (1½ cup) white button
   mushrooms
1 egg
175 g (6 oz) (3 cups) fresh white
   breadcrumbs
pinch thyme
pinch sage
10 g (2 tablespoons) finely
   chopped parsley
salt and pepper to taste

For the ratatouille:
225 g (½ lb) courgettes
2 aubergines
1 red pepper
1 green pepper
2 medium onions
4 tomatoes
oil for frying

For the garnish:
parsley sprigs

1 Preheat the oven to 170°C,
325°F, gas 3.

2 Spread the fat over the turkey
roast, then wrap in foil to make a
parcel and place in a roasting
pan. Put in the oven and roast for
about 2 hours.

3 To make the stuffing: peel and
finely chop the onion. Wipe and
finely chop the mushrooms. Beat
the egg. Mix the stuffing ingredients together with enough of
the beaten egg to bind them all.

4 Wash all the vegetables for the
ratatouille. Trim and slice the
courgettes; slice and chop the
aubergines; deseed and core the
peppers and cut the flesh into
strips; peel and chop the onions;
quarter the tomatoes.

5 Remove the turkey from the
oven and open up the foil. Leave
until cool enough to handle, then
remove the string and the outer
layer of skin. Spread some of the
stuffing in a thick layer over the
turkey roast but leaving the ends
free.

6 Roll out the pastry thickly (5-8
mm, ¼-⅜ in) into a large oblong to
fit the roast and its stuffing. Place
the turkey roast, upside down, on
the pastry, so you can spread
stuffing on the other side as well.

7 Spread over the remaining
stuffing, dampen the ends of the
pastry and fold it over to make a
"pastry parcel", seal the edges
and ends together well, then turn
it over again so the lengthwise
join is underneath. Increase the
oven heat to 190°C, 375°F, gas 5.

8 Brush the parcel with the
remaining beaten egg, and decorate the top with leaves from any
remaining pastry. Brush the
leaves with egg and then bake
the parcel on a greased baking
sheet for about 35 minutes or
until the pastry is golden-brown
and the turkey is cooked. Serve
either hot or cold, garnished with
sprigs of parsley.

9 For the ratatouille: heat the
oil and fry the courgettes, aubergines, peppers and onion until
softened and slightly browned.
Add the tomatoes and cook for a
further 5 minutes. Season to
taste and serve.

Serves 6-8

---

*Turkey Roast with Fruit Sauce –
the mandarin oranges provide a
delicious contrast of flavours*

Turkey Escalopes

An escalope is a thin slice of prime-cut meat (usually veal) which is beaten flat and often fried in shallow fat. Boned chicken and turkey breasts make ideal escalopes, which can also be stuffed and rolled and then fried or braised.

To Prepare Escalopes
Place the meat between 2 pieces of greaseproof (waxed) paper – the moisture helps to prevent sticking – and, using a rolling pin or cutlet bat, beat flat until the meat is doubled in size and almost wafer-thin.

Hawaiian Turkey Escalopes

250 g (9 oz) (1¼ cups) long grain rice
4 turkey escalopes
salt and pepper
2.5 ml (½ teaspoon) ground (powdered) ginger
75 g (3 oz) (⅜ cup) butter or margarine
50 ml (2 fl oz) (¼ cup) white wine
50 g (2 oz) (½ cup) grated fresh or desiccated coconut
5 ml (1 teaspoon) curry powder
60 ml (2¼ fl oz) (¼ cup) stock
15 ml (1 tablespoon) lemon juice
45 ml (3 tablespoons) pineapple juice
60 ml (2¼ fl oz) (¼ cup) soured cream
pinch cayenne pepper
4 slices pineapple, fresh or canned

1 Wash the rice well in several changes of cold water. Cook in boiling, salted water for about 12 minutes or until tender.

2 Meanwhile, rub the salt, pepper and ginger well into both sides of the escalopes.

3 Melt 50 g (2 oz) (¼ cup) fat in a pan, add the escalopes and fry over brisk heat until golden-brown on both sides. Lower the heat, then cook for 15 minutes or until the meat is tender.

4 Pour the wine over the turkey, heat through, then set alight.

5 Meanwhile, melt the remaining fat in a frying pan (skillet), add the coconut and fry until golden-brown. Set aside. Drain the escalopes, then arrange on a serving dish, surrounded by the rice.

6 Stir the curry powder into a little turkey cooking liquid, then return to the pan with the stock, the pineapple juice and lemon juice. Cook over a high heat, stirring with a wooden spoon to loosen the pan juices and sediment. Add the soured cream and cayenne pepper and beat well. Taste, and adjust the seasoning, then add the pineapple and heat through for 1-2 minutes.

7 Arrange the pineapple slices over the escalopes, then pour over the sauce. Sprinkle with the coconut and serve immediately.

Serves 4

Turkey Olives

800 g (1¾ lb) turkey breast
175 g (6 oz) (1½ cups) stoned (pitted) green olives
1 egg
2.5 ml (½ teaspoon) ground (powdered) ginger
salt and pepper
flour, for dredging
25 g (1 oz) (2 tablespoons) butter or margarine
30 ml (2 tablespoons) oil
175 ml (6 fl oz) (¾ cup) sweet white wine
225 ml (8 fl oz) (1 cup) fresh orange juice
100 ml (4 fl oz) (½ cup) chicken stock
75 g (3 oz) (½ cup) stoned (pitted) black (ripe) olives

1 Cut 6 large thin slices from the turkey breast, then beat them between 2 sheets of greaseproof (waxed) paper until very thin.

2 Chop the remaining turkey meat finely. Chop the green olives finely and beat the egg. Put the chopped turkey and half the olives in a bowl, then add the beaten egg, ginger and salt and pepper to taste. Stir well to mix.

3 Divide the mixture equally between the turkey slices, then roll up and secure with wooden cocktail sticks (toothpicks). Dredge the rolls with flour.

4 Heat the fat and oil in a frying pan (skillet), add the turkey rolls and fry gently until browned on all sides. Remove from the pan with a slotted spoon (skimmer), and place in a casserole dish.

5 Add the wine, orange juice and stock to the frying pan (skillet). Bring to the boil, scraping up the sediment from the bottom of the pan with a wooden spoon. Boil for 5 minutes.

6 Meanwhile, preheat the oven to 180°C, 350°F, gas 4.

7 Chop the black olives finely, then sprinkle over the turkey with the remaining green olives. Pour over the sauce, then cover and cook in the preheated oven for about 45 minutes until the turkey is tender when pierced with a skewer.

8 Place the turkey rolls on a warmed serving platter, remove the cocktail sticks (toothpicks) and cut the meat into neat slices.

9 Taste and adjust the seasoning of the sauce, then spoon a little sauce over the meat. Serve hot with the remaining sauce handed separately.

Serves 6

Tip: To make coating the chicken pieces with the breadcrumbs easier, put the crumbs in a paper or polythene bag. After coating the chicken with flour and egg, pop them into the bag and toss. Remove the pieces and shake off the excess breadcrumbs.

Turkey Escalopes with Spring Vegetables

4 turkey escalopes
2 g (1 teaspoon) dried savory
2 g (1 teaspoon) dried thyme
salt and pepper
2 leaves fresh sage
½ bay leaf, imported
225 ml (8 fl oz) (1 cup) milk
450 g (1 lb) young fresh peas
1 lettuce
8 small carrots
8 button (pearl) onions
100 g (¼ lb) smoked streaky bacon
100 g (¼ lb) (½ cup) butter or
  margarine
1 sprig fresh savory
5 ml (1 teaspoon) sugar
1 egg plus 1 egg yolk
15 g (1 tablespoon) paprika
  pepper
100 g (¼ lb) (1 cup) flour
100 g (¼ lb) (1 cup) dried
  breadcrumbs
30 ml (2 tablespoons) soured
  cream

1 Sprinkle both sides of the escalopes with the dried savory, thyme and salt and pepper to taste. Rub the seasonings well into the meat with the fingertips.

2 Put the escalopes in a large shallow dish. Place the sage leaves and bay leaf on top, add a little milk, then leave to marinate for 2 hours.

3 Meanwhile, shell the peas. Wash the lettuce without detaching the leaves, drain thoroughly, then cut into quarters. Peel the carrots, then cut into julienne strips (matchsticks). Peel the small onions. Dice the bacon.

4 Melt half the fat in a frying pan (skillet), add the onions and bacon and fry gently until lightly coloured. Add the peas, carrots, fresh savory, sugar, salt and pepper then cover and cook gently for 1 hour. Add the lettuce for the final 15 minutes cooking.

5 Twenty minutes before the end of cooking, drain the escalopes and dry thoroughly on absorbent paper.

6 Beat the egg lightly with the paprika and salt and pepper. Coat the escalopes first in the flour, then in the beaten egg, then in the breadcrumbs.

7 Melt the remaining fat in a frying pan (skillet). Add the escalopes and fry gently until tender and golden-brown on both sides.

8 Drain the vegetables, reserving the cooking liquid, then arrange on a warmed serving dish.

9 Beat the egg yolk and soured cream together, then stir into the reserved cooking liquid. Cook over low heat until well blended, stirring constantly. Do not allow to boil.

10 Taste and adjust the seasoning of the sauce, then pour over the vegetables. Arrange the escalopes on top and serve immediately.

Serves 4

Stuffed Turkey Rolls

350 g (¾ lb) onions
100 g (¼ lb) (½ cup) butter or
  margarine
salt and pepper
pinch of grated nutmeg
1 egg
200 ml (7 fl oz) (⅞ cup) double
  (heavy) cream
4 large turkey escalopes
4 thin rashers (slices) smoked
  bacon
4 thin slices cheese
30 ml (2 tablespoons) oil
100 ml (4 fl oz) (½ cup) dry white
  wine
350 g (¾ lb) (6 cups) mushrooms
2 shallots

1 Peel the onions and chop finely. Melt 40 g (1½ oz) (3 tablespoons) fat in a frying pan (skillet), add the onions and sprinkle with salt and pepper to taste. Cover and cook over a gentle heat until soft, then add the nutmeg and leave to cool.

2 Transfer the onions to a bowl, then stand in a larger bowl filled with crushed ice. Add the beaten egg and stir well to mix. Leave to chill for a few minutes, then beat in half the cream a little at a time. Leave to chill.

3 Flatten the escalopes with a rolling pin. Sprinkle with salt and pepper.

4 Spread half the onions on the escalopes, then put a rasher (slice) of bacon on each and cover with a slice of cheese. Spread the remaining onions on top, then roll up the escalopes, tucking in the ends to secure the stuffing. Tie with kitchen thread.

5 Heat the oil and 20 g (¾ oz) (1½ tablespoons) of the fat in a heavy-bottomed saucepan. Add the turkey rolls and fry gently until golden-brown on all sides.

6 Pour in the wine, cover and cook gently for 45 minutes until tender, basting occasionally.

7 Meanwhile, wipe the mushrooms, trim the stalks, then slice finely. Peel and chop the shallots. Melt the remaining fat in the frying pan (skillet), add the mushrooms and shallots and cook over brisk heat until the moisture has evaporated. Add salt and pepper to taste.

8 Remove the turkey from the saucepan with a slotted spoon. Remove the thread, then place the turkey on a warmed serving dish and keep hot. Pour the remaining cream into the saucepan, then stir with a wooden spoon to loosen the pan juices and sediment. Add the mushrooms and shallots, then boil for 1-2 minutes stirring constantly.

9 Taste and adjust the seasoning of the sauce, then pour over the turkey and serve immediately.

Serves 4

Look 'n Cook Stuffed Turkey Rolls

1 Ingredients for turkey rolls 2 Soften chopped onions in fat, then add nutmeg 3 Beat half the cream into onion and egg mixture 4 and 5 Beat out escalopes and season. Top them with bacon, cheese and remaining onion 6 Roll up escalopes and secure 7 Fry turkey rolls till golden 8 Pour in

wine, cover and cook gently till tender **9** Sauté
shallots and mushrooms; season **10** and **11** Stir

cream, then mushroom mixture into pan juices;
heat, then pour over turkey rolls

365

Creamed Turkey

40 (1½ oz) (3 tablespoons) butter
  or margarine
1 small onion
175 g (6 oz) (2 cups) button
  mushrooms
25 g (1 oz) (4 tablespoons) flour
350 ml (12 fl oz) (1½ cups) turkey
  or chicken stock
350 ml (12 fl oz) (1¾ cups) double
  (heavy) cream
2.5 ml (½ teaspoon) salt
freshly ground (milled)
  black pepper
2.5 ml (½ teaspoon) chopped
  rosemary
juice 1 lemon
550-700 g (1¼ lb-1½ lb) (3-4 cups)
  leftover cooked turkey

1 Peel and finely chop the onion. Wipe and thinly slice the mushrooms. Cut the turkey meat into small pieces.

2 Heat the fat in a large pan and fry the onion carefully until it is soft. Add the mushrooms and fry for a further 2 minutes.

3 Stir in the flour and cook for a few minutes. Add the stock and then the cream gradually, stirring until the sauce thickens.

4 Stir in the salt, pepper, rosemary, lemon juice and turkey, and simmer over a low heat for 5 minutes. Serve with fluffy rice or on toast triangles if liked.

Serves 6

Turkey Divan

450 g (1 lb) fresh broccoli or 2
  packets frozen broccoli,
  thawed
675 g (1½ lb) (4 cups) cooked
  turkey meat

For the cheese sauce:
40 g (1½ oz) (3 tablespoons) butter
  or margarine
40 g (1½ oz) (6 tablespoons) flour
400 ml (¾ pint) (2 cups) milk

50 g (2 oz) (½ cup) grated cheese
salt and pepper

1 If using fresh broccoli, trim the thick stem ends and cut the large sprigs in half. Cook in boiling salted water for 8-10 minutes or until just tender. If using frozen broccoli, cook according to the package instructions. Drain the broccoli. Cut the cooked turkey meat into strips.

2 To make the cheese sauce: melt the fat in a pan, stir in the flour and cook for 1 minute, stirring continuously. Take the pan off the heat and blend in half the milk. Stir in the rest of the milk, return the pan to the heat and bring to the boil, stirring. Cook for 2 minutes until the sauce is thick.

3 Remove the pan from the heat and stir in half the cheese and seasoning to taste.

4 Preheat the oven to 200°C, 400°F, gas 6.

5 Arrange the broccoli and turkey in layers in a greased ovenproof dish, spoon the cheese sauce over the top and sprinkle with the remaining cheese. Bake in the oven for 15 minutes or until hot and browned.

Serves 4

Tip: Do not overcook the broccoli or the tops will become too soft and break off.

Creamed Turkey – diced turkey meat in a rich cream sauce, flavoured with rosemary

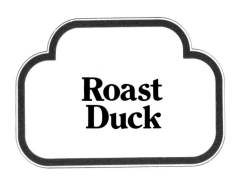

Roast Duck

Of the numerous breeds of edible duck available, probably none is superior to the famous large white Aylesbury ducks. These were formerly bred in large numbers in Aylesbury, Buckinghamshire (hence the name), as well as other English counties and elsewhere.

Aylesbury ducks can weigh as much as $3\frac{1}{2}$ kg (7 lb), but for the cook, the smaller ducklings, up to 2 kg (4 lb), are preferable because they are more tender and less fatty. Ducks more than 1 year old – known as breeders – are too tough for roasting although they can be boiled or braised and used for pies.

If a duck is excessively fatty, pinch the skin together between your forefingers, so it's clear of the flesh, and pierce all over with a sharp knife. This will ensure the fat can run out freely, without the meat juices escaping.

Signs of Quality
You can tell a good-quality duck by the following points: young birds have a clean smell, their feet are a bright yellow colour, the bill and feet are pliable, and there should be plenty of flesh round the breast.

Estimating Quantities
As the ratio of bone to flesh is so much greater in a duck than in other poultry such as chicken, allowance must be made for this when estimating the weight of bird to buy. The following chart is a guide to the average number of portions that can be carved from different weights of bird:

Weight of Bird – undrawn but plucked	Portions without bone – each about 100g ($\frac{1}{4}$ lb)
$2\frac{1}{4}$ kg ($4\frac{1}{2}$ lb)	6
$2\frac{3}{4}$ kg ($5\frac{1}{2}$ lb)	$7\frac{1}{4}$
$3\frac{1}{4}$ kg ($6\frac{1}{2}$ lb)	$9\frac{3}{4}$

Duck with Peaches

1 kg (2 lb) can peach halves
$\frac{1}{2}$ lemon
2.2 kg ($4\frac{1}{2}$ lb) duck, oven-ready
salt and pepper
2 cloves
pinch cinnamon
50 ml (2 fl oz) ($\frac{1}{4}$ cup) white vinegar
40 g ($1\frac{1}{2}$ oz) (3 tablespoons) butter
pinch cayenne pepper

1 Drain the peach halves, reserving the syrup. Squeeze the half lemon, reserving the juice.

2 Season inside the duck with salt and pepper and fill it with 6 half peaches, the cloves, cinnamon and salt and pepper. Then add 30 ml (2 tablespoons) vinegar.

3 Heat the butter in a large pan and when it begins to brown, add the duck.

4 Brown the bird over a low heat, turning it frequently until it is golden-brown on all sides. Cover and leave to cook for about 50 minutes.

5 Add the rest of the vinegar, the other peach halves, sliced, the lemon juice and 150 ml ($\frac{1}{4}$ pint) ($\frac{5}{8}$ cup) of the reserved peach syrup, and finish the cooking (another 20-25 minutes).

6 Before serving, heat a serving dish and sauce-boat. Put the duck in the centre of the dish. Surround it with the peaches.

7 Adjust the seasoning of the sauce, and boost it with a pinch of cayenne pepper. Pour the sauce into the sauce-boat. Serve the duck and sauce simultaneously.

Serves 6

Duck with Peaches – duck dressed up with a succulent but simple sauce made with canned peaches

Duck in Pernod with Mixed Vegetables

2 kg (4 lb) duck, oven-ready
2.5 ml (½ teaspoon) salt
freshly ground (milled) black
  pepper
225 g (½ lb) bacon
1 small turnip
4 carrots
18 small white (pearl) onions
40 g (1½ oz) (3 tablespoons) butter
1 clove garlic
1 bay leaf, imported
2.5 ml (½ teaspoon) thyme
2.5 ml (½ teaspoon) marjoram
3 sprigs parsley
100 ml (4 fl oz) (½ cup) dry
  white wine
45 ml (3 tablespoons) Pernod
454 g (1 lb) canned peas, drained

1 Preheat the oven to 190°C, 375°F, gas 5. Wash the duck and dry it thoroughly. Prick with a fork all over the skin and into the fat underneath it. Season inside and out with salt and pepper and truss it (see pages 102-103).

2 Cut the bacon into small pieces. Peel the turnip and carrots. Cut the turnip into wedges and the carrots into 5 mm (¼ in) pieces. Peel the onions and garlic; crush the latter.

3 Fry the bacon in a large flameproof casserole. When the fat has run from the bacon, remove it and add the butter. When the fat is hot, brown the duck in it and leave it breast side uppermost.

4 Add the turnip wedges, onions, carrots, bay leaf, garlic, thyme, marjoram and parsley. Cover with the lid and braise in the preheated oven for 1 hour.

5 Pour the fat from the pot and add the wine and Pernod. Cover again and cook for a further 20 minutes. Add the peas and cook for 10 minutes longer.

6 Serve the duck whole or cut up into serving pieces. Strain the vegetables and put them round the duck. Skim the surplus fat off the sauce, then sieve (strain) it and serve separately in a sauce-boat.

Serves 6

Honey-glazed Duckling with Grapefruit and Orange

2½ kg (5 lb) fresh duckling, oven-
  ready, with giblets
salt
1 medium carrot
1 medium onion
2 sticks celery
15 ml (1 tablespoon) oil

For the Fruit Sauce:
2 lumps sugar
150 ml (¼ pint) (⅝ cup) fresh orange
  and grapefruit juice, mixed
30 ml (2 tablespoons) (⅛ cup)
  white vinegar
15 ml (1 tablespoon) tomato concentrate (paste)
150 ml (¼ pint) (⅝ cup) dry Madeira
  or sherry
150 ml (¼ pint) (⅝ cup) water
1 chicken stock cube
1 clove garlic
sprig fresh mint
1 bouquet garni

For the Glaze:
125 g (4½ oz) (⅜ cup) liquid honey
25 ml (2 tablespoons) (⅛ cup)
  white vinegar
15 g (½ oz) (¼ cup) arrowroot or
  cornflour (cornstarch)
150 ml (¼ pint) (⅝ cup) cold water
salt and pepper
pinch nutmeg
1 orange
1 grapefruit

1 Preset oven at 200°C, 400°F, gas 6. Wash the duck, drain and wipe dry. Season inside and out with salt only. Leave to absorb for 15 minutes. Scald the neck, winglets and gizzard, and place in a roasting pan.

2 Peel and quarter the carrot and onion, cut the celery in slivers, and place on top of the giblets as a trivet for the duck to sit on.

3 Brush the duck with oil and place it on top of the vegetables. Roast the duck for 35 minutes. Discard most of the fat in the pan and reduce the heat to 180°C, 350°F, gas 4. Cook for another hour, basting from time to time and removing excess fat to prevent it burning. When done, drain the duck of its juices, cavity downwards, lift out and keep warm. Remove all fat from the pan.

4 To make the sauce, place the roasting pan on top of the stove and boil down (evaporate) the gravy for 5 minutes until almost reduced to a glaze. At the same time cook the 2 sugar lumps in a corner of the pan until they turn to caramel; then immediately flood with the orange and grapefruit juices, and the vinegar, and boil for 2 minutes. Stir in the tomato concentrate (paste), wine, water and crumbled stock cube.

5 Peel and crush the garlic, add with the sprig of mint and bouquet garni. Boil for 15 minutes.

6 To glaze the duck, boil the honey and vinegar in a small pan and pour over the duck. Return the duck on a tray to the oven at 180°C, 350°F, gas 4, for 5 minutes to make the glaze. Take out the duck as soon as it is glossy.

7 Blend the arrowroot or cornflour (cornstarch) with the remaining cold water and pour into the sauce to thicken it when boiling. Leave to clear for 5 minutes, then strain and season with salt, pepper, and a pinch of nutmeg.

8 Peel the rind of the orange and grapefruit, without the white pith. Cut it into short, very thin strips. Boil them in water for 10 minutes, rinse, drain and add to the sauce. Skin the segments (sections), remove any pips, and reserve for the garnish.

9 Place the duck on a shallow serving dish. Pour some of the sauce over the duck, with the rest in a sauceboat. Serve the bird, garnished with segments (sections) of orange and grapefruit.

Serves 4

Honey-glazed Duckling, with a decorative garnish of tangy orange slices and grapefruit segments (sections)

Duck with Grapes and Mint

salt and pepper
2.2 kg (4½ lb) duck, oven-ready
50 g (2 oz) (¼ cup) butter
2 carrots
2 onions
150 g (good ¼ lb) streaky bacon
1 lemon
15 ml (1 tablespoon) sugar
100 ml (4 fl oz) (½ cup) stock
  or dry white wine
100 ml (4 fl oz) (½ cup) canned
  grape juice
30 ml (2 tablespoons) vinegar
8 mint leaves
1 kg (2 lb) large white grapes

1 Salt and pepper the inside of the duck and truss it (see pages 102-103).

2 Preheat the oven to 240°C, 475°F, gas 9.

3 Prick all over the skin of the duck with a fork (see page 182). Put the duck onto the grid of the roasting pan and when the oven is very hot, put it in. Leave for 15 minutes to melt the excess fat. Remove the duck from the oven and wipe it with absorbent paper. Turn off the oven and shut the oven door.

4 Melt the butter in a large pan. Add the duck and brown on all sides, turning it frequently without piercing the skin (about 15 minutes).

5 While the duck is sizzling, peel the carrots and onions, and chop them finely. Chop the bacon. Squeeze the juice from the lemon.

6 When the duck is golden-brown, take the pan off the heat and put the duck into the warm oven so that it will not get cold.

7 Put into the large pan the chopped carrots, onions and bacon and brown them.

8 When these ingredients start to get brown, sprinkle with sugar and leave to caramelize slightly.

9 Add the stock or white wine, grape juice, 30 ml (2 tablespoons) lemon juice, the vinegar, pepper and the mint leaves.

10 Put the duck back into this sauce, cover the pan and finish the cooking over a low heat (about 30 minutes). Heat the serving dish and sauce-boat.

11 Meanwhile, wash and dry the grapes, skin and remove the pips.

12 Strain the sauce, then put it back in the pan.

13 Pour the grapes into the sauce and reheat for 1 minute.

14 Carve the duck quickly, and arrange the pieces on the hot serving dish. Take out the grapes with a slotted spoon and garnish the duck with them. Pour the rest of the sauce into the sauce-boat.

15 Serve the duck and sauce together with shell pasta or new potatoes.

Serves 5-6

Potato Straw Nests and Honeycomb Nests

1 kg (2 lb) potatoes
oil for deep frying

1 Peel the potatoes, then without rinsing, slice them with a mandoline (vegetable slicer). Use the comb-shaped blade for the potato straws, and the fluted blade for the honeycomb shapes. With the latter, press the potato flat onto the blade, turning the hand gently to the right, then gently to the left, thus using the whole potato. Do the same with the other potatoes.

2 Heat the oil to 185°C, 360°F.

3 Fill a large nest shape (see pages 164-165) with the potato straws, distributing them equally throughout. Keep it in shape by pressing a smaller one into it. If making honeycomb shapes, overlap the pieces in the larger shaped basket – by doing this, the pieces will lightly weld themselves on top of each other. Then squeeze into it the smaller basket shape.

4 Plunge the filled basket into the fat when quite hot and keep squeezing the two baskets together throughout the cooking ie for 5 to 6 minutes. Cook until the nest comes away by itself when the smaller basket is removed. Leave the nest to drain on absorbent paper.

5 Put into a nest, cherries, prunes (plums), orange quarters, peaches etc; dauphine potatoes; or small pieces of any fried food.

Serves 4

Roast Duckling with Apricot Stuffing

2 kg (4 lb) duckling
apricot stuffing (see recipe on
  page 192)
40 g (1½ oz) (3 tablespoons) butter
45 ml (3 tablespoons) clear honey
25 ml (1 fl oz) vinegar
1 bunch watercress

1 Preheat the oven to 180°C, 350°F, gas 4.

2 Wash and dry the duck well on absorbent paper.

3 Spoon the apricot stuffing into the cavity of the duckling, then truss securely with kitchen thread (see pages 102-103). Place on a rack in a roasting pan, then prick all over the skin with a skewer, taking care not to puncture the flesh itself.

4 Melt the butter until just liquid but not oily.

5 Mix together the vinegar, butter and honey, then brush all over the skin. Roast in the preheated oven for 1½ hours or until the duckling is tender. Brush the juices over the bird again 15 minutes before the end of the cooking time.

6 Remove the trussing thread from the duckling, leave to stand for 15-20 minutes, so the juices can settle, before carving. Then place on a warmed serving platter. Serve at once garnished with watercress.

Serves 4

Look 'n Cook Carving a Duck

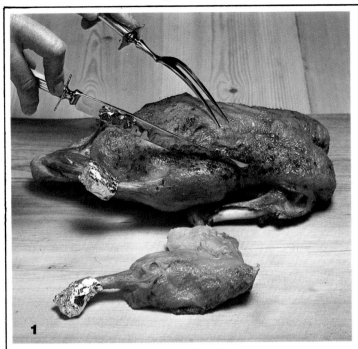

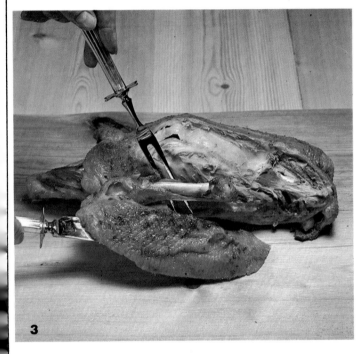

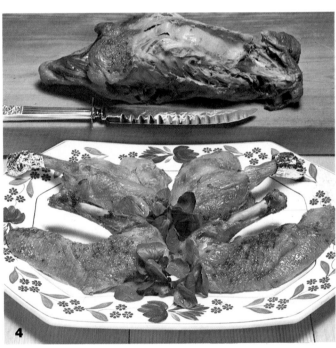

1 The English-style method of carving a duck. First, detach the leg by cutting downwards, parallel to the body wall behind the knee joint. Twist the leg away from the body slightly to expose the ball and socket joint and cut through this to sever the leg completely **2** After removing the 2 legs, carve the breasts. Cut along the centre of the breastbone and then down towards the back, easing the flesh away from the ribcage with the knife. **3** The breastmeat is removed in 1 piece with the wing attached **4** The 4 portions of duck arranged on the serving dish **5** The French-style of carving: the leg is detached in the same way. The winglet is removed next and then the breastmeat is cut into slices, usually about 3 from each breast

Braised Duck with Apricots

2½ kg (5 lb) duck, oven-ready
salt and pepper
pinch (powdered) allspice
50 g (2 oz) (4 tablespoons) butter
 or margarine
15 ml (1 tablespoon) oil
300 ml (½ pint) (1¼ cups) chicken
 or white stock
150 ml (¼ pint) (⅝ cup) dry white
 wine
450 g (1 lb) fresh apricots, or
 canned apricot halves, drained
juice and grated rind 1 lemon
5 ml (1 teaspoon) white vinegar
15 ml (1 tablespoon) apricot
 brandy (optional)
30 ml (2 tablespoons) brandy
 (optional)

1 Preheat the oven to 190°C, 375°F, gas 5.

2 Rub the flesh of the prepared duck with salt, pepper and all-spice.

3 Heat the fat and oil in a large frying pan (skillet), then put in the duck and brown on all sides. Lift it out of the frying pan (skillet) and place in a large flameproof casserole.

4 Pour the stock and wine into the frying pan (skillet) and heat until the liquid reaches boiling point. Remove from the heat and pour this mixture over the duck. Cover the casserole and place in the preheated oven for 1½-2 hours.

5 Meanwhile, wash and halve the apricots, discarding the stones (pits). After the duck has been cooking for 1 hour, add half the fresh or canned apricots to the roasting pan. Baste them with the stock mixture, and leave to cook.

6 When the duck is cooked, lift it onto a serving dish and keep warm. Strain the cooking liquid and skim off all but 15 ml (1 tablespoon) of the fat. Rub the cooked apricots through a sieve (strainer) and reserve the purée.

7 Pour the cooking juices into a small pan, and heat briskly until the liquid has reduced (evaporated) by one-third. Stir in the apricot purée, the lemon rind

and juice, and the white vinegar.

8 Arrange the remaining apricot halves round the duck. Bring the brandies to the boil and immediately pour them over the duck. If liked, the brandy can be set alight for effect. Serve at once, with the sauce in a sauce-boat.

Serves 4

Roast Duckling with Turnips

1.5 kg (3 lb) duckling, oven-
 ready
salt and pepper
100 g (¼ lb) (½ cup) butter
2 carrots
2 onions
2 tomatoes
few sprigs parsley
2 cloves garlic
some chicken giblets
sprig thyme
½ bayleaf, imported
100 ml (4 fl oz) (½ cup)
 reisling
200 ml (6 fl oz) (¾ cup) water
1 kg (2 lb) small turnips
15 g (4 teaspoons) sugar
200 g (7 oz) shallots
15 ml (1 tablespoon)
 cornflour
30 ml (1 fl oz) (2 tablespoons)
 Madeira or dry sherry

1 Preheat the oven to 220°C, 425°F, gas 7. Season the duck inside and outside with salt and pepper. Truss it (see pages 102-103) then spread it with 25 g (1 oz) (2 tablespoons) butter. Place it on one side in a roasting pan.

2 Peel and wash the carrots and the large onions and cut them into large dice. Wash and quarter tomatoes. Wash the parsley. Peel and crush the garlic.

3 When the duck starts to brown, place the giblets round it, together with the carrots and onions. Let them brown slightly. When it has been cooking for 25 minutes, turn the duck onto its other

side. With a small ladle, re-move the fat which has run from the duck. Add the tom-atoes, parsley, garlic, thyme and bayleaf. Pour in 85 ml (3½ fl oz) (7 tablespoons) white wine and the water. Cook for another 25 minutes, basting with juices.

4 Peel and wash the turnips, cutting them into wedges. Place them in a heavy frying pan (skillet) with 40 g (1½ oz) (3 tablespoons) butter, a pinch of salt, half the sugar and just enough water to cover the turnips. Cover with foil. Bring to the boil and cook over a moderate heat. The turnips should be cooked when all the water has evap-orated and they are coated with a sticky brown glaze.

5 Take the duck from the oven and turn it on its back; cook for another 20 minutes, basting several times. If it be-gins to brown too much, cover it with foil.

6 Peel the shallots or baby (pearl) onions and glaze them in the remaining butter and sugar in the same way as for the turnips.

7 When the duck is cooked, put it on a serving dish or in a casserole and keep warm. Pass the cooking juice through a fine mesh strainer into a saucepan. Skim off the fat. Mix the cornflour (corn-starch) with the rest of the white wine. Pour this mixture into the saucepan and mix with a whisk. Cook for 5 min-utes, then add the Madeira to the sauce.

8 Mix together the glazed turnips and the shallots or baby (pearl) onions. Pour the sauce over them. Simmer gently for 4-5 minutes and serve with duck.

Serves 4

Roast Duck with Turnips – a homely meal well suited to serv-ing in an earthenware casserole

Roast Goose

A mature goose weighs between 6-7 kg (12-14 lb), so choose smaller, younger birds to be sure of tenderness. You can recognize tenderness by the pliability of the breastbone and light orange-coloured beak of a young bird.

Before roasting a goose, pinch together the skin on the breast, then prick all over with a fork; this will allow the natural fat to run out during cooking.

Roast Goose with Prune and Apple Stuffing

4-4½ kg (8-9 lb) goose, oven-ready
salt and black pepper
pinch garlic salt
pinch ground (powdered) ginger
goose giblets
1 large carrot
1 large onion
little melted goose fat
25 g (1 oz) (2 tablespoons) tomato concentrate (paste) diluted with 30 ml (1 fl oz) (2 tablespoons) vinegar
1.25 ml (¼ teaspoon) gravy browning
pinch mace
50 ml (2 fl oz) (¼ cup) melted goose fat (optional)
25 g (1 oz) 4 tablespoons) flour (optional)

For the Stuffing:
225 g (½ lb) small sharp eating apples
225 g (½ lb) (1½ cups) canned prunes, with the juice
1 egg
225 g (·½ lb) (4 cups) fresh brown breadcrumbs
50 g (2 oz) (4 tablespoons) melted butter
pinch mixed spice
25 g (1 oz) (2 tablespoons) brown sugar
juice and grated rind 1 lemon

1 Wash, clean and wipe the bird. Thoroughly season it inside and out with salt, pepper, garlic salt and ginger. Prick the skin without touching the flesh (see page 182) to allow the seasoning to penetrate. Leave to stand for 20 minutes.

2 Make the stuffing: peel, core and quarter the apples. Drain the canned prunes, reserving the juice. Remove the stones (pits) from the prunes. Beat the egg. In a bowl, blend the brown breadcrumbs, melted butter, beaten egg, spice, sugar and juice and grated rind of the lemon. Gently but thoroughly combine the prunes and apples with this mixture.

3 Spoon some of the stuffing inside the cavity of the goose and the rest inside the neck cavity (turn the bird on its back to do this). Fold the neck flap over the backbone and secure it with a skewer or kitchen thread. Preheat the oven to 190°C, 375°F, gas 5.

4 Wash the giblets, put them in a pan and cover with cold water. Bring to the boil and then drain and rinse in cold water. Peel and quarter the carrot and onion. Lay them with the giblets in a roasting pan and place the goose on top. Brush a little melted goose fat all over the bird. Roast in the preheated oven for 1 hour, basting from time to time with a little water and the fat of the goose. After 1 hour, turn the bird on its side and cook for a further 15 minutes. Then turn it on the other side and cook for 15 minutes more. Reduce the oven temperature to 170°C, 325°F, gas 3 for the rest of the cooking time. The goose should be ready after a total cooking time of 2½ hours. To test if the bird is cooked, pierce the thickest part of the leg with a skewer: the juices should run clear.

5 When cooked, lift the goose from the pan and drain all its juice into the pan. Keep the goose warm while making the gravy.

6 Remove all the fat from the roasting pan, leaving only the meat juices. Pour the juices into a saucepan. Dilute 150 ml (¼ pint) (⅝ cup) of the reserved prune juice with 150 ml (¼ pint) (⅝ cup) water and add this mixture to the meat juices. Stir in the tomato concentrate (paste) and vinegar, the gravy browning, salt, pepper and the mace. Bring to the boil and boil for 15 minutes. Strain into a bowl.

7 The gravy can be served thin and clear as it is. If preferred, it can be thickened as follows. Mix the melted goose fat and the flour together in a pan and cook until a light brown. Draw the pan off the heat and gradually add the gravy. Return the pan to the heat, bring to the boil and cook for 3 minutes until thickened. Strain the gravy.

8 Carve the goose (see page 167) by removing the legs first; then slice the breast and leg meat as for duck, cutting 4 thin slices from each breast. Garnish each portion with some of the stuffing and serve the gravy separately.

Serves 4

Roast Goose with Apple and Walnut Stuffing

450 g (1 lb) fresh chestnuts
2½ kg (5 lb) goose

For the Stuffing:
450 g (1 lb) (2 cups) pork sausagemeat
2 onions
2 sticks (stalks) celery
50 g (2 oz) (½ cup) shelled walnuts
2 cooking (green) apples
1 egg
50 g (2 oz) (¼ cup) butter or margarine
2 g (1 teaspoon) dried sage
salt and pepper

1 Peel the chestnuts and cook until tender (see page 141).

2 To make the stuffing, fry the sausagemeat gently for about 10 minutes until lightly coloured, stirring occasionally. Remove from the heat and drain off the excess fat.

3 Peel the onions and chop finely. Chop the celery and walnuts. Peel and core the apples, then slice finely. Beat the egg.

4 Melt half the fat in a pan, add the onions, celery and walnuts and fry gently until softened and lightly coloured. Add the apples and cook for a few minutes more.

5 Remove the pan from the heat, then stir in the sausagemeat, beaten egg, sage and salt and pepper to taste.

6 Preheat the oven to 200°C, 400°F, gas 6.

7 Spoon the stuffing into the cavity of the goose, then truss securely with kitchen thread (see pages 102-103). Place the goose on a rack in a roasting pan, prick all over with a skewer, then brush with the remaining fat.

8 Roast in the preheated oven for 1¾ hours or until the juices run clear when the thickest part of the thigh is pierced with a skewer.

9 Five minutes before the end of the cooking time, drain the chestnuts and heat through in a pan of hot water.

10 When the goose is cooked, remove the thread and place the goose on a warmed serving platter. Drain the chestnuts and arrange around the goose.

11 Serve hot with giblet gravy, chestnuts and brussels sprouts.

Serves 6

Roast Goose—straightforward to cook and a splendid dish to serve. A tart sauce like gooseberry helps to take the edge off the natural fattiness of the bird

Guinea Fowl

Guinea Fowl Véronique

Two 1¼ kg (1½ lb) guinea fowl,
  oven-ready
salt and pepper
4 rashers (slices) streaky bacon
  (unsmoked)
50 g (2 oz) (4 tablespoons) butter
25 g (1 oz) (2 tablespoons) butter
  or margarine
25 g (1 oz) (4 tablespoons) flour
300 ml (½ pint) (1¼ cups) dry
  white wine
300 ml (½ pint) (1½ cups) stock
  made with giblets and chicken
  stock cube (see page 000)
pinch nutmeg
100 ml (4 fl oz) (½ cup) double
  (heavy) cream
juice ½ lemon
100 g (¼ lb) white Muscatel grapes

1 Preheat the oven to 200°C, 400°F, gas 6.

2 Wipe the birds inside and out, and season them inside and out with salt and pepper. Derind the bacon; wrap the rashers round the guinea fowl breasts and secure with string. Spread the 50 g (2 oz) (4 tablespoons) butter on top of the birds, then place them in a roasting pan, resting on their sides. Cook on 1 side for 10 minutes, then turn over onto the other side for another 10 minutes, then on their backs for the rest of the cooking time. Baste them with melted fat from time to time. Cook them in the oven for about 45 minutes overall. Remove the bacon rashers (slices) about 20 minutes before the end of cooking.

3 Meanwhile, melt the 25 g (1 oz) (2 tablespoons) butter or margarine in a pan, stir in the flour and mix thoroughly for about 2 minutes until it has a light brown, sandy texture. Gradually pour in the white wine and stock, stirring constantly. Taste and season with salt and nutmeg, and simmer for a further 10 minutes. Strain and reboil for 5 minutes. Stir in the cream and boil to reduce (evaporate) the sauce for another 5 minutes. Then add the lemon juice.

4 When the birds are cooked, quarter them, and place the pieces in a casserole or shallow ovenproof dish; pour over the sauce.

5 To prepare the garnish: skin the grapes and remove the pips, if liked. Scatter the grapes over the guinea fowl and serve at once with boiled rice.

Serves 4

Pot Roast Guinea Fowl

1¼ kg (2½ lb) guinea fowl, oven-
  ready
salt and pepper
pinch mace
50 g (2 oz) (4 tablespoons) butter
25 g (1 oz) (2 tablespoons) lard
1 medium carrot
1 small onion
2 sticks celery
25 ml (1 fl oz) oil
1 bouquet garni

For the Gravy:
1 small rasher (slice) bacon
guinea fowl giblets including
  the neck and gizzard
50 ml (2 fl oz) (¼ cup) dry sherry
300 ml (½ pint) (1¼ cups) water

For the Garnish:
bunch watercress

1 Wash and dry the guinea fowl, then season inside and out with salt, pepper and mace. Smother the breast and legs with a mixture of butter and lard.

2 Peel the carrot and onion, then cut in small cubes. Wash and dice the celery. Heat the oil in a pan, add the vegetables and brown them for 1-2 minutes. Place the vegetables in a casserole large enough to hold the guinea fowl.

3 Preheat the oven to 200°C, 400°F, gas 6.

4 Dice the bacon. Wash the giblets, put in a pan of cold water and bring to the boil. Rinse in cold water and drain. Add them to the vegetables with the diced bacon and bouquet garni. Spoon them over the bottom of the casserole.

5 Place the guinea fowl on the bed of vegetables, cover with a lid and roast in the preheated oven for 30 minutes. During the cooking time turn the bird round to allow its legs and breast to roast evenly and stay moist. Remove the lid after 30 minutes to allow the heat to brown the bird quickly. At this stage add the sherry and cook for another 15 minutes.

6 Remove the bird, and leave it to stand for 15 minutes, then carve in portions (see page 167) and place on a platter. Pour the contents of the casserole into a saucepan with the water and boil it for 15 minutes. Sieve (strain) the gravy and skim off most of the fat; check the seasoning. If the gravy is too pale, add 2.5 ml (½ teaspoon) gravy browning or beef extract. Pour the sauce into a sauce-boat.

7 Garnish the guinea fowl with watercress and serve with bread sauce, and a green salad if liked.

Serves 4

The flesh of the guinea fowl is white and tender, and has a slightly gamey flavour. They are now available all year round, and can be roasted, braised, sautéed, pan fried or grilled. In fact, they are as versatile a bird as a chicken or turkey.

*Guinea Fowl Véronique cooked
in a classic white sauce and
garnished with deseeded
green grapes*

Poultry Stuffings

Cranberry Stuffing

1 medium onion
25 g (1 oz) ($\frac{1}{8}$ cup) butter or
  margarine
225 g ($\frac{1}{2}$ lb) cranberries, fresh or
  frozen and thawed
25 g (1 oz) ($\frac{1}{8}$ cup) honey or sugar
225 g (8 oz) pork or beef
  sausagemeat
100 g ($\frac{1}{4}$ lb) fresh white breadcrumbs
1 beaten egg
salt and pepper
good pinch cinnamon
pinch pepper
juice and grated rind 1 orange
5 g (1 tablespoon) freshly
  chopped parsley

1 Peel the onion and chop finely. Melt the fat in a sauté pan and sauté the onion for 5 minutes until soft but not coloured. Add the cranberries and fry for 2 minutes until lightly cooked. Remove the pan from the heat, add the honey or sugar, and cool.

2 In a bowl combine the sausagemeat, crumbs and beaten egg. Season with salt, pepper, the juice and rind of 1 orange, and parsley.

3 Stir in the cranberry mixture as lightly as possible so as not to crush the cranberries too much.

Use for turkey, capon and guinea fowl.

Apricot Stuffing

50 g (2 oz) dried apricots
100 ml ($\frac{1}{5}$ pint) ($\frac{1}{2}$ cup) dry cider
1 medium onion
50 g (2 oz) ($\frac{1}{4}$ cup) margarine or fat
150 g ($\frac{1}{4}$ lb) (1 cup) fresh white
  breadcrumbs
4 g (1 tablespoon) fresh chopped
  mint and parsley
100 g ($\frac{1}{4}$ lb) pork or beef
  sausagemeat, or mixture of
  both
1 egg
salt and black pepper
pinch mace
pinch allspice

1 Soak the dried apricots in the cider for 2 hours, then drain, reserving the liquid, and chop the apricots. Peel the onion and chop.

2 Heat the fat in a pan and brown the onion slightly for 2 minutes; add the crumbs and apricots, cook for 5 minutes, then remove the pan and cool.

3 Combine all the stuffing ingredients in a bowl, together with the reserved liquid, and blend thoroughly to form a smooth but firm paste.

Use for ducks, geese and guinea fowl

Lemon, Rice and Sultana Stuffing

1 medium onion
75 ml ($\frac{1}{8}$ pint) ($\frac{5}{16}$ cup) oil
75 g (3 oz) long grain rice
50 g (2 oz) white mushrooms
225 ml ($\frac{2}{5}$ pint) (1 cup) hot water
1 chicken stock cube
salt and pepper
50 g (2 oz) sultanas
grated rind and juice 1 lemon

1 Peel and chop the onion. Heat the oil in a heavy-based pan and sauté the onion for 3 minutes without colouring. Add the rice, stirring it into the oil, and cook until translucent – about 5 minutes.

2 Wash, drain and slice the mushrooms, and add to the rice mixture; cook for 1 minute only. Pour in the hot water and crumble in the stock cube. Season to taste with salt and pepper and boil for 20 minutes.

3 Scald and drain the sultanas and stir into the rice mixture, together with the lemon juice and grated rind.
Use for ducks, geese and guinea fowl

Potato and Onion Stuffing

50 g (2 oz) (4 tablespoons) butter
  or margarine
100 g ($\frac{1}{4}$ lb) ($\frac{1}{2}$ cup) onion, chopped
175 g (6 oz) cooked potato, diced
225 g ($\frac{1}{2}$ lb) sausagemeat
salt and pepper
1 egg, beaten
pinch sage and parsley

1 Heat the fat in a pan, add the onions and sauté them until tender but not brown. Add the diced cooked potato, toss together and then leave to cool.

2 Blend the sausagemeat with salt and pepper, the beaten egg and the sage and parsley. Incorporate the cooled potato mixture and season to taste.

Use with all types of poultry

All about Fish

Fish can add variety to your daily menu. There is a wide range of fish (and shellfish) to choose from, with many different tastes and textures, from the kings of fish, salmon and trout, through flat fish, halibut and sole, and oily fish, mackerel and herring, to the tiny whitebait and sardines. Whether planning an everyday meal or a dinner party, there is always a fish to suit the occasion.

Your choice of fish will probably depend on the occasion and how much money you wish to spend but all fish, no matter what the cost, contain many vital nutrients. Fish muscle is made up of protein, fat and water and also contains vitamins and minerals. For example, 225 g (8 oz) herring contains: $23\frac{1}{2}$ g protein; $14\frac{1}{2}$ mg calcium; 200 i.u. vitamin A; 1300 i.u. vitamin D; 2 mg iron; 0.05 mg vitamin B.

Protein Cod is very rich in protein, particularly the liver and the roes. The protein content in salmon and trout is higher still, but a little lower in white fish. A rich egg sauce will increase the protein content in a white fish dish.

All about Fish (continued)

Fat The fat content in fish varies greatly according to species and accounts for the wide variation in calories provided by fish. Fish of the cod family contain less than one per cent fat while halibut has 2 to 5 per cent fat. Fatty fish such as salmon, mackerel or herring are always relatively fatty but the fat content varies with the season and spawning cycle – herring can contain as little as 5 per cent or as much as 22 per cent fat. Fat in fish flesh is not localized, as it is in meat, but is distributed throughout the flesh. In certain areas however, particularly just below the skin, the fat content is higher than elsewhere. The fat of fish is also easily digested.

Vitamins The flesh of fatty fish contains a little vitamin A and is rich in vitamin D. The lean fish have almost no vitamin A or D in the flesh. Fish oils, found in the liver, provide a reliable source of vitamins A and D – these vitamins are more concentrated in the livers of fatty species. Livers of halibut and tuna are especially rich in both vitamins A and D. Fish, like meat, is a good source of niacin and provides riboflavin as well. The proportions of the different vitamins vary with the species and a certain amount is lost in the cooking.

Minerals All fish are good sources of phosphorus, iodine, copper and fluorine. Most of the calcium in fish is found in the bones and, for this reason, it is wise to include the softened bones when eating canned fish. The iron content of fish is rather low and the diet should provide other sources of this mineral. Shellfish, such as oysters and clams, which are eaten whole, provide more iron than other fish.

Fish is cooked and eaten all over the world, whether roasted over a wood fire by a primitive savage, or served in a delicious wine sauce with truffles by a great French chef. The supply of various kinds of fish and their abundance during different seasons of the year is reflected in the market price. Although prices of some fish are high during off-season periods or because of scarcity, on average, fish are an economical food source. Fish can be especially delicious if served with a rich wine sauce to add extra flavour and nutritive value.

In Britain, Australia and the United States, the value of proteins is uppermost in food planning and thus meat is in far greater demand than fish. However, fish is not only nourishing and tasty but also more digestible than meat. Any white fish can be made to emulate meat by adding a rich, creamy egg sauce. To obtain the same benefit as from meat, fish should be eaten in larger quantities – 900 g (2 lb) cod equals 450 g (1 lb) meat.

Whatever the method of preservation, fish nearly always tastes best when it is fresh from the sea. There are exceptions: soles are less tough if allowed to stand on ice for a day or two, and salmon will improve in flavour, if kept on ice for several days.

Choosing and Buying Fish
The quality of fish is largely determined by its freshness. Always make sure that the fish you buy are fresh. Check that the skin is shiny and bright and the scales do not cling tightly. The gills should be a clear bright red, free from shine. They should not be pink, grey or brownish-green. The eyes should be bright, clear and full – not faded, cloudy or sunken. The flesh should be firm and elastic to the touch and should not separate easily from the bone. Above all, the fish should not smell strongly or unpleasantly – it should have only a mild, characteristic odour.

Methods of Cooking Fish
These depend on the nature of the fish and on the recipe. Sometimes a combination of several methods is required to complete one fish dish. The chief methods used are:

Boiling: applicable to large or small pieces, or whole fish which are completely immersed in the cooking liquid.

Boil Point 'Au Bleu': the fish must be alive. It is cooked in clear stock with vinegar.

Poaching: the fish is placed in only a little liquid and the liquor is used as a base for the sauce.

Stewing: a form of poaching. Fish cooked in this way are served as soup in clear broth, or styled 'en matelote', in which case the broth is thickened with a roux or cream.

Shallow frying: the fish is cooked with a little fat in a pan (skillet). When cooked in clarified butter and finished with 'beurre noisette', the method is called 'a la Meunière'.

Deep frying: the fish is completely immersed in fat or oil, usually coated in batter, crumbs or seasoned flour and milk.

Baking: the fish is baked in leaves or foil.

Roasting: cooked in the oven and basted with fat.

Braising: baked in the oven with a little liquor on a bed of root vegetables.

Grilling: cooked on a charcoal grill or grill (broiler).

Au Gratin: the fish is cooked until the moisture has evaporated and the top is browned to form a crust.

In salted water: this procedure varies according to the size and cut of the fish. With whole fish, immerse in cold, salted water or court bouillon, bring to the boil and simmer until the fish is cooked. With cut fish, immerse the fish in boiling, salted water and simmer for a few minutes.

Salt Water Fish

Atlantic	Pacific
Alewives	Anchovies
Bass	Cod:
Catfish	(Black Alaska)
Cod	(Sable Fish)
Cusk	Cod: Gray
Eels	Eulachon
Flounder	Flounder
Haddock	Halibut
Hake	Herring
Halibut	Ling Cod
Herring	Rockfish
Mackerel	Salmon:
Plaice	(Chum)
Pollock	(Cohoe)
Rosefish:	(Pink)
(Ocean Perch)	(Spring)
Salmon:	(Sockeye)
(Atlantic)	Skate
Shad	Sole
Skate	Trout:
Smelts	(Steelhead)
Sole	Tuna:
Swordfish	(Albacore)
Tuna	
Witch	

Poached Fish

Poached Cod Andalouse

25 g (1 oz) (2 tablespoons) butter
25 g (1 oz) (2 tablespoons)
  margarine
8 boneless cod steaks
pinch garlic salt, pepper, paprika
1 large onion, cut into rings
25 g (1 oz) (¼ cup) red pepper, cut
  into strips
2 large white mushrooms, sliced
grated rind and juice 1 lemon
15 ml (1 tablespoon) white wine
  vinegar
75 ml (2½ fl oz) (⅓ cup) dry white
  wine
150 ml (¼ pint) (½ cup) water
1 chicken stock cube
1 celery stalk, chopped
25 g (1 oz) (2 tablespoons) tomato
  concentrate (paste)
1 bouquet garni
150 ml (¼ pint) (⅝ cup) single
  (light) cream or milk
15 g (½ oz) (1 tablespoon) cornflour
  (cornstarch)

1 Preheat the oven to 200°C, 400°F, gas 6. Grease a shallow baking dish with half of the butter and margarine. Arrange the fish steaks in the dish and dot with small pieces of butter. Season with salt, pepper and paprika.

2 Place the onion rings, strips of red pepper and sliced mushrooms over the fish steaks. Sprinkle with grated lemon, lemon juice and vinegar.

3 Place the wine, water, stock cube, chopped celery and tomato concentrate (paste) in a saucepan and boil for 2 minutes. Pour over the fish steaks.

4 Place a bouquet garni on the side and bake in the preheated oven for 18 minutes.

5 Pour the fish liquid into a small saucepan and bring to the boil. Boil for 5 minutes.

6 Blend together the cream and cornflour (cornstarch). Pour into the boiling fish stock, stirring all the time until it thickens. Cook for 5 minutes. Coat the fish evenly with the sauce and serve.

Serves 4

Red Mullets Breton-style

6 fillets medium-sized red
  mullet
1 chicken stock cube
400 ml (14 fl oz) (1¾ cups) water
100 ml (4 fl oz) (6 tablespoons) dry
  white wine
50 g (2 oz) (4 tablespoons) butter
white parts 2 leeks, sliced
2 onions, chopped
30 g (2 oz) (good ½ cup) flour
200 ml (7 fl oz) (⅞ cup) single
  (light) cream
3 sprigs parsley, chopped

1 Preheat the oven to 190°C,

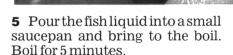
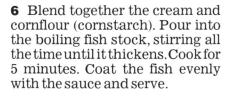

Poached Cod Andalouse — a delicious way of serving cod in a wine sauce flavoured with red pepper, mushrooms and onions

375°F, gas 5. Prepare the stock from the cube and hot water. Butter a flameproof dish and place the fillets of fish on it. Add the stock and white wine and cover with a sheet of aluminium foil.

2 Bring to the boil over a high heat, then cook for 8 minutes in the oven. Adjust the seasoning. Remove the fish to a deep serving dish and keep hot.

3 Heat the butter in a pan and cook the leeks and onions until lightly browned. Add the flour and stir well, with a wooden spoon, for 5 minutes over a low heat.

4 Pour 400 ml (¾ pint) (1¾ cups) of the stock into the pan. Stir until blended and cook a further 5 minutes. Then incorporate the cream and cook carefully for 3 minutes.

5 Pour the sauce over the fish and sprinkle with the chopped parsley.

Serves 6

Fillet of Sole Melone

1 medium onion, chopped
50 g (2 oz) (4 tablespoons) butter
four 75 g (3 oz) soles or plaice,
 filleted
pinch salt and pepper
pinch ground (powdered) ginger
grated rind and juice 1 lemon
150 ml (¼ pint) (⅝ cup) water
1 chicken stock cube
150 ml (¼ pint) (⅝ cup) single
 (light) cream
½ honeydew melon, peeled and
 deseeded
10 g (⅓ oz) cornflour (cornstarch)
480 g (1 lb) mashed potatoes
1 egg yolk
25 g (1 oz) (2 tablespoons) butter
salt and pepper
1 egg, beaten
chopped parsley

1 Preheat the oven to 200°C, 400°F, gas 6. Butter a shallow dish and sprinkle the bottom with the chopped onion.

2 Pound the fish fillets lightly with a rolling pin – to break down the fibres – then season with salt, pepper and ground (powdered) ginger. Fold the fillets in two and lay in the shallow dish. Add the grated lemon rind and lemon juice, the water and crumbled chicken stock cube. Cover with a piece of greaseproof (waxed) paper.

3 Bake on the top shelf of the preheated oven for 15 minutes. When cooked, pour the fish liquor (reduced stock) into a small saucepan. Leave the oven at the same temperature.

4 Boil the fish liquor for 3 minutes and thicken it with the cream and cornflour (cornstarch) which have been blended together. Season.

Fillet of Sole Melone, served with a salad of lettuce, hard-boiled (hard-cooked) eggs, red pepper, celery, carrot and raisins

5 Cut the melon into small cubes.

6 Blend the mashed potatoes with the egg yolk and butter and season. Place in a piping bag and pipe an attractive border around a clean, shallow dish. Dry it in the oven for 6 minutes. Then brush it with beaten egg. Arrange the cooked fish and raw melon cubes in the centre and pour over the cream sauce. Brown in the oven for 8 minutes. Decorate with melon balls and parsley.

Serves 4

Cod Dugleré

25 g (1 oz) (⅛ cup) chopped onions
four 225 g (½ lb) cod steaks
salt and pepper
450 g (1 lb) chopped, peeled
 tomatoes
50 g (2 oz) (4 tablespoons) soft
 butter
150 ml (5 fl oz) (⅝ cup) dry white
 wine
75 ml (3 fl oz) (⅜ cup) fish stock
1 bay leaf, imported
pinch tarragon
juice ½ lemon
pinch cayenne pepper
5 g (1 tablespoon) chopped
 parsley

1 Preheat the oven to 200°C, 400°F, gas 6. Butter a shallow dish and sprinkle with the chopped onions. Place the cod steaks on top and season with salt and pepper.

2 Cover with the coarsely chopped tomatoes and dot with half of the butter.

3 Pour over the wine and fish stock. Add the bay leaf and tarragon.

4 Bake in the preheated oven for 15-20 minutes.

5 Pour the sauce into a saucepan and boil to reduce by half. Season well and add the lemon juice and cayenne pepper.

6 Remove from the heat and stir in the remaining soft butter to cream it.

7 Pour the sauce over the fish and garnish with chopped parsley.

Serves 4

Plaice Belomar

450 g (1 lb) plaice fillets
juice ½ lemon
pinch salt
25 g (1 oz) (2 tablespoons) butter
2 onions, chopped

100 g (¼ lb) (1¼ cups) sliced, white
  mushrooms
100 g (¼ lb) (1 cup) chopped
  gherkins (dill pickles)
50 ml (2 fl oz) (¼ cup) brandy
  (optional)
40 g (1½ oz) (3 tablespoons) tomato
  concentrate (paste)
150 ml (¼ pint) (⅝ cup) single
  (light) cream
freshly ground (milled) black
  pepper

1 Rub the plaice fillets with the lemon juice and lightly sprinkle them with salt.

2 Heat the butter and add the onions and mushrooms. Fry over a low heat.

*Plaice Belomar —
fillets of fish served in a rich
creamy sauce, flavoured with
brandy*

3 Add the gherkins (dill pickles) and pour in the brandy. Set alight and let the flames die down.

4 Stir in the tomato concentrate (paste) and cream. Season with salt and pepper.

5 Fold over the plaice fillets and put them in the sauce. Cover and simmer for 10 minutes.

6 Pour into a serving dish and serve with boiled rice or potatoes.

Serves 4

...illeroy

...arlic

...s and trimmings of several
...les
...onion, thinly sliced
1 carrot, thinly sliced
bouquet garni
225 ml (8 fl oz) (1 cup) dry
  white wine
salt and pepper
8 fillets of sole
40 g (1½ oz) (3 tablespoons) butter
40 g (1½ oz) (6 tablespoons) flour
pinch grated nutmeg
2 eggs plus 2 egg yolks
50 ml (2 fl oz) (¼ cup) soured
  cream
45 ml (3 tablespoons) oil
oil for deep frying
150 g (good ¼ lb) (2 cups) dried
  breadcrumbs

1 Peel the garlic, and stick it with the clove.

2 Put into a saucepan the heads and fish trimmings, onion and carrot slices, bouquet garni, garlic stuck with clove, half the white wine and 300 ml (½ pint) (1¼ cups) water. Season with salt and pepper and leave to boil gently for 25 minutes.

3 Preheat the oven to 220°C, 425°F, gas 7.

4 Butter an ovenproof dish.

5 Season the fillets of sole with salt and pepper. Fold each into 2 with the skin inside. Place on the buttered dish. Pour the rest of the white wine over the fish and cook in the oven for 6 or 7 minutes.

6 As soon as the fillets have stiffened a little, drain them and put them onto a plate.

7 Pour their cooking juice into the fish stock.

8 Strain the fish stock.

9 Heat 40 g (1½ oz) (3 tablespoons) butter in a saucepan over a low heat. Add the flour stirring with a wooden spoon. Cook for a few minutes then gradually add the fish stock, mixing continuously to form a smooth thick sauce.

Then add the grated nutmeg and simmer for 5 minutes.

10 Blend the egg yolks with the cream, and add to the sauce, stirring with a wooden spoon. Heat the sauce for 3 or 4 minutes until it is very thick but do not boil. Take off the heat and leave to cool.

11 Grease your work surface with 15 ml (1 tablespoon) of the oil.

12 When the sauce is almost cold, coat the sole fillets with it.

13 Place the sauce-coated fillets on the work surface and leave to cool. The sauce should be firm and not stick to the fingers.

14 Heat the oil in a deep fat fryer to 190°C, 375°F.

15 Break the remaining 2 eggs into a bowl, and beat in the rest of the oil.

16 Heat a serving dish.

17 Dip the fillets of sole first into the beaten eggs, then into the breadcrumbs. Gently press the breadcrumbs into place.

18 Lower the fillets into the hot oil. Fry until golden and then drain.

19 Arrange the fillets of sole on the serving dish and serve immediately with a tomato sauce.

Serves 4

Poached Haddock with Herbs

675 g (1½ lb) smoked haddock
250 ml (8 fl oz) (1 oz) milk
1 small bunch chervil
1 small bunch parsley
1 small bunch tarragon
1 hard-boiled (hard-cooked) egg,
  finely chopped
juice 3 lemons
5 ml (1 teaspoon) double (heavy)
  cream

salt and pepper
75 g (3 oz) (6 tablespoons) butter
few sprigs parsley

1 Put the haddock in a pan. Add the milk and enough cold water to cover the fish, then simmer for 15 minutes.

2 Meanwhile, chop the herbs finely and put in a bowl with the chopped egg. Stir well to mix.

3 Put the lemon juice and cream in a small pan. Season with salt and pepper. Bring to the boil, then add the butter in small pieces, beating constantly with a whisk. Remove from the heat and stir in egg and herb mixture. Keep hot.

4 Drain the haddock carefully and arrange the fish on a warmed serving dish. Garnish with parsley and serve immediately. Serve the herb sauce separately.

Serves 4

Boiled Turbot

four 275 g (10 oz) turbot steaks
juice 1 lemon
50 g (2 oz) (2 tablespoons) salt
parsley sprigs

1 Preheat the oven to 200°C, 400°F, gas 6.

2 Rub the fish steaks with lemon juice and place in a shallow baking dish. Cover with water and add the salt.

3 Bring to the boil on top of the stove and then place in the oven to simmer for 20 minutes.

4 Garnish the turbot with sprigs of parsley and serve with boiled potatoes and Hollandaise sauce.

Serves 4

Tip: To enhance the delicate flavour of turbot, always serve it with a side sauce such as Hollandaise or prawn sauce. Brill and halibut are both boiled and served in the same way.

Fillets of Plaice Tivoli

four 100 g (¼ lb) fillets of plaice,
  sliced into small pieces
50 g (2 oz) (½ cup) flour
pinch salt and pepper
50 ml (2 fl oz) (¼ cup) oil
50 g (2 oz) (½ cup) sliced, white
  leeks
100 g (4 oz) (⅔ cup) chopped,
  skinned tomatoes
2 chopped mint leaves
1 pinch powdered thyme

150 ml (¼ pint) (⅝ cup) dry cider
  (apple cider)
25 g (1 oz) (3 tablespoons) tomato
  concentrate (paste)
1 chicken stock cube
1 pinch dill

1 Wash and drain the fish fillets
and sprinkle with seasoned flour.

2 Heat the oil in a sauté pan (skillet) and fry the fish fillets for 3
minutes. Remove and keep
warm.

3 Add the leeks and sauté for 3
minutes. Add the chopped
tomatoes, mint, thyme, cider,

*Fillets of Plaice Tivoli
prepared in a tangy apple cider
sauce, with tomatoes and leeks to
complement the delicate flavour
of the plaice*

tomato concentrate (paste) and
stock cube and stir well. Boil for 5
minutes to reduce (evaporate) the
liquid. Season well.

4 Reheat the fish fillets and
place on a warmed serving dish.
Pour over the sauce and serve
with a sprinkling of dill.

Serves 4

Fish Stocks & Sauces

Fish Stocks and Sauces

When making fish stock, do not use the bones of oily fish which are not suitable for white sauces. A fish stock must be neutral with a sweetish taste. Sweating bones and onions in margarine or clarified butter produces a good flavour but tends to colour the sauce.

Fish sauces must always be more acidic than those served with meat and poultry. This can be done by adding the juice of 1 lemon per litre (1¾ pints) (4½ cups) of sauce and also some dry white wine – sweet wine tends to make the sauce grey in colour. Wine vinegar is always preferable to dark vinegar when used with fish stock.

Basic Fish Stock

450 g (1 lb) fish heads, bones and
  trimmings
25 g (1 oz) (2 tablespoons) butter
25 ml (1 fl oz) (⅛ cup) oil
1 carrot, sliced
1 onion, sliced
900 ml (1½ pints) (3⅝ cups) water
300 ml (½ pint) (1¼ cups) dry
  white wine
1 bouquet garni
pinch salt and pepper
1 chicken stock cube

1 Wash the fish heads and trimmings well.

2 Heat the butter and oil in a large pan and add the sliced carrot and onion. Cover and cook gently for 5 minutes.

3 Add the fish trimmings to the

vegetables in the pan. Cook for 5 minutes.

4 Pour in the water and wine and add the bouquet garni. Season. Cook for 15 minutes.

5 Crumble in the stock cube and simmer for 5 minutes.

6 Strain through clean muslin (cheesecloth) or a fine sieve (strainer), cover and cool. Refrigerate until required.

Makes 900 ml (1½ pints) (3⅝ cups)

Tip: Fish stock should always be used the same day.

Basic White Wine Sauce

25 g (1 oz) (2 tablespoons) butter
  or margarine
25 g (1 oz) (4 tablespoons) flour
600 ml (1 pint) (2½ cups) fish stock
50 g (2 oz) (½ cup) chopped
  shallots
150 ml (¼ pint) (⅝ cup) dry white
  wine
4 egg yolks
150 ml (¼ pint) (⅝ cup) single
  (light) cream
pinch salt and pepper
pinch cayenne pepper
juice ½ lemon

1 Melt the fat in a saucepan and stir in the flour. Cook the roux for 3 minutes.

2 Add the fish stock gradually, stirring all the time, until the velouté sauce is smooth. Simmer for 20 minutes.

3 Boil the shallots in the wine until soft and add to the velouté sauce. Simmer for 15 minutes.

4 Blend the egg yolks with the cream and some of the sauce until well mixed. Pour into the velouté sauce and reheat, but do not allow the sauce to boil.

5 Season with salt and pepper and stir in the cayenne pepper and lemon juice.

Makes about 900 ml (1½ pints) (3⅝ cups)

Fillet of Cod Véronique

four 175 g (6 oz) fillets of cod
pinch salt and pepper
50 g (2 oz) (4 tablespoons) butter
150 ml (¼ pint) (⅝ cup) dry white
  wine
300 ml (½ pint) (1¼ cups) velouté
  sauce
50 ml (2 fl oz) (¼ cup) single (light)
  cream
pinch cayenne
juice ½ lemon
150 g (5 oz) skinned, seeded and
  split white Muscat grapes

1 Preheat the oven to 200°C, 400°F, gas 6.

2 Wash and dry the cod fillets. Season with salt and pepper.

3 Butter a shallow baking dish and arrange the fish fillets in it, side by side.

4 Pour in the dry white wine and velouté sauce, and cover with damp greaseproof (waxed) paper.

5 Bake in the oven for 15 minutes. Remove the paper and pour off the liquor into a saucepan. Keep the fish warm.

6 Boil the liquor to reduce (evaporate) by half and stir in the cream, whisking all the time. Season with salt, pepper and cayenne and stir in the lemon juice.

7 Arrange the fish in a clean, shallow dish. Pour over the sauce, and decorate with a border of grapes.

Serves 4

Tips: A fish sauce should always be made with ingredients which will enhance the flavour of the fish used. Aromatic herb sauces are best with oily fish such as sardines, trout or mackerel. The best stock you can make for a fish sauce is usually derived from the liquid in which the fish is poached. A fish liquor of wine and onions, infused with a bouquet garni, can constitute the base for a delicious sauce. Thicken with a liaison of egg yolks and cream, or simply blend with a basic white sauce.

Look'n Cook Making Fish Stock

1 As a preliminary to making Poached Brill (see p. 306) make the fish stock. Ingredients: fish trimmings, butter, carrot, onion, white wine, bouquet garni, salt and pepper **2** Wash the fish and cut off heads, bones and trimmings **3** Heat some butter and oil in a large pan. Add the carrots and onions and cook for 5 minutes. Add the fish trimmings and cook another 5 minutes **4** Add the water and wine and bouquet garni. Cook for 15 minutes, then crumble in the stock cube. Simmer 5 minutes

Braised fish

Haddock with Anchovies

1½ kg (3 lb) haddock
salt and pepper
6 canned anchovy fillets,
  drained
25 g (1 oz) (½ cup) fine
  breadcrumbs
75 g (3 oz)) (6 tablespoons) soft
  butter or margarine
5 g (1 tablespoon) chopped
  parsley
grated rind 1 lemon

1 Preheat the oven to 200°C, 400°F, gas 6.

2 Clean and wash the fish. Season with salt. Make several small incisions across the backbone of the fish with a sharp knife. Cut the anchovy fillets into thin strips and place in the slits.

3 Place the fish in a greased baking dish and sprinkle with the breadcrumbs. Melt 25 g (1 oz) (2 tablespoons) fat and baste the fish.

4 Bake the fish for 20 minutes, basting it occasionally.

5 Cream the chopped parsley with the remaining butter and the grated lemon rind. Season with salt and pepper. Place in the refrigerator until firm but still malleable. Turn onto a sheet of aluminium foil and roll into a cylindrical shape. Refrigerate again. When really cold, cut into thin, round slices.

6 Serve the fish with the rounds of parsley butter and coleslaw tossed in a vinaigrette dressing.

Serves 4

Haddock with Anchovies — served with a salad of finely grated carrot, white cabbage and beetroot (beets) tossed in French dressing

Fillet of Sole Bonne Femme

75 g (3 oz) (6 tablespoons) butter
25 g (1 oz) (¼ cup) chopped shallots
5 g (1 tablespoon) chopped
  parsley
100 g (¼ lb) (1¼ cups) sliced, white
  mushrooms
four 100 g (¼ lb) fillets of sole
salt and pepper
150 ml (¼ pint) (⅝ cup) dry white
  wine
75 ml (3 fl oz) (⅜ cup) fish stock
150 ml (¼ pint) (⅝ cup) velouté
  sauce
juice ½ lemon
pinch cayenne pepper

1 Preheat oven to 200°C, 400°F, gas 6.

2 Butter a shallow baking dish with 15 g (½ oz) butter. Sprinkle with the chopped shallots, parsley and sliced mushrooms.

3 Season the fillets of sole with salt and pepper and arrange them in the baking dish.

4 Add the wine, fish stock and

velouté sauce and heat the dish on top of the stove until the liquor is boiling.

5 Cover the dish and place in the oven for 8 minutes.

6 Keeping the fillets warm, pour the liquor into a pan and boil to reduce (evaporate) by one-third.

7 Cut the butter into small pieces and whisk it in, one piece at a time, until it is all blended and the liquor is creamy.

8 Check the seasoning and add the lemon juice.

9 Place the fish on a flat serving dish and cover with the sauce. Sprinkle with cayenne pepper and place under a grill (broiler) for a few seconds to brown it. Decorate with sautéd button mushrooms.

Serves 4

Tip: To make Sole Bercy, a delicious alternative to Sole Bonne Femme, just follow the recipe as indicated but omit the mushrooms.

Fillet of Lemon Sole Stockholm

50 g (2 oz) (4 tablespoons) butter
25 g (1 oz) ($\frac{1}{8}$ cup) chopped onions
four 175 g (6 oz) fillets of lemon sole
salt and pepper
pinch paprika
150 ml ($\frac{1}{4}$ pint) ($\frac{5}{8}$ cup) dry white wine
300 ml ($\frac{1}{2}$ pint) ($1\frac{1}{4}$ cups) velouté sauce
75 ml (3 fl oz) ($\frac{3}{8}$ cup) single (light) cream
pinch dill
8 peeled, cooked prawns

1 Preheat the oven to 200°C, 400°F, gas 6.

2 Grease a shallow baking dish with butter and sprinkle with chopped onions.

Fillets of Lemon Sole Stockholm, cooked in white wine and cream, and served with whole prawns and buttered rice

3 Arrange the fish fillets in the dish and season with salt, pepper and paprika.

4 Add the wine and cover with a sheet of greaseproof (waxed) paper and bake for 15 minutes.

5 Pour off the fish liquor into a pan and stir in the velouté sauce and cream. Boil for 10 minutes.

6 Check the seasoning and pour over the fish. Sprinkle with dill and garnish with the peeled prawns. Serve with buttered, boiled rice.

Serves 4

Tip: Baking with dry heat is impossible for fish, thus no fish can be 'baked' without a certain amount of moisture. Always remember to add sufficient moisture to make up the loss from evaporation during the cooking process. To ensure that the moisture is retained either baste occasionally or cover the fish with a lid or greaseproof (waxed) paper.

Cod Manuella

eight 100 g (¼ lb) cod fillets
25 g (1 oz) (4 tablespoons) flour
salt and pepper
50 ml (2 fl oz) (¼ cup) oil
1 onion, chopped
1 courgette (zucchini), peeled
  and sliced
3 tomatoes, peeled and chopped
1 red pepper, deseeded and
  chopped
15 g (½ oz) (1 tablespoon) tomato
  concentrate (paste)
15 ml (1 tablespoon) wine
  vinegar
150 ml (¼ pint) (⅝ cup) dry sherry
150 ml (¼ pint) (⅝ cup) water
1 chicken stock cube
pinch garlic salt
5 g (1 tablespoon) chopped
  parsley

1 Clean and wash the cod fillets and cut into small pieces. Season the flour and sprinkle it over the cod.

2 Heat the oil and sauté the onion, sliced courgette (zucchini), chopped tomatoes and red pepper until soft (about 8 minutes).

3 Stir in the tomato concentrate (paste), vinegar, sherry and water. Crumble in the stock cube and boil for 12 minutes, stirring from time to time.

4 Place the fish fillets on top. Season with salt and pepper and cover with a lid. Simmer gently on top of the stove for 12 minutes.

5 Pour into a serving dish and sprinkle with chopped parsley.

Serves 4

Cod Manuella — a Spanish dish in which cod is poached with courgettes (zucchini), tomatoes and red peppers in a delicious sherry sauce

Fish Stuffings

Both stuffings are enough for 4 whole small fish or 4 – 6 fillets.

Mousseline Stuffing

225 g (½ lb) (1 cup) raw finely
  minced (ground) whiting or
  haddock
1 egg white
75 ml (⅛ pint) (⅜ cup) double
  (heavy) cream
salt and pepper

1 Mix the fish paste with the egg white in a bowl. Place inside a larger bowl containing crushed ice and chill for at least 1 hour.

2 Add the double (heavy) cream gradually, stirring all the time and season with salt and pepper.

Herb and Breadcrumbs Stuffing

225 g (½ lb) (1 cup) coarsely
  minced (ground) whiting or
  haddock
5 g (1 tablespoon) chopped
  parsley
1 grated small onion
150 g (5 oz) (1 cup) fresh white
  breadcrumbs
1 whole egg
salt and pepper
pinch of garlic salt

1 Mix the minced (ground) fish, chopped parsley, grated onion and breadcrumbs together.

2 Blend with the beaten egg and season with salt and pepper and the garlic salt. Use as a stuffing for any fish – whole round or flat fish and fillets.

Look'n Cook Making Fish Stuffing

1 Wash the whiting, cutting along the backbone to fillet it **2** Remove the skin from the fillets **3** Chop up the flesh in a mincer (grinder) or blender to obtain a very fine paste. Season with salt and pepper **4** Place the fish paste in a bowl and blend with the egg white. Put this bowl within another larger bowl full of crushed ice. Chill the mixture for at least an hour **5** and **6** Add the double cream, spoonful by spoonful, to the mousseline stuffing. Mix thoroughly with a wooden spoon

Look 'n Cook Stuffed Fillet of Sole (Paupiettes)

7 Flatten the fillets with a wooden mallet or rolling pin or a wide-bladed knife. Season them, turn over and repeat the flattening process **8** Spread the stuffing over the fillets **9** Roll the fillets up from the tail end. Do not squeeze them – the stuffing will ooze out **10** Tie the stuffed fillets round with thread or fine string. Make 2 turns and one knot **11** Butter an ovenproof dish and sprinkle with chopped shallots. Place the stuffed fillets, upright and tightly packed, on top **12** Pour in the white wine and fish stock. Cover with a lid or aluminium foil and cook for 30 minutes in the oven. Make a sauce with the fish liquor and eggs. Pour over the stuffed fillets and serve

Stuffed Fillets of Sole with White Wine Sauce (Paupiettes de Sole)

For the Stuffing:
1 slice bread
225 g (½ lb) whiting fillets
75 g (3 oz) (6 tablespoons) butter
pinch grated nutmeg
1 egg, beaten
salt and pepper

For the Sauce:
eight 75 g (3 oz) fillets of sole
25 g (1 oz) (2 tablespoons)
** chopped shallots**
225 ml (8 fl oz) (1 cup) dry white
** wine**
225 ml (8 fl oz) (1 cup) fish stock
15 g (½ oz) (1 tablespoon) butter
15 g (½ oz) (1 tablespoon) flour
2 egg yolks
juice of 1 lemon
salt and pepper

1 Soak the bread in a little water and mash it with a fork. Put the whiting fillets through the mincer (grinder) or in a blender. (If using a blender, add 15 ml (1-2 tablespoons) water or milk.)

2 Heat 25 g (1 oz) butter in a small saucepan and add the soaked, crumbled bread. Stir with a wooden spoon until blended but do not brown.

3 Melt the remainder of the butter in a small saucepan over a low heat.

4 Mix in a bowl the minced (ground) whiting and breadcrumb mixture. Add the melted butter, grated nutmeg, beaten egg, and season with salt and pepper. Blend well together.

5 Preheat the oven to 200°C, 400°F, gas 6.

6 Flatten the fillets of sole on both sides with a wooden mallet or a rolling pin. (First place the fish between two pieces of greaseproof (waxed) paper or foil, so that it does not stick to the board or the mallet.) Then season them with salt and pepper.

7 Spread the stuffing over the fillets and roll them up from the tail end. Be careful not to squeeze them, or the stuffing will ooze out.

Tie them round with thread or fine string.

8 Butter a small, round ovenproof dish (about 18 cm (6 in) in diameter) and sprinkle with the chopped shallots. Arrange the stuffed fillets on top, standing upright and packed in tightly, very close to each other.

9 Pour over the wine and fish stock. Cover with a lid or aluminium foil and cook in the oven for about 30 minutes.

10 Blend the butter and flour together to make a firm paste.

11 Remove the string from the stuffed fillets. Arrange them on a serving dish and keep warm.

12 Pour off the fish liquor into a saucepan and boil to reduce by one third. Add the butter paste (*beurre manié*), a little at a time, stirring constantly to make a thick, smooth sauce.

13 Beat the egg yolks with the lemon juice and add to the sauce. Adjust the seasoning. Heat gently over a low heat, stirring constantly until the sauce coats the back of the spoon. Do not allow it to boil.

14 Pour the sauce over the stuffed fillets. Serve with crescents of puff pastry (fleurons) and baked potatoes or plain rice.

Serves 4

Tip: Lemon sole or flounder could both be substituted for sole in this dish. Also, a mousseline stuffing could be used, as shown in the step-by-step picture sequence, instead of the coarser breadcrumb-based stuffing.

Fillets of Sole, paupiette – style, may be stuffed with a mixture of either breadcrumbs and fish or minced (ground) whiting and cream

Fish and Wine

Poached Brill or Flounder

1½ kg (3 lb) flounder
50 g (2 oz) (4 tablespoons) butter
  and margarine, mixed
25 g (1 oz) (¼ cup) chopped
  shallot
5 g (1 tablespoon) freshly
  chopped mixed tarragon,
  parsley, chive, mint

For the Fish Stock:
25 g (1 oz) (2 tablespoons)
  butter
25 ml (1 fl oz) (⅛ cup) oil
1 carrot, sliced
1 onion, sliced
300 ml (½ pint) (1¼ cups) water
300 ml (½ pint) (1¼ cups) dry white
  wine
bouquet garni
1 chicken stock cube

For the Sauce:
15 g (½ oz) (2 tablespoons)
  cornflour (cornstarch)
150 ml (¼ pint) (⅝ cup) double
  (heavy) cream
2 egg yolks
25 g (1 oz) (2 tablespoons)
  butter
salt and pepper
juice ½ lemon
pinch cayenne pepper

1 Preheat the oven to 200°C, 400°F, gas 6. Fillet and skin the fish. Wash the fillets and cut them into suitably sized portions. Heavily grease the bottom of a shallow ovenproof dish with the butter and margarine and sprinkle in the chopped shallot and the herbs. Place the fish pieces on top.

2 Make the fish stock: heat the butter and oil together in a pan, add the carrot and onion, cover and cook gently for 5 minutes.

Wash the fish bones, skin and head, add them to the vegetables and cook for 5 minutes more. Stir in the water and wine and add the bouquet garni. Cook the stock for a further 15 minutes, then crumble in the stock cube. Simmer for 5 minutes and then strain the stock over the fish pieces. Cover with buttered greaseproof (waxed) paper and bake in the preheated oven for 15 minutes.

3 Remove the dish from the oven, discard the greaseproof (waxed) paper and lift out the pieces of fish with a slotted spoon. Arrange the fish on a serving dish and keep it warm.

4 Strain the fish stock into a pan and place over a high heat. Boil for 8 minutes until reduced (evaporated) by half.

5 Make the stock: mix the cornflour (cornstarch) with the cream and add to the reduced stock, whisk continuously. Heat gently until the sauce thickens slightly, stirring all the time. Take the pan off the heat and whisk in the egg yolks and the butter, cut into small pieces. Whisk until the ingredients are well incorporated. Season the sauce with salt and pepper and add the lemon juice and cayenne pepper.

6 Pour the sauce over the fish pieces and place under a hot grill (broiler) for a few minutes to brown the top. Serve with boiled new potatoes, cauliflower or asparagus tips.

Serves 6

Tips: If any of the sauce is left over, try blending it with an equal quantity of white sauce and using this to cover mild-flavoured vegetables such as cauliflower, leeks, celery, turnips. You can also use it with hard-boiled (hard-cooked) eggs and with rice.

Many types of fish can be used for this dish, including sole, salmon, cod and tuna. But make sure that you always use dry white wine and fresh herbs.

This dish can also be served cold: allow to cool and blend the sauce with a quarter as much mayonnaise or salad cream. Place the fish on a bed of sliced cold cooked potato and pour over the sauce. Decorate with fresh lettuce leaves, tomatoes and cucumber.

Norwegian Baked Cod with Peppers

450 g (1 lb) cod fillet
salt and pepper
grated rind and juice ½ lemon
150 ml (¼ pint) (⅝ cup) dry white
  wine
½ green pepper
½ red pepper
50 g (2 oz) (4 tablespoons) tomato
  concentrate (paste)
15 g (½ oz) (2 tablespoons) flour
100 ml (4 fl oz) (½ cup) single
  (light) cream
1 onion, chopped
2 cloves garlic, chopped
pinch paprika
pinch chopped thyme
50 g (2 oz) grated (½ cup) Cheddar
  or Parmesan cheese
8 g (2 tablespoons) (⅛ cup) fresh
  breadcrumbs

1 Preheat the oven to 200°C, 400°F, gas 6. Cut the fish into 1 cm (½ in) slices and place them in an ovenproof dish. Season the fish with salt and pepper and add the lemon juice and white wine. Remove the membranes and seeds from the peppers and cut the fish into strips. Place the strips on top of the fish.

2 Mix together the tomato concentrate (paste), grated lemon rind, flour, cream, chopped onion, chopped garlic, paprika and chopped thyme. Pour the mixture over the fish.

3 Sprinkle the fish with the cheese and breadcrumbs and bake in the preheated oven for 20-25 minutes.

Serves 4

Look 'n Cook Poached Flounder

1 To prepare the fish stock,(see page 299). Remove the dish from the oven and discard the greaseproof (waxed) paper **2** Lift the fish pieces from the stock using a slotted spoon and arrange them on a warmed serving dish. Keep them warm **3** Pour the fish stock through a sieve (strainer) into a saucepan and place over a high heat. Boil for 8 minutes until the stock is reduced (evaporated) to half the original quantity **4** Blend the cornflour (cornstarch) with the double (heavy) cream and add this mixture to the reduced stock, whisking all the time. Warm gently, until the sauce thickens slightly **5** Remove the pan from the heat and allow the sauce to cool a little. Cut the butter into small pieces and add them to the sauce with the egg yolks. Whisk until all the ingredients are well blended and the butter has completely melted **6** Spoon the thickened sauce over the fish pieces on the serving dish **7** Finally, place the dish under a hot grill (broiler) for a few minutes to brown the top

Fish au Gratin

The term 'au gratin' means to form a thin crust on the top of certain dishes by browning in the oven or under the grill (broiler).

Baked Tuna au Gratin

50 g (2 oz) (4 tablespoons) butter
25 g (1 oz) (4 tablespoons) flour
300 ml (½ pint) (1¼ cups) milk
2 egg yolks
100 g (¼ lb) (1 cup) grated cheese
salt and pepper
pinch grated nutmeg
450 g (1 lb) (2 cups) canned tuna, drained and flaked
225 g (½ lb) (2 cups) cooked mashed potato

1 Preheat the oven to 200°C, 400°F, gas 6. Make the cheese sauce: melt 25 g (1 oz) (2 tablespoons) of the butter in a pan, add the flour and cook the roux for 1 minute, without browning. Take the pan off the heat and gradually blend in the milk. Return to the heat and cook the sauce until thickened, stirring constantly. Remove from the heat and add 1 egg yolk and 50 g (2 oz) (½ cup) of the grated cheese. Stir until well blended. Add salt and pepper to taste and the nutmeg.

2 Place the tuna in a shallow ovenproof dish, cover with the cheese sauce and sprinkle over the remaining grated cheese.

3 Blend the mashed potatoes with the remaining egg yolk and butter. Pass the potato through a sieve (strainer) and then pipe it in an attractive pattern round the serving dish.

4 Place the dish in the preheated oven for about 12 minutes to brown the top. Serve with French beans or other green vegetables.

Serves 4

Hake Oriental

25 g (1 oz) (2 tablespoons) margarine
4 x 175 g (6 oz) hake fillets, skinned
salt and pepper
pinch paprika
2 g (1 teaspoon) curry powder
1 onion, sliced
5 g (1 tablespoon) desiccated coconut
1 bouquet garni
300 ml (½ pint) (1¼ cups) water
juice 1 lemon
15 g (½ oz) (1 tablespoon) tomato concentrate (paste)
150 ml (¼ cup) (⅝ cup) plain yogurt
15 g (½ oz) (1½ tablespoons) cornflour (cornstarch)
15 ml (1 tablespoon) oil
5 g (1 tablespoon) chopped parsley

1 Preheat the oven to 200°C, 400°F, gas 6. Grease a shallow ovenproof dish with the margarine and place in the fish. Season and add paprika, curry powder, onion, desiccated coconut and bouquet garni.

2 Mix the water, lemon juice and tomato concentrate (paste) and pour over the fish. Bake in the oven for 20 minutes.

3 Lift the fish from the sauce and keep warm. Strain the sauce into a pan and boil it for 10 minutes. Strain again and add the yogurt, cornflour (cornstarch) and oil. Check the seasoning.

4 Place the fish in a shallow dish and coat with the sauce. Sprinkle with the chopped parsley and serve.

Serves 4

Sole au Gratin

6 x 75 g (3 oz) fillets sole
50 ml (2 fl oz) (¼ cup) oil
25 g (1 oz) (⅛ cup) chopped shallots
50 g (2 oz) (¼ cup) chopped onion
200 g (7 oz) (2 cups) chopped mushrooms
100 g (¼ lb) (2 cups) fresh breadcrumbs
15 g (½ oz) (1 tablespoon) tomato concentrate (paste)
1 beef stock cube
150 ml (¼ pint) (⅝ cup) dry white wine
25 g (1 oz) (2 tablespoons) butter
25 g (1 oz) (3 tablespoons) grated Parmesan
5 g (1 tablespoon) chopped parsley
½ lemon

1 Preheat the oven to 200°C, 400°F, gas 6. Clean the sole fillets. Heat the oil in a pan and add the chopped shallots and onions. Cook for about 5 minutes until soft and lightly browned. Add the mushrooms and cook for a further 5 minutes until all the moisture has evaporated. Stir in the breadcrumbs.

2 Mix the tomato concentrate (paste), crumbled beef stock cube and wine and add to the pan. Bring to the boil and cook for 5 minutes to form a sauce.

3 Roll the sole fillets loosely, place them on an ovenproof serving dish and cover with the sauce. Dot the butter on top and bake in the preheated oven for 15-20 minutes.

4 Remove from the oven and sprinkle the dish with the Parmesan and parsley. Return to the oven for 5 minutes to brown the top.

5 Serve with a squeeze of lemon.

Serves 6

Sole au Gratin. This delicious recipe brings out the delicate flavour of the sole

Seafood Salad

25 ml (1 fl oz) ($\frac{1}{8}$ cup) oil
1 small onion, chopped
200 g (7 oz) ($\frac{7}{8}$ cup) long grain rice
$\frac{1}{2}$ litre (1 pint) (2$\frac{1}{2}$ cups) fish stock,
  or water with 1 chicken stock
  cube added
50 g (2 oz) canned anchovy fillets,
  drained
75 ml (3 fl oz) ($\frac{3}{8}$ cup) salad oil
30 ml (1 fl oz) ($\frac{1}{8}$ cup) lemon juice
5 ml (1 teaspoon) anchovy
  essence
pinch freshly ground (milled)
black pepper
500 g (1 lb) (3 cups) shelled
  shrimps
250 g (9 oz) (2$\frac{1}{4}$ cups) (cooked peas)
250 g (9 oz) (2$\frac{1}{4}$ cups) mussels
pinch finely chopped dill

1 Heat the oil in a pan, add the onion and fry for 3-4 minutes. Add the rice and fry for a further 1-2 minutes. Pour on the fish stock, or the water and stock cube, cover and let the rice cook for about 25 minutes or until the liquid has been absorbed. When cooked, transfer to a serving dish.

2 Mash the anchovy fillets and mix them with the salad oil, lemon juice, anchovy essence and pepper. Pour this mixture onto the cooked rice and allow to cool. Place in the refrigerator to chill completely.

3 When ready to serve, add the shrimps, peas and mussels and sprinkle with the dill. Serve with toast for supper or as an appetizer.

Seafood Salad—shrimps, mussels, anchovies and rice make a tasty chilled dish

Serves 4

Moulded Cod and Prawns in Aspic

50 g (2 oz) (¼ cup) short grain rice
300 ml (½ pint) (1¼ cups) fish stock
1 egg yolk
100 g (¼ lb) (⅔ cup) flaked cooked cod
100 g (¼ lb) (¾ cup) shelled prawns
pinch nutmeg
salt and pepper
225 ml (8 fl oz) (1 cup) chicken stock, or water with 1 chicken stock cube added
25 g (1 oz) (¼ cup) gelatine

For the Garnish:
cucumber and lemon slices

1 Put the short grain rice and fish stock in a pan, bring to the boil and simmer for 10 minutes.

2 Add the egg yolk, flaked cod, prawns, nutmeg and salt and pepper and blend well.

3 Put the chicken stock, or water and stock cube, in a pan and bring to the boil. Take off the heat, add the gelatine and stir until dissolved. Allow to cool.

4 Pour half the dissolved gelatine in a 20 cm (8 in) ring mould, place the mould over a bowl of ice and tilt it so that the gelatine coats the sides and base of the mould as it cools.

5 Add the rest of the dissolved gelatine to the fish mixture and blend well. Pour into the mould and leave in the refrigerator for 1 hour to set.

6 Invert the mould over a serving dish and decorate with cucumber and lemon slices.

Serves 6

Tip: Tarragon leaves can also be used to decorate the ring, in which case add 5 ml (1 teaspoon) tarragon vinegar to the fish mixture before chilling.

Moulded Cod and Prawns in Aspic — a perfect picnic treat which can be prepared in advance

Grilled Fish

Grilling (broiling) is one of the best methods of cooking fish. It is especially suited to oily (fat) fish: herring, mackerel, sardine, trout, salmon, shad and others. When grilling a whole, round fish, first clean it, if necessary (the fishmonger will usually do this for you), then descale, wash and dry. If liked, the head and tail can be removed, though it is usual to leave them on both grilled and fried fish. The practice of cutting the tail into a deep V-shape is known as 'Vandyking'. Score the fish on both sides by making 2-3 diagonal cuts with a knife: this helps it to cook evenly, without burning the outside and leaving the inside half-raw. Brush it with oil or clarified butter, sprinkle with salt, a little made mustard or lemon juice – or top with a delicious savoury butter. Line the grill (broiler) with foil so that the fishy smell doesn't linger in your kitchen after cooking. Grill (broil) at a high temperature, turning the fish once, carefully, and brushing the second side with oil. Allow 8 minutes to cook a fish 2.5 cm (1 in) thick. For a special decorative touch, heat a skewer in an open flame till red-hot, then mark the fish with a criss-cross pattern just before serving. Serve grilled fish with a piquant sauce – the sharpness takes the edge off the richness of the fish – or one with a garlic or herb base, or topped with pats of savoury butter, and accompany with plain boiled potatoes or rice.

White fish is also excellent grilled, especially if it has been lightly marinated first to bring out its flavour. Steep it in a mixture of oil, lemon juice or wine vinegar, seasoned with salt and pepper. Add crushed garlic, a little sugar, soya sauce, sliced onion, a pinch of cayenne and fresh herbs such as tarragon, fennel or thyme: the combinations are endless.

Grilled fish is rich in protein and vitamins, and is a vital part of a calory-controlled, low fat diet. Serving fish as kebabs or with an oriental sauce is an original variation on plain grilled fish, and both make excellent party dishes.

Baltic Cod Kebabs

400 g (14 oz) cod fingers or fillets
4 button (pearl) onions
4 firm tomatoes, skinned and halved
4 button mushrooms, washed
2 g (1 teaspoon) chopped dill
1 sprig parsley
1 lemon, cut in wedges

For the Marinade:
75 ml (8 fl oz) (⅜ cup) oil
juice 1 lemon
10 ml (2 teaspoons) Worcestershire sauce
salt and pepper

1 Cut the fish into 2.5 cm (1in) cubes and place in a bowl.

2 Mix the marinade ingredients together and pour over the cubes of cod. Leave to soak in the marinade for 30 minutes.

3 Parboil the button (pearl) onions for 5 minutes.

4 Impale the cod cubes, tomatoes, mushrooms and onions on four long, metal skewers. Brush with the remaining marinade and season.

5 Place under a grill (broiler) for 8-10 minutes. Brush with oil or melted butter from time to time.

6 Sprinkle the cooked kebabs with chopped dill and garnish with parsley and lemon wedges. Serve with tartare sauce and plain boiled rice.

Serves 4

Baltic Cod Kebabs – marinated pieces of cod threaded on skewers with mushrooms, onions and tomatoes

Shallow-fried Fish

Fish, shallow-fried, should be tasty, crisp and fresh. All kinds of fish lend themselves to this method of cooking, from herring or trout to fillets of plaice or sole; and cod or haddock steaks. First clean and dry the fish, scaling and gutting if necessary. Then coat it in seasoned flour, or matzo or corn meal. (This seals in its flavour, and prevents it from sticking to the pan.) Make sure the fish is evenly coated – shake off excess flour. Heat a heavy frying pan (skillet) and pour in enough oil to reach a depth of about ½ cm (¼ in). When the oil is very hot, place the fish in it and fry it quickly, turning it once, for 2 minutes. Lower the heat, and let it cook thoroughly. Drain and dry on absorbent paper. Serve immediately, with a tangy sauce, French fries or creamed potatoes, seasonal vegetables, and a generous wedge of lemon.

You may fry in cooking fats (shortening) or use a mixture of oil and clarified butter. Fish dipped in beaten egg, then rolled in fine breadcrumbs or oatmeal (after being floured) is especially delicious fried. Fried fish is a perennial family favourite – but when it is cooked a là Meunière, it becomes a classic of French cuisine. Coat the fish evenly with seasoned flour, then cook it gently in clarified butter which is seething hot, but not browning. (Add a little oil.) When it is ready, keep the fish hot, squeeze the juice of ½ a lemon over it, and sprinkle with chopped parsley. Melt a little butter until it is frothy and lightly coloured and pour it, hot, over the fish. Fish Meunière can be adapted to a whole range of recipes, and each different garnish – like tomatoes, capers, or shrimps and mushrooms – has its own title in classic French cookery.

Trout with Almonds. Coat the fish with seasoned flour and shallow-fry. Then sprinkle with lightly-toasted, flaked almonds and serve garnished with lemon slices

Fried Salmon with Creamed Mushrooms

25 g (1 oz) (2 tablespoons) butter
75 g (3 oz) (good ¾ cup) flour
75 ml (2½ fl oz) (⅓ cup) liquid
  from canned mushrooms
75 ml (2½ fl oz) (⅓ cup) water
150 ml (¼ pint) (⅝ cup) single
  (light) cream
salt and pepper
15-30 ml (1-2 tablespoons) dry
  sherry
¼ kg (½ lb) (4 cups) canned
  button mushrooms, cut in
  quarters
6 salmon steaks, 225 g (½ lb) each
100 ml (4 fl oz) (½ cup) oil
1 lemon
lettuce leaves

1 Melt the butter in a pan, add 25 g (1 oz) (4 tablespoons) flour and cook the roux for 1 minute. Take the pan off the heat and blend in the canned mushroom liquid, the water and the cream. Cook the sauce for 5 minutes, add salt and pepper and the sherry and simmer for a further 10 minutes. Add the mushrooms and heat for 3 minutes more.

2 Season the rest of the flour and dust the salmon steaks with the flour.

3 Heat the oil in a pan, add the steaks and fry for 4-5 minutes on each side until golden-brown. Place the steaks on a serving dish and spoon a little of the sauce on each one. Garnish with the lemon, cut into an attractive shape, and the lettuce leaves.

Serves 6

Fried Salmon with Creamed Mushrooms. The mushroom, sherry and cream sauce complements the flavour of the salmon

Plaice Fillets with Shrimps (Prawns)

15 g (½ oz) (2 tablespoons) flour
25 g (1 oz) (½ cup) breadcrumbs
salt
2 eggs, well beaten
4 fillets plaice
30 ml (2 tablespoons) oil
125 g (5 oz) (⅝ cup) butter
225 g (½ lb) (1½ cups) shelled
  shrimps (prawns)
1 lemon

1 Put the flour on one plate and the breadcrumbs on another. Add salt to the eggs.

2 Salt the fillets of plaice, and dip them, on both sides, into the flour. Shake them gently to get rid of the excess flour, then dip them into the beaten egg, and lastly into the breadcrumbs. Press the breadcrumbs firmly onto the fish.

3 Put the fillets onto a plate and let them rest for 10 minutes, preferably in the refrigerator.

4 Heat the oil and 40 g (1½ oz) (3 tablespoons) butter in a frying pan (skillet) and fry the fillets of fish for 2 or 3 minutes on each side, turning them carefully with a fish slice or spatula.

5 Remove from the frying pan (skillet) and arrange them on a heated serving dish. Keep hot.

6 Melt 40 g (1½ oz) (3 tablespoons) butter on a low heat in a small saucepan. Pour in the shrimps (prawns) and shake the pan until all are coated with butter (2 or 3 minutes).

7 Arrange a row of shrimps (prawns) down the middle of each fillet and keep hot.

8 Heat the rest of the butter in the same saucepan until it is a nutty brown, and pour this over the fish fillets.

9 Cut the lemon into quarters. Garnish the dish with the lemon quarters and serve very hot.

Serves 4

Plaice Fillets with Shrimps (Prawns) – deep-fried plaice decorated with shrimps (prawns) tossed in melted butter

Look'n Cook Trout Meunière

1 Heat a mixture of butter and oil in a large, oval frying pan (skillet) and, when foaming, add the floured trout. Arrange side by side and cook gently on one side **2** Turn the trout over and cook the other side **3** Arrange the cooked trout on a warmed serving dish and sprinkle with chopped parsley **4** Heat the remainder of the butter in a pan until frothing and pour over the trout **5** Garnish the dish with peeled lemon slices and more chopped parsley. Serve with sautéed mushrooms

Trout Meunière

four 225 g (½ lb) trouts
salt and pepper
50 g (2 oz) (good ½ cup) flour
150 g (5 oz) (⅝ cup) butter
50 ml (2 fl oz) (¼ cup) oil
2 lemons
5 g (1 tablespoon) chopped parsley

1 Wash and dry the trout and season with salt and pepper.

2 Roll the trout in flour and shake off the excess.

3 Heat 50 g (2 oz) (4 tablspoons) butter and the oil in a large, oval frying pan (skillet). When foaming, add the trout and cook gently on both sides.

4 Meanwhile, cut vertical grooves in the skin of a lemon and slice thinly. Peel another lemon and cut into slices.

5 Arrange the cooked trout on a buttered serving dish and sprinkle with the chopped parsley. Keep hot.

6 Heat the remainder of the butter in a pan until it is frothing and pour over the trout. Garnish with the lemon slices.

Serves 4

Tip: Sole or flounder can be used as a substitute for trout. Use the fish whole and do not remove the white skin or take off the fillets. Cook in the same manner as for trout.

Variations

Belle Meunière: Garnish the trout with peeled, seeded tomatoes and sautéed mushrooms.

Bretonne: Garnish the trout with peeled shrimps and sliced sautéed mushrooms.

Doria: Decorate the trout with chopped, sautéed cucumber.

Marseillaise: Garnish with sautéed aubergines (eggplants), tomatoes and garlic butter.

Skate in Black Butter

1 kg (2 lb) skate wings or flounder
1 kg (2 lb) skate wings
100 g (¼ lb) (½ cup) butter
30 ml (2 tablespoons) vinegar
25 g (1 oz) (2 tablespoons) capers
5 g (1 tablespoon) chopped parsley

For the Stock:
½ litre (1 pint) (2½ cups) water
75 ml (3 fl oz) (⅜ cup) vinegar
1 onion, chopped
1 carrot, chopped
1 bouquet garni
salt and pepper

1 Cut the skate into equal sized pieces.

2 Put all the ingredients for the stock in a large pan and boil for 10 minutes (until the onion and carrot are soft).

3 Add the fish and poach for 12 minutes. Remove the skate, drain well and place in a serving dish. Keep hot.

4 Heat the butter in a frying pan (skillet) until it is brown and foaming – almost black. Add the vinegar immediately and pour over the fish.

5 Sprinkle with capers and chopped parsley and serve.

Serves 4

Shallow-fried Mullet

four 225 g (½ lb) red mullet
25 g (1 oz) (2 tablespoons) seasoned flour
50 ml (2 fl oz) (¼ cup) oil
100 g (¼ lb) (½ cup) butter
4 bananas
2 corn cobs
10 g (2 tblspoons) chopped parsley

1 Clean and wash the mullet and pass in seasoned flour.

2 Heat the oil and 50 g (2 oz) (4 tablespoons) butter in a pan (skillet) and cook the mullet

gently on both sides until cooked. Arrange in a serving dish and keep hot.

3 Split the bananas in two and heat the remainder of the butter in a pan. Fry the bananas until soft.

4 Place the corn in a saucepan and cover with water. Boil for 12 minutes, slice into 8 pieces and season.

5 Sprinkle the mullet with chopped parsley and serve with the corn slices and fried bananas.

Serves 4

Goujons of Sole Murat

This famous recipe was created by M. Dinan who was chef to Marshall Murat and later to Napoleon when he was imprisoned on St. Helena.

350 g (¾ lb) fillets of sole
25 g (1 oz) (4 tablespoons) flour
450 g (1 lb) boiled potatoes
225 g (½ lb) canned artichoke bottoms
50 g (2 oz) (4 tablespoons) butter
50 ml (2 fl oz) (¼ cup) oil
salt and pepper
juice 1 lemon
5 g (1 tablespoon) chopped parsley

1 Cut the fillets into strips 3mm (¼ in) wide by 5cm (2 in) long and dredge with flour.

2 Cut the potatoes and artichokes into strips – the same size as the sole strips.

3 Heat the butter and oil in a frying pan (skillet) and sauté the strips of sole, potatoes and artichokes for 8-10 minutes. Cover the pan with a lid and toss from time to time. Season with salt and pepper.

4 Arrange the sautéed strips in a serving dish and sprinkle with lemon juice and chopped parsley.

Serves 4

Deep-fried Fish

Deep-fried fish, coated with crisp batter or egg-and-breadcrumbs and served piping hot, is an irresistible family dish. Deep-frying is a good way of cooking white and oily fish, either whole, if small, or as fillets, strips, fish-balls and made-up mixtures like croquettes, patties and fish cakes.

You need a deep-fat fryer with a basket inside to hold the fish. You can use any vegetable oil or solid cooking fat, but do not mix the two. Never fill the pan more than half-full of oil or fat, as it can very easily froth up and make sure the cooking fat is completely clean.

To prepare fish for frying

1 Egg and crumb method: (see pages 330-331) wash and dry the fish completely – hot fat and water do not mix and spitting will occur. Dust the fish evenly with flour (shake off the excess) and dip it first in beaten egg, then in fine breadcrumbs (they can be white or brown).

2 Batter method: coat the floured fish in a savoury batter (see page 342) seasoned to your taste.

Heat the oil or fat to 190°C, 375°F – check with a frying thermometer or by putting in a cube of bread which should turn brown within 1 minute and the oil or fat bubble round it as soon as it is submerged. Dip the basket into the hot fat or oil (this prevents food sticking to it), then lower the fish into the fryer. Fillets take 3-4 minutes to cook; thicker fish 5-6 minutes. When the fish is crisp and golden, take it out carefully, drain and dry thoroughly on absorbent paper. Serve immediately.

Never overfill the frying basket, as too much food causes a reduction in temperature, resulting in soggy or under-cooked food. And *never* leave the fryer over heat unattended. Make sure the handle is turned inwards and away from you, so there is no danger of knocking it over.

Deep-frying is a particularly tasty way of cooking white fish such as sole or flounder

Fried Perch

oil for deep frying
four 225 g (½ lb) fillets perch
225 ml (8 fl oz) (1 cup) beer (lager)
20 g (¾ oz) (3 tablespoons) flour
bunch parsley
2 lemons
salt

1 Heat the oil to 190°C, 375°F.

2 Clean the fish fillets. Wash and dry them. Put them into a dish and cover with beer (lager).

3 Pour the flour onto a plate, dip the drained fish into it and shake to remove excess flour.

4 Dip the basket into the hot oil and then lower the fish into the basket. Leave until the fish are cooked through and browned (about 4-5 minutes).

5 Wash and dry the parsley and untie the bunch.

6 Wash and dry the lemons. Cut into halves, serrating the edges. Heat a serving dish.

7 When the fish are cooked, drain them and place on a serving dish. Salt them, then arrange the half lemons around the dish.

8 Lower the parsley into the oil. Leave for about 2 seconds, then drain it. Decorate the plate with the parsley.

9 Serve very hot.

Serves 4

Tip: The oil should be very hot, but not boiling. Serve with a fluffy purée of potatoes.

Fried Sardines

16 large fresh sardines
handful rough sea salt
8 g (1 tablespoon) dry
    breadcrumbs
15 ml (1 tablespoon) single
    (light) cream
1 egg, separated
1 clove garlic, chopped
2 shallots, chopped
5 g (1 tablespoon) chopped
    chives
5 g (1 tablespoon) chopped
chervil
salt and pepper
150 g (5 oz) (1¼ cups) flour
oil for deep frying
300 ml (½ pint) (1¼ cups) milk
bunch parsley

1 Wash and dry the sardines. Place them in an earthenware dish. Sprinkle with the sea salt. Leave them for 4 hours in a cool place.

2 Mix the breadcrumbs and cream in a bowl. Add the egg yolk and mix again.

3 Add the garlic, shallots, chives and chervil to the cream and breadcrumbs. Add salt and pepper. Mix thoroughly with a wooden spoon.

4 Pour the flour onto a plate. Heat the oil to 190°C, 375°F.

5 Clean the sardines. Gut them, cut out the backbone and fill with the cream stuffing. Reshape and secure the sardines with a wooden cocktail stick.

6 Put the stuffed sardines back into the earthenware dish, cover with the milk. Then dry them and dip into the flour one by one. Put them into the frying basket. Gently shake the basket to remove excess flour.

7 Lower the basket into the hot oil and fry until brown.

8 Heat a serving dish. Wash the parsley, dry well.

9 When the fish have browned, drain them and arrange on the serving dish.

10 Lower the parsley into the oil. Fry for 2 minutes, then drain it and arrange with the fish.

11 Serve very hot.

Serves 4

Tip: Sprats can be used as an alternative to sardines.

Deep-Fried Sole or Flounder with Courgette (Zucchini) Fritters

115 g (4½ oz) (1 cup + 4 tablespoons)
    flour
2 eggs
400 ml (¾ pint) (1¾ cups) milk
5 g (1 tablespoon) chopped
    parsley
1 garlic clove, peeled and
    crushed
salt and pepper
oil for deep frying
2 large courgettes (zucchini),
    thinly sliced
four 225 g (½ lb) sole or
    flounder fillets
2 lemons

1 Preheat the oven to 140°C, 275°F, gas 1.

2 Prepare the batter for the courgettes (zucchini). Sift 75 g (3 oz) (good ¾ cup) of the flour into a bowl. Add the eggs and mix well together. Gradually stir in 200 ml (7 fl oz) (⅞ cup) of the milk. Add the chopped parsley, garlic and salt and pepper to taste. Mix well.

3 Half fill a deep fat fryer with oil and heat to 190°C, 375°F.

4 Dip courgette (zucchini) slices in flour, then coat with batter and lower into the oil. Cook for 3-4 minutes.

5 When the fritters are well browned, take them out of the oil, drain them on absorbent paper, put them into a heated vegetable dish, and keep them warm in the oven.

6 Rinse and dry the fish fillets. Pour the rest of the milk into a bowl. Spread the rest of the flour on a plate.

7 Dip the fillets into the milk, then coat them in the flour. Shake to remove excess flour. Dip the basket in the hot oil and then lower the fish into the basket and cook until brown on both sides.

8 Cut the lemons into halves (with a zig-zag edge, if liked).

9 Drain the fillets and arrange them on a white napkin on a heated serving dish. Place a lemon half on each fillet. Serve very hot with the courgette (zucchini) fritters.

Serves 4

Tip: The fritter batter should be a lot thicker than pancake (crêpe) batter, so add a little extra flour if necessary.

Fish Tempura

Tempura is the Japanese name for a dish of lightly-fried pieces of meat, fish, poultry or vegetables, served straight from the pan with a soya sauce dip or raw vegetable salads.

900 g (2 lb) fish fillets (eg bonito, bream, mullet, cod, halibut)
juice 1 lemon
50 g (2 oz) (good ½ cup) seasoned flour
oil for deep frying

For the Batter:
150 ml (¼ pint) (⅝ cup) water
1 egg, beaten
15 ml (1 tablespoon) oil
75 g (3 oz) (good ¾ cup) flour
pinch salt and pepper

1 Mix all the ingredients for the batter in a bowl.

2 Cut the fish fillets into small squares, cubes or strips. Sprinkle with the lemon juice and coat in the seasoned flour.

3 Heat the oil to 190°C, 375°F. Dip the fish pieces in the batter and then fry in the hot oil for 3-4 minutes. Drain and dry on absorbent paper. Serve with mayonnaise dips, vegetable salads, and a tartare, horseradish or chilli sauce.

Serves 4

Tartare Sauce
Blend 150 ml (¼ pint) (⅝ cup) mayonnaise with 15 g (½ oz) (1 tablespoon) chopped parsley, gherkins (dill cucumbers) and capers.

Horseradish Sauce
Blend 150 ml (¼ pint) (⅝ cup) mayonnaise with 15 g (½ oz) (1 tablespoon) grated horseradish.

Chilli Sauce
Blend 150 ml (¼ pint) (½ cup) mayonnaise with 2.5 ml (½ teaspoon) Tabasco sauce and 5 g (1 tablespoon) chopped chives.

Red Pepper dip

25 ml (1 fl oz) (⅛ cup) soya sauce
5 ml (1 teaspoon) vinegar
juice 1 orange
1 small onion, finely chopped
salt and pepper
5 g (1 teaspoon) sugar
150 ml (¼ pint) (⅝ cup) mayonnaise
50 g (2 oz) finely chopped red pepper
25 g (1 oz) tangerine segments (sections)

1 Mix together the soya sauce, vinegar, orange juice, onion, salt and pepper and sugar in a blender or a bowl.

2 Lightly blend in the mayonnaise, then add the red peppers and tangerine segments (sections).

Makes 150 ml (¼ pint) (⅝ cup)

Pineapple Dip

150 ml (¼ pint) (⅝ cup) mayonnaise or salad dressing
25 g (1 oz) chopped pineapple
25 ml (1 fl oz) (⅛ cup) soya sauce
1 clove garlic, chopped
75 ml (2½ fl oz) (⅓ cup) pineapple juice

1 Work all the ingredients, except the mayonnaise or salad dressing, in a blender or in a bowl.

2 Blend in the mayonnaise or salad dressing.

Makes 150 ml (¼ pint) (⅝ cup)

Fish-balls Chinese-style

1 onion, peeled
450 g (1 lb) white fish (eg haddock, bream, red mullet, ocean perch, snapper), skinned and

bones removed
100 g (¼ lb) (2 cups) crushed water biscuits or breadcrumbs
5 g (1 teaspoon) sugar
salt and pepper
1 egg, beaten
50 g (2 oz) (good ½ cup) seasoned flour
oil for deep frying

For the Batter:
1 egg
100 g (¼ lb) (1 cup + 2 tablespoons) flour
150 ml (¼ pint) (⅝ cup) flat light beer or water

1 Combine the ingredients for the batter in a bowl to form a smooth but fairly liquid batter. Leave for 20 minutes before using.

2 Grate the onion into a bowl. Mince (grind) the fish and add to the onion. Blend in the crushed biscuits or breadcrumbs, sugar, salt and pepper to taste and the beaten egg. Mince again to obtain a smooth paste.

3 Divide the mixture into small dumplings and coat with seasoned flour, then dip in the batter.

4 Heat the oil to 190°C, 375°F. Then fry the dumplings a few at a time for 3 minutes or until crisp and golden. Drain on absorbent paper. Serve at once with a sweet 'n sour sauce poured over or in a sauce-boat.

Serves 4

Vegetable accompaniments
You can serve almost any raw vegetables with Fish Tempura, such as carrots, turnips and cucumber, all cut in floral shapes. All vegetables must be raw or, at the most, scalded, so that they keep their colour and taste. To scald, plunge into boiling salted water for 30 seconds.

Fish Tempura – small pieces of fish cooked quickly in hot oil and served with various vegetables and sauces

Beer Batter

225 g (½ lb) (2¼ cups) flour
pinch salt
150 ml (¼ pint) (⅝ cup) flat beer
 (lager)
1 egg yolk
150 ml (¼ pint) (⅝ cup) milk
2 egg whites
25 ml (1 fl oz) (⅛ cup) oil

1 Sift the flour and salt into a bowl.

2 Mix the beer (lager), egg yolk and milk together and then blend this mixture into the flour to obtain a smooth batter. Cover the bowl with a cloth and leave the batter to stand at room temperature for 1 hour.

3 When the batter is ready, beat the egg whites until they stand in soft peaks. Add the egg whites and the oil to the batter and use immediately.

Makes about 300 ml (½ pint) (1¼ cups)

Whiting Fritters. The recipe for Beer Batter given above can be used to coat all kinds of fish, meat and vegetables for deep-frying. Try using whiting, as shown here

Vegetable Fritters
Many different vegetables can be deep-fried and served as fritters. Coat the vegetable pieces in seasoned flour, dip them in batter and fry for a few minutes in fat heated to 190°C, 375°F. Try using slices of aubergine (eggplant) cut on the slant or lengthwise strips of courgette (zucchini). Sprouts, cauliflower, broccoli and root vegetables, such as parsnips, carrots, turnips and swedes, make excellent fritters but parboil them first in salted water until tender.

French Fried Onions

450 g (1 lb) large onions, sliced across in rings
150 ml (¼ pint) (⅝ cup) milk
50 g (2 oz) (good ½ cup) plain flour
salt
oil for deep frying

1 Separate the onion slices into rings. Place the rings in a bowl, cover with cold water and leave to soak for 10 minutes. Drain well.

2 Dip the onion rings in the milk and then drain in a colander. Sift the flour and a pinch of salt onto a plate. Coat the onion rings in the seasoned flour.

3 Heat the oil to 190°C, 375°F. Add the onion rings and fry for 3 minutes or until golden. Drain them on absorbent paper and use as a garnish for deep–fried fish.

Makes about 450 g (1 lb)

French Fried Parsley

bunch parsley
oil for deep frying

1 Wash the parsley well, drain and dry on a cloth. The parsley must be as free from moisture as possible.

2 Heat the oil to 200°C, 400°F and add the parsley sprigs. Allow them to fry for only 15 to 20 seconds. Drain and dry on absorbent paper. Use for garnishing fried fish.

Rolled Whiting

4 whiting
2 eggs
30 ml (2 tablespoons) oil
salt and pepper
100 g (¼ lb) (1 cup) flour
200 g (7 oz) fresh bread
oil for deep frying
few sprigs parsley

1 Trim, clean and wash the whiting. Carefully split them along the backbone with a filleting knife. Slip the knife through to separate the two fillets. Cut out the backbone close to the head with kitchen scissors. Dry the fillets.

2 Prepare the coating. Put the eggs, oil and some salt and pepper in a deep plate. Beat with a whisk. Spread the flour on a plate. Make crumbs from the bread, and pour onto another plate.

3 Dip the whiting successively in the flour, the beaten egg and the breadcrumbs. Press on the crumbs gently with the flat of a knife, then roll up the fillets to the outside of either side of the head. Keep them in place with a skewer or cocktail stick. (See step-by-step, pages 330-331.)

4 Heat the oil in the deep fat fryer to 190°C, 375°F.

5 Carefully lower the rolled-up whiting into the hot oil and fry until golden-brown. Drain them on absorbent paper and keep hot.

6 Toss the parsley into the oil and fry for 2 seconds. Drain and decorate the serving dish with it. Serve with a tomato sauce.

Serves 4

Fried Whitebait

450 g (1 lb) whitebait
100 g (¼ lb) (1 cup + 2 tablespoons) flour
250 ml (8 fl oz) (1 cup) milk or beer (lager)
oil for deep frying
1 bunch parsley
2 lemons
salt

1 Clean, wash and dry the fish.

2 Pour the flour into a bowl.

3 Put the fish in a deep dish and soak in the milk or beer (lager).

4 Heat the oil in a deep fat fryer to 190°C, 375°F.

5 Drain the fish in a colander. Shake them, then toss them in the flour. It is best to do this gradually so the flour does not get too wet and clot on the fish. Toss the fish so that they are evenly covered. Then empty them back into the dried colander to remove any excess flour. Wash and dry the parsley. Cut the lemons into quarters.

6 Put the fish into the frying basket and lower into the hot oil. When the fish are golden and have risen to the surface, drain and dry them in absorbent paper. Add salt.

7 Fry the parsley for 2 or 3 seconds. Drain it.

8 Heat a serving dish. Put the fish on it. Decorate with the fried parsley and lemon quarters. Serve immediately.

Serves 4

Tip: It is not practical to clean very small fish, but they should be thoroughly washed.

411

1 Put the whitebait in a container and cover with milk. For a variety of flavour, some of the fish can be soaked in beer (lager) in a separate container **2** Pour the flour into another container. Drain the fish and then, with the hands, toss them in the flour **3** Put the fish in a perforated basket (the one from the frier, for example). Shake the fish to remove any excess flour **4** The fish are now ready for frying **5** Heat the

oil. Lower the basket into the hot, but not smoking oil **6** When the fish are cooked, raise the basket and rest the loops on the handles of the frier, so that the oil can drain **7** Dry the fish on absorbent paper, put them onto a plate and lightly salt them **8** Fry the parsley in the same oil **9** Arrange the fish on a hot serving dish. Decorate with the parsley and lemons cut into quarters

Look'n Cook Fried Fish Fingers

1 Take fillets of plaice, cod or flounder. Cut them into long pieces (fingers). Marinate them in the oil, lemon and parsley mixture **2** Prepare the batter **3** Beat the egg whites until stiff and fold into the batter **4** Heat up the frying oil. Drain the pieces of fish. Dip them in the batter **5** Lower them into the hot oil and let them brown **6** Drain and serve with fried parsley

Fish Croquettes

15 ml (1 tablespoon) oil
1 onion, chopped
1 shallot, chopped
75 g (3 oz) (1 cup) mushrooms,
 chopped
2 sprigs parsley, chopped
225 ml (8 fl oz) (1 cup) milk
25 g (1 oz) (4 tablespoons) flour
salt and pepper
freshly grated nutmeg
225 g (½ lb) (1 cup) minced
 (ground) whiting fillets
oil for deep frying

1 Heat the oil in a pan, add the chopped vegetables and parsley and cook gently without browning. Warm the milk.

2 Stir in half the flour and cook for a few seconds, stirring constantly with a wooden spoon.

3 Stir in the milk gradually. Season with salt and pepper to taste and add a little grated nutmeg.

4 Stir in the minced (ground) fish and cook gently for 10 minutes, stirring constantly. Remove from the heat and leave to cool.

5 Heat the oil to 190°C, 375°F.

6 Shape the fish mixture into croquettes, then roll them in the remaining flour.

7 Deep-fry the croquettes in the hot oil until golden, then drain on absorbent paper and serve hot with a tomato sauce.

Serves 4

Deep-fried Kedgeree in Pastry Casing

150 g (¼ lb) flaked cooked
 haddock
75 g (3 oz) cooked rice
75 g (3 oz) cooked peas
75 g (3 oz) (⅝ cup) diced cooked
 carrots
75 g (3 oz) canned baked beans in
 tomato sauce
75 g (3 oz) (⅜ cup) chopped raw
 onion

1 hard-boiled (hard-cooked) egg,
 coarsely chopped
salt and pepper
pinch curry powder
225 g (½ lb) puff pastry,
 home-made or frozen and
 thawed
oil for deep frying

1 Place the haddock, rice, peas, carrots, baked beans, onion, egg, salt, pepper and curry powder in a bowl and mix thoroughly.

2 Roll out the puff pastry thinly (about 4 mm [⅛ in] thick). Cut the pastry into 4 rounds, each about 15 cm (6 in) in diameter.

3 Place 3 large spoonsful of the kedgeree mixture on each pastry round. Brush the edges of the pastry with water and fold over to make a halfmoon shape and enclose the stuffing. Press the edges together to seal.

4 Heat the oil to 190°C, 375°F. Add the pastry cases and fry for 4 minutes or until golden.

5 Drain and serve with tomato curry sauce or lemon wedges.

Serves 4

Indian Fish Cutlets

225 g (½ lb) cooked rice
225 g (½ lb) any cooked fish
15 g (½ oz) (2 tablespoons) curry
 powder
3 eggs
salt and pepper
50 g (2 oz) (1 cup) fresh
 breadcrumbs
25 g (1 oz) (5 tablespoons)
 desiccated coconut
100 g (¼ lb) (1 cup + 2 tablespoons)
 seasoned flour
oil for deep frying

1 Mince (grind) the rice and fish together twice. Add the curry powder, 1 egg and seasoning and mix well. Form the mixture into 4 cutlet shapes.

2 Beat the remaining eggs. Mix the breadcrumbs and desiccated coconut. Coat the cutlets in the seasoned flour, then dip in the

beaten egg and then roll in the breadcrumbs.

3 Heat the oil to 190°C, 375°F, add the cutlets and fry for 5 minutes. Serve with a wedge of lemon.

Serves 4

Fried Cod Fingers

1 lemon
900 g (2 lb) cod fillets, skinned
60 ml (4 tablespoons) oil
20 g (4 tablespoons) chopped
 parsley and chervil
freshly ground (milled) pepper
 and salt
oil for frying

For the Batter:
100 g (¼ lb) (1 cup + 2 tablespoons)
 flour
2 eggs, separated
100 ml (4 fl oz) (½ cup) beer (lager)

1 Squeeze the lemon. Cut the cod fillets into strips (fingers). Place in earthenware dish. Pour the lemon juice and the oil over them. Sprinkle with the chopped parsley and chervil, some pepper and a little salt. Mix very carefully and leave to soak.

2 Pour the flour into a bowl. Put the egg yolks into the middle with a pinch of salt. Using a whisk, mix in the flour a little at a time. When the batter becomes too thick, dilute it with the beer to obtain a type of thick pancake batter. Leave to stand.

3 Meanwhile, beat the egg whites until firm. Add to the batter and fold in with a metal spoon or spatula, giving a very light batter. Heat the oil in a deep fat fryer to 190°C, 375°F.

4 Drain the cod strips well, dip into the batter and lower into the hot oil.

5 Drain the strips on absorbent paper when they are golden. Serve immediately, very hot, with mayonnaise, a tartare sauce or fried parsley.

Serves 6

Baked Fish

Baking Fish

Baking is one of the most versatile methods of cooking. Fish may be baked simply, with a little butter, lemon juice and parsley; in a variety of different liquids such as stock, wine, apple cider, or cream; or stuffed, in a rich sauce. Baking retains the flavour of the fish supremely well, and cooking smells are kept to a minimum.

Arrange the fish attractively in a casserole – which can also be used as a serving dish. Always preheat the oven. Set it at 180°C, 350°F, gas 4 for dishes to be cooked in a covered casserole; 200°C, 400°F, gas 6 if you want a golden brown or gratinéed surface.

The possibilities for experimenting with different ingredients, herbs and seasonings are almost limitless. Sousing is a form of baking: cook at 180°C, 350°F, gas 4 and allow the fish to cool in its spiced vinegar.

Cooked 'en papillote', the fish is placed on a sheet of aluminium foil or greaseproof (waxed) paper, covered with a garnish, rich or simple. The sheet is folded to make an airtight parcel and the fish cooks in its own juices in the oven. Serve the fish in its wrapping on each plate. This method of cooking is excellent as part of a calorie-controlled diet.

A popular American method of cooking fish is 'planking'. The fish is partially grilled (broiled), then transferred to an oiled oak plank, and baked. The planks imparts a delicious, barbecue-like flavour and aroma – and makes an impressive dish to present to guests, especially if the platter is decorated with a piped border of duchesse potatoes before it is placed in the oven.

Serve boiled or creamed potatoes with baked fish – or make a rice pilaff. A crisp green salad is an excellent accompaniment.

Baked Fish Fillets in Soured Cream

four 150 g (5 oz) fish fillets
salt and pepper
50 ml (2 fl oz) (¼ cup) oil
25 g (1 oz) (4 tablespoons) chopped chives
150 ml (¼ pint) (⅝ cup) soured cream
1 bay leaf, imported
pinch caraway seeds, optional
pinch paprika
sprig parsley
4 lemon wedges

1 Set the oven at 200°C, 400°F, gas 6.

2 Place the fish fillets on a greased, shallow dish. Season with salt and pepper and brush with oil. Bake for 5 minutes in the pre heated oven.

3 Add the chopped chives, soured cream, bay leaf and caraway seeds, cover with a lid, return to the oven and bake for 15 minutes at the same temperature.

4 Serve the fish in the same dish, with boiled new potatoes and turnips. Sprinkle with paprika just before serving and decorate with parsley and lemon wedges.

Serves 4

Baked Mackerel Stuffed with Apple

four 225 g (½ lb) mackerel
100 g (¼ lb) (½ cup) butter
100 g (¼ lb) (1 cup) celery, finely chopped
1 apple, peeled and finely chopped
small onion, chopped
50 g (2 oz) (1 cup) fresh breadcrumbs
5 g (1 tablespoon) chopped parsley
salt and pepper
pinch ground (powdered) ginger
juice and grated rind 1 lemon

1 Preheat the oven to 180°C, 350°F, gas 4.

2 Using a sharp knife, remove the backbones from the fish without damaging the belly. Open out the fish to form a pocket for the stuffing, and clean it thoroughly.

3 Make the stuffing. Melt 50 g (2 oz) (¼ cup) butter in a saucepan and sauté the celery, apple and onion for 4 minutes. Stir in the breadcrumbs and chopped parsley. Season with salt and pepper and add the ginger, grated lemon rind and juice.

4 Spread the filling evenly on each mackerel, and fold over. Melt the remaining butter in a pan and use to brush the mackerel. Wrap them in foil and bake in the oven for 20 minutes.

Serves 4

Baking en Papillote

A papillote is a heart-shaped piece of greaseproof (waxed) paper or aluminium foil, well-oiled or buttered, and folded around the ingredients to be cooked. This method of cooking is advantageous because it ensures that the fish simmers in its own juices and thus does not lose its own distinctive flavour.

Many fish can be cooked in this way – trout, red mullet, sole or herrings to name but a few. Really, the term only implies half-cooking because the fish used is often pre-cooked before it is placed in the paper bag or foil.

Always serve papillotes in their puffed-up paper shells and let your guests cut them open themselves at the table with a knife. If you use aluminium foil, remove the fish from the foil to serve.

Mexican Baked Cod

four 225 g (½ lb) cod steaks
salt and pepper
150 ml (¼ pint) (⅝ cup) medium
  sherry
50 ml (2 fl oz) (¼ cup) grapefruit
  juice
pinch paprika
1 bouquet garni
50 ml (2 fl oz) (¼ cup) oil and
  butter
1 onion, chopped
4 tomatoes, skinned, deseeded
  and chopped
1 red pepper, deseeded and
  chopped
100 g (¼ lb) (¾ cup) corn kernels,
  fresh, canned or frozen and
  thawed
50 g (2 oz) (1 cup) fresh
  breadcrumbs
5 g (1 tablespoon) chopped
  parsley

1 Preheat the oven to 200°C, 400 F, gas 6.

2 Wash and dry the cod steaks. Season with salt and pepper and place in a shallow ovenproof dish. Pour over the sherry and grapefruit juice. Add a pinch of paprika and the bouquet garni.

3 Bake in the oven for 15 minutes.

4 Meanwhile, heat the butter and oil in a saucepan and sauté the chopped onions until soft. Add the tomatoes, red pepper and corn kernels. Season with salt and pepper and simmer for 8 minutes.

5 When the fish are cooked, remove from the oven. Place the cod steaks on a serving dish and keep warm. Drain off the fish liquor and add to the sauce.

Mexican Baked Cod – the cod steaks are cooked in sherry and grapefruit juice and served in a tomato sauce

6 Boil the sauce for 4 minutes, season to taste and remove from the heat. Stir in the bread-crumbs and chopped parsley, and pour over the cod steaks.

7 Serve with boiled potatoes or rice.

Serves 4

Herrings with Apples in Cider

1 kg (2 lb) fresh herrings, filleted
50 g (2 oz) (good ½ cup) flour
15 g (½ oz) (1 tablespoon) prepared
  English mustard
salt and pepper
1 onion, sliced
2 apples, peeled and sliced in
  rings
450 g (1 lb) (3 cups), potatoes
  thinly sliced
300 ml (½ pint) (1¼ cups) dry cider
  (apple cider)
300 ml (½ pint) (1¼ cups) water
15 ml (1 tablespoon) cider
vinegar
1 bay leaf, imported
100 g (¼ lb) (½ cup) butter
5 g (1 tablespoon) chopped
  parsley

1 Preheat the oven to 200°C, 400°F, gas 6.

2 Wash and drain the herring fillets and coat with flour. Spread the mustard on the fleshy side. Season with salt and pepper.

3 Place the fish fillets, side by side, in an oblong, shallow dish and cover with alternate layers of sliced onion, apples and potatoes. Season with salt and pepper.

4 Pour in the cider (apple cider), water and cider vinegar. Add the bay leaf and dot the top with small pieces of butter.

5 Bake in the oven for 45-50 minutes. Sprinkle with parsley before serving.

Serves 4

Polynesian Baked Mackerel

four 225 g (½ lb) mackerel
salt and pepper
50 g (2 oz) (4 tablespoons) butter
100 g (¼ lb) (2 cups) button
  mushrooms, sliced
1 sprig thyme
1 bay leaf, imported
1 lemon

For the Marinade:
150 ml (¼ pint) (⅝ cup) pineapple
  juice
150 ml (¼ pint) (⅝ cup) dry, white
  wine
15 ml (1 tablespoon) soya sauce
1 clove garlic, crushed
1 medium onion, chopped
salt and pepper
5 g (1 teaspoon) sugar

1 Preheat the oven to 200°C, 400°F, gas 6.

2 Clean and wash the fish. Make 4 slits in each mackerel. Season with salt and pepper and place in a shallow dish.

3 Place all the ingredients for the marinade in a blender and liquidize. Transfer the marinade to a pan and boil for 5 minutes.

4 Slice the mushrooms and heat the butter in a small pan. Add the mushrooms and sauté for 1 minute and place around the fish, with the thyme and bay leaf.

5 Pour over the marinade and bake in the oven for 25 minutes. Baste with the liquid from time to time.

6 Serve with wedges of lemon.

Serves 4

Polynesian Baked Mackerel – the mackerel are marinated in pineapple juice and white wine and baked with mushrooms

Portuguese Stuffed Plaice Rolls

eight 100 g (¼ lb) fillets of plaice
  or lemon sole, skinned
50 g (2 oz) (4 tablespoons) butter
225 g (½ lb) (1½ cups) prawns
1 lemon

For the Stuffing:
1 hard-boiled (hard-cooked) egg
1 sprig watercress
50 g (2 oz) (4 tablespoons) butter
50 ml (2 fl oz) (¼ cup) oil
1 onion, chopped
100 g (¼ lb) (2 cups) fresh
  breadcrumbs
1 egg, beaten
juice and grated rind 1 lemon
salt and pepper

For the Sauce:
300 ml (½ pint) (1¼ cups) velouté
  sauce
15 ml (1 tablespoon) tomato
  concentrate (paste)
30 ml (2 tablespoons) dry sherry
juice ½ lemon
salt and pepper

1 Preheat the oven to 180°C, 350°F, gas 4.

2 Tap each fillet gently with a rolling pin to break down the fibres.

3 Chop the hard-boiled (hard-cooked) egg and watercress and mix well with the other stuffing ingredients to form a paste.

4 Spread the stuffing evenly over each fish fillet. Roll up the fillets and place upright in a shallow ovenproof dish. Season, dot with butter and bake for 15 minutes.

5 Meanwhile make the sauce. Boil the velouté and stir in the tomato concentrate (paste), sherry and lemon juice. Season to taste.

6 Pour the sauce over the cooked, rolled fillets and decorate with the prawns and lemon wedges.

Serves 4

Portuguese Stuffed Plaice Rolls are stuffed with breadcrumbs, watercress and lemon and then covered in a sherry sauce

Baked & Braised Fish

Halibut (Flounder) in Wine

four 225g (½lb) halibut steaks,
 about 2cm (1in) thick
½ lemon
salt and pepper
15ml (1 tablespoon) oil
150ml (¼ pint) (⅝ cup) dry
 vermouth

350ml (12 floz) (1½ cups) double
 (heavy) cream
50g (2oz) (4 tablespoons) butter
225g (½lb) (4 cups) button
 mushrooms, sliced
1 onion, chopped
100g (¼lb) (¾ cup) shelled shrimps
 (prawns)
25g (1oz) (2 tablespoons) tomato
 concentrate (paste)
pinch cayenne pepper
15ml (1 tablespoon) brandy

1 Preheat the oven to 200°C, 400°F, gas 6. Rub the steaks with the lemon. Salt and pepper lightly.

2 Place the fish steaks in an oiled ovenproof dish and pour over the vermouth and 300ml (½ pint) (1¼ cups) double (heavy) cream.

3 Cover the dish with aluminium foil and place in the preheated oven for 20 minutes.

4 Heat 25g (1oz) (2 tablespoons) butter in a pan, add the mushrooms and fry for 2 minutes. Add salt and pepper and the rest of the cream. Keep warm.

5 In a separate pan, heat the rest of the butter, add the onion and fry for 4 minutes. Add the remaining ingredients and cook for 2 minutes. Add the mushrooms and cream. Taste and correct the seasoning.

6 Transfer the halibut to a warmed serving dish and cover with the sauce. Serve with boiled potatoes and a green salad.

Serves 6

Halibut in Wine – halibut baked with shrimps in a rich, creamy sauce flavoured with vermouth and brandy

Baked Bass with Mushroom and Olive Stuffing

1 bass (2 kg) (4 lb), cleaned, scaled
300 ml (½ pint) (1¼ cups) dry white wine
300 ml (½ pint) (1¼ cups) water
1 onion, sliced
1 carrot, sliced
1 bouquet garni
1 clove garlic, crushed
1 bulb fennel, sliced
salt and pepper

For the Stuffing:
50 ml (2 fl oz) (¼ cup) oil
1 onion, chopped
225 g (½ lb) (2 cups) chopped mushrooms
225 g (½ lb) (4 cups) fresh breadcrumbs
5 g (1 tablespoon) chopped parsley
4 stoned (pitted) olives, chopped

For the Garnish:
6 button mushrooms
6 black olives, stoned (pitted)
6 green olives, stoned (pitted)
4 tomatoes
1 lemon

1 Preheat the oven to 200°C, 400°F, gas 6. Place the bass in a shallow ovenproof dish and add the wine, water, onion, carrot, bouquet garni, garlic, fennel and seasoning. Cover with grease-proof (waxed) paper and bake in the preheated oven for 30 minutes.

2 Remove the dish from the oven, discard the bouquet garni and lift out the vegetables. Chop them coarsely and put on one side to use in the stuffing. Place the fish on an oval serving dish and reserve the stock. Reduce the oven temperature to 180°C, 350°F, gas 4.

3 Make the stuffing: heat the oil in a pan and add the chopped onion and mushrooms. Cook for 5 minutes and then add the chopped, cooked vegetables, the breadcrumbs, salt and pepper, parsley and chopped olives. Mix well.

4 Cut the tops of the button mushrooms in swirls using a cannelle knife and then boil the mushrooms for 4 minutes in a little of the reserved fish stock.

5 Surround the bass with the stuffing. Decorate with the black and green olives and the cooked mushrooms.

6 Place the 4 tomatoes for the garnish in boiling water for 1 minute, remove and peel off the

Baked Bass with Mushroom and Olive Stuffing is served surrounded by stuffing, and garnished with peeled tomatoes, olives and lemon waterlilies

skins. Cut the lemon in a decorative shape and place the tomatoes and lemon on the dish. Return the dish to the oven for 12 minutes to reheat. Serve with boiled potatoes.

Serves 6

Bass or Snapper à la Dugleré

one 900g (2lb) bass or snapper, cleaned and scaled
55g (2oz) (¼ cup) butter
4 tomatoes, skinned, deseeded and chopped
2 onions, chopped
2 shallots, chopped
1 clove garlic, chopped
1 bouquet garni
salt and pepper

300ml (½ pint) (1¼ cups) dry white wine
15g (½oz) (2 tablespoons) flour
pinch cayenne pepper
5g (1 tablespoon) chopped parsley

1 Wash and dry the fish. Either leave it whole or cut it into 6 steaks. Do not separate these but leave them packed together.

2 Preheat the oven to 190°C, 375°F, gas 5. Liberally grease an oval ovenproof dish with 15g (½oz) (1 tablespoon) of the butter. Arrange half the chopped tomatoes, onions and shallots and the bouquet garni on the bottom of the dish. Place the fish on top. Cover it with the rest of the tomatoes, onions and shallots. Season with salt and pepper. Sprinkle the wine over the top. Cut 25g (1oz) (2 tablespoons) of the butter into small pieces and scatter them over the fish. Cook in the preheated oven for 30 minutes.

The ingredients for Bass or Snapper Dugleré. The bass is cooked in white wine, with tomatoes and shallots

3 When the fish is cooked, transfer it carefully from the cooking dish to a heated oval serving dish. Keep warm.

4 Pour the cooking juices and vegetables into a saucepan and bring to the boil. Boil until reduced (evaporated) by one-quarter. Discard the bouquet garni. Cream the rest of the butter with the flour to make a paste. Whisk this into the cooking juices and simmer until thickened.

5 Correct the seasoning and add the cayenne pepper.

6 Coat the fish with the sauce and serve immediately, sprinkled with the chopped parsley.

Serves 4

Look'n Cook Cooking and Dressing a Salmon

1 Clean, descale and wash the salmon. Place it in a fish kettle or large pan and cover with cold water. Add sea salt and thin slices of lemon with the pith and peel removed. Simmer gently without letting the water boil for 30 minutes. Let it cool in its own liquor until quite cold **2** Drain the cooked salmon **3** Carefully remove the skin with a thin-pointed knife **4** Make some aspic jelly and, when it is melted and almost set, coat the fish with the jelly **5** Decorate the salmon with strips and small pieces of tomato,

tarragon and truffle and coat with more jelly to fix the decorations in place. Remove the decorated salmon from the grid and place on a large serving dish **6** Surround the fish with stuffed tomatoes, stuffed eggs and parsley **7** To serve the fish, cut off fillets, parallel to the backbone, with a knife and fork **8** When all the flesh has been taken off the first side, remove the fish bones by lifting up the backbone from the tail towards the head. Cut off the remaining fillets

Serving poached fish

Serve poached freshwater fish in their own court bouillon in a shallow dish. The court bouillon should always be clear – never cloudy. Serve with sliced carrots, sliced cooked onions and boiled potatoes and garnish with bay leaves and parsley. Alternatively, pour warm melted butter over the fish or, if you prefer a sauce, try a hollandaise and decorate with lemon waterlillies.

Trout Soup Solianka

four 225 g (½ lb) trout
1 litre (1¾ pints) (4½ cups) water
1 bouquet garni
1 chicken stock cube
50 g (2 oz) (4 tablespoons) butter
1 carrot, thinly sliced
1 stick celery, thinly sliced
1 clove garlic, crushed
50 g (2 oz) (¼ cup) flour
15 ml (1 tablespoon) tomato
  concentrate (paste)
salt and pepper
juice 1 lemon
5 g (1 tablespoon) chopped
  parsley and dill
5 g (1 tablespoon) capers
6 stuffed olives, sliced

1 Clean and fillet the fish, and cut each fillet into 3 pieces. Keep the heads, bones and trimmings to make the fish stock.

2 Place the fish bones with a bouquet garni in a saucepan of water, crumble in the stock cube and boil for 20 minutes.

3 Heat the butter in a saucepan and sauté the sliced carrot, celery and garlic for 15 minutes. Add the flour and cook for 3 minutes. Strain off the fish stock and add to the sautéed vegetables. Stir in the tomato concentrate (paste) and boil for 15 minutes until the vegetables are almost soft. Add the fish and simmer for 15 minutes. Season to taste.

4 Stir in the lemon juice, chopped parsley and dill and garnish with the capers and olives. Serve with rye bread and butter.

Serves 4 –6

Poached Trout

four 225 g (½ lb) whole trout
2 carrots, sliced
2 onions, chopped
1 stick celery, thinly sliced
1 bouquet garni
1 sprig mint
6 peppercorns
1 litre (1¾ pints) (4½ cups) water
30 ml (2 tablespoons) vinegar
salt and pepper
2 lemons

1 Clean and wash the fish.

2 Make the court bouillon: place the carrots, onions, celery, bouquet garni, mint and peppercorns in a large saucepan. Add the water and vinegar and

Trout Soup Solianka is garnished with capers and stuffed olives. Serve each dish with a swirl of sour cream

boil for 15 minutes.

3 Place the trout in the court bouillon and simmer for 10 minutes.

4 Cut the lemons into wedges. Arrange the poached trout on a serving dish, pour over a little court bouillon and decorate with the lemon wedges. Serve with boiled, new potatoes and melted butter or hollandaise sauce.

Serves 4

Tip: This basic recipe for court bouillon stock can be used for all poached fish.

Salmon Mousse

450 g (1 lb) salmon, poached
25 g (1 oz) (2 tablespoons) butter
25 g (1 oz) (4 tablespoons) flour
300 ml (½ pint) (1¼ cups) milk
salt and pepper
pinch paprika
5 g (1 tablespoon) tomato
   concentrate (paste)
5 ml (1 teaspoon) anchovy
   essence
juice ½ lemon
50 ml (2 fl oz) (¼ cup) dry sherry
pinch cayenne pepper
300 ml (½ pint) (1¼ cups) whipped
   double (heavy) cream

For the Aspic Jelly:
300 ml (½ pint) (1¼ cups) water
50 g (2 oz) (½ cup) gelatine
1 chicken stock cube
juice ½ lemon

For decoration:
¼ cucumber, sliced
12 peeled prawns
6 stuffed olives

1 Remove the bones and skin from the salmon. Chop the flesh.

2 Heat the butter in a saucepan, add the flour and cook for 2 minutes. Stir in the milk.

3 Place the chopped salmon in the sauce and cook for 10 minutes. Season with salt and pepper and a pinch of paprika. Stir in the tomato concentrate (paste), anchovy essence, lemon juice, sherry and cayenne pepper. Simmer for 8 minutes. Liquidize or pass through a sieve (strainer). Allow the salmon purée to cool a little and stir in the whipped cream.

4 Make the aspic jelly. Boil the water and stir in and dissolve the gelatine, stock cube and lemon juice. Simmer for 5 minutes and allow to cool a little.

5 Stir half of the aspic into the salmon purée.

6 Cover the base of a 1 litre (2 pint) (5 cups) mould with aspic, 4 mm (⅛ in) thick, and allow to set. Then line the sides of the mould with aspic and set.

7 Dip the decorative garnishes –

the cucumber, prawns and olives – in a little tepid aspic and arrange inside the mould on the bottom and sides in an attractive pattern. Allow to set and then dab with the remaining aspic. Allow to set.

8 Pour in the salmon purée and chill in the refrigerator for 2 hours.

9 Stand the mould on a plate and hold under running, slightly tepid tapwater. Gently loosen the mould and ease off. Be careful not to use excessive force or the mousse will break.

10 Garnish with sliced cucumber, prawns and olives.

Serves 6

Savoury Pike with Walnuts

1 kg (2 lb) whole pike, trout or
   bream
salt and pepper
50 g (2 oz) (good ½ cup) flour
50 ml (2 fl oz) (¼ cup) oil
100 g (¼ lb) (1 cup) celery, sliced
100 g (¼ lb) (1 cup) carrots, sliced
100 g (¼ lb) (1 cup) onions, sliced
100 g (¼ lb) (1¼ cups) mushrooms,
   sliced
100 g (¼ lb) (¾ cup) walnuts, chopped
150 ml (¼ pint) (⅝ cup) dry white
   vermouth
150 ml (¼ pint) (⅝ cup) water
1 chicken stock cube
100 g (¼ lb) (1 cup) grated cheese

1 Preheat the oven to 200°C, 400°F, gas 6.

2 Clean the fish and cut either into small pieces across the bone or into steaks. Season with salt and pepper and dredge with flour.

3 Heat the oil in a frying pan (skillet) and brown the fish for 5 minutes on each side. Place the fish pieces in a shallow, ovenproof dish.

4 In the same frying pan (skillet) sauté the celery, carrots, onions and mushrooms for 4

minutes. Pour the sautéed vegetables over the fish pieces and sprinkle with the walnuts. Add the vermouth and water and crumble in the stock cube.

5 Bake in the oven for 30 minutes. Remove and sprinkle with the grated cheese. Place under a hot grill (broiler) until brown and bubbling and serve immediately.

Serves 4

Carp in Mandarin Sauce

1 kg (2 lb) carp or any white fish
1 green pepper, deseeded and cut
   into strips
1 red pepper, deseeded and cut
   into strips
500 ml (1 pint) (2½ cups) court
   bouillon (see page 363)
1 small can mandarin oranges
dash Tabasco sauce
15 g (½ oz) (1 tablespoon) tomato
   concentrate (paste)
50 g (2 oz) (¼ cup) sugar
salt and pepper
15 g (½ oz) (1½ tablespoons)
   cornflour (cornstarch)
75 ml (3 fl oz) (⅜ cup) single (light)
   cream
5 ml (1 teaspoon) horseradish
   cream
4 sprigs watercress

1 Preheat the oven to 200°C, 400°F, gas 6.

2 Clean, wash and fillet the carp.

3 Place the fish fillets in a shallow, ovenproof dish. Cover with the pepper strips and pour in the court bouillon.

4 Open the can of mandarin oranges, strain off the juice into a bowl, retaining the segments (sections) for decoration, and blend in the Tabasco, tomato concentrate (paste) and sugar. Season with salt and pepper. Pour over the fish and bake in the oven for 25 minutes.

5 Drain off the fish liquor, transfer the cooked fish to a clean serving dish and keep hot. Boil the liquor to reduce (evaporate) it by half.

6 Mix together the cornflour (cornstarch) and single (light)

Salmon Mousse is ideal for lunch on hot, summer days or as a mouth-watering dish for any dinner party

cream and stir into the reduced fish liquor. Add the horseradish

cream and heat through.

7 Decorate the fish with the segments (sections) of mandarin oranges and sprigs of watercress. Serve the sauce separately.

Serves 4

427

Salmon Steaks with Spinach

75 g (3 oz) (6 tablespoons) butter
2 carrots, thinly sliced
2 onions, thinly sliced
2 sticks celery, thinly sliced
4 salmon steaks

For the Court Bouillon:
1 onion, cut into quarters
1 stick celery, thinly sliced
few sprigs parsley
1 carrot, thinly sliced
½ bay leaf, imported
450 g (1 lb) fish trimmings
100 ml (4 fl oz) (½ cup) dry white
   wine
½ litre (1 pint) (2½ cups) water
salt and pepper

For the Spinach Purée:
25 g (1 oz) (2 tablespoons) butter
1 kg (2 lb) spinach leaves, washed
   and coarsely chopped
salt and pepper
pinch grated nutmeg
15 g (½ oz) (2 tablespoons) flour
30 ml (2 tablespoons) single
   (light) cream

1 To make the court bouillon, place the onion, celery, parsley, carrot, bay leaf, fish trimmings, white wine and water in a large saucepan. Season with salt and pepper and boil for 20 minutes.

2 Heat the butter in a saucepan and sauté the sliced vegetables over a low heat for 8 minutes, until soft.

3 Strain off the court bouillon. Place the salmon steaks on top of the sautéed vegetables and cover with the court bouillon. Simmer for 15 minutes.

4 Make the spinach purée: heat the butter in a sauté pan and sweat the spinach for 10 minutes over a low heat. Season with salt, pepper and nutmeg.

5 Sprinkle with the flour and stir in the cream. Simmer for several minutes.

6 Remove the skin and bones from the salmon steaks and arrange on a large serving dish. Heap the spinach purée on one side of the dish, and the sautéed vegetables on the other. Garnish the salmon steaks with thin strips of carrot and lemon slices. Serve with a hollandaise or shrimp sauce.

Serves 4

Tips: Fish trimmings may be bought from a fishmonger. Alternatively, buy 450 g (1 lb) of a cheap white fish such as whiting.

Sorrel makes an excellent substitute for spinach.

Crayfish Bordelaise

36 crayfish
2 carrots, diced
2 onions, chopped
4 shallots, chopped
juice ½ lemon
100 g (¼ lb) (½ cup) butter
sprig of thyme
½ bay leaf, imported
bouquet garni
150 g (6 oz) (1½ cups) mushrooms,
   chopped
salt and pepper
pinch cayenne pepper
pinch paprika
45 ml (3 tablespoons) brandy
150 ml (¼ pint) (⅝ cup) dry, white
   wine
300 ml (½ pint) (1¼ cups) water
1 chicken stock cube
25 g (1 oz) (3 tablespoons)
   cornflour (cornstarch)
225 ml (8 fl oz) (1 cup) single
   (light) cream
20 g (¾ oz) (1½ tablespoons)
   tomato concentrate (paste)
5 g (1 tablespoon) parsley,
   chopped

1 Clean and gut the crayfish. Gently twist and pull out the fin from under the tail.

2 Sprinkle the chopped carrots, onions and shallots with lemon juice.

3 Heat 50 g (2 oz) (¼ cup) butter in a sauté pan. Add the chopped vegetables, thyme and bay leaf and cook over a low heat (with the lid on).

4 Meanwhile, heat the remaining butter and sauté the chopped mushrooms.

5 Add the crayfish to the sautéed vegetables and season with salt and pepper, cayenne pepper and paprika. Sauté briskly over a high heat, stirring frequently, until the crayfish have turned red all over.

6 Add the brandy, sautéed mushrooms, wine and water. Crumble in the stock cube and cook for 15 minutes over a moderate heat. Then drain the crayfish, arrange in a deep serving dish and keep hot.

7 Boil the sauce to reduce (evaporate) it by half. Blend the cornflour (cornstarch) with a little cream and stir into the reduced sauce. Add the remainder of the cream and the tomato concentrate (paste). Boil for a few minutes, over a high heat. Correct the seasoning.

8 Pour the sauce over the crayfish, sprinkle with chopped parsley and serve.

Serves 6

Tips: All crustaceans such as lobster, crawfish and large prawns can be cooked in a similar manner. It is the shell – not the flesh – which gives the sauce its distinctive flavour. The sauce can be made into a bisque, a kind of shellfish soup, by mixing it with béchamel or velouté sauce and adding lobster meat or prawns and so on. Crayfish Bordelaise may be served as an appetizer or as a main dish. The usual accompaniment is boiled rice.

Salmon Steaks with Spinach are garnished with spinach purée and sautéed vegetables and served with a hollandaise sauce

Fish Dumplings

Forcemeats are usually made from minced (ground) cheap white fish, such as whiting or coley, and combined with breadcrumbs or a thick white sauce, egg yolks and seasonings. Shellfish can also be used but if you want to economize, mix it with a cheaper fish. Use the forcemeat for stuffing whole fish or paupiettes or shape into dumplings, cover with fish stock and poach for 10 minutes. Serve the dumplings hot as a garnish for fish dishes or cold as an hors d'oeuvre.

Basic Fish Forcemeat

450 g (1 lb) minced (ground) white fish
150 ml (¼ pint) (⅝ cup) thick white sauce
50 g (2 oz) (4 tablespoons) butter, softened
salt and pepper
pinch grated nutmeg
2 eggs, beaten
juice ½ lemon

1 Pound the minced (ground) fish to a paste with a rolling pin or liquidize.

2 Add the thick white sauce and butter and blend well. Season with salt and pepper and nutmeg.

3 Beat in the eggs and then add the lemon juice.

4 Use as a stuffing for fish or shape into dumplings and poach.

Serves 4

Tip: Serve the dumplings with a sauce. Wine or shellfish flavoured sauces such as shrimp, prawn or lobster sauces are delicious. Dumplings are an ideal way of using up left-over fish, or making a little fish go a long way. Any fish can be used.

Quenelles

450 g (1 lb) raw fish
50 g (2 oz) (4 tablespoons) butter or margarine
100 g (¼ lb) (1 cup + 2 tablespoons) flour
100 ml (4 fl oz) (½ cup) water
salt and pepper
pinch grated nutmeg
2 egg whites
300 ml (½ pint) (1¼ cups) double (heavy) cream
300 ml (½ pint) (1¼ cups) fish stock
5 g (1 tablespoon) chopped parsley

1 Skin and bone the fish and mince (grind) the fish flesh twice.

2 Melt the fat in a pan, add the flour and cook the mixture for 3 minutes, stirring continuously. Add the water and mix well to form a stiff paste. Leave to cool.

3 Add the minced (ground) fish to the paste and either pound with a rolling pin or liquidize.

4 Season with salt and pepper and grated nutmeg and mix in the egg whites. Chill the mixture thoroughly by placing in the refrigerator or freezer.

5 When the mixture is icy cold, blend in the cream and shape the mixture into quenelles. Take a spoonful at a time, about 25 g (1 oz), and, using two spoons, shape the mixture until it is oval.

6 Place the quenelles in a large, greased pan or baking dish. Cover with the fish stock – the quenelles should be totally immersed.

7 Bring the stock to the boil, and then simmer on top of the stove for 10 minutes until the quenelles are cooked.

8 Place the quenelles in a shallow serving dish and cover with Nantua sauce (see page 374). Sprinkle with chopped parsley and serve with boiled rice or duchesse potatoes.

Serves 6

Mushroom Fish Stuffing

225 g (½ lb) minced (ground) white fish, eg whiting, haddock
4 soft herring roes
75 g (3 oz) (1½ cups) fresh breadcrumbs
75 ml (3 fl oz) (⅜ cup) milk
50 g (2 oz) (4 tablespoons) butter
50 g (2 oz) (¼ cup) shallots, chopped
75 ml (3 fl oz) (⅜ cup) dry white wine
150 g (5 oz) (1¼ cups) mushrooms, chopped
5 g (1 tablespoon) chopped parsley
salt and pepper
2 eggs, beaten
juice ½ lemon

1 Blend the minced (ground) fish with the soft herring roes, breadcrumbs and milk. Mince (grind) again or place in a blender and liquidize.

2 Melt the butter in a pan and sweat the shallots for 2 minutes with the lid on. Add the wine and chopped mushrooms, and boil for 3 minutes.

3 Pour onto the fish mixture and stir in the chopped parsley and salt and pepper. Blend well and gradually add the eggs and lemon juice until all the moisture has been absorbed by the breadcrumbs and fish. If the mixture is too moist, add more crumbs – it should be of a firm, but moist consistency.

4 Use as a stuffing for fish or poach as dumplings.

Serves 4

Tip: Use this mushroom fish stuffing in savoury, stuffed pancakes. Make the pancakes and roll up the stuffing inside. Cover with a cheesey Mornay sauce, sprinkle with grated cheese and place under a hot grill (broiler) until the pancakes are bubbling and golden-brown.

Quenelles are delicious fish dumplings, usually served in a Nantua sauce with plain, boiled rice

Salmon Loaf

1½ litres (2½ pints) (6¼ cups) water
pinch salt
100 g (¼ lb) (½ cup) long grain rice
225 g (½ lb) canned salmon,
  drained
1 red pepper, deseeded and
  chopped
10 stoned (pitted) green olives
4 hard-boiled (hard-cooked)
  eggs, chopped
50 ml (2 fl oz) (¼ cup) mayonnaise
5 ml (1 teaspoon) tomato
  concentrate (paste)
juice ½ lemon
50 g (2 oz) (4 tablespoons) butter,
  softened
1 small lettuce, washed and
  dried
small pinch parsley

1 Boil the water in a saucepan and add the salt and rice. Cook for about 20-25 minutes, drain and cool.

2 Flake the salmon with a fork. Add the chopped red pepper and olives, rice and hard-boiled (hard-cooked) eggs.

3 Blend the mayonnaise with the tomato concentrate (paste) and lemon juice, and stir in the salmon mixture.

4 Grease inside an oblong mould (or cake tin) with the butter. Pour in the salmon mixture, pressing it well down. Chill in the refrigerator for 2 hours.

5 Cover a serving dish with the lettuce leaves and turn out the salmon loaf onto them. Decorate with parsley and serve immediately.

Serves 4

Salmon Pastry Envelopes

225g (½lb) (2 cups) mushrooms,
  chopped
juice ½ lemon
450g (1lb) canned salmon
50g (2oz) (4 tablespoons) butter

6 shallots or onions, peeled and
  chopped
25g (1oz) (4 tablespoons) flour
100ml (4fl oz) (½ cup) single
  (light) cream
2 eggs, beaten
4 sprigs parsley, chopped
450g (1lb) puff pastry, frozen and
  thawed

1 Preheat the oven to 180°C, 350°F, gas 4.

2 Place the chopped mushrooms in a small bowl and pour over the lemon juice.

3 Drain the salmon and put aside the fish juice in a small bowl. Remove the bones and pound the flesh finely with a rolling pin or pestle.

4 Heat the butter in a frying pan (skillet). Add the shallots or onions and the mushrooms which have been soaked in lemon juice. Sauté for 3 minutes, then add the salmon, stirring briskly over high heat.

5 Stir in the flour and cook for 3 minutes, then add the salmon juice and cream, stirring all the time. Stir in 1 beaten egg and the chopped parsley when the sauce has thickened, and remove from the heat.

6 Roll out the puff pastry, 4mm (⅛in) thick, and cut into rectangles 7cm (3in) across by 10cm (4in) long.

7 Place some of the salmon filling on the middle of each rectangle and moisten the pastry edges. Fold over and pinch together to seal the parcels. Brush with beaten egg.

8 Place the parcels on a greased baking (cookie) sheet and bake for 15-20 minutes. Serve hot or cold.

Serves 6

Coulibiac

Coulibiac is a traditional, hot, Russian fish pie usually made with salmon, although turbot is an acceptable substitute. It is served with sour cream.

50 g (2 oz) (4 tablespoons) butter
1 medium onion, chopped
225 g (½ lb) (1 cup) long grain rice
1 litre (1¾ pints) (4¼ cups) water
1 chicken stock cube
900 g (2 lb) puff pastry, frozen and
  thawed
225 g (½ lb) canned salmon, flaked
juice 1 lemon
100 g (¼ lb) (1¼ cups) mushrooms,
  sliced
salt and pepper
2 hard-boiled (hard-cooked)
  eggs, sliced
1 egg, beaten

1 Preheat the oven to 200°C, 400°F, gas 6.

2 Heat the butter in a saucepan and sauté the onion until soft. Add the rice and simmer for 3 minutes until transparent. Add the water and crumble in the stock cube. Bring to the boil, then simmer for 20 minutes, until the rice is cooked.

3 Roll out the pastry into an oblong shape on a floured board until it is 4 mm (⅛ in) thick. Place a layer of the cooked rice in the centre, then a layer of salmon. Pour over the lemon juice and top with the sliced mushrooms. Season with salt and pepper. Cover with more rice and arrange the slices of hard-boiled (hard-cooked) eggs along the top.

4 Wrap the pastry over so that it resembles a bread loaf and place on a greased baking (cookie) sheet. Brush the top with beaten egg and make a decorative pattern with a fork.

5 Bake in the oven for 30 minutes. Serve with a dish of sour cream or shrimp sauce.

Serves 6

Tips: Coulibiac can be served with a sour cream sauce – *smitana*. To make this, just boil up a few shallots in a cup of white wine, stir in some sour cream and season with salt and pepper. Another way to make Coulibiac is to use Danish yeast pastry instead of puff pastry.

All about Joints of Lamb
Roast Shoulder of Lamb

Lamb used to be referred to as 'spring lamb' when it was only home-produced. However, the advent of refrigeration meant that it could be shipped around the world and eaten at all times of the year. Lamb is only called 'lamb' from five months to a year and a half, after that it is referred to as mutton.

Choosing Lamb

You should always look carefully at the colour and texture of the meat when buying lamb. Good quality lamb is light pink and lean with firm fat – the younger the animal, the paler the meat. In an older animal it may be light red. The colour of the fat varies too. Freshly killed young lamb, available in the spring and early summer, has a creamy fat, while the fat of imported lamb is firm and white.

Cuts of Lamb

The cuts of lamb, unlike beef, are international and thus the same throughout the world. Lamb is easy to cook as it has a distinctive flavour and natural fat. Thus most cuts are tender and not tough. In England, the United States and Australia, most people prefer their lamb well cooked. However, in France and Europe it is usually eaten slightly underdone and still pink in the centre. Lamb is very versatile and most cuts can be cooked by both dry and moist cooking methods. In this issue we concentrate on the joints of lamb. These are traditionally roasted but they can also be boiled and pot-roasted.

Loin: This is a prime cut which is usually roasted, either on the bone or boned, stuffed and rolled. The loin is also cut up and served as chops. Other cooking methods for loin are pot-roasting and braising. When cooking loin, you should allow 350 g (¾ lb) per person on the bone, and 100-175 g (4-6 oz) off the bone.

Leg: This is another joint which is usually roasted, braised or pot-roasted. It is often boned and stuffed but the meat can also be cut off the bone and used in stews and casseroles, pies and kebabs. If you intend to roast a leg joint,

always allow 350 g (¾ lb) meat on the bone per person.

Shoulder: This is a large joint which is often more flavoursome than the leg. It is also inclined to be more fatty. Shoulder can be stuffed with various exciting stuffings and roasted. Allow 350 g (¾ lb) on the bone per person.

Breast of Lamb: This is a cheap and rather fatty cut which is often boned, stuffed and rolled. It is then roasted or braised, stewed or boiled. You should allow 225-350 g (8-12 oz) per person, on the bone.

Best End of Neck: This is inexpensive and probably the most versatile joint of all. It is the cut next to the loin and can be roasted, stewed or braised. Allow 350 g (¾ lb) per person.

Chops: These are cut from the loin; the ones nearest to the leg are known as the chump chops. They are usually grilled (broiled) or fried but they are also often used in casseroles. Allow 1-2 chops per person.

Cutlets: These come from the best end and can be grilled (broiled) or fried. They have little lean meat and a longish bone. Allow 1-2 per person.

Neck, Middle and Scrag End: These are all cheap cuts which are suitable for stews and casseroles. They have little meat and a high proportion of fat and bone. Allow 225-350 g (8-12 oz) meat on the bone per person.

Sauces and Stuffings

Roast lamb is traditionally served with mint sauce or jelly, redcurrant jelly, Cumberland or onion sauce. Lamb is delicious when stuffed. Be adventurous and try some new fruity stuffings, made with apricots, prunes, apples and dried fruit. Rice can be used for stuffing lamb – try mixing it with herbs and nuts for a change from the usual thyme and parsley or sage and onion.

Crown Roast of Lamb

This is a very special and well-known lamb dish which always looks impressive at dinner parties. Most butchers will prepare a

crown roast for you if you give them a couple of days' warning. It consists of two pieces of best end which are usually taken from opposite sides of the animal. It is served stuffed in the centre and the bones are decorated with cutlet frills.

Roasting Lamb

Lamb joints are usually roasted. Always roast with the thickest layer of fat on top so that the joint will be automatically basted during cooking. You can try dusting the basted skin of the lamb with seasoned flour. This will absorb excess fat and make the top crisp and golden.

Herbs and Lamb

Herbs go very well with lamb and you should try roasting or casseroling it with different herbs and combinations. Thyme, oregano, marjoram, basil, savory, rosemary, parsley and mint all enhance its flavour. Garlic is also a good flavouring – try rubbing your joint with it, or inserting a clove into the meat itself. Do not overdo the flavouring as lamb has a rather delicate flavour and you may disguise it altogether. Herbs should only be used to complement it.

Storing Lamb

The cheapest way to buy lamb, of course, is to buy in bulk and store it in your freezer. However, if you cannot afford to do this, uncooked meat should keep in the refrigerator for 3-4 days. It will keep best if placed immediately below the freezing compartment. Do not store the lamb in its wrapping paper. Instead, put it on a plate and cover with some thin polythene – leave the ends open for ventilation. Always wrap cooked lamb before placing in a refrigerator, otherwise it will dry out. If you do not have a refrigerator, store the meat in a very cool place and wrap it well to protect it from flies.

Two examples of the varied dishes which can be made from lamb joints: a stuffed roast leg, and cutlets from the best end served with caper sauce

434

Leg of Lamb

Traditionally served, a roast leg of lamb with roast potatoes, peas, mint sauce, redcurrant jelly, or cranberry sauce, is very popular.

We also realise that you may want to know of other unusual ways of cooking a leg of lamb and so we offer you many different and interesting recipes. We show you how to add a delicate flavour by inserting slivers of garlic into cuts in the flesh. In another recipe we explain how to lard a leg of lamb with bacon strips to give a gamey venison flavour. Lamb can be marinated and spread with a sauce made with sour cream before cooking as a change. Or it can be served, Spanish-style, with tomatoes and olives and flavoured with rosemary.

You will know when a leg of lamb is cooked because the juice will run clear if the meat is pierced with a sharp knife. If you use a meat thermometer, the internal temperature of the meat (not near a bone) should read 87°C, 180°F.

To calculate cooking times, allow 20 minutes per 450 g (1lb), and 20 minutes over for a joint on the bone. Allow 25 minutes if the joint is boned, and 30 minutes if the joint is boned and stuffed and make sure you add the weight of the stuffing to the weight of the joint. When you buy a leg of lamb, allow 350 g (¾lb) for each person for meat on the bone, and 100 g-175 g (4-6 oz) if the joint has been boned.

Pot Roast Lamb

salt and pepper
2 kg (4 lb) leg of lamb, boned, rolled and tied
2 cloves garlic
50 g (2 oz) (4 tablespoons) butter
30 ml (2 tablespoons) oil

3 carrots, sliced
3 onions, sliced
3 leeks, sliced
450 ml (16 fl oz) (2 cups) beef stock
450 g (1 lb) (2 cups) cooked flageolet or lima beans
350 ml (12 fl oz) (1½ cups) water
7 ml (½ tablespoon) cornflour (cornstarch)

1 Season the leg of lamb and insert slices of garlic into cuts in the flesh.

2 Heat 25 g (1oz) (2 tablespoons) butter and the oil in a casserole, and brown the lamb all over for 8 minutes. Remove. Brown the carrots, onions and leeks in the same fat for 5 minutes. Pour off the fat. Return the lamb to the casserole. Add the stock and bring to the boil, and simmer for 2 hours.

3 Reheat the beans in the rest of the butter and season with salt and pepper. Keep warm.

4 When the meat is cooked, remove from the casserole and keep warm. Pour off the fat, add 300 ml (½ pint) (1¼ cups) of the water and boil for 5 minutes. Thicken with the cornflour (cornstarch) mixed with the rest of the water. Boil for 5 minutes, strain and season.

5 To serve, slice the meat and arrange on a dish, surrounded by the beans. Serve the sauce separately.

Serves 8

Roast Lamb with Lemon Sauce

1½ kg (3 lb) leg of lamb
2 cloves garlic, sliced
salt and pepper
50 ml (2 fl oz) (¼ cup) oil
50 g (2 oz) (4 tablespoons) butter
2 carrots, sliced
2 sticks celery, sliced
1 onion, chopped
2 lemons

275 ml (9 fl oz) (1⅛ cup) water
100 g (¼ lb) (½ cup) sugar
15 ml (1 tablespoon) vinegar
7 ml (½ tablespoon) cornflour (cornstarch)

1 When buying the leg of lamb, ask the butcher to cut out the aitchbone (pelvic bone) and to trim the knuckle.

2 Preheat the oven to 200°C, 400°F, gas 6.

3 Make cuts in the flesh and insert the slices of garlic. Season the leg, smother with the oil and butter and place in a roasting tin on a bed of carrots, celery, onion, 1 sliced lemon and the aitchbone.

4 Roast for 1¼ hours (allowing 20 minutes per 450 g (1lb) and 20 minutes over) basting from time to time. When cooked, rest the meat for 15 minutes, then remove and place on a clean dish and keep warm.

5 Make the gravy. During the roasting time, cut the other lemon into segments, and simmer for 8 minutes in 225 ml (8 fl oz) (1 cup) of the water with the sugar and vinegar.

6 When the joint has been removed, put the roasting tin on top of the stove over a gentle heat for 2 minutes to allow the sediment to settle. Carefully pour off the fat, leaving the sediment and juices. Cook for 3 minutes until brown, then add 300 ml (½ pint) (1¼ cups) of lemon liquid (add water if necessary to make up the amount). Stir and scrape the tin to loosen the browned sediment, and cook for 8 minutes. Thicken with the cornflour (cornstarch) mixed with 45 ml (3 tablespoons) of the water. Cook for 5 minutes to clear. Strain.

7 To serve, decorate the leg of lamb with a frill round the bone, and pour a little sauce over it. Arrange the lemon segments on top. Serve the rest of the sauce separately. Serve with boiled rice, sprinkled with chopped parsley.

Serves 6

An unusual and different way of serving roast leg of lamb is on a bed of beans

Braised Lamb in Wine

4 cloves garlic
2 kg (4 lb) leg of lamb
100 ml (4 fl oz) (½ cup) oil
2 onions, chopped
2 carrots, diced
100 ml (4 fl oz) (½ cup) white wine
1 litre (1¾ pints) (4½ cups) stock
bouquet garni
salt and pepper

1 Preheat the oven to 200°C, 400°F, gas 6.

2 Cut each clove of garlic into four and insert each into a gash cut in the leg of lamb.

3 Heat the oil in a frying pan (skillet) and brown the lamb on all sides for 8 minutes. Remove and place in a casserole.

4 Brown the onions and carrots and add to the lamb.

5 Pour the white wine and stock into the casserole. Add the bouquet garni, salt and plenty of pepper and bring to the boil. Cover and put in the oven for 2 hours.

6 When the meat is cooked, remove from the casserole and keep warm. Strain the liquid from the casserole into a saucepan. Remove the fat and boil until only 300 ml (½ pint) (1¼ cups) remains.

7 The lamb may be served sliced, with a little sauce poured over it, or whole to be carved at table.

Serves 6-8

Festive Leg

225 g (½ lb) canned pineapple rings with juice
2 kg (4 lb) leg of lamb
salt and pepper
glacé cherries for decoration

1 Preheat the oven to 200°C, 400°F, gas 6.

2 Remove the juice from the can of pineapple rings.

3 Put the lamb in a roasting tin and pour the pineapple juice over. Season with salt and pepper.

4 Roast in the preheated oven, allowing 20 minutes per 450 g (1 lb) and 20 minutes over, basting occasionally with the juice.

5 When cooked, place on a dish and garnish with halved pineapple rings with a cherry between each. Serve with roast potatoes.

Serves 6-8

Stuffed Leg of Lamb

25 g (1 oz) (2 tablespoons) currants
75 g (3 oz) (6 tablespoons) butter
1 onion, chopped
4 apples, peeled, cored and diced
175 g (6 oz) (¾ cup) long grain rice
salt and pepper
2 kg (4 lb) leg of lamb, boned
100 ml (4 fl oz) (½ cup) oil
100 ml (4 fl oz) (½ cup) stock
juice 1 lemon

1 Preheat the oven to 200°C, 400°F, gas 6.

2 Soak the currants in water.

3 Heat the butter in a frying pan (skillet). Fry the onion gently, add the apples and cook until all the liquid evaporates.

4 Boil the rice for 10 minutes.

5 Mix the onion and apples with the drained currants and the rice. Season with salt and pepper. Stuff the leg with the mixture and sew up the opening. Season and brush with oil.

6 Roast for 2¼ hours in all, 35 minutes at 200°C, 400°F, gas 6 and for 1 hour 40 minutes with the temperature reduced to 180°C, 350°F, gas 4.

7 When the leg is cooked, remove from the pan and put on a serving dish. Make a gravy with the juices in the pan and the stock and flavour with lemon juice.

Serves 6-8

Normandy Lamb

1 clove garlic
2 kg (4 lb) leg of lamb
salt and pepper
5 ml (1 teaspoon) thyme
75 g (3 oz) (6 tablespoons) butter
225 ml (8 fl oz) (1 cup) cider
5 ml (1 teaspoon) flour
50 ml (2 fl oz) (¼ cup) calvados, (apple brandy) or brandy
150 ml (5 fl oz) (⅔ cup) single (light) cream

1 Preheat the oven to 200°C, 400°F, gas 6.

2 Insert the clove of garlic, peeled, into the knuckle end of the leg of lamb with the point of a knife. Salt and pepper the meat generously and sprinkle with thyme. Rub in well so that the flavours sink into the meat.

3 Heat the butter, reserving 5 ml (1 teaspoon), in a casserole. Add the lamb and brown all over for 8 minutes. Cover and cook, allowing 20 minutes per 450 g (1 lb) and 20 minutes over, basting with half of the cider from time to time.

4 Blend the 5 ml (1 teaspoon) flour with the 5 ml (1 teaspoon) butter for a "beurre manié" to thicken the gravy later on.

5 When the lamb is cooked, pour on the calvados (apple brandy) or brandy and flame. Then place the meat on a serving dish and keep warm.

6 Pour the remainder of the cider into the pan. Boil for 2 minutes, scraping the casserole to loosen the browned sediment.

7 Add the cream and stir for 1 minute, then add the "beurre manié" and cook gently until it thickens.

8 Serve the sauce separately with the lamb.

Serves 6-8

Stuffed Leg of Lamb. The stuffing is a tasty mixture of raisins, apple and onion

Glazed Lamb with Sherry Sauce

1.75 kg (3½ lb) boned leg of
  lamb
150 g (5 oz) streaky bacon,
  chopped or minced
50 g (2 oz) (1 cup) breadcrumbs
1 egg, beaten
salt and pepper
pinch dried thyme and rosemary
300 ml (½ pint) (1¼ cups) dry sherry
300 ml (½ pint) (1¼ cups) water
3 carrots, cleaned and chopped
2 sticks celery, chopped
few sprigs each fresh parsley
  and tarragon
1 clove garlic, crushed
30 ml (2 tablespoons) oil
50 g (2 oz) (4 tablespoons) butter
150 ml (¼ pint) (⅔ cup) sour cream
15 ml (1 tablespoon) made
  mustard
1 egg yolk
5 ml (1 teaspoon) chopped fresh
  parsley

1 Ask the butcher to bone the leg of lamb for you. Mix the bacon, breadcrumbs, egg, seasoning and herbs to a paste and use it to stuff the leg. Tie the meat into shape with fine string and marinate it for 5 hours or overnight in the sherry, water, vegetables, fresh herbs and garlic, turning it from time to time to soak all sides.

2 Preheat the oven to 200°C, 400°F, gas 6. Drain the joint from the marinade and dry it. Brush it with the oil and butter, season with a pinch of salt and pepper, and roast for 35 minutes.

3 Meanwhile drain the vegetables from the marinade, reserving both. Place the vegetables under the joint and continue to roast for 15 minutes.

4 Reduce the oven temperature to 180°C, 350°F, gas 4. Pour the marinade around the joint, cover and cook for 1 hour.

5 Mix the sour cream, mustard, egg yolk and parsley. Remove the meat from the oven and pour the vegetables and cooking liquid into a pan. Turn the oven up to 220°C, 425°F, gas 7. Spread the sour cream mixture over the joint and return to the oven for 10 minutes until it is golden-brown.

6 Meanwhile boil the marinade to reduce (evaporate) it to a thicker consistency. Strain the vegetables out and pour the sauce into a sauce-boat. Serve the meat on a heated dish with the sauce.

Serves 8

Leg of Lamb Minorca

1.75 kg (3½ lb) leg of lamb
2 cloves garlic
salt and pepper
2 sprigs fresh rosemary
2 onions, chopped
3 carrots, quartered
30 ml (2 tablespoons) oil
75 g (3 oz) (6 tablespoons) butter
300 ml (½ pint) (1¼ cups) rosé wine
25 g (1 oz) (2 tablespoons) tomato
  concentrate (paste)
100 g (¼ lb) (1 cup) sliced button
  mushrooms
12 stuffed green olives
15 g (½ oz) (1½ tablespoons)
  cornflour (cornstarch)
45 ml (3 tablespoons) water
12 small tomatoes

1 Remove the aitchbone (pelvic bone) or ask the butcher to do it for you, and keep it. Cut the garlic into slivers and insert them into slits on the surface of the meat. Season with salt and pepper, and rosemary sprigs.

2 Preheat the oven to 190°C, 375°F, gas 5. Place the onions and carrots in a roasting pan with the bone. Brush the joint with oil and 50 g (2 oz) (4 tablespoons) of the butter and set it on the vegetables. Roast for 45 minutes.

3 Add the wine and tomato concentrate (paste), cover and continue to cook for 45 minutes.

4 Remove the meat from the roasting pan and keep it warm. Take the bone and carrots from the liquid. Boil the liquid to reduce (evaporate) it.

5 Fry the mushrooms in the rest of the butter for 5 minutes. Add to the sauce with the green olives. Thicken the sauce with the cornflour (cornstarch) dissolved in the water.

6 Grill (broil) the tomatoes for 5 minutes. Arrange them around the joint on a serving dish. Impale 2 tomatoes on a kebab skewer with a few stuffed olives and stick it into the meat to decorate. Pour the sauce over the joint and serve.

Serves 6-8

Lamb Espagnola

2 kg (4 lb) leg or shoulder of lamb
2 cloves garlic, crushed
5 ml (1 teaspoon) mixed dried
  herbs
few sprigs fresh rosemary
60 ml (4 tablespoons) sherry
60 ml (4 tablespoons) water
12 small onions or shallots,
  peeled
6 stuffed green olives, sliced

1 Place the lamb in a roasting pan. Spread the crushed garlic and dried herbs evenly over the surface and arrange rosemary sprigs on top and underneath. Pour the sherry over the meat and leave it to stand for 3 hours.

2 Preheat the oven to 190°C, 375°F, gas 5. Add the water to the roasting pan and arrange the peeled, whole onions around the joint. Roast in the oven for 20 minutes per 450 g (1 lb) and 20 minutes more, basting from time to time.

3 Set the lamb on a heated serving dish and arrange the onions around it. Stir the sliced olives into the cooking juices and pour the liquid over the joint.

Serves 6-8

*Leg of Lamb Minorca. The
joint is covered
with a sauce of mushrooms
and olives*

Shoulder of Lamb

Shoulder of lamb is a popular cut which has a higher proportion of fat than the leg but greater flavour. The joint is sold both on the bone and with the bones removed, ready for stuffing.

Shoulder of lamb can be used in four main ways: cut into blade-bone chops which can be grilled (broiled) or braised; as a stuffed joint to be roasted or braised; cut into cubes for stews, curries or blanquettes; and minced to make meatballs, burgers or sausages which can be grilled (broiled), fried or baked.

For the traditional roast joint, allow 350 g (¾ lb) weight on the bone per person and a cooking time of 20 minutes per 450 g (1 lb) plus an extra 20 minutes. Spread the meat with a little butter and oil and season with salt and pepper. Roast at 200°C, 400°F, gas 6 for the first 30 minutes, then reduce the temperature to 180°C, 350°F, gas 4 for the rest of the cooking time.

Lamburgers Capucine

725 g (1½ lb) (3 cups) minced raw
  shoulder of lamb
1 onion, chopped
1 egg
salt and pepper
50 g (2 oz) (1 cup) breadcrumbs
25 g (1 oz) (¼ cup) flour
4 slices (rashers) bacon, scalded
50 g (2 oz) (4 tablespoons) butter
50 ml (2 fl oz) (¼ cup) oil
100 g (¼ lb) (1 cup) sliced
  mushrooms
1 green pepper, sliced

1 Combine the meat, onion, egg, seasoning, breadcrumbs, and flour and shape into 4 burgers. Wrap each with a rasher (slice) of

bacon and secure with kitchen thread.

2 Heat the butter and oil in a pan, add the lamburgers, cover with a lid and cook for 8-10 minutes, turning from time to time until golden-brown and cooked through.

3 Lift from the pan, remove the thread and place on a warmed serving plate. Fry the mushrooms and pepper in the same pan for 4 minutes and use to garnish the lamburgers.

Serves 4

Variation

Preheat the oven to 200°C, 400°F, gas 6. Combine the lamb, onion, eggs, seasoning, breadcrumbs and flour in the same way as for the lamburgers. Cut four thick slices from a marrow (large zucchini) and remove the seeds. Parboil the rings in salted water, drain and place in a casserole dish. Fill the rings with the lamb mixture, cover and bake in the preheated oven for 20 minutes.

Andorran Shoulder of Lamb

2 kg (4 lb) shoulder of lamb,
  bones and fat removed
25 g (1 oz) (2 tablespoons) butter
30 ml (1 fl oz) (2 tablespoons) oil
225 ml (8 fl oz) (1 cup) stock
225 ml (8 fl oz) (1 cup) dry white
  wine
100 ml (4 fl oz) (½ cup) anisette

For the Stuffing:
225 g (½ lb) sausagemeat
1 egg, beaten
15 ml (1 tablespoon) brandy
  (optional)
100 g (¼ lb) (1 cup) chopped
  mushrooms
2 sprigs thyme, finely chopped
  sprig rosemary, finely chopped
15 ml (1 tablespoon) chopped
  parsley
1 shallot, chopped
1 clove garlic, peeled and
  chopped

salt and pepper
25 g (1 oz) (2 tablespoons) butter
15 ml (1 tablespoon) oil

For the Tomato Sauce:
45 ml (3 tablespoons) oil
1 onion, chopped
700 g (1½ lb) tomatoes, skinned
  and chopped
1 clove garlic, peeled
1 chilli, deseeded and chopped
1 sugar lump
1 sprig thyme

1 To make the stuffing, mix all the ingredients, except the butter and oil, together in a bowl.

2 Heat the butter and oil in a pan, add the stuffing and cook for 7-8 minutes until golden-brown.

3 Spread the lamb flat on the work surface. Spread the stuffing over the meat, taking it to within 3 cm (1¼ in) of the edge. Roll up the meat and secure with kitchen string.

4 Heat the butter and oil in a heavy-bottomed pan and fry the meat until golden-brown all over. Pour in the stock and white wine, cover and leave to cook over a low heat for 2¼ hours.

5 Meanwhile, prepare the tomato sauce. Heat the oil in a pan add the onion, tomatoes, garlic, chilli, sugar and thyme and season with salt and pepper. Cook over a high heat until golden-brown, then reduce the heat, cover and cook over a low heat for 40 minutes.

6 Pour the sauce through a fine conical strainer, cover and return to a low heat. If the sauce becomes too thick, add a few spoonfuls of the cooking liquor from the meat.

7 When the meat is cooked, transfer it to a heated serving dish and pour the sauce into a sauceboat.

8 Just before serving, warm the anisette, sprinkle it over the meat and set it alight. Serve with rice, noodles or French beans.

Serves 6-8

*In front, Roast Shoulder of
Lamb and, behind,
Andorran Shoulder of Lamb and
Lamburgers Capucine*

Spring Lamb in Mushroom Sauce

2 kg (4 lb) shoulder of Spring
  lamb, boned
salt and pepper
pinch thyme
450 g (1 lb) (5 cups) button
  mushrooms
150 g (5 oz) ($\frac{2}{8}$ cup) butter
2 large onions, chopped
15 g ($\frac{1}{2}$ oz) (2 tablespoons) flour
30 ml (2 tablespoons) double
  (heavy) cream
50 g (2 oz) (1 cup) fresh
  breadcrumbs
30 ml (2 tablespoons) oil
225 g ($\frac{1}{2}$ lb) (2 cups) pearl
  onions
bouquet garni
150 ml ($\frac{1}{4}$ pint) ($\frac{2}{8}$ cup) stock

1 Cover the working surface
with a cloth and lay the meat out
on it, skin downwards. Open up
the meat and season the inside

Spring Lamb in Mushroom Sauce
is stuffed, rolled and
roast, then carved and served
with mushrooms and onions

with the salt and pepper and
thyme. Roll the shoulder and
put aside while preparing the
stuffing.

2 Wash, dry and chop half of the
button mushrooms. Melt 25 g
(1 oz) (2 tablespoons) butter in a
saucepan and fry the onions and
mushrooms over a low heat until
soft.

3 Remove the onions and mushrooms from the pan and liquidize
in a blender to form a purée.

4 Return the purée to the pan
and add the flour. Cook for 1
minute over a low heat, stirring all
the time. Gradually, stir in the
cream, then the breadcrumbs.
Correct the seasoning.

5 Preheat the oven to 200°C,
400°F, gas 6.

6 Unroll the shoulder of lamb,

spread with the onion and mushroom mixture, then roll it up
again and tie it with string.

7 Place the lamb on a roasting
tray and smother it with oil and
75 g (3 oz) (6 tablespoons) of the
butter. Season well and place in
the oven. After 35 minutes, reduce
the temperature to 180°C, 350°F°,
gas 4. Continue to roast gently for
another 1$\frac{1}{2}$ hours.

8 Heat the remaining butter in a
pan and fry the rest of the mushrooms and the pearl onions until
golden-brown. Add the bouquet
garni, season and pour in the
stock. Cover and cook over a low
heat for 15 minutes.

9 When the lamb is cooked,
carve it and serve on a heated
serving dish, surrounded by the
mushroom and onion garnish.

10 If you like, you can make a
gravy with the meat juices and
the stock and pour it over the
meat.

Serves 6

444

Shoulder of Lamb with Apricot Stuffing

2 kg (4 lb) shoulder of lamb, boned
salt and pepper
30 ml (2 tablespoons) oil
50 g (2 oz) (4 tablespoons) butter
150 ml (¼ pint) (⅝ cup) chicken stock
60 ml (4 tablespoons) syrup from canned apricots
15 ml (1 tablespoon) wine vinegar
15 g (½ oz) (1½ tablespoons) cornflour (cornstarch)
12 canned apricot halves

For the Apricot Stuffing:
100 g (¼ lb) (¾ cup) dried apricots
100 g (¼ lb) (½ cup) pork sausagemeat
100 g (¼ lb) (½ cup) beef sausagemeat
50 g (2 oz) (1 cup) fresh white breadcrumbs
1 egg, beaten

1 Soak the dried apricots for several hours or overnight in water. When they are soft, drain and chop finely.

2 Preheat the oven to 200°C, 400°F, gas 6. Blend the ingredients for the stuffing to make a thick smooth paste.

3 Spread the boned shoulder of lamb open, season, and cover the inside evenly with stuffing. Roll it up and tie it into shape with fine string. Place in a roasting pan and brush with oil and butter.

4 Roast the meat for 20 minutes, then lower oven heat to 180°C, 350°F, gas 4. Continue to cook for 1½ hours, basting frequently.

5 Remove the meat from the roasting pan and drain off the excess fat. Add the stock, syrup and vinegar, season, and boil for several minutes to evaporate. Thicken with the cornflour (cornstarch) dissolved in a little water.

6 Place the stuffed lamb on a serving dish or carving board and surround it with the canned apricot halves. Serve each portion with an apricot half and the sauce poured over.

Serves 8

Shoulder of Lamb is especially satisfying when stuffed with Chestnuts (on the left) or Apricots (on the right)

Shoulder of Lamb with Chestnut Stuffing

salt and pepper
2 kg (4 lb) boned shoulder of lamb
30 ml (2 tablespoons) oil
50 (2 oz) (4 tablespoons) butter
150 ml (¼ pint) (⅝ cup) stock
For the Chestnut Stuffing:
225 g (½ lb) (1 cup) sausagemeat
225 g (½ lb) (1 cup) canned chestnuts, drained and chopped
1 egg, beaten
25 g (1 oz) (¼ cup) flour
15 ml (1 tablespoon) sherry

1 Preheat oven to 200°C, 400°F, gas 6. Blend stuffing ingredients.

2 Season the lamb and spread the stuffing evenly over the inside. Roll and tie. Brush with oil and butter and roast, basting frequently, for 1¾ hours. After 20 minutes reduce the oven heat to 180°C, 350°F, gas 4.

3 Remove the meat from the pan and drain off excess fat. Add the chicken stock, season, and boil for 5 minutes to evaporate. Serve the gravy with the meat.

Serves 8

Breast of Lamb

Breast of lamb is usually considered a 'poor man's joint', being one of the cheapest cuts of lamb. There is no need for it to taste impoverished, however; carefully cooked, it is worthy of a place on any rich man's table.

Breast of lamb should be boned – the butcher will usually do this – and it is generally stuffed, rolled and roasted. Because lamb breast contains little lean meat it is best stuffed with a sausagemeat mixture, but a wide variety of flavours can be incorporated. Rich and fruity stuffings may be used. The stuffing should be spread on the inner side of the breast, or placed in a 'pocket' between the meat and inner skin layers. Season the meat well before stuffing.

Norfolk Parcel

1 kg (2 lb) boned breast of lamb,
   cut in 4 equal pieces
30 ml (2 tablespoons) oil
25 g (1 oz) (2 tablespoons) butter

For the Stuffing:
2 large onions, chopped
25 g (1 oz) (2 tablespoons) fat
150 ml ($\frac{1}{4}$ pint) ($\frac{5}{8}$ cup) chicken
   stock
225 g ($\frac{1}{2}$ lb) (1 cup) sausagemeat
100 g ($\frac{1}{4}$ lb (2 cups) fresh
   breadcrumbs
salt and pepper
15 ml (1 tablespoon) fresh sage,
   finely chopped
15 ml (1 tablespoon) chutney

1 Trim any excess fat from the meat, and beat it lightly with a rolling pin or meat mallet. Preheat the oven to 200°C, 400°F, gas 6.

2 To make the stuffing, fry the onion gently in the fat until soft but not browned. Add the stock

Norfolk Parcel makes a meaty meal. Tie it as shown at right, and roast it to juicy crispness as seen above

and boil for 5 minutes, until the liquid is well reduced (evaporated). Remove from the heat and stir in the sausagemeat, breadcrumbs, a pinch of salt and pepper, the sage and the chutney. Blend well to make a thick paste.

3 Divide the stuffing into 4 and spread it over the pieces of meat. Place the pieces of meat on top of each other to make a sandwich, and tie them together neatly with fine string. Season with salt and pepper and brush the oil and butter over the top and sides.

4 Roast the meat parcel in the oven for 20 minutes. Then turn the oven temperature down to 180°C,

350°F, gas 4 for 1½-2 hours, basting the meat frequently. Place the meat on a heated serving dish. Strain fat from the cooking juices and pour the rest over the meat. Serve.

Serves 6

Saddle of Lamb

The saddle is cut from the best end to the end of the loins and includes the chump chops and the kidneys. This large joint usually weighs about 3½ kg (7 lb). A short saddle weighs about 1-2½ kg (2-5 lbs) and is without the chump chops.

To roast, the saddle should be skinned and the kidneys removed. Any excess fat and sinews should but cut away. The flaps should be cut off, leaving about 15 cm (6 in) on each side, so that they meet in the middle. The aitchbone (pelvic bone) should be removed. The saddle may also be cooked by pot-roasting or braising.

There are two ways of carving a saddle on the bone. It may be carved lengthways, either side of the backbone, or a deep cut is made on both sides of the backbone and the whole section of meat freed from the bone. The meat is then cut in thick slices.

Waipura

1¼ kg (2½ lb) saddle of lamb, boned and skinned
7 ml (½ tablespoon) chopped parsley
1 clove garlic, crushed
salt and pepper
one 350 g (¾ lb) pork fillet
50 g (2 oz) (4 tablespoons) butter

1 Ask the butcher to bone and skin the saddle of lamb.

2 Preheat the oven to 200°C, 400°F, gas 6.

3 Sprinkle the meat with the parsley, garlic, salt and pepper, and use the pork fillet to fill the cavity left by the removal of the backbone. Roll up and tie with string.

4 Place in a roasting tin, and

smother with the butter. Roast for ½ hour, then reduce the heat to 180°C, 350°F, gas 4 for 1¼ hours (allowing 30 minutes to 450 g (1 lb) and 20 minutes over).

5 When cooked, rest for 15 minutes. Make a gravy from the juices in the pan. Serve with roast potatoes and a green salad.

Serves 6

Soubise Saddle of Lamb

1¼ kg (2½ lb) saddle of lamb
salt and pepper
50 g (2 oz) (4 tablespoons) butter
225 g (½ lb) (1 cup) onion purée
500 ml (1 pint) (2½ cups) thick white sauce
2 egg yolks
75 ml (5 tablespoons) white wine
15 g (½ oz) (1½ tablespoons) grated Parmesan cheese
slices of truffle for decoration (optional)

1 Preheat the oven to 200°C, 400°F, gas 6.

2 Place the saddle in a roasting tin. Season and spread with butter. Roast for ½ hour, then reduce the heat to 180°C, 350°F, gas 4 for 40 minutes (allowing 20 minutes for every 450 g (1 lb) and 20 minutes over).

3 Mix the purée of onions with the white sauce and egg yolks, and season.

4 Remove the loins by making a deep cut along the backbone and slipping the knife underneath. Carve them into thick slices.

5 Increase the oven temperature to 220°C, 425°F, gas 7.

6 Spread the slices of meat with half of the sauce and sandwich together to the original shape and place on the bones.

7 Dilute the remainder of the sauce with the white wine and pour over the saddle. Sprinkle with Parmesan cheese. Brown in the oven for 8 minutes until golden-brown. This can be

decorated with slices of truffle (optional).

Serves 4

Britannia Saddle of Lamb

1¼ kg (2½ lb) saddle of lamb
100 ml (4 fl oz) (½ cup) brandy
5 ml (1 teaspoon) mixed spice
75 g (3 oz) (6 tablespoons) butter
225 g (½ lb) (1 cup) minced lean pork
100 g (¼ lb) (½ cup) minced liver
150 g (5 oz) (2½ cups) white breadcrumbs
2 eggs, beaten
20 g (4 tablespoons) chopped parsley
10 g (2 tablespoons) chopped fresh mint
2 ml (1 teaspoon) rosemary
salt and pepper
350 g (¾ lb) pieces belly of pork fat
100 g (¼ lb) ox tongue, cut in strips

1 When buying the saddle of lamb, ask the butcher to bone it completely, leaving enough flap to wrap under the saddle and enclose the stuffing.

2 Remove the underfillets and marinate them with a little of the brandy and mixed spice for ½ hour. Sauté them in 25 g (1 oz) (2 tablespoons) of the butter for 5 minutes.

3 Make the stuffing by mixing the minced lean pork and liver with the breadcrumbs, eggs and chopped parsley, mint, rosemary and brandy. Season with salt and pepper.

4 Preheat the oven to 200°C, 400°F, gas 6.

5 Spread the pieces of belly of pork fat on a board and place a layer of stuffing on top, then arrange a few strips of ox tongue and the underfillets and continue until all is used. Wrap in the belly of pork fat to make a sausage shape, the same length as the saddle and about 7.5 cm (3 in) in diameter.

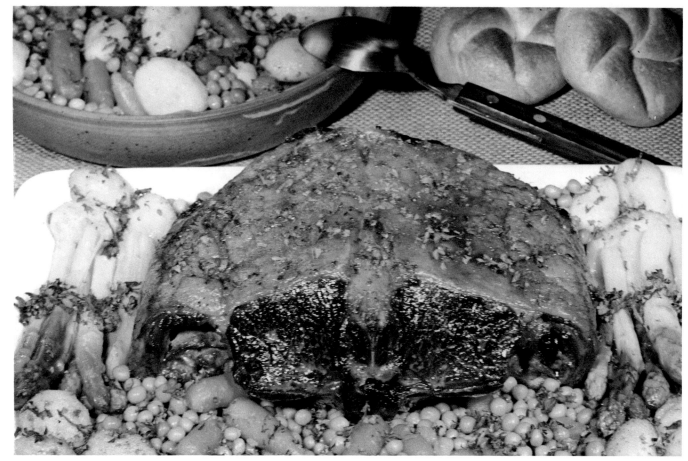

6 Turn the saddle upside down on the board, and place the filling inside. Cover with the two flaps of the saddle. Season and tie firmly with string at 2.5 cm (1 in) intervals.

7 Place the saddle in a roasting tin and smother with the rest of the butter and roast for 30 minutes, then reduce the heat to 180°C, 350°F, gas 4 for 1¼ hours (allowing 30 minutes to 450 g (1 lb) and 30 minutes over).

8 Remove the saddle, discard the string, and keep warm. Make gravy from the juices in the pan. Serve with mint jelly and redcurrant sauce.

Serves 4

Springtime Saddle of Lamb

1¼ kg (2½ lb) saddle of lamb
salt and pepper

Springtime Saddle of Lamb is a delicious combination of the best meat and the best vegetables of the season

75 g (3 oz) (6 tablespoons) butter
225 g (½ lb) French beans
12 asparagus spears
225 g (½ lb) small carrots
5 ml (1 teaspoon) sugar
3 small onions, peeled
225 g (½ lb) (2 cups) peas
450 g (1 lb) new potatoes
sprig mint
15 ml (1 tablespoon) chopped
  parsley
1 head celery
6 tomatoes

1 Preheat the oven to 200°C, 400°F, gas 6.

2 Place the saddle in a roasting pan. Season with salt and pepper and smother it with 50 g (2 oz) (4 tablespoons) of the butter. Roast for ½ hour, then reduce the heat to 180°C, 350°F, gas 4 for 40 minutes, basting from time to time.

3 Meanwhile, head and tail the French beans. Scrape the asparagus and tie in bundles.

4 Put the carrots in a saucepan with the sugar and onions, and cover with water. Boil for 15 minutes. Add the peas and cook for 8 minutes until the water has almost evaporated. Then add the remaining butter.

5 Boil the new potatoes with the mint, until cooked, and drain. Mix with the carrots and peas, season with salt and pepper and sprinkle with parsley. Keep warm.

6 Boil the asparagus in salted water for 15 minutes, drain, remove the string, and keep warm.

7 Boil the celery in salted water for 15 minutes, drain and keep warm.

8 Drop the tomatoes in boiling water for 2 minutes, then skin and warm in the oven.

9 When ready to serve, arrange the saddle on a large dish and surround with the asparagus, celery, tomatoes, new potatoes, carrots, onions, peas and French beans. Sprinkle with chopped parsley.

Serves 4

Best End of Lamb

The neck of lamb is seldom sold as a complete joint and is more usually divided into three: the scrag and middle, which are best used for stewing, and the best end which can be cooked in a number of ways but is particularly good roasted.

Two best end joints are used to make the traditional crown roast and guard of honour. The joints are chined (your butcher will do this) and the ends of the rib bones are stripped of skin and fat; the bone tips then form the points of the crown or the interlacing blades of the guard of honour.

Crown Roast of Lamb

2 best ends of lamb, chined
10 ml (2 teaspoons) butter
1 cooking (green) apple, peeled, cored and chopped
225 g (½ lb) pork sausagemeat
30 ml (2 tablespoons) fresh breadcrumbs
15 ml (1 tablespoon) chopped parsley
15 ml (1 tablespoon) finely chopped mint or 2.5 ml (½ teaspoon) mixed herbs
glacé cherries

1 Preheat the oven to 180°C, 350°F, gas 4. Trim the skin and fat from the ends of the rib bones so that 2.5 cm (1 in) of the bone protrudes. Place the two joints back to back with the bones curving upwards and outwards. Secure with kitchen thread.

2 Heat the butter in a pan and sauté the apple. Add the sausagemeat, cook for 2-3 minutes, then stir in the rest of the ingredients.

3 Place the stuffing in the cavity of the crown. Cover the tips of the bones with foil and roast in the preheated oven for 30 minutes per 450 g (1 lb) plus 30 minutes.

4 Decorate the bone ends with cutlet frills and glacé cherries and serve with roast potatoes.

Serves 6-8

Guard of Honour

2 best ends of lamb, chined
salt and pepper
few parsley sprigs

A decorative, delicious Crown Roast of Lamb makes an eye-catching centrepiece for that very special occasion

1 Preheat the oven to 180°C, 350°F, gas 4.

2 Trim the skin and fat from the ends of the rib bones so that about 7.5 cm (3 in) of bone protrudes. Stand the joints together in a roasting pan with the bone ends criss-crossing. Secure with kitchen thread.

3 Sprinkle with salt and pepper, cover the ends of the bones with foil, and bake in the preheated oven for about 1½ hours.

4 Decorate with the parsley sprigs and serve with creamed potato and peas.

Serves 6-8

Braised Stuffed Lamb

1.2 kg (2½ lb) best end, boned
50 ml (2 fl oz) (¼ cup) oil
25 g (1 oz) (2 tablespoons) butter
450 g (1 kg) small onions
350 g (¾ lb) carrots, quartered
1 beef stock cube
300 ml (½ pint) (1¼ cups) water
15 g (½ oz) (1½ tablespoons)
  cornflour (cornstarch)

Guard of Honour looks as grand and festive as its name suggests, and would honour a special dinner party

For the Stuffing:
25 g (1 oz) (2 tablespoons) butter
  or margarine
75 g (3 oz) (6 tablespoons)
  chopped onion
350 g (¾ lb) sausagemeat
5 ml (1 teaspoon) chopped
  parsley
pinch mixed herbs
pinch thyme
salt and pepper
1 egg

1 Preheat the oven to 200°C, 400°F, gas 6.

2 Prepare the stuffing: heat the fat in a pan, add the chopped onion and cook for 5 minutes. Mix in the sausagemeat, herbs and seasoning and blend well. Cover with a lid and cook for 5 minutes more. Remove from the heat and blend in the egg to make a smooth paste.

3 Spread the stuffing over the meat, roll up and secure with kitchen thread. Brush with a little oil and brown in the preheated oven for 20 minutes.

4 After this time, reduce the heat to 180°C, 350°F, gas 4 and continue cooking for one hour more, brushing with more oil if necessary.

5 Meanwhile, heat the butter in a pan and sauté the small onions until brown (about 4 minutes). Cover the onions with water and boil for 8 minutes until tender. Drain and keep hot.

6 Boil the carrots in salted water for about 20 minutes until tender. Drain and keep hot.

7 Twenty minutes before the meat has finished cooking, dissolve the beef stock cube in the water and pour it over the meat. Return the meat to the oven for the rest of the cooking time.

8 When the meat is cooked, lift it from the roasting pan, transfer to a serving dish and keep hot while preparing the gravy.

9 Place the roasting tin with the cooking juices on top of the cooker and boil for 5 minutes. Season, strain and thicken with the cornflour (cornstarch) dissolved in 90 ml (6 tablespoons) of water.

10 Surround the meat with the carrots and onions, pour over a little of the gravy and serve the rest in a sauce-boat.

Serves 6

Carving Lamb

Carving may look easy but it is more skilful than it appears. It is very important that you have a really sharp carving knife, with a 25 cm (10 in) blade. Always sharpen the knife before carving with a traditional steel or an electric knife sharpener. You may have an electric carving knife – these are really good and enable you to carve meat very thinly and thus it will go further.

Always use a carving fork with a thumb guard and, if possible, place the joint of meat on a spiked carving dish so that it does not slip. Allow the meat to stand for about 15 minutes before carving it. Carve thin, consistent slices in order to obtain the best flavour. When possible, cut the lamb against the grain. This will give you more tender slices.

When a joint is carved well, it looks more attractive and the meat goes further. Each joint needs different carving and there are no hard and fast rules. It depends on the position of the bones and the way in which the meat and fat are distributed. You will probably find that it is much easier to carve if you are standing up. Always use a long, even sawing action and keep the blade at the same angle. Do not press down on the meat too much or you will squeeze out the juices. Serve the carved meat on very warm plates.

Leg of Lamb: Carve the leg with the round side uppermost, inserting the fork near the knuckle. Make the first cut down to the bone diagonally. Cut out a thick wedge-shaped slice, then carve slices from either side of the cut. Turn the joint over and carve in long slices parallel to the leg bone.

Shoulder of Lamb: Carve the shoulder downwards towards the knuckle end. Turn over and carve downwards in long slices.

Loin of Lamb: Ask your butcher to cut through the sections of the backbone, then it can be divided into chops.

Best End of Neck of Lamb: Your butcher will chine this joint for you (saw along the backbone to release the meat from the bone). Remove the chined bone from the cooked meat and carve between the ribs.

Look'n Cook Carving Shoulder of Lamb

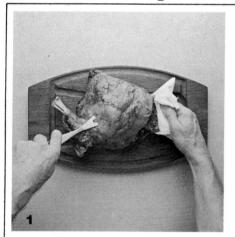
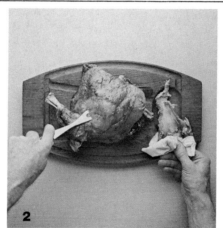
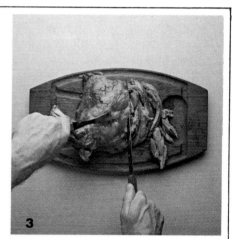

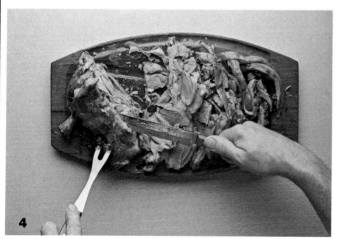
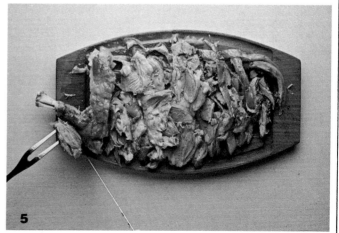

1 Using your left hand, insert the carving fork into the shoulder. With your right hand, grip the exposed blade bone **2** Twist the blade bone until free and then pull out **3** Carve downwards diagonally from one end to the other **4** Turn and slice parallel until you reach the bone at the end **5** The finished carved joint

451

Look'n Cook Carving Leg of Lamb

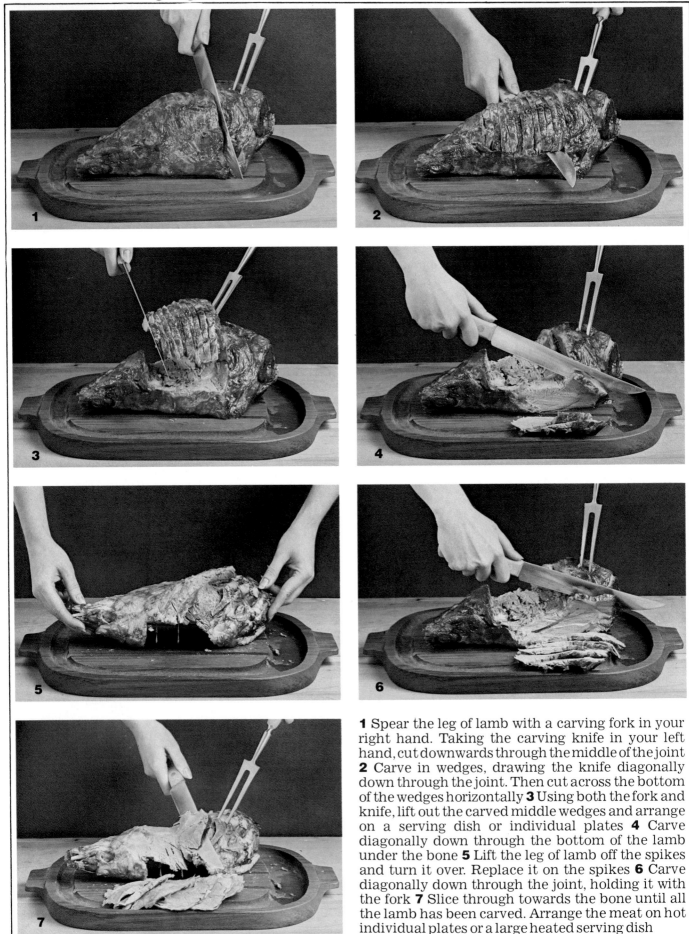

1 Spear the leg of lamb with a carving fork in your right hand. Taking the carving knife in your left hand, cut downwards through the middle of the joint **2** Carve in wedges, drawing the knife diagonally down through the joint. Then cut across the bottom of the wedges horizontally **3** Using both the fork and knife, lift out the carved middle wedges and arrange on a serving dish or individual plates **4** Carve diagonally down through the bottom of the lamb under the bone **5** Lift the leg of lamb off the spikes and turn it over. Replace it on the spikes **6** Carve diagonally down through the joint, holding it with the fork **7** Slice through towards the bone until all the lamb has been carved. Arrange the meat on hot individual plates or a large heated serving dish

Look'n Cook Carving Loin and Best End of Lamb

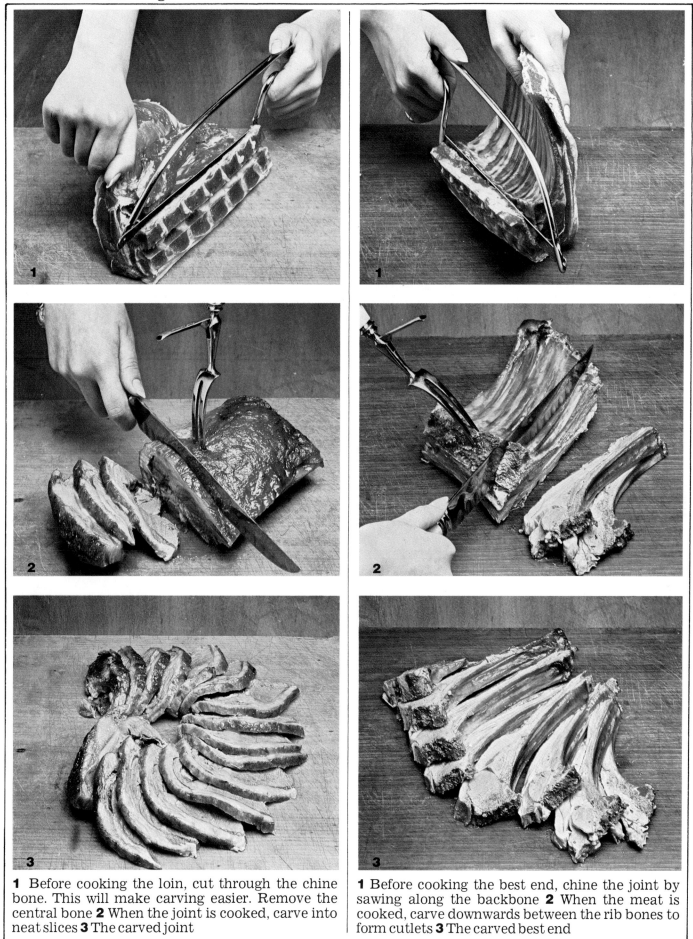

1 Before cooking the loin, cut through the chine bone. This will make carving easier. Remove the central bone **2** When the joint is cooked, carve into neat slices **3** The carved joint

1 Before cooking the best end, chine the joint by sawing along the backbone **2** When the meat is cooked, carve downwards between the rib bones to form cutlets **3** The carved best end

Loin of Lamb

The loin of a lamb is half of the saddle, cut lengthways through the spine. It is a meaty and well-flavoured cut and is hence quite expensive. It may be roasted on the bone or with the bone removed – the butcher will do this for you. When boned, with the long flap of the breast, it is sometimes stuffed and rolled, tied in shape with string and roasted. It is also used without the breast flap.

Beswick Lamb

1½ kg (3 lb) loin of lamb, boned
25 g (1 oz) (2 tablespoons) butter
30 ml (1 fl oz) (2 tablespoons) oil
450 g (1 lb) garden peas
1 sprig mint
6 spring onion (scallion) bulbs
50 ml (2 fl oz) (¼ cup) sherry
juice 1 orange

For the Stuffing:
2 slices bacon, chopped
2 lamb's kidneys, skinned, cored
  and chopped
50 g (2 oz) (4 tablespoons) butter
1 onion, finely chopped
100 g (¼ lb) (1 cup) chopped
  mushrooms
salt and pepper
5 ml (1 teaspoon) tomato
  concentrate (paste)
50 g (2 oz) (1 cup) fresh
  breadcrumbs

1 To make the stuffing, fry the chopped bacon and kidney in the butter for 3 minutes. Then stir in the onion and cook another 3 minutes. Add the mushrooms and fry 2 minutes. Season, stir in the tomato concentrate (paste) and the breadcrumbs, and stir to bind all ingredients together to a loose mixture, adding a little melted butter if necessary. Allow the stuffing to cool.

Beswick Loin of Lamb is served with peas and redcurrant jelly for a dinner party or an extra special occasion

2 Preheat the oven to 200°C, 400°F, gas 6. Spread the stuffing on the inside of the loin of lamb, roll up the meat and tie it with fine string. Place it in a roasting pan, brush with butter and oil and season. Roast it for 1-1½ hours.

3 Boil the peas in salted water with a sprig of mint and the spring onion (scallion) bulbs until tender. Drain and pile the peas on a heated serving dish.

4 When the meat is cooked, carve it into slices and arrange them on the bed of garden peas.

5 Strain off excess fat from the cooking juices. Pour the sherry and orange juice into the roasting pan and boil for 3 minutes. Season to taste. Pour the sauce into a sauce-boat and serve with the meat, peas, and some redcurrant or cranberry jelly.

Serves 8

Kebabs and Grills

Shish kebab are the Turkish words for cooked meat (kebab) on the skewer (shish). In Turkey and all over the Middle East people eat shish kebab at home, in cafés, and even from street vendors. There, lamb is the most usual meat and a shish kebab of lamb's liver and kidneys is considered the greatest delicacy. In Turkey the meat is separated by pieces of mutton fat. In England we use pieces of bacon. The fat from the bacon is needed to moisten the chunks of lean meat as they are grilled (broiled) and the kebabs need to be brushed with oil.

The meat is usually mixed with vegetables, such as onions, mushrooms, green peppers and tomatoes. If using small whole tomatoes it is wise to put them on either end of the skewer so that they receive less heat and remain firm. Fruit makes an interesting addition, and chunks of pineapple, firm apricots and pieces of peach or apple grill well.

Kebabs are always marinated in a mixture of wine, oil and vinegar with additions of garlic and herbs. Using a marinade helps to tenderize the meat as well as impart extra flavour. It is important that the cubes of meat should be the same size so that they will be cooked at the same time.

Lemon Kebabs

2 rashers (slices) streaky bacon
550 g (1¼ lb) leg of lamb, cut in 2.5 cm (1 in) cubes
4 onions, quartered
2 tomatoes, quartered
1 green pepper
8 bay leaves
8 mushrooms
50 ml (2 fl oz) (4 tablespoons) oil

Lemon Kebabs are colourful and ideal to prepare for a party or when your friends drop in unexpectedly

5 ml (1 teaspoon) cornflour (cornstarch)
45 ml (1½ fl oz) (3 tablespoons) water
225 g (½ lb) (1 cup) long grain rice, boiled
25 g (1 oz) (2 tablespoons) butter

1 Scald the bacon in boiling water for ½ minute. Drain and dry on absorbent paper. Cut into strips 2.5 cm (1 in) wide.

2 Soak the lamb cubes (which may be cut in half if preferred) and the bacon strips in the marinade for 3 hours. Drain and dry on absorbent paper.

3 Impale on skewers the lamb and bacon alternately with the onions, tomatoes, green pepper, bay leaves, and mushrooms.

4 Brush the kebabs with oil.

5 Cook under a grill (broiler) or over charcoal for 8 minutes.

6 Meanwhile, boil the marinade for 5 minutes until 300 ml (½ pint) (1¼ cups) is left. Thicken with the cornflour (cornstarch) mixed with water and cook for 2 minutes until clear. Season.

7 Serve the kebabs on a bed of plain boiled rice mixed with the butter and seasoned, with the sauce separately.

8 To serve each guest, place some rice on a plate and then arrange the meat and garnish on the rice, removing the skewer carefully.

Serves 4

Look'n Cook Mixed Grill Kebabs

1 The ingredients 2 Cut the shoulder of lamb into cubes and prepare the beef, kidneys and streaky bacon 3 Prepare the marinade and soak the meat for 3 hours. Drain and dry on absorbent paper 4 Cut the tomatoes in quarters, trim the spring onions (scallions) and cut the pepper into squares 5 Impale the ingredients on the skewers alternating the meat with the garnish 6 Brush with oil and grill (broil) over charcoal

Mixed Grill Kebabs

4 rashers (slices) of streaky bacon
4 lamb's kidneys, quartered
450 kg (1 lb) lamb shoulder, cut
  into 16 cubes
100 g ($\frac{1}{4}$ lb) rump steak, cut into
  4 cubes
12 spring onions (scallions)
1 green pepper, deseeded
4 tomatoes, quartered
15 ml (1 tablespoon) oil
5 ml (1 teaspoon) cornflour
  (cornstarch)
45 ml (1$\frac{1}{2}$ fl oz) (3 tablespoons)
  water
pinch cayenne or chilli pepper

For the Marinade:
300 ml ($\frac{1}{2}$ pint) (1$\frac{1}{4}$ cups) vermouth
30 ml (1 fl oz) (2 tablespoons) oil
15 ml (1 tablespoon) vinegar
6 crushed black peppercorns
1 bay leaf
pinch tarragon
pinch thyme

1 Scald the bacon in boiling water for $\frac{1}{2}$ minute. Drain and dry.

2 Mix the marinade.

3 Skin the kidneys and remove the core. Put the meat in the marinade for 3 hours.

4 Trim the spring onions (scallions) and cut the green pepper into squares.

5 Impale the meat on the skewers, wrapping some of the pieces of kidney in bacon, with the onions, peppers and tomatoes.

6 Brush with oil and cook under the grill (broiler) for 8 minutes.

7 Boil the marinade for 5 minutes. Thicken with the cornflour (cornstarch) and water and boil for 2 minutes. Season.

8 Serve with rice and the sauce.
Serves 4

Spanish Kebabs with Olives

2 rashers (slices) streaky bacon
2 loin chops, cut in cubes
2 tomatoes
2 mushrooms
6 olives
15 ml (1 tablespoon) oil
5 ml (1 teaspoon) cornflour
  (cornstarch)
45 ml (1$\frac{1}{2}$ fl oz) (3 tablespoons)
  water

For the Marinade:
200 ml (6 fl oz) ($\frac{3}{4}$ cup) tomato juice
90 ml (3 fl oz) ($\frac{3}{8}$ cup) dry sherry
juice 1 lemon
15 ml (1 tablespoon) oil
15 ml (1 tablespoon) vinegar
1 chilli
1 red pepper
1 onion
2 cloves garlic
pinch oregano

Spanish Kebabs with Olives are an attractive and quick meal for busy working mothers to prepare and cook

salt and pepper

1 Scald the bacon in boiling water for $\frac{1}{2}$ minute. Drain and dry.

2 Liquidize all the ingredients for the marinade.

3 Marinate the bacon and lamb for 1 hour. Drain and dry.

4 Impale the meat and bacon, rolled, on two of the skewers, and put the tomatoes, mushrooms and olives on the other skewers. Brush with the oil.

5 Cook the meat under the grill (broiler) for 8 minutes, and the garnish for 5.

6 Meanwhile, boil the marinade until 300 ml ($\frac{1}{2}$ pint (1$\frac{1}{4}$ cups) remains. Thicken with the cornflour (cornstarch) and water.

7 Serve the kebabs on rice .

Serves 2

Chops and Cutlets

Chops and Cutlets

Chops are cut across the saddle and split in the middle of the backbone. Each chop includes the meat of the loin and a small piece of the fillet as well. Lamb loin chops correspond to T-bone steaks in beef. A chop cut across the saddle is a chop royale and can be either cut single, 2.5 cm (1 in) thick, or double, 4 cm (1½ in) thick.

When boned, a chop or cutlet becomes a noisette – a little 'nut' of tender meat, or in butcher's terms, the 'eye' of the meat. When boned and rolled (like a Tournedos in beef) it is called a rosette.

The chump chops are the cheapest because they include part of the aitch bone. There are only 2 or 3 on each animal. They are usually cut slant-wise and weigh 275 g (10 oz) each.

Cutlets are cut from the 13 ribs of the lamb. There are 7 at the best end and it is usual for the butcher to remove one bone without meat, leaving 6 cutlets of equal thickness. The butcher should chine the cutlets. This means that he removes the backbone.

In double cutlets, the rib is cut between two bones and the butcher will then usually remove one rib bone. If wished, the cutlet may then be flattened slightly to make a wider piece of meat.

Lamb Cutlets Reform

4 double cutlets
175 g (6 oz) (3 cups) breadcrumbs
30 ml (2 tablespoons) chopped
 ham
10 ml (2 teaspoons) chopped
 parsley
salt and pepper
pinch clove
175 g (6 oz) (1¾ cups) seasoned
 flour
2 eggs, beaten
100 g (¼ lb) (½ cup) butter

For the Reform Sauce:
25 g (1 oz) carrot, finely chopped
25 g (1 oz) onion, finely chopped
25 g (1 oz) celery, finely chopped
½ bay leaf
sprig thyme
15 g (½ oz) (1 tablespoon)
 margarine
15 ml (1 tablespoon) lemon juice
6 peppercorns, crushed
300 ml (½ pint) (1¼ cups) brown
 sauce
15 ml (1 tablespoon) port
15 ml (1 tablespoon) redcurrant
 jelly

For the Garnish:
½ small cooked beetroot
hard-boiled white of ½ egg
1 gherkin
1 mushroom
15 g (½ oz) ham
15 g (½ oz) tongue

1 When you buy the double cutlets ask the butcher to remove one of the bones from each.

2 To make the Reform Sauce: gently fry the carrot, onion, celery, bay leaf and thyme in the margarine in a pan for 3 minutes. Drain off the fat. Add the lemon juice and crushed peppercorns, and cook until the liquid has evaporated by two thirds.

3 Add the brown sauce, and simmer for ½ hour. Remove any scum from the surface.

4 Add the port and redcurrant jelly. Bring to the boil and strain through a fine sieve. Keep warm.

5 Prepare the garnish by cutting the ingredients into matchsticks.

6 Put the breadcrumbs, ham, parsley, seasoning and pinch of clove in a basin and mix well.

7 Flatten each cutlet slightly, and dip each in the seasoned flour, and in the beaten egg.

8 Press the breadcrumb mixture well into both sides of the cutlets. If you like, add a professional touch by making criss-cross lines on each side with the blade of a knife.

9 Heat the butter in a pan and sauté the cutlets for 4-5 minutes on each side.

10 Just before serving, add the garnish to the sauce and reheat. Serve separately, with the cutlets placed on a dish.

Serves 4

Worcestershire Cutlets

4 double cutlets
20 asparagus spears
30 ml (2 tablespoons) oil
2 strips red pepper

For the Sauce:
150 ml (¼ pint) (⅝ cup) tomato
 sauce
150 ml (¼ pint) (⅝ cup) brown
 sauce
10 ml (2 teaspoons)
 Worcestershire sauce
30 ml (2 tablespoons) pineapple
 juice
salt and pepper

1 When you buy the cutlets, ask the butcher to remove one bone. Scrape the tip of the remaining bone clean.

2 Scrape the asparagus and boil for 15 minutes. Drain and keep warm.

3 To make the sauce, heat the tomato and brown sauces. Add the Worcestershire sauce and pineapple juice. Check the seasoning. Keep warm.

4 Season the cutlets, brush with oil and grill (broil) or sauté for 4-5 minutes on each side.

5 Place the cutlets on a serving dish, with a paper frill on each bone tip, and garnish with the asparagus decorated with the strips of pepper. Serve the sauce separately.

Serves 4

Worcestershire Cutlets with asparagus may look plain but taste delicious in their spicy, tangy gravy

Chops Royale

4 double chops
25 ml (1 fl oz) (2 tablespoons) oil
salt and pepper
pinch mace
4 large onions
100 g ($\frac{1}{4}$ lb) (1 cup) flour
100 ml (4 fl oz) ($\frac{1}{2}$ cup) milk
oil for deep frying
4 mushrooms
4 tomatoes
bunch watercress

1 Brush the chops with oil, season with salt and pepper and a pinch of mace, and grill (broil) for 12-15 minutes, turning once.

2 Meanwhile, cut the onions into rings, dip in flour, then milk, then flour again, and deep fry for $\frac{1}{2}$ minute. Drain on absorbent paper.

3 Brush the mushrooms with oil and grill for 2 minutes. Make two cross cuts on the top of each tomato, brush with oil and grill for 2-3 minutes until the skin blisters.

4 When ready to serve, garnish the chops with the mushrooms, tomatoes, onion and watercress.

Serves 4

Chops with Barbecue Sauce

1 onion, chopped
1 stick celery, chopped
1 clove garlic, crushed
25 g (1 oz) (2 tablespoons) butter
5 ml (1 teaspoon) dry mustard
5 ml (1 teaspoon) demerara sugar
2.5 ml ($\frac{1}{2}$ teaspoon) Tabasco
300 ml ($\frac{1}{2}$ pint) (1$\frac{1}{4}$ cups) tomato juice
5 ml (1 teaspoon) Worcestershire sauce
juice $\frac{1}{2}$ lemon
5 ml (1 teaspoon) vinegar
1 bay leaf
4 double chops, grilled

1 Fry the onion, celery and garlic

Chops Royale are a great idea for barbecue parties along with kebabs and different sauces and spicy dips

in the butter for 5 minutes. Add the remaining ingredients and simmer for 15 minutes. Remove the bay leaf.

2 Serve the chops on a dish and the sauce separately.

Serves 4

Noisettes Provençale

1 best end of neck, including the two cutlets of the middle neck, to give 6 noisettes

100 ml (4 fl oz) ($\frac{1}{2}$ cup) oil

For the Provençale Sauce:
225 g ($\frac{1}{2}$ lb) onions, sliced
1 clove garlic
5 ml (1 teaspoon) flour
15 ml (1 tablespoon) tomato concentrate (paste)
150 ml ($\frac{1}{4}$ pint) ($\frac{5}{8}$ cup) stock
225 g ($\frac{1}{2}$ lb) tomatoes, skinned, deseeded and chopped
bouquet garni
salt and pepper

1 Bone the noisettes of lamb by holding the best end upright and with a sharp knife gently and carefully detaching and scraping the meat from the top to the middle of the back bone until the meat is detached. Roll the belly flap round the meat and secure with cocktail sticks or string.

2 In a frying pan (skillet) gently fry the sliced onions and clove of garlic for 5 minutes in 25 ml (1 fl oz) (2 tablespoons) of the oil. Sprinkle on the flour and cook for 1 minute. Stir in the tomato concentrate (paste) and stock and simmer for 10 minutes. Add the tomatoes, bouquet garni and seasoning and simmer for 15 minutes until the sauce is thick. Remove the bouquet garni and check the seasoning.

3 Season the noisettes with salt and pepper and fry for 12-15 minutes in the rest of the oil. When cooked, remove the sticks or string.

4 To serve, place the sauce on a dish and put the noisettes on top. Serve with plain boiled potatoes.

Serves 3

Noisettes with Cream Cheese

1 best end of neck
salt and pepper
75 ml (3 fl oz) ($\frac{3}{8}$ cup) oil
75 g (3 oz) ($\frac{1}{2}$ cup) cream cheese
4 rashers (slices) streaky bacon
1 large onion, chopped
225 g ($\frac{1}{2}$ lb) fresh or canned
  tomatoes
5 ml (1 tablespoon) chopped basil

1 Bone the best end of neck to give 4 noisettes. Fold the belly flap round and tie up with string. Season with salt and pepper. Put half the oil in a frying pan (skillet) and brown the noisettes on both sides. Cool.

1 How to bone a noisette. Holding the best end of neck upright, carefully detach and scrape the meat from the tip to the middle of the backbone until the meat is detached 2 Roll the belly flap round the meat and secure with cocktail sticks (or pieces of string may be used) at intervals of 2.5 cm (1 in), and cut the noisettes 2.5 or 4 cm (1 or 1½ in) thick 3 Noisettes of Lamb served with a rich delicious Provençale Sauce

2 Preheat the oven to 190°C, 375°F, gas 5.

3 Spread each noisette with some of the cream cheese, and wrap each in a rasher (slice) of bacon, held in place with a cocktail stick.

4 Place in a roasting pan, with the oil from the frying pan (skillet) and bake for 45 minutes in the oven.

5 Put the rest of the oil in a frying pan (skillet) and gently fry the onion for 5 minutes. If the tomatoes

1

are fresh, skin them. Add the tomatoes to the pan. Season with salt and pepper. Add the basil and simmer for 15 minutes. Sieve the sauce, check the seasoning and keep warm.

6 When ready to serve, place the noisettes on a dish, having removed the string and cocktail stick. Serve the sauce separately. Serve with boiled potatoes, or with noodles tossed in butter.

Serves 2

2

3

1 The ingredients of the curry: lamb, apple, orange, pineapple, banana, onion, garlic, rice, desiccated coconut **2** Peel, core and dice the apple. Cut orange peel into matchstick strips **3** Peel and finely chop the onion and the garlic. Chop the parsley **4** With a pestle and mortar crush the mustard seed and black pepper and mix the garlic with them **5** Pour hot water on to the desiccated coconut and leave to stand **6** Heat the oil in a heavy pan and put the lamb pieces in it to brown **7** Turn the pieces while cooking until coloured on all sides **8** Add the onions and diced apple to the pan and stir to mix with the meat

9 and **10** Add the spices; stir well **11** Mix in the parsley and orange rind **12** Boil the coconut in the water for 2 minutes. Strain through a cloth, squeezing to obtain all the juice **13** Pour the coconut liquid into the curry **14** Add salt and check seasoning. Leave to cook gently **15** Boil the rice in salted water until it is tender **16** Slice the bananas and chop some pineapple **17** Serve the curry in a large dish with the rice, fruit and chutney placed in individual side dishes

Lamb Curry with Coconut

1 large apple
rind 1 orange
1 large onion
4 cloves garlic
10 g (2 tablespoons) chopped
   fresh parsley
5 ml (1 teaspoon) each: mustard
   seed, black pepper
225 ml (8 fl oz) (1 cup) hot water
100 g (¼ lb) (1¼ cups) desiccated
   coconut
50 ml (2 fl oz) (¼ cup) oil
675 g (1½ lb) lean lamb (shoulder
   or leg) cut in 3 cm (1¼ in) cubes
5 ml (1 teaspoon) each: ground
   (powdered) fenugreek,
   turmeric, coriander, cumin
2.5 ml (½ teaspoon) each: cayenne
   pepper, ginger
salt
225 g (½ lb) (1 cup) rice
2 bananas
3 slices pineapple

1 Peel, core and dice the apple. Slice the orange rind into matchstick strips. Peel and chop the onion and garlic; chop the parsley.

2 Crush the mustard seed and pepper and add the garlic to them. Pour hot water on to the desiccated coconut and let it stand.

3 Heat the oil in a heavy pan and gently fry the pieces of lamb, stirring to turn them and brown them on all sides. Meanwhile boil the water and coconut for 2 minutes, then strain through a clean cloth, squeezing the coconut to extract all the juices.

4 Stir in the apple, onion, and all the spices, stirring to spread them over the meat. Add the parsley and orange rind.

5 Pour the coconut liquid in to the curry, add a pinch of salt and adjust seasoning to taste. Bring to boil and cover. Simmer over low heat for 40-50 minutes until lamb is cooked, stirring from time to time and adding a little water if it becomes dry.

6 Boil the rice in salted water until it is just tender. Rinse and drain.

7 Peel and slice the bananas; cut the pineapple into small chunks. Put rice, bananas and pineapple into side dishes. Transfer the curry to a large serving dish. Serve at once with fruit chutney and other curry accompaniments.

Serves 6

Chicken Dhansak

175 g (6 oz) (1 cup) lentils
4 chicken joints
50 g (2 oz) (½ cup) flour seasoned
   with pinch each: salt, pepper,
   cumin, paprika, dry mustard
50 ml (2 fl oz) (¼ cup) oil
2 medium onions, chopped
2 cloves garlic, crushed
2.5 ml (½ teaspoon) each: cumin,
   dry mustard, paprika,
   turmeric, ground cardamom
7 g (¼ oz) (½ tablespoon) tomato
   concentrate (paste)
450 ml (¾ pint) (1⅞ cups) chicken
   stock
1 bay leaf, imported
salt
50 g (2 oz) (⅓ cup) raisins
175 g (6 oz) (¾ cup) long grain rice
pinch turmeric

1 Soak the lentils in water overnight. Rinse and drain.

2 Dredge the chicken joints in the seasoned flour, and fry them in the oil in a heavy pan for 12 minutes, covered. Turn the joints from time to time to brown evenly. Transfer the chicken to a casserole dish.

3 Preheat the oven to 180°C, 350°F, gas 4. In the same pan and oil used to fry the chicken joints, gently fry the onion and garlic 4 minutes until soft. Add the spices and cook 1 minute. Stir in the tomato concentrate (paste), the chicken stock, bay leaf and a pinch of salt, bring to the boil, and simmer 10 minutes.

4 Meanwhile cook the lentils for 10 minutes in boiling salted water. Drain. Add the lentils and the raisins to the curry sauce. Pour the sauce over the chicken joints cover and braise in the oven for 25 minutes.

5 While the chicken is in the oven, boil the rice in salted water and a pinch of turmeric until it is tender.

6 Arrange the rice on a large warmed serving dish and place the chicken and lentils in the middle. Serve at once with curry accompaniments such as red and green peppers, egg, banana slices, peanuts, and cucumber in yogurt.

Serves 4

Tips: Since cooked rice keeps well and can be re-cooked in a number of ways, it is not a bad idea to make a large quantity at one time and to save any leftovers. Cold rice may be stored in a covered dish in a refrigerator for several days without any ill effects. A good way to use up cold rice is to butter it. For each 100 g (¼ lb) (1½ cups) cooked rice, melt 20 g (¾ oz) (1½ tablespoons) butter in a heavy pan. Add the rice and stir well. Cover the pan tightly and heat very gently, shaking frequently, for 5 minutes or until rice is steaming. The buttered rice may be flavoured with chopped red or green peppers, cucumber, mushrooms, hard-boiled eggs, shredded cooked chicken or other cold foods. Season with salt and pepper, and spice with a dusting of cumin, paprika, coriander or nutmeg. Colour it yellow by adding a pinch of turmeric to the butter, or red with a little tomato concentrate (paste). Alternatively, mix in a few spoonfuls of plain yogurt for a cool creamy taste.

Minced Lamb

Oriental Lamb Puffs

450 g (1 lb) (2⅔ cups) left over roast meat
1 onion, chopped
1 clove garlic, crushed
25 g (1 oz) pineapple, cubed
100 g (¼ lb) (2 cups) breadcrumbs
1 egg
15 ml (1 tablespoon) chopped ginger
15 ml (1 tablespoon) soya sauce
salt and pepper
50 g (2 oz) (½ cup) seasoned flour
oil for deep frying

For the Batter:
100 g (¼ lb) (1¼ cups) flour
1 egg

300 ml (½ pint) (1¼ cups) milk mixed with water

1 Make the batter and beat until smooth.

2 Mince together the meat, onion, garlic and pineapple and combine with the breadcrumbs, egg, ginger, soya sauce and seasoning.

3 Divide into 20 balls, coat in seasoned flour and the batter and fry at 190°C, 375°F, for 2 minutes until golden-brown.

Serves 4

Minced Lamb Cutlets with Asparagus

225 g (½ lb) (1 cup) minced raw lamb from the shoulder

Oriental Lamb Puffs are crispy deep-fried lamb fritters served with a tomato sauce on a bed of boiled rice

225 g (½ lb) (1 cup) sausagemeat
50 g (2 oz) (1 cup) breadcrumbs
1 egg
1 small onion, chopped
25 g (1 oz) (2 tablespoons) raisins
15 ml (1 tablespoon) fresh parsley
15 ml (1 tablespoon) corn kernels
1 red pepper, ¼ cut in strips, ¾ chopped
50 g (2 oz) (½ cup) seasoned flour
75 ml (3 fl oz) (⅜ cup) oil
12 asparagus spears

For the Sauce:
1 onion, chopped
1 rasher (slice) streaky bacon, diced
1 clove garlic
15 ml (1 tablespoon) flour
30 ml (2 tablespoons) tomato concentrate (paste)
150 ml (¼ pint) (⅝ cup) white wine
300 ml (½ pint) (1¼ cups) stock
1 bay leaf

1 Combine the lamb and sausagemeat and breadcrumbs with the egg, onion, raisins, parsley, corn kernels and ¼ of the chopped red pepper. Divide into 6 portions and shape each into a "cutlet" shape. Dip in seasoned flour and brown in 50 ml (2 fl oz) (¼ cup) of the oil for 6 minutes. Then place in a casserole.

2 To make the sauce, heat 25 ml (1 fl oz) (⅛ cup) of the oil and fry the onion, bacon, garlic and half of the diced red pepper for 5 minutes. Sprinkle on the flour, add the tomato concentrate (paste), white wine and stock. Season and add the bay leaf. Simmer for 5 minutes.

3 Preheat the oven to 190°C, 375°F, gas 5.

4 Pour the sauce over the cutlets and braise in the oven for 30 minutes.

5 Meanwhile, scrape the asparagus, tie, and boil for 15 minutes.

6 When ready to serve, arrange the cutlets in a dish, pour the sauce over and garnish with the asparagus and strips of red pepper.

Serves 4

Minced Lamb Cutlets are easily prepared but can be made into an extra special dish by garnishing with asparagus

Kiwi Eggs

450 g (1 lb) (2 cups) minced lamb
1 large onion, grated
25 g (1 oz) (1 cup) fresh
  breadcrumbs
few drops Worcestershire sauce
salt and pepper
2 eggs, beaten
4 hard-boiled eggs
25 g (1 oz) (⅓ cup) dried
  breadcrumbs
oil for deep frying

1 Mix together in a bowl the minced lamb, grated onion, breadcrumbs and Worcestershire sauce. Season with the salt and pepper and bind the mixture with one of the beaten eggs.

2 Divide the mixture into four portions and mould each around a hard-boiled egg. Dip in the rest of the beaten egg, then coat with breadcrumbs.

3 Heat the oil in a deep fat fryer and, when hot, fry the kiwi eggs for 5-7 minutes until crisp and golden-brown. Cool and cut into halves or quarters. Serve with a green or mixed salad.

Serves 4

Sicilian-style Lamb Loaf

50 g (2 oz) (4 tablespoons) lard
  (shortening)
3 bay leaves
6 slices very lean ham
450 g (1 lb) (2 cups) minced lamb
175 g (6 oz) (¾ cup) minced lamb's
  liver
50 g (2 oz) (¼ cup) texturized
  vegetable protein
75 ml (3 fl oz) (⅜ cup) warm water
1 egg, beaten
30 ml (2 tablespoons) dry sherry
1 small onion, chopped
1 clove garlic, crushed
50 g (2 oz) (½ cup) corn kernels
50 g (2 oz) (½ cup) cooked peas
¼ red pepper, chopped
50 g (2 oz) (⅓ cup) diced gherkin

Look'n Cook Kiwi Eggs

1 Mix together the minced lamb, chopped onions, and breadcrumbs in a bowl. Season with salt and pepper and Worcestershire sauce and bind with the beaten egg **2** Divide the mixture into four and mould it around each hard-boiled egg **3** Dip each Kiwi Egg in beaten egg and coat with breadcrumbs. Deep fry in hot oil for 5-7 minutes

salt and pepper
15 ml (1 tablespoon) wine
  vinegar
juice and grated rind 1 lemon
1 orange, thinly sliced
12 juniper berries

1 Grease an oblong 750 ml (1¼ pints) (3 cups) ovenproof dish with the lard (shortening).

2 Preheat the oven to 180°C, 350°F, gas 4.

3 Place 3 bay leaves in the bottom of the dish, then line with the slices of ham.

4 In a large bowl, mix together the lamb and liver. Soak the texturized vegetable protein in the warm water and add to the bowl. Bind with the beaten egg.

5 Mix in the sherry, onion, garlic, corn kernels, cooked peas, red pepper and gherkin. Season with the salt and pepper and stir in the wine vinegar and lemon juice and rind.

6 Place the filling in the lined dish and stand the dish in a shallow tray, half-filled with water.

7 Bake in the oven for 1¼ hours. Remove and cool. Then chill in the refrigerator and, when cold, decorate with the slices of orange and juniper berries. Serve it sliced like a meatloaf for lunch or a picnic.

Serves 8

Lamb Turnovers

225 g (½ lb) puff pastry, fresh or
  frozen and thawed
150 g (5 oz) (⅝ cup) minced cooked
  lamb
25 g (1 oz) (1½ tablespoons) apple
  chutney
25 g (1 oz) (2 tablespoons) diced
  apple
15 ml (1 tablespoon) grated
  onion
1 egg, beaten
salt and pepper
pinch cumin

Look'n Cook Lamb Braid

1 Mix the minced lamb, onions, breadcrumbs, tomato concentrate (paste), Worcestershire sauce and beaten egg together. Season with salt and pepper **2** Roll out the pastry and place the lamb mixture in the centre **3** With a sharp knife, cut strips diagonally from the centre to the edge of the pastry along each side and dampen the edges with water **4** Fold the end strips over and fold the others alternately across the filling **5** Place on a baking (cookie) sheet, brush with eggwash and bake 30 minutes

1 Roll out the pastry on a floured surface, 3 mm (⅛ in) thick and, using a saucepan lid, cut out 4 circles.

2 Preheat the oven to 200°, 400°F, gas 6.

3 In a large bowl, mix together the minced lamb, chutney, diced apple and grated onion. Bind with most of the beaten egg (put a little of it aside to glaze the pastry). Season with salt and pepper and a pinch of cumin.

4 Divide the mixture into four portions and place one in the centre of each pastry circle. Wet the edges of the pastry with water and fold over, pressing the edges firmly together. Then crimp the edges.

5 Place the turnovers on a greased baking tray (cookie sheet) and bake on the middle shelf of the oven for 20 minutes until well-risen and ·golden-brown.

Serves 4

Lamb Braid

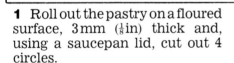
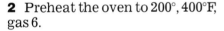

450 g (1 lb) (2 cups) minced lamb
2 onions, chopped
25 g (1 oz) (½ cup) fresh
  breadcrumbs
15 g (½ oz) (1 tablespoon) tomato
  concentrate (paste)
15 ml (1 tablespoon)
  Worcestershire sauce
2 eggs, beaten
salt and pepper
225 g (½ lb) puff pastry, fresh or
  frozen and thawed

1 Mix together the minced lamb, onions, breadcrumbs, tomato concentrate (paste), Worcestershire sauce and one of the beaten eggs. Season with salt and pepper.

2 Roll out the pastry on a floured surface, 3 mm (⅛ in) thick, into an oblong.

3 Place the lamb mixture in the centre and, with a knife, cut diagonal strips from the centre to

the edges along each side. Dampen the edges with a little water.

4 Fold the pastry at each end and then fold the strips over alternately so that they meet in the centre.

5 Preheat the oven to 220°C, 425°F, gas 7.

6 Place the Lamb Braid on a greased baking tray (cookie sheet) and brush with the remaining beaten egg. Bake in the oven for 15 minutes, then reduce the temperature to 180°C, 350°F, gas 4. Cook for a further 30 minutes. Serve hot with fresh vegetables.

Serves 4

Tip: To make this dish more economical and to give it a smoother texture, try mixing pork sausagemeat with the minced lamb. For a different flavour, why not add a little chopped liver? The addition of herbs such as rosemary, or even spices, make the Lamb Braid taste delicious.

Lamb en Croûte

Both lamb joints and cutlets can be served en croûte in crisp golden puff pastry. If you use a boneless leg of lamb or loin joint, then make sure that the meat is well cooked before encasing it in the pastry. Cutlets need only be quickly browned on each side.

Lamb Capricio Pie

450 g (1 lb) shortcrust (pie crust)
225 g (½ lb) (1 cup) minced cooked lamb
175 g (6 oz) (¾ cup) pork sausagemeat
100 g (¼ lb) (½ cup) minced cooked lamb's liver
1 small onion, chopped
8 stuffed olives, sliced
2 eggs, beaten
150 ml (¼ pint) (⅝ cup) dry sherry
75 g (3 oz) (1½ cups) fresh breadcrumbs

salt and pepper
pinch curry powder

1 Preheat the oven to 200°C, 400°F, gas 6.

2 Roll out the shortcrust (pie crust) dough, 3 mm (⅛ in) thick and 40 cm (16 in) long by 20 cm (8 in) wide.

3 Cut the pastry into 2 squares and use one to line a greased square cake tin (pan). Prick the pastry all over with a fork and bake blind for 15 minutes. Remove from the oven and cool.

4 Meanwhile, mix all the other ingredients together in a large bowl. Reserve a little beaten egg for glazing the pie.

5 Fill the baked pastry (pie crust) case with the filling and cover with the uncooked square of dough. Crimp the edges of the pie together and glaze with beaten egg.

6 Bake in the oven for 20 minutes. Serve cold with salad.

Serves 6-8

Lamb Cutlets en Croûte stretch a little meat around a large family – serve them with fresh garden vegetables

Lamb Cutlets en Croûte

4 lamb cutlets
25 g (1 oz) (2 tablespoons) butter
15 ml (1 tablespoon) oil
1 small onion, chopped
25 g (1 oz) (¼ cup) chopped mushrooms
15 g (½ oz) (¼ cup) fresh breadcrumbs
5 ml (1 teaspoon) mixed herbs
salt and pepper
1 egg, beaten
225 g (½ lb) puff pastry, fresh or frozen and thawed
few sprigs parsley

1 Trim the cutlets to expose 5 cm (2 in) bone at the narrow end. Melt the butter and oil in a frying pan (skillet) and brown the cutlets on both sides. Drain on absorbent kitchen paper and cool.

2 Cook the onions and mushrooms in the remaining butter and oil until soft. Place in a bowl with the breadcrumbs and herbs and mix together well. Season with the salt and pepper and bind with some of the beaten egg.

3 Preheat the oven to 220°C, 425°F, gas 7.

4 Roll out the pastry on a floured surface into a large oblong, 3 mm (⅛ in) thick. Cut into 4 strips.

5 Season the cutlets with salt and pepper and spread each with the stuffing mixture on one side only. Wrap a strip of pastry around each cutlet, working from one end to the other and seal the ends well.

6 Brush with the remaining beaten egg and place on a baking tray (cookie sheet). Bake in the oven for 15 minutes, then reduce the heat to 180°C, 350°F, gas 4. Continue cooking for another 15 minutes until golden-brown, then remove and arrange on a serving dish. Garnish with sprigs of parsley and serve with buttered peas and carrots and roast potatoes.

Serves 4

All about Lamb Stews and Casseroles

...ing Hotpot

Lamb Stews

Stews have the great merit of being suitable for cooking in advance, for reheating or freezing.

A stew is a combination of meat and vegetables cooked on top of the stove. There are three kinds of stew, one brown and two white. For the brown stew the meat is always seared first to seal the juices. It is then thickened by flour sprinkled on the meat or by a roux or cornflour (cornstarch).

The stew may be given a good brown colour by the addition of 1.25 ml (¼ teaspoon) of commercial "browning", made from caramel, or you can use the same amounts of black treacle and vinegar to darken the stew without sweetening it.

In a white stew, the meat is first boiled in water. A roux is added to the stew and diluted with the stock, mixed with some milk. The stew may be further enriched with cream or a liaison of egg yolks and cream.

The other type of white stew is a fricasée in which the meat is lightly pan fried to sear, but not to colour. The meat is then dredged with flour and liquid added.

A sauté is another variety of stew in which the meat is cooked as dry as possible. The meat is browned and cooked, with a lid on, in its own juices until almost tender.

Stews are cooked on top of the stove and it is necessary to use a heavy cast-iron dish. However, even with one, it is difficult with a gas cooker to prevent the meat burning.

If you do not have a suitable dish, it may be best to start the stew in a saucepan on top of the stove, and then to put the meat and vegetables in an ovenproof dish and finish the cooking in the oven.

Haricot Bean Lamb Stew

550 g (1¼ lb) stewing lamb
25 g (1 oz) (2 tablespoons) lard (shortening)
2 rashers (slices) streaky bacon
8 button onions
1 clove garlic, crushed
25 g (1 oz) (¼ cup) flour
900 ml (1½ pints) (3¾ cups) stock
salt and pepper
bouquet garni
225 g (½ lb) (1⅓ cups) dried haricot beans, soaked overnight
1 carrot, chopped
1 large onion, chopped
15 g (½ oz) (1 tablespoon) tomato concentrate (paste)
15 ml (1 tablespoon) vinegar
15 ml (1 tablespoon) chopped parsley

1 Cut the meat into cubes.

2 Heat the lard (shortening) in a pan and add the bacon, diced (keep the bacon rind to cook with the beans) and the button onions. Colour slightly and remove from the pan.

3 In the same pan, brown the meat. Drain off half the fat, add the garlic and flour and stir for 1 minute.

4 Add the stock and bring to the boil. Season, skim off any scum. Add the bouquet garni, cover with a lid and simmer for 1½ hours.

5 Preheat the oven to 180°C, 350°F, gas 4.

6 Drain the soaked haricot beans, reserving the liquid. Put the beans in clean water and bring to the boil. Throw the water away. Put the beans in an ovenproof dish with the chopped carrot, onion, bacon rinds, tomato concentrate (paste) and vinegar. Add some of the original liquid to cover and bake in the oven for 1 hour. When the beans are tender, remove the bacon rinds, and season with salt and pepper.

7 To serve, either combine the beans with the meat in one dish, or serve separately, sprinkled with chopped parsley.

Serves 4

Lamb and Pasta Stew

salt and pepper
2 courgettes (zucchini), cut in chunks
50 ml (2 fl oz) (¼ cup) oil
4 chump chops
1 onion, chopped
25 g (1 oz) (¼ cup) flour
25 g (1 oz) (2 tablespoons) tomato concentrate (paste)
300 ml (½ pint) (1¼ cups) stock
juice 2 oranges
15 ml (1 tablespoon) thin strips of orange peel
225 g (½ lb) pasta wheels
15 ml (1 tablespoon) chopped fresh mint
few mint leaves

1 Sprinkle salt on the courgettes (zucchini) and leave for ½ hour. Wash off the bitter juices and dry.

2 Preheat the oven to 180°C, 350°F, gas 4.

3 Heat the oil and brown the chops. Remove from the pan and place in an ovenproof dish.

4 In the same pan, fry the onion for 3 minutes; stir in the flour and cook for 1 minute. Add the tomato concentrate (paste) and cook for 1 minute. Stir in the stock and orange juice and boil for 15 minutes. Season with salt and pepper and strain over the chops.

5 Meanwhile, blanch the strips of orange peel in boiling water for 6 minutes. Drain and add to the meat.

6 Put the meat in the oven to cook for 1 hour.

7 During this time, boil the pasta for 8 minutes. Drain and add to the stew with the courgettes (zucchini) 15 minutes before the end of the cooking time.

8 When ready to serve, check the seasoning, sprinkle with chopped mint and garnish with a few whole leaves for decoration.

Serves 4

Lamb and Pasta Stew is a good way of serving lamb with mint and oranges which makes an ideal lunch or supper dish

Lamb Stew with Celery and Pepper

1 kg (2 lb) lean stewing lamb cut
  into 2.5 cm (1 in) cubes
50 ml (2 fl oz) (¼ cup) oil
2 onions, chopped
1 red pepper, diced
1 stick celery, diced
15 g (½ oz) (1 tablespoon) tomato
  concentrate (paste)
75 ml (2½ fl oz) (⅓ cup) medium
  sherry
salt and pepper
pinch ground (powdered) mace
600 ml (1 pint) (2½ cups) beef
  stock
15 g (½ oz) (1½ tablespoons)
  cornflour (cornstarch)
60 ml (2¼ fl oz) (⅓ cup) cold water
2.5 ml (½ teaspoon) gravy
  browning (optional)
200 g (7 oz) (1 good cup) long
  grain rice

1 Brown the meat in the oil in a heavy-based casserole. Add the onions, pepper and celery and fry gently for 4 minutes.

2 Add the tomato concentrate (paste), sherry and seasoning. Stir. Add the meat stock.

3 Cover and stew gently for 1½ hours on a low heat or until the meat is tender.

4 To thicken, prepare a roux by combining the cornflour (cornstarch) and water to a smooth paste. Add the browning, if used, and pour the roux into the stew. Stir and simmer for 10 minutes.

5 Cook the rice in boiling, salted water. Serve the casserole steaming hot on a bed of rice.

Serves 6

Lamb Stew with Celery and Pepper tastes as good as it looks with meaty chunks and vegetables on a bed of rice

Lamb Stew Jardinière

75 ml (3 fl oz) (⅜ cup) oil
900 g (2 lb) leg of lamb cut into
  2.5 cm (1 in) cubes
1 onion, chopped
25 g (1 oz) (2 tablespoons) tomato
  concentrate (paste)
1 beef stock cube
300 ml (½ pint) (1¼ cups) cider
900 ml (1½ pints) (3⅞ cups) water
salt and pepper
225 g (½ lb) pearl onions
225 g (½ lb) (2⅓ cups) peas
5 ml (1 teaspoon) sugar
15 g (½ oz) (1 tablespoon) butter
225 g (½ lb) baby carrots,
  quartered
225 g (½ lb) turnips, cut in strips
25 g (1 oz) (¼ cup) flour

1 Heat 50 ml (2 fl oz) (¼ cup) of the oil in a pan and brown the lamb for 8 minutes. Place the meat in a casserole.

2 In the same oil, fry the chopped onion until tender. Stir in the tomato concentrate (paste), and cook for 1 minute. Add the stock cube, cider and water and season. Boil for 10 minutes.

3 Pour the sauce over the meat. Cover and simmer for 1½ hours.

4 Boil the pearl onions and peas until tender in water seasoned with salt, pepper and half the sugar. Drain, toss in butter and keep warm.

5 Boil the carrots and turnips separately in water seasoned as for the peas and onions. Drain.

6 Mix the remaining oil and flour over a low heat for 3-4 minutes. Add a little of the stew gravy, stir and simmer for 10 minutes.

7 Pour into the stew and stir on a low heat for 5 minutes.

8 Pour the stew into the centre of a shallow dish and surround with the vegetables.

Serves 6

Latin American Bean Stew

225 g ($\frac{1}{2}$ lb) (1$\frac{1}{3}$ cups) haricot beans, soaked overnight
2 litres (3$\frac{1}{2}$ pints) (9 cups) water
50 ml (2 fl oz) ($\frac{1}{4}$ cup) oil
1 kg (2 lb) lean shoulder of lamb, cut in cubes
1 large onion, chopped
1 stick celery, sliced
2 aubergines (eggplants), peeled and cubed
1 bay leaf
3 cloves garlic, chopped
2 red chillies, sliced
50 g (2 oz) (4 tablespoons) tomato concentrate (paste)
150 ml ($\frac{1}{4}$ pint) ($\frac{5}{8}$ cup) white wine
salt and pepper
15 g ($\frac{1}{2}$ oz) (1$\frac{1}{2}$ tablespoons) cornflour (cornstarch), optional

1 Place the beans in a pan, add 900 ml (1$\frac{1}{2}$ pints) (3$\frac{3}{4}$ cups) of the water and bring to the boil. Remove any scum as it rises, reduce the heat and simmer for 1 hour until almost tender.

2 Meanwhile, heat the oil in a flameproof casserole and cook the lamb for 5 minutes to brown it. Add the onion and celery and cook for a further 2 minutes. Add the aubergines (eggplants), bay leaf, garlic and chillies and cook for 1 minute. Stir in the tomato concentrate (paste), the rest of the water and the wine and simmer for 1$\frac{1}{2}$ hours.

3 Drain the haricot beans and add them to the stew after the 1$\frac{1}{2}$ hours. Season and simmer for 20 minutes.

4 If liked, thicken the stew with the cornflour (cornstarch) mixed with 75 ml (2$\frac{1}{2}$ fl oz) ($\frac{1}{3}$ cup) water.

5 Serve the stew in the casserole dish.

Serves 6

Oriental Stew (left) and Latin American Bean Stew (right) are just two of the delicious stews made with lamb

Variation

Oriental Stew

1 Omit the haricot beans from the recipe for Latin American Bean Stew and cook the lamb in the same way but leave to simmer for 1$\frac{3}{4}$ hours.

2 Meanwhile, mix 150 ml ($\frac{1}{4}$ pint) ($\frac{5}{8}$ cup) pineapple juice, 5 ml (1 teaspoon) sugar, 15 ml (1 tablespoon) vinegar and 30 ml (2 tablespoons) soya sauce together in a pan. Add 225 g ($\frac{1}{2}$ lb) (4 cups) button mushrooms and 1 red pepper, diced. Bring to the boil and boil for 5 minutes.

3 Add the mushroom and pepper mixture to the lamb stew $\frac{1}{2}$ hour before it has finished cooking.

4 Heat 25 ml (1 fl oz) (2 tablespoons) oil and a pan and stir fry 225 g ($\frac{1}{2}$ lb) bean shoots for 1-2 minutes.

5 Stir the bean shoots into the stew, check the seasoning and garnish with 6 olives. Serve with toasted peanuts.

Lamb and Prawns Spanish-style

50 ml (2 fl oz) (¼ cup) oil
1 kg (2 lb) boned middle lamb
  cutlets, cut in small, thin slices
1 large onion, sliced
12 stuffed olives, sliced
2 cloves garlic, chopped
300 ml (½ pint) (1¼ cups) water
150 ml (¼ pint) (⅝ cup) medium
  sherry
1 bay leaf
pinch saffron
100 g (¼ lb) (½ cup) long grain rice
225 g (½ lb) tomatoes, skinned,
  deseeded and chopped
1 small red pepper, deseeded
  and chopped
175 g (6 oz) (1⅜ cups) peeled
  prawns
175 g (6 oz) (1½ cups) sliced
  mushrooms
salt and pepper
15 ml (1 tablespoon) chopped
  parsley

1 In a large sauté pan, heat the oil and cook the lamb for 8 minutes, covered with a lid.

2 Add the onion, cook for 1 minute, then add the olives, garlic, water, sherry, bay leaf and saffron, and bring gently to the boil. Reduce the heat and simmer for ½ hour.

3 Add the rice, tomatoes and pepper and simmer for 20 minutes.

4 Add the prawns and mushrooms, season and cook for 4 minutes more. Sprinkle with the chopped parsley and serve.

Serves 6

Lamb Bourguignonne

900 g (2 lb) lean shoulder of
  lamb, cut in 2½ cm (1 in) cubes
50 ml (2 fl oz) (¼ cup) oil
3 rashers (slices) bacon, diced
2 onions, chopped

Lamb Bourguignonne is a dish for special occasions which is marinated in red wine then served on a bed of rice

25 g (1 oz) (2 tablespoons) tomato
  concentrate (paste)
5 ml (1 teaspoon) molasses or
  dark treacle
150 g (5 oz) (⅝ cup) long grain rice
50 g (2 oz) (4 tablespoons) butter
6 mushrooms, sliced
salt and pepper
pinch mixed spice

For the Marinade:
300 ml (½ pint) (1¼ cups) red wine
150 ml (¼ pint) (⅝ cup) water
1 bay leaf
2 cloves garlic, crushed
bouquet garni
30 ml (1 fl oz) (2 tablespoons)
  vinegar

1 Mix the ingredients for the marinade. Place the lamb in a bowl, pour over the marinade and leave to soak for 3 hours.

2 Lift the meat from the marinade and dry it. Heat the oil in a pan and cook the lamb and bacon for about 6 minutes until browned. Add the onions and cook for a further 3 minutes.

3 Add the marinade, tomato concentrate (paste) and molasses or treacle and bring to the boil. Reduce the heat and simmer for 1½ hours.

4 Meanwhile, cook the rice in boiling salted water, drain and mix with half of the butter.

5 Sauté the mushrooms in the rest of the butter for 2 minutes.

6 When the stew has finished cooking, discard the bay leaf and bouquet garni. Add the mushrooms, check the seasoning and add a pinch of mixed spice. Arrange the boiled rice on a serving dish and pour the lamb bourguignonne over it.

Serves 6

Lamb Portuguese

1.2 kg (2¼ lb) lamb from the leg, loin or shoulder, cut into 2.5 cm (1 in) cubes
25 g (1 oz) (4 tablespoons) flour
salt and pepper
50 ml (2 fl oz) (¼ cup) oil
225 g (½ lb) (1 cup) chopped onion
50 g (2 oz) (4 tablespoons) tomato concentrate (paste)
900 ml (1½ pints) (3¾ cups) water
225 ml (8 fl oz) (1 cup) red wine
45 ml (1½ fl oz) (3 tablespoons) vinegar
bouquet garni
pinch fresh rosemary
pinch summer savory
1 clove garlic, chopped
225 g (½ lb) (1¼ cups) haricot beans, soaked overnight

1 Roll the lamb in the flour seasoned with salt and pepper. Shake to remove any excess.

2 Heat the oil in a heavy-based casserole dish and lightly brown the meat. Add the onion and stir over a moderate heat for 5 minutes.

3 Add the tomato concentrate (paste) water, wine and vinegar. Stir. Add the bouquet garni and season with salt, pepper, rosemary, summer savory and garlic. Cover and stew over a low heat for 1 hour.

4 While the stew is cooking, boil the soaked haricot beans in salted water for 10 minutes. Remove the scum from the surface, reduce the heat and simmer for a further 40 minutes.

5 Drain the beans and add to the casserole. Check the seasoning. Cook for a further ½ hour or until the meat and beans are tender.

Serves 6

Tips: Dishes described as "Portuguese" are strongly flavoured with tomato. You may either increase or decrease the amount of tomato concentrate (paste) used according to taste. Ideally, fresh tomatoes should be used. In this recipe, you may substitute 450 g (1 lb) of skinned, deseeded and chopped tomatoes for the tomato concentrate (paste).

Lamb Blanquette

1 kg (2 lb) lamb from the shoulder cut into 2.5 cm (1 in) cubes
2 onions, medium
2 cloves
½ head celery, diced
1 bay leaf
pinch fresh thyme
salt and pepper
150 ml (¼ pint) (⅝ cup) dry white wine
25 g (1 oz) (2 tablespoons) butter
25 g (1 oz) (4 tablespoons) flour
juice ½ lemon
2 cloves garlic, crushed
pinch cayenne pepper
2 egg yolks
75 ml (2½ fl oz) (⅓ cup) single (light) cream
5 ml (1 teaspoon) chopped parsley

1 Place the lamb in a large saucepan. Stud each onion with a clove and add to the meat with the celery, bay leaf, thyme, salt and pepper. Pour in the wine and enough water to cover the ingredients. Cover and cook on a low heat for 1½ hours.

2 Strain, reserving 550 ml (1 pint) (2½ cups) of the stock. Remove the onions and place the celery and meat in a casserole dish.

3 Melt the butter and stir in the flour. Simmer on a low heat and continue to stir until a smooth paste is formed. Bring the reserved stock to the boil and gradually add to the roux sauce, stirring all the time. Check the seasoning. Stir in the lemon juice, crushed garlic and cayenne pepper.

4 Beat the egg yolks and cream together in a bowl. Add 150 ml (¼ pint) (⅝ cup) of the sauce to the mixture and blend well.

5 Gradually pour the mixture into the sauce, stirring all the time. Simmer for 5 more minutes.

6 Add the sauce to the meat and reheat. Sprinkle with chopped parsley and serve.

Serves 4

Lamb Bordelaise

150 g (5 oz) mushroom caps
450 g (1 lb) potatoes
100 ml (4 fl oz) (½ cup) oil
675 g (1½ lb) lean lamb from the shoulder, cut into 2.5 cm (1½ in) cubes
salt and pepper
1 onion, chopped
bouquet garni
4 cloves garlic, chopped
300 ml (½ pint) (1¼ cups) beef stock
150 ml (¼ pint) (⅝ cup) dry white wine
oil for deep frying
15 ml (1 tablespoon) chopped parsley

1 Thoroughly wash the mushroom caps. Drain, dry and cut into quarters.

2 Peel, wash and cut the potatoes into balls, 2.5 cm (1 in) in diameter, with a potato or melon baller.

3 Heat the oil in a pan and add the meat. Cover and sauté for 12 minutes or until browned. Season. Add the onion and bouquet garni. Stir and cook for 5 more minutes.

4 Add the mushrooms and garlic and cook for a further 2 minutes. Remove any excess fat from the pan.

5 Add the stock and wine. Stir and cook on a low heat for 40 minutes or until tender.

6 About 10 minutes before the lamb is ready to serve, heat the deep fat fryer to 190°C, 375°F, and deep-fry the potato balls for 4 minutes or until cooked and golden-brown. Drain and keep warm.

7 Pour the lamb into a shallow meat dish. Serve garnished with the chopped parsley and surrounded by the potato balls.

Serves 4

Spicy Lamb Curry

50 ml (2 fl oz) (¼ cup) oil
1 kg (2 lb) middle neck lamb
  cutlets
1 large onion, chopped
1 apple, peeled, cored and sliced
500 ml (1 pint) (2½ cups) water
50 g (2 oz) (⅝ cup) desiccated
  coconut
10 ml (2 teaspoons) curry powder
pinch cumin
pinch paprika
25 g (1 oz) (4 tablespoons) flour
50 g (2 oz) (4 tablespoons) tomato
  concentrate (paste)
150 ml (¼ pint) (⅝ cup) pineapple
  juice
1 bay leaf
50 g (2 oz) (3 tablespoons) mango
  chutney
salt and pepper
75 g (3 oz) (½ cup) almonds

For the Garnish:
2 bananas, sliced
100 g (¼ lb) (1¼ cups) desiccated
  coconut
100 g (¼ lb) (½ cup) pineapple
  chunks
100 g (¼ lb) (⅜ cup) mango chutney
100 g (¼ lb) (⅜ cup) peach chutney

1 Heat the oil in a heavy saucepan and fry the lamb cutlets for 8 minutes until browned. Remove.

2 Fry the onion and apple until soft.

3 Meanwhile, bring the water to the boil and soak the coconut in it for 3-4 minutes.

4 Add the curry powder, cumin, paprika, flour and tomato concentrate (paste) to the pan. Cook for 3 minutes.

5 Add the coconut water, pineapple juice and bay leaf and bring to the boil, stirring all the time. Add the mango chutney and seasoning and simmer for 1½ hours.

6 Sprinkle with the almonds and serve with boiled rice, bananas, coconut, pineapple, mango and peach chutney arranged around the curry in small bowls.

Serves 4-6

Spicy Lamb Curry is served in the traditional manner, and surrounded by sambals, chutneys, coconut and boiled rice

Lamb Curry

1 kg (2 lb) shoulder of lamb
30 ml (2 tablespoons) oil
2 large onions, sliced
30 ml (2 tablespoons) curry
  powder
15 ml (1 tablespoon) turmeric
5 ml (1 teaspoon) ground
  (powdered) ginger
150 ml (¼ pint) (⅝ cup) beef stock
salt and pepper
15 g (½ oz) (1 tablespoon) tomato
  concentrate (paste)
50 g (2 oz) (3 tablespoons) mango
  chutney
25 g (1 oz) (2 tablespoons) raisins
150 ml (¼ pint) (⅝ cup) sour cream
50 g (2 oz) (⅜ cup) split almonds
½ lemon, sliced

1 Cut the lamb off the bone and remove the fat. Cut it into 2.5 cm (1 in) cubes.

2 Heat the oil in a heavy saucepan and fry the onions until soft. Add the lamb and brown it all over.

3 Stir in the curry powder, turmeric and ginger. Cook for 3 minutes.

4 Stir in the stock and season with the salt and pepper. Add the tomato concentrate (paste) and bring to the boil, stirring all the time.

5 Add the mango chutney and raisins and simmer, covered with a lid, for 45 minutes until the meat is tender.

6 Stir in the sour cream and most of the almonds. Simmer gently for 10 more minutes.

7 Arrange the curry on a serving dish, surrounded by a ring of boiled rice. Sprinkle with the remaining almonds and decorate with slices of lemon. Serve with sambals such as coconut, mango chutney, sliced tomatoes, bananas, chopped apple, cucumber and segments (sections) of orange.

Serves 4-6

Lamb Casseroles

A casserole differs from a stew in being cooked in the oven rather than on top of the cooker, and in containing considerably less liquid. A casserole can be made using better cuts of meat, such as chops, and so takes less time to cook than a stew.

A hotpot is a form of casserole which is cooked in clear broth and relies upon the inclusion of potatoes, beans or lentils for its thickening.

Types of meat suitable for hotpots include middle neck cutlets or diced shoulder of lamb, and all cuts of mutton.

Lancashire Hotpot

675 g (1½ lb) middle neck of lamb, cut in chops
15 ml (1 tablespoon) seasoned flour
25 ml (1 fl oz) (2 tablespoons) oil
4 medium onions, sliced
2 lamb's kidneys, skinned, cored and sliced
225 g (½ lb) (2 cups) sliced mushrooms
1 parsnip, sliced
675 g (1½ lb) potatoes, sliced
550 ml (1 pint) (2½ cups) stock

1 Preheat the oven to 180°C, 350°F, gas 4.

2 Trim any excess fat from the lamb chops and coat them in the seasoned flour.

3 Heat the oil in a pan, add the lamb and cook for a few minutes until browned on both sides.

4 Arrange the lamb, onions, kidneys, mushrooms, parsnip and potatoes in layers in a large casserole, finishing with a layer of potatoes. Pour in the stock and cover.

5 Bake in the preheated oven for 2 hours. After this time, remove the lid and cook for a further ½ hour to brown the potatoes.

Serves 4

Casserole of Lamb Polish-style

675 g (1½ lb) stewing lamb, cut into cubes
75 ml (3 fl oz) (⅜ cup) oil
2 onions, chopped
5 ml (1 teaspoon) paprika

Lancashire Hotpot is a famous old English dish which was traditionally made with oysters, now a luxury food

pinch caraway seeds
25 g (1 oz) (¼ cup) flour
25 g (1 oz) (2 tablespoons) tomato concentrate (paste)
600 ml (1 pint) (2½ cups) water
1 bay leaf
salt and freshly milled (ground) black pepper
675 g (1½ lb) new potatoes
4 fresh tomatoes, skinned, halved and deseeded
150 ml (¼ pint) (⅝ cup) sour cream or yogurt

1 Preheat the oven to 190°C, 375°F, gas 5.

2 Remove any fat from the meat. Heat the oil in a heavy casserole and add the meat. Cover and cook for 8 minutes, stirring from time to time, until the meat is evenly browned. Add the chopped onions and cook for 2 minutes more.

3 Sprinkle in the paprika, caraway seeds and flour and add the tomato concentrate (paste). Stir

and cook for 1 minute. Pour in the water and add the bay leaf. Bring to the boil, season and place in the preheated oven for ¾-1 hour.

4 Meanwhile, boil the potatoes in salted water for about 20 minutes or until tender.

5 Five minutes before the casserole has finished cooking, remove from the oven and add the drained potatoes. Decorate with the halved tomatoes and return to the oven for the rest of the cooking time.

6 Serve the casserole with the sour cream or yogurt poured over the top or served separately.

Serves 6

Casserole of Lamb Polish-style is nourishing and cheap but the sour cream topping turns it into something very special

Yugoslavian Casserole

2 onions, thinly sliced
2 peppers, deseeded and sliced
150 ml (¼ pint) (⅝ cup) oil
4 tomatoes, skinned, deseeded and chopped
salt and pepper
100 g (¼ lb) (½ cup) long grain rice
800 g (1¾ lb) shoulder, cubed
300 ml (½ pint) (1¼ cups) hot water
5 ml (1 teaspoon) paprika

1 Gently fry the onions and peppers in 45 ml (3 tablespoons) of the oil for 10 minutes. Add the tomatoes, cook for 2 minutes and season. Place half the mixture in a flameproof casserole.

2 Preheat the oven to 180°C, 350°F, gas 4. Heat 45 ml (3 tablespoons) oil in the pan and fry the rice for 2 minutes. Add the rice to the casserole and cover with the rest of the tomatoes.

3 Brown the meat in the rest of the oil, season and add to the casserole. Add the water, cover and bring to the boil. Cook in the oven for 1½ hours.

4 Sprinkle with the paprika and serve.

Serves 5

Lamb and Cabbage Casserole

1½ kg (3 lb) boneless shoulder of lamb
30 ml (1 fl oz) (2 tablespoons) oil
1 kg (2 lb) cabbage
10 ml (2 teaspoons) salt
450 ml (¾ pint) (1⅞ cups) hot beef stock
1 bay leaf
a little freshly chopped parsley

1 Cut the lamb into cubes. Heat the oil in a flameproof casserole, add the lamb and fry briskly until browned on all sides. Remove from the pan and pour off the oil.

2 Wash and trim the cabbage, separating the leaves. Put the lamb and cabbage in alternate layers in the casserole, sprinkling each layer with salt.

3 Pour in the stock, add the bay leaf and bring to the boil. Reduce the heat, cover and cook gently for 1½ hours or until the lamb is tender, adding a little more water if the meat becomes dry during cooking.

4 Remove the bay leaf, taste and adjust the seasoning. Sprinkle with the parsley and serve hot.

Serves 6

Look'n Cook Chump Chops Catalania

1 The ingredients: lamb chump chops, potatoes, tomatoes, courgettes (zucchini), onions, garlic, parsley, white wine, milk and cheese **2** Dredge the chops with flour and shallow fry until browned on both sides. Place them in a shallow ovenproof dish **3** Blanch the courgettes (zucchini) and cover the chops **4** Fry the onions until soft, then add the chopped tomatoes, garlic, water, wine, stock cube

5 and seasoning. Simmer for 5 minutes **5** Pour the tomato and wine mixture over the courgettes (zucchini) in the dish **6** Cover with a layer of thinly sliced blanched potatoes, overlapping each other **7** Make a basic roux and then a white sauce by adding milk. Stir in a little cheese and then pour the sauce over the potatoes **8** Sprinkle with the remaining cheese, then bake for about 45 minutes

Chump Chops Catalania

6 lamb chump chops
25 g (1 oz) ($\frac{1}{4}$ cup) seasoned flour
50 ml (2 fl oz) ($\frac{1}{4}$ cup) oil
3 onions, sliced
4 tomatoes, skinned, deseeded
  and chopped
1 clove garlic, crushed
150 ml ($\frac{1}{4}$ pint) ($\frac{5}{8}$ cup) white wine
150 ml ($\frac{1}{4}$ pint) ($\frac{5}{8}$ cup) water
1 chicken stock cube
salt and pepper
bouquet garni
4 courgettes (zucchini), sliced
450 g (1 lb) potatoes
150 ml ($\frac{1}{4}$ pint) ($\frac{5}{8}$ cup) white sauce
75 g (3 oz) ($\frac{3}{4}$ cup) grated Cheddar

1 Dredge the lamb chops in the seasoned flour. Heat the oil in a frying pan (skillet) and fry the lamb chops until well-browned on both sides. Remove them from the pan and arrange in the bottom of a shallow ovenproof dish.

2 Preheat the oven to 180°C, 350°F, gas 4.

3 In the same oil, fry the onions until soft, then add the chopped tomatoes and garlic. Pour in the wine and water and crumble in the stock cube. Season with salt and pepper and add the bouquet garni. Simmer for about 5 minutes.

4 Meanwhile, blanch the courgettes (zucchini) in boiling water for 3-4 minutes and arrange over the lamb chops in the dish.

5 Pour the tomato and wine mixture over the top.

6 Blanch the potatoes in boiling water for 4 minutes. Cut in thin slices and arrange them, overlapping, across the top of the dish.

7 Heat the white sauce and stir in 50 g (2 oz) ($\frac{1}{2}$ cup) of the grated cheese. Blend and pour the sauce over the potatoes. Sprinkle with the remaining grated cheese.

8 Bake in the oven for 45 minutes.

Serves 6

Lamb and Rice Casserole is an exciting new idea for serving lamb with cooked rice and fresh vegetables

Lamb and Rice Casserole

30 ml (2 tablespoons) oil
50 g (2 oz) (4 tablespoons) butter
2 onions, chopped
2 large carrots, chopped
1 stick celery, chopped
2 leeks, cleaned and sliced
6 lamb chops
25 g (1 oz) (4 tablespoons)
  seasoned flour
sprig thyme
1 bay leaf
salt and pepper
pinch nutmeg
550 ml (1 pint) (2$\frac{1}{2}$ cups) water
1 chicken stock cube
350 g ($\frac{3}{4}$ lb) (1$\frac{1}{2}$ cups) rice
100 g ($\frac{1}{4}$ lb) (1 cup) peas

1 Heat the oil and butter in a flameproof casserole dish. Gently fry the onions, carrots, celery and leeks until tender, stirring from time to time.

2 Preheat the oven to 190°C, 375°F, gas 5.

3 Dredge the lamb chops in the seasoned flour. Remove the fried vegetables from the casserole and keep warm. Shallow-fry the lamb chops until well-browned on both sides. Return the vegetables to the casserole, add the thyme, bay leaf, salt and pepper and nutmeg.

4 Pour in the water and crumble in the stock cube. Bring to the boil, check the seasoning, then bake in the oven for 30 minutes.

5 Remove and stir in the rice. Bring to the boil on top of the stove, add the peas and cover with a lid. Replace in the oven and bake for a further 20 minutes until the rice is tender. If necessary, you can add extra stock during cooking if the rice absorbs too much liquid.

Serves 6

Algerian Lamb Casserole

50 ml (2 fl oz) (¼ cup) oil
1 kg (2 lb) lamb cutlets
450 g (1 lb) onions, sliced
450 g (1 lb) potatoes, peeled and
  thinly sliced
500 ml (1 pint) (2½ cups) water
150 ml (¼ pint) (⅝ cup) white wine
bouquet garni
pinch cumin
salt and pepper
1 bay leaf

1 Preheat the oven to 180°C, 350°F, gas 4.

2 Heat the oil in a flameproof dish and brown the lamb cutlets on both sides. Add the onions and fry until soft.

3 Cover with the sliced potatoes, water and white wine. Add the bouquet garni, cumin and salt and pepper. Stir in the bay leaf and cover with a lid.

Algerian Lamb Casserole brings a taste of North Africa to your dinner table, flavoured with wine and cumin

4 Bake in the oven for 1¼-1½ hours until the lamb is tender and the potatoes are cooked through. Check the seasoning and serve with cooked fennel, celery, carrots or pumpkin.

Serves 4-6

Tips: The Algerians usually serve this dish with couscous, a type of semolina which is cooked in twice its volume of stock with boiled vegetables such as celery, fennel, carrots, chickpeas and squashes. You can make a spicy sauce from the stock with harissa paste. Just crush a clove of garlic and mix with 2.5 ml (½ teaspoon) cumin, 25 g (1 oz) (2 tablespoons) tomato concentrate (paste), 2.5 ml (½ teaspoon) oil and a good pinch of chilli powder. Mix in a little salt and dilute into the stock with a pinch of basil.

North African Cooking
Lamb and mutton are widely eaten in North Africa and are usually roasted over glowing charcoal fires. Meat is seasoned and flavoured with delicate herbs and spices and served with a cool yogurt dressing. Oregano and cumin are ideal for enhancing the flavour of lamb. Stews, hotpots and casseroles are popular as they can be cooked in a single pot over an open fire, thus conserving fuel. Aubergines (eggplants) are the most widely eaten vegetables and are stuffed, puréed, stewed and fried. You can try making a delicious lamb casserole with aubergines (eggplants), cumin, cinnamon and wine. Add a generous sprinkling of herbs and whatever vegetables you fancy. Chick peas can be used to pad it out.

484

Casserole of Lamb Basquaise

1 kg (2 lb) shoulder of lamb
50 ml (2 fl oz) ($\frac{1}{4}$ cup) oil
3 large onions, quartered
1 green pepper, deseeded and cut
  in strips
150 g (5 oz) ($\frac{2}{3}$ cup) diced raw
  streaky bacon
4 large mushrooms, sliced
2 cloves garlic, crushed
150 ml ($\frac{1}{4}$ pint) ($\frac{5}{8}$ cup) dry white
  wine
300 ml ($\frac{1}{2}$ pint) (1$\frac{1}{4}$ cups) water
1 chicken stock cube
bouquet garni
sprig tarragon
4 large tomatoes, skinned,
  deseeded and chopped
salt and pepper
25 g (1 oz) (3 tablespoons)
  cornflour (cornstarch)

1 Cut the lamb into 1 cm ($\frac{1}{2}$ in) cubes.

2 Preheat the oven to 190°C, 375°F, gas 5.

3 Heat the oil in a saucepan and fry the onions and pepper until soft. Add the lamb and bacon, cover with a lid and cook for 3 minutes. Then add the sliced mushrooms and garlic.

4 Pour the wine and water into the pan and crumble in the stock cube. Add the bouquet garni, tarragon and chopped tomatoes and season with salt and pepper.

5 Transfer to a flameproof casserole dish, cover with a lid and cook in the oven for 1$\frac{1}{4}$ hours. The meat should be tender and the liquid reduced.

6 Mix the cornflour (cornstarch) with a little of the liquid from the casserole and stir into the dish. Bring to the boil on top of the stove, stirring all the time, until the sauce thickens. Serve the casserole with boiled rice or roast potatoes.

Serves 6

Tip: For a different flavour, try substituting red wine, dry sherry or vermouth for white wine in this casserole. The addition of basil or oregano will give it a taste of the Mediterranean.

Dijon Lamb Hotpot

30 ml (1 fl oz) (2 tablespoons) oil
6 lamb cutlets
2 sticks celery, sliced
4 carrots, sliced
1 swede, cut in chunks
2 onions, chopped
300 ml ($\frac{1}{2}$ pint) (1$\frac{1}{4}$ cups) water
150 ml ($\frac{1}{4}$ pint) ($\frac{5}{8}$ cup) dry white
  vermouth
pinch marjoram
pinch thyme
salt and pepper
pinch cumin
15 ml (1 tablespoon) vinegar
15 ml (1 tablespoon) honey
1 chicken stock cube
5 ml (1 teaspoon) made Dijon
  mustard

1 Heat the oil in a frying pan

Dijon Hotpot comes all the way from France with tasty lamb cutlets in an unusual wine and mustard flavoured sauce

(skillet) and fry the cutlets for about 5 minutes until browned.

2 Preheat the oven to 190°C, 375°F, gas 5.

3 Place the browned cutlets in an ovenproof dish and cover with the vegetables. Pour in the water and vermouth. Sprinkle in the herbs and season with salt and pepper. Stir in the cumin, vinegar and honey. Crumble in the stock cube.

4 Cover with a lid and bake in the oven for 1$\frac{1}{2}$ hours until the meat and vegetables are tender.

5 Stir the mustard into the stock until well blended with the liquid. Serve hot with boiled rice or potatoes.

Serves 6

Tip: If you prefer a casserole-type dish in a thick sauce to a hotpot such as this one which is served in a thin gravy, you can always thicken the liquid with cornflour (cornstarch).

Turkish-style Moussaka

6 small aubergines (eggplants)
salt and pepper
100 ml (4 fl oz) (½ cup) oil
450 g (1 lb) tomatoes, skinned,
  deseeded and chopped
2 onions, chopped
100 g (¼ lb) (1¼ cups) sliced
  mushrooms
675 g (1½ lb) (3 cups) minced
  lamb
3 cloves garlic, crushed
30 ml (2 tablespoons) chopped
  parsley
2 eggs, beaten
50 g (2 oz) (½ cup) flour

1 Preheat the oven to 220°C,
425°F, gas 7.

2 Slice 4 of the aubergines (eggplants) in half. Make an incision
around the sides with a knife.
Then make a criss-cross pattern.

3 Season them with salt and
pepper and fry in 30 ml (2 tablespoons) of the oil for a few
minutes. Scoop out the pulp.

4 Heat 15 ml (1 tablespoon) of oil
in a pan and sauté the tomatoes.

5 Using the same amount of oil,
fry the onions until tender in
another pan. Meanwhile, sauté
the mushrooms in 15 ml (1 tablespoon) oil.

6 In a large bowl, mix together
the lamb and garlic with the
sautéed onions and mushrooms,
and one third of the cooked
tomatoes. Mix in the crushed
garlic and parsley and bind with
the beaten eggs, and 25 g (1 oz)
(4 tablespoons) flour.

7 Peel the remaining aubergines
(eggplants) and slice thinly. Season and toss in the remaining
flour. Fry them in the rest of the
oil for 1 minute.

8 Grease a deep ovenproof dish
and line the sides with the aubergine (eggplant) skins. Fill the dish
with alternate layers of the
lamb mixture and fried sliced
aubergines (eggplants). Cover the
top with more skins.

9 Bake in a bainmarie for 45
minutes. Surround with the remaining tomato pulp.

Serves 6

Greek-style Moussaka

2 aubergines (eggplants), peeled
  and sliced
2 courgettes (zucchini), sliced
5 ml (1 teaspoon) salt
15 g (½ oz) (2 tablespoons) flour
oil for deep frying
450 g (1 lb) potatoes, sliced
6 tomatoes, skinned and sliced
50 g (2 oz) (½ cup) grated cheese

For the Filling:
50 ml (2 fl oz) (¼ cup) oil
1 onion, chopped
450 g (1 lb) (2 cups) minced lamb
1 clove garlic, crushed
25 g (1 oz) (4 tablespoons) flour
25 g (1 oz) (2 tablespoons) tomato
  concentrate (paste)
pinch each oregano and mace
salt and pepper
150 ml (¼ pint) (⅝ cup) stock

For the Cheese Sauce:
300 ml (½ pint) (1¼ cups) white
  sauce
50 g (2 oz) (½ cup) grated cheese
1 egg yolk
juice and rind 1 lemon

1 Sprinkle the aubergines (eggplants) and courgettes (zucchini)
with salt. Leave 10 minutes, then
wash and dry.

2 Parboil the courgettes (zucchini) for 3-4 minutes. Coat the
aubergines (eggplants) with flour
and deep fry for 30 seconds.

3 Make the filling. Heat the oil
and fry the onion until soft. Add
the lamb, garlic, flour, tomato
concentrate (paste), herbs and
seasoning. Pour in the stock,
boil, then simmer for 10 minutes.

4 Blanch the potatoes.

5 Preheat the oven to 190°C,
375°F, gas 5.

6 Place alternate layers of the
meat mixture, courgettes (zucchini), aubergines (eggplants),
tomatoes and potatoes in a deep
casserole.

7 Make the white sauce, stir in
the cheese, egg yolk and lemon
juice and rind. Simmer gently,
then pour over the moussaka.
Sprinkle with grated cheese and
bake for 30 minutes.

Serves 6

Lamb Cobbler

50 ml (2 fl oz) (¼ cup) oil
1 onion, chopped
675 g (1½ lb) (3 cups) minced lamb
100 g (¼ lb) (½ cup) chopped lamb's
  liver
25 g (1 oz) (4 tablespoons) flour
50 g (2 oz) (4 tablespoons) tomato
  concentrate (paste)
300 ml (½ pint) (1¼ cups) stock
salt and pepper
pinch rosemary
5 ml (1 teaspoon) made mustard
25 g (1 oz) (2 tablespoons)
  chopped gherkin

For the Topping:
350 g (¾ lb) (3⅜ cups) self raising
  flour
pinch salt
100 g (¼ lb) (½ cup) butter
75 ml (3 fl oz) (⅜ cup) water
15 ml (1 tablespoon) milk

1 Heat the oil in a pan and sauté
the onion until soft. Add the lamb
and liver and cook for 5 minutes.

2 Stir in the flour and tomato
concentrate (paste) and cook for
2-3 minutes. Then pour in the
stock and add the salt and pepper
and rosemary.

3 Preheat the oven to 190°C,
375°F, gas 5.

4 Mix the mustard and gherkin
into the lamb mixture and pour
into a shallow ovenware dish.
Leave to cool.

5 Meanwhile, make the topping.
Sift the flour and salt together
and rub in the butter. Add enough
water to form a stiff dough.

6 Knead the dough a little on a
floured board and roll out ½ cm
(¼ in) thick. With a round pastry
cutter cut the dough into rounds
to form small scones. Arrange
these scones, overlapping each
other, around the top of the casserole dish. Brush with milk.

7 Bake in the oven for 30
minutes.

Serves 6

486

All about Pork

Sautéed Pork Cutlets

Pork has a distinctive flavour which is quite different from other meats. As well as giving us tasty joints and chops, the pig also provides us with bacon, gammon, ham and many types of sausage.

Choosing Pork
The lean meat should always be pale pink in colour, without gristle and firm to the touch. It should be marbled a little with milky-white fat, and the outer fat should be firm and white. If you are buying a joint with skin or rind, make sure that there are no hairs and that it is not too thick. If you like crackling on your roast, ask the butcher to score the rind for you.

Storing Pork
Pork is available all the year round, fresh or frozen. Of course, if you have a freezer you would be well advised to buy in bulk. Joints and chops will store in a freezer for about 4 months. Pork can be stored in a refrigerator for 2-3 days, or in a cool place for about 24 hours.

Cuts of Pork
Pork is available in a variety of cuts and should always be cooked thoroughly. It can be roast, grilled (broiled), fried, casseroled, cured, boiled and made into sausages. Here are the best known cuts:

Loin: This is usually considered to be the choicest cut, it is also the most expensive. It can be roasted whole on the bone or boned, rolled and stuffed. It is also cut up into loin and chump chops. When roasting loin, allow 225 g (½ lb) on the bone per person, and 100-175 g (4-6 oz) boned per person.

Fillet: This is another expensive cut which is lean and tender. It is usually roasted either on the bone or boned and stuffed. It comes from the top end of the hind leg and can also be cut into steaks.

Leg: This is a very large joint which is often cut in two and then roasted. It can be roasted on the bone or stuffed and rolled. Generally, it has more flavour when roasted on the bone.

Spare Ribs: These are usually associated in most people's minds with Chinese and Oriental cooking. However, they are growing ever more popular in the West.

They are usually roasted or marinated or grilled (broiled). They should not be confused with spare rib chops which come from the belly.

Chops: Chump and loin chops both come from the loin and are about 2.5 cm (1 in) thick. They are usually grilled (broiled), fried or baked. Sometimes they include the kidney as well.

Cutlets: These lean pieces of meat are taken from the spare rib and have very little bone. Like chops, they can be fried, grilled (broiled) or casseroled.

Blade: This is a cheaper joint which can be roasted or braised on or off the bone.

Belly: This is a very fatty cut which can be roasted as a joint or cut into slices. Because it is so fat, it is cheap and sold either fresh or salted.

Hand: This joint comes from the foreleg and is sold both fresh and salted. It is suitable for roasting, braising and stewing. If you are a crackling lover, this is the cut for you as it has a very large area of rind.

Sucking Pig: This is a young pig which is slaughtered between three weeks and two months. It can be spit-roasted.

Sauces and Flavourings
Pork is traditionally served with apple or gooseberry sauce. Spices such as cloves and paprika go well with pork in either a marinade or a tart apple sauce. Herbs such as thyme, sage, rosemary and garlic all enhance the flavour of pork. Pork is a favourite meat in oriental dishes and is often served with ginger, soya sauce or pineapple. You can make a delicious marinade for a joint or chops with these ingredients. Or why not try cooking your roast the Italian way? Just make some small cuts in the lean meat and insert some slivers of garlic. Sprinkle with oregano and roast as normal. The end result tastes and looks delicious. Or you can try making a sticky glaze for a roast joint with honey, orange or pineapple juice and spices such as powdered cloves, ginger or cinnamon.

Chops and Cutlets

Both loin and chump pork chops come from the loin. Pork chops can be grilled (broiled), fried or casseroled in many different ways. In this section, we give you recipes for all three. Pork chops are most economical when served in a sauce or casserole to make them go further.

Fruity Pork Chops

four 175 g (6 oz) pork chops
salt and pepper
50 ml (2 fl oz) (¼ cup) oil
pinch oregano
½ red pepper, cut in strips
100 g (¼ lb) (½ cup) long grain rice
225 g (½ lb) green grapes, halved

1 Sprinkle the pork chops with salt and freshly ground (milled) black pepper.

2 Heat the oil in a frying pan (skillet) and gently fry the chops until brown on both sides. Sprinkle in the oregano.

3 Add the strips of red pepper and fry until soft.

4 Meanwhile, cook the rice in boiling salted water until tender, but still firm.

5 Add the halved grapes to the pork and peppers and heat through.

6 Arrange the rice on a heated serving dish and pile the chops in the centre. Spoon the peppers and grapes over the top and serve.

Serves 4

Fruity Pork Chops are served on a bed of plain rice with sautéed strips of red pepper and juicy green grapes

Barbecued Pork Cutlets

50 ml (2 fl oz) ($\frac{1}{4}$ cup) oil
6 pork cutlets
50 g (2 oz) (4 tablespoons) butter
1 small onion, chopped
100 ml (4 fl oz) ($\frac{1}{2}$ cup) water
25 g (1 oz) (2 tablespoons) brown sugar
2.5 ml ($\frac{1}{2}$ teaspoon) made mustard
salt and pepper
15 ml (1 tablespoon) vinegar
15 g ($\frac{1}{2}$ oz) (1 tablespoon) tomato concentrate (paste)
2 tomatoes, skinned, deseeded and chopped
5 ml (1 teaspoon) Worcestershire sauce
70 ml (2$\frac{1}{2}$ fl oz) ($\frac{1}{3}$ cup) tomato ketchup (catsup)
pinch paprika

1 Heat the oil and fry the pork cutlets until well browned on both sides.

2 Meanwhile, make the barbecue sauce. Melt the butter in a saucepan and fry the onion until soft. Add the water and stir in the brown sugar, mustard, seasoning and vinegar. Bring to the boil, then simmer for 5 minutes.

3 Add all the remaining ingredients, stir well and simmer for 15 minutes.

4 Serve the pork cutlets with the barbecue sauce on a bed of plain boiled rice.

Serves 6

Tips: You can make the sauce more interesting by adding sliced mushrooms or peppers. If you like red-hot food, why not add a few drops of chilli sauce? Or you can make a more fruity version with cooked plums, pineapple or fresh chopped peaches and apricots.

You can remove the meat from the chops, of course, and use it skewered as kebabs. Or why not try marinating the chops in soya sauce, pineapple juice, oil and garlic for a more oriental flavour?

Pork in Cider brings the flavour of the countryside to your dinner table with its fresh vegetables and fruity taste

Pork in Cider

100 ml (4 fl oz) ($\frac{1}{2}$ cup) oil
2 carrots, diced
2 onions, diced
1 clove garlic, crushed
2 shallots, chopped
1 stick celery, thinly sliced
50 g (2 oz) ($\frac{1}{2}$ cup) flour
3 tomatoes, skinned, deseeded and chopped
300 ml ($\frac{1}{2}$ pint) (1$\frac{1}{4}$ cups) dry cider
bouquet garni
225 g ($\frac{1}{2}$ lb) (1 cup) canned, creamed corn kernels
salt and pepper
six 225 g ($\frac{1}{2}$ lb) pork cutlets
15 ml (1 tablespoon) chopped parsley

1 Heat half of the oil in a saucepan and gently fry the carrots, onions, garlic, shallots and celery until tender.

2 Sprinkle in half of the flour, stir and cook for 1 minute. Add the tomatoes and cider and bring to the boil. Add the bouquet garni and corn kernels and season with

490

salt and pepper. Simmer for 15-20 minutes.

3 Coat the cutlets in the remaining seasoned flour and heat the rest of the oil in a pan. Shallow fry the cutlets for about 10 minutes until browned on both sides.

4 Preheat the oven to 180°C, 350°F, gas 4.

5 Remove the cutlets from the pan and arrange in an ovenproof dish. Cover with the sauce and check the seasoning. Bake in the covered ovenproof dish for 20 minutes.

6 Sprinkle with parsley and serve with boiled new potatoes.

Serves 6

Tip: If you have no cider, you can always use apple juice or white wine or a mixture of both. Fresh sliced apples will increase the fruity flavour. Fresh corn on the cob or canned corn kernels will give the casserole a more crunchy texture.

Pork with Rice and Peppers is an easy and tasty dish to prepare which is ideal for quick, filling family meals

Pork with Rice and Peppers

6 pork cutlets
50 g (2 oz) ($\frac{1}{2}$ cup) seasoned flour
50 ml (2 fl oz) ($\frac{1}{4}$ cup) oil
1 onion, chopped
1 green pepper, deseeded and cut in strips
1 red pepper, deseeded and cut in strips
1 clove garlic, crushed
100 ml (4 fl oz) ($\frac{1}{2}$ cup) water
salt and pepper
175 g (6 oz) ($\frac{3}{4}$ cup) long grain rice
50 g (2 oz) (4 tablespoons) butter

1 Coat the pork cutlets in the seasoned flour. Heat the oil in a frying pan (skillet) and cook the cutlets for about 10 minutes until browned on both sides.

2 Remove the cutlets and keep warm. Sauté the onion, green and red peppers and garlic until soft. Then return the cutlets to the pan and add the water and seasoning. Bring to the boil, then simmer, covered with a lid, for 20 minutes.

3 Meanwhile, cook the rice in boiling salted water until tender. Drain and place in a buttered mould. Press it down firmly and trim out on to a serving dish.

4 Surround the moulded rice with the cutlets, peppers and onions and serve immediately.

Serves 6

Tips: You can use either pork chops or cutlets for this dish. It tastes especially delicious if served in a tomato sauce. Just add some skinned, deseeded and chopped tomatoes, tomato concentrate (paste), sliced mushrooms and a pinch of basil. For a special occasion, try substituting white wine or dry sherry for the water.

491

Pork Chops with Cider Cream Sauce

4 pork chops
15 g ($\frac{1}{2}$ oz) (2 tablespoons) flour
salt and pepper
50 g (2 oz) (4 tablespoons) butter
1 large onion, chopped
175 g (6 oz) (1$\frac{1}{2}$ cups) sliced
  mushrooms
300 ml ($\frac{1}{2}$ pint) (1$\frac{1}{4}$ cups) dry cider
50 ml (2 fl oz) ($\frac{1}{4}$ cup) double
  (heavy) cream
15 ml (1 tablespoon) chopped
  parsley

1 Coat the pork chops in half the flour seasoned with salt and pepper. Melt the butter in a large frying pan (skillet) and fry the pork chops slowly until cooked through. Remove the chops from the pan and keep them warm.

2 Add the onion to the meat cooking juices and fry gently for 3 minutes.

3 Stir in the mushrooms and cook for another 3 minutes.

4 Stir in the rest of the flour and cook for 1 minute. Take the pan off the heat and stir in the cider to make a smooth sauce. Return the pan to the heat and stir for 1 minute.

5 Over a low heat, stir in the cream and season with salt and pepper. Heat to just below boiling point. Pour the sauce over the pork chops, garnish with the chopped parsley, and serve at once.

Serves 4

Pork Chops a l'Orange

4 thick pork chops
1 onion, finely chopped
50 g (2 oz) (4 tablespoons) butter
60 ml (2$\frac{1}{4}$ fl oz) (4 tablespoons) oil
50 g (2 oz) (1 cup) fresh
  breadcrumbs
salt and pepper

Pork Chops with Cider Cream Sauce – an impressive combination, enriched with thick cream and sliced mushrooms

good pinch dried sage
grated rind and juice 1 orange
30 ml (2 tablespoons) flour
300 ml ($\frac{1}{2}$ pint) (1$\frac{1}{4}$ cups) chicken
  stock

1 Cut a pocket in each pork chop by making a slit in the same direction as the bone, cutting from the fat side through to the bone.

2 Gently fry the chopped onion in half of the butter and oil for 5 minutes until softened but not browned.

3 Stir in the breadcrumbs, salt and pepper to taste, sage, and the grated orange rind, so that the mixture absorbs the cooking fats and forms a thick paste. If necessary, remove from the heat and use the milk to bind the mixture.

4 Preheat the oven to 170°C, 325°F, gas 3. Stuff $\frac{1}{4}$ of the breadcrumb mixture into each chop, securing if necessary with a cocktail stick. Arrange the chops in an ovenproof dish and keep warm.

5 Heat the rest of the butter and oil in the pan, scraping up any residue. Fry the flour for 3 minutes. Remove from the heat and stir in the stock and orange juice and bring to the boil, stirring all the time.

6 Pour the sauce over the chops, cover, and cook in the oven for 15 minutes. Serve with buttered green beans.

Serves 4

Joints of Pork

The following recipes show just how many ways there are of serving roast pork apart from with the traditional apple sauce and crackling.

Pork with Pineapple

75 g (3 oz) (6 tablespoons) butter
70 ml (2½ fl oz) (⅓ cup) oil
1 kg (2 lb) best end of pork
salt and pepper
150 ml (¼ pint) (⅝ cup) water

1 small pineapple, cut into chunks, or 225 g (½ lb) canned pineapple pieces, drained

For the Gravy:
15 ml (1 tablespoon) flour
70 ml (2½ fl oz) (⅓ cup) water
30 ml (1 fl oz) (2 tablespoons) Worcestershire sauce
70 ml (2½ fl oz) (⅓ cup) pineapple juice
15 ml (1 tablespoon) cornflour (cornstarch)

1 Preheat the oven to 190°C, 375°F, gas 5. Melt the butter in a saucepan and combine it with the oil.

2 Remove the back spine bone from the joint and all the rind from the pork itself. Season the meat with salt and pepper and brush all over with half the butter

Pork with Pineapple – crisp, roast best end of pork with fresh or canned pineapple chunks in a delicious, golden gravy

and oil mixture. Place the pork on a rack in a roasting pan and roast in the oven for 1½ hours or until the meat is well cooked. Baste from time to time with the water, to ensure the meat does not dry out.

3 Meanwhile heat the remaining butter and oil in a pan and fry the pineapple pieces for 3 minutes on both sides or until it is golden. Remove from the pan and keep warm.

4 When the meat is cooked, prepare the gravy. Remove most of the fat from the meat juice. Add the flour and stir over a low heat for 3-4 minutes until browned. Add the water, Worcestershire sauce, and the pineapple juice. Bring to the boil and simmer for 5 minutes, stirring all the time. Thicken with the cornflour (cornstarch) mixed with a little water. Check the seasoning.

5 Place the meat on a heated serving tray, surround it with the pineapple pieces and, just before serving, pour over the gravy.

Serves 8

Braised Leg of Pork

1½ kg (3 lb) joint of pork, from the thick part (cushion) of the leg
300 ml (½ pint) (1¼ cups) dry white wine
70 ml (2½ fl oz) (⅓ cup) brandy
2 shallots, sliced
1 clove garlic, crushed
2 carrots, sliced
1 bay leaf
sprig thyme
sprig parsley
salt and pepper
25 g (1 oz) (2 tablespoons) fat
25 g (1 oz) (½ cup) brown breadcrumbs
50 ml (2 fl oz) (¼ cup) water
5 ml (1 teaspoon) cornflour (cornstarch)

1 Preheat the oven to 230°C, 450°F, gas 8. Trim the pork all round. Remove all the rind and some of the fat.

2 Place it in a large bowl and cover it with the wine, brandy, shallots, garlic, carrots, bay leaf, thyme and parsley. Cover and allow the meat to marinate for 6 hours, turning it from time to time.

3 Wipe it, season it to taste with salt and pepper and place it in a roasting pan. Add the fat and sear the meat in the oven for 30 minutes. Strain off any excess fat.

4 Reduce the heat to 180°C, 350°F, gas 4. Add the vegetables and herbs and baste the meat with the marinating liquor from time to time, until it is cooked. The cooking time will depend on the weight of the leg. Allow at least 30 minutes per 450 g (1 lb). When cooked, sprinkle the meat with the brown breadcrumbs.

5 Strain the juices into a saucepan. Season, add the water and boil it for 5 minutes. If necessary, thicken with the cornflour (cornstarch) mixed with a little water.

Serve the sauce in a gravyboat with the meat.

Serves 8-10

Pork with Rosemary

1 kg (2 lb) lean boned shoulder or loin of pork
salt and pepper
150 g (5 oz) (⅝ cup) butter
1 carrot, sliced
1 large onion, chopped
1 stick celery, diced
350 g (¾ lb) mushrooms
300 ml (½ pint) (1¼ cups) water
150 ml (¼ pint) (⅝ cup) dry white wine
2 sprigs rosemary
1 clove garlic, crushed

1 Preheat the oven to 190°C, 375°F, gas 5. Season the meat.

Pork with Rosemary – an unusual way of serving a joint by pot-roasting in white wine with mushrooms and celery

2 Melt half of the butter in a flameproof casserole. Add the meat and brown it on all sides. Remove the casserole from the heat.

3 In a separate pan heat the remaining butter. Add the carrot and sauté for 5 minutes. Add the onion and celery and sauté for a further 5 minutes. Finally add the mushrooms, cover and cook on a low heat for 2 minutes.

4 Pour the contents of the pan into the casserole. Add the water, wine, one rosemary sprig and the garlic. Check the seasoning. Cover and cook in the oven for 1½ hours or until the meat is well cooked.

5 Serve garnished with the second sprig of rosemary.

Serves 6

Stuffed Pork with Aubergines (Eggplants)

1.2 kg (2½ lb) boneless loin of pork, rind and some fat removed
salt and pepper
450 g (1 lb) onions, chopped
1 clove garlic, crushed
30 ml (1 fl oz) (2 tablespoons) oil
8 tomatoes, skinned, deseeded and chopped
5 ml (1 teaspoon) chilli powder
50 g (2 oz) (⅓ cup) seedless raisins
175 g (6 oz) cooked rice
1 egg, beaten
150 ml (¼ pint) (⅝ cup) dry white wine
150 ml (¼ pint) (⅝ cup) stock
2 aubergines (eggplants), peeled and sliced
25 g (1 oz) (¼ cup) flour
oil for deep frying

1 Preheat the oven to 190°C, 375°F, gas 5. Cut the pork almost in half lengthways and season.

2 Fry the onions and garlic in the oil until soft. Add the tomatoes and chilli powder and simmer for 5 minutes. Add the raisins.

3 Blend half the tomato mixture with the rice and egg and place the stuffing on the pork. Fold over the meat and tie at intervals. Place in a roasting pan and cook in the oven for 1 hour.

4 Pour out the fat which has collected in the roasting pan. Mix the remaining tomato mixture with the wine and stock and add to the pan. Return to the oven for 30 minutes or until the meat is cooked. Baste occasionally, adding more wine to the sauce if it becomes too thick.

5 Meanwhile, soak the aubergines (eggplants) in salted water for 15 minutes, then drain and dry. Coat in the flour and deep fry until golden. Keep warm.

6 Remove the string from the joint and place the meat in a serving dish. Pour the sauce round it and add the aubergine (eggplant) slices.

Serves 6-8

Stuffed Pork with Aubergines (Eggplants). A tomato and chilli mixture is used in both the sauce and the filling

Pork with Prune and Almond Stuffing

1 kg (2 lb) boned fillet of pork, rind and some fat removed
salt and pepper
100 g (¼ lb) (½ cup) long grain rice

For the Stuffing:
100 g (¼ lb) (¾ cup) stoned (pitted) prunes, cooked
50 g (2 oz) (½ cup) flaked almonds
100 g (¼ lb) (2 cups) fresh breadcrumbs
1 egg
pinch mixed spice

For the Gravy:
300 ml (½ pint) (1¼ cups) stock
½ beef stock cube
5 ml (1 teaspoon) cornflour (cornstarch)
100 ml (4 fl oz) (½ cup) port or dry sherry (optional)

1 Preheat the oven to 190°C, 375°F, gas 5.

2 Spread the meat flat and season the inside. Combine the ingredients for the stuffing and place along the centre of the meat. Roll up and secure with string. Season the outside of the meat and roast in the preheated oven for 1¼ hours, basting from time to time with a little water.

3 Meanwhile, cook the rice in boiling salted water until tender. Drain and keep warm.

4 Place the stock in a pan, crumble in the stock cube and bring to the boil. Add the cornflour (cornstarch), mixed with a little water, and cook for a few minutes more. Season the gravy and add the port or sherry, if used.

5 Place the rice on a serving dish and lay the roast pork on the top. Serve with the gravy and apple sauce.

Serves 6

Tip: You can substitute other nuts such as chopped walnuts for the almonds in the stuffing.

Pork with Prune and Almond Stuffing, on a bed of rice, is served with a deliciously rich wine-flavoured gravy ▶

Look'n Cook Crown Roast of Pork

1 Remove the chine bones from the two pork joints **2** Cut 4 cm (1½ in) of the fat from the ends of the bones **3** Trim away the sinew from between the bones **4** Bend the two joints round to form the crown shape and secure with string **5** Place the crown in a roasting pan and brush all over with the melted butter **6** Wrap aluminium foil round the ends of the bones to prevent them burning during the cooking **7** Heat the rest of the butter in a frying pan (skillet), add the onion and celery and fry until they are soft **8** Add the

sausagemeat and cook until the fat runs out of the meat **9** Drain the excess fat from the pan **10** Add the breadcrumbs, rosemary, parsley, seasoning and stock and mix well **11** Place the stuffing mixture in the centre of the crown and cover with a circle of aluminium foil to prevent it drying out. Roast in the oven, allowing 30 minutes per 450g (1lb) **12** Remove from the oven, discard the pieces of foil and place a cutlet frill on the end of each bone **13** Garnish joint with peas and roast potatoes and serve

Crown Roast of Pork

2 loins of pork, each containing
  8 chops, chined
50 g (2 oz) (4 tablespoons) melted
  butter
1 onion, finely chopped
2 sticks celery, finely chopped
225 g (½ lb) (1 cup) pork
  sausagemeat
100 g (¼ lb) (2 cups) fresh
  breadcrumbs
5 ml (1 teaspoon) rosemary
30 ml (2 tablespoons) finely
  chopped parsley
2.5 ml (½ teaspoon) thyme
salt and pepper
50 ml (2 fl oz) (¼ cup) chicken
  stock

1 Remove the chine bone from the loins. Cut 4 cm (1½ in) of the fat away from the ends of the bones. Trim away the sinew from between the bones.

2 Bend the 2 loins round to form the crown and secure with string. Place the crown in a roasting pan and brush all over the outside with the melted butter. Wrap pieces of aluminium foil round the ends of the bones to prevent them burning.

3 Preheat the oven to 180°C, 350°F, gas 4. Prepare the stuffing: heat the remaining butter in a frying pan (skillet) add the onion and celery and fry until they are soft.

4 Add the sausagement and cook until all the fat has run out of the meat. Drain the excess fat from the pan.

5 Stir in the breadcrumbs, rosemary, parsley, thyme, seasoning and stock and mix.

6 Place the stuffing in the centre of the crown and cover the stuffing with a circle of foil.

7 Roast the crown in the oven, allowing 30 minutes per 450 g (1 lb).

8 Before serving, remove the pieces of foil and place a cutlet frill on the end of each bone. Serve the crown roast garnished with peas and roast potatoes.

Serves 8

Loin of Pork
Spanish-style

450 g (1 lb) haricot beans, soaked
  overnight
2 cloves garlic, crushed
1 bay leaf
50 ml (2 fl oz) (¼ cup) olive oil
2 onions, sliced
1 kg (2 lb) boned loin of pork,
  cubed
225 g (½ lb) chorizo (spicy Spanish
  sausage), cut in 2 cm (¾ in) slices
225 g (½ lb) smoked streaky
  bacon, cut in small strips
3 tomatoes, skinned, deseeded
  and chopped
15 ml (1 tablespoon) paprika
pinch saffron
1 litre (1¾ pints) (4½ cups) boiling
  water
salt and pepper
350 g (¾ lb) runner beans,
  trimmed and cut in 3 cm (1¼ in)
  lengths
small round cabbage, quartered
6 eggs

1 Drain the haricot beans, rinse and place in a pan. Cover with fresh cold water and add 1 clove of garlic and the bay leaf. Bring to the boil, reduce the heat and simmer for 1 hour.

2 Heat the oil in a pan and add the onion, pork, chorizo, bacon, the remaining garlic and the tomatoes. Add the paprika and saffron and cook gently for 7 or 8 minutes, stirring constantly.

3 Pour in the boiling water, season with salt and pepper and cook over a low heat for 45 minutes.

4 When the haricot beans have cooked for 1 hour, drain and add them to the pork and simmer for a further 30 minutes.

5 Add the runner beans and cabbage and cook for 20 minutes.

6 Meanwhile, cook the eggs in boiling water for 10 minutes, cover with cold water and then remove the shells.

7 Transfer the pork mixture to a heated serving dish and garnish with the hard-boiled eggs. Serve very hot.

Serves 6

Pork Orloff

50 g (2 oz) (4 tablespoons)
  margarine
few bacon rinds
1½ kg (3 lb) loin of pork in 1 piece
1 onion
1 carrot, sliced
1 bay leaf
bouquet garni
salt and pepper
45 ml (3 tablespoons) grated
  Parmesan cheese
25 g (1 oz) (2 tablespoons) butter,
  cut in pieces

For the Purée:
50 g (2 oz) (4 tablespoons)
  margarine
15 ml (1 tablespoon) oil
4 onions, chopped
450 g (1 lb) mushroom caps, diced
150 ml (¼ pint) (⅝ cup) thick white
  sauce
150 ml (¼ pint) (⅝ cup) double
  (heavy) cream
pinch grated nutmeg
45 ml (3 tablespoons) grated
  Parmesan cheese

1 Heat the margarine in a pan, add the bacon rinds and pork and cook until browned. Add the onion, sliced carrot, bay leaf, bouquet garni and seasoning and then cover with water. Cover the pan and cook slowly for 1¾ hours.

2 Meanwhile, make the purée. Heat the margarine and oil in a pan and gently fry the chopped onion for 10 minutes, without browning. Add the diced mushrooms and cook for 1 minute.

3 Strain off the fat and add the white sauce and cream. Mix well and season with salt, pepper and nutmeg. Stir in the cheese and cook for 3 minutes. Cool.

4 Preheat the oven to 230°C, 450°F, gas 8. Lift the pork from the pan and carve it into thick slices. Spread each slice with purée and replace the slices to resemble the original joint.

5 Cover with the remaining purée and sprinkle with the grated Parmesan cheese and the pieces of butter. Return to the oven for 5-10 minutes to brown.

Serves 6-8

8

9

10

1 Score the rind of the boned pork with a very sharp knife and set the joint aside **2** Peel and finely chop the onion **3** Fry the onion in the butter over a gentle heat until soft and lightly golden in colour **4** Finely chop the apricots and walnuts and mix with the onion, breadcrumbs, parsley and salt and pepper to taste **5** Bind with the egg and mix well **6** Place the stuffing on the inner side of the meat and press it down well **7** Roll the meat up and tie it tightly with string **8** Brush the skin all over with the oil **9** Rub the skin well with salt to ensure a crisp crackling **10** Serve the stuffed pork with boiled, sliced leeks

Pickled Pork with Saffron Rice

1½ kg (3 lb) pork loin, boned
15 ml (1 tablespoon) saltpetre
450 g (1 lb) sea salt
5 ml (1 teaspoon) powdered
  ginger
salt and pepper
4 cloves
450 g (1 lb) (2 cups) long grain rice
1.25 ml (¼ teaspoon) powdered
  saffron
50 g (2 oz) (4 tablespoons) butter

1 Buy the pork loin the day before the dish is to be served. Rub saltpetre over it. Put a layer of sea salt in an earthenware bowl. Lay in the meat and cover it with the rest of the salt. Leave it for 24 hours in a cool place.

2 Remove the pork from the salt, wash it thoroughly in cold water and dry it.

3 Preheat the oven to 190°C, 375°F, gas 5. Spread out a cloth and put the meat onto it, fat side down. Sprinkle with the ginger and pepper to taste. Roll it up, seasoned side inside, tying it tightly with string.

4 Using the point of a very sharp knife, cut the fat in criss-cross lines forming a diamond pattern. Stud the meat with the 4 cloves and season with pepper.

5 Pour 100 ml (4 fl oz) (½ cup) of warm water into a roasting pan containing a rack. Place the meat on the rack and roast in the oven for about 1¼ hours or until cooked through.

6 Put the rice into a pan with 1.2 litres (2 pints) (5 cups) cold water, the saffron and salt to taste. Cover and cook for 20 minutes, until the rice is tender and the water absorbed. Add the butter, season with pepper and fluff up with a fork.

7 Arrange the sliced pork on the rice to serve.

Serves 8

Tip: You can use ordinary table or cooking salt for curing the pork instead of sea salt.

Boned Blade of Pork with Apricot and Walnut Stuffing

2 kg (4 lb) blade or shoulder of
  pork, boned
1 onion, finely chopped
15 g (½ oz) (1 tablespoon) butter
50 g (2 oz) (⅔ cup) dried apricots,
  soaked in water overnight and
  finely chopped
12 walnut halves, finely chopped
50 g (2 oz) (1 cup) fresh white
  breadcrumbs
15 ml (1 tablespoon) chopped
  parsley
salt and pepper
1 egg
15 ml (1 tablespoon) oil
5 ml (1 teaspoon) salt

1 Preheat the oven to 230°C, 450°F, gas 8. Score the rind of the pork with a very sharp knife.

2 Fry the onion gently in the butter until lightly golden.

3 Mix together the apricots, walnuts, onion, breadcrumbs, parsley and salt and pepper to taste. Mix in the egg.

4 Place the stuffing on the inner side of the meat. Roll up the meat and tie tightly with string. Place in a greased roasting pan, brush with the oil and rub the salt into the skin.

5 Roast for 30 minutes or until the surface has crackled. Turn the oven to 190°C, 375°F, gas 5, and roast for a further hour.

Serves 6

Flemish Pork with Red Cabbage

1 kg (2¼ lbs) best end rib of pork,
  or loin
salt and pepper
good pinch mixed spice
60 ml (2¼ fl oz) (4 tablespoons) oil
1 small red cabbage, shredded
1 onion, chopped
1 clove garlic, finely chopped
100 ml (4 fl oz) (½ cup) vinegar
2 apples, peeled, cored and
  thinly sliced
15 ml (1 tablespoon) sugar
5 ml (1 teaspoon) chopped
  parsley
½ beef stock cube dissolved in
  300 ml (½ pint) (1¼ cups) water
15 ml (1 tablespoon) tomato
  concentrate (paste)
10 ml (2 teaspoons) cornflour
  (cornstarch), mixed with water

1 Preheat the oven to 190°C, 375°F, gas 5. Remove the rind from the pork and season with salt, pepper and mixed spice. Brush with oil and place on a rack in a roasting pan. Roast in the preheated oven for 1¼ hours, basting frequently with 225 ml (8 fl oz) (1 cup) water.

2 Place the cabbage in an earthenware bowl with the onion, garlic, vinegar and 550 ml (1 pint) (2½ cups) water. Leave to stand for 15 minutes.

3 Add the apples to the cabbage with the sugar and seasoning. Transfer to a stainless steel pan, bring to the boil and simmer for 20 minutes.

4 Transfer the pork to a serving dish. Surround with the cabbage in its liquid and sprinkle with parsley.

5 Pour off the fat from the roasting pan, retaining the meat juices. Add the stock and tomato concentrate (paste), bring to the boil and simmer for 5 minutes. Add the cornflour (cornstarch) to the pan and simmer for 1 minute, stirring. Season and strain into a sauce boat or jug to serve.

Serves 6

Tips: To save time, instead of pickling a best end or loin of pork, you can buy a gammon or back bacon joint. If you are not a lover of red cabbage, don't ignore this recipe. You can substitute white Savoy cabbage and omit the vinegar. However, if you do use red cabbage and want to make this dish extra special, use red wine instead of water.

Pork Piedmontese

50 ml (2 fl oz) (¼ cup) oil
675 g (1½ lb) lean pork, cut into
  cubes
15 g (½ oz) (2 tablespoons) flour
15 g (½ oz) (1 tablespoon) tomato
  concentrate (paste)
300 ml (½ pint) (1¼ cups) water
150 ml (¼ pint) (⅝ cup) dry white
  wine
85 ml (3 fl oz) (⅜ cup) single (light)
  cream
juice 1 lemon
pinch oregano
salt and pepper
3 medium courgettes
  (zucchini)

For the Stuffing:
100 g (¼ lb) calves liver
salt and pepper
15 g (½ oz) (2 tablespoons) flour
30 ml (1 fl oz) (2 tablespoons) oil
1 onion, chopped
50 g (2 oz) bacon, finely sliced
50 g (2 oz) mushrooms, finely
  sliced

Pork Portuguese, served with rice pilaff, is a tasty way of serving pork in white wine with tomatoes, celery and peppers

15 ml (1 tablespoon) Parmesan
  cheese
50 ml (2 fl oz) (¼ cup) dry white
  wine
85 ml (3 fl oz) (⅜ cup) double
  (heavy) cream

1 Preheat the oven to 180°C, 350°F, gas 4. Heat the oil in a pan. Add the meat and brown for 12 minutes. Sprinkle in the flour and stir. Cook for one minute, then add the tomato concentrate (paste), water and wine. Bring to the boil and simmer for 15 minutes. Stir in the cream, lemon juice and oregano. Season and transfer to a casserole. Bake in the preheated oven for one hour or until the meat is tender.

2 Meanwhile cut the courgettes (zucchini) in half lengthways. Cook them for 5 minutes in boiling salted water. Drain and keep warm.

3 If necessary remove the mem-

brane from the liver. Cut it into small cubes and roll in seasoned flour.

4 In a separate pan, heat the oil. Add the onion and sauté until it is soft. Add the bacon, liver, mushrooms and Parmesan cheese and cook for 5 minutes on a moderate heat. Pour in the wine and cream. Stir and simmer for a further 5 minutes. Check the seasoning.

5 With a spoon scoop out the seeds from the courgette (zucchini) halves. Place them on a warm serving dish and spoon the stuffing mixture into the cavities. Surround with the hot pork casserole and serve.

Serves 6

Tips: You can use this tasty stuffing for other vegetables besides courgettes (zucchini). Try using it in aubergines (eggplants) or even red and green peppers. To give it an even richer, more distinctive flavour, substitute a fortified wine such as sherry or port for the white wine.

Pork Paupiettes Braised in Beer

450 g (1 lb) lean loin of pork
salt and pepper
25 g (1 oz) (2 tablespoons) fat
100 g (¼ lb) carrots
450 g (1 lb) small onions
25 g (1 oz) (4 tablespoons) flour
15 ml (1 tablespoon) tomato
  concentrate (paste)
400 ml (14 fl oz) (1¾ cups) brown
  stock
300 ml (½ pint) (1¼ cups) light beer
bouquet garni

For the Stuffing:
30 ml (2 tablespoons) chopped
  onion
15 ml (1 tablespoon) oil
50 g (2 oz) (1 cup) white
  breadcrumbs
5 ml (1 teaspoon) chopped
  parsley
pinch thyme
½ egg to bind
25 g (1 oz) chopped apricots
25 g (1 oz) chopped walnuts
10 ml (2 teaspoons) butter

1 Cut the meat across the grain into 4 thin slices and pound them. Trim to approximately 12.5 cm × 10 cm (5 in × 4 in) and chop the trimmings into small pieces. Season the meat slices.

2 Prepare the stuffing. Sauté the onion in the oil until it is soft. Combine the onion with all the other ingredients and mix in the chopped pork trimmings. Spread a quarter of the stuffing down the centre of each meat slice. Roll them up and secure with string.

3 Heat the fat in a pan. Add the paupiettes and lightly brown them all over. Then add the carrots and onions and continue cooking until the meat is golden all over. Remove from the heat.

4 Drain off the fat and pour 25 g (1 oz) (2 tablespoons) into a clean pan. Add the flour and stir on a low heat until you have a brown roux. Mix in the tomato concentrate (paste) and allow to cool. Boil the stock and add it to the pan with the beer. Bring the sauce to the boil, remove any scum, season and pour over the meat.

5 Add the bouquet garni, cover and allow to simmer on a low heat for 1-1½ hours.

6 Remove the string and place the paupiettes on a warm serving dish. Surround with the vegetables and pour over the sauce.

Serves 4

Pork Alentago

675 g (1½ lb) lean pork tenderloin,
  boned
200 ml (6 fl oz) (¾ cup) dry white
  wine
2 cloves garlic, crushed
2 bay leaves
5 ml (1 teaspoon) paprika
salt and pepper
2 slices bacon, diced
4 slices white bread
1 clove garlic, halved
30 ml (1 fl oz) (2 tablespoons) oil
275 g (10 oz) canned mussels or
  clams, drained

1 Cut the pork into 2.5 cm (1 in) cubes.

2 Combine the wine, garlic, bay leaves and paprika in a bowl. Season with the salt and pepper and add the pork. Cover tightly with plastic or foil and refrigerate for 24 hours.

3 Fry the bacon in a heavy frying pan (skillet) until the fat runs out.

4 Drain the pork cubes, dry them thoroughly and brown in the bacon fat. Cover and cook over a very low heat for 30 minutes.

5 Strain the marinade and add the liquid to the pan. Simmer uncovered for 20 minutes.

6 Meanwhile, remove the crusts from the bread and rub with the garlic clove. Heat the oil in a pan and sauté the bread until it is brown. Place the bread slices in a shallow casserole and keep warm.

7 Add the mussels or clams to the pork and marinade and heat through. Pour the pork and shellfish over the bread and serve.

Serves 4

Pork Canton

675 g (1½ lb) lean minced pork
50 g (2 oz) (½ cup) chopped onions
salt and pepper
1.25 ml (¼ teaspoon) fresh root
  ginger, chopped
1 egg, beaten
30 ml (1 fl oz) (2 tablespoons) oil

For the Sauce:
50 g (2 oz) (½ cup) chopped onion
2 sticks celery, diced
30 ml (2 tablespoons) cornflour
  (cornstarch)
1.25 ml (¼ teaspoon) fresh root
  ginger, chopped
25 g (1 oz) (2 tablespoons) sugar
15 ml (1 tablespoon) soya sauce
225 ml (8 fl oz) (1 cup) chicken
  stock
100 ml (4 fl oz) (½ cup) peach juice
50 ml (2 fl oz) (¼ cup) vinegar
225 g (½ lb) canned peaches,
  drained and diced

1 Combine the pork, onion, salt, pepper and ginger in a bowl. Bind with the beaten egg.

2 Roll the mince mixture into balls approximately 4 cm (1½ in) in diameter.

3 Heat the oil in a frying pan (skillet) and cook the meatballs for about 10 minutes or until done. Remove the meat from the pan and drain well.

4 Prepare the sauce. Drain all but 15 ml (1 tablespoon) of fat from the pan. Sauté the onion and celery in the fat until the onion is transparent.

5 Combine the remaining ingredients, except the peaches, and pour into the pan. Stir and cook until the sauce is thick and clear.

6 Finally add the meatballs and diced peaches. Cover and simmer gently for 10 minutes to allow the sauce flavour to impregnate the meat. Serve with hot rice or noodles.

Serves 6

*Pork Paupiettes Braised in Beer
are stuffed with fruit,
nuts and herbs and cooked in a
tasty, beer-flavoured stock*

Oriental Pork

Sweet'n Sour Pork

450 g (1 lb) pork tenderloin,
  cubed
30 ml (1 fl oz) (2 tablespoons)
  sherry
15 ml (1 tablespoon) soya sauce
1.25 ml (¼ teaspoon) sugar
5 mm (¼ in) piece fresh root
  ginger, grated
salt and pepper
4 celery sticks, sliced
1 red pepper, deseeded and diced
8 spring onions (scallions), cut
  into 5 cm (2 in) pieces
¼ English cucumber, cut into
  wedges
45 ml (2 fl oz) (3 tablespoons) oil
225 g (½ lb) canned pineapple
  chunks with juice

50 g (2 oz) (6 tablespoons)
  cornflour (cornstarch)
50 ml (2 fl oz) (¼ cup) vinegar
100 ml (4 fl oz) (½ cup) sweet white
  wine
15 ml (1 tablespoon) brown sugar
oil for deep frying

1 Mix the pork with the sherry,
soya sauce, sugar and ginger. Add
pepper to taste and mix well.
Marinate for 30 minutes.

2 Fry the vegetables in the oil
until soft but not brown. Drain the
pineapple reserving the juice and
add the chunks to the pan. Stir-fry
for 2 minutes.

3 Mix 30 ml (2 tablespoons) of the
cornflour (cornstarch) with the
vinegar, and stir in to the pan with
pineapple juice, wine and sugar.
Season and simmer for 2 minutes,
stirring.

4 Heat the oil for deep frying.
Remove the pork from the
marinade and add the marinade
to the sauce.

5 Coat the pork in the remaining

*Pork and Bamboo Shoots. Sliced
pork tenderloin stir-fried
with onion and garlic
in a pineapple and ginger sauce*

cornflour (cornstarch) and fry it in
the hot oil. Drain well.

6 Serve the pork on a bed of fried
noodles with the sauce poured
over.

Serves 4

Pork and Bamboo Shoots

45 ml (2 fl oz) (3 tablespoons) oil
1 onion, chopped
1 clove garlic, crushed
450 g (1 lb) pork tenderloin,
  thinly sliced
225 g (½ lb) bamboo shoots, thinly
  sliced
5 ml (1 teaspoon) cornflour
  (cornstarch)
2.5 ml (½ teaspoon) powdered
  ginger
5 ml (1 teaspoon) soya sauce
2.5 ml (½ teaspoon) anchovy
  essence
150 ml (¼ pint) (⅝ cup) pineapple
  juice
pepper

1 Heat the oil in a frying pan
(skillet) and fry the onion and
garlic until soft but not brown.
Add the pork and stir-fry until
browned.

2 Add the bamboo shoots to the
pan, cover and cook gently for 10
minutes.

3 Mix the cornflour (cornstarch),
ginger, soya sauce and anchovy
essence with enough pineapple
juice to make a smooth paste.
Add to the pan with the remaining juice and simmer gently,
uncovered, for 15 minutes.

4 Season with pepper and serve
with boiled rice and Kumquat
pickle.

Serves 4

*Sweet'n Sour Pork — traditional
Chinese Food, which is
becoming increasingly popular in
countries all over the world.
Serve it on a bed of fried
noodles, with fried rice, boiled
noodles and chopped mangoes*

Spareribs Tahiti

900 g (2 lb) pork spareribs
100 ml (4 fl oz) (½ cup) vinegar
300 ml (½ pint) (1¼ cups) water
200 ml (6 fl oz) (¾ cup) tomato
 ketchup (catsup)
175 g (6 oz) (¾ cup) brown sugar
7.5 ml (1½ teaspoons) soya sauce
2 large pinches salt
25 g (1 oz) (3 tablespoons)
 cornflour (cornstarch)
60 ml (2¼ fl oz) (4 tablespoons)
 water

1 Preheat the oven to 170°C, 325°F, gas 3. Divide the meat into individual ribs. Pour the vinegar and water over them in a roasting pan and bake for 1 hour. Skim off any fat from the liquid, strain the liquid and reserve.

2 Stir the ketchup (catsup), brown sugar, soya sauce and salt into the cooking liquid. Mix the cornflour (cornstarch) with the 60 ml (2¼ fl oz) (4 tablespoons) of water and add to the liquid. Stir over heat to thicken.

3 Pour the sauce over the spareribs and return them to the oven to bake for 30 minutes or until browned. Serve immediately with rice.

Serves 4

Stir-fried Pork with Nuts

225 g (½ lb) pork tenderloin
4 small carrots, cut in
 matchstick strips
45 ml (2 fl oz) (3 tablespoons) oil
good pinch salt
1 onion, thinly sliced
1 clove garlic, crushed
2 thin slices fresh root ginger,
 peeled and finely chopped
½ red pepper, deseeded and sliced
25 g (1 oz) (¼ cup) blanched
 almonds or cashew nuts
100 ml (4 fl oz) (½ cup) chicken
 stock
30 ml (1 fl oz) (2 tablespoons) soya
 sauce

15 ml (1 tablespoon) sherry
15 g (½ oz) (1½ tablespoons)
 cornflour (cornstarch)

1 Cut the pork into thin slices across the grain of the meat. Blanch the carrots in boiling water for 4 minutes, refresh in cold water and drain.

2 Heat half the oil in a pan. Add the pork and salt and stir-fry for 3 minutes. Remove the meat from the pan with a perforated spoon and keep warm.

3 Heat the rest of the oil in the pan. Add the onion, garlic and ginger, and stir-fry for 1 minute. Then add the pepper, carrot and nuts and stir-fry for another minute. Add the stock, soya sauce and sherry, and bring to the boil, stirring.

4 Lower the heat and return the pork to the pan. Cover and cook gently for about 5 minutes or until the pork is tender.

5 Mix the cornflour (cornstarch) to a paste with a little water, and stir it into the pan until the sauce thickens. Serve at once.

Serves 3

Pacific Pork

675 g (1½ lb) pork tenderloin
25 g (1 oz) (¼ cup) flour
25 g (1 oz) (2 tablespoons) fat
225 ml (8 fl oz) (1 cup) pineapple
 juice
100 g (¼ lb) (½ cup) crushed canned
 pineapple
2.5 ml (½ teaspoon) each: salt,
 pepper, powdered ginger,
 allspice
15 g (½ oz) (1½ tablespoons)
 cornflour (cornstarch)
30 ml (1 fl oz) (2 tablespoons)
 water

1 Preheat oven to 180°C, 350°F, gas 4. Cut the tenderloin into 6 pieces, and coat them with flour.

2 Melt the fat in a frying pan (skillet) and brown the pork lightly. Transfer the pork to an ovenproof

dish. Combine the pineapple juice and fruit, salt, pepper, ginger and allspice. Pour the mixture over the meat and bake uncovered for 45 minutes or until the meat is tender.

3 Remove the meat to a serving dish and keep warm. Pour the rest of the cooking liquid into the pan and thicken with the mixture of cornflour (cornstarch) and water. Pour the sauce over the meat and serve.

Serves 6

Pork Vindaye

450 g (1 lb) spare rib chops or
 blade of pork
2 onions
2 cloves garlic
1 red pepper
30 ml (1 fl oz) (2 tablespoons) oil
10 ml (2 teaspoons) vinegar
15 ml (1 tablespoon) curry
 powder
10 ml (2 teaspoons) powdered
 ginger
salt
225 ml (8 fl oz) (1 cup) water

1 Cut the meat into large chunks or, if using spare rib chops, remove excess fat and cut them in half.

2 Finely chop the onions and garlic. Deseed the red pepper and chop. Mix these together with the oil and vinegar and pound to a paste with a pestle and mortar.

3 Stir in the curry powder, ginger and a good pinch of salt. Coat the pieces of meat with this mixture and place them in a large saucepan. Pour in the water, cover, and simmer for 2 hours. Serve with golden rice – boiled with a pinch of turmeric to colour it.

Serves 4

*Pork Vindaye – large chunks
of pork cooked gently in
a spicy curry-flavoured coating
until succulently tender*

Saté

This is a traditional Indonesian dish of small pork kebabs served with a spicy peanut sauce, always featured among the many accompaniments on an Indonesian rice table.

450 g (1 lb) pork fillet
50 ml (2 fl oz) (¼ cup)
  soya sauce
50 ml (2 fl oz) (¼ cup) sherry
1 clove garlic, crushed
1 thin slice fresh root ginger,
  finely chopped
5 ml (1 teaspoon) curry
  powder
30 ml (1 fl oz) (2 tablespoons) oil
100 g (¼ lb) (⅔ cup) fresh peanuts,
  finely chopped
5 ml (1 teaspoon) honey
few drops chilli sauce
5 ml (1 teaspoon) tomato ketchup
  (catsup)
5 ml (1 teaspoon) lemon juice
50 g (2 oz) (¼ cup) peanut butter
5 ml (1 teaspoon) cornflour
  (cornstarch)

1 Cut the pork into 3 cm (1¼ in) cubes. Mix together the soya sauce, sherry, garlic, ginger, curry powder and oil, and marinate the pork pieces in this for 3 hours, basting from time to time.

2 Strain the meat from the marinade and thread the pieces on to kebab skewers. Grill (broil) the kebabs, turning frequently, until browned on all sides.

3 Meanwhile, pour the marinade into a saucepan and add the rest of the ingredients except the cornflour (cornstarch). Heat gently, stirring to blend them into a smooth sauce. Thicken if required with the cornflour (cornstarch) mixed with a little water.

4 Take the cooked pork from the kebab skewers. Arrange the meat around a heated serving dish, and pour the peanut sauce into the middle. Use cocktail sticks to dip the meat pieces into the sauce. Serve with Indonesian Rice.

Serves 4

Indonesian Rice

100 g (¼ lb) (½ cup) long grain rice
pinch turmeric
30 ml (1 fl oz) (2 tablespoons) oil
50 g (2 oz) (⅓ cup) fresh peanuts,
  skinned
5 ml (1 teaspoon) cumin seeds
25 ml (1½ tablespoons) desiccated
  coconut
salt and pepper

1 Boil the rice in salted water with a pinch of turmeric. Rinse and drain.

2 Heat the oil in a frying pan (skillet). Add the rice and stir-fry for 3 minutes. Add the other ingredients, stir well and fry for another 3 minutes.

Serves 4

A traditional Indonesian Rice Table with the famous Saté (foreground), Indonesian Rice (centre), king prawns, curried chicken and bean sprouts

All about Sausages

1 Gutsleberwurst
2 Sulzwurst
3 Bierwurst
4 Salami special
5 Leberrotwurst
6 Aalrauchmettwurst
7 Chorizo
8 Peppered salami

Sausages come in a wide variety of flavours and sizes. Most are based on minced pork. How many times have you stood in a delicatessen or continental *charcuterie* and gazed longingly at the colourful display of sausages and been tempted to buy, but, through ignorance of their names or cooking methods, turned away empty-handed? The wealth of choice is overwhelming. In this issue, we show you how to cook sausages from the most humble chipolata (link sausage) to the more exotic continental varieties. There are ideas for serving hot and cold sausages in new exciting ways and also recipes for making your own at home.

The history of sausages goes back about 5,000 years. There is evidence that the Sumerians, Assyrians and ancient Greeks all ate sausages. The Romans were real sausage lovers and our own word 'sausage' is, in fact, derived from a Latin word, *salsisium*. Sausages became very popular at Roman feasts and orgies but were later outlawed by the early Christian church for obvious reasons! It was the Romans who introduced the black pudding into their colony of Britain and, of course, it still survives today. Early sausages were much more tasty and spicy than the sausages of today. Among the ingredients were mixed herbs, peppercorns, pine kernels and cumin. However, even in those days there were some unscrupulous butchers who tried to substitute horsemeat for pork.

Sausages have remained popular through the centuries and today there are at least 500 different varieties which can be made. They are made on a worldwide scale, not only in Europe but also in the Middle East and even China. There are smoked sausages such as frankfurters and Viennas, dry sausages such as salami, chorizo and mortadella, as well as the uncooked pork and beef varieties we fry or grill (broil) until they are brown and sizzling.

Nowadays, most sausages are made not only of meat and fat, seasoned with salt, pepper and herbs, but also breadcrumbs stuffed into blanched intestines. With a new process, modern technology can now even make a sort of artificial sausage skin.

The Germans and Italians are probably the world's biggest sausage producers and consumers. They use beer, spices, onions, aromatic herbs, garlic and even kidneys and tongue in their sausages. The Germans claim that they alone produce 1458 different sausages.

There are six classifications of sausages: fresh; smoked; cooked; dry; new conditioned; and cooked specialities.

Storing Sausages
You can store salted and smoked varieties of sausages in the freezer for long periods of time. Sausages will keep in the refrigerator for a few days or may be stored in a cool place such as a larder. As long as the air is cool, you can hang them up in the traditional way. But protect them from flies and other insects.

Serving Sausages
Sausages are more versatile than most of us realise, and grilling (broiling) or frying them for breakfast or a snack meal are not the only ways of serving them. In this issue of *Look 'n Cook*, we show you how to casserole and stew them, and even make your own. Mustard is the traditional accompaniment to sausages and nowadays there are many varieties and blends to choose from. Mustard can flavour a sausage casserole as well as being smeared along the tops of fried sausages. Home-made tomato and spicy barbecue sauces also go well with sausages, as well as the bottled ketchup (catsup).

Flavourings for Sausages
You can now buy sausages in all sorts of different shapes and flavours. If you plan to be really adventurous and make your own sausages, then there are many herbs, spices and even alcohol which you can use to vary the flavour. Apart from the obvious salt and pepper, you can use spices such as paprika, cayenne pepper and chilli powder for a hot, spicy result. Mace, nutmeg, cloves, garlic, cinnamon and allspice can also be used. Many commercially produced and packaged sausages and chipolatas (link sausages) now contain herbs. You can use nearly all herbs in sausage-making, particularly sage and thyme. Rosemary, parsley, basil, marjoram and sorrel can all be used. In addition to herbs and spices, you can also use wine and even brandy.

Making your own Sausages
Making sausages is really a very simple business and far less complicated than it may sound. Of course it is easier to go to your local supermarket and buy a packet off the shelf, but the home-made sort are far more tasty and very rewarding. Also, you have more freedom of choice in that you can choose your ingredients more selectively and blend in your favourite herbs and spices and flavourings for a really tasty result. You don't need any expensive equipment – a mincer, especially an electric one, can be a boon, but as long as you chop the ingredients finely you can make reasonable sausages.

Opposite are some of the attractive, delicious sausages you can buy in most food halls of big stores or delicatessens. Nowadays, most shops offer a wide range of home-produced and continental sausages at very reasonable prices so you can afford to be a little adventurous and try some to eat cold or cooked, in a variety of ways. The names are often difficult to pronounce but don't be put off by this. In the pictures on the following pages, we identify the different sausages and give you some useful information on their flavour, cooking methods and serving. Using this, you will soon learn to recognize the different varieties.

The sausages which may be eaten cold constitute a large group, and many of its members are very well known and popular. They have all been cooked, either by being cured and smoked at very low temperatures, or by boiling.

These cooking processes preserve the meat so that the sausages may be kept for some time without deterioration – a week or more in a dry, airy, cool place.

Once they have been cut open it is safer to store them in a refrigerator. To serve, cut in thin slices with a sharp knife and remove the outer skin. Arrange

Salami and Corn Salad, a light and appetizing buffet dish. The presentation of cold meats is always important

the slices overlapping on a platter, or fold them into a roll and secure with a cocktail stick. Sausages may be cut straight across to give rounds, or on a slant to give oval slices. The thick sausages may also be diced.

Salami and Corn Salad

450 g (1 lb) German and Italian salami, thinly sliced
4 small corn cobs
225 g ($\frac{1}{2}$ lb) cauliflower florets
1 red pepper, cut in strips
$\frac{1}{2}$ cucumber, sliced
225 g ($\frac{1}{2}$ lb) (2 cups) pickled cocktail onions

1 Arrange half of the salami slices, overlapping, around a dish. Roll up the remaining slices and arrange in an inner ring.

2 Boil the corn cobs in water for 8 minutes.

3 Boil the cauliflower florets for 5 minutes only.

4 Pile all the vegetables in the centre of the salami.

Serves 6

Types of Sausages

1 Salami la is a hard, spicy sausage which will keep for months.

2 Leberrotwurst contains minced (ground) meat and bacon.

3 Chorizo is a Spanish sausage flavoured with red pepper.

4 Salami special is spicy, garlic flavoured, and net-covered.

5 Aalrauch mettwurst has been smoked over fish bones.

6 Gutsleberwurst is a coarse liver sausage, lightly seasoned.

7 Haas Bauernsalami is one of the spiciest of salamis.

8 Land salami is mild, made of pork and beef with no garlic.

9 Regensburger Knackwurst may be cooked and served hot.

10 Bierwurst is spicy, containing garlic and peppers.

11 Cervelas fine is mild and smooth, and will keep well.

12 Negroni – a dry smoked sausage with peppercorns.

13 Schinkenplockwurst is a sausage of smoked pickled pork.

14 Liver sausage is mild and smooth textured.

15 Schinken-sülzwurst is like a brawn and contains mushrooms.

16 Frankfurters may be reheated or served cold as canapés.

17 Katenrauchwurst is made of pork smoked for a long time.

18 Farmer's salami is smoked dry and hard, with various spices.

19 Pepper salami has a peppercorn coating for extra flavour.

Hot Sausages

Most of the Continental pork sausages available to us on the market are delicious simmered, baked or grilled (broiled) to serve hot.

They may be cut in chunks and added to soups and casseroles, chopped for sauces and stews, sliced for pizzas and quiches.

Allow 100 g ($\frac{1}{4}$ lb) per person of freshly ground meat sausage or the smoked varieties, and slightly less for the spicier, drier types.

Sausage and Vegetable Casserole

100 g ($\frac{1}{4}$ lb) ($\frac{1}{3}$ cup) red kidney
  beans, soaked overnight
$\frac{1}{4}$ small green cabbage, shredded
2 potatoes, peeled and sliced
2 carrots, peeled and chopped
1 large leek, sliced
2 onions, peeled and sliced
2 beef stock cubes dissolved in
  900 ml (1$\frac{1}{2}$ pints) (4 cups) boiling
  water
salt and pepper
450 g (1 lb) pork chipolata (link)
  sausages

1 Put the kidney beans into a large saucepan with the cabbage,

Sausage and Vegetable Casserole with juicy cabbage, carrots and beans, makes a big tasty meal just right for winter days

potatoes, carrots, leak, onion, stock and seasoning. Bring to the boil, reduce the heat and simmer for 1 hour.

2 Twist each sausage into three, to give chains of three small sausages. Add to the casserole and simmer for a further 15 minutes, or until the sausages are coked.

3 Serve with crusty bread.

Serves 4

Ham Sausage with Sauerkraut

25 g (1 oz) (2 tablespoons) cooking
  fat
1 onion, chopped

450 g (1 lb) canned sauerkraut
6 juniper berries
bouquet garni
salt and pepper
450 g (1 lb) smoked ham sausage, in one piece
$\frac{1}{2}$ ham stock cube, dissolved in 300 ml ($\frac{1}{2}$ pint) (1$\frac{1}{4}$ cups) boiling water
450 g (1 lb) baby carrots
25 g (1 oz) (2 tablespoons) butter

1 Preheat the oven to 180°C, 350°F, gas 4. Melt the fat in a pan and fry the onion until soft but not brown.

2 Wash and drain the sauerkraut and add to the onion, with the juniper berries, bouquet garni and seasoning. Stir over a medium heat for 3 or 4 minutes. Turn into a casserole dish, lay the whole sausage on top and pour over the stock.

3 Cover the casserole and cook in the preheated oven for about 35 minutes, or until the sausage is heated through.

4 Cook the carrots in boiling salted water for 15 minutes. Drain and toss in the butter.

5 Remove the juniper berries and bouquet garni from the casserole. Arrange the sausage and sauerkraut on a heated serving

Ham Sausage with Sauerkraut – the fatty content of the sausage is complemented by the crisp, acid sauerkraut

dish, cut the sausage in thick slices and garnish with the baby carrots.

Serves 4

Tip: The juniper berries give this dish a delicate gin flavour. If juniper berries are not available, add 15 ml (1 tablespoon) gin with the ham stock.

Hot Dogs

6 finger rolls
6 frankfurter sausages
30 ml (2 tablespoons) strong made mustard
15 ml (1 tablespoon) tomato concentrate (paste)
10 ml (2 teaspoons) tomato ketchup (catsup)

1 Preheat the oven to 180°C, 350°F, gas 4.

2 Split the finger rolls along one

side and open them out. Put them in the oven to warm through, but do not allow them to dry out.

3 Place the sausages in a pan of hot water and simmer gently for 10 minutes.

4 Combine the mustard, tomato concentrate (paste) and ketchup (catsup) in a bowl and beat well.

5 Spread the cut surfaces of the warmed rolls with the mustard mixture, put a hot frankfurter inside each roll and serve immediately.

Serves 6

Tip: An excellent accompaniment to hot dogs is, of course, sliced, fried onion. And any hot spread or sauce can be used instead of the mustard – try a spicy tomato or barbecue sauce.

Pan-fried toasties
Use your favourite spicy sausage for this quick and easy pan-fried sandwich. Butter 2 slices of white bread. Cover one slice with 25 g (1 oz) thinly sliced sausage, a little tomato relish and 25 g (1 oz) ($\frac{1}{4}$ cup) grated cheese. Fry it on both sides until the cheese is melted and the sandwich is golden-brown.

Sausages and Pastry

Pastry makes a good accompaniment to sausages since it can stretch any dish to make it more economical and it can turn ordinary 'bangers' into special party dishes when baked in golden flaky or puff pastry. There are, of course, classic sausage and pastry dishes, such as sausage rolls and in this section we feature another standard, Easter Pie, which is beautifully easy to make using our step-by-step guide.

Dickens Pies

100 g (¼ lb) (½ cup) mincemeat
225 g (½ lb) cooked pork sausages, skinned and chopped
2 eggs
350 g (¾ lb) puff pastry

1 Preheat the oven to 220°C, 425°F, gas 7. Combine the mincemeat, sausages and 1 egg.

2 Roll out the pastry to 3 mm (⅛ in) thickness and cut into twelve 7.5 cm (3 in) rounds. Place a spoonful of the mixture in the centre of 6. Roll the remaining rounds to enlarge them to 10 cm

Sausage Pie is meaty and satisfying, and any leftovers will taste just as good when eaten cold the next day

(4 in). Dampen the edges of the filled rounds with water and cover with the larger pieces. Press the edges to seal and place on a greased baking sheet. Brush with the remaining egg, beaten, and allow to rest for 20 minutes.

3 Bake in the preheated oven for 20 minutes and serve hot or cold.

Makes 12 pies

Sausage Cheese Flan

225 g (½ lb) shortcrust (piecrust)
225 g (½ lb) beef and pork chipolata (link) sausages

150 ml (¼ pint) (⅝ cup) white sauce
2 eggs
salt and pepper
pinch cayenne pepper
**50 g (2 oz) (½ cup) grated Cheddar
  cheese**

1 After making the shortcrust (piecrust), allow it to rest for 20 minutes.

2 Prick the sausages and grill (broil) them for 4 minutes to brown the outsides.

3 Preheat the oven to 200°C, 425°F, gas 7. Grease a 20 cm (8 in) flan tin. Roll out the dough to 3 mm (⅛ in) thickness and use it to line the flan tin. Prick the dough with a fork and bake blind in the preheated oven for 12 minutes. Cool. Reduce the oven temperature to 180°C, 350°F, gas 4.

4 Combine the white sauce and the eggs, season to taste and add half of the cheese. Pour the mixture into the flan and arrange the sausages on top. Sprinkle with the rest of the cheese and bake for 30 minutes.

Serves 4

*Sausage Cheese Flan combines
hearty sausages with
a light and tasty cheese mixture,
to make a perfect supper*

Sausage Pie

450 g (1 lb) shortcrust (piecrust)
**25 g (1 oz) (2 tablespoons) lard
  (shortening)**
**225 g (½ lb) beef and pork
  chipolata (link) sausages**
3 eggs
**100 g (¼ lb) (½ cup) pork
  sausagemeat**
**15 ml (1 tablespoon) chopped
  parsley**
1 onion, chopped
**45 ml (3 tablespoons) fresh white
  breadcrumbs**
**30 ml (1 fl oz) (2 tablespoons)
  brandy or sherry**
salt and pepper
pinch paprika
pinch mace or nutmeg
pinch garlic salt

1 Preheat the oven to 190°C, 375°F, gas 5. Roll out the dough to

3 mm (⅛ in) thickness and divide into two. Grease a 20 cm (8 in) pie tin with the lard (shortening) and line the bottom with one piece of the dough. Trim, and prick the base with a fork.

2 Grill (broil) the sausages for 3 minutes to brown the outsides. Cut into thick chunks and allow to cool.

3 Beat 2 of the eggs and combine with the sausagemeat, parsley, onion, breadcrumbs, brandy or sherry, salt, pepper, paprika, mace or nutmeg, and garlic salt. Blend in the chunks of sausage and place the mixture in the pie tin.

4 Cover with the remaining piece of dough. Beat the remaining egg and use to glaze the surface of the pie. Decorate with pastry trimmings and brush again with the beaten egg. Flute the edges of the pie with a fork to seal.

5 Bake in the preheated oven for 40 minutes and serve hot or cold.

Serves 6

Sausage and Mushroom Pie

450 g (1 lb) pork sausages
50 g (2 oz) ($\frac{1}{4}$ cup) butter
2 onions, sliced
40 g (1$\frac{1}{2}$ oz) (6 tablespoons) flour
300 ml ($\frac{1}{2}$ pint) (1$\frac{1}{4}$ cups) milk
300 ml ($\frac{1}{2}$ pint) (1$\frac{1}{4}$ cups) stock
salt and pepper
100 g ($\frac{1}{4}$ lb) (1 cup) sliced button
 mushrooms
350 g ($\frac{3}{4}$ lb) puff pastry
1 egg, beaten

1 Preheat the oven to 200°C, 400°F, gas 6.

2 Prick the sausages and grill (broil) them until golden.

3 Heat the butter in a pan and gently fry the onions for 5 minutes. Stir in the flour and cook for 1 minute more.

4 Gradually blend in the milk and stock and bring to the boil. Stir until thickened and then add the seasoning and mushrooms.

5 Place the sausages in a pie dish and pour over the mushroom sauce. Roll out the puff pastry cover the dish with it and trim off any excess pastry. Brush the top with the beaten egg and bake the pie for 40 minutes. Serve piping hot.

Serves 6

Tip: This pie can be stored in the freezer. Freeze it uncooked, and when ready to use, cook in an oven preheated to 220°C, 425°F, gas 7 for 45-50 minutes.

Vary the vegetables used in the sauce – try sweetcorn kernels, carrots or peas.

Sausage Rolls

450 g (1 lb) (2 cups) pork
 sausagemeat
450 g (1 lb) puff pastry
1 egg, beaten

Sausage and Mushroom Pie holds a rich chunky filling in a creamy sauce, topped with a light pastry shell

1 Preheat the oven to 220°C, 425°F, gas 7.

2 Roll the sausagemeat into a long strip 60 cm (24 in) long.

3 Roll out the pastry to 3 mm ($\frac{1}{8}$ in) thickness and cut it into 2 strips 30 cm x 10 cm (12 in x 4 in). Cut the sausagemeat in half and place one half on each strip of pastry. Brush the edge of the pastry with beaten egg and fold over. Crimp the edge with a fork. Cut into pieces about 6.5 cm (2$\frac{1}{2}$ in) long and brush with beaten egg.

4 Place the rolls on a greased baking sheet and bake for 15 minutes. Serve hot.

Makes 16 sausage rolls

Savoury Bouchées

1 small onion, chopped
30 ml (1 fl oz) (2 tablespoons) oil
1 clove garlic, chopped
225 g ($\frac{1}{2}$ lb) (1 cup) pork
 sausagemeat
50 ml (2 fl oz) ($\frac{1}{4}$ cup) dry sherry
salt and pepper
15 ml (1 tablespoon) chopped
 parsley
450 g (1 lb) puff pastry
25 g (1 oz) (2 tablespoons) lard
 (shortening)
1 egg, beaten
6 stuffed olives

1 Preheat the oven to 220°C, 425°F, gas 7.

2 Fry the onion in the oil for 3 minutes. Add the garlic and meat

and cook for 15 minutes, covered with a lid. Add the sherry, seasoning and parsley and keep the mixture hot while making the bouchée cases.

3 Roll out the pastry to 3 mm (⅛ in) thickness. Cut 12 rounds using a 6.5 cm (2½ in) cutter. Grease a baking sheet with the lard (shortening) and place 6 rounds on the sheet. Press a 4 cm (1½ in) cutter into the centre of the remaining rounds to give 6 rings. Dampen the edge of the rounds with water and place the rings on top. Press together to seal. Brush the tops with the beaten egg and bake in the oven for 15 minutes until golden and puffy.

4 Fill the bouchées with the sausage mixture, top each one with a stuffed olive and serve hot.

Makes 6

Sausage Rolls, left, and Savoury Bouchées, right, are ideal party dishes, tasty and neat for eating with your fingers

Easter Pie

450 g (1 lb) (4½ cups) flour
9 eggs
225 g (½ lb) (1 cup) butter or margarine, softened
675 g (1½ lb) (3 cups) pork sausagemeat
15 ml (1 tablespoon) chopped parsley
2.5 ml (½ teaspoon) salt
pinch freshly ground (milled) black pepper
5 ml (1 teaspoon) mixed spice
pinch cayenne pepper
1 egg yolk, beaten
25 g (1 oz) (2 tablespoons) lard (shortening)

1 Form the flour into a ring on the work surface. Break in 2 eggs and add the softened butter. Mix together with the fingers, adding 15-30 ml (1-2 tablespoons) water, and knead the dough for 2-3 minutes until smooth. Roll the dough into a ball and place it in a cool place or in the refrigerator for 30 minutes.

2 Cook 5 of the eggs in boiling water for 10 minutes, drain and cover them with cold water to cool.

3 In a bowl, combine the sausagemeat with 2 of the eggs and the parsley, salt, pepper, mixed spice and cayenne. Mix well.

4 Shell the hard-boiled eggs to prevent them discolouring; cover them with cold water until needed.

5 Halve the dough and roll out each piece to a rectangle about 5 mm (¼ in) thick.

6 Place half of the meat mixture along the centre of one piece of dough and arrange the hard-boiled eggs along the top of the meat. Cover the eggs with the rest of the meat mixture, making sure the eggs are well covered at the sides.

7 Brush the border of dough round the meat with the egg yolk and lay the second piece of dough over the top. Trim off the excess dough and crimp the edges of the parcel with the fingers to seal. Pinch together at intervals to produce a fluted edge. Preheat the oven to 180°C, 350°F, gas 4.

8 Brush the whole parcel with more egg yolk. Roll out the dough trimmings to 3 mm (⅛ in) thickness and cut out decorative leaf shapes. Arrange some into roses and place the roses and the leaves on the top of the Easter Pie. Brush the decorations with more beaten egg yolk.

9 Grease a baking sheet with the lard (shortening) and place the pie on the sheet. Bake in the pre-heated oven for 1 hour. Allow to cool and decorate with sprigs of parsley. Serve cold.

Serves 8

Look'n Cook Easter Pie

1 The ingredients **2** Form the flour into a continuous ring on the work surface. Break in 2 of the eggs **3** Add the softened fat and a little water and mix with the fingers. Knead the dough for 2-3 minutes until smooth. Roll the dough into a ball and place it in the refrigerator for 30 minutes. Meanwhile, cook 5 of the eggs in boiling water for 10 minutes. Drain and cover with cold water to cool **4** Combine the sausagemeat,

2 of the eggs, parsley, salt, pepper, mixed spice and cayenne **5** Mix the ingredients well **6** Shell the eggs and, to prevent them discolouring, cover them with cold water until needed **7** Cut the dough in half and roll out each piece into a rectangle 5 mm ($\frac{1}{2}$ in) thick **8** Place half of the meat mixture along the centre of one piece of dough **9** Arrange the hard-boiled eggs in a row along the top of the meat

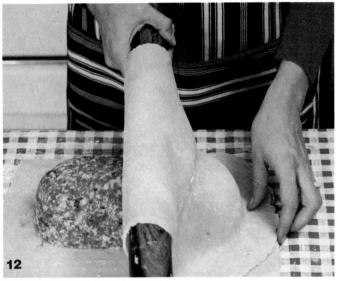

10 Cover with the rest of the sausagemeat mixture, making sure that the eggs are well covered at the sides **11** Brush the border of dough round the meat with the beaten egg yolk **12** Cover the meat with the second piece of dough **13** Trim the edges of the dough with a knife **14** and **15** Crimp the edges with the fingers to seal and then pinch the dough together at invervals to produce a fluted edge **16** Brush all

over the outside of the pie with the egg yolk **17** Roll out the dough trimmings to 3 mm ($\frac{1}{8}$ in) thickness and cut out decorative leaf shapes. Form some of the leaves into roses and arrange the roses and leaves on the top of the pie. Brush with egg yolk **18** Bake the pie for 1 hour and then allow to cool. Transfer to a serving dish and decorate the dish with sprigs of parsley. Serve cold

All about Ham and Bacon

Ham steaks with pineapple

Who could resist a delicious joint of pearly pink, succulent ham as in our cover picture? In this issue we deal with ham, gammon and bacon and give you exciting recipes for all three. But first we must distinguish between them.

Both gammon and ham come from the hind leg of the pig, whereas bacon comes from the body. Gammon is cut from a side of bacon after brining and may be smoked or unsmoked. Ham is removed from the hind leg before salting and is then cured. Some hams such as Parma ham (prosciutto) are smoked and then eaten raw. Bacon is the salted flesh of the pig which may be smoked or unsmoked. Smoked bacon keeps longer than the unsmoked green types. Bacon, ham and gammon are all sold as joints and steaks or slices.

Choosing Ham, Bacon and Gammon
When buying cooked sliced ham, it should have pink coloured flesh and very white fat. Make sure that it is moist and not dried out. Bacon should smell pleasant and have firm white fat and pink lean flesh. If unsmoked, the rind should be pale and creamy; if smoked, a golden-brown. Never buy gammon slices and steaks which are less than 5 mm ($\frac{1}{4}$ in) thick.

Storing Bacon and Ham
Store bacon and ham in a cool place such as a refrigerator or larder. Always wrap it in foil or polythene to keep it fresh and protect it from insects. Greaseproof (parchment) paper is not very satisfactory as it will allow the bacon to dry out. You can store bacon and ham for up to a week in a refrigerator. Or if you are fortunate enough to have a freezer you can, of course, freeze it.

Types of Ham
There are many different types and varieties of ham which you can buy, both imported and home-produced. The principal British varieties are York, Wiltshire and Suffolk sweet-cure ham. York ham is dry-salt cured and mildly smoked and is probably the best known. The Wiltshire ham is even milder and the

Suffolk variety is much sweeter. In the United States you can buy country hams such as the Virginia and Kentucky varieties. These may be cured in many ways. Of course, there are also the smoked hams which are thinly sliced and eaten raw such as the famous Italian Parma ham (prosciutto) and the French Bayonne ham which is salted and smoked with herbs.

Glazes for Bacon and Gammon
Your joint will taste even more delicious if you make a glaze for it. Boil the joint for half the cooking time, then bake in the oven and, half an hour before removing the cooked joint, score the fat in a diamond pattern. Stud each diamond with a clove and baste with a glaze. You can make a glaze with a little honey mixed with orange juice and grated rind or pineapple juice and brown sugar. You can even add some wine or cider and spices such as ginger, allspice or powdered cloves. Maple or golden syrup mixed with spices makes a sweeter alternative.

Cuts of Bacon
These tend to vary from country to country and may be either smoked or unsmoked. Although most people tend to associate bacon rashers (slices) with breakfast-time and the delicious aroma of sizzling bacon wafting around the house, bacon can be served in a variety of ways and in different dishes. It comes in slices, steaks and joints which can be fried, grilled (broiled), roasted or boiled depending on the cut. The breakfast slices are back, streaky or middle cut, all of which may be smoked or green. Back is the leanest, streaky is streaked through with fat while middle cut consists of long rashers (slices) of streaky and back combined. Collar and hock are the commonest bacon joints. They tend to be fairly inexpensive and are suitable for boiling. Collar can also be roasted or braised. Usually they are boned and prepared by the butcher or supermarket and therefore there is little effort involved in cooking them. They can be eaten either hot or cold and there is very little waste on them.

Ham Joints

Ham joints are both economical and versatile. Don't fall into the trap of thinking that you can only serve them cold with salad. They can be served hot or cold with a variety of flavourings, glazes and sauces – fruity ones are especially good. Syrup or honey mixed with fruit juice and spices makes a delicious glaze, and should give the meat itself a subtle flavour.

Ham with Cranberries

2 kg (4 lb) ham joint
cloves for decoration

For the Glaze:
100 g ($\frac{1}{4}$ lb) ($\frac{1}{2}$ cup) butter
100 g ($\frac{1}{4}$ lb) ($\frac{3}{8}$ cup) golden syrup
5 ml (1 teaspoon) cinnamon
pinch chilli powder
5 ml (1 teaspoon) made mustard

For the Cranberry Sauce:
350 g ($\frac{3}{4}$ lb) (3 cups) cranberries
25 g (1 oz) (2 tablespoons)
  brown sugar
200 ml (6 fl oz) ($\frac{3}{4}$ cup) water
pinch ground ginger
5 ml (1 teaspoon) arrowroot

1 Soak the ham in cold water overnight. Drain, place in a large saucepan and cover with water. Bring to the boil, then simmer for about 1$\frac{1}{4}$ hours.

2 Remove the ham from the pan and carefully peel off the skin and trim any excess fat. With a knife, make a criss-cross pattern across the fat. Place a clove in the centre of each diamond.

3 Preheat the oven to 180°C, 350°F, gas 4.

4 Make the glaze. Place all the ingredients except the mustard in a pan and bring to the boil. Boil the glaze for 2-3 minutes, then remove from the heat and add the mustard.

5 Pour the glaze over the ham so that it is coated evenly. Place the ham in a shallow roasting tray and bake in the oven for about 30 minutes until crisp and golden-brown.

6 Meanwhile, make the cranberry sauce. Place the cranberries, sugar, 150 ml (¼ pint) (⅝ cup) of the water and ginger in a pan and bring to the boil. Boil for 5 minutes. Mix the arrowroot with the remaining water and stir into the sauce. Boil for another 3-4 minutes until the mixture is clear.

7 Serve the glazed ham hot or cold with the cranberry sauce and a coleslaw salad.

Serves 8

Glazed Ham with Cranberries has a crisp, golden exterior, studded with cloves, and is served with fresh cranberry sauce

Maple Baked Ham

1½ kg (3 lb) ham joint
1 onion
6 peppercorns
1 bay leaf
cloves for decoration
100 g (¼ lb) (⅜ cup) maple syrup
2.5 ml (½ teaspoon) ginger
pinch nutmeg
pinch allspice

1 Place the ham in a large pan, cover with cold water and bring to the boil. Remove the scum from the top and add the onion, peppercorns and bay leaf. Simmer, covered with a lid, for 1½ hours. Leave to cool in the liquid, then drain.

2 Remove the skin and score the fat in a criss-cross pattern. Stud each diamond shape with a clove.

3 Preheat the oven to 190°C, 375°F, gas 5.

4 Mix together the maple syrup and spices. Place the ham in a roasting pan and brush with the glaze.

5 Bake for about 1 hour until the ham is crisp and well glazed.

Serves 8-10

Cinnamon Ham with Apricots

2 kg (4 lb) ham, soaked, cooked and derinded
225 g (½ lb) canned apricot halves, drained

For the Glaze:
5 ml (1 teaspoon) made mustard
50 g (2 oz) (4 tablespoons) softened butter
50 g (2 oz) (3 tablespoons) honey
pinch powdered cinnamon
pinch powdered ginger
30 ml (1 fl oz) (2 tablespoons) brandy

1 Preheat the oven to 190°C, 375°F, gas 5. Combine the mustard with the softened butter, honey, cinnamon, ginger and brandy. Place the ham in a roasting pan, spread the glazing mixture over the surface of the meat and place in the oven for 5-8 minutes to caramelize the glaze.

2 Remove the ham from the oven and decorate with the drained apricot halves. Serve cold with a salad of lettuce, celery and apple mixed with a yogurt dressing.

Serves 8

Tip: A cooked ham can be glazed in a number of ways and is therefore a very versatile dish to prepare. The basic glaze can be varied to include the ingredients you have or the flavours you prefer. In this recipe, for instance, try using a different spirit and change the fruit used for decoration – try peaches, oranges or papaws.

York Ham with Orange

7½ kg (15 lb) York ham
24 cloves
100 g (¼ lb) (½ cup) Demerara sugar
pinch powdered cinnamon
10 ml (2 teaspoons) mustard powder

550 ml (1 pint) (2½ cups) white wine
bouquet garni
2 onions, sliced
2 carrots, sliced
50 g (2 oz) (4 tablespoons) tomato paste
15 ml (1 tablespoon) cider vinegar
25 g (1 oz) (3 tablespoons) cornflour (cornstarch)
150 ml (¼ pint) (⅝ cup) water
4 oranges, sliced
8 glacé or cocktail cherries

1 Cover the ham with cold water and leave to soak for 6 hours.

2 Drain and rinse the ham and place it in a large pan. Cover with cold water and bring to the boil, removing any scum as it rises. Simmer for 3½ hours or until tender.

3 Remove the ham and allow it to cool slightly. Peel off the skin and place the ham in a deep roasting pan. Allow to cool completely.

4 Preheat the oven to 180°C, 350°F, gas 4. Make regular criss-cross lines, 2.5 cm (1 in) apart, on the surface of the ham and press a clove into each intersection.

5 Mix the sugar, cinnamon and mustard powder and sprinkle this mixture over the ham. Place in the oven for 1 hour.

6 After the ham has cooked for 20 minutes, pour over the wine and add the bouquet garni, onions, carrots, tomato paste and vinegar and return the pan to the oven for the remaining 40 minutes. Baste the meat frequently to prevent it drying out.

7 Lift the ham from the pan and keep it warm while preparing the sauce. Pour the contents of the roasting pan into a saucepan and boil for 10 minutes. Thicken with the cornflour (cornstarch) mixed with the water.

8 Place the ham on a serving dish and decorate it with the orange slices and cherries. Decorate the end of the knuckle bone with a paper frill. Strain the sauce and serve it with the ham.

Serves 25-30

Tip: Score the oranges from one end to the other before slicing: this will give the slices a decorative serrated edge.

Ham Mousse

30 ml (2 tablespoons) powdered gelatine
30 ml (1 fl oz) (2 tablespoons) medium sherry
70 ml (2½ fl oz) (⅓ cup) stock
225 g (½ lb) (1 cup) minced cooked ham
150 ml (¼ pint) (⅝ cup) white sauce
salt and pepper
pinch grated nutmeg
pinch paprika
150 ml (¼ pint) (⅝ cup) double (heavy) cream
15 ml (1 tablespoon) oil

1 Place the gelatine in a bowl, pour over the sherry and leave to soak for a few minutes to soften the gelatine.

2 Bring the stock to the boil and pour it over the gelatine. Stir until dissolved.

3 Stir the ham and the white sauce into the gelatine and stock mixture and then season with salt and pepper. Add a pinch of grated nutmeg and paprika.

4 Transfer the mixture to a pan and bring to the boil. Simmer for 5 minutes, then allow to cool.

5 Once the ham mixture is cold, whip the cream until it is stiff and fold it in.

6 Oil a 900 ml (1½ pint) (3¾ cup) mould and place the ham mixture in it. Place in the refrigerator for at least 2 hours to chill it thoroughly.

7 Turn the mousse onto a flat plate and serve with a salad of lettuce and avocado, garnished with orange and grapefruit segments (sections).

Serves 4

York Ham with Orange. What an impressive centrepiece for a buffet or reception — and one you can easily make yourself ➤

Look'n Cook Ham Ile de France

1 Some of the main ingredients: a semi-salted leg of ham, a salted bacon breast, lettuce, peas, butter, egg, seasoning **2** Place the ham in a pot and cover with water. Bring to the boil, reduce the heat and simmer for 4 hours **3** and **4** Remove the brown ends of the lettuce stalks. Peel the carrots and onions. Cut the bacon breast into strips and cut the carrots into matchsticks. Blanch the bacon strips

5 and **6** Immerse each lettuce in boiling water for 2 minutes. Drain. Holding them by the stalks, plunge each one into cold water 3 or 4 times to remove any sand. Drain again, press the leaves together and secure with string **7** Fry the bacon in a flameproof dish. Arrange the lettuces on top. Cover and cook for 45 minutes **8** Cook the carrots and onions separately in butter and water

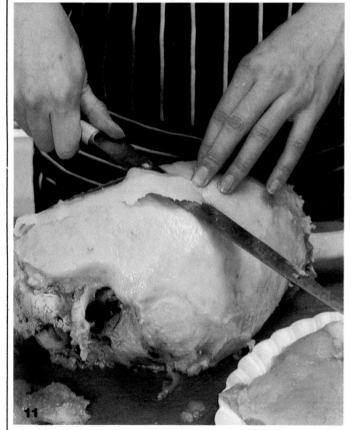

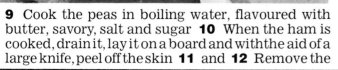

9 Cook the peas in boiling water, flavoured with butter, savory, salt and sugar **10** When the ham is cooked, drain it, lay it on a board and with the aid of a large knife, peel off the skin **11** and **12** Remove the excess fat from the meat. Place the leg in a large roasting pan and pour over the Madeira. Ensure that the whole leg has a coating of the wine before baking. Place in the oven to glaze **13** While the ham is

cooking, baste it frequently with the Madeira. When ready it should have a golden glaze **14** Halve the lettuces lengthways. Remove the stalks carefully with a knife and fold each portion in half **15** Heat

the ham juices with half the cream. Whisk the remaining cream with the egg yolk and add this to the sauce **16** Arrange the vegetables around the ham and serve the peas and sauce separately

Ham Ile de France

one 6 kg (13 lb) leg of ham
6 large lettuces
675 g (1½ lb) carrots, peeled
225 g (½ lb) bacon breast
100 g (¼ lb) (½ cup) butter
450 g (1 lb) small onions
salt and pepper
15 ml (1 tablespoon) sugar
950 g (2 lb) (6½ cups) peas
pinch savory
300 ml (½ pint) (1¼ cups) Madeira
275 ml (9 fl oz) (1⅛ cups) single
  (light) cream
1 egg yolk

1 Cover the ham with water and simmer for 4 hours.

2 Trim the stalks of the lettuces. Cut the carrots into matchsticks. Cut the bacon into strips and blanch in boiling water for 30 seconds. Refresh and drain.

3 Plunge each lettuce into boiling water for 2 minutes and drain. Holding the stalk, dunk each into cold water 3-4 times to remove the sand. Press the leaves together and tie with string.

4 Melt 25 g (1 oz) (2 tablespoons) butter in a pan. Fry the bacon for 5 minutes, place the lettuces on top, cover with water and simmer for 45 minutes.

5 Place the carrots and onions in separate pans and just cover them with water. Add seasoning, 5 ml (1 teaspoon) sugar and 25 g (1 oz) (2 tablespoons) butter to each pan. Cover and simmer, until the water has evaporated. Keep

Cold Glazed Ham is surrounded by orange cups stuffed with rice, olives and fresh fruit in a tangy vinaigrette dressing

warm. Cook the peas in water seasoned as for the carrots and onions, but add the savory.

6 Preheat the oven to 190°C, 375°F, gas 5. When the ham is cooked, skin it and remove the excess fat. Smear it with Madeira and glaze in the oven for 30 minutes, basting frequently.

7 Drain and cut the lettuces in half lengthways. Remove the stalks and fold each portion in half. Place the meat on a serving dish with the lettuce, carrots and onions. Drain the peas and bacon and combine in a bowl.

8 Pour the ham juices into a pan, add half the cream and boil for 2 minutes. Blend the remaining cream with the egg yolk and gradually stir it into the pan. Season, strain and serve with the meat and vegetables.

Serves 12-14

Fiesta Ham

2 kg (4 lb) joint of ham
450 ml (¾ pint) (1⅞ cups) apple juice
1 onion, finely sliced
freshly ground (milled) black pepper
30 ml (1 fl oz) (2 tablespoons) honey
3 eating (dessert) apples
25 g (1 oz) (2 tablespoons) Demerara sugar
25 g (1 oz) (2 tablespoons) butter
30 ml (1 fl oz) (2 tablespoons) oil
12 stuffed green olives

1 Cover the ham joint with cold water and leave to soak for 12 hours. Drain.

2 Place the ham in a pan and pour over the apple juice. Add the onion and pepper, cover and simmer, allowing 20 minutes per 450 g (1 lb) plus 20 minutes.

3 Preheat the oven to 220°C, 425°F, gas 7. Remove the ham from the pan and allow to cool slightly. Remove the skin and score the fat diagonally in a diamond pattern. Place the ham in a shallow ovenproof dish and brush the surface with the honey. Place in the preheated oven for about 15 minutes until golden-brown.

4 Core the apples and, leaving them unpeeled, cut them across in rings. Toss the apple rings in the sugar.

5 Heat the butter and oil in a pan and fry the apple rings, turning once, until golden.

6 Place the ham on a serving dish and surround it with the apple rings. Place each olive on a cocktail stick and push the sticks into the meat in the centre of the scored diamond shapes. Serve.

Serves 10

Tips: Apples combine well with other fruit such as blackberries, blackcurrants and black cherries, so try reducing the amount of apple juice and making up the difference with another fruit juice; add a pinch of cinnamon, too. And for more festive occa-sions, try adding 30 ml (2 tablespoons) apple brandy to the juice which is poured over.

Mustard Ham

one 6 kg (12 lb) ham
300 ml (½ pint) (1¼ cups) stock
150 ml (¼ pint) (⅝ cup) pineapple juice
40 g (1½ oz) (4 tablespoons) dry mustard powder
15 ml (1 tablespoon) cornflour (cornstarch)
2 egg yolks
30 ml (2 tablespoons) Dijon mustard
100 g (¼ lb) (1½ cups) fine dry breadcrumbs

1 Soak the ham in cold water for 6 hours, changing the water frequently.

2 Preheat the oven to 150°C, 300°F, gas 2. Place the ham in a roasting pan, with the fat side uppermost, and bake in the pre-heated oven for about 6 hours or until cooked. Mix the stock and pineapple juice and use to baste the ham from time to time.

3 Remove the ham from the oven and allow to cool slightly. Remove the rind and most of the fat from the joint and place the meat in a roasting pan. Increase the oven temperature to 220°C, 425°F, gas 7.

4 In a bowl, mix the dry mustard, cornflour (cornstarch), egg yolks and Dijon mustard and beat until smooth. Spread the mixture over the top and sides of the ham.

5 Sprinkle over the bread-crumbs and place the joint in the oven for about 20 minutes or until the top is browned and crisp.

Serves 24

Tips: This recipe is sufficient for a large number of people, but if your numbers are a little more conservative, cut the finished joint into 3 and freeze the smaller pieces. If well sealed, the joints should keep for up to 6 months.

Ham Porte Maillot

one 2½ kg (5 lb) ham
salt and pepper
450 g (1 lb) carrots, cut in sticks 4 cm x 5 mm (1½ in x ¼ in)
450 g (1 lb) turnips, cut in sticks 4 cm x 5 mm (1½ in x ¼ in)
450 g (1 lb) green beans
450 g (1 lb) (4 cups) frozen peas
15 ml (1 tablespoon) sugar
300 ml (½ pint) (1¼ cups) medium sherry
100 g (¼ lb) (½ cup) butter

1 Cover the ham with cold water and leave to soak for 6 hours, changing the water frequently.

2 Place the ham in a large pan and cover generously with cold water. Simmer, allowing 40 minutes per kg (2 lb).

3 Bring a large pan of salted water to the boil, add the carrots and cook for 8 minutes. Add the turnips and cook for a further 5 minutes. Add the beans and peas. When all the vegetables are cooked, drain them, run cold water over them and drain again.

4 Just before the ham has finished cooking, preheat the oven to 190°C, 375°F, gas 5.

5 Lift the ham from the pan. Peel off the rind and place the ham in a deep ovenproof dish. Sprinkle it with the sugar and place in the oven for 5 minutes to caramelize the sugar. Pour over the sherry and return to the oven for a further 5 minutes, basting occasionally and taking care not to let it burn.

6 Meanwhile, melt the butter in a pan and add the drained veg-etables, salt and pepper. Heat through, stirring from time to time.

7 Place the ham on a large serv-ing dish, with the vegetables. Pour the sauce from the dish into a sauce-boat and serve hot.

Serves 10-12

Cold Glazed Ham

300 ml (½ pint) (1¼ cups) water
30 ml (2 tablespoons) powdered
  gelatine
25 g (1 oz) (2 tablespoons) sugar
15 ml (1 tablespoon) port
salt and pepper
2 kg (4 lb) cooked ham
1 green leek leaf
4 oranges
350 g (¾ lb) (4½ cups) cooked rice
1 small onion, chopped
8 stuffed green olives, chopped
5 ml (1 teaspoon) chopped
  parsley
30 ml (1 fl oz) (2 tablespoons)
  vinaigrette dressing
6 lettuce leaves

1 Make the aspic: boil the water
and remove the pan from the
heat. Dissolve the gelatine and
sugar in the water. Add the port,
season and allow to cool. Brush
the ham with half the aspic and
allow it to set.

2 Scald the leek leaf and cut it
into strips. Remove the skin from
one orange and cut out 25 small
petal shapes. Dip these in the
remaining aspic and decorate the
ham with a floral pattern. Allow
to set before recoating the meat.

3 Making zig-zag incisions, cut
3 oranges into halves. Remove
the fruit and white flesh from the
skins. Dice the fruit and combine
it with the rice, onion, olives, seasoning and parsley. Toss this
mixture in the vinaigrette and
spoon it into the orange halves.

4 Place the ham on a bed of lettuce leaves. Surround with the
orange salads and serve.

Serves 6

Glazed Knuckle of Ham
with Pineapple

two 675 g (1½ lb) ham knuckles,
  boned, soaked overnight
bouquet garni
100 g (¼ lb) (½ cup) brown sugar

*Glazed Knuckle of Ham with
Pineapple cleverly imitates the
real fruit and makes a tasty,
attractive dish for buffet parties*

15 ml (1 tablespoon) made
  mustard
100 g (¼ lb) (½ cup) butter
5 ml (1 teaspoon) mixed spice
salt and pepper
cloves for decoration
2 canned pineapple rings
225 g (½ lb) canned pineapple
  pieces, drained

For the Sauce:
50 g (2 oz) (4 tablespoons) sugar
50 ml (2 fl oz) (¼ cup) vinegar
70 ml (2½ fl oz) (⅓ cup) medium
  sherry
300 ml (½ pint) (1¼ cups) beef stock
150 ml (¼ pint) (⅝ cup) pineapple
  juice
15 ml (1 tablespoon) rum
6 coriander seeds, crushed
10 ml (2 teaspoons) cornflour
  (cornstarch)
70 ml (2½ fl oz) (⅓ cup) water

1 Drain and wrap each knuckle
in a piece of muslin (cheesecloth).
Secure with string. Place them in
a large pot and cover with water.
Add the bouquet garni, bring to
the boil and simmer for 1 hour.
Remove from the heat and allow
the meat to cool in the liquid.

2 Blend the sugar, mustard, butter, mixed spice and seasoning in
a bowl.

3 Drain and dry the hams.
Spread them with the glaze and,
with a knife, make a lattice pattern all over. Stud each intersection of lines with a clove. Preheat
oven to 190°C, 375°F, gas 5.

4 Place them in a roasting tray
and braise in the preheated oven
for 20 minutes or until the glaze is
golden.

5 While the ham is baking, prepare the sauce. Boil the sugar and
vinegar, stirring all the time until
the sugar has caramelized. Still
stirring, add the sherry, stock,
pineapple juice, rum, coriander
seeds and seasoning. Boil for 10
minutes and thicken with the
cornflour (cornstarch) mixed
with the water.

6 Remove the ham from the
oven. Heat the tip of a skewer
over a flame and singe the lines of
the pattern to a dark brown. (This
is optional and purely for decoration.)

7 Place a pineapple ring on top
of each knuckle, surround with
pineapple pieces and serve with
the hot sauce.

Serves 6

Ham with Chablis

7 ml (1½ teaspoons) butter
four 5 mm (¼ in) thick slices
 cooked York ham
200 ml (6 fl oz) (¾ cup) Chablis or
 other dry white wine
350 g (¾ lb) (3¾ cups) trimmed and
 finely sliced mushrooms
1 clove garlic, chopped
2 shallots, chopped
salt and pepper
250 ml (8 fl oz) (1 cup) soured
 cream

1 Preheat the oven to 200°C,
400°F, gas 6.

2 Butter an ovenproof dish and
place the slices of ham in it. Pour
in 50 ml (2 fl oz) (¼ cup) of the
Chablis, cover the dish and place
in the oven for 10 minutes.

3 Place the mushrooms, garlic
and shallots in a sauté pan, pour
over the rest of the wine and season. Bring quickly to the boil,
then simmer for 10 minutes.

4 Add the soured cream and boil
for 5 minutes.

5 Remove the ham from the
oven and add the cooking juices
to the mushrooms. Boil the sauce
again for 5 minutes.

6 Place the slices of ham in a
deep serving dish, pour over the
sauce and serve hot.

Serves 4

Cranberry Glazed Ham

30 ml (1 fl oz) (2 tablespoons)
 melted butter
10 ml (2 teaspoons) made
 mustard
black pepper
4 ham steaks
100 g (¼ lb) (1 cup) cranberries
225 g (½ lb) (1 cup) sugar
grated rind and juice 1 orange

1 Mix the butter, mustard and
pepper. Brush the steaks with the
mixture and grill (broil) on one
side for 5 minutes. Turn over,
brush again and grill (broil) until
tender.

2 Mix the cranberries, sugar and

*Ham Florentine. The slices of
ham surround a spinach and
cream filling and are served with
a rich, Madeira-flavoured sauce*

orange rind and juice in a pan.
Leave to stand for 5 minutes.

3 Simmer the cranberries gently
for 5 minutes until hot.

4 Garnish the ham with the
cranberries and serve with
noodles.

Serves 4

Ham Florentine

25 ml (1 fl oz) (2 tablespoons) oil
50 g (2 oz) (4 tablespoons) butter
1 carrot, diced
1 onion, chopped
50 g (2 oz) streaky bacon,
 derinded and cubed
30 ml (2 tablespoons) flour
300 ml (½ pint) (1¼ cups) chicken
 stock
100 ml (4 fl oz) (½ cup) Madeira
salt and pepper
pinch thyme
1 bay leaf
2 kg (4 lb) spinach, cooked and
 chopped
100 ml (4 fl oz) (½ cup) double
 (heavy) cream
6 thick slices cooked ham

1 Heat the oil with half the butter and fry the carrot, onion and
bacon until slightly browned.
Sprinkle in the flour and cook for 2
minutes more, stirring. Mix in the
stock and Madeira, season and
add the thyme and bay leaf. Cover
and cook for 25 minutes.

2 Preheat the oven to 200°C,
400°F, gas 6. Mix the spinach with
the cream and seasoning. Divide
the spinach between the slices of
ham and roll them up. Place in an
ovenproof dish greased with the
rest of the butter.

3 Strain the sauce and pour half
over the rolls. Place in the oven for
10 minutes, then serve with the
rest of the sauce.

Serves 6

*Ham with Chablis is expensive
to make but never fails
to impress your guests at that
special occasion or dinner*

Ham and Leek Mornay

4 young leeks
4 large slices ham
25 g (1 oz) (2 tablespoons) butter
300 ml (½ pint) (1¼ cups) béchamel
   sauce
100 g (¼ lb) (1 cup) grated Cheddar
   cheese
salt and pepper

1 Preheat the oven to 190°C, 375°F, gas 5. Trim and remove the outer leaves of the leeks. Cut off the green part and cook them for 15 minutes in boiling salted water.

2 Roll a slice of ham around each leek. Grease a shallow ovenproof casserole dish with half the butter, and place the leeks inside. Add 75 g (3 oz) (¾ cup) of the cheese to the béchamel sauce and season it.

3 Pour the cheese sauce over the leeks. Sprinkle with the remaining cheese and dot with the rest of the butter.

4 Bake in the preheated oven for 15 minutes and serve.

Serves 4

Ham and Apple Casserole

50 g (2 oz) (4 tablespoons) butter
2 onions, sliced
2 apples, peeled, cored and sliced
4 gammon steaks
25 g (1 oz) (4 tablespoons) flour
300 ml (½ pint) (1¼ cups) dry cider
150 ml (¼ pint) (⅝ cup) chicken
   stock
salt and pepper
pinch powdered clove
2.5 ml (½ teaspoon) mustard
   powder
225 g (½ lb) (2 cups) canned corn
   kernels, drained
75 g (3 oz) (½ cup) raisins
100 g (¼ lb) mushrooms, washed
   and sliced

1 Preheat the oven to 190°C, 375°F, gas 5. Melt the butter in a pan. Fry the onions and apples

until soft. Add the gammon slices and brown on both sides. Transfer the ham to a flameproof casserole.

2 Add the flour to the pan and stir over a low heat for 2 minutes. Add the cider and stock and bring to the boil, stirring all the time.

3 Simmer and add the seasoning, mustard, corn kernels, raisins and mushrooms. Cook for 1 more minute and pour the contents of the pan into the casserole dish. Cover and cook in the oven for 45 minutes or until well cooked.

Serves 4

Ham Jambalaya

50 ml (2 fl oz) (¼ cup) oil
450 g (1 lb) cooked ham, diced
1 onion, finely chopped
2 cloves garlic, crushed
1 tomato, peeled, deseeded and
   chopped
450 g (1 lb) (2 cups) long grain rice
750 ml (1¼ pints) (3 cups) water
1 chicken stock cube
pinch turmeric
salt and pepper
400 g (14 oz) canned pineapple
   pieces with their juice
175 g (6 oz) (1 cup) peeled prawns
   (shrimps)
1 egg
40 g (1½ oz) (⅔ cup) fine dry
   breadcrumbs
25 g (1 oz) (2 tablespoons) butter

1 Heat the oil in a saucepan, add the ham and fry gently for 5 minutes. Add the onion, garlic and tomato and fry for 5 more minutes. Add the rice, water, stock cube, turmeric, salt and pepper.

2 Drain the pineapple pieces, and retain 150 ml (¼ pint) (⅝ cup) of the juice. Add this to the pan.

3 Bring to the boil, cover and cook gently for 15 minutes.

4 Stir in the prawns (shrimps) and heat through. Check the seasoning. Place the rice on a serving dish.

5 Dry the pineapple pieces. Beat the egg. Dip the pineapple in the egg and roll each piece in the breadcrumbs.

6 Melt the butter in a frying pan (skillet), add the pineapple pieces and fry until golden on both sides.

7 Spoon the pineapple on to the rice and serve.

Serves 6

Ham with Wine and Tomato

50 g (2 oz) (4 tablespoons) butter
6 large slices cooked ham
6 shallots, chopped
70 ml (2½ fl oz) (⅓ cup) dry white
   wine
4 tomatoes, skinned, deseeded
   and chopped
10 ml (2 teaspoons) tomato paste
salt and pepper
150 ml (¼ pint) (⅝ cup) double
   (heavy) cream
1 sprig parsley

1 Preheat the oven to 190°C, 375°F, gas 5. Grease a small baking dish with a little butter. Roll the ham slices into cylinders and place them side by side in the dish. Dot the ham with 15 ml (1 tablespoon) of butter and place it in the oven for 15 minutes or until heated through.

2 Meanwhile, gently heat the remaining butter in a frying pan (skillet) and sauté the shallots for 3 minutes.

3 Add the wine and boil for 2 minutes before adding the tomatoes and tomato paste. Season. Allow the sauce to boil for 5 more minutes while gradually stirring in the cream. Check the seasoning.

4 Pour the sauce over the ham, and garnish with the parsley.

Serves 6

Ham with Wine and Tomato is served with a quickly made onion and tomato sauce which is enriched with wine and cream

Bacon and Olives en Croûte

900 g (2 lb) collar of bacon,
  soaked overnight
450 g (1 lb) frozen puff pastry,
  thawed
25 g (1 oz) (2 tablespoons)
  Demerara sugar
10 ml (2 teaspoons) French
  mustard
8 stuffed green olives, chopped
a little beaten egg

1 Place the soaked bacon in a saucepan. Cover with cold water, bring to the boil and simmer for 1 hour.

2 Remove the bacon from the pan and leave to cool slightly. Remove the skin and excess fat and allow to become quite cold.

3 Preheat the oven to 220°C, 425°F, gas 7. Roll the pastry out to a circle large enough to wrap the bacon.

4 Mix the sugar, mustard and olives and spread on top of the bacon. Place it sugar side down on the pastry. Fold the pastry up over the joint, sealing the seams together with beaten egg.

5 Place the joint, seams downwards on a flat baking (cookie) sheet. Make a small hole in the top and decorate with leaves made from pastry trimmings. Brush with egg.

6 Bake for 25-30 minutes, until the pastry is golden.

Serves 6

Bacon and Olives en Croûte proves how versatile bacon can be, and looks and tastes good as well as being economical

Bacon and Chestnuts en Croûte

1½ kg (3 lb) forehock bacon,
  soaked overnight
15 ml (1 tablespoon) butter
1 onion, chopped
225 g (½ lb) (1 cup) canned
  unsweetened chestnut purée
60 ml (2¼ fl oz) (4 tablespoons)
  crunchy peanut butter
1.25 ml (¼ teaspoon) chopped
  fresh thyme
good pinch mixed spice
salt and pepper
10 ml (2 teaspoons) clear honey
2 eggs, beaten
675 g (1½ lb) frozen puff pastry,
  thawed

1 Place the soaked bacon in a saucepan. Cover with cold water, bring to the boil and simmer for 1½ hours.

2 Remove the bacon from the pan. Cool. Remove the skin and excess fat and allow to become quite cold.

3 Preheat the oven to 220°C, 425°F, gas 7. Melt the butter in a small pan and fry the onion until soft. Drain and mix with the chestnut purée, peanut butter, thyme, spice, seasoning, honey and half of the beaten egg to bind.

4 Roll the pastry out to a circle large enough to wrap the bacon.

5 Spread the mixture over the top and sides of the bacon and place it, chestnut side down, on the pastry. Fold the pastry up over the joint, sealing the seams together with a little beaten egg.

6 Turn onto a flat baking (cookie) sheet. Make a small hole in the top and decorate with leaves made from pastry trimmings. Brush all over with beaten egg.

7 Bake for 30-35 minutes, or until the pastry is golden-brown.

Serves 8-10

Bacon and Chestnuts en Croûte is a welcome change from the usual Sunday joints-serve it hot with a delicious brown gravy

Smoked Ham

Salted and smoked hams, including Virginia, Kentucky and Dijon, are boiled to serve either hot or cold as a much-prized dish. The curing of hams is a very specialized industry. The meat is covered with a mixture of salt, saltpetre and sugar and left for three days. It is then put into brine, washed and dried and finally smoked in a special chamber. It is usually necessary to soak smoked ham before cooking in order to remove the very salty flavour.

The best known and most popular variety of smoked ham is prosciutto from Parma in Italy. These pigs are fed on whey from the local cheese which contributes to its delicate flavour. Parma ham (prosciutto) is bought from the grocer or delicatessen, thinly sliced and ready to eat without further preparation or cooking. It must be kept well-covered in the refrigerator to prevent it from drying out.

Parma Ham Antipasto

Wafer thin slices of translucent smoked ham wrapped loosely around fresh fruits must be the most refreshing and simple starter.

The ingredients should be touched as little as possible and the starters served straight away for them to be seen and eaten at their best. Each of the following fruit preparations is enough for 4 servings.

1 Peel 1 large or 2 small papaws, deseed and cut into wedges. Wrap 1 or 2 slices of ham around each and garnish with thin slices of lemon and parsley sprigs.

2 Cut 8 fresh figs in half. Form 4 ham slices into cornet shapes and fill and garnish with the halved figs.

3 Remove the peel and seeds from half a small ripe honeydew melon. Slice it into 4 wedges and garnish each wedge with 1 or 2 slices ham and thinly sliced orange.

4 Halve two tiny cherantais melons, deseed and garnish each with 1 slice ham and a few seedless green grapes.

5 Peel 1 avocado pear, cut it into quarters lengthwise and brush it with lemon juice to keep it white. Arrange each quarter on a plate with 1 or 2 slices ham and garnish with black olives.

6 Peel 2 dessert pears, cut them in half lengthwise and remove the core using a teaspoon. Brush each half with lemon juice, fill with halved and deseeded black grapes and arrange each on a plate with a cornet of ham.

7 Peel and halve 2 peaches or nectarines, roll 1 or 2 slices ham around each half and garnish with tiny sprigs of watercress.

8 Halve 4 dessert plums and remove the stones (pits). Arrange on the plate with slices of ham and garnish with orange sections (segments).

Parma Ham Antipasto is a tasty, traditional north Italian appetizer which can be served with figs, melon slices or papaws

Pasta is the generic term for products made from a dough of durum flour, or semolina, mixed with eggs, oil and water. It is economical to use as there is no waste. It can be made at home and we give you the recipe below. It is sometimes blended with spinach to produce a green pasta or tomato concentrate (paste) to produce red.

Pasta can be bought everywhere and there are many different sizes for different uses. The very small varieties of pasta can be used as a garnish in soup; there are other varieties such as noodles to be cooked plain as an accompaniment to a meat dish, or the pasta can be used for a main composite dish. Perhaps the most well known is Spaghetti Bolognese with minced beef and chicken livers. Other varieties of pasta can be used to wrap around meat such as ravioli, or cannelloni.

Pasta has been made for thousands of years – the Chinese were making it 6,000 years ago and travellers and explorers gradually introduced it into the west. Some stories say that Marco Polo brought it back with him from his travels, but historical research has shown that pasta was being eaten in Rome in 1284 some years before Marco Polo returned.

The Italians have made pasta their national dish and, apart from the well known spaghetti, macaroni and ravioli, have thought of many delightful names for the different shapes they now produce. What other country would think of making pasta in the shape of butterflies (farfallette), shells (conchiglie), spirals (fusilli), wagon wheels (ruote) and even the alphabet letters our children love to find in soup?

Pasta is simple to cook in boiling salted water, and if you add a little oil to the water the pasta will not stick. The cooking time varies from 5 minutes for vermicelli to 18 minutes for thick macaroni. When cooked, it should be drained, returned to the pan with a knob of butter and some pepper. Pasta can be kept indefinitely in a cool store cupboard, and is therefore an excellent food to have tucked away for unexpected guests.

The Italians cook pasta until it is *al dente* which means "to the tooth". They like to be able to bite into it, and tend to prefer to eat it rather dry, tossed in a little oil, and sprinkled with grated Parmesan cheese.

Basic Noodle Paste for Pasta

See pages 552-553 for step-by-step illustrations for this recipe

450 g (1 lb) (4½ cups) plain bread flour
2 eggs, beaten
100 ml (4 fl oz) (½ cup) tepid water
7 g (¼ oz) (½ tablespoon) salt
10 ml (2 teaspoons) oil

1 Sift the flour into a circle. In the well, put the eggs, water, salt and oil.

2 If you wish, blend in a vegetable to colour the pasta at this stage.

3 With your fingertips, work into a soft dough and shape into a ball.

4 On a floured surface, knead the dough until smooth and elastic. Wrap in a damp cloth and rest for 30 minutes.

5 Roll out to 3 mm (⅛ in) thick and cut into the desired shapes.

6 Sprinkle a sheet of paper with flour or semolina and arrange the pasta on it and put in a warm place to dry.

7 When ready to cook, bring a large pan of water to the boil, add 25 g (1 oz) (2 tablespoons) salt and 5 ml (1 teaspoon) of oil to prevent the pasta from sticking. Boil until the pasta is of the desired softness.

8 Drain, and return to the pan and mix with oil if you wish. Place in a serving dish and serve immediately.

Makes 450 g (1 lb) paste
Serves 6-8

Pasta Soups

Three Bean Spaghetti Soup

100 g (¼ lb) (½ cup) dried red kidney beans, soaked overnight
100 g (¼ lb) (½ cup) dried haricot beans, soaked overnight
2 onions, sliced
25 ml (1 fl oz) (2 tablespoons) oil
25 g (1 oz) (2 tablespoons) tomato concentrate (paste)
900 ml (1½ pints) (3¾ cups) stock
salt and pepper
175 g (6 oz) (1 cup) shelled broad beans
100 g (¼ lb) (1 cup) sliced mushrooms
100 g (¼ lb) (½ cup) spaghetti rings

1 Simmer the dried beans, without salt, in water until soft – in separate pans, to avoid the red beans colouring the white. When soft, season with salt and drain.

2 Gently fry the onions in a flameproof casserole in the oil for 3 minutes. Add the tomato concentrate (paste) and fry for 1 minute. Stir in the stock, season, and bring to the boil, then simmer for 5 minutes.

3 Add the broad beans, mushrooms and pasta rings. Simmer for 10 minutes. Add the pre-cooked dried beans and heat through. Check the seasoning, then serve.

Serves 6

Three Bean Spaghetti Soup is nourishing and warming on cold winter days and makes a tasty meal in itself

The addition of pasta to soup makes it both more visually attractive and more nutritious. We give you recipes for thin soups such as Watercress and Vermicelli, and Chicken Noodle Soup – these will make good first courses for a dinner. There are also recipes for more substantial soups such as Three Bean Spaghetti Soup and Minestrone. These will make a quick and simple family meal if eaten with bread, cheese and fruit.

Minestrone Soup

50 g (2 oz) (4 tablespoons) pork fat
50 g (2 oz) (⅓ cup) diced bacon
25 g (1 oz) (⅕ cup) chopped onion
white 1 leek, shredded
1.8 litres (3 pints) (7½ cups) water
1 carrot, finely diced
1 turnip, finely diced
1 potato, finely diced
1 celery stalk, finely diced
50 g (2 oz) (¾ cup) shredded cabbage
2 tomatoes, skinned, deseeded and chopped
50 g (2 oz) diced French beans
50 g (2 oz) (½ cup) fresh peas
50 g (2 oz) rice or vermicelli
1 clove garlic, peeled
25 g (1 oz) (2 tablespoons) ham fat
pinch basil or marjoram
2 g (1 teaspoon) chopped parsley

1 Melt the pork fat in a large pan, add the diced bacon, chopped onion and shredded leek and cook gently for 5 minutes.

2 Add the water and bring to the boil. Add the carrot, turnip, potato, celery, cabbage and tomatoes. Cook for a further 25 minutes.

3 Add the French beans, the peas, and the rice or vermicelli and simmer gently for a further 45 minutes, skimming carefully from time to time.

4 Pound the garlic with the ham fat, the basil or marjoram, and the chopped parsley. Add this mixture to the soup, boil for 5 minutes and serve.

Serves 6

Tip: For extra flavour, a pinch of saffron powder can be added with the bacon and chopped onion.

Chicken Consommé Vermicelli

350 g (¾ lb) chopped or minced (ground) beef
pinch salt
1 egg white
1.8 litres (3 pints) (7½ cups) cold chicken stock
175 g (6 oz) chopped mixed vegetables (onion, carrot, celery, leek)
bouquet garni
3-4 peppercorns
2 raw chicken legs
75 g (3 oz) vermicelli

1 Thoroughly mix together the beef, salt, egg white and 300 ml (½ pint) (1¼ cups) of the cold chicken stock in a thick-bottomed pan.

2 Add the chopped vegetables, the rest of the stock, the bouquet garni, peppercorns and chicken legs.

3 Bring slowly to the boil over a gentle heat, stirring occasionally. Allow to boil rapidly for 5-10 seconds, then reduce the heat to a gentle simmer. Leave to simmer very gently for 1½-2 hours without stirring.

4 Meanwhile, cook the vermicelli in boiling salted water for 5 minutes, and drain.

5 When the soup is cooked, lift out the chicken legs, strain the soup through double muslin (cheesecloth) and remove all the fat from the surface with absorbent kitchen paper. Adjust the seasoning. Remove the skin and bones from the chicken legs and dice the meat. Add the chicken meat to the soup and bring it back to the boil. Add the vermicelli, allow it to warm through, and serve.

Serves 6

Tip: To enrich the vermicelli, you can cook it in a little of the

strained soup rather than the salted water.

For economy, the chicken legs can be replaced by 2 chicken stock cubes.

Watercress and Vermicelli Soup

225 g (½ lb) watercress
1.8 litres (3 pints) (7½ cups) water
225 g (½ lb) (1½ cups) sliced potatoes
1 small onion, sliced
salt and pepper
2 egg yolks
75 g (3 oz) vermicelli

1 Clean the watercress and reserve a few of the top leaves. Place the rest of the watercress in a pan, add the water, potatoes and onion and bring to the boil. Reduce the heat and simmer for about 15 minutes or until the potatoes are tender. Season to taste.

2 Whisk the egg yolks in a bowl and then gradually add the hot soup, whisking all the time. Return the soup to the pan and reheat, without boiling, until the soup is the consistency of custard.

3 Meanwhile, cook the vermicelli in boiling salted water for about 5 minutes and drain. Boil the reserved watercress leaves in salted water for 3 minutes and drain.

4 Add the vermicelli to the reheated soup, garnish with the boiled watercress leaves and serve.

Serves 6

Tip: The egg yolks add nutritional value to the soup, but they can be omitted if preferred.

Watercress and Vermicelli Soup is a sophisticated soup to serve at parties and special lunches and occasions

Pasta

To make spaghetti, the basic pasta is dried in long, thin, round strands which vary in thickness and length; the very fine strands are known as vermicelli.

As with all pasta, the time for which it is cooked depends upon the texture you prefer. Ten minutes' cooking will produce spaghetti which is just cooked but still firm (*al dente*), while cooking for 15 minutes will make the pasta quite soft.

The traditional way of serving spaghetti is to drain it well, then toss it in butter, either plain or garlic-flavoured, and then top it with grated cheese. Parmesan is the usual choice because it is so dry, but other hard cheeses such as Cheddar and Gruyère can also be used. For the best results, grate cheese which has been left unwrapped in the refrigerator for a few days and so is very dry.

Bolognese Sauce

50 ml (2 fl oz) (¼ cup) oil
1 onion, chopped
1 stick celery, chopped
1 clove garlic, chopped
225 g (½ lb) (1 cup) minced beef
50 g (2 oz) (¼ cup) minced chicken
  or calves' liver
25 g (1 oz) (4 tablespoons) flour
25 g (1 oz) (2 tablespoons) tomato
  concentrate (paste)
1 beef stock cube
300 ml (½ pint) (1¼ cups) water
50 ml (2 fl oz) (¼ cup) dark sherry
  or Marsala
pinch each oregano, paprika and
  mace
salt and pepper

1 Heat the oil in a pan and sauté the onion, celery and garlic for 5 minutes until lightly browned.

2 Add the minced beef and liver and cook for a further 5 minutes.

3 Sprinkle in the flour and cook for 1 minute. Stir in the tomato concentrate (paste) and cook for 1 minute more. Dissolve the beef stock cube in the water and add the liquid to the pan with the sherry or Marsala. Add the oregano, paprika, mace and seasoning and simmer for a further 15 minutes.

Makes ½ litre (1 pint) (2½ cups)

Spaghetti Amalfi

3 aubergines (eggplants), diced
salt
50 ml (2 oz) (¼ cup) oil
1 onion, chopped
1 clove garlic, peeled and
  chopped
1 green pepper, deseeded and
  diced
2 mushrooms, sliced
25 g (1 oz) (4 tablespoons) flour
25 g (1 oz) (2 tablespoons) tomato
  concentrate (paste)
150 ml (¼ pint) (⅝ cup) water
1 chicken stock cube
pinch each basil, paprika, curry
  powder
pepper
225 g (½ lb) spaghetti
25 g (1 oz) (2 tablespoons) butter
50 g (2 oz) (½ cup) grated cheese

1 Sprinkle the diced aubergines (eggplants) with salt and leave to stand for 30 minutes. Rinse and dry.

2 Heat the oil in a pan and fry the onion and garlic for 5 minutes without browning. Add the pepper, aubergines (eggplants) and mushrooms and simmer for 3 minutes more. Sprinkle in the flour and add the tomato concentrate (paste) and water. Crumble in the chicken stock cube and add the basil, paprika, curry powder and salt and pepper. Simmer for 12 minutes until thick.

3 Meanwhile, cook the spaghetti in salted water, drain and add the butter and grated cheese. Mix well.

4 Place the spaghetti on a serving dish, cover with the aubergine (eggplant) sauce and serve.

Serves 4

Spaghetti Flan

175 g (6 oz) shortcrust (pie crust)
100 g (¼ lb) spaghetti, broken into
  short lengths
60 ml (4 tablespoons) tomato
  ketchup (catsup)
4 rashers (slices) bacon
1 onion, chopped
25 g (1 oz) (2 tablespoons) butter
3 eggs, beaten
salt and pepper

1 Preheat the oven to 200°C, 400°F, gas 6. Line a flan dish with the pastry (dough), prick the base with a fork and bake blind in the oven for 10 minutes. When cooked, remove and reduce the oven temperature to 190°C, 375°F, gas 5.

2 Cook the spaghetti in boiling salted water until tender, then drain and mix with the tomato ketchup (catsup).

3 Chop 3 of the bacon rashers (slices). Fry the chopped bacon and the onion gently in the butter for 5 minutes.

4 Remove from the heat and mix in the spaghetti in tomato sauce, the beaten eggs, and the seasoning. Pour the mixture into the flan case. Cut the remaining rasher (slice) of bacon into strips and arrange them in a lattice pattern over the top of the flan. Bake in the oven for 30 minutes.

Serves 4-6

Spaghetti Amalfi is served with a delicious tomato and aubergine (eggplant) sauce, and sprinkled with Parmesan

Spaghetti San Remo

100 g (¼ lb) spaghetti
45 ml (3 tablespoons) oil
2 onions, thinly sliced
2 cloves garlic, chopped
125 g (¼ lb) bacon slices, cut in
  1 cm (⅜ in) strips
225 g (½ lb) (2½ cups) button
  mushrooms
5 anchovy fillets
salt and pepper
6 stuffed green olives
5 g (1 tablespoon) chopped
  parsley
50 g (2 oz) (½ cup) grated
  Parmesan cheese

1 Boil the spaghetti in salted water for 15 minutes until cooked *al dente*.

2 Meanwhile heat the oil in a frying pan (skillet) and fry the onions 3 minutes. Add the garlic and fry 1 minute. Stir in the bacon, mushrooms, and anchovy fillets, and cook for another 5 minutes. Season with salt and pepper.

3 Drain the spaghetti and rinse quickly with hot water. Place it in a heated serving dish. Pile the bacon mixture on top and garnish with the stuffed olives. Sprinkle with parsley and Parmesan cheese, and serve immediately.

Serves 2

Spaghetti with Clams

48 clams (or cockles)
bouquet garni
450 g (1 lb) spaghetti

Spaghetti San Remo has all the flavour and colouring of Italy – serve it hot with a salad and Parmesan cheese

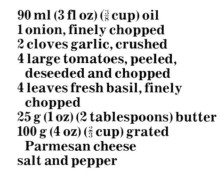

90 ml (3 fl oz) (⅜ cup) oil
1 onion, finely chopped
2 cloves garlic, crushed
4 large tomatoes, peeled,
  deseeded and chopped
4 leaves fresh basil, finely
  chopped
25 g (1 oz) (2 tablespoons) butter
100 g (4 oz) (⅔ cup) grated
  Parmesan cheese
salt and pepper

1 Wash the clams thoroughly in cold water and rinse 3 times to deposit the sand. Put them in a large saucepan, cover with water and add the bouquet garni. Boil them for 5 minutes until all the shells are open. Remove them from the shells, and rinse in cold water.

2 Boil the spaghetti in salted water for 10-15 minutes until cooked *al dente*. Drain and rinse.

3 To make the sauce, heat the oil and fry the onions 4 minutes until soft. Add the garlic and fry 1 minute. Stir in the tomatoes and basil and season. Simmer for 8 minutes.

4 Reheat the spaghetti in the butter and stir in ½ of the Parmesan. Mix the clams with the sauce and continue to simmer until they are hot. Pour the spaghetti into a warmed serving dish, and stir in the clams and sauce gently. Sprinkle the rest of the Parmesan over the dish or serve it separately. Serve at once.

Serves 8

Pesto Sauce
Finely chop 25 g (1 oz) fresh basil leaves, 2 cloves garlic and 50 g (2 oz) (¼ cup) pine kernels. Mix them together and add 50 g (2 oz) (½ cup) grated Parmesan cheese. Gradually beat in 100 ml (4 fl oz) (½ cup) olive oil, and season. Serve with plain cooked spaghetti.

Spaghetti with Clams comes from Calabria in southern Italy – try substituting mussels instead of using clams

1 Weigh the flour **2** Sift to remove any lumps **3** Add two eggs, water, oil and salt **4** Add sieved cooked spinach at this stage to blend with the noodle dough to make green pasta **5** Or, combine tomato concentrate (paste) to make red pasta. Use the fingertips to make the dough **6** Knead each piece of dough on a floured surface until smooth and elastic and roll into a ball. Wrap in a damp cloth and rest for 30 minutes **7** Roll out the spinach dough very thinly to 3 mm ($\frac{1}{8}$ in) thick **8** Roll out

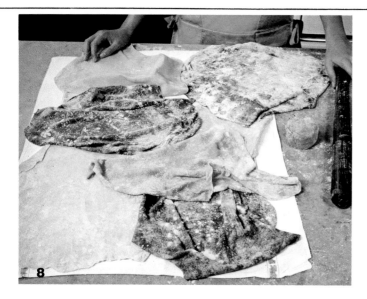

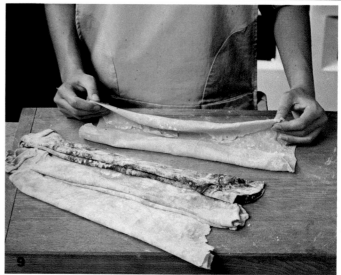

each ball of dough **9** Roll up each piece **10** Cut with a sharp knife into strips for noodles **11** Sprinkle a sheet of paper with flour or semolina and place the pasta on it and dry in a warm place **12** When ready to cook, boil a large amount of water in a pan, add salt and oil, and the pasta. Cook until "al dente" or as desired **13** Strain and place in a bowl **14** Mix gently with butter and pepper and serve with grated cheese or a sauce

Lasagne

Lasagne consists of flat sheets (about 13 cm (5 in) square) or wide strips of pasta. It may be white, brown (wholemeal) or green (spinach-flavoured). It is usually cooked in layers with meat and sauce, and topped with grated cheese.

Lasagne Verde

175 g (6 oz) green lasagne
salt

15 g ($\frac{1}{2}$ oz) (1 tablespoon) butter
600 ml (1 pint) (2$\frac{1}{2}$ cups) thick Bolognese Sauce (see p. 548)
600 ml (1 pint) (2$\frac{1}{2}$ cups) white sauce
50 g (2 oz) ($\frac{1}{2}$ cup) grated cheese

1 Boil the green lasagne in salted water for 5 minutes or until tender. Rinse in cold running water, drain and dry.

2 Preheat oven to 190°C, 375°F, gas 5. In a buttered ovenproof dish arrange a layer of lasagne, topped by a layer of Bolognese Sauce and then one of white sauce. Repeat. Sprinkle the grated cheese over the top and bake for 30 minutes. Serve hot.

Serves 6

Spiced Lamb Lasagne is an ideal lunch or suppertime snack, served piping hot with a fresh, mixed or green salad

Bacon and Mushroom Lasagne

175 g (6 oz) streaky bacon, thinly sliced
1 onion, chopped
30 ml (2 tablespoons) oil
25 g (1 oz) ($\frac{1}{4}$ cup) flour
15 g ($\frac{1}{2}$ oz) (1 tablespoon) tomato concentrate (paste)
salt and pepper
600 ml (1 pint) (2$\frac{1}{2}$ cups) meat stock
100 g ($\frac{1}{4}$ lb) (1 cup) chopped mushrooms
175 g (6 oz) lasagne
300 ml ($\frac{1}{2}$ pint) (1$\frac{1}{4}$ cups) white sauce
100 g ($\frac{1}{4}$ lb) (1 cup) grated cheese

1 Reserve 3 slices of bacon and chop the rest. Fry the chopped bacon with the onion in the oil until soft. Stir in the flour and cook for 1 minute. Stir in the

tomato concentrate (paste), season, and add the stock. Stir in the mushrooms, bring to the boil, cover and simmer for 10 minutes.

2 Boil the lasagne in salted water for 5 minutes or until tender and rinse thoroughly in running cold water. Drain and dry.

3 Preheat oven to 190°C, 375°F, gas 5. Arrange the bacon mixture and the lasagne in layers in an ovenproof dish, starting with bacon and finishing with lasagne. Cut the three remaining slices of bacon in half and arrange them over the dish. Pour over the white sauce, and sprinkle with the grated cheese. Bake in the oven for 30 minutes. Serve piping hot with grilled (broiled) tomatoes.

Serves 6

Spiced Lamb Lasagne

1 onion, finely chopped
30 ml (2 tablespoons) oil
450 g (1 lb) (2 cups) minced lamb, raw or cooked
7 g (1 tablespoon) chilli powder
1 green pepper, deseeded and chopped
15 g ($\frac{1}{2}$ oz) (1 tablespoon) tomato concentrate (paste)
salt and pepper
450 ml ($\frac{3}{4}$ pint) (1$\frac{7}{8}$ cups) meat stock
50 g (2 oz) ($\frac{1}{3}$ cup) raisins
175 g (6 oz) lasagne sheets
150 ml ($\frac{1}{4}$ pint) (1 cup) plain yogurt
1 egg
15 g ($\frac{1}{2}$ oz) (1 tablespoon) chopped walnuts
1 small red pepper, deseeded and cut in rings

1 Fry the onion in the oil for 3 minutes until softened. Add the minced lamb and stir to brown it. Add $\frac{2}{3}$ of the chilli powder and cook for 1 minute. Add the green pepper, tomato concentrate (paste), seasoning, stock and raisins. Bring to the boil, cover, and simmer for 15 minutes if using cooked lamb, or 40 minutes if using raw lamb.

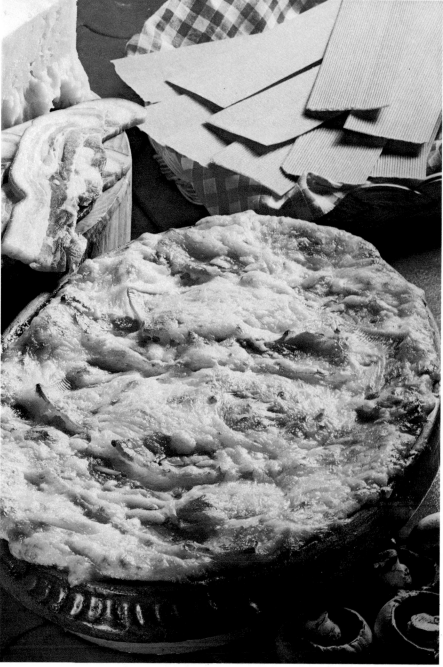

Bacon and Mushroom Lasagne is an exciting variation on the traditional dish: layers of bacon and mushrooms

2 Boil the lasagne sheets in salted water for about 5 minutes or until just tender. Wash the lasagne briskly under cold running water to remove the starch and separate the sheets. Drain and dry the sheets on a clean cloth or paper towel.

3 Preheat the oven to 190°C, 375°F, gas 5. Spoon a layer of meat sauce into the bottom of an ovenproof dish. Cover with a layer of lasagne. Repeat until the sauce

and lasagne are all used, finishing with a layer of sauce on top.

4 Beat together the yogurt, egg, and chopped walnuts, adding the rest of the chilli powder. Pour the yogurt mixture over the top of the dish. Arrange the rings of red pepper over the yogurt. Return to the oven and cook for another 20 minutes. Serve immediately with a crisp green salad.

Serves 6

Tip: Extra flavour may be given to lasagne dishes by brushing the pasta layers with butter while making up the dish.

Ravioli

Ravioli are small pasta dumplings, stuffed with savoury fillings: beef, chicken, veal, spinach, eggs and cheese can all be used in different combinations. They are usually served as an appetizer in a rich tomato sauce. Once the basic method of making ravioli has been learned – and it is quite easy – you will find that you can experiment with your own favourite combinations of fillings and flavours. A good tip to remember is that ravioli cooked and left overnight in the refrigerator with its accompanying sauce, will be extra tender the next day.

The traditional way of serving ravioli is to drain it well, then toss it in butter, either plain or garlic-flavoured, and then top it with grated cheese.

Ravioli

For the filling you can use one kind of meat alone or a combination, such as pork and veal.

450 g (1 lb) noodle paste
15 ml (1 tablespoon) oil
100 g (¼ lb) (½ cup) finely chopped onion
225 g (½ lb) (1 cup) minced pork, veal, beef or chicken
100 g (¼ lb) (¼ cup) cooked spinach
salt and pepper
pinch ground (powdered) nutmeg
1 egg, beaten

1 Divide the paste into two equal portions. Roll each into a rectangle, 3 mm (⅛ in) thick. Leave to rest in a cool place.

2 Heat the oil in a frying pan (skillet). Gently fry the onion until it is soft but not coloured. Remove

Ravioli Sophia are stuffed with cheese and spinach purée, and served with a typical Italian tomato and mushroom sauce

and lightly fry the meat. Drain and place in a bowl with the onion and the spinach, from which all water has been squeezed. Season with salt, pepper and nutmeg. Mince finely and bind with the beaten egg.

3 Either spoon the filling, or pipe it, in little walnut-sized heaps at 4 cm (1½ in) intervals along one half of the paste. Brush with water between the fillings and cover with the second layer of paste. Mark the paste over the fillings with a pastry cutter turned upside down. Then, using a ruler

and a serrated pastry wheel or ravioli cutter, cut the ravioli into squares. Line a baking tray (cookie sheet) with greaseproof (parchment) paper and sprinkle with uncooked semolina. Place the squares on it and leave to dry for 1 hour.

4 Bring a large pan of water to the boil. Add the ravioli and boil for 8 minutes. Refresh in cold water and drain.

5 Preheat the oven to 190°C, 375°F, gas 5. Place the ravioli in a buttered casserole and cover with tomato sauce. Sprinkle with grated cheese and bake for 20 minutes.

Makes 16

Ravioli Marinara with Aubergine (Eggplant)

2 aubergines (eggplants), sliced
salt
oil for deep frying
450 g (1 lb) noodle paste

For the Filling:
50 g (2 oz) (4 tablespoons) butter
50 g (2 oz) ($\frac{1}{2}$ cup) flour
100 ml (4 fl oz) ($\frac{1}{2}$ cup) water
175 g (6 oz) ($\frac{3}{4}$ cup) minced raw
  cod or other white fish
100 g ($\frac{1}{4}$ lb) (1 cup) peeled prawns,
  finely chopped
pinch each salt and pepper
pinch sugar
juice $\frac{1}{2}$ lemon
pinch parsley and basil
1 egg, beaten

For the Sauce:
300 ml ($\frac{1}{2}$ pint) (1$\frac{1}{4}$ cups) tomato
  sauce
50 ml (2 fl oz) ($\frac{1}{4}$ cup) single (light)
  cream
50 g (2 oz) ($\frac{1}{2}$ cup) grated Cheddar
  cheese

1 Sprinkle the aubergines (eggplants) with salt and put on one side for 20 minutes.

2 Roll out the noodle paste as described in the basic recipe for ravioli.

3 To make the filling, heat the butter in a pan, add the flour and cook to a pale roux. Gradually pour on the water to form a stiff paste. Take off the heat and stir in the fish and the prawns. Season, add the sugar, lemon juice and herbs. Finely add the beaten egg.

4 Prepare, fill and cook the ravioli as described in the basic recipe.

5 Wipe the aubergines (eggplants) dry and dust lightly with flour. Heat the oil and deep fry for 30 seconds. Preheat the oven to 190° C, 375° F, gas 5. Prepare the tomato sauce as described in the recipe on page 548. Stir in the cream. Butter a shallow casserole and arrange the aubergines (eggplants) in two rows with the ravioli in its sauce in the middle. Sprinkle with the grated cheese and bake for 12 minutes.

Ravioli Sophia

450 g (1 lb) noodle paste

For the Filling:
175 g (6 oz) ($\frac{3}{8}$ cup) spinach purée
100 g ($\frac{1}{4}$ lb) ($\frac{2}{3}$ cup) cottage cheese
50 g (2 oz) ($\frac{1}{3}$ cup) grated
  Parmesan cheese
2 egg yolks, beaten
25 g (1 oz) (4 tablespoons) flour
pinch salt and pepper
grated rind $\frac{1}{2}$ lemon

For the Sauce:
300 ml ($\frac{1}{2}$ pint) (1$\frac{1}{4}$ cups) tomato
  sauce
100 g ($\frac{1}{4}$ lb) (1 cup) chopped
  mushrooms

1 Roll out the noodle paste as

Ravioli Marinara with Aubergine (Eggplant) makes a tasty meal which can be served as an appetizer

described in the previous recipe.

2 Squeeze all excess water from the spinach purée. In a bowl, combine it with the two cheeses, egg yolks, flour, salt, pepper and grated lemon rind.

3 Make and cook the ravioli as described in the previous recipe.

4 To make the sauce, follow the recipe described on page 548 for Fettuccine Napolitana, but add chopped mushrooms with the onions. Bake as in previous recipe.

Serves 6

Cannelloni

The very name 'cannelloni' is colourful and conjures up an image of Italy. Cannelloni are hollow pasta tubes, usually 10 cm (4 in) long and 5 cm (2 in) in diameter. They can be stuffed with a variety of meat, cheese or vegetable mixtures and are then coated with a sauce and baked. They are often topped with grated cheese. Always blanch the cannelloni in boiling salted water, to which has been added 15 ml (1 tablespoon) oil, for 5 minutes. The oil will prevent the cannelloni tubes sticking together. Cannelloni can be served both as an appetizer or as a main course with a green salad.

Cannelloni with Olives

6 tubes cannelloni
15 ml (1 tablespoon) oil
1 onion, chopped
225 g (½ lb) (1 cup) minced beef
15 g (½ oz) (1 tablespoon) tomato concentrate (paste)
2 g (1 teaspoon) basil
7 g (1 teaspoon) sugar
8 stuffed olives
salt and pepper
1 tomato, thinly sliced

For the Sauce:
300 ml (½ pint) (1¼ cups) white sauce
2.5 ml (½ teaspoon) made mustard
salt and pepper
100 g (¼ lb) (1 cup) grated cheese

Cannelloni with Olives makes a nourishing meal for lunch or supper, stuffed with minced beef in a cheesy sauce

1 Blanch the cannelloni in a pan of salted boiling water for 5 minutes. Drain and place under running cold water until cool.

2 Heat the oven to 190°C, 375°F, gas 5.

3 Heat the oil in a frying pan (skillet) and fry the onion until soft. Add the minced beef and cook until brown. Stir in the tomato concentrate (paste), basil and sugar.

4 Chop 6 olives and add them to the beef mixture and season with salt and pepper.

5 Using a piping (decorator's) bag or spoon, fill the cannelloni tubes with the mixture. Place in a shallow ovenproof dish.

6 Heat the white sauce and flavour with the mustard and salt and pepper. Stir in most of the cheese, reserving a little for the top.

7 Pour the sauce over the cannelloni and sprinkle with the

remaining cheese. Bake in the oven for 20 minutes.

8 Decorate the top with the remaining sliced olives and tomato and serve hot.

Serves 3-6

Tip: This dish can be served as an appetizer, in which case allow one cannelloni tube per person. If serving as a main course, allow two per person.

Cannelloni Fries

8 tubes cannelloni
15 ml (1 tablespoon) oil
1 red pepper, deseeded and
  chopped
100 g (¼ lb) (1 cup) chopped
  mushrooms
300 ml (½ pint) (1¼ cups) white
  sauce
100 g (¼ lb) (1 cup) chopped ham
salt and pepper
50 g (2 oz) (1 cup) fresh
  breadcrumbs
50 g (2 oz) (½ cup) flour
1 egg, beaten
100 g (¼ lb) (1½ cups) fine dried
  breadcrumbs
oil for deep frying

For the Ratatouille:
150 ml (¼ pint) (⅝ cup) oil
1 clove garlic, peeled and
  crushed
1 onion, sliced
225 g (½ lb) tomatoes, peeled,
  deseeded and chopped
1 small green or red pepper,
  deseeded and chopped
1 aubergine (eggplant),
  quartered
3 courgettes (zucchini), sliced
15 g (½ oz) (1 tablespoon) tomato
  concentrate (paste)
pinch thyme
1 bay leaf, imported
salt and pepper

1 Cook the cannelloni in boiling salted water for 5 minutes. Drain and place under a running cold tap.

2 Heat the oil in a frying pan (skillet) and fry the chopped

Cannelloni Fries are an unusual way of serving stuffed cannelloni with ratatouille and are ideal for lunches

pepper until soft. Add the mushrooms and fry for a further 3 minutes.

3 Heat the white sauce and stir in the onion and mushroom mixture and the ham. Season with salt and pepper and mix in the fresh breadcrumbs.

4 Dry the cannelloni on absorbent paper and fill the tubes with the sauce. Dredge the stuffed tubes with flour and then coat with the beaten egg and crumbs. Chill for 1 hour.

5 Meanwhile make the ratatouille. Heat the oil in a pan and fry the garlic and onion for 5 minutes, then add the tomatoes and green (or red) pepper. Add the aubergine (eggplant) and courgettes (zucchini). Stir in the tomato concentrate (paste),

thyme and bay leaf and season. Cover the pan and simmer for 30-45 minutes.

6 Heat the oil and deep fry the cannelloni until crisp and golden. Drain on absorbent paper. Arrange the cannelloni on top of the ratatouille in a serving dish and serve.

Serves 4

Tip: Other stuffings can be used for both fried and baked cannelloni. Try using a Bolognese sauce or a ricotta cheese and spinach stuffing. If ricotta is not available, use cottage cheese instead. Just mix together equal quantities of cheese and spinach purée and season with salt and pepper. Any kind of meat can be used to stuff cannelloni – chicken, ham, veal, pork or minced beef. For different flavours, try using corn kernels, pimentos, parsley or anchovies. Fish stuffings are delicious – try prawns, tuna or white fish in a creamy sauce.

Pasta Salads

Pasta makes a delicious addition to salads of all types and blends well with acidic salad dressings such as mayonnaise, salad cream and French dressing.

Here are recipes for making pasta salads mixed with meat and fresh vegetables.

Pasta with Avocado and Lemon Sauce

225 g (½ lb) large pasta shells
salt and pepper
50 ml (2 fl oz) (¼ cup) oil and
  vinegar dressing
1 large ripe avocado pear
juice and grated rind 1 lemon
1 clove garlic, finely chopped
10 g (2 teaspoons) sugar
45-60 ml (3-4 tablespoons) stock
  or milk
4 spring onions (scallions),
  chopped
10 g (2 tablespoons) chopped
  parsley

1 Cook the pasta shells in boiling seasoned water until tender. Drain thoroughly and, while still warm, toss lightly in the oil and vinegar dressing.

2 Cut the avocado pear in half, discard the stone and scoop out the flesh. Mix the avocado flesh with the lemon juice, lemon rind, salt and pepper, garlic, sugar and stock or milk and then blend until smooth either in an electric blender or by pushing the mixture through a sieve.

3 Stir in the spring onions (scallions) and parsley, and then stir the avocado and lemon sauce into the pasta. Serve as an appetizer or an accompaniment to cold meat.

Serves 4

Oriental Pasta Salad

175 g (6 oz) (1¼ cups) pasta shapes
  or short-cut macaroni
salt and pepper
175 g (6 oz) fresh or canned bean
  sprouts
2 carrots, grated or thinly
  sliced
½ small cucumber, cut in thin
  diagonal slices
175 g (6 oz) (1 cup) canned
  pineapple chunks, drained
  (reserve the juice)

Pasta with Avocado and Lemon Sauce is a super appetizer or is delicious served with cold ham, chicken or salmon

For the Dressing:
90 ml (6 tablespoons) oil
90 ml (6 tablespoons) orange
  juice
30 ml (2 tablespoons) reserved
  pineapple juice
15 ml (1 tablespoon) soya sauce
pinch ground (powdered) ginger

For the Garnish:
4 spring onions (scallions)

1 Cook the pasta in boiling salted water until just tender. Meanwhile, mix all the dressing ingredients.

2 Drain the pasta and while it is still warm, mix it with the dressing. Allow to cool.

3 Add the bean sprouts, carrot, cucumber and pineapple chunks to the pasta and toss lightly together.

4 Trim the spring onions (scallions) to within 5 cm (2 in) of the bulbs. Chop the green parts finely and sprinkle over the salad.

5 With a sharp knife, make several cuts in the onion bulbs from the stem end towards the root end, stopping 5 mm ($\frac{1}{4}$ in) from the bottom. Place the bulbs in iced water until they open out into 'water lilies'. Use to garnish the salad.

Serves 4-6

Ratatouille Pasta

3 aubergines (eggplants)
salt and pepper
300 ml ($\frac{1}{2}$ pint) (1$\frac{1}{4}$ cups) oil
2 medium onions, sliced
3 cloves garlic, peeled and

Oriental Pasta Salad brings a touch of the Orient to your dinner table – refreshing, fruity and very exotic

crushed
225 g ($\frac{1}{2}$ lb) tomatoes, skinned, deseeded and chopped
2 red or green peppers, deseeded and chopped
6 courgettes (zucchini), quartered
bouquet garni
225 g ($\frac{1}{2}$ lb) (1$\frac{2}{3}$ cups) macaroni

For the Dressing:
45 ml (3 tablespoons) oil
15 ml (1 tablespoon) vinegar
1 small onion, chopped

1 Quarter the aubergines (eggplants), sprinkle them with salt and leave for about 20 minutes. Rinse and dry.

2 Heat half the oil in a pan and fry the sliced onions for a few minutes until lightly coloured, then add the garlic. Fry for 5 minutes

more then add the tomatoes, and peppers.

3 In a separate pan, fry the aubergines (eggplants) and courgettes (zucchini) for a few minutes in the rest of the oil. Drain and add to the other pan. Season with salt and pepper, add the bouquet garni and simmer for 30 minutes.

4 Meanwhile, cook the macaroni in boiling salted water until tender. Mix the dressing ingredients. Drain the cooked pasta, refresh in cold water and toss in the dressing.

5 When the ratatouille is cooked, remove the bouquet garni and blend the mixture with the pasta. Allow to cool and serve.

Serves 6

Tip: This dish is very versatile: you can serve it hot or cold and try varying the pasta – perhaps using pasta shells.

Meat and Pasta

Beef Fritters with Spaghetti Creole Sauce

50 g (2 oz) (½ cup) flour
2 eggs, beaten
50 g (2 oz) cornflakes, crushed
15 g (½ oz) chopped almonds
oil for deep frying
225 g (½ lb) spaghetti
50 g (2 oz) (4 tablespoons) butter
50 g (2 oz) (½ cup) grated cheese

For the Fritters:
225 g (½ lb) (1 cup) minced beef
100 g (¼ lb) (½ cup) minced pork
100 g (¼ lb) (1 cup) chopped
  mushrooms
100 g (¼ lb) (½ cup) chopped onion
1 egg
50 g (2 oz) (1 cup) fresh
  breadcrumbs
5 g (1 tablespoon) chopped
  parsley
1 clove garlic, chopped
salt and pepper
pinch paprika

For the Sauce:
25 ml (1 fl oz) (⅛ cup) oil
1 small onion, chopped
25 g (1 oz) (3 tablespoons) diced
  bacon
25 g (1 oz) (4 tablespoons) flour
1 dried chilli
75 g (3 oz) (6 tablespoons) tomato
  concentrate (paste)
500 ml (1 pint) (2½ cups) water
1 beef stock cube, crumbled
bouquet garni
2 mint leaves

1 Combine all the ingredients for the fritters and divide into 8 balls. Roll them in the flour, then dip in the beaten egg and roll in the cornflakes and almonds. Heat the oil to 190°C, 375°F and fry the fritters for 4 minutes.

2 Cook the spaghetti in boiling salted water for 10-12 minutes,

then drain, season and add the butter and cheese. Mix well and keep warm.

3 Next make the sauce. Heat the oil in a pan and fry the onion and bacon for 5 minutes. Add the flour and cook for 1 minute more.

4 Add the remaining ingredients, bring to the boil and simmer for 15 minutes.

5 Season the sauce and strain. Blend half the sauce with the cooked spaghetti.

6 Arrange the fritters in a circle on a plate and pour the spaghetti in its sauce into the centre. Serve the rest of the sauce separately.

Serves 4

Spaghetti Chinese-style

50 ml (2 fl oz) (¼ cup) oil
1 onion, shredded
225 g (½ lb) cooked lean pork, cut
  in strips
1 red pepper, cut in strips
1 green pepper, cut in strips
225 g (½ lb) bean shoots
15 ml (1 tablespoon) soya sauce
15 ml (1 tablespoon) vinegar
2.5 ml (½ teaspoon) sugar
salt and pepper
225 g (½ lb) cooked spaghetti

1 Heat the oil in a pan and fry the onion for 3 minutes. Add the pork, peppers and bean shoots and cook for 6 minutes.

2 Add the soya sauce, vinegar, sugar and seasoning.

3 Add the cooked spaghetti and stir-fry until hot.

Serves 4

Veal Oregano

salt and pepper
1½ kg (3 lb) best end of veal
100 ml (4 fl oz) (½ cup) oil
150 ml (¼ pint) (⅝ cup) dry
  vermouth

300 ml (½ pint) (1¼ cups) water
2 carrots, chopped
2 onions, chopped
1 stick celery, chopped
150 g (5 oz) (¾ cup) diced bacon
  rashers (slices)
50 g (2 oz) (½ cup) flour
50 g (2 oz) (4 tablespoons) tomato
  concentrate (paste)
1 clove garlic, crushed
5 g (1 tablespoon) basil
5 g (1 tablespoon) oregano
bouquet garni
225 g (½ lb) spaghetti
50 g (2 oz) (4 tablespoons) butter
50 g (2 oz) (½ cup) grated Gruyère
  cheese
12 black olives
2 globe artichokes, boiled and
  quartered

1 Preheat the oven to 190°C, 375°F, gas 5.

2 Season the joint of veal. Brush with 50 ml (2 fl oz) (¼ cup) oil and roast for 1½ hours. Baste with the vermouth and water frequently. Remove and keep hot.

3 Heat the rest of the oil in a saucepan and gently fry the chopped vegetables and bacon for 8 minutes on a low heat, covered with a lid.

4 Sprinkle with flour and make a roux. Stir in the tomato concentrate (paste). Cook for 2 minutes, add the garlic and juices from the roasting pan to make a thin sauce. Season and add half of the herbs, and the bouquet garni and boil for 20 minutes. Strain and keep hot.

5 Boil the spaghetti for 10 minutes in salted water. Drain, and toss in butter, and keep warm.

6 Carve the meat between the ribs into cutlets and arrange on a dish. Surround with the spaghetti, sprinkled with cheese and decorated with 6 black olives, and quarters of cooked globe artichokes. Pour a little sauce on the meat and sprinkle with basil and oregano. Serve the remainder of the sauce with the olives.

Serves 6

All about Rice

Rice with Mushrooms and Scrambled Egg

Rice is a cereal which grows in the Far East, China and the United States. Rice originated in India and China and was later introduced into ancient Egypt and Greece. It gradually became popular in Europe. Rice needs heat and humidity to grow well and early European attempts to cultivate it generally met with failure. Nowadays, rice is becoming increasingly popular and many people are substituting it for other starchy foods such as potatoes.

There are several varieties of rice. The best known are the white polished and brown unpolished. Most people in the West eat the white polished varieties but brown rice is much better for you. It is the whole unpolished grain with only the inedible husk and a little bran removed. It has an unusual chewy texture and a slightly nutty flavour. Wild rice is wrongly named since it is not really a cereal but the green seeds of a grass which grows wild in the United States. It is usually eaten with game.

Rice comes in different grain sizes – long, medium and short. The long grain is the most familiar. It is used in savoury dishes such as curries, risottos, paellas and salads. Medium grain is generally used for stuffings, croquettes and moulds and, of course, short grain for sweet puddings and desserts.

Cooking Rice

Rice is very versatile and can be boiled or fried, served plain, coloured or mixed with chopped meats, fish or vegetables. Always wash rice before cooking it. The best way is to place it in a colander or strainer under a running cold tap. Boil in a pan of salted water. Use 500 ml (1 pint) (2½ cups) water for each 50 g (2 oz) (¼ cup) rice. Allow 50 g (2 oz) (¼ cup) uncooked rice per person and remember that rice trebles in bulk during cooking. Add the rice to the pan when the water is boiling and boil white rice for 12-15 minutes until soft but firm; brown rice takes longer, about 25 minutes. Drain the cooked rice and rinse in hot water to remove

all traces of the starch. The rice should be dry, not soggy, and slightly fluffy in texture. You can serve the rice immediately but it is better to return it to the empty pan with a knob of butter. Cover the pan with a lid and leave the rice to dry out for about 10 minutes. The grains should be separate, not sticking together.

Colouring and Flavouring Rice

Cooked rice can be coloured, and therefore made more attractive, by adding saffron or turmeric and mixing well with a fork. Turmeric is cheaper than saffron, but take care not to use too much as it has a very distinctive flavour. For a different flavour, try cooking rice in stock instead of water. Use fresh stock or add a stock cube to the cooking water.

Rice Salads

Never worry about cooking too much rice – it will never waste. Rice can be stored in an airtight container in a refrigerator for up to a week. It can be reheated, or a better way is to use up cold leftover rice in a salad. Just toss it with a vinaigrette dressing or some thinned mayonnaise. You can mix in cooked meat such as ham, chicken or bacon; flaked fish such as salmon or tuna; shellfish, prawns and lobster; or chopped up peppers, spring onions (scallions) and herbs. For a Chinese flavour, fry up the cold rice with onions, mushrooms, corn kernels, peppers, bean sprouts and peas. Add some chicken and prawns and lay thinly cut strips of cooked omelette across the top.

Famous Rice Dishes

Rice forms the basis of many famous ethnic dishes, the most famous of which are the Italian *risotto*, the eastern *pilau* (or pilaff) and the Spanish *paella*. All these dishes are main meals in themselves. Risotto and pilau are often confused in many people's minds but really they are quite different. Risotto is much moister and not so highly spiced as a pilau, also it is always served with grated cheese. A paella, unlike risottos and pilaus, is cooked in a sauté pan (skillet) and all the ingredients are cooked together.

Soups and Appetizers

Rice need not only be served as an accompaniment to a main course. It can also form the basis of many exciting soups and starters. Try mixing it with chopped fruits, salad vegetables and prawns, pile it into individual dishes and serve as an appetizer. Below, we give you some delicious recipes and ideas.

Curry and Rice Soup

450 g (1 lb) onions, chopped
25 g (1 oz) (2 tablespoons) butter
30 ml (2 tablespoons) oil
7 g (1 tablespoon) curry powder
25 g (1 oz) (2 tablespoons) desiccated coconut
15 g (½ oz) (2 tablespoons) flour
1½ litres (2½ pints) (6 cups) stock
1 stick celery, thinly sliced
75 g (3 oz) (⅜ cup) long grain rice
salt and pepper

1 Fry the onions in the butter and oil in a heavy saucepan, until soft. Add the curry powder and coconut and cook for a further minute. Add the flour and cook for 1 minute. Pour in the stock and bring to the boil, stirring all the time.

2 Add the celery and rice and season with salt and pepper. Boil gently for 35 minutes until the rice is tender, covered with a lid, and then serve.

Serves 6

Tip: Another idea for a soup with rice is to use canned tomato soup and add cooked rice, pimentos and diced tomatoes. Or why not try a quick bisque? Just add a pinch of paprika, some cooked rice and prawns to canned tomato soup.

Prawn and Melon Cocktail

2 tomatoes, peeled, deseeded and chopped
1 green pepper, deseeded and chopped
½ fresh melon, scooped into balls
½ cucumber, chopped
75 g (3 oz) (½ cup) seedless raisins
50 g (2 oz) (½ cup) stuffed green olives, sliced
175 g (6 oz) (1 cup) peeled prawns
450 g (1 lb) boiled rice
few crisp lettuce leaves, shredded
4 slices cucumber
4 sprigs parsley

For the Dressing:
45 ml (3 tablespoons) vinegar
100 ml (4 fl oz) (½ cup) salad oil
2.5 ml (½ teaspoon) dry mustard
salt and freshly ground (milled) black pepper

1 Mix together the tomatoes, green pepper, melon, cucumber, raisins, olives and prawns. Add the cold, cooked rice.

2 Combine together the ingredients for the dressing and beat well. Toss the vegetable and prawn mixture lightly in the dressing.

3 Place the shredded lettuce leaves in the bottom of some individual cocktail glasses and top with the rice mixture. Garnish with the cucumber slices and sprigs of parsley.

Serves 4

Tip: If you wish you can serve the prawn and melon cocktails over crushed ice, either in the bowl or on a plate below. To make the cocktails even more attractive you can garnish them with whole prawns and wedges of lemon. Try mixing in some lemon juice for a tangy flavour.

Prawn and Melon Cocktails make a tangy start to any meal, garnished with olives and served on a bed of crushed ice

Risotto Rosso

15 ml (1 tablespoon) oil
50 g (2 oz) (4 tablespoons) butter
1 large onion, chopped
1 red pepper, deseeded and
  chopped
225 g (½ lb) (1 cup) long grain rice
15 g (½ oz) (1 tablespoon) tomato
  concentrate (paste)
salt and pepper
pinch each oregano and basil
600 ml (1 pint) (2½ cups) fish stock
  or water
100 g (¼ lb) (¾ cup) peeled prawns
2 large tomatoes, peeled,
  deseeded and chopped
pinch paprika

1 Heat the oil and half of the butter in a large frying pan (skillet). Gently fry the onion and red pepper for 4 minutes until soft but not browned.

2 Add the rice and stir while cooking for 3 minutes. Stir in the tomato concentrate (paste) and season with salt and pepper and a pinch of oregano and basil. Pour in the fish stock or water, bring to the boil, and simmer for 10 minutes.

3 Stir in the peeled prawns and the chopped tomato and continue to simmer gently for 10 minutes or until the rice is tender. Transfer to a warmed serving dish, stir in the rest of the butter, and sprinkle with a pinch of paprika before serving.

Serves 4

Curried Fish Risotto

100 g (¼ lb) (1 cup) dried kidney
  beans, soaked overnight
6 spring onions (scallions),
  shredded lengthways
15 ml (1 tablespoon) oil
50 g (2 oz) (4 tablespoons) butter
1 large onion, chopped
1 green pepper, split, deseeded
  and sliced
225 g (½ lb) (1 cup) long grain rice
2.5 ml (½ teaspoon) each of
  turmeric and coriander
pinch each of mace, ginger,
  cayenne pepper
600 ml (1 pint) (2½ cups) fish stock
  or water
50 g (2 oz) (⅓ cup) sultanas
  (seedless white raisins)
1 bay leaf, imported
225 g (1 lb) cod or other firm
  white fish, filleted and cut in
  5 cm (2 in) chunks

1 Boil beans in salted water until tender. Rinse and drain. Decorate with the spring onions (scallions).

2 In a heavy frying pan (skillet) heat the oil and ½ the butter. Gently fry the onion and green pepper 3 minutes until softened. Stir in the rice and cook for 3 minutes.

3 Add the spices, fish stock or water, sultanas (seedless white raisins) and bay leaf. Bring to the boil and simmer gently for 10 minutes. Add the fish pieces, cover again and cook for 15 minutes, checking from time to time that the rice is not sticking.

4 When the fish is cooked and the rice tender, check the seasoning and turn into a heated serving dish. Stir in the rest of the butter and serve immediately with a salad of kidney beans and spring onions (scallions).

Serves 4

Paella Cartagena

50 ml (2 fl oz) (¼ cup) oil
1 large onion, chopped
½ red pepper, deseeded and diced
1 breast of chicken, skinned
  boned and diced
225 g (½ lb) (1 cup) long grain rice
600 ml (1 pint) (2½ cups) chicken
  stock
salt and pepper
pinch paprika
small pinch saffron
2 cloves garlic, crushed
2 chorizo sausages (spiced
  smoked Spanish sausages)
6 frozen scampi, thawed
24 fresh mussels, washed and
  scraped
75 g (3 oz) (¾ cup) cooked garden
  peas
4 tomatoes, skinned, deseeded
  and chopped
5 g (1 tablespoon) chopped
  parsley

1 Heat the oil in a large, heavy frying pan (skillet) or if possible, a 2-handled paella pan. Shallow fry the onion and red pepper until soft. Add the diced chicken and fry, stirring, until just browned.

2 Stir in the rice and cook for 4 minutes until it starts to turn opaque. Add the chicken stock, salt and pepper, paprika, a small pinch of saffron and the garlic. Bring to the boil and simmer over low heat for 15 minutes.

3 Add the sausage (cut into thick slices), scampi, and mussels. Cover with a lid and cook for 5 minutes. Stir in the peas and tomatoes and cook for another 3 minutes.

4 Check the seasoning, sprinkle with chopped parsley, and serve the paella at once in the paella pan or a large dish.

Serves 6

Tips: The principle of a paella (a dish which originated in Moorish Spain) is that the ingredients are added to the dish according to the time required to cook them, starting with those that take longest.

A paella should contain 4 or 5 different meats at least, including chicken and sausage, shellfish such as mussels, scampi or large prawns, squid, crayfish, and other meats such as pork fillet or duck.

Paella is characteristically coloured and flavoured with a small pinch of saffron, but a pinch of turmeric may be used instead to give the golden colour required.

Curried Fish Risotto makes an unusual alternative to the traditional dish, served with kidney beans

Dolmades

8 cabbage leaves
450 g (1 lb) (2 cups) minced beef
1 medium onion, chopped
50 ml (2 fl oz) (¼ cup) oil
50 g (2 oz) cooked rice
2 g (1 teaspoon) mixed herbs
salt and pepper
300 ml (½ pint) (1¼ cups) tomato
  sauce

1 Preheat the oven to 180°C, 350°F, gas 4.

2 Boil the cabbage leaves in salted water for 5 minutes. Drain and dry on absorbent paper.

3 Put the mince with the chopped onion in a saucepan and fry gently in the oil until the meat is brown, about 10 minutes.

4 Add the cooked rice, herbs, and seasoning.

5 Divide the filling between the cabbage leaves, roll up and place close together in a baking dish just big enough to hold them. Pour the tomato sauce over, cover with a lid, and bake for 40 minutes. Serve hot as an appetizer or as a main dish with plain, boiled rice.

Serves 4

Tip: Traditional Greek Dolmades consists of lamb wrapped up in vine leaves, blanched for 5 minutes, and flavoured with mint. You may be able to try this with vine leaves yourself to enjoy the authentic taste. You can buy them in cans in delicatessens.

Salonika Cutlets

225 g (½ lb) (1 cup) minced beef
225 g (½ lb) (1½ cups) cooked rice
1 egg, beaten
1 onion, chopped
salt and pepper
grated peel 1 lemon
50 g (2 oz) (⅓ cup) sultanas
  (seedless white raisins)
50 g (2 oz) (½ cup) seasoned flour
50 ml (2 fl oz) (¼ cup) oil

1 Mix the beef, rice, egg, onion, salt and pepper, grated lemon peel and sultanas (seedless white raisins) together and form into four triangular 'cutlets,' 1 cm (½ in) thick.

2 Dredge with the seasoned flour.

3 Heat the oil in a frying pan (skillet) and fry for 8 minutes on each side until golden.

4 Serve with boiled rice and a tomato sauce. Fried marrow fritters would go well with this dish.

Serves 4

Keftedhes Kebab

450 g (1 lb) (2 cups) minced beef
1 onion, chopped
50 g (2 oz) cooked rice
50 g (2 oz) (1 cup) breadcrumbs
1 egg, beaten
salt and pepper
50 ml (2 fl oz) (¼ cup) oil

For the Barbecue Sauce:
15 g (½ oz) (1 tablespoon) sugar
15 ml (1 tablespoon) vinegar
pinch cayenne pepper
300 ml (½ pint) (1¼ cups) tomato
  sauce

1 Preheat the oven to 200°C, 400°F, gas 6.

2 Mix the beef, onion, rice, breadcrumbs, egg and seasoning together.

3 Divide into four and mould on to short skewers in long, oval shapes.

4 Heat the oil in a frying pan (skillet) and brown for 15 minutes covered with a lid.

5 Meanwhile, add the sugar, vinegar and cayenne pepper to the tomato sauce and boil for 5 minutes.

6 Arrange the kebabs in a shallow dish, pour the sauce over and heat through in the oven for 10 minutes.

7 Serve with plain, boiled rice.

Serves 4

Calypso Chicken with Rice

80 ml (3 fl oz) (6 tablespoons)
  white wine
300 ml (½ pint) (1¼ cups) white
  sauce, made with chicken stock
4 chicken portions
7 g (1½ tablespoons) oregano
15 ml (1 tablespoon) lemon juice

For the Rice:
175 g (6 oz) (¾ cup) patna rice
50 g (2 oz) (¼ cup) chopped onion
1 clove garlic, peeled and
  chopped
25 ml (1 fl oz) (2 tablespoons) oil
100 g (¼ lb) red or green pepper,
  chopped
100 g (¼ lb) (½ cup) corn kernels
salt and pepper
50 g (2 oz) (2½ tablespoons) diced
  mango chutney

1 Preheat the oven to 190°C, 375°F, gas 5.

2 Stir the white wine into the white sauce and simmer for 10 minutes.

3 Place the chicken in an ovenproof dish. Pour the sauce over and sprinkle with oregano. Bake for 1½ hours.

4 Meanwhile, make the rice. Boil the rice in salted water for 20 minutes. Drain and run hot water through the rice in a sieve to remove any trace of starch.

5 Sauté the onion and garlic in the oil gently for 5 minutes.

6 Stir in the chopped peppers and corn kernels. Cook for 3 minutes.

7 Mix with the rice, season with salt and pepper. Mix in the chutney. Keep warm.

8 When ready to serve, add the lemon juice to the chicken. Put the rice in a dish, and place the chicken on top.

Serves 4

Reading from the top clockwise: Yogurt and Cucumber Soup, Almond Fritters, Keftedhes and Dolmades, and Calypso Chicken with Rice. These are all traditional Greek dishes which you could try out at home

Rice with Spices

Because of its bland flavour, rice – especially polished white rice – blends very happily with spices. Although curry powder is a useful item in any kitchen cupboard, it is worthwhile experimenting with the common spices (listed opposite) and some of the less familiar ones. Do not be afraid to try new spices and combinations, but use them sparingly at first, and keep a note of quantities so that you can repeat your successes. Spices should be added to the fat and fried for a few minutes before the cooking liquid is added.

Turkey Rajah

1 small turkey (or large roasting chicken)
75 ml (3 fl oz) (⅓ cup) oil
5 ml (1 teaspoon) each salt, black pepper, paprika
2.5 ml (½ teaspoon) powdered ginger

For the Rice:
225 g (½ lb) (1 cup) long grain rice
600 ml (1 pint) (2½ cups) water
100 g (¼ lb) (⅔ cup) diced pineapple
12 black grapes, halved and deseeded
rind 1 orange, cut in matchstick strips

For the Sauce:
1 onion, chopped
1 clove garlic, crushed
30 ml (2 tablespoons) oil
15 g (½ oz) (2 tablespoons) flour
5 ml (1 teaspoon) each turmeric and coriander
2.5 ml (½ teaspoon) each mustard powder and ginger
pinch each cinnamon and cayenne
6 cardamom seeds

Turkey Rajah uses the whole bird and so will make an impressive dinner party dish

600 ml (1 pint) (2½ cups) chicken stock
15 ml (1 tablespoon) vinegar
15 ml (1 tablespoon) honey
15 ml (1 tablespoon) tomato concentrate (paste)
juice 1 orange

1 Preheat the oven to 200°C, 400°F, gas 6. In a roasting pan brush the turkey with the oil and rub the salt, pepper, paprika and ginger evenly into the skin. Roast for 25 minutes per 450 g (1 lb), turning the oven down to 180°C, 350°F, gas 4 after the first ½ hour.

2 Cook the rice in the boiling salted water until tender. Rinse and drain.

3 Fry the onion and garlic in the oil for 4 minutes until soft. Stir in the flour and fry 1 minute. Add the spices, stir to blend and cook 1 minute. Pour in the rest of the sauce ingredients, bring to the boil and simmer for 20 minutes until the sauce is thickened, stirring frequently.

4 When the turkey is cooked, mix the cooked rice with the pineapple, halved grapes and orange rind. Place the roasted turkey in the middle of a large serving dish and arrange the rice around it. Pour the sauce over the turkey, reserving some in a sauce boat. Serve immediately with curry side dishes – yogurt, poppadums, sliced raw onion and fruit chutney.

Serves 6-8

Tip: The spices in this recipe can be replaced by commercial curry powder, if desired.

All about Spices

Commercial curry powders are so cheap and easily available that many cooks get into the habit of using them in so-called Indian dishes. In fact the genuine Indian cuisine never uses a prepared curry powder, but different combinations of spices,Buy spices fresh, in small quantities. Store them in glass jars in a dark, dry place.

Cardamom
Tiny dark seeds in a greenish-buff bean-sized pod, cardamoms have a delightful mild flavour and are very aromatic. Several seeds, used whole, impart a delicate flavour to meat, vegetables, cakes and sweet dishes. In India the seeds are chewed to sweeten the breath.

Cayenne and Paprika
Cayenne, a bright orange-red pepper, is the dried and powdered form of chilli peppers – small red or green pods of *Capsicum frutescens*. Chillies are extremely hot and become even hotter when dried. They are closely related to the red and green bell or sweet peppers, from which the much milder spice paprika is made. Cayenne is widely used in curries, but should be added very sparingly, according to taste; it also provides red colouring. Paprika may be used where colour and flavour are required without the scorching pungency of cayenne.

Cinnamon
The dried inner bark of a tree grown mainly in Sri Lanka, cinnamon has a warm, spicy, sweet flavour well suited to sweet dishes eggs, cream cheese and butter.

Cloves
Cloves are the dried buds of a tree related to the myrtle and grown in the tropics, especially in Zanzibar. Cloves have a warmly pungent, spicy aroma, excellent in a wide variety of dishes from fruit pies to marinades for meat and fish.

Coriander
Coriander spice consists of the dried seeds of an unbelliferous plant from the Mediterranean. They may be used whole or powdered. Coriander is a pleasantly sweet, aromatic spice used in curries and savoury dishes, cakes and desserts.

Cumin
A very important spice in Indian, Oriental and African cooking, cumin has a slightly bitter but pleasant flavour and is strongly aromatic. The small brown seeds are used whole (as in pickles, or even some Dutch cheeses) or powdered. It goes particularly well with lamb and vegetables such as cabbage.

Ginger
Powdered ginger is most frequently used in Indian cookery, while the Chinese make use of the fresh root from which the spice comes. Ginger has a superbly strong, hot, aromatic flavour which is widely used in both savoury and sweet dishes throughout the world.

Mace and Nutmeg
Different parts of the same fruit, mace and nutmeg are aromatic spices similar in flavour; mace has a lighter, more orangey taste, while nutmeg is warm and bittersweet. Nutmeg is the seed of the tree *Myristica fragrans,* and mace is the seed covering. Nutmeg can be bought powdered but is best if ground from the whole seed as needed. It is used in meat recipes but mostly in sweet and milky dishes. Mace blades may be used whole, as in pickles, or powdered in meat and fish dishes and sauces.

Turmeric
Most characteristic of all spices used in curry, turmeric comes from the root of a plant related to ginger. Turmeric is a very mild-flavoured spice, faintly bitter and only slightly aromatic. Its main effect is in colouring food yellow as it contains a strong dye chemical.

Lamb and Nut Korma

50 g (2 oz) cashew nuts
3 dried chillies
2.5 ml (½ teaspoon) cinnamon
pinch powdered cardamom
5 ml (1 teaspoon) ginger
pinch cloves
2 cloves garlic, crushed
10 ml (2 teaspoons) coriander
5 ml (1 teaspoon) cumin
150 ml (¼ pint) (⅝ cup) water
2 onions, chopped
50 g (2 oz) (4 tablespoons) butter
150 ml (¼ pint) (⅝ cup) yogurt
675 g (1½ lbs) lean lamb, cubed
grated rind ½ lemon
10 ml (2 teaspoons) lemon juice
2.5 ml (½ teaspoon) turmeric

1 Grind the nuts and chillies in a liquidizer; add water if needed.

2 Mix the cinnamon, cardamom, ginger, cloves, garlic, coriander and cumin. Add the nuts and chillies, and mix with the water to a paste.

3 Fry the onion gently for 5 minutes in the butter. Add the paste and yogurt and fry until the oil separates.

4 Add the lamb, lemon rind and juice, and turmeric. Cover and simmer for 1 hour.

Serves 4

Pork Goulash with Sour Cream

675 g (1½ lb) pork fillet, cubed
salt and pepper
25 g (1 oz) (4 tablespoons) paprika
25 g (1 oz) (2 tablespoons) butter
1 large onion, chopped
25 g (1 oz) (4 tablespoons) flour
150 ml (¼ pint) (⅝ cup) chicken
  stock
100 g (¼ lb) (1¼ cups) mushrooms
8 tomatoes, chopped
150 ml (¼ pint) (⅝ cup) sour cream

1 Toss the pork in the seasoning and half the paprika.

2 Brown the meat in butter in a casserole, and remove.

3 Fry the onion for 5 minutes and remove.

4 Add the flour and remaining paprika and fry for 3 minutes.

5 Add the stock, stir and bring to the boil.

6 Return the pork and onion to the casserole, add the mushrooms and tomatoes, cover and simmer for 45 minutes.

7 Add the sour cream.

Serves 4

Chicken Tandoori

grated rind 1 lemon
90 ml (6 tablespoons) lemon juice
10 ml (2 teaspoons) salt
4 chicken quarters
5 ml (1 teaspoon) coriander
2.5 ml (½ teaspoon) cumin
5 ml (1 teaspoon) ginger
1 clove garlic, crushed
10 ml (2 teaspoons) paprika
pinch cayenne
300 ml (½ pint) (1¼ cups) yogurt
15 ml (1 tablespoon) vinegar
50 g (2 oz) (4 tablespoons) butter

1 Mix the lemon rind, 30 ml (2 tablespoons) of the juice, and the salt. Make gashes in the flesh of the chicken and rub in the mixture.

2 Mix the coriander, cumin, ginger, garlic, paprika and cayenne. Blend with the rest of the lemon juice, add the yogurt and vinegar. Spread over the chicken and cover. Marinate over night in a refrigerator.

3 Preheat the oven to 200°C, 400°F, gas 6.

4 Place the chicken on a rack in a roasting tin for 15 minutes. Baste with the remaining marinade and the butter.

5 Reduce the heat to 180°C, 350°F, gas 4 and cook for 1 hour, then increase the heat again to 200°C, 400°F, gas 6 for 15 minutes to dry the chicken pieces.

Serves 4

Lamb Biriani

675 g (1½ lb) diced lean lamb
1.2 litres (2 pints) (5 cups) water
sprig coriander or parsley
3 chillies, red and green
50 ml (2 fl oz) (¼ cup) oil
50 g (2 fl oz) (4 tablespoons)
  butter
4 onions
450 g (1 lb) patna rice
5 ml (1 teaspoon) turmeric
15 ml (1 tablespoon) coriander
  seeds
pinch cumin
2 cloves garlic, crushed
salt and pepper
8 crushed cardamoms
100 g (¼ lb) (⅔ cup) seedless raisins
4 canned lychees
sprig watercress

1 Scald the lamb in boiling water for 5 minutes. Drain and place in a saucepan with the fresh water, the coriander or parsley, and the chillies. Simmer for 1½ hours. Remove the meat, keep the stock.

2 Heat half of the oil and butter and fry two chopped onions for 5 minutes. Add the rice and cook for 1 minute. Add half the turmeric, coriander, cumin, and garlic. Fry for 1 minute. Add the stock and season. Cover and simmer for 20 minutes.

3 Heat the remaining oil and butter and brown the meat. Sprinkle with the rest of the spices and raisins and brown for 3 minutes.

4 Preheat oven to 190°C, 375°F, gas 5.

5 Slice the remaining onions and fry separately until golden.

6 Mix the meat and rice in a dish and cover with the onions. Reheat in oven for 15 minutes. Garnish with lychees and watercress.

Serves 4

Reading clockwise: Pork Goulash with Sour Cream, Lamb and Nut Korma with rice, Lamb Biriani and Tandoori Chicken

Sautéed Chicken with Cumin

5 ml (1 teaspoon) cumin
5 ml (1 teaspoon) paprika
5 ml (1 teaspoon) cardamom
1 clove garlic, crushed
pinch mustard powder
salt and pepper
1 chicken, cut in pieces
75 ml (2½ fl oz) (⅓ cup) oil
2 large onions, chopped
5 ml (1 teaspoon) flour
300 ml (½ pint) (1¼ cups) stock
15 ml (1 tablespoon) soya sauce
15 g (½ oz) (1 tablespoon) tomato
  concentrate (paste)
225 g (½ lb) (¾ cup) mango chutney
pinch cayenne
225 g (½ lb) (1 cup) rice
25 g (1 oz) (2 tablespoons) butter
1 green pepper, deseeded
2 large tomatoes
75 g (3 oz) (1 cup) deccicated
  coconut
2 bananas
15 ml (1 tablespoon) lemon juice

1 Blend the spices, garlic, mustard, salt and pepper together and rub all over the chicken pieces.

2 Heat half of the oil and fry the onions. Sprinkle with any spices left over from the chicken and cook for 1 minute. Add the flour and stir for 1 minute. Add the stock, soya sauce and tomato concentrate (paste) and simmer for 15 minutes. Strain and check the seasoning. Add 15 ml (1 tablespoon) of the mango chutney and a pinch of cayenne.

3 Preheat the oven to 200°C, 400°F, gas 6.

4 In a sauté pan, heat the rest of the oil and fry the chicken until brown for 12 minutes, covered with a lid, turning the pieces over. Place the chicken in a casserole with the sauce.

5 Bake for 20 minutes, basting with the sauce.

6 Meanwhile cook the rice in salted water for 20 minutes. Drain and wash to remove starch. Stir in the butter and keep warm.

Sautéed Chicken with Cumin is highly spiced and served with boiled rice, sambals and crisp, fried poppadums

7 Prepare the following sambais, in separate bowls as accompaniments to the chicken. Dice the pepper, slice the tomatoes, and place the coconut in a bowl (if you wish toast the coconut in the oven first for extra flavour). Slice the bananas, and sprinkle with lemon juice to prevent them turning brown. Put the remaining mango chutney in a bowl.

8 When ready to serve put the chicken in a dish, and place on the table with the rice and sambals.

Serves 4

Sweet and Sour Chicken

50 ml (2 fl oz) (¼ cup) vinegar
75 g (3 oz) (⅜ cup) sugar
15 g (½ oz) (1 tablespoon) tomato
  concentrate (paste)
30 ml (2 tablespoons) soya sauce
150 ml (¼ pint) (⅝ cup) pineapple
  juice

300 ml (½ pint) (1¼ cups) water
1 onion, quartered
1 green pepper, cut in squares
175 g (6 oz) (1 cup) chopped
  pineapple
10 g (⅓ oz) (1 tablespoon) cornflour
  (cornstarch)
4 tomatoes, quartered
salt and pepper
4 chicken joints, cooked

1 Preheat the oven to 200°C, 400°F, gas 6.

2 Mix the vinegar, sugar, tomato concentrate (paste), soya sauce, pineapple juice and 225 ml (8 fl oz) (1 cup) of the water in a pan.

3 Add the onion, pepper and pineapple and bring to the boil. Mix the cornflour (cornstarch) with the rest of the water and add to the pan.

4 Boil, stirring for 1 minute to thicken. Add the tomatoes and season.

5 Pour the sauce over the chicken joints and heat through in the oven for 20 minutes.

Serves 4

*Sweet and Sour Chicken and
boiled rice bring a
taste of the Orient to your
dinner table*

Papaw Maori

50 ml (2 fl oz) (¼ cup) oil
1 large onion, chopped
1 clove garlic, chopped
175 g (6 oz) (¾ cup) long grain rice
600 ml (1 pint) (2½ cups) chicken
  stock
100 g (¼ lb) (⅔ cup) diced, cooked
  chicken
90 ml (3 fl oz) (⅜ cup) pineapple
  juice
salt and pepper
50 g (2 oz) (⅓ cup) chopped
  pineapple
4 papaws, split and deseeded
lemon wedges

1 Heat the oil and fry the onion and garlic for 3 minutes.

2 Add the rice and stir for 1 minute until it becomes translucent. Add the stock, chicken,

pineapple juice and seasoning. Bring to the boil and simmer for 20 minutes until the rice is tender. Add the chopped pineapple and heat for 2 minutes.

3 To serve, fill the cavity of the papaws with the hot rice mixture. Garnish with the lemon wedges.

Serves 4

Sweet and Sour Variations
There are many Sweet and Sour Dishes. Try using cubes of lean pork which you first marinate in a mixture of soya sauce, sherry, salt, sugar and pepper. After 20 minutes, the meat is dipped in a batter of flour, egg, water and salt, and deep fried until golden-brown. The pieces are then mixed with other vegetables which have been stir fried. This can also be done using a whole fish. Make gashes in the skin, rub in the marinade and proceed as for the pork.

Wild Rice

Wild rice is not strictly a cereal but a grass which grows wild in the north of the United States. Unfortunately, it is expensive and classed as a luxury food. However, if you do get the opportunity to try it, it is well worthwhile. Wild rice has a delicate, nutty flavour with a slightly crunchy texture. It is the harvesting process which makes wild rice so prohibitively expensive. It is traditionally harvested by American Indians who take their boats through the marshes and knock the wild rice plants as they pass. The grains are released and fall into the boat.

Wild rice should be served with game birds, venison or capon. It can also form the basis of a tasty risotto. Alternatively, you can make a ring of wild rice and fill the centre with mushrooms or chicken livers in a creamy sauce. Always soak wild rice overnight to obtain the best results. You do not need to use much as it expands to four times its normal size when cooked. To make it go further, you can mix it with brown or white rice. Always wash it well before cooking and place in boiling water with a pinch of salt for about 40 minutes, until tender.

Savoury Wild Rice Manitoba

175 g (6 oz) (¾ cup) wild rice
750 ml (1¼ pints) (3 cups) water
salt and pepper
50 g (2 oz) (¼ cup) butter
2 onions, chopped
100 g (¼ lb) (⅔ cup) seedless raisins
75 g (3 oz) (½ cup) flaked almonds
pinch cinnamon

1 Soak the wild rice overnight, drain and wash well.

2 Bring the water to the boil in a saucepan, season and add the wild rice. Boil gently for 40 minutes until tender.

3 Meanwhile, heat the butter in a frying pan (skillet) and shallow-fry the onions until golden. Add the raisins, flaked almonds, cinnamon and season with salt and pepper.

4 Add the strained, cooked wild rice and heat through. Serve with game.

Serves 4-6

Tip: Wild rice can be mixed with a variety of vegetables such as cooked peas, corn kernels, lentils and beans. Try mixing in some chopped cooked meat or poultry. They can be stir-fried in oil or butter and served as a savoury first course or as an accompaniment to game.

Capon and Wild Rice

one 2½ kg (5 lb) capon
salt and pepper
30 ml (2 tablespoons) oil
100 g (¼ lb) (½ cup) butter
175 g (6 oz) (¾ cup) wild rice, which has been soaked overnight
1 onion, chopped
750 ml (1¼ pints) (3 cups) water

For the Gravy:
neck, gizzard and giblets of the capon
300 ml (½ pint) (1¼ cups) water
1 chicken stock cube
bouquet garni

1 Preheat the oven to 200°C, 400°F, gas 6.

2 Rub the capon, both inside and out with the salt and pepper. Then rub with the oil and half of the butter. Roast the capon for 1 hour, basting from time to time.

3 Meanwhile, wash the wild rice thoroughly. Heat the remaining butter in a saucepan and gently fry the onion for about 5 minutes until soft. Add the wild rice, cook for 1 minute, then add the water and season with salt and pepper. Bring to the boil and boil gently for 40 minutes, until tender.

4 Make the gravy by boiling together the capon's giblets, neck and gizzard with the water. Crumble in the stock cube, add salt and pepper and the bouquet garni and boil for 10 minutes.

5 Serve the wild rice and gravy separately with the capon. Serve with cranberry sauce and garnish the capon with sprigs of watercress. Serve with green vegetables such as sautéed courgettes (zucchini), broccoli or sprouts.

Serves 6

Wild Rice with Shallots and Green Peppers

225 g (½ lb) (1 cup) wild rice
1 litre (1¾ pints) (4 cups) water
1 chicken stock cube
pinch salt
50 g (2 oz) (¼ cup) butter
2 shallots, finely chopped
½ small green pepper, chopped
1 stick celery, chopped
50 g (2 oz) (½ cup) chopped walnuts
freshly ground (milled) black pepper

1 Soak the wild rice in water overnight, drain and wash well.

2 Put the water, stock cube and salt in a saucepan, bring to the boil and add the rice. Cook for about 40 minutes until tender.

3 Melt the butter and sauté the shallots, green pepper and celery for 3 minutes.

4 Add the walnuts, pepper and wild rice and serve as a dressing for game.

Serves 6

Capon and Wild Rice is a special dish for dinner parties, served with cranberry sauce and pear and apple purée

Rice Stuffings

Using rice in stuffings is a good way of adding carbohydrate and nutrients.

The rice used must always be at least half cooked and some fat should be included in the stuffing ingredients so that the rice remains separate and does not become sticky.

Tomatoes Stuffed with Rice

12 large firm tomatoes
10 g (2 teaspoons) sugar
salt and pepper
100 ml (4 fl oz) ($\frac{1}{2}$ cup) oil
2 onions, chopped
1 bunch parsley, chopped
300 g (11 oz) (1$\frac{3}{4}$ cups) long grain
  rice
25 g (1 oz) (2 tablespoons)
  currants
50 g (2 oz) (2 tablespoons) pine
  nuts
10 g ($\frac{1}{3}$ oz) (2 tablespoons) dried
  breadcrumbs

1 Preheat the oven to 200°C, 400°F, gas 6. Cut a lid from the stalk end of each tomato and scoop out the centres of the tomatoes. Discard the seeds and cut the pulp into dice. Sprinkle the insides of the tomatoes with sugar, salt and pepper.

2 Heat 60 ml (4 tablespoons) of the oil in a pan and cook the onion until softened. Add the parsley and tomato pulp and cook over a low heat until most of the moisture has evaporated.

3 Meanwhile, cook the rice in boiling salted water.

4 Add the currants and pine nuts to the rice. Add the onion and tomato mixture.

5 Fill the tomatoes with the rice

mixture. Place them in an oven-proof dish and sprinkle with the breadcrumbs and the rest of the oil. Bake in the oven for 15 minutes. Serve very hot.

Serves 6

Stuffed Papaws

3 firm ripe papaws
50 g (2 oz) (4 tablespoons) butter
1 small onion, thinly sliced
1 stick celery, finely chopped
1 tomato, skinned, deseeded and
  chopped
7 g (1 tablespoon) chopped
  almonds
350 g ($\frac{3}{4}$ lb) (1$\frac{1}{2}$ cups) minced beef
5 ml (1 teaspoon) curry powder
100 ml (4 fl oz) ($\frac{1}{2}$ cup) water
salt and pepper
175 g (6 oz) cooked rice
5 g (1 tablespoon) dried
  breadcrumbs

Tomatoes Stuffed with Rice are a delicious appetizer or the ideal accompaniment to salads and grills

1 Preheat the oven to 200°C, 400°F, gas 6. Peel and halve the papaws and scoop out the seeds.

2 Heat half the butter in a pan and fry the onion and celery for 1 minute. Add the tomato and chopped almonds and fry lightly for a few minutes.

3 Add the minced beef, curry powder, water and seasoning and simmer for 5 minutes. Stir in the cooked rice.

4 Place the papaw halves on an ovenproof dish and fill them with the stuffing mixture. Sprinkle with the breadcrumbs and the rest of the butter, melted. Bake in the preheated oven for 20 minutes.

Serves 6

Spring Rolls with Ginger Rice

225 g ($\frac{1}{2}$ lb) puff pastry
oil for deep frying

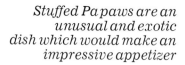

For the Ginger Rice:
225 g (½ lb) (1 cup) long grain rice
½ litre (1 pint) (2½ cups) water
5 ml (1 teaspoon) salt
15 g (½ oz) (1½ tablespoons) chopped ginger
10 g (⅓ oz) (2 teaspoons) chopped onion
15 g (½ oz) (1 tablespoon) butter

For the Filling:
25 ml (1 fl oz) (⅛ cup) oil
175 g (6 oz) (¾ cup) minced beef
1 small onion, chopped
5 ml (1 teaspoon) curry powder
salt and pepper
1 egg
25 g (1 oz) (½ cup) breadcrumbs

1 Prepare the rice: put the rice, water and salt in a pan and bring to the boil. Stir once and cover. Simmer for 15 minutes or until the rice is tender and the liquid has been absorbed.

2 Meanwhile, prepare the filling. Heat the oil in a pan and cook the minced beef and onion for 5 minutes. Add the curry powder, salt and pepper and mix. Remove from the heat and cool. Blend in the egg and the breadcrumbs.

3 Roll out the puff pastry to 3 mm (⅛ in) thickness and cut into oblongs 7 × 10 cm (3 × 4 in). Place a spoonful of the meat mixture on each oblong of pastry and roll up.

4 Heat the deep fat to 190°C, 375°F and fry the rolls for 5 minutes.

5 Meanwhile, fry the ginger and the onion in the butter for a few minutes.

6 Drain the rice and mix with the ginger and onion. Drain the spring rolls and serve them with the ginger rice.

Serves 6

Spring Rolls with Ginger Rice can be served on their own as a snack or with sweet and sour Chinese dishes

Maltese Rice Mould

15 ml (1 tablespoon) oil
175 g (6 oz) carolina rice
100 ml (4 fl oz) (½ cup) water
pinch salt
850 ml (1½ pints) (3¾ cups) milk
25 g (1 oz) (4 tablespoons)
   powdered gelatine
50 g (2 oz) (¼ cup) castor sugar
5 drops orange essence
2 drops orange colouring
4 blood oranges
4 egg yolks
30 ml (2 tablespoons) Grand
   Marnier or Curaçao
150 ml (¼ pint) (⅝ cup) double
   (heavy) cream, whipped
20 glacé cherries

1 Preheat the oven to 180°C, 350°F, gas 4. Oil a 1.2 litre (2 pint) jelly mould.

2 Place the rice, water and salt in an ovenproof dish and bake for 12 minutes until the water has been absorbed. Add the milk and bake for a further 30 minutes, covered with foil.

3 Meanwhile, mix the gelatine, castor sugar, orange essence and orange colouring.

4 Remove the rice from the oven and blend in the gelatine mixture. Peel 1 orange thinly and cut the rind into thin strips.

Maltese Rice Mould is a superb blend of oranges, cream and rice, ringed with cherries

Place in a pan, cover with water and boil for 5 minutes. Drain, rinse and refresh. Blend into the rice with the egg yolks. Stir the rice over a gentle heat, without boiling, for about 4 minutes until thickened. Add the liqueur.

5 Remove from the heat and when completely cold, fold in the whipped cream. Fill the mould and chill for 2 hours until firm.

6 Peel the oranges, removing the white pith and cut into segments (sections).

7 Turn out the rice mould and decorate with the orange segments (sections) and the glacé cherries.

Serves 8

Look 'n Cook Polentina

1 Boil the milk and sprinkle in the cornmeal. Simmer for 5 minutes and stir until it thickens **2** Remove from the heat, season, and add the egg yolks and butter **3** Stir until the butter melts **4** Pour the hot cornmeal porridge on to a greased baking tin **5** When cold turn out on a board and cut into triangles **6** Meanwhile sauté the onions, peppers and mushrooms. Add the sliced ham and cook **7** Add the baked beans **8** Arrange the vegetables and ham in a dish surrounded by the triangles of cornmeal gnocchi and reheat in the oven at 200°C, 400°F, gas 6 for 10 minutes. Serve hot

582

Polentina

500 ml (1 pint) (2½ cups) milk
100 g (¼ lb) (¾ cup) cornmeal
salt and pepper
pinch mace
2 eggs yolks
50 g (2 oz) (4 tablespoons) butter
25 ml (1 fl oz) (2 tablespoons) oil
1 onion, sliced
4 mushrooms, sliced
1 green pepper, deseeded and
  chopped
1 chilli, chopped
100 g (¼ lb) ham
100 g (¼ lb) (½ cup) baked beans in
  tomato sauce

1 Boil the milk and sprinkle on the cornmeal and stir. Cook for 5 minutes simmering until thick and like porridge. Season with salt, pepper and mace.

2 Remove from the heat and add the egg yolks and butter. Stir until the butter has melted.

3 Pour the mixture into a greased shallow dish. Smooth with a palette knife and cool.

4 When cold, turn out on a board and cut into triangles.

5 Heat the oil and sauté the onion for 3 minutes, then add the mushrooms, pepper and chilli. Cook for 4 minutes. Add the ham, cut in strips, and the baked beans and simmer for 4 minutes. Season.

6 Preheat the oven to 200°C, 400°F, gas 6.

7 Place the mixture in a dish with the triangles of cornmeal arranged round the edge. Reheat for 10 minutes, and serve hot.

Serves 4

Tortillas with Avocado Guacomole Dip

100 g (¼ lb) (¾ cup) cornmeal
100 g (¼ lb) (1⅛ cups) flour
5 ml (1 teaspoon) salt
5 ml (1 teaspoon) baking powder
40 g (1½ oz) (3 tablespoons) lard
  (shortening)
90 ml (3 fl oz) (⅜ cup) water
1 egg

For the Dip:
2 avocados, chopped
15 g (½ oz) (1 tablespoon) minced
  onion
15 ml (1 tablespoon) lemon juice
75 g (3 oz) (⅓ cup) cream cheese
100 g (¼ lb) (½ cup) celery, chopped
5 ml (1 teaspoon) chilli powder
2.5 ml (½ teaspoon) salt

1 Sift the cornmeal, flour, salt and baking powder. Rub in the lard (shortening) until the mixture is like breadcrumbs.

2 Add some of the water with the egg, to form a stiff dough. Knead it for a few minutes and then let it rest for ½ hour.

3 Take pieces the size of a walnut, and roll out to 15 cm (6 in) circles, 3 mm (⅛ in) thick.

4 Preheat the oven to 200°C, 400°F, gas 6.

5 Heat a heavy cast-iron griddle or frying pan (skillet), ungreased, until a drop of water sizzles on the surface. Cook each tortilla for 1 minute on each side until brown flecks appear. When cooked, keep warm in the oven, wrapped in foil.

6 To make the dip, mix the avocados, onion and lemon juice in an electric blender until smooth.

7 Beat the cream cheese until light and add to the avocado mixture. Add the celery, chilli powder and salt.

8 Serve immediately as a dip for the tortillas.

Serves 4

Tortillas with Avocado Guacomole Dip is typically Mexican. The Dip is mild and creamy in texture

Old Crusader Frumenty

The word, frumenty, is derived from the latin frumentum *meaning corn. The dish is of Turkish origin and was brought back to England by the Crusaders in the thirteenth century. The Arabs call this dessert 'Azure'.*

225 g (½ lb) (¾ cup) cracked wheat
1¼ litres (2 pints) (5 cups) water
500 ml (1 pint) (2½ cups) milk
300 ml (½ pint) (1¼ cups) single (light) cream
175 g (6 oz) (½ cup) honey
50 g (2 oz) (⅓ cup) sultanas (seedless white raisins)
50 g (2 oz) (⅓ cup) currants
15 g (½ oz) (2 tablespoons) candied peel

grated rind and juice 1 lemon
few drops vanilla essence
few drops orange water essence
few drops rose water essence

For the Thickening:
75 g (3 oz) (9 tablespoons) cornflour (cornstarch)
3 egg yolks
150 ml (¼ pint) (⅝ cup) milk

For the Decoration:
150 ml (¼ pint) (⅝ cup) double (heavy) cream
1 pomegranate, cut in wedges
1 stick angelica, cut in strips
4 glacé cherries
8 walnuts

1 Soak the cracked wheat in the water for 1 hour. Transfer to a

Frumenty is a traditional dish which was brought back to England by the Crusaders in the thirteenth century

saucepan and bring to the boil, then reduce the heat and simmer with the lid on for 30 minutes. Add the milk and cream and bring back to the boil.

2 Blend together the cornflour (cornstarch), egg yolks and milk in a bowl. Then stir into the wheat mixture until it thickens. Bring to the boil and cook for 4 minutes.

3 Remove from the heat and sweeten with the honey. Add the dried fruits, candied peel, lemon rind and juice and essences. Cool and pour into a glass dish.

4 Whip the cream until stiff and pipe in rosettes around the top of the bowl in a decorative pattern. Decorate with the pomegranate wedges, angelica, glacé cherries and walnuts. Chill and serve.

Serves 6

All about Batters, Custards and Rice Desserts

Individual Crème Caramels

Pancakes

It has been the custom to leave pancake batter to stand for a while before cooking, but experiments have shown that this makes no difference to the final results. Cooked pancakes will keep for a week if wrapped in greaseproof (parchment) paper and stored in the refrigerator. Reheat the pancakes in a lightly greased hot pan, turning once.

Basic Pancakes

100 g (¼ lb) (1⅛ cups) flour
2.5 ml (½ teaspoon) salt
1 egg
300 ml (½ pint) (1¼ cups) milk
oil for frying

1 Sieve the flour and salt into a bowl. Add the egg and half of the milk and beat thoroughly until smooth. Mix in the remaining milk and beat until bubbly.

2 Put the oil for frying in a heat-proof jug. Pour a little of the oil

Basic Pancakes, cooked to perfection and served with spoonfuls of your favourite jam, are served as a warming breakfast dish

into a 15 cm (6 in) frying pan (skillet) over a fairly high heat. Tilt the pan to coat with oil, then pour any excess back into the jug.

3 When the pan is hot, pour in a little batter, tilting the pan to thinly coat the base. Cook quickly, shaking the pan and loosening the edge with a palette knife, until the underside is golden-brown. Toss the pancake and cook the second side.

4 Slide the cooked pancake out on to a plate and keep warm, covered with a second plate. Repeat with the remaining batter, to make 8-10 pancakes.

5 Fold the pancakes into quarters and serve with jam.

Serves 4

Brandy and Orange Pancakes

1 quantity Basic Pancake batter
finely grated rind 1 orange
50 g (2 oz) (¼ cup) sugar
50 g (2 oz) (¼ cup) butter
juice 2 oranges
90 ml (6 tablespoons) brandy

1 Make up the pancake batter, adding the grated orange rind with the egg, and make the pancakes following the instructions for the Basic Pancake recipe. Fold the pancakes in quarters.

2 Gently heat the sugar in a frying pan (skillet), shaking the pan, until the sugar is golden-brown. Remove the pan from the heat and add the butter, orange juice and half of the brandy.

3 Place the folded pancakes in the pan and simmer for a few minutes, spooning the sauce over.

4 Warm the remaining brandy, pour it over the pancakes, ignite and serve immediately.

Serves 4

Brandy and Orange Pancakes are a variation of the famous Crêpes Suzette. You can prepare this dish well in advance

Pear Pancake Gâteau

1½ quantities Basic Pancake
  batter
25 g (1 oz) (2 tablespoons) butter
25 g (1 oz) (4 tablespoons) flour
300 ml (½ pint) (1¼ cups) milk
2 pears, peeled, quartered and
  cored
25 g (1 oz) (2 tablespoons)
  pistachios
25 g (1 oz) (2 tablespoons) sugar
few drops almond essence
100 (¼ lb) (⅜ cup) apricot jam

1 Make the pancakes following
the instructions for the Basic
Pancake recipe (see page 1314).
Pile the pancakes flat and keep
them warm between two plates
while making the sauce.

2 Preheat the oven to 190°C,
375°F, gas 5. Melt the butter in a
pan, stir in the flour and cook over
a low heat for 2 minutes. Gradually stir in the milk, bring to the
boil and simmer for 3 minutes,
stirring continuously.

3 Slice the pears thinly. Skin and
chop the pistachios. Add the
pears and pistachios to the sauce
with the sugar and almond
essence and warm through.

4 Place a pancake on a serving
dish and spread it evenly with
10 ml (2 teaspoons) of the jam and
some of the sauce. Lay another
pancake on top and spread with
jam and sauce. Continue to layer
pancakes in the same way, finishing with a plain pancake.

5 Place the gâteau in the oven for
10 minutes to heat through. Serve
hot, cut into wedges.

Serves 8

*Pear Pancake Gâteau — wafer-
thin pancakes layered with
sweet apricot jam and a delicious
pear and pistachio nut sauce*

3 When all the pancakes are
cooked put a scoop of ice-cream
on to each and fold the pancake in
half. Serve immediately with the
lemon sauce poured over.

Serves 4

Lemon Surprise Pancakes

150 ml (¼ pint) (⅝ cup) sour cream
25 g (1 oz) (2 tablespoons) castor
  (fine granulated) sugar
finely grated rind and juice 1
  lemon

1 quantity Basic Pancake batter
5 ml (1 teaspoon) powdered
  ginger
8-10 scoops vanilla ice-cream

1 Make the lemon sauce by mixing together the sour cream,
sugar, lemon rind and juice.

2 Make up the pancake batter,
adding the ginger with the flour.
Make the pancakes following the
instructions for the Basic Pancake recipe (see page 1314). Pile
the pancakes flat and keep them
warm between two plates.

Apple-Pear Pancakes

1 quantity Basic Pancake batter
5 ml (1 teaspoon) cinnamon
2 red apples

Chocolate Walnut Pancakes

1 quantity Basic Pancake batter

For the Walnut Filling:
50 g (2 oz) (⅓ cup) sultanas or seedless raisins
45 ml (2 fl oz) (3 tablespoons) rum
50 g (2 oz) (4 tablespoons) butter
175 g (6 oz) (1 cup) very finely chopped walnuts
175 g (6 oz) (¾ cup) castor (fine granulated) sugar
few drops vanilla essence
45 ml (2 fl oz) (3 tablespoons) single (light) cream

For the Chocolate Sauce:
100 g (¼ lb) plain chocolate
10 ml (2 teaspoons) cornflour (cornstarch)
225 ml (8 fl oz) (1 cup) milk
10 ml (2 teaspoons) castor (fine granulated) sugar
45 ml (2 fl oz) (3 tablespoons) single (light) cream
2.5 ml (½ teaspoon) cinnamon

1 First make the walnut filling: soak the sultanas or seedless raisins in the rum for 15 minutes. Soften the butter and blend in the walnuts, sugar, vanilla and cream. Mix well, then add the rum and fruit.

2 Make the chocolate sauce: break the chocolate into a small pan and add 45 ml (2 fl oz) (3 tablespoons) cold water. Stir over a gentle heat until melted and smooth. Blend the cornflour (cornstarch) with a little of the milk and stir into the chocolate with the sugar and remaining milk. Gradually bring to the boil and simmer for 5 minutes, stirring. Remove from the heat and stir in the cream and cinnamon.

3 Make the pancakes following the instructions for the Basic Pancake recipe (see page 1314). Put a little of the walnut filling on to each cooked pancake, roll up the pancakes and transfer to a heated serving dish. Cover and keep warm.

4 Gently reheat the chocolate sauce and pour it over the pancakes. Serve immediately.

Serves 4

---

3 pears
50 g (2 oz) (¼ cup) sugar
15 ml (1 tablespoon) cornflour (cornstarch)
juice 1 orange
45 ml (2 fl oz) (3 tablespoons) apricot jam
sugar for sprinkling

1 Make up the pancake batter adding the cinnamon with the flour. Make the pancakes following the instructions for the Basic Pancake recipe (see page 1314). Pile the pancakes flat and keep them warm between two plates while making the filling.

2 Quarter the apples and pears, remove the cores and cut the fruit into chunks.

Apple-Pear Pancakes are easy to prepare and are sure to become a firm favourite with your family for suppers in winter

3 Place the sugar in a pan with 300 ml (½ pint) (1¼ cups) cold water and stir over a low heat until dissolved. Blend the cornflour (cornstarch) with the orange juice and stir into the pan with the apricot jam. Bring to the boil and simmer for 3 minutes, stirring continuously.

4 Put some of the filling in the middle of each pancake, roll up the pancakes and transfer to a heated serving dish. Sprinkle with a little sugar and serve.

Serves 4

Custards

Custard is made from a base of milk and egg yolks. It must be cooked gently and stirred frequently to prevent it curdling. Once you have perfected the art of making a good custard you can flavour and sweeten it to taste, use it as a filling for pastries and cakes or simply as an accompaniment to your favourite stewed fruit. The following recipes will give you some idea of the many ways you can enhance the simple charm of this underrated dessert.

Crème Brulée

25 g (1 oz) (2 tablespoons) butter
6 egg yolks
100 g (¼ lb) (½ cup) castor (fine granulated) sugar
550 ml (1 pint) (2½ cups) single (light) cream
40 g (1½ oz) (3 tablespoons) demerara sugar

1 Preheat the oven to 150°C, 300°F, gas 2. Grease a 900 ml (1½ pint) (3¾ cup) shallow oven-proof dish with the butter.

2 In a bowl, cream the egg yolks and sugar. Bring the cream almost to the boil and stir it very gradually into the egg mixture. Strain the custard into the shallow dish. Stand the dish in 2.5 cm (1 in) cold water on a roasting tray and bake in the oven for 1-1½ hours or until the custard has set firm.

3 Remove the custard from the oven and let it cool. Chill it overnight in the refrigerator.

4 About 1 hour before serving, sprinkle the top with the demerara sugar. Brown it very quickly under the grill (broiler), turning the dish occasionally so that the sugar melts evenly. Allow it to cool until the sugar topping becomes crisp. Serve with a bowl of whipped cream.

Serves 6

Confectioner's Custard

50 g (2 oz) (½ cup) flour
4 eggs
75 g (3 oz) (⅜ cup) sugar
550 ml (1 pint) (2½ cups) milk

1 Sieve the flour. Separate the eggs and place the yolks in a bowl – you will not need the whites.

2 Add the sugar to the egg yolks and whisk the mixture until it creams and has increased in bulk. Add the sieved flour all at once and whisk in.

3 Bring the milk to the boil in a thick-bottomed saucepan. Gradually whisk the milk into the egg mixture. Return the mixture to the saucepan and bring slowly to the boil, whisking continually. Cook gently until it becomes a smooth cream – the flour will stop it curdling.

Makes about 900 ml (1½ pints) (3¾ cups)

Zuppa Inglese

6 eggs
300 g (11 oz) (1⅜ cups) castor (fine granulated) sugar
15 ml (1 tablespoon) grated orange rind
65 g (2½ oz) (⅝ cup) flour
75 g (3 oz) (⅝ cup) cornflour (cornstarch)
15 ml (1 tablespoon) butter
pinch salt

For the Filling:
225 g (½ lb) candied fruits
85 ml (3 fl oz) (⅜ cup) maraschino
15 ml (1 tablespoon) kirsch
300 ml (½ pint) (1¼ cups) confectioner's custard

For the Meringue:
3 egg whites
50 g (2 oz) (¼ cup) castor (fine granulated) sugar
25 g (1 oz) (2 tablespoons) icing (confectioners') sugar

1 The day before the meal, make the cake. Separate the egg whites from the yolks and place them in separate bowls. Add the sugar to the yolks and beat them until thick and creamy. This should take about 8 minutes of constant beating by hand. Add the orange rind, flour and cornflour (cornstarch) and mix well.

2 Preheat the oven to 170°C, 325°F, gas 3. Grease a 20 cm (8 in) cake tin (pan) with the butter.

3 Add a pinch of salt to the egg whites and whisk them until they are stiff. Fold the egg whites gently into the cake mixture. Pour the mixture into the cake tin (pan) and place it in the oven for 25 minutes. The cake should be just coloured when the cooking time is over. Turn the cake out on a rack and leave it to cool.

4 On the day of the meal, dice the candied fruits. Place them in a bowl with the maraschino and kirsch and leave to soak for 2 hours. Drain the fruits, reserving the liquid, and stir them into the confectioner's custard.

5 Cut the cake into 2 layers. Pour half the reserved liquid over each layer. Spread the bottom layer with the confectioner's custard and place the other layer on top.

6 Preheat the oven to 170°C, 325°F, gas 3.

7 Prepare the meringue. Whisk the egg whites until they start to whiten. Add the castor (fine granulated) sugar and continue beating until stiff. Cover the cake with large swirls of the meringue, using a piping (decorator's) bag or large spoon. Sprinkle the meringue with the icing (confectioners') sugar.

8 Place the cake on the top shelf of the oven for 6-8 minutes to lightly brown the meringue. Remove from the oven and allow to cool. Chill in the refrigerator and serve.

Serves 6-8

Look'n Cook Confectioner's Custard

1 Separate the eggs and place the yolks in a bowl. You will not need the whites **2** Add the sugar to the yolks and whisk until they are creamy **3** Whisk in the sieved flour **4** Bring the milk to the boil, whisk-ing occasionally to stop a skin forming **5** Gradually whisk it into the egg mixture **6** Return the custard to the saucepan and whisk gently over a low heat until it is smooth

Basic Baked Egg Custard

550 ml (1 pint) (2½ cups) milk
3 eggs
25 g (1 oz) (2 tablespoons) castor (fine granulated) sugar
5 ml (1 teaspoon) grated nutmeg

1 Preheat the oven to 170°C, 325°F, gas 3.

2 Heat the milk gently in a saucepan. Take care that it does not boil.

3 Meanwhile, whisk the eggs and sugar together in a mixing bowl.

4 Pour on the hot milk, stirring continuously. Then pour the custard into a greased ovenproof dish and sprinkle over the grated nutmeg.

5 Place the dish in the preheated oven and bake until set (about 45 minutes).

Serves 4

Pear and Almond Custard

4 pears, peeled, cored and quartered
300 ml (½ pint) (1¼ cups) water
150 g (5 oz) (⅝ cup) castor (fine granulated) sugar
50 g (2 oz) (⅜ cup) blanched almonds
few drops almond essence
2 egg yolks
25 g (1 oz) (3 tablespoons) cornflour (cornstarch)
300 ml (½ pint) (1¼ cups) single (light) cream
4 glacé cherries
15 ml (1 tablespoon) flaked almonds

1 Place the pears, water and sugar together in a saucepan and bring to the boil. Poach until the pears are tender.

Pear and Almond Custard tastes as good as it looks with its fresh juicy pears in a delicately flavoured almond custard

2 Strain off the syrup and liquidize with the blanched almonds and almond essence.

3 Blend the egg yolks, cornflour (cornstarch) and 30 ml (2 tablespoons) of the cream together in a bowl. Then stir in the syrup and the rest of the cream.

4 Reheat in a saucepan to boiling point, then allow to cool.

5 Divide the pears between four attractive glasses and pour in the almond custard.

6 Decorate with glacé cherries and flaked almonds. Chill before serving.

Serves 4

Tips: If fresh pears are out of season or unavailable you can always substitute canned pears.

To blanch almonds, just pour boiling water over them and leave for a few minutes. Remove the skins by squeezing the end of each nut – the almond will then pop out!

Baked Custard Tarts

225 g (½ lb) shortcrust (pie crust),
  fresh or frozen and thawed
butter for greasing
400 ml (14 fl oz) (1¾ cups) milk
2 cm (1 in) piece vanilla pod, or
  few drops vanilla essence
3 eggs
15 ml (1 tablespoon) castor
  (fine granulated) sugar
5 ml (1 teaspoon) grated nutmeg

1 Preheat the oven to 200°C,
400°F, gas 6.

2 Roll out the shortcrust (pie
crust) dough 3 mm (⅛ in) thick.
Grease some tartlet tins (muffin
pans) and line with the dough.
Prick the bottoms and put aside
in a cool place.

3 Place the milk and vanilla pod
or vanilla essence in a saucepan
and heat through.

4 Meanwhile, cream together
the eggs and sugar until light and
creamy. Pour on the hot milk, stirring well, and then strain through
a sieve. Leave it to become cold.

5 When cold, pour the custard
into the prepared tartlet tins
(muffin pans). Leave about 5 mm
(¼ in) spare at the top of each tin
(pan).

6 Sprinkle the tarts with grated
nutmeg and bake in the oven for
about 20 minutes until cooked
and golden. Serve cold with
cream.

Serves 4-6

Tips: You can flavour these
delicious tarts with a few drops of
your favourite liqueur – orange
liqueurs are particularly good. Or
add some coffee essence or cocoa
powder. Another idea is to stir
some chestnut purée into the
custard mixture.

Also, be careful not to overcook
these tarts. As soon as the custard
rises and feels firm, the tarts are
cooked. It is easy to overcook and
allow them to become watery. It
helps if you place the tartlet tins
(muffin pans) on a hot baking
(cookie) sheet, in the oven.

*Oeufs en Neige aux Oranges has
its egg whites floating
on top of a creamy custard which
is flavoured with oranges*

Oeufs en Neige aux Oranges

4 eggs, separated
pinch salt
200 g (7 oz) (1 cup) castor (fine
  granulated) sugar
500 ml (18 fl oz) (2¼ cups) milk
2 oranges
50 ml (2 fl oz) (¼ cup) curaçao

1 Beat the egg whites with a
pinch of salt until they form stiff
peaks. Beat in 100 g (¼ lb) (½ cup) of
the sugar, a little at a time.

2 Bring a pan of water to the boil
and drop the meringue, a few
tablespoonfuls at a time, into the
water. Simmer for about 10
minutes until cooked through.
Remove, drain and dry on a clean
cloth. Repeat until all the meringue is used up.

3 Meanwhile, heat the milk and
grate the rind and squeeze the
juice of 1 orange. Add the grated
rind to the milk.

4 Cream together the egg yolks
with the remaining sugar and
gradually whisk in the hot milk
away from the heat. When all the
milk is added, return the mixture
to the saucepan and gently
reheat, stirring all the time, until
the custard is thick and coats the
back of a spoon. Cool a little, then
stir in the orange juice and
curaçao. Pour into a serving dish.

5 With a cannelling knife, make
vertical grooves at regular
intervals around the remaining
orange. Then slice it thinly, horizontally. Decorate the top of the
custard with the meringues and
arrange the slices of orange
around the sides of the dish to
form an attractive border.

Serves 4

Tip: As a variation on this dish,
you can make it go further by
pouring the orange custard on to
a layer of sponge soaked in sherry,
or crushed macaroons sprinkled
with an orange-flavoured liqueur.

Another way of cooking the
whisked egg white meringue is to
drop the spoonfuls into the hot
milk which you intend to use for
the custard.

Look'n Cook Oeufs à la Neige

1 and **2** Separate the eggs and place the yolks and whites in different bowls **3** Add half the sugar to the egg yolks and whisk them to a cream **4** and **5** Whisk the egg whites until stiff, add the remaining sugar and continue to whisk until they are very stiff **6** Heat the milk and vanilla essence in a large saucepan. Drop 4 tablespoonfuls of the meringue into the hot (not boiling) milk and poach them for 5 minutes on

594

either side **7** Remove and place them to drain on a clean cloth **8** Bring the milk to the boil and gradually whisk it into the egg yolks **9** and **10** Return the custard to the saucepan and cook it gently, stirring continually, until it coats the spoon **11** and **12** Strain it and pour it into 4 individual serving dishes. Let it cool. Place a poached meringue on top, chill and serve

Oeufs à la Neige

5 eggs
150 g (5 oz) (⅝ cup) castor (fine granulated) sugar
750 ml (1¼ pints) (3 cups) milk
few drops vanilla essence

1 Break the eggs and place the whites and yolks in separate bowls.

2 Add half the sugar to the yolks and whisk them until they are creamy. Whisk the egg whites until they are stiff, add the remaining sugar and continue to whisk until the meringue is very stiff.

3 Bring the milk and vanilla to the boil, reduce the heat and drop 4 tablespoonfuls of the meringue mixture into the saucepan. Let the meringues poach for 5 minutes on either side. Remove them with a draining spoon and place them on a clean cloth to dry.

4 Return the milk to the boil and gradually whisk it into the egg yolk mixture. Return this mixture to the saucepan and cook it over a low heat, stirring constantly with a wooden spoon until the custard is smooth and coats the spoon.

5 Strain the custard and pour it into 4 individual serving dishes. Allow the custard to cool. Place a poached meringue on top of each dish and chill in the refrigerator for 1 hour before serving.

Serves 4

Almond Coffee Cream

2 eggs
150 g (5 oz) (⅝ cup) castor (fine granulated) sugar
225 ml (8 fl oz) (1 cup) double (heavy) cream
100 g (¼ lb) (¾ cup) almonds

Almond Coffee Cream is a smooth, rich dessert, topped with almonds and garnished with rich coffee-flavoured sweets

50 ml (2 fl oz) (¼ cup) cold black coffee
100 g (¼ lb) (¾ cup) icing (confectioners') sugar

For the Garnish:
24 coffee-flavoured sweets

1 Separate the eggs and place the yolks in a bowl. You will not need the whites.

2 Place the bowl containing the egg yolks in a basin of hot, but not boiling, water. Add the sugar to the yolks and whisk the mixture thoroughly for 3 minutes. Gradually pour in 50 ml (2 fl oz) (¼ cup) of the cream and continue to whisk until the mixture is thick and smooth.

3 Preheat the oven to 200°C, 400°F, gas 6. Place the almonds in a small saucepan with just enough water to cover them. Bring the water to the boil and remove the saucepan from the heat. Drain and refresh the almonds and peel off their skins. Chop them into fine slithers. Wrap them in aluminium foil and place in the preheated oven for 2 minutes. Allow them to cool in the foil.

4 Reserve 15 ml (1 tablespoon) of the almond slithers and mix the rest into the egg mixture.

5 Whip the remaining cream and stir in the black coffee. Gently fold in the icing (confectioners') sugar. Mix this coffee cream with the egg yolk mixture.

6 Pour the cream into 4 individual serving dishes. Place them in the refrigerator to chill for at least 4 hours. Sprinkle with the reserved almonds, garnish with the coffee-flavoured sweets and serve.

Serves 4

Cabinet Pudding

150 g (5 oz) sponge cake
75 g (3 oz) (⅜ cup) glacé cherries
15 g (½ oz) angelica
15 ml (1 tablespoon) butter
15 ml (1 tablespoon) sugar
For the Custard:
3 eggs
50 g (2 oz) (¼ cup) castor (fine granulated) sugar
few drops vanilla essence
550 ml (1 pint) (2½ cups) milk

1 Cut the sponge cake into 1 cm (½ in) cubes and place them in a bowl. Quarter the glacé cherries and cut the angelica into small strips. Carefully mix them both with the cake cubes.

Cabinet Pudding, a traditional British dessert, is a tasty mixture of sponge cake and glacéd fruits set in an egg custard

2 Butter the inside of six 150 ml (¼ pint) (⅝ cup) moulds and sprinkle each with a little sugar. Divide the cake mixture between the 6 moulds. Preheat the oven to 200°C, 400°F, gas 6.

3 Prepare the custard. In a bowl, cream together the eggs, sugar and vanilla essence. Heat the milk, without letting it boil, and blend it thoroughly with the egg mixture. Pass the custard through a strainer and divide it between each of the 6 moulds. Allow 30 minutes for the custard to soak through the cake.

4 Place the moulds in a roasting tin (pan) with 4 cm (1½ in) of water. Bake them in the oven for 30 minutes or until they are set. Turn them out on to a serving dish and serve immediately with a bowl of whipped cream.

Serves 6

Coffee Banana Custard

3 eggs
30 ml (2 tablespoons) sugar
15 ml (1 tablespoon) instant
  coffee granules
550 ml (1 pint) (2½ cups) milk
2 bananas
grated chocolate to decorate

1 Whisk together the eggs, sugar and coffee. Warm the milk and pour onto the egg mixture, stirring well.

2 Strain the mixture into a heavy-bottomed pan and stir over a gentle heat with a wooden spoon until the custard thinly coats the back of the spoon. Do not allow it to boil. Cool slightly.

3 Slice the bananas thinly and divide between 4 individual glass serving dishes.

4 Pour the warm coffee custard over the bananas and sprinkle the tops with grated chocolate. Serve immediately.

Serves 4

Tip: Orange Strawberry custard can be made following the recipe above. Omit the instant coffee granules and grated chocolate from the ingredients. Put a few strips of thinly pared orange rind in the milk when it is warmed, cover the pan and leave to infuse for 10 minutes before pouring onto the egg mixture. Slice some fresh strawberries into the serving dishes and decorate the tops with finely grated orange rind.

Whisky Sabayon

6 egg yolks
175 g (6 oz) (¾ cup) castor
  (fine granulated) sugar
pinch grated nutmeg
85 ml (3 fl oz) (⅜ cup) whisky
juice 1 lemon
grated rind and juice 1 orange

1 Whisk together the egg yolks, sugar and nutmeg in a large bowl.

2 Add the whisky, place the bowl over a pan of hot water and whisk until the mixture is thick.

3 Add the lemon and orange juice and continue to whisk over the pan of hot water until the mixture is thick and pale.

4 Remove the bowl from the heat and whisk until the mixture is cool. Spoon into 4 individual glass serving dishes, and decorate each with a little grated orange rind. Serve chilled.

Serves 4

Pear Brioche – yeasty, rich brioche stuffed with fresh chopped pears, crisp macaroons and kirsch-flavoured custard

Pear Brioche

350 g (¾ lb) (3¾ cups) flour
5 ml (1 teaspoon) salt
20 g (¾ oz) fresh yeast
45 ml (3 tablespoons) castor (fine
  granulated) sugar
85 ml (3 fl oz) (⅜ cup) milk
2 eggs, beaten
50 g (2 oz) (¼ cup) butter

For the Filling:
3 egg yolks
1 whole egg
50 g (2 oz) (½ cup) flour
75 g (3 oz) (⅜ cup) sugar
550 ml (1 pint) (2½ cups) milk
30 ml (1 fl oz) (2 tablespoons)
  kirsch

4 ripe pears
6 almond macaroons, crushed
175 g (6 oz) (½ cup) apricot jam

1 For the brioche: sieve the flour and salt into a warmed bowl. Blend the yeast with 5 ml (1 teaspoon) of the sugar, and add to the flour with the milk, beaten eggs, and the remaining sugar. Beat well until the dough is smooth and elastic. Work the butter into the dough.

2 Cover the bowl with greased polythene and leave to rise in a warm place for 40 minutes. Preheat the oven to 220°C, 425°F, gas 7.

3 Stir the dough well and turn into a lightly greased charlotte mould or cake tin (pan). Cover and leave to prove for 15 minutes.

4 Bake for 50 minutes, until golden-brown. Turn out on to a wire rack to cool.

5 For the filling: place the egg yolks, whole egg, flour and sugar in a bowl and mix well together. Heat the milk and pour on to the egg mixture, stirring. Return the mixture to the pan and stir continuously over a medium heat until the mixture comes to the boil. Remove from the heat

---

Lemon Sabayon is a smooth and creamy custard dessert, made with fresh lemons, orange liqueur, egg yolks, sugar and milk

immediately, add the kirsch and cool.

6 Peel, core and dice the pears. Stir the pears and crushed macaroons into the cooled custard.

7 Turn the oven to 190°C, 375°F, gas 5. Remove a slice from the top of the brioche and scoop out some of the inside, leaving a hole almost large enough to hold the pear custard. Wrap the brioche loosely in aluminium foil and place in the oven for about 15 minutes to warm through.

8 Meanwhile melt the apricot jam in a pan with 30 ml (2 tablespoons) water. Gently reheat the pear custard.

9 Stand the brioche on a heated serving dish and pour over the melted jam, coating the inside generously, and allowing a little to drizzle down the outsides. Fill the brioche with the heated pear custard and serve immediately.

Serves 6

Lemon Sabayon

4 egg yolks
1 whole egg
50 g (2 oz) (¼ cup) castor (fine granulated) sugar
finely grated rind and juice 1 lemon
15 ml (1 tablespoon) Cointreau
300 ml (½ pint) (1¼ cups) sweet vermouth

1 Place the egg yolks, whole egg and sugar together in a bowl and whisk for 5 minutes.

2 Whisk in the lemon rind and juice, Cointreau and vermouth.

3 Place the bowl over a pan of hot water and continue to whisk until the mixture is thick and pale.

4 Remove the bowl from the heat and whisk until the mixture is cool. Spoon into 4 individual glass dishes and serve chilled.

Serves 4

Queen of Puddings

550 ml (1 pint) (2½ cups) milk
175 g (6 oz) (¾ cup) castor
  (fine granulated) sugar
225 g (½ lb) (4 cups) cakecrumbs
grated rind 2 lemons
2 eggs, separated
225 g (½ lb) (¾ cup) apricot jam

1 Preheat the oven to 180°C, 350°F, gas 4. Heat the milk and 50 g (2 oz) (¼ cup) of the sugar gently in a saucepan. Stir in the cakecrumbs and lemon rind and remove from the heat. Beat in the egg yolks.

2 Pour half the mixture into a greased earthenware dish and bake it in the oven for 30 minutes or until set.

3 Heat the apricot jam in a saucepan and spread half over the top of the set custard. Top up the dish with the remaining egg yolk mixture and return it to the oven for a further 30 minutes or until it is thoroughly set.

4 Cover the top of the pudding with the rest of the jam. Whisk the egg whites with 75 g (3 oz) (⅓ cup) of the remaining sugar until they are stiff.

5 Raise the oven temperature to 190°C, 375°F, gas 5. Pile the whisked meringue on to the pudding and sprinkle with the remaining sugar. Return to the oven and bake for 5 minutes or until the meringue is golden. Serve immediately.

Serves 6

Crème Caramel

30 ml (1 fl oz) (2 tablespoons)
  water
100 g (¼ lb) sugar cubes

Crème Caramel is a classic French dessert which is always a favourite at parties with its creamy texture and caramel top

4 eggs
50 g (2 oz) (¼ cup) sugar
4 drops vanilla essence
550 ml (1 pint) (2½ cups) milk

1 Make the caramel. Bring half of the water and the sugar cubes to the boil in a heavy-based saucepan. When they begin to caramelize, add the remaining water and reboil until the water and caramel mix.

2 Line the mould as shown on the opposite page.

3 Preheat the oven to 180°C, 350°F, gas 4. Cream together the eggs, sugar and vanilla essence. Heat the milk, without letting it boil, and gradually whisk it into the egg mixture. Strain this cream and pour it into the mould. Place the mould in a roasting tin (pan), half-filled with water, and bake for 1 hour, or until set.

4 Chill thoroughly before turning out the caramel on to a serving dish. Pour any caramel remaining in the mould around the dish and serve.

Serves 6

Look'n Cook Lining a Crème Caramel Mould

1 Hold the rim of the mould with a clean cloth to prevent your hands burning and pour in the caramel **2** and **3** Tip Land rotate crème mould so the base is covered in caramel **4** and **5** Tip the mould so it is almost on its side and continue to rotate it until all the sides are well coated **6** When the interior of the mould is completely coated, pour off and discard the excess caramel

Rice Desserts

Rice pudding is not a name that conjures up visions of exotic culinary delights; for many people it is a reminder of school or institutional cooking that they prefer to forget. However, rice pudding is not only easy, cheap and nutritious – it can also be delicious and impressive. Even a basic rice pudding can be varied in many ways. Try adding beaten egg; spices such as cinnamon; raisins or chopped candied fruits; or cream. Serve it with unusual fruits such as mango, papaw or passion fruit.

Basic Rice Pudding

50 g (2 oz) (¼ cup) short grain rice
25 g (1 oz) (2 tablespoons) butter
25 g (1 oz) (2 tablespoons) castor (fine granulated) sugar
550 ml (1 pint) (2½ cups) milk
pinch grated nutmeg

1 Preheat the oven to 150°C, 300°F, gas 2.

2 Wash the rice in a colander under running water, and drain. Grease an ovenproof dish with some of the butter.

3 Place the rice and sugar in the dish. Pour in the milk and top with the rest of the butter, cut in small pieces. Dust with freshly grated nutmeg.

4 Bake in the oven for 2 hours, stirring the pudding after ½ hour. Serve hot or cold.
Serves 4

Banana Rice Caramel

100 g (¼ lb) (½ cup) short grain rice
900 ml (1½ pints) (3½ cups) milk
100 g (¼ lb) lump sugar
15 ml (1 tablespoon) water
4 bananas
100 g (¼ lb) (½ cup) castor (fine granulated) sugar
few drops vanilla essence
4 eggs, beaten

1 Place the rice in a pan of cold water and bring it to the boil. Refresh with cold water and drain.

2 Bring the milk to the boil in a pan and add the rice. Cook for about 40 minutes until the rice is

Banana Rice Caramel is served either hot or cold. Your children will adore the flavour of the bananas and sticky toffee

very tender, and has absorbed the milk.

3 Meanwhile, make the caramel by melting the lump sugar in the water, stirring constantly. Boil to 160°C, 315°F, when it starts to colour. Remove the pan from the heat and dip its base at once into cold water to stop the sugar cooking further.

4 Pour the caramel into a mould. Holding the mould with a cloth, turn it so that the caramel is distributed over the sides. Allow the caramel to cool to a sticky consistency.

5 Preheat the oven to 180°C, 350°F, gas 4. Peel and slice 3 bananas. Arrange the slices over the bottom of the mould and in one row around the sides.

6 When the rice is cooked, stir in the castor (fine granulated) sugar and the vanilla essence. Fold in the beaten eggs. Pour the mixture into the mould lined with caramel and banana.

7 Bake the rice in a bain-marie in the oven for 40 minutes. Turn out the mould on to a serving dish. Peel and slice the remaining banana and arrange the slices around the pudding. Serve hot or cold.

Serves 4-6

Mandarin Condé

60 g (2½ oz) (⅜ cup) rice
550 ml (1 pint) (2½ cups) milk
50 g (2 oz) (¼ cup) castor (fine granulated) sugar
3 drops vanilla essence
15 ml (1 tablespoon) candied orange peel cut in small strips
225 g (½ lb) (1 cup) canned mandarin segments
50 g (2 oz) (½ cup) glacé cherries

For the Apricot Glaze:
50 g (2 oz) (¼ cup) apricot jam
25 g (1 oz) (2 tablespoons) sugar
300 ml (½ pint) (1¼ cups) water

Mandarin Condé is a substantial dessert with the tangy flavour of mandarins providing a contrast to the creamy rice

10 ml (2 teaspoons) cornflour (cornstarch)
15 ml (1 tablespoon) Cointreau

1 Place the rice in a pan of cold water. Bring to the boil. Rinse and refresh in cold water.

2 Bring the milk to the boil in a pan. Add the rice and cook until it is soft and has absorbed the milk.

3 Stir in the sugar and vanilla essence and add the pieces of candied orange peel. Moisten a mould and pour the rice into it. Press it down level and firmly, and leave it to cool.

4 To make the apricot glaze, heat the jam, sugar and water gently until they are melted and smooth. Add the cornflour (cornstarch), dissolved in a little water, and boil for 2 minutes until the glaze clears. Stir in the Cointreau.

5 When the rice is cold and set, turn it out on a serving dish. Arrange the mandarin segments on top of, and around, the rice. Place a whole glacé cherry in the middle and halved cherries in the mandarin segments around the rice. Pour the apricot glaze over the middle of the rice so that it flows down the sides. Serve cold.

Serves 4-6

Tip: The orange liqueur used to flavour the apricot glaze can, of course, be varied – Grand Marnier or curaçao would be equally delicious. Or, for economy, the Cointreau can be replaced by orange essence, but this is much stronger so use only 2-3 drops.

Look'n Cook Rice Condé with Apricots

1 Place the rice in a saucepan of cold water and bring it to the boil **2** Refresh the rice in cold water and leave it until it is quite condé **3** Drain the rice through a colander **4** Bring the milk to the boil and pour the rice into it **5** Bring the mixture back to the boil, then cover the pan and place it in a preheated oven. Bake for about 40 minutes until the rice is completely cooked **6** Add the vanilla essence and mix

well **7** Gently stir in the castor (fine granulated) sugar **8** Dampen a shallow cake tin (pan). Pour the rice into it and press it down firmly and evenly **9** Allow the rice to cool. Turn it out on a serving dish **10** Decorate the top with the apricot halves **11** Glaze the top of the fruit with the apricot glaze **12** Decorate the dish with glacé cherries and candied angelica

Rice Condé with Apricots

100 g (¼ lb) (½ cup) short or long
  grain rice
750 ml (1¼ pints) (3 cups) milk
few drops vanilla essence
100 g (¼ lb) (½ cup) castor (fine
  granulated) sugar
75 g (3 oz) (¼ cup) apricot jam
10 ml (2 teaspoons) kirsch
12 canned apricot halves
6 glacé cherries
1 stick candied angelica

1 Preheat the oven to 170°C,
325°F, gas 3.

2 Place the rice in a saucepan of
cold water and bring it to the boil.
Drain, refresh in cold water, and
drain again through a colander.

3 In an ovenproof pan or casserole, bring the milk to the boil.
Add the rice and bring it back to
the boil. Cover the pan or casserole and place it in the oven.
Cook for 1 hour or until the rice
has absorbed all the milk.

4 Remove the rice from the oven.
Gently stir in the vanilla essence
(do not add too much) and the
sugar with a fork.

5 Moisten a shallow cake tin
(pan) with cold water and pour
the rice into it. Press it down
firmly and make an even flat surface. Leave to cool.

6 Melt the apricot jam in a pan
over low heat and stir in the
kirsch.

7 Place a serving dish over the
rice mould and turn it over so that
the rice comes out of the pan in
one piece. Arrange the canned
apricot halves over the top and
pour the melted apricot glaze
over them. Decorate with the
glacé cherries and the candied
angelica, cut in short strips. Serve
cold.

Serves 4-6

Tip: Do not add sugar to the milk
while it is cooking, as this will
prevent the rice from swelling up.
You could substitute other fruit
for the apricots in this recipe: try
using peaches, pears, cherries or
papaws.

Empress Rice Pudding

750 ml (1¼ pints) (3 cups) milk
75 g (3 oz) (⅜ cup) short grain rice
100 g (¼ lb) (½ cup) castor (fine
  granulated) sugar
3 drops vanilla essence
25 g (1 oz) (¼ cup) powdered
  gelatine
25 g (1 oz) (¼ cup) diced mixed
  candied fruit and peel
150 ml (¼ pint) (⅝ cup) whipping
  cream
2 egg whites
9 glacé cherries to garnish

1 In a saucepan, bring the milk
to the boil. Wash the rice and add

---

*Empress Rice Pudding is a creamy
and colourful dessert, and
is decorated with delicious diced
candied fruits and mixed peel*

---

it to the milk. Simmer until the
rice is tender and has absorbed
the milk.

2 Stir the sugar gently into the
rice. Blend in the vanilla essence.

3 Dissolve the gelatine in a little
hot water. Allow to cool and add
to the rice. Add the diced candied
fruit and peel, and mix well.

4 Allow to cool. Beat the cream
lightly and fold it into the rice.

5 Beat the egg whites until stiff.
Fold them into the rice. Moisten a
ring mould (tube pan) with cold
water and pour the rice mixture
into it. Place the ring mould (tube
pan) in the refrigerator and chill
until the mixture is set firm.

6 Turn the rice pudding out on to
a serving dish. Place the glacé
cherries around the top to decorate and serve.

Serves 4-6

All about Cheesecakes, Sponge Desserts and Meringues

Apricot Cheesecake

Cheesecakes

Cheesecakes are becoming increasingly popular and you can easily make your own at home. They are Jewish in origin and come from Russia and Central Europe. Nowadays, we tend to associate them with American cooking. Cheesecakes can be either baked or set with gelatine. They are nearly always served cold. There is a wide range of attractive and delicious cheesecake recipes to choose from. They may be made with cream, cottage, curd or ricotta cheese on a base of rich pastry (pie crust), sponge cake or biscuit crumbs.

You can top cheesecakes with whipped cream, fresh or crystallized fruit, or a fruit glaze. You can sprinkle a layer of fresh fruit, such as raspberries, or dried fruits between the base and the cheesecake mixture. Cream and curd cheese have rather a bland flavour, therefore the grated rind and juice of a lemon or orange are often added. In Italy, grated Parmesan cheese is sometimes mixed into the cheesecake for extra flavour.

Cheesecakes freeze particularly well and thus you can make one in advance, freeze it until you need it, and decorate just before serving with fruit, cream or a glaze.

Pineapple Cheesecake

225 g (½ lb) ginger biscuits (cookies)
100 g (¼ lb) (½ cup) butter
100 g (¼ lb) (⅔ cup) cream cheese
100 g (¼ lb) (½ cup) crushed pineapple
50 g (2 oz) (¼ cup) castor (fine granulated) sugar
15 ml (1 tablespoon) lemon juice
50 ml (2 fl oz) (¼ cup) water
15 g (½ oz) (2 tablespoons) powdered gelatine
150 ml (¼ pint) (⅝ cup) double (heavy) cream
4 pineapple rings
6 glacé cherries
angelica to decorate

1 Crush the ginger biscuits (cookies). This is best done by placing them in a paper or greaseproof (parchment) paper bag. Secure the end and flatten with a heavy rolling pin.

2 Place the crushed biscuits (cookies) in a basin. Heat the butter in a saucepan and mix well with the melted butter.

3 Spread the biscuit (cookie) mixture over the base of a 20 cm (8 in) diameter shallow loose-bottomed cake tin (pan).

4 Blend together the cream cheese, crushed pineapple and sugar. Stir in the lemon juice.

5 Warm the water and dissolve the gelatine. Stir well until it is dissolved. Cool a little, then add to the cream cheese mixture.

6 Whip the cream until stiff and fold in with a metal spoon. Pour the cheesecake mixture over the biscuit base and level off the top. Chill in the refrigerator for about 3 hours, until firm and set.

7 Remove the cheesecake from the mould and place on an attractive serving plate.

8 Cut the pineapple rings into chunks and slice the glacé cherries in half. Slice the angelica to make two thin 'stems' and four diamond-shaped 'leaves.'

9 Next make two flowers using the pineapple chunks as 'petals,' the cherry centres and angelica 'stems' and 'leaves.' Arrange these flowers on the top of the cheesecake. Place the remaining pineapple and cherries alternately around the base to form a decorative border.

Serves 6

Tips: You can use curd cheese instead of cream cheese in this recipe. To give it a more lemony, sharper flavour, add a little grated lemon rind.

Chocolate Orange Cheesecake

225 g (½ lb) sweetmeal biscuits (graham crackers)
100 g (¼ lb) (½ cup) butter
pinch cinnamon
butter for greasing
50 ml (2 fl oz) (¼ cup) milk
75 g (3 oz) chocolate
225 g (½ lb) (1⅓ cups) cream cheese
50 ml (2 fl oz) (¼ cup) water
25 g (1 oz) (¼ cup) powdered gelatine
juice and grated rind 1 orange
150 ml (¼ pint) (⅝ cup) double (heavy) cream, whipped
3 glacé cherries
chocolate buttons to decorate

1 Crush the sweetmeal biscuits (graham crackers) as described above. Melt the butter and blend with the crushed biscuits (crackers) and cinnamon.

2 Grease the bottom of a loose-bottomed 20 cm (8 in) cake tin (pan) and line the sides with greaseproof (parchment) paper.

3 Spread the biscuit (cracker) mixture over the base of the tin (pan).

4 Place the milk and chocolate in a saucepan and heat gently, stirring until the chocolate melts. Mix well with the cream cheese.

5 Heat the water and dissolve the gelatine. Reheat until you have a clear jelly (gelatin)-like substance.

6 Stir the gelatine into the cream cheese with the orange rind and juice. Fold in the whipped cream, and then pour the mixture into the tin (pan).

7 Chill in the refrigerator for 3 hours until set and firm. Remove the cheesecake from the tin (pan) and place on a serving plate. Decorate the top with halved glacé cherries and chocolate buttons before serving.

Serves 6-8

Pineapple Cheesecake (top) and Chocolate Orange Cheesecake (below) are equally good to look at and great to eat

Redcurrant Cheesecake

75 g (3 oz) (6 tablespoons) butter
45 ml (1½ fl oz) (3 tablespoons)
  golden syrup or honey
175 g (6 oz) (6 cups) cornflakes
2 eggs, separated
50 g (2 oz) (¼ cup) castor (fine
  granulated) sugar
225 g (½ lb) (1⅓ cups) cream cheese
50 ml (2 fl oz) (¼ cup) lemon juice
30 ml (1 fl oz) (2 tablespoons)
  water
30 ml (2 tablespoons) powdered
  gelatine
150 ml (¼ pint) (⅝ cup) double
  (heavy) cream
225 g (½ lb) (2 cups) redcurrants
50 ml (2 fl oz) (¼ cup) melted
  redcurrant jelly

1 Preheat the oven to 180°C, 350°F, gas 4.

2 In a saucepan, melt the butter and golden syrup (or honey) together. Stir in the cornflakes until they are well coated. Press the mixture around the base of a lightly greased, 20 cm (8 in) flan case with a loose bottom. Bake for 10 minutes. Allow to cool.

3 Cream the egg yolks with the sugar in a bowl. Beat in the cream cheese. Add the lemon juice gradually, and beat until soft and smooth.

4 Heat the water and melt the gelatine in it. Add this to the cheese mixture and stir until well blended. Allow to cool nearly to setting point.

5 In separate bowls, beat the egg whites and the double (heavy) cream until they are both stiff. Gradually fold the cream into the cheese mixture. Then gently fold in the beaten egg whites.

6 Pour the mixture into the flan case and allow it to set. When set, lift the bottom out of the flan case

Redcurrant Cheesecake has a smooth, creamy texture and is topped with a colourful and fruity, fresh redcurrant glaze

and slide the cheesecake on to a serving dish.

7 Wash and pick over the redcurrants (if they are not very ripe, cook them for 5 minutes in a little water and sugar, then drain). Arrange them over the top of the cheesecake and cover with the melted redcurrant jelly. Serve cold.

Serves 6

Apple and Raisin Cheesecake

sweet shortcrust (pie crust)
  dough made with 225 g (½ lb) (2¼
  cups) flour
225 g (½ lb) sweet apples
50 g (2 oz) (¼ cup) butter
1 egg
50 g (2 oz) (¼ cup) castor (fine
  granulated) sugar

30 ml (2 tablespoons) flour
150 g (5 oz) ($\frac{5}{8}$ cup) cream cheese
50 ml (2 fl oz) ($\frac{1}{4}$ cup) single (light) cream
2 drops vanilla essence
50 g (2 oz) ($\frac{1}{3}$ cup) raisins
150 ml ($\frac{1}{4}$ pint) ($\frac{5}{8}$ cup) whipping cream

1 Preheat the oven to 200°C, 400°F, gas 6. Roll the shortcrust (pie crust) dough on a floured board to 5 mm ($\frac{1}{4}$ in) thick. Lightly grease a flan case and line it with the dough. Prick the bottom and bake blind for 15-20 minutes.

2 Meanwhile, peel, core and thinly slice the apples. Melt the butter in a pan and cook the apple slices over gentle heat for a few minutes until tender. Strain and allow to cool.

3 To make the cheesecake filling, beat the egg with the sugar. Blend in the flour. Add the cream cheese and beat until soft. Gradually beat in the cream and vanilla essence. Finally, fold in the raisins.

Apple and Raisin Cheesecake is layered with fruit to help make it light and moist, and is garnished with whipped cream

4 Remove the flan case from the oven and lower the oven temperature to 190°C, 375°F, gas 5. Let the flan cool and then pour in half the cheesecake mixture. Cover it with a layer of apple slices. Pour the rest of the mixture over the top. Bake for 30 minutes.

5 Beat the whipping cream until stiff. Remove the cheesecake from the oven and turn it out of the flan case. When it is cool, top with whipped cream and serve.

Serves 6

Tip: To give the apple slices a delicious flavour, cook them with 5 ml (1 teaspoon) powdered cinnamon. Other seasonal fruits, such as plums or pears, could be substituted for the apples.

Mock Cheesecake

200 g (7 oz) (1$\frac{1}{2}$ cups) biscuit (cookie) crumbs
25 g (1 oz) (2 tablespoons) castor (fine granulated) sugar
50 g (2 oz) ($\frac{1}{4}$ cup) butter, melted
4 eggs, separated
300 ml ($\frac{1}{2}$ pint) (1$\frac{1}{4}$ cups) sweetened condensed milk
grated rind and juice 2 lemons

1 Preheat the oven to 190°C, 375°F, gas 5. In a mixing bowl beat together the biscuit (cookie) crumbs, sugar and melted butter. Line a flan case with the mixture.

2 Beat the egg yolks. Stir in the condensed milk, lemon rind and juice. Beat the egg whites until stiff. Fold the whites into the mixture and pour it into the flan case. Bake for 15-20 minutes in the preheated oven, cool and serve.

Serves 6

Apricot Cheesecake

425 g (15 oz) canned apricots in
  syrup
1 packet orange jelly (jello)
450 g (1 lb) (2⅔ cups) cottage
  cheese
25 g (1 oz) (2 tablespoons) castor
  (fine granulated) sugar
150 ml (¼ pint) (⅝ cup) double
  (heavy) cream, whipped
100 g (¼ lb) ginger biscuits
  (cookies), crushed
25 g (1 oz) (2 tablespoons)
  demerara sugar
50 g (2 oz) (¼ cup) butter, melted

For the Decoration:
40 g (1½ oz) (2 tablespoons)
  apricot jam
425 g (15 oz) canned apricots in
  syrup
15 g (½ oz) flaked almonds

1 Make up the syrup from the
canned apricots to 300 ml (½ pint)
(1¼ cups) with water. Bring to the
boil, add the jelly (jello) and stir to
dissolve. Cool.

2 Sieve the apricots and cheese
and stir in the cooled jelly (jello)
and sugar. Fold in the cream.

3 Line the base of a 20 cm (8 in)
cake tin (pan) with non-stick
paper. Pour in the mixture and
chill to set.

4 Combine the biscuits
(cookies), demerara sugar and
butter, sprinkle over the set mixture and press down with a spoon.

5 Melt the jam with 15 ml (1
tablespoon) of the apricot syrup,
sieve and cool. Turn out the
cheesecake and decorate with the
apricots. Brush with the jam glaze
and sprinkle with almonds.

Serves 8

Avocado Orange Cheesecake

175 g (6 oz) (1¼ cups) biscuit
  (cookie) crumbs
50 g (2 oz) (¼ cup) butter, melted

1 avocado
50 ml (2 fl oz) (¼ cup) lemon juice
75 g (3 oz) (½ cup) cream cheese
150 ml (¼ pint) (⅝ cup) sour cream
1 orange
25 g (1 oz) (2 tablespoons) castor
  (fine granulated) sugar
7 ml (1½ teaspoons) powdered
  gelatine dissolved in 15 ml
  (1 tablespoon) water
1 egg white

1 Mix the crumbs with the butter, and press the mixture evenly
into the base of a lightly greased
flan case. Place in the refrigerator
and chill until set.

---

*Avocado and Orange Cheese-
cake has a deliciously unusual
flavour, and would be the
perfect choice for a summer buffet*

---

2 Peel, stone (pit) and mash ¾ of
the avocado. Thinly slice the
remaining ¼ and dip the slices in
lemon juice; reserve for garnish.

3 Beat the cream cheese, sour
cream, and remaining lemon
juice into the mashed avocado.
Grate the rind of ½ the orange and
add. Stir in the sugar.

4 Combine the gelatine with the
avocado mixture. Beat the egg
white until stiff and fold in.

5 Pour the mixture on to the
crumb crust and chill until set.
Remove the flan from the ring.
Peel and slice the rest of the
orange, and decorate the top of
the cheesecake with orange slices
and the reserved avocado slices.

Serves 6

Trifles

The dictionary defines a 'trifle' as a paltry, insignificant thing; and as a dessert. A classic trifle dessert, however, is far from insignificant. At its best it is light but lavish, somewhat alcoholic and highly decorative. The trifle was developed in Great Britain in the eighteenth century, from the Elizabethan dish of syllabub. A trifle should have four layers: the first of sponge cakes soaked in sherry and fruit juice; then a layer of fruit; then one of custard, and a topping of whipped cream. The modern, less rich and filling versions often substitute jelly (jello) for one of these layers, and do not include sherry. Whatever the layers contain, trifles are easy and popular with old and young alike.

Country Trifles

50 g (2 oz) packet jelly (jello)
225 g (½ lb) (1 cup) canned fruit salad or cocktail with syrup
75 g (3 oz) (½ cup) muesli
30ml (2 tablespoons) custard powder
25 g (1 oz) (2 tablespoons) sugar
500 ml (1 pint) (2½ cups) milk

For the Topping:
150 ml (¼ pint) (⅝ cup) double (heavy) cream
25 g (1 oz) (2 tablespoons) muesli
2 glacé cherries

1 In a pan dissolve the jelly (jello) in 150ml (¼ pint) (⅝ cup) boiling water. Stir in the syrup from the can of fruit salad. Measure the liquid and make it up to 300ml (½ pint) (1¼ cups) with cold water.

2 Divide the fruit salad and the muesli between four single-serving sundae glasses. Pour the jelly (jello) into the glasses. Leave them in a cool place or in the refrigerator until set.

3 Mix the custard powder with the sugar and 50ml (2 fl oz) (¼ cup) of the milk in a bowl, until smooth. Heat the rest of the milk in a pan until almost boiling. Stir in the custard powder mixture and return the pan to the heat, stirring while it comes to the boil. Cook for 1 minute, stirring constantly. Withdraw the pan from the heat. Dampen a circle of greaseproof (parchment) paper and lay it on the custard while it cools. Leave until almost cold.

4 When the custard is nearly set, pour it over the jelly (jello) in the sundae glasses. Spread it level

Country Trifles — delicious layers of meusli, fruit salad, jelly (jello) and custard, topped with rosettes of cream

and chill until the custard is firm.

5 Whip the cream until stiff and place it in a piping (decorator's) bag. Pipe the cream in rosettes around the edge of the custard. Place the muesli for the topping inside the cream border in each glass. Put a glacé cherry on top of each trifle and serve cold.

Serves 4

Tip: To vary the trifles, you could arrange canned mandarin segments over the top and perhaps sprinkle a little orange-flavoured liqueur, such as Grand Marnier or curaçao, over the fruit before adding the jelly (jello). Allow 5 ml (1 teaspoon) of the liqueur per portion.

1 The ingredients: sponge cake, sherry, brandy, eggs, milk, jam, ratafias, glacéd fruits and almonds **2** Split the sponge cakes and spread with raspberry jam. Sandwich them together and cut into squares **3** Place the sponge squares, ratafias and split almonds in a glass bowl. Mix the sherry, brandy and essences (optional) and pour over the cake **4** In a bowl combine the egg yolks, cornflour (cornstarch) and a little milk. Pour on the boiling milk and stir. Return to the pan and reheat until thickened **5** Pour the custard over the cakes and leave in a cool place to set **6** Whip the cream until stiff and spread it over the set custard. Make a swirling pattern on it and decorate with glacé cherries and strips of candied angelica **7** The finished dish should be served cold. Almonds and ratafias may also be used to decorate the top

Christmas Cake Trifle

225-350 g (½-¾ lb) leftover
  Christmas or fruit cake
30 ml (1 fl oz) (2 tablespoons)
  brandy
450 g (1 lb) ripe pears
550 ml (1 pint) (2½ cups) custard
150 ml (¼ pint) (⅝ cup) whipping
  cream

1 Cut or break the cake into chunks. Place them in a glass bowl and sprinkle with brandy. Peel, core and slice the pears. Mix them with the cake.

2 Pour the custard over the cake and fruit and leave to set. Decorate with whipped cream.

Serves 6-8

Tipsy Trifle

2 plain sponge cakes, 20 cm
  (8 in) in diameter
100 g (¼ lb) (⅜ cup) raspberry jam
12 ratafias
30 ml (2 tablespoons) split
  blanched almonds
150 ml (¼ pint) (⅝ cup) sherry
30 ml (1 fl oz) (2 tablespoons)
  brandy
2 drops each lemon and orange
  essence (optional)
4 egg yolks
10 ml (2 teaspoons) cornflour
  (cornstarch)
450 ml (16 fl oz) (2 cups) milk
50 g (2 oz) (¼ cup) castor (fine
  granulated) sugar
150 ml (¼ pint) (⅝ cup) whipping
  cream
6 glacé cherries
two 10 cm (4 in) stems candied
  angelica

1 Split the sponge cakes horizontally and spread them liberally with jam on the inside face. Sandwich them together again and cut into squares.

2 Arrange the sponge squares, ratafias and almonds in the base of a large glass bowl.

3 Measure the sherry into a jug

and add the brandy, and fruit essences, if wished. Pour over the cake and leave to soak.

4 In a bowl beat together the egg yolks, cornflour (cornstarch) and 30 ml (1 fl oz) (2 tablespoons) of the milk. Meanwhile, bring the rest of the milk to the boil in a pan. Gradually pour the hot milk into the bowl, beating all the time. Pour the mixture back into the pan and reheat, without boiling, to thicken.

5 Pour the custard over the cakes and leave in a cool place to set. Whip the cream until stiff and spread it evenly on top of the set custard.

6 Decorate the top with a swirling pattern and arrange the glacé cherries and 'leaves' of angelica as decoration. Serve well chilled.

Serves 6-8

Chocolate Orange Trifle

1 chocolate Swiss roll (jelly roll)
30 ml (1 fl oz) (2 tablespoons)
  Grand Marnier
2 oranges
550 ml (1 pint) (2½ cups) chocolate
  custard
150 ml (¼ pint) (⅝ cup) whipping
  cream
6 glacé cherries, halved
50 g (2 oz) grated chocolate

1 Cut the Swiss roll (jelly roll) into slices about 2 cm (¾ in) thick. Arrange them to line a glass dish as evenly as possible. Sprinkle them with Grand Marnier.

2 Grate the rind of one of the oranges and reserve. Peel both oranges and cut them in thin slices across the segments, removing any pips (seeds). Cut the slices in half and arrange them over the slices of cake.

3 Pour the custard over the orange and cake slices and chill to set. Beat the cream until thick, then fold in the grated orange rind. Decorate the top of the trifle with whipped cream, halved

glacé cherries and grated chocolate. Serve cold.

Serves 6

Apple Trifle

1 kg (2 lb) cooking (green) apples
juice and grated rind 1 lemon
100 g (¼ lb) (½ cup) castor (fine
  granulated) sugar
20 trifle sponges
30 ml (1 fl oz) (2 tablespoons)
  sherry (optional)
100 g (¼ lb) (⅜ cup) blackberry jelly
150 ml (¼ pint) (⅝ cup) whipping
  cream
8 glacé cherries
two 10 cm (4 in) stems candied
  angelica

1 Peel and core the apples and cut them in slices. Place them with 15 ml (1 tablespoon) water and the lemon juice and grated rind in a pan, cover and cook gently for 5 minutes until tender. Pass them through a sieve and return the purée to the pan with the sugar. Cook gently, stirring frequently, until the sugar is melted and the mixture thickened. Allow to cool.

2 Place a layer of trifle sponges on the base and sides of a glass dish. Sprinkle with the sherry, if used. Pour the apple purée into the bowl and chill.

3 Melt the blackberry jelly over low heat, stirring. Pour it over the apple. Leave to set.

4 Beat the cream until stiff and place it in a piping (decorator's) bag. Pipe the cream in rosettes around the dish where the trifle sponges meet, and in the middle. Cut the glacé cherries in half and the candied angelica in diamond-shaped 'leaves,' and use them to decorate the cream rosettes. Serve immediately or chill until ready to serve.

Serves 8

Apple Trifle contains a lovely mixture of apple, sponges and blackberry jelly, and it is topped with cream and fruits

Sponge Desserts

The following delicious sponges, filled with flavoured creams, soaked in sweet syrups and often covered with exotic fresh fruits, are rich and luxurious. They make impressive desserts for special occasions and are well worth the small extra effort involved in preparing them.

Peach Chantilly

butter for greasing
2 large eggs
50 g (2 oz) (¼ cup) castor (fine granulated) sugar
50 g (2 oz) (good ½ cup) flour, sieved
4 large ripe peaches
75 g (3 oz) (⅜ cup) sugar
30 ml (2 tablespoons) Cointreau
300 ml (½ pint) (1¼ cups) double (heavy) cream, whipped
225 g (½ lb) (¾ cup) strained apricot jam
5 ml (1 teaspoon) arrowroot
75 g (3 oz) (½ cup) flaked almonds

1 The day before serving, make the sponge. Preheat the oven to 190°C, 375°F, gas 5. Grease an oblong cake tin (pan) with butter and line its base with greaseproof (parchment) paper.

2 Place the eggs and castor (fine granulated) sugar in a bowl over a saucepan of hot water. Whisk until the mixture is pale and thick. Remove the bowl from the heat and continue to whisk until the mixture cools. Fold in the sieved flour and turn the cake mixture into the tin (pan). Bake in the oven for 25 minutes and turn the cake out onto a rack to cool overnight.

3 The following day cut the cake lengthways into 3 layers. Bring a saucepan of water to the boil and

Peach Chantilly is sandwiched together with layers of fresh peaches, orange liqueur, and stiffly whipped cream

scald the peaches in it for 30 seconds. Drain them and peel off their skins. Halve them and remove their stones (pits).

4 Preheat the oven to 190°C, 375°F, gas 5. Place the peach halves in a shallow ovenproof dish with 200 ml (6 fl oz) (¾ cup) water, the sugar and Cointreau. Cover and bake in the oven for 20 minutes. Allow the peaches to cool in their syrup.

5 Place ⅔ of the cream in a bowl and the rest in a piping (decorator's) bag fitted with a star nozzle. Chill the bag of cream in the refrigerator.

6 Drain the peach halves, straining the syrup into a saucepan. Cut 3 peach halves into thin slices.

Blend the slices with the cream in the bowl.

7 Build up the cake in the following way. Spread the bottom and middle layers of the cake with ⅓ of the apricot jam and half the cream and sliced peach mixture. Sandwich them together and finish with the third piece of cake. Arrange the remaining peach halves along the top of the cake.

8 Heat the syrup, stirring in the remaining apricot jam and 30 ml (1 fl oz) (2 tablespoons) water. Blend the arrowroot with 15 ml (1 tablespoon) water and stir it into the syrup. Boil for 3 minutes.

9 Using a spoon, coat the peaches and cake with the syrup. Apply the flaked almonds to the sides of the cake with your hand and pipe the reserved cream along the top rim. Chill the cake for 2 hours and serve.

Serves 6-8

shaped piece 5 cm (2 in) deep. Soak the cake with ⅔ of the wine syrup. Fill the cavity with half the cream and half the raspberries. Replace the cone and baste with the remaining syrup. Decorate with the remaining cream and raspberries.

Serves 6-8

Strawberry Sponge Ring

lard for greasing
175 g (6 oz) (¾ cup) butter
175 g (6 oz) (¾ cup) castor (fine granulated) sugar
3 eggs
175 g (6 oz) (1¾ cups) self-raising flour, sieved
300 ml (½ pint) (1¼ cups) double (heavy) cream, whipped
30 ml (1 fl oz) (2 tablespoons) kirsch
175 g (6 oz) (½ cup) strained apricot jam
70 ml (2½ fl oz) (⅓ cup) water
350 g (¾ lb) (2 cups) fresh strawberries, hulled

1 Preheat the oven to 170°C, 325°F, gas 3. Grease a 1½ litre (3 pint) (7 cup) gugelhopf mould with the lard.

2 Whisk together the butter and sugar until light and fluffy. Beat in the eggs, one at a time, adding 15 ml (1 tablespoon) of the flour with each egg. Gently fold in the rest of the flour. Turn into the mould and bake it in the oven for 1¼ hours. Cool the cake on a rack.

3 In a bowl blend the whipped cream and half the kirsch.

4 Place the apricot jam, remaining kirsch and water in a pan. Stirring continually, slowly bring to the boil. Brush the cooled cake with the hot syrup.

5 Place the cake on a serving dish. Pile the whipped cream into the centre and decorate it with half the strawberries. Arrange the rest around the dish and serve.

Serves 6-8

Tipsy Cake

2 eggs
2 egg yolks
265 g (9½ oz) (1 cup + 3 tablespoons) castor (fine granulated) sugar
2 egg whites
grated rind 1 lemon
75 g (3 oz) (¾ cup) plain flour
25 g (1 oz) (3 tablespoons) arrowroot
pinch salt
225 ml (8 fl oz) (1 cup) sweet white wine
15 ml (1 tablespoon) brandy
300 ml (½ pint) (1¼ cups) double (heavy) cream, whipped
225 g (½ lb) (1¾ cups) raspberries

1 Line the base of a greased 20 cm (8 in) cake tin (pan) with greaseproof (parchment) paper. Preheat the oven to 180°C, 350°F, gas 4.

Strawberry Sponge Ring looks exotic, but is really a simple combination of a sponge cake, cream and juicy strawberries

2 Place the eggs, egg yolks and 225 g (½ lb) (1 cup) of the sugar in a bowl over a pan of hot water. Whisk the mixture until it is thick. Whisk the egg whites until stiff and fold them into the egg mixture with the lemon rind.

3 Sift together the flour, arrowroot and salt and fold into the mixture. Turn it into the tin (pan) and bake in the oven for ¾-1 hour. Turn the cake onto a rack to cool.

4 Boil the remaining sugar with 50 ml (2 fl oz) (¼ cup) of water for 1 minute, stirring constantly. Let the syrup cool and add the wine and brandy.

5 When the cake has cooled, cut around the top, using a serrated edge knife to remove a cone

Look'n Cook Chantilly Cream

1 and **2** Measure 50 ml (2 fl oz) (¼ cup) of the cream and the same quantity of milk into a bowl. Blend well **3** Add the rest of the cream and whisk it gently, using a circular movement from the wrist, until it begins to thicken **4** and **5** Add the sugar all at once and then the vanilla essence **6** Rapidly whisk the cream until it is very firm and forms peaks **7,8** and **9** Decorate the Mirabelle Gâteau (see page

10

1360): spoon half of the cream on to the bottom layer of the cake and spread it evenly with a knife. Arrange the prepared mirabelle plums on the bed of cream and sandwich them with the top cake layer. Fill a piping (decorator's) bag, fitted with a star nozzle, with the remaining cream. Decorate the top of the cake with swirls of cream **10** and **11** Decorate with a glacé cherry and 4 pieces of angelica

Raspberry Torte

175 g (6 oz) (¾ cup) butter
175 g (6 oz) (¾ cup) castor (fine
  granulated) sugar
3 eggs
175 g (6 oz) (good 1½ cups)
  self-raising flour, sieved
finely grated rind 1 orange

For the Filling and Topping:
25 g (1 oz) (3 tablespoons)
  cornflour (cornstarch)
40 g (1½ oz) (3 tablespoons) sugar
300 ml (½ pint) (1¼ cups) milk
300 ml (½ pint) (1¼ cups) double
  (heavy) cream
30 ml (2 tablespoons) Cointreau
450 g (1 lb) (3 cups) raspberries

1 Preheat the oven to 190°C, 375°F, gas 5.

2 Cream the butter and castor (fine granulated) sugar together until light and fluffy, then beat in the eggs, one at a time, adding a spoonful of the flour with each to prevent curdling. Fold in the orange rind and remaining flour.

3 Divide the mixture between two greased and lined 20 cm (8 in) sandwich tins (pans). Bake for 25–30 minutes, until well-risen and firm to the touch. Turn out and cool on a wire rack.

4 Prepare the filling: blend the cornflour (cornstarch) and sugar to a smooth paste with a little of the milk. Heat the remaining milk and pour onto the cornflour (cornstarch), stirring well. Return

Raspberry Torte is a treat for anyone with a sweet tooth. Its layers of soft sponge are interspersed with cream and fruit

to the pan, bring to the boil and simmer for 3 minutes, stirring continuously. Dampen a piece of greaseproof (parchment) paper and place it on the custard. Cool completely.

5 Whip the cream until thick. Remove the paper from the cold custard and fold in 45ml (3 tablespoons) of the cream. Fold half of the Cointreau and half of the raspberries into the custard. Fold the remaining Cointreau into the cream.

6 Split the cold sponge cakes in half and sandwich them together with the custard mixture, so that there are four layers of sponge and three of filling. Transfer to a serving plate.

7 Spread the cream over the top of the cake, making a thick border, 4cm (1½ in) wide, around the edge. Fill the centre with the remaining raspberries.

Serves 8

Fruity Layer Gâteau

ingredients for sponge as in
  Raspberry Torte
300 ml (½ pint) (1¼ cups) double
  (heavy) cream, whipped
icing (confectioners') sugar
15 ml (1 tablespoon) rum
45 ml (3 tablespoons) lemon curd
450 g (1 lb) assorted canned fruit,
  drained

1 Prepare and cook the sponge following the instructions for the Raspberry Torte.

2 Sweeten the cream to taste with icing (confectioners') sugar and add the rum.

3 Split the cold sponge cakes in half and spread 3 with lemon curd. Sandwich and decorate with the cream and fruit.

Serves 8

Fruity Layer Gâteau looks exotic, but is simple and quite economical to prepare, using canned fruit with cream

Coffee Rum Gâteau

175 g (6 oz) (¾ cup) butter
175 g (6 oz) (¾ cup) castor (fine granulated) sugar
3 eggs
175 g (6 oz) (good 1½ cups) self-raising flour
50 g (2 oz) (¼ cup) sugar
300 ml (½ pint) (1¼ cups) hot strong black coffee
30 ml (2 tablespoons) rum
300 ml (½ pint) (1¼ cups) double (heavy) cream
few drops vanilla essence
30 ml (2 tablespoons) toasted flaked almonds

1 Preheat the oven to 190°C, 375°F, gas 5.

2 Cream the butter and castor (fine granulated) sugar together until light and fluffy. Beat in the eggs, one at a time, adding a spoonful of the flour with each to prevent curdling. Sieve the remaining flour and fold it into the mixture with a metal spoon.

3 Turn the mixture into a 20 cm (8 in) plain ring mould (tube pan). Bake for 25-30 minutes, until well risen and firm to the touch. Turn out and cool on a wire rack.

4 Dissolve the sugar in the hot coffee, add the rum and leave to cool.

5 When the cake is cold, return it to the clean mould and pour over the coffee. Leave to stand until all the liquid is absorbed, then turn onto a serving plate.

6 Whip the cream with the vanilla essence until it is just thick. Mask the cake completely with the cream and sprinkle with the toasted almonds to decorate. Serve chilled.

Serves 6-8

Apricot-Almond Gâteau is not difficult to make. It is decorated with ratafia biscuits and then topped with canned apricots

Pear and Chocolate Sponge

175 g (6 oz) (¾ cup) butter or margarine
175 g (6 oz) (¾ cup) castor (fine granulated) sugar
3 eggs
175 g (6 oz) (good 1½ cups) self-raising flour
60 ml (4 tablespoons) chopped walnuts
6 canned pear halves, drained
7 walnut halves
For the Chocolate Buttercream:
225 g (½ lb) (1⅔ cups) icing (confectioners') sugar
225 g (½ lb) (1 cup) butter
20 ml (4 teaspoons) cocoa powder
few drops vanilla essence

1 Preheat the oven to 190°C, 375°F, gas 5.

2 Cream the fat and castor (fine granulated) sugar until light and

fluffy, then beat in the eggs, one at a time, adding a spoonful of the flour with each. Sieve the remaining flour and fold in with a metal spoon.

3 Divide the mixture between two greased and lined 20 cm (8 in) sandwich tins (pans). Bake for 25-30 minutes. Turn out and cool on a wire rack.

4 Make the chocolate buttercream: sieve the icing (confectioners') sugar and cream it with the butter until light and fluffy. Blend the cocoa powder with a little boiling water, and stir into the butter and sugar with a few drops of vanilla essence.

5 Split each sponge in half. Spread 3 of them with $\frac{1}{2}$ of the buttercream. Sandwich together, with the plain sponge on top.

6 Spread the top and sides of the cake with buttercream. Press the chopped nuts on to the sides. Arrange the pears over the top and decorate with swirls of buttercream and the walnut halves.

Serves 8

Pear and Chocolate Sponge is a delicious gâteau which you could serve either as a dessert or for a special afternoon tea

Apricot-Almond Gâteau

175 g (6 oz) ($\frac{3}{4}$ cup) butter or margarine
175 g (6 oz) ($\frac{3}{4}$ cup) castor (fine granulated) sugar
3 eggs
175 g (6 oz) (good 1$\frac{1}{2}$ cups) self-raising flour
50 g (2 oz) ($\frac{1}{2}$ cup) ground almonds
75 g (3 oz) ratafias
450 g (1 lb) canned apricot halves, drained
30 ml (2 tablespoons) apricot jam

For the Almond Filling:
350 g ($\frac{3}{4}$ lb) (2$\frac{1}{2}$ cups) icing (confectioners') sugar
175 g (6 oz) ($\frac{3}{4}$ cup) butter or margarine
30 ml (2 tablespoons) milk
few drops almond essence

1 Preheat the oven to 190°C, 375°F, gas 5. Cream the fat and

sugar until light, then beat in the eggs, one at a time, adding a spoonful of the flour with each. Add the almonds, then sieve the remaining flour and fold in with a metal spoon.

2 Divide the mixture between two greased and lined 20 cm (8 in) sandwich tins (pans). Bake for 25-30 minutes. Turn out and cool.

3 Make the almond filling: cream the icing (confectioners') sugar with the fat until light and fluffy. Beat in the milk and almond essence.

4 Sandwich the cold sponge cakes with half the almond filling, and spread the rest over the top and sides.

5 Press the ratafias on to the sides of the cake. Drain the apricot halves, reserving 30 ml (2 tablespoons) of the syrup and arrange the apricot halves, cut side down, over the top of the cake. Melt the jam with the reserved apricot syrup and use to brush over the apricots.

Serves 8

Apple and Hazelnut Gâteau

100 g (¼ lb) (½ cup) butter
100 g (¼ lb) (½ cup) castor (fine granulated) sugar
2 eggs, separated
50 g (2 oz) (½ cup) ground hazelnuts, toasted
100 g (¼ lb) (1 cup + 2 tablespoons) self-raising flour
pinch salt
15 ml (1 tablespoon) milk

For the Filling:
450 g (1 lb) sharp dessert apples
30 ml (2 tablespoons) apricot jam
juice and grated rind 1 lemon
45 ml (3 tablespoons) sugar
45 ml (3 tablespoons) brandy
300 ml (½ pint) (1¼ cups) double (heavy) cream

1 Preheat the oven to 190°C, 375°F, gas 5. Cream the butter and sugar until light and beat in the egg yolks. Stir in ¾ of the hazelnuts. Fold in the flour and salt with the milk. Stiffly whisk the egg whites and fold in with a metal spoon.

2 Turn the mixture into a greased and floured 20 cm (8 in) cake tin (pan), and bake for 25 minutes, until the cake has shrunk slightly from the sides of the tin (pan) and is firm. Cool on a wire rack.

3 Peel, core and slice the apples, and place in a small pan with the jam, lemon rind and juice. Cover and cook gently until the apples are soft. Cool.

4 Dissolve the sugar in a small pan with 45 ml (3 tablespoons) water, bring to the boil and boil until syrupy. Stir in 30 ml (2 tablespoons) of the brandy and cool.

5 Whip the cream until thick and fold in the remaining brandy.

6 Split the cold cake and sprinkle each half with some of the syrup. Sandwich the sponges with some of the cream and the apples. Moisten the cake with the remaining syrup.

7 Decorate with the remaining cream and reserved hazelnuts.

Serves 6-8

Strawberry Cream Gâteau

75 g (3 oz) (good ¾ cup) flour
2.5 ml (½ teaspoon) powdered cinnamon
pinch salt
3 eggs
100 g (¼ lb) (½ cup) castor (fine granulated) sugar
finely grated rind ½ lemon
300 ml (½ pint) (1¼ cups) double (heavy) cream
few drops vanilla essence
350 g (¾ lb) strawberries, hulled
6 macaroons, crushed
175 g (6 oz) (½ cup) redcurrant jelly
15 ml (1 tablespoon) orange juice

1 Preheat the oven to 180°C, 350°F, gas 4. Sieve the flour with the cinnamon and salt.

2 Break the eggs into a bowl and gradually whisk in the sugar. Stand the bowl over a pan of hot water and whisk until thick and pale in colour. Remove from the heat and continue to whisk until cool.

3 Fold in the sieved flour and the grated lemon rind. Pour the mixture into a greased and lined 20 cm (8 in) cake tin (pan). Bake in the preheated oven for 15-20 minutes. Turn out and cool on a wire rack.

4 Whip the cream with a few drops of vanilla essence and divide between two bowls. Slice one-quarter of the strawberries and mix with one bowl of the cream. Use to sandwich the sponge cakes together.

5 Use the remaining cream to pipe a decorative border around the top of the cake and to spread around the sides. Press the crushed macaroons on to the sides.

6 Heat the redcurrant jelly with the orange juice until completely dissolved. Allow to cool, without setting. Arrange the remaining strawberries over the top of the cake inside the cream border, and brush with the redcurrant glaze.

Serves 8

Chocolate Rum Gâteau

150 g (5 oz) (1¼ cups) flour
25 g (1 oz) (4 tablespoons) cocoa powder
2.5 ml (½ teaspoon) salt
10 ml (2 teaspoons) baking powder
150 g (5 oz) (⅝ cup, firmly packed) soft brown sugar
2 eggs, separated
85 ml (3 fl oz) (⅜ cup) oil
85 ml (3 fl oz) (⅜ cup) milk
2.5 ml (½ teaspoon) vanilla essence
50 ml (2 fl oz) (¼ cup) rum
150 ml (¼ pint) (⅝ cup) single (light) cream
150 ml (¼ pint) (⅝ cup) double (heavy) cream
75-100 g (3-4 oz) grated chocolate

1 Preheat the oven to 180°C, 350°F, gas 4.

2 Sieve together the flour, cocoa powder, salt and baking powder and stir in the sugar.

3 Mix together the egg yolks, oil, milk and vanilla essence and beat with the flour mixture to a smooth batter.

4 Whisk the egg whites until stiff and peaking and fold in to the batter with a metal spoon.

5 Divide the mixture between two 20 cm (8 in) greased and lined sandwich tins (pans) and bake for about 30 minutes until well risen and firm to the touch. Turn out and cool on a wire rack.

6 Return the cold cakes to the clean tins (pans) and sprinkle with the rum. Leave to stand until all the rum has been absorbed.

7 Whip the creams together until thick. Use a little less than half to sandwich the sponges together, then transfer the cake to a serving plate. Spread the remaining cream over the top and sides. Press the chocolate on to the sides and sprinkle over the top.

Serves 8

Strawberry Cream Gâteau and Chocolate Rum Gâteau are two quite different treats which just cannot fail to impress

Meringue Desserts

Meringue desserts are always popular and although they look impressive, they are really very easy to make. There are three different types of meringue:

Swiss Meringue is the one that most people know about and is used for meringue shells and the topping on most hot meringue puddings.

American Meringue is another topping for meringue pies, but cream of tartar and vinegar are added to the meringue mixture.

Cooked Meringue is made with icing (confectioners') sugar and is hard and powdery. It is suitable for gâteaux or as a topping for desserts.

Most of our recipes are made with the Swiss meringue mixture. A balloon whisk is best if you are to obtain a stiff, shiny meringue – electric and rotary whisks can be used with some success but the results will not be as good. However, they do save you time and arm-ache!

Strawberry Meringue Flan

3 egg whites
175 g (6 oz) (¾ cup) castor (fine granulated) sugar
225 g (½ lb) (1⅓ cups) strawberries
300 ml (½ pint) (1¼ cups) double (heavy) cream
30 ml (1 fl oz) (2 tablespoons) Cointreau

1 Preheat the oven to 130°C, 250°F, gas ½, or even lower, if possible.

2 Cover a baking (cookie) sheet with some silicone (non-stick) paper. Draw a circle of 20 cm (8 in) diameter on the paper.

3 Whisk the egg whites until stiff, then whisk in half of the sugar. When stiff, fold in the remaining sugar with a metal spoon.

4 Spread some of the meringue over the circle to make the base of the flan. Fill a piping (decorator's) bag, fitted with a large star nozzle, with the rest of the meringue and pipe large, attractive rosettes around the base to form the sides of the flan. Bake in the oven until dry and white (about 1½-2 hours). Do not allow the meringue to brown. Cool the meringue case on a rack.

5 Hull and wash the strawberries. Whip the cream until stiff and stir in the Cointreau.

6 Place a layer of cream inside the base of the meringue and pile the strawberries on top. Place the rest of the cream in a jug and serve separately.

Serves 4-6

Tips: You can fill this meringue case with any fresh fruit. Peaches, raspberries, bananas and papaws are all suitable. To make it more attractive, you can pipe rosettes of cream across the top and around the sides of the meringue case. Another idea is to soak the fruit in brandy or a liqueur before filling the case. Be careful to drain them thoroughly, though, as the liqueur will make the meringue soggy.

If you prefer, you can make individual meringue cases so that your guests can have one each. This is a good idea for parties and buffets. Just draw smaller circles on the non-stick paper and pipe the meringue as before.

Flamed Pineapple Meringue

2 whole eggs
6 egg yolks
100 g (¼ lb) (¾ cup) icing (confectioners') sugar
100 g (¼ lb) (1 cup + 2 tablespoons) flour, sieved
225 ml (8 fl oz) (1 cup) pineapple juice
750 ml (1¼ pints) (3 cups) milk
5 ml (1 teaspoon) vanilla essence
10 slices pineapple
50 g (2 oz) (¼ cup) butter, softened
150 ml (¼ pint) (⅝ cup) white rum

For the Meringue:
4 egg whites
100 g (¼ lb) (¾ cup) icing (confectioners') sugar

1 In a mixing bowl, blend together the whole eggs, egg yolks and icing (confectioners') sugar. Whisk well, then mix in the flour. Stir in the pineapple juice.

2 Heat the milk in a heavy saucepan and, when boiling, pour it over the egg and pineapple mixture, stirring all the time. Add the vanilla essence and pour back into the saucepan.

3 Return the pan to the heat and boil for several minutes, stirring continuously, until it thickens. Then remove from the heat.

4 Cut 2 of the pineapple slices into cubes and mix into the crème pâtissière. Then stir in the butter and 50 ml (2 fl oz) (¼ cup) of the rum.

5 Preheat the oven to 200°C, 400°F, gas 6.

6 Beat the egg whites until stiff. Gradually add the sugar, beating all the time until stiff and shiny.

7 Spread the crème pâtissière over the base of an ovenproof dish. Arrange the remaining pineapple slices on top and then cover with the meringue. Place in the oven and bake until the meringue is cooked and golden.

8 Just before serving, heat the rest of the rum in a small saucepan. Pour it over the meringue, set it alight, and serve the flaming dish to your guests.

Serves 8

Tip: There are a number of variations on this dish which you can try. You can substitute brandy or another spirit for rum and can even use alternative fruits for the filling.

Strawberry Meringue is filled with delicious orange liqueur flavoured cream and then topped with juicy strawberries

Quick Vacherin

150 ml (¼ pint) (⅝ cup) double
  (heavy) cream
few drops vanilla essence
1 meringue base
12-16 scoops ice-cream
  (raspberry ripple or
  strawberry)
450 (1 lb) (2⅔ cups) strawberries,
  hulled
8 pink oval-shaped meringues
8 brown oval-shaped meringues

1 Whip the cream until thick and
fold in the vanilla essence. Transfer to a piping (decorator's) bag
fitted with a large star nozzle.

2 Place the meringue base on a
serving plate and cover with the
ice-cream. Pile the strawberries
on top, reserving a few for decoration.

3 Stand the pink and brown
meringues alternately around
the sides, pressing on to the ice-
cream to secure.

4 Pipe the cream in swirls
around the meringues and over
the strawberries, and decorate
with the reserved strawberries.
Serve immediately.

Serves 6-8

Coconut Pyramids

lard for greasing
2 egg whites
150 g (5 oz) (⅝ cup) castor (fine
  granulated) sugar
150 g (5 oz) (1½ cups) desiccated
  coconut

1 Preheat the oven to 140°C,
275°F, gas 1. Grease a baking
(cookie) sheet and cover with rice
paper.

2 Whisk the egg whites until
they are stiff and peaking, and
fold in the sugar and coconut with
a metal spoon.

3 Pile the mixture onto the prepared baking (cookie) sheet in 12
small pyramids and press into a

neat shape. Bake in the oven for
¾-1 hour until the pyramids are
pale fawn. Cool on a wire rack.

Makes 12

Cherry Alaska Tarts

175 g (6 oz) sweetmeal biscuits
  (cookies)
40 g (1½ oz) (3 tablespoons) castor
  (fine granulated) sugar
5 ml (1 teaspoon) powdered
  ginger
75 g (3 oz) (⅜ cup) margarine

For the Filling:
2 egg whites
75 g (3 oz) (⅜ cup) castor (fine
  granulated) sugar
350 g (¾ lb) canned cherries,
  drained
2 pieces bottled stem ginger,
  finely chopped
15 ml (1 tablespoon) stem ginger
  syrup
6 scoops vanilla ice-cream

1 Preheat the oven to 180°C,
350°F, gas 4.

2 Crush the biscuits (cookies)
finely and stir in the sugar and
powdered ginger. Melt the margarine and mix well with the
crumbs. Divide the mixture between six 10cm (4in) fluted flan
cases, and, using the back of a
teaspoon, press the mixture
firmly and evenly over the base
and sides.

3 Bake in the preheated oven for
10 minutes. Allow to cool in the
flan cases.

4 Increase the oven temperature
to 230°C, 450°F, gas 8. Remove the
cold biscuit (cookie) bases from
the flan cases and place on an
upturned baking (cookie) sheet.

5 Make the filling: whisk the egg
whites until they are softly peaking, add half the sugar and continue to whisk until glossy and
firm. Gently fold in the remaining
sugar with a metal spoon.

6 Divide the cherries between
the biscuit (cookie) bases and
sprinkle with the finely chopped

stem ginger and the syrup. Put a
scoop of ice-cream on top and
cover the ice-cream and fruit
completely with the meringue.
Put into the oven for 2-3 minutes
until the outside of the meringue
just begins to brown.

7 Slide each Alaska Tart on to an
individual serving plate and
serve immediately.

Serves 6

Cream Meringues

2 egg whites
100 g (¼ lb) (½ cup) castor (fine
  granulated) sugar
150 ml (¼ pint) (⅝ cup) double
  (heavy) cream

1 Preheat the oven to 110°C,
225°F, mark ¼. Line a baking
(cookie) sheet with aluminium
foil or non-stick paper.

2 Whisk the egg whites until
they are softly peaking, add half
the sugar and continue to whisk
until the mixture is glossy and
firm. Fold in the remaining sugar
with a metal spoon.

3 Transfer the mixture to a piping (decorator's) bag fitted with a
large star nozzle, and pipe 10-12
swirls on to the prepared baking
(cookie) sheet. Alternatively,
spoon the mixture in neat
mounds.

4 Dry the meringues in the cool-
est part of the oven for 2-3 hours,
until the meringues are firm and
crisp, but still white. If the meringues begin to brown, prop open
the oven door a little.

5 Remove the meringues from
the paper and cool on a wire rack.

6 Whip the cream until it is just
thick and use to sandwich the
meringue shells in pairs.

Makes 5 or 6

Blackcurrant Meringue Pie

100 g ($\frac{1}{4}$ lb) (1 cup + 2 tablespoons)
  flour
pinch salt
5 ml (1 teaspoon) powdered
  cinnamon
50 g (2 oz) ($\frac{1}{4}$ cup) softened butter
50 g (2 oz) ($\frac{1}{4}$ cup) castor (fine
  granulated) sugar
2 eggs, separated
2 drops vanilla essence
350 g ($\frac{3}{4}$ lb) canned blackcurrants
5 ml (1 teaspoon) arrowroot
40 g ($1\frac{1}{2}$ oz) (3 tablespoons) sugar

For the Topping:
100 g ($\frac{1}{4}$ lb) ($\frac{1}{2}$ cup) castor
  (fine granulated) sugar
2.5 ml ($\frac{1}{2}$ teaspoon) powdered
  cinnamon

1 Sieve the flour, salt and cinnamon on to the table. Make a well in the centre and in this, place the butter, castor (fine granulated) sugar, egg yolks and vanilla.

2 With the finger-tips of one hand, blend together the butter, sugar and egg yolks until well mixed, then work in the flour. Knead lightly until smooth, then wrap and chill for about 1 hour.

3 Meanwhile, make the filling. Pour off half the juice from the blackcurrants, using a little to blend with the arrowroot. Place the remaining blackcurrants and juice in a pan with the sugar and bring to the boil. Add the blended arrowroot and simmer for 3 minutes, stirring continuously. Cool.

4 Preheat the oven to 190°C, 375°F, gas 5. Roll out the pastry and use to line an 18 cm (7 in) flan ring, set on a baking (cookie) sheet. Line with greaseproof (parchment) paper, fill with baking beans and bake in the preheated oven for 15 minutes. Remove the paper and beans and bake for a further 5 minutes, or until a pale biscuity colour. Leave to cool in the flan ring.

5 Reduce the oven temperature to 150°C, 300°F, gas 2. Pour the blackcurrant mixture into the pie shell.

6 Make the topping: whisk the egg whites until stiff and peaking. Add 10 ml (2 teaspoons) of the sugar and whisk until firm, then fold in the remaining sugar and the cinnamon with a metal spoon. Pile the meringue on top of the pie to completely cover the filling and bake in the oven for 30 minutes.

7 Serve warm or cold.

Serves 5 or 6

Tip: If blackcurrants are not available, you can replace them by the same weight of stoned (pitted) black cherries, blackberries or damsons.

Swiss Peach Meringue, topped with meringue pyramids, has a Swiss (jelly) roll base with peaches, custard and macaroons

Swiss Peach Meringue

1 swiss roll (jelly roll)
4 almond macaroons, crushed
30 ml (2 tablespoons) brandy
2 peaches, stoned (pitted),
  skinned and sliced
45 ml (3 tablespoons) custard
  powder
40 ml ($2\frac{1}{2}$ tablespoons) sugar
450 ml ($\frac{3}{4}$ pint) (2 cups) milk

For the Topping:
2 egg whites
100 g ($\frac{1}{4}$ lb) ($\frac{1}{2}$ cup) castor
  (fine granulated) sugar
15 ml (1 tablespoon) flaked
  almonds

1 Slice the swiss roll (jelly roll) and arrange the slices around the

100 g (¼ lb) (½ cup) glacé or
  maraschino cherries
100 ml (4 fl oz) (½ cup) maraschino
  liqueur
50 ml (2 fl oz) (¼ cup) rum
For the Meringue Topping:
2 egg whites
pinch salt
30 ml (2 tablespoons) icing
  (confectioners') sugar

1 Preheat the oven 180°C, 350°F,
gas 4.

2 Add half of the sugar to the egg
yolks and beat together until
light and fluffy. Sieve the flours
together and fold into the egg
yolk mixture with a metal spoon.

3 Whisk the egg whites and salt
in a separate bowl until they are
stiff and peaking. Add the remaining sugar, a little at a time, beating
well after each addition.

4 Carefully fold the egg whites
into the yolk mixture and pour
into a 20 cm (8 in) greased and
floured cake tin (pan). Bake in the
preheated oven for 20 minutes.
Increase the oven temperature to
190°C, 375°F, gas 5, and bake for a
further 10 minutes. Do not turn off
the oven as it will be needed at a
later stage. Turn out the cooked
cake on to a cooling rack and
leave to cool completely.

5 Cut the cherries into small
pieces and place them in a bowl
with the maraschino and rum for
15 minutes. When the cake is cold,
slice it in half through the middle
and sandwich together again
with the cherries and their liquid.
Place on a flat ovenproof serving
dish.

6 Prepare the meringue topping: whisk the egg whites with
the salt and sugar until thick and
firm. Spread the mixture evenly
over the top and sides of the cake,
and bake in the hot oven for 8-10
minutes until golden-brown.

7 Cool the cake completely
before serving.

Serves 6

Tip: For a crisper, crunchier topping, sprinkle some crushed
toasted peanuts over the meringue before baking. The filling can
also be altered – try using cubed
pineapple or papaw instead of the
cherries.

sides and base of a heatproof serving bowl. Sprinkle over the
macaroons, then moisten with
the brandy. Arrange the sliced
peaches over the top.

2 Make the custard: blend the
custard powder and sugar with a
little of the milk. Bring the rest of
the milk to the boil and pour on
to the custard mixture, stirring.
Return to the pan and simmer for
3 minutes, stirring. Cool slightly,
then pour gently over the peaches
and sponge.

3 Whisk the egg whites until
they are stiff and peaking. Add
10 ml (2 teaspoons) of the sugar
and whisk until firm. Carefully
fold in the remaining sugar with a
metal spoon. Transfer the mixture to a piping (decorator's) bag
fitted with a star-shaped nozzle
and cover the custard with peaks
of meringue.

4 Stud some of the peaks

*Créole Meringue Cake has all the
colour and exciting flavours
of South America and the French
Caribbean where it originated*

with the flaked almonds and
place under a hot grill (broiler)
until golden-brown. Serve
immediately.

Serves 4 or 5

Créole Meringue Cake

200 g (7 oz) (1 cup) castor
  (fine granulated) sugar
4 eggs, separated
25 g (1 oz) (4 tablespoons) flour
60 g (2½ oz) (7½ tablespoons)
  cornflour (cornstarch)
pinch salt

All about Tarts, Flans and Pies

Apple Bakewell Tart

Tarts and Flans

Tarts and flans are tremendously versatile; whether rich in protein or light and fruity, from practical weekday puds to sophisticated party desserts, there's something suitable for every occasion. Try some of our more unusual combinations – curd cheese filling in an almond flavoured crust, rich egg nog in a chocolate flavoured case, or even a shell of ice-cream filled with creamy coffee and honey.

Wholemeal Yogurt Flan

wholemeal shortcrust (pie crust)
  made with 175 g (6 oz) (1⅝ cups)
  wholemeal flour
3 fresh peaches
300 ml (½ pint) (1¼ cups) natural
  yogurt
225 g (½ lb) (1⅓ cups) cottage
  cheese
45 ml (3 tablespoons) clear honey
2.5 ml (½ teaspoon) vanilla
  essence

1 Preheat the oven to 200°C, 400°F, gas 6.

2 Roll out the wholemeal dough and use it to line a 20 cm (8 in) flan ring. Set on a baking (cookie) sheet. Bake blind for 20 minutes. Allow to cool.

3 Peel and halve the peaches, remove the stones (seeds) and slice the fruit neatly.

4 Mix together the yogurt and cottage cheese and pass through a sieve. Stir in the honey and vanilla essence.

5 Arrange two-thirds of the sliced peaches in the cold flan shell and spoon the yogurt mixture over. Top with the remaining sliced peaches and chill in the refrigerator for several hours.

Serves 6

Crunchy Peanut Tart

shortcrust (pie crust) made with
  175 g (6 oz) (1⅝ cups) flour
3 eggs
60 ml (4 tablespoons) golden
  syrup
50 g (2 oz) (¼ cup) butter
2.5 ml (½ teaspoon) vanilla
  essence
100 g (¼ lb) unsalted peanuts,
  chopped

1 Preheat the oven to 200°C, 400°F, gas 6.

2 Roll out the dough and use it to line a 20 cm (8 in) flan ring set on a baking (cookie) sheet. Line with paper and fill with baking beans and bake blind for 15 minutes. Remove the paper and beans and bake for a further 5 minutes. Remove from the oven and reduce the oven temperature to 170°C, 325°F, gas 3.

3 Beat the eggs and syrup together. Melt the butter and add it with the vanilla essence and peanuts to the egg mixture. Pour into the flan shell.

4 Bake for 30 minutes, cool slightly then remove the flan ring. Serve warm or cold.

Serves 6

Strawberry Cream Flan

shortcrust (pie crust) made with
  175 g (6 oz) (1⅝ cups) flour
350 g (¾ lb) (2 cups) strawberries
150 ml (¼ pint) (⅝ cup) double
  (heavy) cream
150 ml (¼ pint) (⅝ cup) single (light)
  cream
25 g (1 oz) (2 tablespoons) castor
  (fine granulated) sugar
30 ml (2 tablespoons) strawberry
  jam
10 ml (2 teaspoons) water

1 Preheat the oven to 200°C, 400°F, gas 6.

2 Roll out the dough and use it to line a 20 cm (8 in) flan ring, set on a baking (cookie) sheet. Line with paper, fill with baking beans and bake blind for 15 minutes. Remove the paper and beans and bake for a further 5 minutes. Cool, then remove the flan ring.

3 Hull the strawberries and slice them. Whip the creams together and fold in the sugar and half of the strawberries. Spoon into the flan shell and decorate with the remaining sliced strawberries.

4 Melt the jam with the water, sieve and brush over the strawberries to glaze. Serve chilled.

Serves 6

Tarte Tatin

sweet shortcrust (pie crust)
  made with 175 g (6 oz) (1⅝ cups)
  flour
1 kg (2 lb) sweet dessert apples
75 g (3 oz) (⅜ cup) butter
150 g (5 oz) (⅝ cup) castor (fine
  granulated) sugar

1 Preheat the oven to 200°C, 400°F, gas 6.

2 Make the filling: peel, quarter and core the apples, then cut them into slices.

3 Grease a 20 cm (8 in) flan tin (pan) with half of the butter and sprinkle with half of the sugar. Arrange the apple slices over, then sprinkle with the remaining sugar and dot with the remaining butter.

4 Roll out the dough thinly, and cut a neat circle a little larger than the flan tin (pan). Place the circle over the apples, tucking the edge inside the flan tin (pan), and bake in the preheated oven for 25-30 minutes until the dough is cooked and the apples have caramelized.

5 Invert the tart on to a serving plate and serve warm.

Serves 6

Tarte Tatin is baked upside down and then inverted on to the plate to reveal its sticky, golden caramelized filling

Russian Apricot Tart

sweet shortcrust (pie crust)
  made with 225 g (½ lb) (2¼ cups)
  flour
450 g (1 lb) fresh apricots
100 g (¼ lb) (½ cup) brown sugar
5 ml (1 teaspoon) mixed spice
beaten egg to glaze

1 Preheat the oven to 200°C,
400°F, gas 6.

2 Roll out two-thirds of the
dough and use it to line a 23 cm
(9 in) flan tin (pan). Prick the base
with a fork.

3 Halve the apricots and remove
the stones (pits). Arrange them,
cut-side down, in the case, and
sprinkle with the sugar and spice.

4 Roll out the remaining dough
and cut into strips 1 cm (½ in) wide,
using a ravioli cutter. Lay the
strips, lattice-fashion, across the
tart, sealing the ends of the strips
to the tart edge with a little water.

5 Brush the strips with beaten
egg to glaze, place the flan tin

*Russian Apricot Tart is
a very attractive dessert with
its lattice pattern of
crinkle-cut strips of crisp pastry*

(pan) on a baking (cookie) sheet
and bake in the preheated oven
for 25-30 minutes.

Serves 6

Chocolate Egg Nog Flan

150 g (5 oz) (good 1¼ cups) flour
45 ml (3 tablespoons) drinking
  chocolate powder
50 g (2 oz) (4 tablespoons)
  margarine
40 g (1½ oz) (3 tablespoons) lard
30 ml (1 fl oz) (2 tablespoons) cold
  water

For the Filling:
75 g (3 oz) (6 tablespoons) castor
  (fine granulated) sugar
2 eggs
25 g (1 oz) (4 tablespoons) flour

300 ml (½ pint) (1¼ cups) milk
5 ml (1 teaspoon) vanilla essence
150 ml (¼ pint) (⅝ cup) single
  (light) cream
15 ml (1 tablespoon) rum
grated nutmeg

1 Preheat the oven to 200°C,
400°F, gas 6. Sieve the flour and
drinking chocolate and add the
fats, cut into pieces. Rub in until
the mixture resembles fine
breadcrumbs. Mix to a firm
dough with the water.

2 Knead the dough lightly and
roll out to fit a 20 cm (8 in) flan ring.
Bake blind for 20 minutes.

3 Make the filling: place 50 g
(2 oz) (¼ cup) of the sugar in a bowl
with 1 egg and 1 egg yolk. Beat
well and mix in the flour. Warm
the milk with the vanilla essence
and pour on to the egg mixture,
stirring. Return to the pan and
stir over gentle heat until thickened. Pour into the case, cool,
then chill.

4 Whisk the remaining egg white
until stiff and peaking, then
whisk in the rest of the sugar.
Whip the cream with the rum and

fold gently into the egg whites. Spread the mixture over the filling and sprinkle with nutmeg.

Serves 6

Lemon Breeze Tart

75 g (3 oz) (⅜ cup) margarine
175 g (6 oz) sweetmeal biscuits (cookies), crushed
40 g (1½ oz) (3 tablespoons) castor (fine granulated) sugar
300 ml (½ pint) (1¼ cups) canned sweetened condensed milk
finely grated rind and juice 2 large lemons
150 ml (¼ pint) (⅝ cup) single (light) cream

1 Preheat the oven to 180°C, 350°F, gas 4.

2 Melt the margarine and stir in the crushed biscuits (cookies) and sugar. Using the back of a metal spoon, press the mixture into the base and up the sides of a 20 cm (8 in) flan ring set on a baking (cookie) sheet. Bake for 10 minutes, then cool in the ring.

3 Combine the condensed milk and lemon rind and juice and stir until the mixture thickens. Add the cream, pour into the cooled flan case and chill for 2 hours.

Serves 6

Blackcurrant Surprise Tart

sweet shortcrust (pie crust) made with 225 g (½ lb) (2¼ cups) flour

Blackcurrant Surprise Tart has a hidden layer of lemon curd which makes a sweet contrast to the sharper fruit

60 ml (4 tablespoons) lemon curd
450 g (1 lb) (4 cups) blackcurrants or blueberries, topped and tailed
100 g (¼ lb) (½ cup) sugar
45 ml (3 tablespoons) cornflour (cornstarch)
beaten egg to glaze

1 Preheat the oven to 190°C, 375°F, gas 5.

2 Roll out two-thirds of the dough and use to line a 23 cm (9 in) flan tin (pan). Prick the base and spread with the lemon curd.

3 Fill the tart with the blackcurrants, sprinkling with the sugar and cornflour (cornstarch).

4 Roll out the remaining dough and cut into strips 1 cm (½ in) wide. Lay the strips, lattice-fashion, across the tart, sealing the ends to the tart edge with water.

5 Brush the strips with beaten egg to glaze, place the flan tin (pan) on a baking sheet and bake in the oven for 30-40 minutes.

Serves 6

Mint Chocolate Flan

75 g (3 oz) bitter chocolate
15 ml (1 tablespoon) butter
175 g (6 oz) (1⅓ cups) crushed ginger biscuits (cookies)
3 egg yolks
100 g (¼ lb) (½ cup) castor (fine granulated) sugar
30 ml (2 tablespoons) crème de menthe
10 ml (2 teaspoons) powdered gelatine
30 ml (1 fl oz) (2 tablespoons) water
few drops green food colouring
150 ml (¼ pint) (⅝ cup) double (heavy) cream, whipped

1 Melt the chocolate and butter in a pan and blend in the biscuit (cookie) crumbs. Grease a 20 cm (8 in) flan case and spread the crumb mixture evenly over the base and sides, pressing it firmly down. Chill in the refrigerator.

2 In a bowl, beat together the egg yolks, sugar and crème de menthe until smooth and thick.

3 Sprinkle the gelatine over the water in a small bowl and stand it in a pan of hot water. Stir until the gelatine has dissolved. Allow it to cool slightly and gradually beat it into the egg mixture. Fold in the food colouring and the whipped cream. When the mixture is about to set, pour it into the flan crust. Chill until set, and serve.

Serves 6

Apricot Marshmallow Tart

450 g (1 lb) fresh apricots, stoned (pitted)
175 g (6 oz) (¾ cup) sugar
30 ml (2 tablespoons) cornflour (cornstarch)
5 ml (1 teaspoon) each ground cinnamon and nutmeg
shortcrust (pie crust) made with 175 g (6 oz) (1¾ cups) flour
100 g (¼ lb) bought marshmallows

1 Place the apricots in a pan with a little water and ⅔ of the sugar. Cook gently over low heat until the fruit is soft.

2 Blend the rest of the sugar, the cornflour (cornstarch) and the spices with a little water. Add this to the fruit and cook until the mixture thickens.

3 Roll out the dough and line a greased 20 cm (8 in) flan case. Preheat the oven to 220°C, 425°F, gas 7.

4 Pour the fruit mixture into the uncooked flan. Roll out the left-over trimmings of dough and cut into ½ cm (¼ in) strips. Arrange these in a lattice pattern over the top of the fruit mixture.

5 Bake the tart in the middle of the oven for 25-30 minutes. Remove it from the oven and place a marshmallow in each square of the lattice pattern. Return to the oven for 5 minutes until the marshmallow is lightly browned. Serve with cream or custard.

Serves 6

Tip: This tart can be made with a variety of other seasonal fruits. Try gooseberries, cherries, greengages or plums, adapting the spices to taste.

Egg Custard Tart

shortcrust (pie crust) made with 175 g (6 oz) (1⅝ cups) flour
2 eggs
25 g (1 oz) (2 tablespoons) sugar
300 ml (½ pint) (1¼ cups) milk
5 ml (1 teaspoon) ground nutmeg

1 Roll out the dough on a floured board and line an 18 cm (7 in) flan case. Preheat the oven to 220°C, 425°F, gas 7.

2 In a bowl, beat the eggs with the sugar. Warm the milk in a pan and pour it on to the egg mixture, stirring. Strain the custard into the uncooked flan shell and sprinkle the nutmeg evenly over the top.

3 Bake in the middle of the oven for 10 minutes. Reduce the oven temperature to 180°C, 350°F, gas 4 and cook for 20 minutes more, or until the custard is set. Cool and serve.

Serves 4-6

Tutti Frutti Tart

225 g (½ lb) flaky pastry, fresh or frozen and thawed
7 large strawberries
1 banana
1 sweet orange
1 peach, or 6 canned peach slices
50 g (2 oz) canned cherries
1 lemon
100 g (¼ lb) (⅜ cup) apricot jam
15 ml (1 tablespoon) water

1 Preheat the oven to 220°C, 425°F, gas 7. Roll out the pastry to 3 mm (⅛ in) thick. Grease a 20 cm (8 in) fluted flan case and line it with the pastry. Bake blind for 20 minutes until the flan shell is crisp and golden-brown. Allow to cool.

2 Prepare the fruit: wash and hull the strawberries, peel and slice the banana. Cut the orange into thin slices and remove any pips (seeds); cut the slices in quarters. Peel and slice the peach, if using a fresh one. Drain the canned cherries. Thinly slice the lemon and quarter the slices.

3 In a pan melt the apricot jam with the water. Pass through a sieve.

4 Arrange the fruit in the flan shell as illustrated, filling ⅙ of the flan with each fruit and finishing with a strawberry in the middle. Pour the apricot glaze over the top. Chill and serve with whipped cream.

Serves 6

Tutti Frutti Tart is a genuine Italian showpiece that is simple to make, and can be filled with a variety of fresh fruits

Apricot Cheese Flan

275 g (10 oz) (2¾ cups) flour
pinch salt
5 ml (1 teaspoon) powdered
  cinnamon
75 g (3 oz) (6 tablespoons) butter
50 g (2 oz) (¼ cup) lard
70 ml (2½ fl oz) (⅓ cup) water
350 g (¾ lb) (2 cups) cream cheese
100 g (¼ lb) (½ cup) castor (fine
  granulated) sugar
5 ml (1 teaspoon) grated orange
  rind
30 ml (2 tablespoons) orange
  juice
30 ml (2 tablespoons) double
  (heavy) cream
1 kg (2 lb) canned apricot halves
  with syrup
30 ml (2 tablespoons) strained
  apricot jam
15 ml (1 tablespoon) arrowroot
225 g (½ lb) (1⅓ cups) strawberries,
  hulled

1 Preheat the oven to 200°C, 400°F, gas 6.

2 Sieve the flour with the salt and cinnamon into a bowl and rub in the butter and lard until it resembles fine breadcrumbs. Add the water and mix to a firm dough.

3 Knead the dough on a floured board until it is smooth. Roll it out to a thickness of 5 mm (¼ in) and use it to line a 30 x 20 cm (12 x 8 in) flan dish. Remove the trimmings and roll them into strips long enough to cover the rims of the flan dish. Brush the rims with a little water and arrange the strips on top. Flute the strips with a knife and prick the bottom with a fork, before baking the flan blind for 20 minutes. Allow it to cool in the dish.

4 Meanwhile, blend together the cream cheese, castor (fine granulated) sugar, orange rind, juice, and cream.

5 Strain the syrup from the apricots into a saucepan and drain the halved apricots on absorbent paper.

6 Gently heat the syrup and stir in the apricot jam. Mix the arrowroot with a little syrup and stir it back into the saucepan. Boil for 1-2 minutes until the syrup is clear.

7 Spread the cream cheese mixture over the bottom of the flan and arrange the apricot halves in rows, hollow side upwards, on top. Spoon over the syrup and garnish with the strawberries. Chill and serve.

Serves 8-10

Kirklebride Easter Baskets

shortcrust (pie crust) made with
  100 g (¼ lb) (1⅛ cups) flour
50 g (2 oz) (¼ cup) butter
50 g (2 oz) (¼ cup) sugar
1 egg
30 ml (2 tablespoons) flour
50 g (2 oz) (⅔ cup) ground almonds
12 canned apricot halves, well
  drained
150 ml (¼ pint) (⅝ cup) double
  (heavy) cream, whipped
12 angelica strips

1 Roll out the dough on a lightly floured board. Using a 6.5 cm (2½ in) fluted cutter, stamp out 12 rounds. Place the rounds in 12 patty tins (pans).

2 Cream the butter and sugar together and beat in the egg. Blend in the flour and ground almonds and divide the mixture between the 12 pastry cases. Bake them in the oven for 20 minutes. Remove and allow them to cool.

3 Place an apricot half on top of each tartlet. Fill a piping (decorator's) bag, fitted with a small star nozzle, with the cream. Pipe rosettes of cream around each apricot. Bend each stick of angelica to form the shape of a handle and insert in the tartlets.

Makes 12 tartlets

Kirklebride Easter Baskets are filled with a creamy and smooth almond butter filling, then topped with apricot halves

Apricot Cheese Flan; a colourful combination of canned apricots and strawberries conceals a layer of cream cheese

Banana Cream Flan

sweet shortcrust (pie crust)
  made with 175 g (6 oz)
  (1⅝ cups) flour
8-10 sugar lumps
2 large oranges
4-5 ripe bananas
300 ml (½ pint) (1¼ cups) double
  (heavy) cream

1 Preheat the oven to 200°C, 400°F, gas 6.

2 Roll out the dough and use to line a 20 cm (8 in) flan ring set on a baking (cookie) sheet. Line with paper, fill with baking beans and bake for 15 minutes. Remove the paper and beans and bake for a further 5 minutes. Remove the flan ring when the flan is cool.

3 Rub the sugar lumps over the orange rind until they are well soaked with the oil. Crush them in a small bowl and add enough orange juice to make a syrup.

4 Slice the bananas, moisten with a little of the orange syrup and spoon into the flan.

5 Whip the cream until it is just thick, and add the remaining orange syrup. Spread the cream thickly over the bananas.

Serves 6

Almond Curd Cake

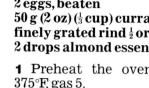 ★ ⧗

75 g (3 oz) (⅜ cup) butter
25 g (1 oz) (2 tablespoons) lard
175 g (6 oz) (1⅝ cups) flour
40 g (1½ oz) (⅜ cup) ground
  almonds
40 g (1½ oz) (3 tablespoons) castor
  (fine granulated) sugar
1 egg yolk
15-30 ml (1-2 tablespoons) water
few drops vanilla essence

For the Filling:
50 g (2 oz) (¼ cup) butter
50 g (2 oz) (¼ cup) castor (fine
  granulated) sugar

275 g (10 oz) (1⅔ cups) curd cheese
2 eggs, beaten
50 g (2 oz) (⅓ cup) currants
finely grated rind ½ orange
2 drops almond essence

1 Preheat the oven to 190°C, 375°F, gas 5.

2 Make the pastry: rub the fat into the flour, add the almonds and sugar and bind with the egg yolk, water and vanilla essence.

3 Roll out the pastry and use to line a 20 cm (8 in) flan ring, set on a baking (cookie) sheet.

4 Prepare the filling: cream together the butter and sugar until light. Sieve the curd cheese and stir into the butter and sugar with the beaten eggs, currants, orange rind and almond essence. Pour into the flan case.

5 Bake in the preheated oven for 30 minutes. Cool slightly before removing the flan ring, and serve warm or cold.

Serves 6

Meringue Mincemeat Tart

 ★ ⧗

sweet shortcrust (pie crust)
  made with 175 g (6 oz)
  (1⅝ cups) flour
450 g (1 lb) (1½ cups) mincemeat
1 egg white
50 g (2 oz) (¼ cup) castor (fine
  granulated) sugar
glacé cherries and angelica

1 Preheat the oven to 200°C, 400°F, gas 6.

2 Roll out the dough and use it to line a 20 cm (8 in) flan ring set on a baking (cookie) sheet. Bake blind for 20 minutes. Remove from the oven and reduce the temperature to 170°C, 375°F, gas 3.

3 Fill the flan shell with the mincemeat.

4 Whisk the egg white until it is softly peaking, add half of the sugar and continue to whisk until the mixture is glossy and forms peaks. Gently fold in the remain-

ing sugar and transfer to a piping (decorator's) bag, fitted with a large star nozzle. Pipe a border of swirls just inside the flan edge and bake in the oven for 15-20 minutes, until set and biscuity coloured. Decorate with pieces of glacé cherry and angelica.

Serves 6

Mincemeat Party Tarts

 ★ ⧗

shortcrust (pie crust) made with
  175 g (6 oz) (1⅝ cups) flour
450 g (1 lb) (1½ cups) mincemeat

For the Toppings:
50 g (2 oz) (¼ cup) unsalted (sweet)
  butter
50 g (2 oz) (¼ cup) castor (fine
  granulated) sugar
15 ml (1 tablespoon) brandy
100 g (¼ lb) marzipan

1 Preheat the oven to 190°C, 375°F, gas 5.

2 Make the brandy butter: cream the butter thoroughly. Beat in the sugar a little at a time and continue to beat until the mixture is white. Gradually beat in the brandy, then chill until quite firm.

3 Roll out the marzipan about 5 mm (¼ in) thick and cut 8 or 9 circles with a 5 cm (2 in) fluted cutter.

4 Roll out the dough thinly and use to line 16-18 tartlet tins (pans). Prick the bases with a fork and bake in the preheated oven for 8 minutes. Put a heaped teaspoonful of mincemeat into each tartlet and bake for a further 6-8 minutes until the mincemeat is hot and the pastry lightly golden. Cool slightly on a wire rack.

5 Top half of the warm mincemeat pies with a swirl of brandy butter. Cover the other pies with marzipan lids.

Makes 16-18

Meringue Mincemeat Tart (in the background) and Mincemeat Party Tarts taste good at Xmas or at any other time of year

Look'n Cook Apple Bakewell Tart

1 The ingredients: shortcrust (pie crust) dough, apples, flour, sugar, ground almonds, eggs, butter, Tia Maria **2** Roll out the dough to line a greased 20 cm (8 in) flan case **3** Prick the base of the flan with a fork **4** Peel and core the apples and slice them in rings. Fry them gently in butter and honey until tender **5** Lay the apple slices in the flan shell **6** Beat the margarine and sugar. Add the beaten eggs, Tia

10

Maria, flour and ground almonds to make a thick paste **7** With a palette knife, spread the paste evenly over the layer of apple rings **8** Cut the dough trimmings into narrow strips. Lay these in a lattice pattern across the flan **9** Brush the lattice strips with beaten egg. Dust the flan with icing (confectioners') sugar and bake in a moderate oven for 30-40 minutes **10** Cool, and serve with custard or cream

Apple Bakewell Tart

shortcrust (pie crust) made with
  225 g (½ lb) (2¼ cups) flour
2 apples
15 ml (1 tablespoon) butter
15 ml (1 tablespoon) honey
100 g (¼ lb) (½ cup) margarine
100 g (¼ lb) (½ cup) sugar
2 eggs, beaten
30 ml (2 tablespoons) Tia Maria
50 g (2 oz) (½ cup) flour
100 g (¼ lb) (¾ cup) ground
  almonds
15 ml (1 tablespoon) icing
  (confectioners') sugar

1 On a floured board, roll out the shortcrust (pie crust) dough to ½ cm (¼ in) thick, and line a 20 cm (8 in) fluted flan case. Prick the base of the flan with a fork.

2 Peel and core the apples and cut them in rings. Cook them in a frying pan (skillet) with the butter and honey for 5-10 minutes until tender. Lay the apple slices in the base of the flan.

3 Preheat the oven to 190°C, 375°F, gas 5.

4 In a mixing bowl, cream together the margarine and sugar until fluffy. Reserve 10 ml (2 teaspoons) of the beaten egg and mix the rest of the egg into the margarine and sugar. Add the Tia Maria.

5 Fold in the flour and the ground almonds and mix to a thick, smooth paste. Spread the paste evenly over the layer of apples in the flan.

6 Cut the dough trimmings into strips 1 cm (½ in) wide and lay these in a lattice pattern across the flan. Brush the lattice strips with the reserved beaten egg and sprinkle the flan with the icing (confectioners') sugar. Bake for 30-40 minutes, allow to cool and serve with cream.

Serves 6-8

Tip: The traditional Bakewell Tart does not include fruit, but a layer of jam. The tart may also be iced with a thin layer of glacé icing instead of the lattice pattern.

Another idea is to add 25 g (1 oz) (2 tablespoons) currants to the almond paste.

Mandarin Crisp

225 g (½ lb) (1 cup) crushed ginger
  biscuits (cookies)
25 g (1 oz) (2 tablespoons) butter
50 g (2 oz) bitter chocolate
50 g (2 oz) orange-flavoured
  jelly (jello)
150 ml (¼ pint) (⅝ cup) hot water
150 ml (¼ pint) (⅝ cup) evaporated
  milk
grated rind ½ orange
100 g (¼ lb) canned mandarin
  segments

1 Place the biscuit (cookie) crumbs in a bowl. Melt the butter and chocolate together and mix them into the crumbs. Lightly grease a 23 cm (9 in) flan case and spoon the crumb mixture into it, pressing it evenly and tightly around the sides and base. Chill in the refrigerator until set.

2 Melt the jelly (jello) in a pan with the water. In a bowl, beat the evaporated milk until thick. Fold in the grated orange rind and the melted jelly (jello).

3 When the mixture is nearly set, pour it into the crumb shell. Drain the mandarin segments and arrange them over the top. Chill until set firm. Serve garnished with whipped cream.

Serves 6-8

Foolish Tart

450 g (1 lb) rhubarb
100 g (¼ lb) (½ cup) sugar
30 ml (2 tablespoons) water
pinch powdered ginger
2.5 ml (½ teaspoon) powdered
  cinnamon
one 25 cm (10 in) bought sponge
  flan shell
100 g (¼ lb) (⅜ cup) apricot jam

150 ml (¼ pint) (⅝ cup) double
(heavy) cream

1 Wash the rhubarb thoroughly and cut it into 3 cm (1¼ in) lengths. Place it with the sugar, water, ginger and cinnamon in a pan, cover and cook over low heat until the fruit is soft and pulpy. Strain off any excess water and mash the fruit pulp to a purée.

2 Place the sponge flan shell on a serving dish. Spread the base and sides with apricot jam.

3 Beat the cream until stiff. Fold in the rhubarb purée and pour the mixture into the flan shell. Chill the flan in the refrigerator until the filling is set, and serve.

Serves 6-8

Pineapple Flan

shortcrust (pie crust) made with
  225 g (½ lb) (2¼ cups) flour
8 canned pineapple rings
300 ml (½ pint) (1¼ cups)
  confectioner's custard
7 strawberries

1 Preheat the oven to 190°C, 375°F, gas 5.

2 Roll out the shortcrust (pie crust) on a floured board, and line a 23 cm (9 in) flan case.

3 Finely chop one of the pineapple rings, and mix it into the confectioner's custard. Pour the custard into the flan. Bake for 30-40 minutes until the flan is just golden-brown. Remove from the flan case and allow to cool.

4 Drain the rest of the canned pineapple rings and arrange them in an overlapping circle around the flan. Place a strawberry in the middle of each pineapple ring. Serve with cream or custard.

Serves 6

Pineapple Flan is a golden delight, with different textures — crisp pastry, a creamy filling, and fresh juicy pineapple

Apricot Cream Tartlets

shortcrust (pie crust) dough
  made with 175 g (6 oz) (1⅝ cups)
  flour
1 egg white
50 g (2 oz) (¼ cup) castor (fine
  granulated) sugar
300 ml (½ pint) (1¼ cups)
  confectioner's custard
100 g (¼ lb) (⅜ cup) apricot jam

1 Preheat the oven to 190°C,
375°F, gas 5. Roll out the shortcrust (pie crust) to line 6 small
tartlet tins (pans). Bake blind for
8-10 minutes, then remove from
the oven.

2 Meanwhile, beat the egg white
until stiff. Gradually fold in the
sugar. Place the mixture in a
piping (decorator's) bag.

3 Fill the base of the tartlets with
confectioner's custard. Spread
apricot jam on top of each one.
Pipe rosettes of meringue around

*Apricot Cream Tartlets are
very light and simple, containing
a creamy filling topped
with swirls of fluffy meringue*

the edge of each tart. Return to
the oven for 5 minutes until the
meringue is just coloured. Allow
to cool and serve.

Serves 6

Mirabelle Tart

shortcrust (pie crust) made with
  225 g (½ lb) (2¼ cups) flour
450 g (1 lb) mirabelle plums
150 ml (¼ pint) (⅝ cup) sweet white
  wine
150 ml (¼ pint) (⅝ cup) water
300 g (11 oz) (1⅓ cups) castor (fine
  granulated) sugar
5 egg yolks
100 g (¼ lb) (1⅛ cups) flour

450 ml (¾ pint) (1⅞ cups) milk
few drops vanilla essence

1 Preheat the oven to 200°C,
400°F, gas 6. Roll out the dough to
line a 25 cm (10 in) flan case and
bake blind for 15-20 minutes.
Remove from the oven and cool.

2 Meanwhile, place the plums,
white wine, water, and 50 g (2 oz) (¼
cup) of the sugar in a pan. Simmer
gently over low heat for about 5
minutes until the plums are tender. Leave them to cool in the
syrup.

3 In a mixing bowl, beat the egg
yolks, then gradually add the
flour and the rest of the sugar.
Pour in the milk, beating all the
time to produce a smooth mixture. Add the vanilla and a little of
the plum syrup. Place in a pan
and heat gently, stirring, until the
mixture thickens.

4 Pour the thickened custard
into the base of the flan shell. With
a perforated spoon, drain the
plums and arrange them on top of

648

the custard mixture. Chill and serve cold.

Serves 6-8

Rice Tart

50 g (2 oz) (¼ cup) butter
50 g (2 oz) (¼ cup) lard
225 g (½ lb) (2¼ cups) flour
15 ml (1 tablespoon) brandy, sherry or rum
15 ml (1 tablespoon) single (light) cream or sour cream
15 ml (1 tablespoon) water
75 g (3 oz) (⅜ cup) sugar
pinch salt

For the Filling:
150 g (5 oz) (⅝ cup) short-grain rice
750 ml (1¼ pints) (3 cups) milk

2 eggs, separated
pinch salt
50 g (2 oz) (¼ cup) sugar
2.5 ml (½ teaspoon) ground cinnamon
25 g (1 oz) (1½ tablespoons) finely chopped almonds

1 Rub the butter and lard into the flour in a mixing bowl. Make a well in the middle and pour in the alcohol, cream or sour cream, water, sugar and salt. Blend and knead lightly to a dough. Leave in a cool place for 1 hour.

2 Meanwhile, wash the rice for the filling and cook it in a pan of boiling water for 3 minutes. Drain and rinse in cold water.

3 Place the milk in a pan and bring it to the boil. Add the rice and cook over very low heat for

---

Mirabelle Tart is bubbling with sunny golden mirabelle plums set in a smooth, creamy base of confectioner's custard

about 10 minutes. Stir in the egg yolks, salt, sugar, ground cinnamon and chopped almonds.

4 In a bowl beat the egg whites until stiff. Fold them into the rice mixture.

5 Preheat the oven to 180°C, 350°F, gas 4. On a floured board roll out the shortcrust (pie crust) dough and use it to line a 23 cm (9 in), lightly greased flan case. Pour the rice mixture into the flan case. Bake in the oven for about 45 minutes. Serve hot or cold.

Serves 6

Tip: This flan goes well with fresh or canned fruit, such as plums or mandarins. To make an Apple and Rice Flan, halve the quantities for the filling and cover the base of the flan with slices of peeled, cored cooking (green) apples sprinkled with sugar, then top with the rice.

Chocolate Meringue Flan

sweet shortcrust (pie crust)
  made with 225 g ($\frac{1}{2}$ lb) (2$\frac{1}{4}$ cups)
  flour
25 g (1 oz) (3 tablespoons)
  cornflour (cornstarch)
25 g (1 oz) ($\frac{1}{4}$ cup) cocoa powder
150 g (5 oz) ($\frac{5}{8}$ cup) castor (fine
  granulated) sugar
450 ml ($\frac{3}{4}$ pint) (1$\frac{7}{8}$ cups) milk
50 g (2 oz) ($\frac{1}{4}$ cup) butter
3 egg yolks
few drops vanilla essence
For the Meringue:
3 egg whites
75 g (3 oz) ($\frac{3}{8}$ cup) castor (fine
  granulated) sugar

1 Preheat the oven to 200°C, 400°F, gas 6. Prepare a 20 cm (8 in) flan case and bake it blind. Let it cool.

2 In a mixing bowl, blend together the cornflour (corn-starch), cocoa powder and sugar. Warm the milk and add it gradually to this mixture. Return it to the pan and cook, stirring, over gentle heat until the mixture thickens.

3 Remove the pan from the heat. Stir in the butter and egg yolks and flavour with a little vanilla essence. Pour the mixture into the flan case.

4 In another bowl beat the egg whites until stiff. Gradually add the sugar. Spoon the meringue over the chocolate filling. Bake for about 15 minutes until the meringue is crisp and golden on top. Cool before serving.

Serves 6

Amandine Tarts, crunchy with almonds and garnished with cherries, can be served either at dinner or at a tea party

Amandine Tarts

sweet shortcrust (pie crust)
  made with 100 g ($\frac{1}{4}$ lb) (1$\frac{1}{8}$ cups)
  flour
50 g (2 oz) ($\frac{1}{4}$ cup) butter
50 g (2 oz) ($\frac{1}{4}$ cup) castor (fine
  granulated) sugar
1 egg, beaten
50 g (2 oz) ($\frac{3}{8}$ cup) ground almonds
30 ml (2 tablespoons) flour
few drops almond essence
50 g (2 oz) ($\frac{3}{8}$ cup) flaked almonds
50 g (2 oz) ($\frac{1}{4}$ cup) apricot jam
6 glacé cherries

1 Preheat the oven to 190°C, 375°F, gas 5.

2 On a floured board roll out the dough to $\frac{1}{2}$ cm ($\frac{1}{4}$ in) thick and line 6 greased and floured tart tins (pans). Bake blind for 20 minutes, then remove from the oven, leaving the oven on.

3 Meanwhile cream the butter with the sugar until pale and fluffy. Gradually add the egg. Then beat in the ground almonds, sifted flour, and flavour with a little almond essence.

4 Fill the half-cooked tart shells with the almond paste. Cover with flaked almonds and return to the oven for 10 minutes or until the dough is cooked.

5 Melt the apricot jam in a pan over low heat, adding a little water if necessary. Sieve. Top each tart with a glacé cherry and spread with apricot glaze. Cool before serving.

Serves 6

Cherry Meringue Flan

shortcrust (pie crust) dough made with 225 g (½ lb) (2¼ cups) flour
300 ml (½ pint) (1¼ cups) confectioner's custard

Cherry Meringue Flan is a real party special, with rings of big luscious cherries set within snowy meringue peaks

10 ml (2 teaspoons) kirsch
1 egg white
50 g (2 oz) (¼ cup) castor (fine granulated) sugar
2 drops vanilla essence
450 g (1 lb) canned morello cherries

1 Preheat the oven to 200°C, 400°F, gas 6. Roll out the short-crust (pie crust) to ½ cm (¼ in) thickness and line a greased 25 cm (10 in) flan dish. Prick the dough and bake blind for 20 minutes.

2 Meanwhile flavour the confectioner's custard with the kirsch. Spread it over the base of the cooled flan case.

3 Beat the egg white until stiff and fold in the sugar. Flavour with vanilla essence. Place in a piping (decorator's) bag and pipe around the flan and in the middle. Arrange the cherries in a double ring on the flan.

4 Return the flan to the oven for 5 minutes so that the meringue is just tinged with gold. Let it cool before serving.

Serves 6-8

Edinburgh Tart

shortcrust (pie crust) made with 225 g (½ lb) (2¼ cups) flour
50 g (2 oz) (¼ cup) butter, melted
50 g (2 oz) (¼ cup) sugar
50 g (2 oz) (½ cup) chopped candied peel
15 ml (1 tablespoon) seedless raisins
50 g (2 oz) (½ cup) flour
2 eggs, beaten

1 Preheat the oven to 190°C, 375°F, gas 5. Roll out the dough to line a 20 cm (8 in) flan case.

2 Mix the butter, sugar, peel, raisins and flour. Stir in the eggs and pour into the pastry case. Bake for 40 minutes, cool and serve.

Serves 6

Pies

Covered pies are easy to make and can be filled with a variety of fruity fillings. You can use ordinary common or garden fruits like apples, pears and plums or more exotic tropical fruits such as mangoes and pineapple. Serve a fruit pie with a jug of freshly made hot custard or some whipped cream. Pies can be made with either puff or short-crust (pie crust) pastry. For extra special results, try adding some ground almonds or cinnamon to the shortcrust (pie crust) pastry mix. The flavour of apple and pear pies is more interesting if you add a pinch of cinnamon and some cloves.

Spicy Apple Pie

1-1½ kg (2-3 lb) cooking (green) apples
butter for greasing
2.5 ml (½ teaspoon) cinnamon
100 g (¼ lb) (½ cup) demerara sugar
4 cloves
grated rind and juice 1 lemon
45 ml (3 tablespoons) water
sweet shortcrust (pie crust) made with 225 g (½ lb) (2¼ cups) flour
10 ml (2 teaspoons) milk
25 g (1 oz) (2 tablespoons) castor (fine granulated) sugar

1 Peel, core and thinly slice the apples. Butter a deep pie dish and arrange the apples inside in layers with the cinnamon and demerara sugar. Spike some apple slices with the cloves and sprinkle the grated lemon rind and juice over the top. Add the water.

2 Preheat the oven to 200°C, 400°F, gas 6. Roll out the dough to the diameter of the pie dish and use to cover the pie. Trim around the edge and seal firmly. Crimp and decorate it if you wish. Make a small incision in the top of the pie with a sharp knife.

3 Brush with milk and sprinkle with sugar. Bake in the oven and reduce the temperature to 180°C, 350°F, gas 4 after 10 minutes. Bake for another 20 minutes until the pie is cooked and golden-brown. Serve hot, or cold, with cream.

Serves 6

Pumpkin Pie

225 g (½ lb) pumpkin, peeled and deseeded
225 g (½ lb) cooking (green) apples, peeled and cored
100 g (¼ lb) (⅔ cup) currants
25 g (1 oz) (¼ cup) chopped mixed peel
5 ml (1 teaspoon) mixed spice
butter for greasing
50 g (2 oz) (¼ cup) soft brown sugar
15 ml (1 tablespoon) water
shortcrust (pie crust) made with 175 g (6 oz) (1⅝ cups) flour
5 ml (1 teaspoon) milk
25 g (1 oz) (2 tablespoons) castor (fine granulated) sugar

1 Cut the pumpkin and apples into cubes and mix with the currants, mixed peel and spice.

2 Grease a deep pie dish and fill with the fruit mixture. Sprinkle over the soft brown sugar and add the water.

3 Preheat the oven to 200°C, 400°F, gas 6. Roll out the dough to a large circle, the same diameter as the pie dish. Wet the rim of the dish and cover with the dough. Trim and crimp the edges and make a small hole in the top. Brush with milk and sprinkle with sugar.

4 Bake in the oven for 10 minutes, then reduce the temperature to 180°C, 350°F, gas 4 and bake for a further 30 minutes until crisp and golden-brown. Serve with whipped cream.

Serves 6

Spiced Date and Pear Pie

100 g (¼ lb) (½ cup) butter or margarine
100 g (¼ lb) (1 cup) wholemeal flour
100 g (¼ lb) (½ cup) oats
water to mix
butter for greasing
100 g (¼ lb) dates, stoned (seeded) and chopped
1 kg (2 lb) dessert pears, peeled, cored and sliced
2.5 ml (½ teaspoon) cinnamon
grated rind and juice ½ lemon
50 g (2 oz) (¼ cup) soft brown sugar
5 ml (1 teaspoon) milk
25 g (1 oz) (2 tablespoons) castor (fine granulated) sugar

1 Rub the fat into the flour and oats with your fingertips. Then mix in enough water to make a stiff pastry dough. Roll out half of the dough on a floured surface and use it to line an 18 cm (7 in) greased shallow pie dish.

2 Preheat the oven to 220°C, 425°F, gas 7.

3 Place the dates, pears, cinnamon, lemon rind, juice and brown sugar inside the pie. Roll out the remaining dough to make a lid. Cover the pie, then trim and crimp the edges. Brush the lid of the pie with milk and sprinkle over the castor (fine granulated) sugar.

4 Bake in the oven for 10 minutes, then reduce the temperature to 190°C, 375°F, gas 5 for the remaining 20 minutes. Remove the pie when it is crisp and golden-brown. Serve the pie hot with a jug of whipped cream or hot custard.

Serves 6

Tips: If fresh pears are not available you can make this pie using the same weight of drained canned pears. Also, if you prefer plain pastry, you can make it with ordinary white flour instead of wholemeal flour.

Rhubarb Pie

shortcrust (pie crust) made with
  350 g ($\frac{3}{4}$ lb) ($3\frac{3}{8}$ cups) flour
10 sticks rhubarb cut into 1.25
  cm ($\frac{1}{2}$ in) slices
350 g (12 oz) ($1\frac{1}{2}$ cups) sugar
25 g (1 oz) (2 tablespoons) butter
grated rind 1 orange
30 ml (2 tablespoons) cornflour
  (cornstarch)
50 ml (2 fl oz) ($\frac{1}{4}$ cup) orange juice
2.5 ml ($\frac{1}{2}$ teaspoon) cinnamon
1 egg yolk
30 ml (1 fl oz) (2 tablespoons)
  milk
25 g (1 oz) ($\frac{1}{4}$ cup) icing
  (confectioners') sugar

1 Preheat the oven to 200°C,
400°F, gas 6. Roll out the dough on
a floured board to a thickness of
5 mm ($\frac{1}{4}$ in). Use half to line the
bottom and sides of a 23 cm (9 in)
pie plate.

2 Arrange the rhubarb over the
bottom of the dish. Add the sugar,
butter and orange rind.

3 Blend the cornflour (cornstarch) with the orange juice and
pour it over the other ingredients.
Sprinkle with the cinnamon and
cover with the second round of
dough. Brush the top with the egg
yolk mixed with milk and bake
the pie in the oven for 30 minutes
or until the crust is golden.

4 Dust with the icing (confectioners') sugar and serve.

Serves 6

Rum and Date Pie

350 g ($\frac{3}{4}$ lb) ($3\frac{3}{8}$ cups) flour
275 g (10 oz) ($1\frac{1}{4}$ cups) butter
50 g (2 oz) ($\frac{1}{4}$ cup) castor (fine
  granulated) sugar
1 egg yolk
30 ml (1 fl oz) (2 tablespoons) cold
  water
butter for greasing
100 g ($\frac{1}{4}$ lb) chopped dates
50 g (2 oz) chopped preserved
  ginger

30 ml (1 fl oz) (2 tablespoons) rum

1 Preheat the oven to 200°C,
400°F, gas 6. Sift the flour into a
bowl. Cut 225 g ($\frac{1}{2}$ lb) (1 cup) of the
butter into pieces and rub it into
the flour until the mixture resembles fine breadcrumbs. Stir in
10 ml (2 teaspoons) of the sugar.
Blend the egg yolk and water
together and tip into the flour,
mixing quickly to form a firm
dough. Turn the dough on to a
floured board and knead lightly
until it is smooth. Roll out the
dough to a thickness of 5 mm ($\frac{1}{4}$ in).

2 Line a well-buttered pie plate
with half the dough and cover it
with the dates and ginger.

3 Cream together the remaining
butter and sugar and the rum and
spread it over the filling.

4 Cover with the remaining
dough and bake the pie in the
preheated oven for 15 minutes.
Reduce the heat to 180°C, 350°F,
gas 4 and bake for a further 30
minutes.

Serves 6

Orange Raisin Pie

shortcrust (pie crust) made with
  225 g ($\frac{1}{2}$ lb) ($2\frac{1}{4}$ cups) flour
350 g ($\frac{3}{4}$ lb) (2 cups) raisins
30 ml (1 fl oz) (2 tablespoons)
  orange juice
40 g ($1\frac{1}{2}$ oz) (2 tablespoons) golden
  syrup
30 ml (2 tablespoons) icing
  (confectioners') sugar

1 Preheat the oven to 220°C,
425°F, gas 7.

2 Roll out the dough on a lightly
floured board to a thickness of
5 mm ($\frac{1}{4}$ in). Use half to line a 20 cm
(8 in) pie plate. Trim the edges.

3 In a bowl, blend together the
raisins, orange juice and golden
syrup. Spread the mixture evenly
over the pie plate. Sprinkle the
rims of the plate with a little
water and arrange the remaining
dough, being careful not to
stretch it, over the top. Seal the

rims with your fingers and cut off
any trimmings.

4 Bake the pie on the middle
shelf of the oven for 25-30 minutes.
Sprinkle with the icing (confectioners') sugar and serve.

Serves 6

Apple and Blackberry Pie

450 g (1 lb) cooking (green)
  apples
225 g ($\frac{1}{2}$ lb) ($1\frac{1}{2}$ cups) blackberries
350 g ($\frac{3}{4}$ lb) prepared flaky
  pastry
butter for greasing
75 g (3 oz) ($\frac{3}{8}$ cup) sugar
15 ml (1 tablespoon) water
beaten egg for glazing

1 Peel, core, quarter and cut the
apples into slices. Remove the
stalks from the blackberries and
wash them thoroughly.

2 Preheat the oven to 200°C,
400°F, gas 6.

3 Roll out the dough on a floured
board to a thickness of 5 mm ($\frac{1}{4}$ in).
Use half the dough to line a but-
tered 900 ml ($1\frac{1}{2}$ pint) ($3\frac{3}{4}$ cup) pie
dish. Cut off and reserve the
trimmings. Cover the base with
half the apples and blackberries.
Add the sugar and water and then
the remaining fruit.

4 Dampen the rim of the pie
plate and cover the pie with the
remaining dough. Seal and flute
the edges. Decorate the top with 5
leaves made from the reserved
pastry trimmings and brush it
with the beaten egg. Place the
dish on a baking (cookie) sheet
and bake it for 10 minutes in the
preheated oven. Reduce the heat
to 180°C, 350°F, gas 4 and cook for a
further 30 minutes. If the dough
colours too quickly cover it with a
sheet of paper. Serve hot.

Serves 6-8

Greengage Pie

175 g (6 oz) (1⅝ cups) flour
pinch salt
40 g (1½ oz) (3 tablespoons) butter
40 g (1½ oz) (3 tablespoons) lard
30 ml (2 tablespoons) water

For the Filling:
675 g (1½ lb) greengage plums
100 g (¼ lb) (½ cup) sugar
30 ml (2 tablespoons) water
5 ml (1 teaspoon) ground
  cinnamon

1 Sift the flour and salt into a bowl. Rub in the butter and lard until the mixture resembles fine crumbs. Gradually add the water, stirring with a palette knife, until the dough starts to stick together. Knead lightly and set aside for 15 minutes.

2 Wash the fruit and remove any pieces of stalk. Arrange them in a large pie dish and sprinkle with the sugar, water and cinnamon.

3 Preheat the oven to 220°C, 425°F, gas 7. Roll out the dough to ½ cm (¼ in) thick, about 2.5 cm (1 in) larger in diameter than the pie dish. Cut a strip the width of the dish rim, dampen the rim and stick the strip round. Dampen the strip and lay the rest of the dough across the pie. Cut off any excess and crimp the edges with a fork. Use leftover dough to make leaves to decorate the top.

4 Bake for 15 minutes, then lower oven heat to 180°C, 350°F, gas 4. Bake for 20-30 minutes until the fruit is cooked. Serve hot or cold, with whipped cream.

Serves 6

Greengage Pie would be ideal for Sunday lunch, with its light pastry shell and filling of tender, juicy, hot greengages

Exotic Pie

350 g (¾ lb) (3⅜ cups) flour
pinch salt
75 g (3 oz) (⅜ cup) butter or
  margarine
75 g (3 oz) (⅜ cup) lard
15 ml (1 tablespoon) castor (fine
  granulated) sugar
50 ml (2 fl oz) (¼ cup) water

For the Filling:
175 g (6 oz) (1 cup) strawberries
225 g (½ lb) lychees
1 kg (2 lb) pineapple
3 bananas
2 mangoes
juice ½ lemon
50 ml (2 fl oz) (¼ cup) rum
25 g (1 oz) (2 tablespoons)
  demerara sugar

1 Sift the flour into a mixing bowl with the salt. Rub in the butter or margarine and the lard to make fine crumbs. Add the sugar. Stir with a knife while adding the water, little by little, until the mixture begins to stick together. Knead lightly to form a smooth dough. Leave it to rest for 15 minutes.

2 Prepare the fruit: wash and hull the strawberries. If using fresh lychees, peel them. Peel the pineapple and remove the dark spots, and cut into cubes. Peel and slice the bananas. Cut the mango flesh into chunks.

3 Preheat the oven to 200°C, 400°F, gas 6. Roll out the dough on a floured board to cover a large, 2 litre (3½ pint) (9 cup) pie dish. Mix the fruit and arrange them in the dish. Sprinkle with the lemon juice, rum and demerara sugar. Place the dough over the top, cut off any excess around the sides and crimp the edges. With the point of a sharp knife, cut out a star shape from the middle of the dough. Bake in the oven for 20-25 minutes; serve hot or cold.

Serves 8

Tip: Before serving, pour thick cream through the star-shaped hole into the pie underneath.

Exotic Pie owes its name to the filling of unusual fruits including lychees, pineapple, mango, and banana

Raspberry Pie

675 g (1½ lb) (5 cups) raspberries
butter for greasing
15 ml (1 tablespoon) cornflour
 (cornstarch)
50 g (2 oz) (¼ cup) castor (fine
 granulated) sugar
pinch nutmeg
few drops almond essence
shortcrust (pie crust) made with
 225 g (½ lb) (2¼ cups) flour
5 ml (1 teaspoon) milk
sugar for dusting

1 Preheat the oven to 200°C, 400°F, gas 6. Wash, drain and hull the raspberries. Place them in a deep buttered pie dish and sprinkle the cornflour (cornstarch) between the layers – this will thicken the syrup. Add the sugar, nutmeg and almond essence.

2 Roll out the dough on a floured surface to the diameter of the pie dish. Dampen the edges of the pie dish and cover the top with the dough. Trim and crimp the edges and make a small hole in the top with a sharp knife. Brush with milk.

3 Bake in the oven and, after 10 minutes, reduce the temperature to 180°C, 350°F, gas 4. Cook for a further 20 minutes until crisp and golden. Just before serving, dust generously with sugar.

Serves 6

Crusty Plum Pie

butter for greasing
675 g (1½ lb) plums
100 g (¼ lb) (½ cup) castor (fine
 granulated) sugar
2.5 ml (½ teaspoon) cinnamon

Raspberry Pie is just right for feeding the family whatever the weather — serve it cold with cream or hot with custard

15 ml (1 tablespoon) water
shortcrust (pie crust) made with
 225 g (½ lb) (2¼ cups) flour
5 ml (1 teaspoon) milk
sugar for dusting

1 Grease a deep pie dish and preheat the oven to 200°C, 400°F, gas 6.

2 Fill the pie dish with the plums, castor (fine granulated) sugar, cinnamon and water.

3 Roll out the shortcrust (pie crust) to the diameter of the pie dish. Cover the pie with the dough lid. Trim and crimp the edges, then brush lightly with the milk and dust with sugar.

4 Place in the oven and, after 10 minutes, reduce the temperature to 180°C, 350°F, gas 4. Bake for another 20 minutes until crisp and golden. Serve with cream or custard.

Serves 6

Tip: You can always use green-gages in this pie for an unusual variation – cook them in exactly the same way.

Index